Get the eBook FREE!

(PDF, ePub, Kindle, and liveBook all included)

We believe that once you buy a book from us, you should be able to read it in any format we have available. To get electronic versions of this book at no additional cost to you, purchase and then register this book at the Manning website.

Go to https://www.manning.com/freebook and follow the instructions to complete your pBook registration.

That's it!
Thanks from Manning!

Machine Learning for Tabular Data

Machine Learning for Tabular Data

XGBoost, Deep Learning, and AI

Mark Ryan
Luca Massaron

Foreword by Antonio Gulli

MANNING
SHELTER ISLAND

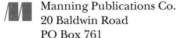

Manning Publications Co.
20 Baldwin Road
PO Box 761
Shelter Island, NY 11964

Development editor:	Doug Rudder
Technical editor:	Vadim Borisov
Review editor:	Kishor Rit
Production editor:	Andy Marinkovich
Copy editor:	Kari Lucke
Proofreader:	Jason Everett
Technical proofreader:	Dwipam Katariya
Typesetter:	Tamara Švelić Sabljić
Cover designer:	Marija Tudor

ISBN 9781633438545
Printed in the United States of America

To the memory of my niece Anna Joy, who set a great example by combining curiosity about the natural world with an abiding dedication to its Creator.
—Mark Ryan

To the memory of John Paul Mueller, a long-time collaborator and friend, with whom we authored many marvelous books to illustrate and share the wonders of computers and technology.
—Luca Massaron

brief contents

contents

foreword

Machine Learning for Tabular Data dives into a critical area of machine learning: working with tabular data. From the spreadsheets you use every day to the databases that power businesses, tabular data is everywhere. It's the hidden gem hiding in plain sight.

This book goes beyond just theory. It equips you to leverage the power of tabular data by teaching you machine learning techniques specifically designed for it. You'll learn how to make sense of your data, uncover patterns, and build real-world applications—all with the added benefit of clear and interpretable results.

Machine Learning for Tabular Data gets you coding and implementing. Unlike many resources that focus solely on model training, this book takes you on a complete journey through the world of machine learning with tabular data. Packed with practical coding examples, the book guides you through the entire machine learning life cycle: wrangling messy data, building models, evaluating performance, and seamlessly deploying them into a professional public cloud environment using MLOps best practices.

And this book goes the extra mile by sharing valuable insights and practical experience, condensing a wealth of knowledge into a single resource. It's the perfect companion for anyone who wants to dive in and start making a real impact with their tabular data.

Part 1 takes you on a journey through machine learning (ML) for tabular data including the data in spreadsheets, CSV files, and databases. This part starts with basics (ML vs deep learning for tabular data) and then explains both approaches.

Part 2 explores ML with gradient boosting, a powerful technique that established in industry for dealing with tabular data. You'll learn about different and best practices and even test a real-world example.

Part 3 delves into deep learning for tabular data, covering everything from getting started to deployment, including building an ML pipeline for production use. Finally, the book compares gradient boosting and deep learning to help you choose the right approach for your needs. This is my favorite part of the whole book.

I hope you enjoy this excellent book and the best practices and practical tips in it to get the most out of tabular data.

—Antonio Gulli,

Google Sr Director, CTO Office, AI, Search and Cloud

preface

This book covers the intersection of two topics that we are passionate about: machine learning and tabular data. We appreciate the importance of tabular data—that is, data in rows and columns that reside in a variety of repositories, from the humble spreadsheet to the most sophisticated relational databases.

Even with the tidal wave of nontabular data in the past two decades, just about every business and government on the planet depends on tabular data. When Manning approached us about the opportunity to write a book to describe the latest techniques for analyzing tabular data with machine learning, including both classical methods like gradient boosting *and* deep learning, we couldn't pass it up. When the generative AI revolution kicked into high gear during the development of this book, we embraced the chance to weave generative AI into the narrative of the book.

We hope that our book gives you practical advice and concrete approaches so you can learn more about the intersection of these two critical topics—machine learning and tabular data.

acknowledgments

This book was a multiyear effort that required the dedication and cooperation of dozens of talented people.

Mark Ryan: I would like to acknowledge Sercan Arik at Google for reviewing my chapters for the initial MEAP version of this book. I would also like to acknowledge my manager Brett Johnson and the director of my area, Helen Slattery, for the opportunities they have provided and for their support during my time at Google. I am indebted to my family for their support and to Dr. Laurence Mussio for his advice and encouragement. Finally, I would like to thank Luca for sharing his immense skill and his patience in the process of creating this book. I have learned so much from Luca and I consider myself privileged to share a byline with him.

Luca Massaron: I would like to warmly thank my family, Yukiko and Amelia, for their support and loving patience as I prepared this new book in a long series. A special thanks to Antonio Gulli for reading our book and writing an exceptional foreword and for all his invaluable advice. Finally, a big thank you to my coauthor, Mark, for having me involved in this project, which I enjoyed and from which I've learned so much.

Last but not least, thank you to all the reviewers who took the time to share their valuable feedback: Adi Shavit, Aqsa Fulara, Dwipam Katariya, Giovanni Alzetta, Giri Swaminathan, Gregory Grimes, Harcharan Kabbay, Jose Antonio Martinez, Keith Kim, Khaing Win, Martin Czygan, Maxim Volgin, Nick Vazquez, Ninoslav Cerkez, Oliver Korten, Richard Meinsen, Said Ech-Chadi, Sergio Govoni, Simon Tschöke, Thiago Britto Borges, Thomas Seeber, Tirthankar Chakravarty, Tomáš Šipka, and Vaijanath Rao, your suggestions helped make this a better book.

about this book

This book describes how you can use machine learning approaches, including classical approaches based on gradient boosting, deep learning, and generative AI, to extract valuable insights from tabular data (structured data organized in rows and columns) that you can apply to your job. You will learn about the defining characteristics of tabular data, best practices for applying machine learning to tabular data, and how to take a model you have trained on tabular data and make it available for others to use. You will also learn the pros and cons of classical machine learning and deep learning when it comes to solving tabular data problems. Throughout the book, you will learn to expedite the analysis process by using generative AI.

Who should read this book?

This book is intended for an audience that spans data scientists, AI/machine learning engineers, and business stakeholders. To get the most out of this book, you should have a basic grounding in classical machine learning techniques and exposure to deep learning. The code examples that appear throughout this book use Python, and most are designed to be run in hosted Jupyter Notebook environments such as Google Colab. You will get the most out of these code examples if you have already been exposed to standard Python methods of working with tabular data, such as the pandas and NumPy packages. In addition to the standalone examples designed to be run in Jupyter Notebooks, chapters 10 and 11 include examples that run in the Google Cloud environment. You don't need to already know Google Cloud to enjoy these examples—we'll tell you everything you need to know from the very start—but if you have already done some work in one of the major cloud environments (AWS, Azure, or Google Cloud), you will have a head start with the examples in these two chapters.

How this book is organized: A roadmap

Machine Learning for Tabular Data has 12 chapters organized into three parts.

Part 1 introduces the fundamental concepts of tabular data and compares approaches for dealing with tabular data:

- Chapter 1 defines tabular data and introduces two approaches for making predictions based on tabular data.
- Chapter 2 describes the defining characteristics of tabular data and key concepts for investigating a given tabular dataset.
- Chapter 3 compares the relative strengths and weaknesses of classic machine learning and deep learning when it comes to dealing with tabular data.

Part 2 describes the classic machine learning approaches available and specifically explains how to use one gradient boosting technique, XGBoost, to get optimal results:

- Chapter 4 shows you how to use classic machine learning algorithms to make predictions based on tabular datasets.
- Chapter 5 describes the go-to approach for machine learning with tabular data: tree-based methods and gradient boosting in particular.
- Chapter 6 describes how to get the most out of classic machine learning approaches, particularly gradient boosting, by optimizing the preparation and selection of features and by optimizing the hyperparameters that control the model training process.
- Chapter 7 shows you the complete process of applying one of the gradient boosting approaches, XGBoost, to a challenging tabular dataset.

Part 3 shows you how to train a deep learning model with tabular data, how to deploy a trained model, and how deep learning stacks up against a classic machine learning approach in an apples-to-apples comparison:

- Chapter 8 describes the various software stacks that are available for applying deep learning to tabular data and summarizes the strengths and weaknesses of the stacks.
- Chapter 9 uses a coding example to illustrate key tips and tricks for getting the most out of deep learning applications trained with tabular data.
- Chapter 10 shows you how to integrate the model that you trained in chapter 9 in a simple web application served from a local machine and how to deploy the same model in a popular managed cloud environment, Google Cloud.
- Chapter 11 shows you how to automate the model training and deployment steps by using the machine learning pipeline facilities of Vertex AI in Google Cloud, as well as how you can take advantage of generative AI to simplify the task of creating a machine learning pipeline.

- Chapter 12 ties the whole book together by comparing the gradient boosting approach from chapter 7 with a deep learning approach and showing you how to get optimal results by combining the two approaches.
- Finally, two appendices closely examine aspects that were not possible to fully illustrate in detail in the chapters. Appendix A offers an overview of the key hyperparameters used by each classical machine learning algorithm discussed in the book, offering typical values to be tested by optimization methods. Appendix B deals with the k-nearest neighbors algorithm and support vector machines, two classical machine learning algorithms that have recently seen an increase in usage thanks to new approaches and tools, such as the NVIDIA RAPIDS library that leverages GPUs to speed up algorithm execution.

If you are interested in learning about both major approaches for dealing with tabular data (classic machine learning and deep learning), we recommend that you read the chapters in sequence. If you are primarily interested in classic machine learning approaches, we suggest that you read part 1, part 2, and chapter 12. If you are primarily interested in deep learning approaches, we suggest that you read part 1 and then part 3.

About the code

This book contains many examples of source code both in numbered listings and in line with normal text. In both cases, source code is formatted in a `fixed-width font` to separate it from ordinary text. Sometimes, code is also in **bold** to highlight code that has changed from previous steps in the chapter, such as when a new feature is added to an existing line of code.

In many cases, the original source code has been reformatted; we've added line breaks and reworked indentation to accommodate the available page space in the book. In rare cases, even this was not enough, and listings include line-continuation markers (➥). Additionally, comments in the source code have often been removed from the listings when the code is described in the text. Code annotations accompany many of the listings, highlighting important concepts.

The code examples throughout this book illustrate key points and provide starting points for your own investigations. You can get executable snippets of code from the liveBook (online) version of this book at https://livebook.manning.com/book/machine-learning-for-tabular-data. The complete code for the examples in the book is available for download from the Manning website at www.manning.com, and from GitHub at https://github.com/lmassaron/Machine-Learning-on-Tabular-Data.

The code examples in all the chapters, with the exception of chapters 10 and 11, are designed to be run in a hosted Jupyter Notebook environment such as Kaggle or Google Colab. Chapter 10 includes an example that needs to be run on a local system as well as examples to run in Google Cloud. The examples in chapter 11 are designed to be run in Google Cloud.

liveBook discussion forum

Purchase of *Machine Learning for Tabular Data* includes free access to liveBook, Manning's online reading platform. Using liveBook's exclusive discussion features, you can attach comments to the book globally or to specific sections or paragraphs. It's a snap to make notes for yourself, ask and answer technical questions, and receive help from the authors and other users. To access the forum, go to https://livebook.manning .com/book/machine-learning-for-tabular-data/discussion. You can also learn more about Manning's forums and the rules of conduct at https://livebook.manning.com/ discussion.

Manning's commitment to our readers is to provide a venue where a meaningful dialogue between individual readers and between readers and the authors can take place. It is not a commitment to any specific amount of participation on the part of the authors, whose contribution to the forum remains voluntary (and unpaid). We suggest you try asking the authors some challenging questions lest their interest stray! The forum and the archives of previous discussions will be accessible from the publisher's website for as long as the book is in print.

about the authors

MARK RYAN is the AI Lead of the Developer Knowledge Platform at Google. Mark has a Bachelor of Mathematics in computer science from the University of Waterloo and a master's of science in computer science from the University of Toronto. He is the author of two books: *Deep Learning with Structured Data* and *Deep Learning with fastai Cookbook*. Mark enjoys investigating under-explored applications of machine learning, including using generative AI to modernize COBOL systems, the intersection of relational databases and machine learning, and the topic of this book: machine learning with tabular data. Beyond machine learning, Mark is interested in the history of technology and enjoys reading about how different breakthroughs, from railways to mobile phones, have changed society.

LUCA MASSARON is a data scientist with more than a decade of experience in transforming data into smarter artifacts, solving real-world problems, and generating value for businesses and stakeholders. He is the author of best-selling books on AI, machine learning, and algorithms. Luca is also a 3× Kaggle Grandmaster, who reached number 7 in the worldwide competition rankings, and a Google Developer Expert in machine learning.

about the cover illustration

The figure on the cover of *Machine Learning for Tabular Data*, titled "La Marchande de Gateaux," or "The Cake Seller," is taken from a book by Louis Curmer published in 1841. Each illustration is finely drawn and colored by hand.

In those days, it was easy to identify where people lived and what their trade or station in life was just by their dress. Manning celebrates the inventiveness and initiative of the computer business with book covers based on the rich diversity of regional culture centuries ago, brought back to life by pictures from collections such as this one.

Part 1

Introducing machine learning for tabular data

This opening section of the book aims to provide you with a solid foundation for understanding how to work with tabular data. The chapters in this section explore the unique characteristics of tabular data, the different modeling approaches (machine learning vs. deep learning), and the best practices for exploratory data analysis and preparation. By reading these chapters, you will acquire a good understanding of the peculiarities of working with tabular data. You will be prepared to tackle more advanced techniques in the following sections.

Chapter 1 introduces tabular data. The chapter explains what tabular data is, why it's important, and how it differs from other kinds of data, such as images, audio, and text. We also introduce machine learning and deep learning concepts, and we try to unravel the controversy about using deep learning methodologies on tabular data. The chapter concludes by reviewing the unique characteristics of tabular data, which require a specific and distinct approach to analysis and modeling.

Chapter 2 explores the structure and characteristics of tabular data, highlighting potential problems and remedies to common problems with real-world data. We offer guidance on how to find tabular data in online and offline sources, especially inside business organizations. This chapter also presents a complete demonstration of how to perform an effective exploratory data analysis.

Chapter 3 compares and contrasts machine learning and deep learning approaches based on three key criteria—simplicity, transparency, and efficacy—highlighting the strong and weak points of each one. We also introduce the Airbnb datasets that we will use throughout the book.

After completing part 1, you will be ready to explore both classical and advanced machine learning methods for tabular data!

Understanding tabular data

This chapter covers

- What tabular data is
- Why tabular data matters
- The distinction between deep learning and non-deep learning approaches to tabular data
- What people think about using deep learning with tabular data
- Characteristics of tabular data that distinguish it from other kinds of data, like image, sound, or text data

Tabular data is central to our modern lives and, for most of us, to our work lives. Tabular data exists in spreadsheets as CSV files and in the tables of relational databases, it populates analysis and reports, and it can be the fuel for training machine learning models. Machine learning models trained on your tabular business can successfully solve many useful problems, such as predicting inventory requirements in retail outlets or predicting the price of market commodities.

In this chapter, we introduce the process of selecting the appropriate modeling approach for tabular data problems. We present two main approaches: deep learning and classical machine learning. Then, from the data perspective, we look at some of the unique considerations you face when using tabular data with machine learning models.

1.1 What is tabular data?

For the purposes of this book, *tabular data* is simply data that is organized in rows and columns. A collection of tabular data can be called a *tabular dataset* or a *table*. All the entries in a row are related to a common data point or an observation. Each row is autonomous from the other rows and completely describes a specific condition. The columns represent attributes for that data point, and they are often mentioned as variables (a more statistical term) or features (a term more typical of machine learning). All the entries in a column have a common data type, such as integer, string, or floating point number. The columns in a table usually have a common type.

Consider a table that contains information about currencies used in a set of nations, as shown in figure 1.1.

Each column in the table has the information for all countries
for one aspect of currency (the attributes of the observations).

Each row in the table has details about the currency for a single country (our observations).

Country	Currency name	Currency nicknames	Currency symbol	ISO 4217 code	Units per US Dollar
Australia	Australian Dollar		$	AUD	1.45
Canada	Canadian Dollar	buck, loonie, piasse	$	CAD	1.29
New Zealand	New Zealand Dollar	gold coin	$	NZD	1.61
South Africa	Rand	buck	R	ZAR	16.78
United Kingdom	Pound Sterling	quid	£	GBP	0.83
United States	US dollar	buck, greenback	$	USD	1.0

Figure 1.1 An example of tabular data

Columns in this table contain values of different types:

- Country, Currency name, Currency symbol, and ISO 4217 code are all *categorical columns* because valid values for these columns come from a finite, relatively small set of values.

- Currency nicknames are free-form text columns because they can contain a range of values or no value at all, depending on the country.
- Units per US Dollar is a continuous column because it contains real number values.

We will explore more details about the characteristics of tabular data in chapter 2. Tabular data can reside in a variety of physical formats:

- *Standalone files,* including CSV files and spreadsheet files such as Excel and Google Sheets files.
- *Tables in relational databases,* such as
  - Open-source databases, such as Postgres (https://www.postgresql.org/) and MySQL (https://www.mysql.com/)
  - On-premise vendor databases, such as SQL Server (https://mng.bz/MD2W) and Oracle (https://www.oracle.com/ca-en/database/)
  - Cloud-native databases, such as Google Cloud Spanner (https://cloud.google.com/spanner), AWS Aurora (https://aws.amazon.com/rds/aurora/), and Snowflake (https://www.snowflake.com/)

NOTE You may have heard the term *structured data* used interchangeably with *tabular data.* However, these two terms are not synonymous. For example, people sometimes refer to data that has a degree of structure but is not tabular, such as nested JSON, as structured data. Structured data, also encompasses relational data, time series data, graph data, and spatial data, any of which might also be represented in tabular form. To avoid any confusion, we will use the term *tabular data* exclusively in this book.

Now that we have established what tabular data is, what isn't tabular data? This is an important question because the differences between tabular data and nontabular data help explain one of the key questions answered in this book: Are there situations where you should use deep learning with tabular data? The following are some examples of data that is not tabular:

- Images
- Videos
- Audio
- Text
- Sensor data in JSON format, such as data generated by Internet of Things devices
- Social media streaming data

Can you think of one thing all these nontabular data types have in common? If you answered, "They have all been very successfully used to train deep learning models," you would be absolutely right. Indeed, in the last 10 years, one groundbreaking model after another has been created using various nontabular datasets. In this book, we'll explore why deep learning hasn't set the world of tabular data on fire in the same way and under what circumstances it makes sense to apply deep learning to tabular data.

1.2 *The world runs on tabular data*

According to the article "Structured vs Unstructured Data" (https://mng.bz/5g7Z), up to 90% of all the digital data in the world is nontabular, and the proportion that is nontabular is increasing every year. If this is true, then why read a book about applying machine learning methods to tabular data? While it's probably true that only a small portion of the world's data is tabular, this portion is absolutely essential. Every bank, every insurance company, every government agency, every retailer, every manufacturer—all of them run their core activities on tabular data. Such predominance is dictated, first, because its format as a table arranged in rows and columns makes tabular data easy to input, retrieve, manage, and analyze. Second, tabular data is supported by many business software and applications, such as spreadsheets, databases, and business intelligence tools.

In addition to their core activities, these organizations depend on tabular data to monitor their progress and detect problems. As you live a modern life as a consumer, an employee, and a citizen, your daily activities generate updates in hundreds, even thousands, of tables.

For three years, one of the authors of this book had the privilege of running the worldwide support function for one of the largest relational database products in the world. Around the clock, seven days a week, this job exposed the width and breadth of organizations that ran on tabular data. It also exposed what happens when the tabular data systems fail. Shoppers across an entire continent couldn't use their credit cards, trucks were backed up for miles at the border, freight trains stopped running, retail websites crashed on Black Friday, and factories creating artificial hearts ground to a halt. It is no exaggeration—the world runs on tabular data and on structured data in general.

Tabular data is everywhere, and it is critically important. For many of us, our jobs revolve around tabular data. Because of this, understanding how to efficiently apply machine learning (and, where appropriate, deep learning) to tabular data is a very useful skill. In this book, you will learn techniques to unlock the potential of tabular data.

1.3 *Machine learning vs. deep learning*

Both deep learning and classical machine learning methods aim to map input data to a prediction. However, they take different approaches, as deep learning methods have been designed to mimic the behavior of a biological brain, whereas other machine learning techniques are often based on statistical optimizations or similarity comparisons. However, apart from the different approaches taken, they also imply a profoundly different way to make good use of data.

In classical machine learning approaches, feature transformation and engineering are king because, no matter the model you adopt, you will always need to apply appropriate transformations to your data based on data characteristics and the knowledge domain the data comes from (Is it business data? Does it represent any social, economic, or physical phenomena?). The following are some reasons why feature engineering is so essential in classical machine learning:

- *Relevant information extraction*—Not all raw data is equally relevant for a specific task. Feature engineering helps identify and extract the most informative aspects of the data, discarding irrelevant or noisy parts. By focusing on the relevant features, the model can concentrate on learning the essential patterns, leading to better generalization and improved performance.
- *Data representation*—Different models have different requirements in terms of data representation. Feature engineering allows you to convert the data into a suitable format that fits the model's assumptions and limitations. This step guarantees that the model can learn effectively from the data and make accurate predictions.
- *Addressing nonlinearity*—In many real-world problems, the relationships between the features and the target variable may not be linear. Feature engineering can help transform the data to address nonlinearities, making it easier for linear models to approximate complex relationships.
- *Domain-specific knowledge*—In some cases, domain experts may have valuable insights about the data that can be used to engineer relevant features. Incorporating domain knowledge can significantly improve the model's performance in specific applications.

On the other hand, deep learning approaches rely on *representation learning*, which is their ability to internally and automatically process the data into a meaningful form for solving the problem at hand. Representation learning capabilities of deep learning models allow them to transform the data into a more compact and meaningful format that captures relevant features and patterns for a specific task. In fact, during the learning process, thanks to the fact that all input features interact in a nonlinear way with the others, deep learning models discover by themselves intricate patterns and dependencies in the data that may not be apparent through manual feature engineering, and they manage to develop hierarchical representations of the input data, starting from basic features and gradually building up to more complex and abstract ones.

Therefore, classical machine learning primarily centers on thorough and effective feature engineering, whereas deep learning models for tabular data are much more focused on the architecture of the arrangement of the layers of neurons and on the characteristics of individual neurons. This dichotomy constitutes a fundamental aspect of our book: upcoming chapters not only emphasize the distinction between classical machine learning and deep learning models but also introduce different ways to frame data problems and find solutions based on this distinction.

While it may not be completely orthodox to simplify the terminology in such a way, throughout the book, we use the generic term *machine learning* or *classical machine learning* for all the machine learning approaches but neural networks and use *deep learning* for neural network-based approaches.

We will cover basic and more advanced machine learning models based on popular packages such as

- Basic machine learning models available in Scikit-learn (https://scikit-learn .org/) and in GPU-specialized libraries [such as NVIDIA Rapids (https:// developer.nvidia.com/rapids)]:
  - Linear regression
  - Logistic regression
  - Generalized linear models
- Some tree-based methods available in Scikit-learn are
  - Bagging ensembles of weak predictors
  - Random forest
  - Extremely randomized trees
- Histogram-based gradient-boosted approaches, including
  - XGBoost eXtreme Gradient Boosting (https://github.com/dmlc/xgboost)
  - Microsoft's LightGBM (https://github.com/Microsoft/LightGBM)
  - HistGradientBoosting from Scikit-learn

For deep learning, we will cover a range of architectures that are effective with tabular data implemented in TensorFlow or PyTorch deep learning frameworks:

- Shallow networks with categorical embeddings (directly implemented using one of the available deep learning frameworks)
- fastai tabular (https://docs.fast.ai/tabular.model.html)
- PyTorch Tabular (https://github.com/manujosephv/pytorch_tabular)
- TabNet (https://arxiv.org/abs/1908.07442)
- SAINT (https://arxiv.org/abs/2106.01342)
- DeepTables (https://github.com/DataCanvasIO/deeptables)

You will see this distinction between machine learning and deep learning throughout this book as we explore both approaches and advise when to use each approach to solve tabular data problems.

1.4   *What makes tabular data different?*

We know that deep learning approaches dominate solving problems involving many types of data that we could define as "nontabular" or "unstructured" because of their great variety of characteristics, sizes, and modalities that you cannot constrain in a rows/columns data model. Typical examples of unstructured data that have been successfully tackled by deep learning are

- Audio
- Video
- Images
- Text

Here, contrary to structured tabular data problems, you don't have anything near the typical matrix-shaped format but different files or instances containing a multitude of information in an unordered way. Before deep learning revolutionized the way unstructured data is modeled, unstructured data that we wanted to use for a predictive model had to be brought back into a structured data format by carefully creating well-defined and specific features (a procedure called feature engineering). For each type of unstructured data problem, researchers and practitioners took years to find the best features to be extracted from the data to feed a machine learning model and then obtain satisfactory predictive results.

Thanks to their representational power, deep learning models can handle all the necessary transformations to turn unstructured data into a viable prediction, in an end-to-end fashion, directly from input to solution. Given this background, you might expect deep learning models to be even more effective on tabular data, but this has not been the case up to now.

There are, in truth, various reasons that can explain the challenge that deep learning faces with tabular data problems. The first reason involves the actual directions of academic research and private investment in new technologies and methodologies. As we mentioned, in the past, researchers spent time and effort finding the best way to turn unstructured data into structured data to fit the machine learning paradigm of the time. Nowadays, the same efforts are spent on advancing deep learning, concentrating particularly on unstructured data because it is more easily available in public repositories and more "uniform" than tabular data, thus bringing more research success.

Image repositories such as ImageNet (https://image-net.org/index.php) and open text corpora such as Wikipedia or the Common Crawl's web archive (https://commoncrawl.org/) are easily available to both academic researchers and practitioners to train or refine their deep learning models. As for tabular data, there is no equivalent in terms of a common open-source data repository. On the contrary, tabular data is dispersed into a multitude of private databases, each one showing an even higher degree of variability than unstructured data because each database has its own data collection rules and structure of features.

In addition to the fact that open-source tabular datasets representing real-world business problems are generally harder to find, you must also consider a second reason. Open-source tabular datasets are usually smaller in size and often quite different from the data that is owned privately by businesses and governments. Consequently, the lack of data usually causes neural networks to underperform. In addition, there is no golden rule to benchmark one's progress because using a particular kind of data is limited to a specific problem in the vast domain of tabular data problems. For any researcher, it is much more challenging to generalize best practices starting from a tabular dataset, or even a limited choice of them, than to do the same using images, audio, or texts that are universally available and accepted as a reference benchmark.

Being difficult to access and extremely varied in the type of information they contain, tabular datasets present a further limitation for deep learning solutions: you cannot think of any pretrained solutions because you cannot get a hold of all the kinds of tabular problems. Once you develop a deep learning model for images and text problems, you can make it available to the public and expect other academics or practitioners to find it useful for their problem after tweaking it a bit. This is technically called *transfer learning* because you can successfully apply, with a limited additional modeling effort, the deep learning network trained on a problem to another similar task. Such an opportunity has strongly driven the diffusion of deep learning models in their pretrained form in recent years.

In conclusion, the lack of generalizable tabular examples, a great variety of kinds of tabular data, and more attention from academics on unstructured data have led to feature engineering playing a different role between machine learning and deep learning:

- In machine learning, feature engineering can yield much more predictive power for tabular data than algorithms themselves, and it is commonly regarded more as an art than a science.
- In deep learning, on the contrary, academics and practitioners tend to rely too much on representation learning and let the network deal with everything instead of using feature engineering themselves and demonstrating how deep learning, given the same data framework as a machine learning algorithm, can learn a solution in a different and useful way.

Truly, as demonstrated by recent studies, tabular data characteristics such as redundant features, skewed distributions, and irregular patterns of the prediction target pose a challenge to neural networks. We will discuss this in more detail in chapter 5, when dealing specifically with the gradient boosting models. All the same, we assert that both machine learning and deep learning models are viable ways to solve tabular data problems, and deep learning will grow in importance as practitioners and researchers put more effort into testing architectures and solutions on more realistic tabular data than those that are easily available today.

1.5   *Generative AI and tabular data*

Generative AI—in particular, large language models (LLMs)—are capable assistants in various tasks related to text production and processing. Generally speaking, LLMs have proven to be a breakthrough solution for a certain range of tasks, such as

- *Generation*—Generate text such as the next token, words to complete a phrase, up to generate a text from an instructional prompt
- *Extraction*—Named entity recognition, sentence segmentation, keyword extraction, topic modeling, named entity recognition, semantic relationship extraction
- *Classification*—Language, intention, sentiment, semantics, and even tricky problems such as sarcasm, irony, negation
- *Transformation* of the text—Translations, corrections, style modifications, paraphrasing, summarization

- *Comprehension*—Leading to question and answering, reasoning, knowledge completion

Many of these tasks can extend to the work of a data scientist or a data engineer. LLMs can support the user in activities such as feature engineering, coding functions, and visualization instructions (for instance, using commands from the matplotlib package), providing analytical advice, helping interpret results, and presenting them synthetically for charts and reports. One notable practical application of LLMs in tabular data is automating textual data-related tasks. When dealing with textual variable fields, they can engineer new features by summarizing, categorizing, and identifying key themes. They can also develop the code to process the same text in Python, for instance, by creating functions or figuring out the correct regular expression for text processing.

Besides supporting the user and being a useful assistant, LLMs can also play a more direct and active role in analytics. Recent applications for ChatGPT (the Advanced Data Analytics API) also provide direct data analysis in CSV format, followed by other data-related tasks, including summarization, preprocessing, analysis, visualization, and report generation. At each step, the tool can provide the Python code to execute and obtain the same results, it runs the code for you and provides some visualizations in charts and tables. This aligns with the expected capabilities for TableGPT or other tools such as MediTab. TableGPT (https://arxiv.org/pdf/2307.08674.pdf) is a new framework that utilizes LLMs to enhance human interaction with tabular data. It enables users to interact with tables using commands expressed in natural language and perform various tasks such as question answering, data manipulation, data visualization, report generation, and automated prediction. MediTab (https://arxiv.org/pdf/2305.12081 .pdf), instead, works on medical tabular data by consolidating tabular samples, aligning out-domain data with the target task, and expanding the training data. Faced with prediction tasks based on textual data, it even demonstrated performances superior to classical machine learning algorithms such as XGBoost.

Generally speaking, LLMs do not offer comparable performance in prediction tasks on tabular data, as demonstrated by the TABLET benchmark (https://arxiv.org/ pdf/2304.13188.pdf). In assessing LLMs' performance relative to fully supervised models, the paper compared Flan-T5 11b and ChatGPT using 4-shot examples compared with XGBoost trained on the entire dataset. The XGBoost model, when applied to all the data, achieved an average F1 score of 0.94 on the prediction tasks. In contrast, ChatGPT averaged a score of 0.68, and Flan-T5 11b achieved a score of 0.66 using the F1 score. This analysis highlights that there is still a significant margin for improvement in predictive tasks for LLMs involving tabular data with multimodal types (text and numbers) and that such tools continue to excel in executing instructions, particularly when working with textual inputs and producing textual outputs. A tool such as llm-classifier (https://github.com/lamini-ai/llm-classifier) works and surprises because it can use the information already contained in the used LLM but cannot acquire much additional information typical of tabular problems.

In sum, generative AI is not yet the solution when dealing with tabular data, not only due to performance reasons but also for other crucial aspects, such as

- *Cost*—Generative AI models often require intensive GPU resources, leading to higher operational costs.
- *Scalability*—The resource-intensive nature of generative AI models, particularly their reliance on GPUs, can hinder scalability.
- *Latency and throughput*—Larger models tend to increase processing time per request, affecting latency and throughput.
- *Bias*—Generative AI models may inherit biases from the data they were trained on, potentially perpetuating or amplifying existing biases.
- *Flexibility*—Adapting generative AI models to custom tasks often necessitates extensive retraining, limiting their flexibility.
- *Determinism*—The inherent complexity of generative AI models can make it challenging to control and predict their output, affecting determinism.
- *Explainability*—The complexity of generative AI models can hinder explainability, making it difficult to understand how they operate and produce results.

Acknowledging such present limitations for generative AI to handle tabular data problems, we will focus on the core classical machine learning and deep learning techniques for learning from tabular data and on how to prepare this data for analysis correctly and properly. However, we will also reserve some space to deal with generative AI tools such as ChatGPT, Google Gemini, and Gemini for Google Cloud because we recognize generative AI's transformative force in the tabular data field. Based on our experience in the field, we do not foresee any replacement by LLMs or other generative tools of the classical machine learning algorithms or the deep learning architecture specialized in tabular data because of the advantages that such consolidated tools offer, both in terms of performance and control. Instead, we recognize how LLMs and other generative AI models can support and enhance tabular data processing, analysis, and modeling, helping practitioners become more proficient and performative in their tabular data projects.

Summary

- Tabular data is data organized in rows and columns, such as data in CSV files or relational database tables.
- Structured data is sometimes used as an alternative term for tabular data, but it is a broader concept, including JSON formatted data.
- Tabular data makes up a small portion of all the digital data in the world, but it has an enormous effect on our lives.
- Compared to other types of data (e.g., images, video, text, audio), the type of data that most jobs revolve around is tabular data, so learning how to efficiently

apply machine learning/deep learning to tabular data is a useful skill that many people can apply to their jobs.

- In this book, we simply refer to machine learning approaches excluding neural networks (going from linear regressions to gradient boosting methods) as *classical machine learning* or just *machine learning* to distinguish them from deep learning.

- Compared to deep learning with other types of data (e.g., images, video, text, audio), deep learning with tabular data gets little attention from academic researchers.

- Conventional wisdom is to use a gradient boosting approach like XGBoost with tabular data.

- There's a lively debate in social media about whether or not there is a place for deep learning in solving problems involving tabular data. In this book, we don't pick a side in this debate. Instead, we try to objectively describe why you would use machine learning or deep learning for a given tabular data problem and the best practices to use for each approach.

- Tabular data has some unique characteristics not shared by other types of data, such as images, video, or text. These characteristics include a lack of large open-source datasets that represent the kinds of tabular datasets that you would see in real-world business problems.

- Generative AI, especially LLMs, significantly affects how AI is perceived, diffused across individuals and organizations, and utilized. LLMs can help automate various tasks related to tabular data analysis and modeling, especially when related to textual inputs and outputs.

Exploring
tabular datasets

2

This chapter covers

- Row and column characteristics in a tabular dataset
- Possible pathologies and remedies for tabular datasets
- Finding tabular data externally on the internet and internally in organizations
- Exploring data to solve common problems in tabular data

Tabular data may consist of practically anything—from low-level scientific research to consumer behavior on a website to the statistics in your fantasy sports league. In the end, though, the commonalities in tabular data prevail over differences, and you can achieve most of your data analysis job just by applying standard approaches and tools even without a lot of domain expertise.

In this chapter, we'll look at how to gather and prepare tabular datasets. We'll also take on a practical data analysis exploration that shows the steps you can take to look at data from different viewpoints: by rows, by columns, under the light of the relationship between features, and considering their overall distribution in the dataset. For that example, we will use a simple toy dataset, the Auto MPG Data Set, a dataset freely available on the UCI Machine Learning website (https://archive.ics.uci.edu/dataset/9/auto+mpg).

2.1 *Row and column characteristics*

Depending on the domain, it is incredible how much variety you will find in tabular data. That is because tabular data is the rule, not the exception, in the world of data, and that has been true since the very beginning. Tabular data has been collected for thousands of years into tables and records, from grain accounting in ancient Egypt to parish births, weddings, and deaths in medieval Europe, up to our days in modern national countries and their bureaucracies. It wasn't until the 1960s that we began collecting data in computerized databases, which gave the term *tabular* a more electronic connotation. The widespread adoption of relational databases since the 1970s has popularized tabular data, making it ubiquitous and used for every possible application. In relational databases, data tables can be combined by the values of specific columns acting as joining keys. Such an innovation allowed computers to store more information in less disk space, guaranteeing the technology's success and widespread diffusion.

You can look at open data repositories or data science competitions, such as Kaggle, which routinely feature tabular data competitions to give you an idea of the current sheer variety of tabular data. For instance, in the last two years, Kaggle organized the Tabular Playground Series (https://mng.bz/pK2z), a series of competitions inspired by most common machine learning problems involving tabular datasets and using synthetic data devised by generative AI, as we will discuss more later in the chapter. Although the Tabular Playground competitions use generated data, the examples and the original data they took inspiration from are selected from real-world examples such as

- Probability and amount of insurance claims
- Loan defaults in the banking sector
- Product testing
- E-commerce sales
- Environment sensor data
- Biological and genomic data
- Ecological measurements

However, despite the variety of real-world applications and underlying knowledge domains, every tabular dataset shares the same structure of a matrix of rows and columns with values in numeric, time or dates, and textual forms. Such applies to all tabular datasets, regardless of their features. While domain knowledge is essential for devising optimal feature engineering for predictive algorithms, the basic structure of tabular data remains consistent across all domains. Such universality justifies the need for a book on tabular data, as examples and techniques can be easily transferred between domains.

Diving deeper into details, in a data table, also called a dataset, you have rows of values, and each row represents a unit of your analysis, which, in statistical terms, can be mentioned as a statistical unit or an observation. If you are analyzing DNA samples, for example, each row in your table represents a sample. If you are analyzing industrial products, each row will be a product. The principle is the same, and the nature of the represented units can significantly vary.

2.1.1   *The ideal criteria for tabular rows*

The only limit to remember for rows in a tabular dataset is that examples should be independent unless you are working with time predictions (time series analysis) or other time-related problems. That's the IID principle that you may have heard about before. IID is an acronym for "independent and identically distributed," meaning that your samples should have been drawn independently, where each drawing doesn't influence or carry information of the subsequent ones. Identically, that means that you always draw in the same way from the same data distribution.

Let's consider a simple example of IID: a coin flip. Each time we flip a coin, the outcome is independent of all the previous flips, and the probability of getting heads or tails is the same for each flip. In other words, the coin flips are identically distributed, according to Bernoulli distribution. If we were to generate a dataset by flipping the same coin repeatedly, the resulting data would be IID. The property of being identically distributed allows us to simplify the modeling and analysis of the data. For example, it allows us to randomly sample the data when creating cross-validation folds. It allows us to assume that predictive algorithms will not memorize and replicate the order of the data presented. Typical examples of non-IID are sales data from multiple stores, where sales from the same store tend to be very correlated and not necessarily with other stores' dynamics or school survey data, where each class presents similar characteristics due to shared interests or experiences, introducing non-IID characteristics into the data. In these instances, the data exhibits distinctive characteristics that deviate from the assumption of independence and identical distribution because the samples derive from specific groups (stores or school classes), but similar situations also arise when the data is hierarchically organized, when you deal with repeated measures when you basically measure the same example multiple times with different but correlated results, or when there is any temporal dependency, typical of time series, where being non-IID is not a problem.

In figure 2.1, we compare how non-IID and IID situations differ when you compare distributions as a plotted series. You can observe an IID behavior in a feature on the left panel. It is based on randomly combining dice rolls with coin flips. On the right panel, you can examine a non-IID behavior: just notice the jump appearing after a certain number of samples, implying something changed in how the distribution was generated or in how you sampled its values.

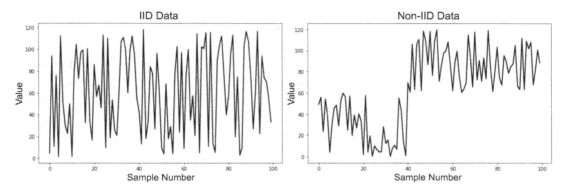

Figure 2.1 **Comparison of IID and non–IID data sequences. The left chart shows IID data, while the right chart illustrates non-IID data, highlighting the sequential correlation patterns.**

Even if we don't know about the details of the distribution we are drawing from, which can be safely imagined as the result of some kind of unknown process, to have IID data, we should always be picking examples with no relation to each other and examples we presume are derived from the same situation or process. Non-IID data can affect your analysis in different ways. In particular, it can affect

- *Bootstrapping*, which is sampling with repetition from a sample until we obtain a new sample of the same size as the original, and *subsampling*, which is sampling without repetition from a sample until obtaining a new sample of the desired size. Both sampling procedures are affected because you may oversample or distort certain data signals, and dependency structures will be messed up. We will return to such sampling procedures because some learning algorithms discussed in chapter 4 use bootstrapping or subsampling.
- *How your model learns*, because it can pick unwanted relationships among the samples that won't be helpful at prediction time when test samples will be different from training one and not related to them. For instance, all learning algorithms based on stochasitc gradient descent (SDG) and mini-batch gradient descent, including deep learning, are affected by the order you present the samples to the algorithm. Consider how non-IID data, which has an intrinsic, hidden order, may affect the results from similar algorithms.
- *Cross-validation*, which is the most efficient testing method for validating your machine learning models and may provide inflated estimates when data is non-IID, because your algorithm may learn to cluster cases based on their relationship specifically in the training set.

Data that is not IID can be detected based on analysis of the data generation process and exploration because

- In non-IID data, each sample is likely to exhibit some form of association with at least one other sample found within the same dataset. This often occurs because you are thinking of analyzing different units, but the units are the same. For instance, in medical analysis, you may be analyzing multiple medical records and thinking that your unit of analysis is the records themselves, which are distinct. In reality, you are analyzing the health data from the same patients at different times: the actual analysis units should be the patients, not the records. A very similar situation happened to the team of Prof. Andrew Ng (see https://mng.bz/OBGE for details) when they prepared the data for a paper by using a dataset of 100,000 x-rays from 30,000 patients, and, as they split it separating training and test data, they didn't consider how the x-rays of the same patient could end up a part in the training set and a part in the test set, hence inflating all the results and distorting all the insights derived from the analysis.

- The measures in your data represent heterogeneous distributions. This typically happens with the passage of time and its consequent changes that reflect on the data at many levels. For instance, when analyzing the balance sheets of different companies, it is important to note that even if the companies are distinct, they may not represent the same distribution if they are from different years. This is because the macroeconomic situation is mutable and can change the characteristics of the companies and their sectors over time (i.e., the characteristics of the distribution you want to represent).

Since every analysis is based on some expected distribution assumptions, data being IID is paramount for proper estimates in statistics and regression analysis. In machine learning, even if the methods are data-driven and nonparametric, IID data is strongly recommended, though, in practice, it is hardly found in real-world datasets. One fundamental limit of machine learning algorithms is that they are aware of the relations between features and the target but cannot figure out the relations between the rows. Machine learning algorithms are column-aware but not row-aware. Hence, it is necessary to adequately provide supplemental features to support the work of machine learning algorithms. Therefore, if two features are correlated, the algorithm will expect such correlation to derive from their relationship, independent of the interference of other features, not because of time or because of another hidden feature that affected the sampling. In other words, when data is not IID, the learning algorithm will learn patterns based on time or relationship among samples as if they were some kind of feature-based relationship.

Times series and every kind of longitudinal data representing phenomena over time are typically not IID. In time series, each observation is autocorrelated, meaning that each target value is correlated with the previous ones, as well as the features, called covariates in statistics, that can explain the target. Given your business data problem and how you collect or assemble the data, you must know how time affects your observations and try to control its effect using time-based features. Thanks to time-based features, your model can determine how time affects the values of the other features and your target. Usually, a time feature and lagged features based on time will solve the situation. Essentially, you can have two scenarios here:

- Each row has a date or a time interval. You can use it as a feature after appropriate transformation—for instance, converting dates to Unix time, a continuous numeric feature. In such a case, you are running a time series analysis and need to use proper cross-validation strategies for time series.

- You pivot multiple rows related to different times, creating time-based features. For instance, you can have the value of a feature at different moments in time and create a separate feature for each of such moments (such as sales_month_1, sales_month_2, and so on). In this case, you just fall back to having IID data and can proceed to analyze without much more formality.

Cross-sectional data, typically in tabular form, may not be naturally IID even when drawn from the same period. This is because interactions among the analysis units and their membership in specific groups can create subtle dependencies between observations, often called "leakage" of information. This leakage can cause unexpected transmission of predictive information from features to the target during training, and it probably won't work the same way during prediction when the represented situations are different. To address this problem, it is necessary to create features that explicitly capture the different memberships between rows and their relationships. For instance, if you are working with data from different companies, failing to provide information about their country of origin or operations, as well as their sector, may create a leakage for your machine learning algorithm that could learn and exploit implicit orderings in the data that won't be replicable at prediction time. In addition, even if you can label the examples in your training data with their correct group, if you cannot replicate the same in your test data, it is important to segregate the groups in cross-validation so that each group appears only in the training or validation folds. Failure to do so can cause inflated prediction cross-validation estimates because the machine learning algorithm can exploit autocorrelation within groups.

When cross-sectional data is used to compare different time periods, the data may not be independent even if the interactions among units and groups are absent. In this case, the order of observations matters, and we need to consider the time series dependencies between the observations. This means that the data is non-IID, and the usual assumptions of independence may not hold. To deal with this situation, we can use time series models to handle the temporal dependencies between observations. Time series models consider that observations taken at different points in time are likely to be correlated, and they can use this correlation to make better predictions. Using appropriate time series models and techniques, we can obtain accurate predictions even when dealing with non-IID data.

As a final general suggestion about how to prepare your data from the point of view of rows, consider the following:

- Verify how time affects your data. Consider using time features and modeling time in your analysis, using lags and moving averages, as customary in time series analysis, to control changes due to time alone.

- Be aware of what you represent in rows because groups and relationships among them can affect your model results in training, validation, and testing.

- If hidden groups exist in your data, explicitly represent any grouping variable in a feature.

- In cross-validation, if your data contains groups, just prefer group cross-validation so they are never split between training and validation folds (https://mng.bz/YDgA).

- If time is a determinant in your model, use time-based validation (https://mng.bz/GeGO).

In the next section, we discuss the ideal criteria that should characterize tabular columns and what each data type implies regarding data processing.

2.1.2   *The ideal criteria for tabular columns*

If the sampling of the cases, arranged in rows, presents some challenges, remember it is in the columns of your data table, which are also called the features, that most information resides and where most of your attention should focus next. A column is characterized by carrying homogeneous information related to its represented rows. For instance, if you are building a real estate evaluation dataset and your rows represent houses, columns may be related to the house's surface area (i.e., how many square meters and market evaluation expressed by a recent sale price). By being homogeneous, you can expect that each of these columns will carry only the information it is designated to. For instance, you shouldn't find sale prices or other information in the surface column. In addition, you should also expect that the column values are uniquely related to the unit that is represented by each row.

Before delving into data structures suitable for handling a dataset of rows and columns, however, you need to first recognize the five types of data that can populate columns and the best way to handle each of them (see table 2.1).

Table 2.1   Types of data in a tabular dataset

Type	Description
Numeric features	Integers for count data, such as when enumerating sales by day for a product: [105, 122, 91, ... 124]
	Floats for measurements, such as when enumerating sales income by day for a product: [1000.50, 1230.00, 950.80, ..., 1200.00]
Ordinal features	Integers (or floats without decimals) for rankings or ordered levels: [0, 1, 2, 3, ..., 999]
	Sometimes ordinal features can be verbally expressed by strings underling some ordered effect such as with Likert-like agreement or preference scales: ["strongly disagree," "disagree," "neither agree nor disagree," "agree," "strongly agree"]

Table 2.1   Types of data in a tabular dataset (*continued*)

Type	Description
Low categorical features	Since they express a quality, they can be a string (called "labels") or integers associated with the original labels; in that case you have a conversion dictionary available: {0: "red," 1:"green," 2: "blue"}
High categorical features	The same as low categorical features but with a large number of label (e.g., US area codes or zip codes: https://postal-codes.net/united-states)
Dates	They can be a string or already encoded in data formats such as "2022-03-04", "Feb 15, 1957 11:45 PM" or "6/12/2022" (there are many date standards and conventions)

Knowing each of them is the basic step in building a dataset and properly processing data to be fed into a machine learning algorithm. Each algorithm will require each type of data to be specially prepared for its best understanding and consequent predictive performance.

You have *numeric features* when your data is expressed by a floating number or an integer representing a counting of some value. Accordingly to statistics, features represented as floating numbers are often distinguished into ratio or interval scales. The distinction is that ratio scales, representing a measurement of something real, like unit sales or money, have an absolute real zero and are only positive. Interval scales are instead abstract or arbitrary measurements; their units can represent anything. In interval scales, the zero value is arbitrary, and the values can be negative. For instance, interval scales are the measure of temperature in Fahrenheit or Celsius degrees. You can turn a ratio scale into an interval one by simple transformations like subtracting the mean, which is a centering operation, and dividing by the standard deviation, which is a standardization operation. In such a fashion, you make the zero value, as well as the scale, arbitrary.

Integer numbers, when the feature is a numeric one, are only ratio scales. However, integers can also be used for ordinal and even categorical features. If you need more clarification about the meaning of a numeric feature expressed in integers, start checking if the numbers are not continuous and if there are many distinct values. When such conditions are satisfied, you can be almost confident that you are dealing with a numeric feature. Numeric features don't need much processing, and for machine learning purposes, you won't care much if they are ratio or interval scale. All you must consider is that they represent a single kind of measurement. For instance, if you are measuring monetary values in your dataset, you cannot create a column representing dollars, euros, and pounds together: for your numeric feature to be usable, you need one measurement type for each column. Also, you need to ascertain that you don't have too many missing numbers in your numeric features and that their values vary enough to be useful. You should avoid low variance or constant features in your data.

Ordinal features are always made up of integers, usually representing rankings and ratings or scores. For instance, as an example of an ordinal feature, just think of the ratings in terms of stars for products sold on e-commerce platforms. Being numbers, ordinal features are pretty similar to numeric values, yet they require different treatment, and you cannot work with them in exactly the same way. First, if numeric values are a scale where each value is equidistant to the next and previous ones, there is no guarantee that the distance between the value points is always constant in an ordinal scale. For instance, as in a long-distance running competition, first and second place may differ by a few seconds. However, a second place and a third place may differ by many minutes.

In the same way, in an ordinal scale representing some underlying numeric measure, some adjacent points can be numerically very near to each other, and others may be numerically very distant. An ordinal scale just tells you about an order, which means that a value comes before the next one and after the previous one. Hence, without making a significant approximation, you cannot process it as if it were purely numeric, for instance, by computing mean and standard deviation. From a certain point of view, you can consider ordinals as categorical features with meaningful ordering.

Categoricals are features constituted by labels: each unique value in a categorical feature represents a quality referred to in the example. We can find these labels expressed as strings, in this case, we are unequivocally working with a categorical feature, or as integer numbers, and in this case, we shouldn't mistake it for an ordinal. Even the missing value can be treated as a label among the others. Hence, missing values are more easily dealt with in categorical features. We distinguish between *low cardinality* and *high cardinality* categorical features based on the number of unique values found in the column. The distinction is helpful because high cardinality categorical features are challenging to handle for deep learning and machine learning algorithms and require a more complex treatment than low cardinality ones. No clear threshold exists for classifying a categorical as low or high cardinality. However, having more than a dozen unique values usually poses a challenging time for the analyst. Throughout the book, we will discuss specialized strategies to handle categorical features called encodings. For the moment, just keep in mind a special type of categorical feature—one with a single label and values representing the presence or absence of the label, usually 0 for the absence and 1 for the presence of the quality. Such features are called binary features or, using a more statistical term, dichotomous variables.

Dates are very commonly found in many business data and databases since time is essential information to be monitored for a business to work its processes and resources properly. Dates also vary a lot since several date formats depend on the country, type of business application, or adoption of particular standards. For this reason, some efforts have been made to standardize the dates—for instance, proposing the ISO 8601 standard (https://mng.bz/zZQQ), but we are still far from having a common standard. It is essential to know that dates may be reported as columns as they are already processed for better clarity into separated columns containing their cyclical components, which are days, months, hours, days of the week, and noncyclical ones—for instance, years. They can also be transformed into a numeric continuous value representing the flow of time; Unix time is the best example, representing the number of seconds that have elapsed since 00:00:00 UTC on January 1, 1970, excluding leap seconds. Finally, dates require some understanding of used conventions for treating missing information because, in certain applications, it is customary to avoid void or null values and instead prefer applying a date far in the past or future to represent that the time value is missing or unknown.

2.1.3 *Representing rows and columns*

When organizing a tabular dataset, it is important to ensure that each row is identifiable and uses appropriate data types for numeric, ordinal, categorical, and date values, which may include float, integer, string, datetime, and sometimes even boolean for binary features. To handle this mix of data types efficiently, the pandas DataFrame is the best data structure available in Python. It is an ordered collection of columns that provides a flexible and efficient way to manage and manipulate tabular data. You can learn more about the pandas DataFrame at https://mng.bz/0Qw6.

In listing 2.1, we create a small tabular dataset from scratch with four rows, representing four individuals, and four columns, representing numeric and categorical features that characterize them, using a data dictionary. We also define a list containing their names to be used as a reference for accessing their information. We then use pandas to convert the dictionary to a DataFrame, a two-dimensional table-like data structure, and assign the labels.

Listing 2.1 Creating a simple tabular dataset

```
import pandas as pd
data = {'gender': ['male', 'female', 'male', 'female'],
        'age': [25, 30, 27, 29],
        'education_level': ['Bachelor', 'Master', 'Bachelor', 'PhD'],
        'income': [50000, 60000, 55000, 70000]}          Creates a dictionary of data
index = [ 'Bob ', 'Alice', 'Charlie', 'Emily']
df = pd.DataFrame(data, index=index)                     Creates a row index
print(df)
print(df.iloc[1])          Prints row 1               Creates a pandas DataFrame
print(df.loc['Alice'])                                 from the dictionary
                           Prints the row
                           whose label is Alice
```

The output for the print(df) command should look like the following:

```
         gender  age education_level  income
Bob        male   25        Bachelor   50000
Alice    female   30          Master   60000
Charlie    male   27        Bachelor   55000
Emily    female   29             PhD   70000
```

Notice that the rows are labeled with the example names and the columns are labeled with the feature names. You can access both rows and columns by their labels or index numbers, starting from zero. Therefore, we can access Alice's information by both means of its row index, which is 1, or by its name label:

```
gender            female
age                   30
education_level   Master
income             60000
Name: Alice, type: object
```

This is made possible by pandas (https://pandas.pydata.org/), which is a Python package dedicated to data processing that allows you to quickly and smoothly load data from multiple sources; slice it based on columns or rows or on both at the same time (an operation known as *dicing*); handle missing values; add, rename, compute, group, and aggregate features; and pivot, reshape, and finally visualize your processed data. Apart from its super helpful data processing functionalities, it is also particularly renowned because of its data structures, Series, and DataFrames, the most widely used data formats for tabular data operating with Python.

In a pandas DataFrame, apart from the table of data, you also have an index for columns so that you can name them and for rows, helping you in the operations of identification and filtering. In addition, you can efficiently perform selections and various operations, such as combining columns or replacing missing values. Recently, even the popular machine learning package Scikit-learn, which has long accepted pandas DataFrames as input for its algorithms, has taken steps to maintain such data structure along all its pipelines. Now all outputs, instead of being transformed data into Numpy arrays, which are matrices homogeneous by type, can be maintained as pandas DataFrames. For more details about how this works and how it can affect how you use the package, see https://mng.bz/nR54. A de facto standard for tabular data, pandas DataFrames will be extensively used throughout the book, where we will show how to apply more useful transformations for dealing with common tabular data characteristics and problems.

After discussing the ideal characteristics of rows and columns in a tabular dataset, the next section will explore what can go wrong and the implications and remedies.

2.2   *Pathologies and remedies*

As a general rule, you must always strive to avoid certain conditions among your features, no matter what their kind, which we previously briefly mentioned when discussing each type of column you may have in a dataset.

Previous data from data science competitions can help us see what could go wrong with a tabular dataset. Let's take, for instance, the Madelon dataset (https://archive .ics.uci.edu/ml/datasets/Madelon), which is remembered after so many years as a very challenging data problem because of its specific characteristics that made prediction hard. The Madelon dataset is an artificial dataset generated using an ad hoc algorithm developed by Isabel Guyon (https://guyon.chalearn.org/), who joined Google Brain in 2022 as a director. The data has been presented at a contest at the NIPS 2003 conference, the seventh Annual Conference on Neural Information Processing Systems. She placed errors in data in the form of random noise and the target by having a part of the labels flipped. She added redundant and highly collinear features, clustered observations along the vertices of a five-dimension hypercube without providing information, and finally inserted irrelevant information. That made many data scientists strive to wrap their heads around the problem at the time. See https://mng.bz/ga4V for more details about the generative process of the synthetic dataset if you are interested.

More recently, Kaggle competitions such as Don't Overfit (https://www.kaggle.com/competitions/overfitting), Don't Overfit II (https://www.kaggle.com/competitions/dont-overfit-ii), Categorical Feature Encoding Challenge I and II (https://www.kaggle.com/competitions/cat-in-the-dat and https://mng.bz/jpyP), extending the problem to categorical features and missing data, proved that when there are too many problems in data, even the most powerful machine learning algorithms can do very little.

Starting from such practical examples, generally speaking, the conditions you have to care about the most in tabular data are

- Avoiding constant or quasi-constant columns
- Avoiding duplicated or highly collinear columns
- Avoiding irrelevant features and prioritize features that demonstrate high predictive power
- Dealing with rare categories or with far too many labels with categoricals
- Spot incongruencies and misplaced, flipped, or distorted values
- Avoiding too many missing cases in a column and handling existing ones
- Excluding leakage features

Let's go through each of these from a theoretical and practical point of view using some artificial data. More real-world examples and commands for the detection and resolution of such conditions will be illustrated in our example in the paragraph concluding the chapter. It is pretty challenging to present examples for each of them or find a single real-world dataset distributed to the public containing all such bad data examples (actually, such examples are abundant in private repositories). Public datasets are often curated enough to have most of such data traps already expunged.

2.2.1 Constant or quasi-constant columns

Avoid constant or quasi-constant columns. As a rule of thumb, the variance shouldn't approximate zero for numeric features, and the majority class shouldn't be over 99.9% for categorical features. All this is paramount because machine learning algorithms can learn only from how empirical conditional expectations of your target vary with respect to your features. No change in the features implies no conditional change on your target from which to learn. Constant features result in more cumber to be handled by numerical processes behind learning algorithms, and quasi-constant features may even result in some overfitting because the minimal nonconstant part may be deterministically associated with some target output. The solution is to drop constant or quasi-constant columns.

Listing 2.2   Dropping zero variance features

```
import pandas as pd
from sklearn.preprocessing import OrdinalEncoder
from sklearn.feature_selection import VarianceThreshold

data = pd.DataFrame({"feature_1":['A' for i in range(15)],
                     "feature_2":['B' if i%2==0 else 'C'
                                  for i in range(15)],
                     "feature_3":[i**2 for i in range(15)]})
ord_enc = OrdinalEncoder()
data[data.columns] = ord_enc.fit_transform(data)
var_threshold = VarianceThreshold(threshold=0)

clean_data = var_threshold.fit_transform(data)
print(var_threshold.variances_)
print(clean_data.shape)
```

An ordinal encoder will transform your data from string labels to ordered numeric ones.

The VarianceThreshold class will filter all features whose variance is equal to or below the selected threshold.

You can have the variances of all features represented by the .variances_ attribute,

2.2.2   *Duplicated and highly collinear features*

Avoiding duplicated or highly collinear columns is helpful because if information redundancy makes your learning more robust, there are some caveats. Most importantly, it renders learning more complicated and computationally expensive. First, duplicated features are useless as constant ones and should be discarded immediately because they just waste memory space and computation time. The discourse is different for highly collinear ones. No matter whether we are talking about numeric features, where you measure collinearity by correlations, or categorical ones, where you measure collinearity by association measures based on chi-square statistics when a set of features are very strongly associated, it is because

- One is the causative feature of the other. For instance, in a dataset related to academic results, time spent studying and test scores are highly correlated because time spent is one of the determinants of good test scores, as many studies have determined.
- They all reflect a latent feature that causes or influences them. For instance, in a dataset about cars, performance and emissions are partially determined by the type of fuel used. Even if the fuel characteristics are not recorded in the data and their relationship is not apparent, the performance and emissions features will be strongly associated with each other.

In the first situation, the solution is simple because you just have to keep the causative feature and drop all the others. Nothing in the data itself will tell you which is the causative feature, and you basically can figure out which is the one only by domain knowledge, theoretical deductions, or causal analysis, which requires additional modeling and experimentation. The latter case is a bit more sophisticated because, even if you can figure out the causative feature, you don't have it among your data and must decide which feature to keep. Again, domain knowledge can help you make decisions. Data analysis can also contribute with hints based on the association with the target and the data quality of the features at hand, using a mix of fewer errors, fewer missing data, and fewer outliers. Keeping only the feature most associated with the target or the one with the highest quality is the best choice.

Listing 2.3 Finding multicollinear numeric features

> Adds more correlated features to the dataset: we pick the first five features, and we duplicate them at the end of the dataset after having added some noise, so they are not the same as the original ones.

> Creates a synthetic dataset: the make_classification command will create a sample dataset of twenty slightly correlated features (see https://mng.bz/eynQ)

```
import numpy as np
from sklearn.datasets import make_classification
from statsmodels.stats.outliers_influence import variance_inflation_factor

np.random.seed(0)                                        Sets the seed for reproducibility
X, _ = make_classification(n_redundant=0,
                           n_repeated=0,
                           random_state=0)
X = np.hstack([X, X[:,:5] + np.random.random((X.shape[0],5))])

vif = [variance_inflation_factor(X, i) for i in range(X.shape[1])]
print(np.round(vif,2))

for a in range(X.shape[1]):
    for b in range(X.shape[1]):
        if a < b:
            r = np.corrcoef(X[:, a], X[:, b])[0][1]
            if np.abs(r) > 0.90:
                print(f"feature {a} and {b} have r={r:0.3f}")
```

> The threshold to report collinearity is evaluated in absolute value (correlation will be negative if a feature is reversed). In addition, depending on the stage of the analysis, you can set this to 0.90, 0.95, or even 0.99.

> The correlation coefficient is computed using the NumPy function np.corcoef (https://mng.bz/8Olw).

> Checking for correlated features by iterating through a correlation matrix, we compute only the correlation coefficients of the lower triangle of the matrix.

> Computes the variance inflation factor to spot the features that have the least unique contribution

---

In the previous example, we deal with highly collinear numeric features in a synthetic dataset. We use two approaches: the variance inflation factor and the Pearson correlation coefficient. The variance inflation factor (VIF) is a typical analysis preparatory to linear models, a family of models to be discussed in chapter 4, which aims at quantifying how much of a feature informative continent is actually to be found in other features. A VIF is, therefore, more extensive in scope than a correlation coefficient, which is a bivariate analysis, an analysis between two variables at a time. Instead, the VIF tries to pounder the role of a feature with respect to all the others. VIFs are powerful in terms of highlighting potentially less contributing features. Still, they won't reveal what feature is related to others or which must be removed. The higher a VIF's value, which starts from 1 and goes to infinity, the more multicollinear the considered feature. In our example, since higher VIF values indicate a less unique contribution of the feature, we can quickly spot that the first and last five features of the dataset are more problematic:

```
[14.98 13.64 11.85 13.12 15.75  1.2   1.41  1.19  1.46  1.31  1.38  1.3   1.19
  1.24  1.63  1.28  1.45  1.23  1.15  1.16 18.86 16.79 15.39 16.45 17.82]
```

However, you need the following one-by-one comparison by correlation analysis to determine which features you can narrow down the problem. By using a threshold set to 0.99, you will figure out only almost identical features. By setting the bar lower to 0.90 or 0.95, you will reveal features whose unique contribution is minimal:

```
feature 0 and 20 have r=0.966
feature 1 and 21 have r=0.963
feature 2 and 22 have r=0.947
feature 3 and 23 have r=0.958
feature 4 and 24 have r=0.964
```

At this point, it is up to you to evaluate what feature to keep between two highly collinear ones. In any case, even if you have to decide what features to drop based on collinearity, selecting features based on quality is something you always consider to later treat only with useful features. Generally speaking, when facing multiple errors that cannot be corrected, such as recording or measurement errors, a high volume of missing data, and outlying measures, a feature should be kept only if it shows an interesting and unique association with the target.

2.2.3   *Irrelevant features*

The same goes for irrelevant features, which make little sense for your problem and have little or no association with the target. At this stage, you just need to rule out improbable features that you know do not apport any information to your problem based on domain knowledge or simple statistical univariate tests, such as correlation or chi-square analysis, as we will demonstrate in the latter part of this chapter.

Selecting features has been widely used to reduce computing requirements during training, help in having a more interpretable model, and improve predictive performance on test data since irrelevant features create false signals and disturbances to machine learning algorithms, both classic and neural networks. Chapter 6 of this book will discuss feature selection in-depth and present tools suitable for selecting a working subset of your initial features.

We will focus especially on those tools based on testing the behavior of features being reshuffled or randomized (by random replacements of their values). The idea is to build a model for your problem and then shuffle each feature to check if the results change too much and the predictive performances decrease. Features, whose randomization does not affect the model performance, are likely to be irrelevant or carry redundant information available elsewhere among the features. Hence, they can be safely dropped, enhancing memory handling and training/prediction times.

2.2.4 *Missing data*

Missing data is a critical factor that must be considered, as it can affect any data source and pose nuisances for many learning algorithms. Deep learning models and numerous machine learning algorithms cannot handle missing data directly. However, certain specialized machine learning algorithms, such as XGBoost and LightGBM, can reasonably manage missing information without requiring any intervention. These algorithms assume the value that was previously deemed more useful in similar situations when confronted with a missing value. For more information, see https://mng .bz/EaxO.

Apart from these specialized algorithms, missing values are usually addressed through a process known as imputation. This involves using the information present in the same column (simple univariate imputation) or in all other available columns (multivariate imputation) to determine a reasonable replacement value or class. Imputing data by multivariate imputation is sometimes more effective, even for XGBoost and LightGBM algorithms. We will discuss multivariate imputation in more detail in chapter 6 of the book.

Please take notice now that if you are dealing with missing data at the early stages of data preparation, missingness may be a piece of information in itself. For instance, if you work with a relational database query and are left or right joining (or full outer joining) tables, you will produce missing cases when cases don't match. In such a situation, a missing case will mean no match with the conditions expressed in a certain database table, which can be precious information.

In other cases, a missing case will mean something specific relative to how the data has been generated, such as in census data, where you don't get answers relative to income if the answerer is too rich or poor because the necessity of being socially acceptable influences answers. Creating a binary feature indicating if a value is missing can help keep track of such patterns. See the MissingIndicator in the Scikit-learn package for more details on this kind of processing: https://mng.bz/EaxO.

2.2.5 *Rare categories*

On the side of categoricals, dealing with too many labels or rare categories in a feature are two conditions that must be addressed as soon as possible, possibly at extraction time. We have already mentioned high cardinality categorical features in the chapter.

Instead, you have rare categories in the context of categorical variables when specific categories occur infrequently or have very few instances in the dataset.

Rare categories increase the possibility of overfitting at training time and can usually be dealt with by aggregating them, thus forming a larger class. Domain knowledge may guide such aggregations, suggesting similar rare categories to aggregate into larger ones.

When, instead, the problem is that there are way too many categories, the most appropriate solution is target encoding, which is mostly effective for gradient boosting, or using embeddings, which works the best for deep learning approaches. We will discuss how these approaches work and how to effectively implement them in chapters 6 and 7.

2.2.6   *Errors in data*

Spotting incongruencies, misplaced, flipped, or distorted values is instead a topic of its own because fixing such a problem mostly depends on your knowledge of the application domain and the recording procedures for the data you are handling. Many errors may happen when a phenomenon is observed in the real world and recorded in data. Errors can range from inescapable measurement errors because of the instruments and sensors we use to an extensive catalog of possible mismatches, underestimates, and overestimates that will make the recording completely unreliable. More than a single error here and there, you should look for systematic errors. These errors almost always happen in certain situations and bias parts of the information. Knowing the data schema and the meaning of the data you are dealing with is the only reasonable remedy for such problems. It may sound very general and vague advice because it is, in reality, but you can only try to understand your data to the best of your ability and not leave anything for granted. Don't believe that machine learning algorithms are robust and can fix all the errors in the data: systematic errors can limit the ability of your models to generalize and provide reliable predictions.

2.2.7   *Leakage features*

Finally, the last point of concern you should deal with is the presence of leakage features. You have leakage when some predictive information that shouldn't be involved in the model training temporarily inflates results, rendering poor results at subsequent prediction time. Leakage can happen at row and feature levels. We have already discussed row leakage when dealing with non-IID rows, which occurs when some samples are associated with others because of time mediation or the mediation of some other feature. Now it is time to discuss feature-level leakage, which is a more common problem than expected when extracting data from business databases.

The key principle is to ensure temporal consistency in the features used for modeling. Ideally, the features should align with or precede the target variable in time. In the best scenario, no feature should be created or generated after the target variable's own time point. This temporal alignment helps to avoid potential data leakage and ensures that the model is making predictions based on information that would have been available at the time of prediction. You need a model able to predict the present or the future, but you cannot do that if the necessary features you have trained the model on are to be produced at a time point following the prediction itself.

When training, it is easy to break this constraint because you are taking everything from the past, and many information sources used for building your training data may not be properly documented in regard to the creation or modification time. Take, for instance, the example of a business offering loans using a machine learning algorithm. Knowing how late the payments have been may provide a tremendous predictive feature at training time, but reasoning how such a feature would be unavailable when granting the loan or not—since it is a future behavior near to the time the target will be defined—renders it a useless, misleading feature because of future leakage. As a proposed solution for this problem, we suggest closely verifying the generative times for features and targets, if possible, and checking if the target comes after the features or vice versa. Frequently, such information is readily available, depending on how data storage is organized in your company. For instance, your data could have specific metadata showing the date and time when an insertion or an update has happened, or your database administrator has perhaps set up a particular timestamp field to snapshot the moment some changes occur.

In the next section, after discussing ideal conditions in tabular data and what could happen when they are not met, we will get nearer to real-world data by discussing how to find tabular data on the internet and in your organization.

2.3 Finding external and internal data

Suppose you need to find some dataset for a machine learning project. Following the instructions in this section, you are guaranteed to find what you need if it is available and accessible on the internet. In fact, not only has the number and quality of data repositories increased over time, but now we have new search and aggregation tools such as Google Dataset Search and Kaggle Datasets that allow us to specifically detail what we are looking for and obtain a list of results to choose from. But let's start from the beginning.

Finding the data you need always comes after defining the project and its purposes. Whether your objectives are business-related or academic, only after you have framed the goals clearly can you decide what kind of data you need to assemble. It is not linear because you'll usually need to reiterate various times between objectives, data, and available resources. Still, data always comes after having a well-defined purpose and before any engineering, like building a pipeline, which is a sequence of data processing steps from the data repository to where the computations are executed, or any further modeling action. Necessarily, in the middle between provisioning data and processing it, there is the phase of data understanding, which is the concluding topic of our chapter.

Since machine learning models need a target—that is, something to predict such as a number for a regression problem or a class or label for a classification problem—you will first be concerned with finding one or more outputs for your problem. Then, all machine learning models need some other information—a set of predictors or features called predictors—to be used to predict your target outputs. It is a process where you map some data (the predictors) to other data (the outputs). Since without any target you cannot even start your project, whereas, on the other end, you may begin with an incomplete set of predictors and increase them along the way, do always start locating your target first and then be concerned with your predictors.

Finding suitable data for your machine learning models and processing it correctly in the data preparation and data pipelining phases is one of the activities data scientists spend more time and effort on—and actually where they get stuck the most. At this time, you will need to invest efforts in terms of getting the data out of the repositories where it is stored after having understood how it is organized (the data scheme) and how to properly bring it all together into a single dataset in a way that is usable for your project.

2.3.1   *Using pandas to access data stores*

Usually, you can find both the target and the predictors in the same data store, if not in the same table or file. Still, sometimes you may find all parts of your necessary data scattered around and they need to be adequately assembled before any usage. You may find such data inside or outside of your organization. A common scenario when locating data resources within an organization is to find them scattered among Excel files, stored in *normalized form* in a data warehouse (DWH), or left unmanaged in data streams. As for DWH, information is organized into multiple tables to minimize redundancy and improve data integrity, scalability, performance, and ease of maintenance. This condition is called a *normalized schema*, where information has been broken down into smaller, more focused tables containing a single subject area or entity. Typically, in such a situation, you can find three types of tables to be assembled:

- *Event tables (transaction tables or fact tables)* are designed to hold records of specific business events measured at a particular moment. Examples of such events could be an order placed in an e-commerce platform, a credit card transaction in banking, a doctor's visit in healthcare, or a user's clickstream on the internet. These tables can take various forms depending on the type of business and the specific events being tracked.

- *Item tables* (also known as product tables) are a type of table found in a DWH that provides detailed information about specific business products or events. For example, an item table might contain information, such as description, prices, and stock levels, about the individual product items purchased as part of a customer order or the drug prescriptions problems during patient–doctor visits. The purpose of an item table is to provide more in-depth data to be used for analysis and decision-making purposes.

- *Dimension tables* store additional descriptive information to add context to the data in other tables, such as a person's birth date or location or a product's category. When using a dimension table, caution is essential because its information may have been changed or updated over time. Data updating can happen in two ways: by maintaining a history of changes by creating a new record for each modification with an attached date or by simply overwriting old data with new data. In the latter case, you may be using data that can act as noise for your models since its rows are temporally misaligned, or it can leak information from the future, affecting your model's capabilities to predict correctly.

Similarly, when dealing with Excel files, you often encounter scattered and denormalized data. In such cases, as with DWH, you face the challenge of working with similar tables and the identical need to consolidate and assemble them into a coherent structure. For such an assembling task between event tables, item tables, and dimension tables, there are different tools available on the market—some of them even of the no-code type, where you operate without scripting but using icons and point-and-click actions, for instance. Historically, SQL has been the elective tool for programmers to gather and combine multiple data sources. Still, SQL is the best choice today when all your data resides in a relational database. It can help you structure a series of queries and temporary tables until you arrive at a final data table to download or directly feed to a machine learning algorithm. When there are multiple sources and we need to check and visualize intermediate results, however, pandas, our choice in the first place for handling diverse data types, is again the tool we suggest to master. Pandas has a lot of functionalities that mimic and extend those of SQL queries. Selecting, filtering, aggregating, ordering, and processing are as easy on pandas as on a relational database, and they follow the same principles, though sometimes based on different terms. For instance, indexes in DataFrames are assimilable to primary keys in relational databases. In addition, pandas DataFrames present further characteristics that make them more versatile and powerful than SQL for data science tasks:

- An API that is common to other tools makes it easy to switch from pandas, which were created for use on a single CPU, to multiprocessing or distributed computing.
- You can achieve processing and data exploration at the same time. In particular, it is straightforward to plot the data you have prepared, as we will see at the end of this chapter.
- You have more control of all the changes and the necessary manipulation steps that should happen on the data, which also means that it is easier to make an error, allowing you to store away intermediate results and preserve some data characteristics, such as data types and data ordering, which is instead sometimes hard to achieve in SQL.

Let's imagine having three tables in a data warehouse, each containing different information about a company's products. These tables need to be joined to create an analysis or train a machine learning model, as shown in figure 2.2.

The task is a quite simple example that would require a SQL query to return a dataset combining the three of them:

```
SELECT df1.product_id, df1.product_name, df1.price,
df2.product_description, df2.category, df3.manufacturer, df3.weight
FROM df1
JOIN df2 ON df1.product_id = df2.product_id
JOIN df3 ON df1.product_id = df3.product_id;
```

Table df1		
product_id	product_name	price
1	Product A	10.99
2	Product B	20.99
3	Product C	15.99
4	Product D	8.99

Table df2		
product_id	product_description	category
1	A great product	Category A
2	A high-quality product	Category B
3	A reliable product	Category C
4	An affordable product	Category D

Table df3		
product_id	manufacturer	weight
1	Manufacturer A	1.5
2	Manufacturer B	2.0
3	Manufacturer C	1.8
4	Manufacturer D	1.2

Figure 2.2   **Three simple tables describing products' features**

However, the same could be easily achieved in pandas using the merge function, keeping control of the various stages where the data is merged and having it ready for further transformations to render it suitable to machine learning.

Listing 2.4   Merging datasets in pandas

```
import pandas as pd
df1 = pd.DataFrame({'product_id': [1, 2, 3, 4],
                    'product_name': ['Product A',
                                     'Product B',
                                     'Product C',
                                     'Product D'],                    The first
                    'price': [10.99, 20.99, 15.99, 8.99]})           table,
df2 = pd.DataFrame({'product_id': [1, 2, 3, 4],                      containing
                    'product_description': ['A great product',       prices
                                            'A high-quality product',
                                            'A reliable product',    The second
                                            'An affordable product'], table,
            'category': ['Category A', 'Category B',                 containing
                         'Category C', 'Category D']})               descriptions
df3 = pd.DataFrame({'product_id': [1, 2, 3, 4],
                    'manufacturer': ['Manufacturer A', 'Manufacturer B',
                                     'Manufacturer C', 'Manufacturer D'],
                    'weight': [1.5, 2.0, 1.8, 1.2]})                 The third table,
merged_df = pd.merge(df1, df2, on='product_id')                      containing
merged_df = pd.merge(merged_df, df3, on='product_id')                makers and
print(merged_df)                                                     characteristics
```

Merges the previous two joined tables with the third one

Merges the first two tables

One limitation to doing this in pandas for every use case is computational efficiency because the package is slow. See, for instance, the following Stack Overflow answer:

https://mng.bz/N1x1. There are also scalability problems since pandas cannot handle data larger than your computer's available memory. Such limitations exist because the package has been coded with functionalities in mind, not performance. Consequently, most of the functions found on pandas are written in plain Python, and they make little access to optimized compiled routines—mainly routines written in Fortran and C++, as, for instance, NumPy, another popular matrix and array manipulation package, does. However, thanks to its popular API, you can learn and start with your projects using just pandas and then scale up to more powerful tools. As stated in the previous point, different products have more or less compatibility with pandas:

- Dask (https://www.dask.org/) is an open-source Python library that presents both low-level and high-level interfaces for the user. It is designed to run on computer clusters. Dask can also work in multiprocessing mode on multiple CPU processors, and it handles out-of-core tasks easily. In these tasks, you process more data than your RAM can handle by working it by chunks living on the disk. This data structure copies the pandas DataFrame API but is much more capable of handling many rows.

- Ray (https://www.ray.io/) is a low-level framework that parallelizes Python code across processors or clusters. It is ideal as a backend for other high-end solutions, such as Modin.

- Modin (https://github.com/modin-project/modin) is perhaps the most compatible tool with Pandas API. It works just by a simple replacement such as `import modin.pandas as pd`, and it performs best with Ray as a backend.

- Vaex (https://vaex.io/) is a Python library for lazy out-of-core DataFrames (similar to pandas). You can also visualize and explore big tabular datasets on your stand-alone machine or a server. Being lazy, it can optimize its operations and reach a performance of up to a billion objects/rows processed per second.

- RAPIDS (https://rapids.ai/) is a collection of libraries for using GPUs' computational capabilities on large matrices. It offers cuDF, a partial replacement for pandas. Data processing can improve efficiency (time to compute), not scalability, because GPUs must access your memory to determine what to calculate.

- Spark (https://spark.apache.org/) is a solution for map-reduce, a big data processing technique, graph algorithms, streaming data, and SQL queries working on single-node machines or clusters. It offers various packages and a DataFrame data structure similar to pandas. It is the solution best suited to handling massive quantities of tabular data.

- Polars (https://www.pola.rs/) is designed as a high-performance DataFrame library. It has been written in Rust, which allows for faster execution, comparable to C/C++, and distributable computations. Polars also has better memory management and large dataset handling and uses a columnar storage format. Columnar storage formats are more efficient for storing and accessing dense data, which is the most typical kind of tabular data. In contrast, row-based storage formats are more efficient for storing and accessing mostly sparse data (pandas uses a row-based storage format). Polars and pandas have similar APIs. However, there are differences because Polars can operate both in eager mode, where commands are executed immediately, or lazy mode, where commands are executed upon a specific command. Still under development, Polars is rapidly gaining traction in the data science community.

Based on your usage of pandas and the dimensions of your tabular data, you may find each one of these projects interesting. As a general suggestion, we advise you to check if your pandas functions are available in each of the products mentioned previously so you won't have to refactor your code and then evaluate the best solution for the size of your data.

2.3.2 *Internet data*

Now that we have created a plan for acquiring and assembling your data from various data storage sources such as relational databases, DWHs, and data lakes, we need to provide you with guidance on where to find additional sources of information on the internet. These sources will help you apply the deep learning and machine learning algorithms outlined in this book and allow you to test these algorithms on different datasets or even benchmark your models. In other words, we will help you locate online resources that can be used to increase and enhance the data you have already acquired.

Concerning where to look for sources, there are specialized websites where tabular data is collected and routinely used by researchers and practitioners. The best example is the UCI Machine Learning Repository (https://archive.ics.uci.edu/). The machine learning community has long used this website for educational purposes and research on machine learning algorithms. We can also quote OpenML (https://www.openml.org/), the repository used by Scikit-learn, as a source for its examples. It is supported by the Open Machine Learning Foundation, a nonprofit organization whose mission is to make machine learning simple, accessible, collaborative, and open. It is also sponsored by private companies, such as Amazon, and universities. In both cases—UCI and OpenML—you can download each dataset following the instructions provided or by directly accessing the URL of the data itself. When we use datasets from these sources, we will provide the Python code snippet to download the data directly for you to work on.

Apart from these open repositories, many other websites offer a shorter selection of open data—data provided freely for academic, scientific, or even commercial usage (but you have to check the usage license they came with). Governments, the scientific community, and sometimes even private companies grant such data to the public. You can get lucky and get some interesting datasets for your work by consulting the Harvard University Dataverse free data repository at https://dataverse.harvard.edu/ or by browsing the Dataset subreddit https://www.reddit.com/r/datasets/. In both cases, it is an excellent way to stumble across something interesting, but it may also be disappointing if you seek specific data and need help finding it. Suppose your search revolves around data relative to the public or macroeconomic sphere, such as transportation, energy, political participation, commerce, industrial production, consumption, and so on. In that case, the open data portals should provide hints on where to look for open data-sets. The two best portals are Data Portals (http://dataportals.org/), which covers the world, and Open Data Monitor (https://opendatamonitor.eu/), which specializes in the European region. Another good source is the National Statistical Service. You can browse for specific countries in this comprehensive list provided by the United States Census Bureau (https://mng.bz/eynQ).

Apart from these specific examples, the best way to come into contact with the type of open data you search is undoubtedly through the dataset search engine provided by Google, which can be found at https://datasetsearch.research.google.com/. The Google Dataset Search, comprising many possible sources and scattered repositories, should give you access to what you are looking for through its search results.

Figure 2.3 shows the results from Dataset Search from Google, where we asked for a dataset relative to credit scoring data.

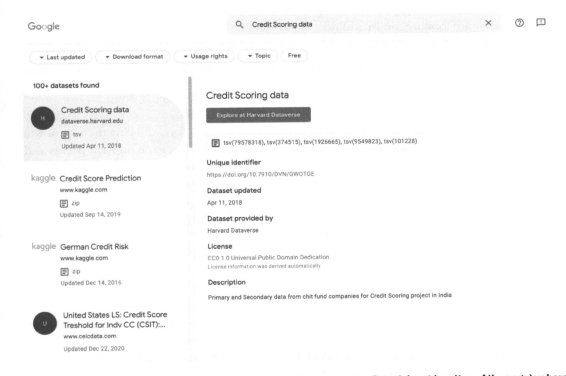

Figure 2.3 What Google Dataset Search returns for credit scoring data. Search input box (top of the page): where you input your search string as you would do in a search engine. Result display panel (left panel): where you can browse the results found by the search engine. Result display (center right page): where key information of the dataset is displayed. You are provided with links to reach the data.

It is not unusual to look for outside data to start a project when you don't have similar data available in your systems or want to experiment with some idea or machine learning model. For instance, let's pretend you need to find external credit scoring data for your project to build a model from scratch based on external data. Credit scoring is a computed quantification of a person's or business's creditworthiness. Building a credit scoring model helps you run any business successfully, such as mortgages, auto loans, credit cards, and private loans, where you have to offer, extend, or deny credit. Credit scoring can be used for risk-based pricing—that is, for setting a fair price for credit, given the risks of not repaying.

Looking, for instance, for credit scoring data as you would on the Google search engine will open up a panel on the left side of the browser listing a series of datasets that could satisfy your request. You can filter the results by recency of the data, format, license (a point to be addressed if you want to make commercial use of the data), costs, and category of interest. On the right panel, a description of the key characteristics of the chosen dataset will appear, with a link allowing you to access the original repository where the data is stored and documented. To download the data, follow the instructions on each landing page you will be pointed to.

To our knowledge, Google Dataset Search is the best tool for finding the data you need or are looking for. In addition, we would like to point out another resource made available by Google through Kaggle, a company devoted to data science competitions that was acquired by Google in 2017. As you will surely notice, the search engine often returns datasets hosted on the Kaggle platform using Google Dataset Search. Apart from offering a competition platform, Kaggle offers a dataset hosting service called Kaggle Datasets, found at https://www.kaggle.com/datasets.

Kaggle Datasets is part of a service offered to platform users, allowing them to download data freely (sometimes because they open-sourced it) in exchange for points and rank in the gamified Kaggle system. The gaming formulation also pushes for data to be uploaded soon. Hence, you will find the latest data around, and you can expect them to be updated often. The result is an impressive collection of data that is not all that easy to find elsewhere, ranging from economic statistics to transaction collections that are helpful in building recommender systems from scratch. Depending on the engagement of the Kaggle user who posted the dataset and that of the community, you may find documentation, data analysis, machine learning models, and discussion associated with the data.

If you can find what you are looking for, you can download the data from the Kaggle Dataset directly, using the download button shown in figure 2.4, after registering with the website. Registering also allows you to install and use the `kaggle-api` command (https://github.com/Kaggle/kaggle-api) to download datasets from the shell. For instance, after having installed it, you can download the German Credit Risk data by the command

```
kaggle datasets download -d uciml/german-credit
```

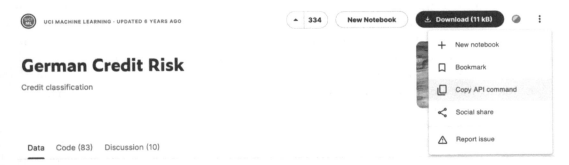

Figure 2.4   Options on the German Credit Risk page at Kaggle Datasets (menu on the right). Easily download the entire dataset with the Kaggle API command from the top-down menu. You can find the command by requiring it directly on the screen from the menu associated with the page, as shown in the figure.

2.3.3   *Synthetic data*

In the scenario when you have already managed to acquire some datasets but need to increment your tabular data available, we have to mention synthetic data generation, which won't create any data from scratch but can effectively increment and improve the existing datasets that you have available at hand, making using machine learning and deep learning models that require a more significant number of examples to run properly feasible. Synthetic data generation is a generative AI application and a growing field because it can

- Overcome data scarcity by inflating the number of tabular examples available
- Provide data diversity by enhancing portions of the data, such as in the case of the minority class in an unbalanced classification problem
- Generate edge cases so that it can provide you with data examples that you cannot frequently encounter and that you can use to test your designed systems
- Preserve privacy because it helps to generate tabular data with the same characteristics as the original one but with no privacy problem because all the represented data is fictitious

In recent times, data generation has made great leap forwards, thanks to the first generative AI experiments with Generative Adversarial Networks (GANs) and Variational Autoencoders (VAEs), two deep learning architectures that were the spearhead of generative AI a few years ago.

GANs were introduced by Ian Goodfellow and his colleagues in 2014. They consist of a couple of deep neural networks—namely a generator and a discriminator—trained simultaneously and made to interact by challenging the discriminator to guess the generative work of the generator against the original examples. It is an unsupervised process, though. Given enough time and computation, the continuous comparison between the generator and discriminator should lead the generator to mimic the real-world distribution of the original examples used for comparison by the discriminator. This is indeed smart and amazing, if you consider that the generator never sees any instance of the data it should resemble because it builds its work from purely random noise. This process works extremely well both for images and tabular data.

VAEs consist of an encoder and a decoder. Their function is to compress input data using the encoder to a state called the latent space, where the data information is highly condensed. Subsequently, the decoder decompresses the data with high fidelity and reconstructs the original data. The underlying idea is that if the compression-decompression process is effective, then the latent space encapsulates the core distributional information of the data, enabling the generation of new data. The architecture of VAEs is designed so that inputs are taken by the encoder and passed through a sequence of layers, which may consist of the same number of neurons or a decreasing number, until reaching a layer representing the latent space. This layer serves as the starting point for the decoder.

How these deep learning approaches generate good data is proven by how a data science competition platform such as Kaggle uses synthetic data for its competitions. Due to the lack of tabular data competitions, Kaggle has recently launched a series of competitions based on synthetic data that don't have anything to envy from traditional ones based on curated original data. The Tabular Playground Series has been a feature of Kaggle for the last two years and still continues to this day (https://www.kaggle.com/competitions).

In listing 2.5, we use the sdv package to generate 10,000 additional examples from the original German Credit Risk dataset, made up of 1,000 samples that we presented in the previous section. To install the sdv package on your system, use the following shell command:

```
pip install sdv
```

The sdv package, from an MIT initiative, is a set of open-source tools devised to help individuals and enterprises generate synthetic data starting from some original one. Such tools use classical statistical methods, such as the Gaussian copulas that can reproduce the distribution of multiple variables simultaneously, and deep learning. The deep learning tools are based on GANs and VAEs. In our example, we found that a VAE architecture can better and more easily mimic the data at hand. You can find more information about the sdv package on the GitHub page of the project (https://github.com/sdv-dev/SDV) or by reading the reference paper illustrating the methodology: Neha Patki, Roy Wedge, Kalyan Veeramachaneni, "The Synthetic Data Vault," IEEE DSAA 2016 (https://mng.bz/ga4V).

Listing 2.5　Generating a synthetic dataset

```
import pandas as pd
from sdv.metadata import SingleTableMetadata   ◄─── Imports from sdv the function to
                                                    generate metadata from your original
```

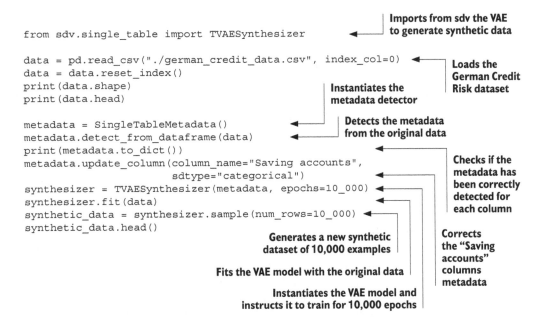

```
from sdv.single_table import TVAESynthesizer
```
Imports from sdv the VAE to generate synthetic data

```
data = pd.read_csv("./german_credit_data.csv", index_col=0)
data = data.reset_index()
print(data.shape)
print(data.head)
```
Loads the German Credit Risk dataset

Instantiates the metadata detector

```
metadata = SingleTableMetadata()
metadata.detect_from_dataframe(data)
print(metadata.to_dict())
metadata.update_column(column_name="Saving accounts",
                       sdtype="categorical")
synthesizer = TVAESynthesizer(metadata, epochs=10_000)
synthesizer.fit(data)
synthetic_data = synthesizer.sample(num_rows=10_000)
synthetic_data.head()
```
Detects the metadata from the original data

Checks if the metadata has been correctly detected for each column

Corrects the "Saving accounts" columns metadata

Generates a new synthetic dataset of 10,000 examples

Fits the VAE model with the original data

Instantiates the VAE model and instructs it to train for 10,000 epochs

The script takes a while to complete since a certain number of iterations over the original data is necessary for the VAE to develop a good latent representation of the original characteristics and distributions of the data. Once completed, the sampled examples from the new synthetic data resemble the sample from the original data, but if you need more formal proof, you must resort to an adversarial validation evaluation, where a machine learning algorithm is challenged to distinguish between the original data and the generated one. A machine learning algorithm is more apt at detecting even subtle patterns in data; hence, if it can be confused when distinguishing between original and generated data, the generated data is assumed to be of good quality. In the following listing, we show how to proceed with setting up adversarial validation for the synthetic data derived from the German Credit Risk data.

Listing 2.6 Testing a synthetic dataset using adversarial validation

```
from sklearn.ensemble import RandomForestClassifier
from sklearn.model_selection import cross_val_predict
from sklearn.metrics import roc_auc_score

X = pd.concat([synthetic_data, data])
categorical_columns = [
    "Sex", "Housing", "Saving accounts",
    "Checking account", "Purpose"]
X_encoded = pd.get_dummies(X, columns=categorical_columns)
X= X.drop("index", axis="columns")
y = [0] * len(synthetic_data) + [1] * len(data)

model = RandomForestClassifier()
```
Concatenates original and synthetic data together

Encodes categorical features into dummy variables

```
cv_preds = cross_val_predict(
    model,
    X_encoded,
    y,
    cv=5,                          Classifies if the example is
    n_jobs=-1,                     original or synthetic
    method="predict_proba"
)                                                                    Computes the
roc_adv_score = roc_auc_score(y_true=y, y_score=cv_preds[:, 1])  ◄── ROC AUC
print(f"roc auc adv score: {roc_adv_score:0.3f}")                    score for the
                                                                     classification
```

The area under the receiver operating characteristic (ROC AUC) score, also known as the area under the curve (AUC), is a metric used to evaluate the performance of a machine learning algorithm in a binary classification problem. It measures the algorithm's ability to distinguish between positive and negative instances based on the predicted probabilities assigned to each observation. A score of 1 indicates a perfect classifier, while a score of 0.5 suggests a model that performs no better than random guessing. You can learn more about this metric by consulting https://mlu-explain .github.io/roc-auc/, part of the Machine Learning University, an education initiative from Amazon to teach machine learning theory.

In this case, the ROC AUC score is approximately 0.567, which indicates that the synthetic data is almost indistinguishable from the original data.

In the next section, we will complete our overview of tabular data by exploring a tabular dataset retrieved from the UCI Machine Learning Repository and Kaggle Datasets. Many of the problems we quoted in the previous paragraphs will be spotted as we analyze the data, and some remedies will be implemented.

2.4   *Exploratory data analysis*

Assembling the dataset into a data matrix arranged by rows and columns is just the starting point of a longer process. The data is then examined, explored, transformed, and finally fed into a model. Studying and exploring data are crucial stages of the process because they give you an idea of what you may have missed in the assembling phase and what can be done for your specific predictive problem. *Exploratory data analysis* (EDA) is often associated more with the feature engineering phase—more in the case of using classical machine learning approaches for tabular. Usually, EDA is instead almost completely ignored when using deep learning. We want to stress that EDA shouldn't be limited to helping create features. It is an overall process of exploration to discover how the data can be used at its best.

EDA certainly has a statistical flavor since it was suggested by one of the most prominent statisticians of the 20th century, John W. Tukey, in his 1977 masterpiece, *Exploratory Data Analysis*. In his work, Tukey claimed that statistical work doesn't come from simply modeling and hypothesis testing based on theoretical assumptions. According to Tukey, data by means of EDA can also tell you what is possible in scientific and engineering problems and hint you at the best ways to curate your data. There are no predefined blueprints for an EDA. Still, smart usage of statistical description and tests and the graphical representation of the features alone and in their relationship with others can tell you how to act on the data. In general, first, employing descriptive statistics and plots, you examine every single feature, called the univariate approach in statistics. You then examine how features relate to each other, called the bivariate approach. Finally, you try to get a glimpse of all the features together using multivariate techniques and dimensionality reduction ones, such as t-SNE and UMAP.

In this phase, just after assembling your data into a tabular matrix, EDA can do the following:

- Inform you about the characteristics of the data, such as numeric, ordinal, high/ low categorical, and date features.
- Give you an idea of the values of each feature and how they are distributed. This is especially useful when working with neural networks, where value scales are important.
- Tell you if there are missing values because neural networks and some machine learning algorithms are deemed to fail in the presence of missing data.
- Locate outliers and clusters of values due to errors and mistakes in extraction and assembling.
- Spot rare categories that can be eliminated or aggregated.

We will show you how to achieve such explorations using simple pandas commands since we deem an EDA process fully guided by an analyst's reasoning more effective than an automated one. However, you can also use automatic data exploration tools if the number of features to explore is vast and you need to save time. Later, you can integrate the automatic EDA with specific and focused custom data explorations. Among the open-source packages for automatic EDA, there are a few notable ones that we would like to suggest you try, and all of them are valid solutions that are easy to learn and use:

- AutoViz (https://github.com/AutoViML/AutoViz)
- Sweetviz (https://github.com/fbdesignpro/sweetviz)
- Pandas Profiling (https://mng.bz/DMxw)

In the following chapters, we will reprise EDA to complete the panorama with the further explorations you may need depending on the techniques (machine learning or deep learning) you want to apply to your data for predictive purposes.

2.4.1 *Loading the Auto MPG example dataset*

Now, as an example of how a simple EDA can hint at ideas and solutions for further processing your data and taking necessary remediation steps when adapting it to the model you want to use, we can go for the Auto MPG Data Set, a dataset freely available on the UCI Machine Learning repository (https://archive.ics.uci.edu/ml/datasets/ auto+mpg). The dataset, assembled by Ernesto Ramos and David Donoho, originates from the StatLib library maintained at Carnegie Mellon University. Previously, it was

featured in the 1983 American Statistical Association Exposition (https://mng.bz/
IYa8) and the works of Ross Quinlan. Ross Quinlan is a major contributor to the development of the decision tree algorithm and the creator of the C4.5 ID3 algorithms.
He quotes this dataset in his 1993 paper "Combining Instance-Based and Model-Based
Learning" (https://mng.bz/BXx8), a true milestone paper on regression problems in
machine learning. For our purposes, it is a simple, manageable example because of its
mixed set of features and some missing data to be handled in the mpg and horsepower
features.

The following is a list of the available features in the dataset:

- mpg: continuous
- cylinders: multivalued discrete
- displacement: continuous
- horsepower: continuous
- weight: continuous
- acceleration: continuous
- model year: multivalued discrete
- origin: multivalued discrete
- car name: string (unique for each example, it can be used as an index in a pandas
  DataFrame)

In our example, the list is short, but the available features can last dozens of pages in
most complex tabular datasets.

To upload our example dataset, we can refer to the code in the following listing that
will connect to the UCI repository, and it will dump the data into a pandas DataFrame.

Listing 2.7 Download of Auto MPG Data Set from UCI repository

**StringIO reads and writes
an in-memory string buffer.**

**Requests is an HTTP library
that can help you recover
data from the web.**

```
from io import StringIO
import requests
import pandas as pd

url = "https://archive.ics.uci.edu/ml/machine-learning-databases/auto-mpg/"
data = "auto-mpg.data-original"
columns = ["mpg", "cylinders", "displacement", "horsepower", "weight",
           "acceleration", "model_year", "origin", "car_name"]

colspecs = [(0, 4), (6, 9), (12, 17), (23, 28), (34, 39),
            (45, 49), (52, 55), (57, 59), (61, -2)]

data_ingestion = StringIO
```

**Derived from the
documentation on
the UCI machine
learning repository**

**Fixed-width data requires
providing each feature with its
start and end position in the input.**

```
(requests.get(url + data).text)
```

→ The dataset is read from the web by requests.get() and then turned into a string buffer.

```
data = pd.read_fwf(data_ingestion,
colspecs=colspecs,
names=columns)
```

→ pd.read_fwf reads a table of fixed-width formatted lines into a DataFrame.

The Auto MPG data set is stored in a fixed-width text file, where values are on the same line, separated by a certain number of spaces or a tab. The return carriage at the end of the row signals the end of an example. The following is a sample of the text file that the request library retries for us from the UCI Machine Learning repository:

```
18.0   8.   307.0   130.0   3504.   12.0   70.   1.   "chevrolet chevelle malibu"
15.0   8.   350.0   165.0   3693.   11.5   70.   1.   "buick skylark 320"
18.0   8.   318.0   150.0   3436.   11.0   70.   1.   "plymouth satellite"
...
31.0   4.   119.0   82.00   2720.   19.4   82.   1.   "chevy s-10"
```

This explains why we must use a fixed-width reader such as pandas `read_fwf` and specify the character position where we expect each value to start and end. More commonly, you can find other datasets organized as CSV files. If the same dataset had been stored in CSV format, it would look like the following:

```
"mpg","cylinders","displacement","horsepower","weight","acceleration",
"model_year","origin","car_name"
18.0,8.0,307.0,130.0,3504.0,12.0,70.0,1.,"chevrolet chevelle malibu"
15.0,8.0,350.0,165.0,3693.0,11.5,70.0,1.,"buick skylark 320"
18.0,8.0,318.0,150.0,3436.0,11.0,70.0,1.,"plymouth satellite"
...
31.0,4.0,119.0,82.0,2720.0,19.4,82.0,1.,"chevy s-10"
```

In CSV files, the values of the features are not placed in fixed positions in rows; they vary in position but not in order of sequence, and you find them separated because of a special character denominated as a separator. In our example, it is the comma. Please also notice that textual data, such as strings or dates, is often delimited between quotes to avoid confusion if the text contains the separator.

In such a case, you have to use the pandas `read_csv` reader, which can handle CSV files. Depending on the situation, your data may be stored as a JSON file or an XML file, but there are readers also for such formats in pandas (see table 2.2).

Table 2.2 Common data reading methods in pandas

Function	Description
read_csv	Loads delimited data from a file, URL, or file-like object Uses a comma as the default delimiter
read_json	Reads data from a JSON string representation

Table 2.2   Common data reading methods in pandas (*continued*)

Function	Description
read_xml	Imports shallow XML documents as a DataFrame
read_html	Reads all tables found in the given HTML document
read_excel	Reads tabular data from an Excel XLS or XLSX file

2.4.2   *Examining labels, values, distributions*

All you have to do is understand what kind of data you are reading from the internet or your local disk and use the appropriate readers among the ones offered by pandas: each will be automatically handled by the proper function.

As we already have a databook for the dataset (just read "attribute information" at https://archive.ics.uci.edu/ml/datasets/Auto%2BMPG), we can immediately take note in specific variables about what features are numeric, ordinal, and categorical:

```
numeric_feats = ["mpg", "displacement", "horsepower", "weight",
"acceleration"]
ordinal_feats = ["cylinders", "model_year"]
categorical_feats = ["origin", "car_name"]
```

In different cases with other datasets, you have to discover such information through your data exploration. The variables will have to be populated by your discoveries. Hence, if we do not know the characteristics of our features, we should discover them through first data exploration, which can be quickly accomplished by a few manual pandas commands followed by some deductions. For instance, we could ask for a sample of the first rows and immediately get an idea of the data we are dealing with. We get just the top five rows using the .head(n) method:

```
data.head(5)
```

The results are shown in figure 2.5.

	mpg	cylinders	displacement	horsepower	weight	acceleration	model_year	origin	car_name
0	18.0	8.0	307.0	130.0	3504.0	12.0	70.0	1.	chevrolet chevelle malibu
1	15.0	8.0	350.0	165.0	3693.0	11.5	70.0	1.	buick skylark 320
2	18.0	8.0	318.0	150.0	3436.0	11.0	70.0	1.	plymouth satellite
3	16.0	8.0	304.0	150.0	3433.0	12.0	70.0	1.	amc rebel sst
4	17.0	8.0	302.0	140.0	3449.0	10.5	70.0	1.	ford torino

Figure 2.5   Results from the data.head(5) command

In this example, many features are floats without decimal parts, which hints at them being integers. Integers may also point out a numeric, ordinal, or categorical feature. Requiring the number of distinct values for each feature is the second step in our example:

```
data.nunique()
```

The returned results are

```
mpg             129
cylinders         5
displacement     84
horsepower       92
weight          356
acceleration     96
model_year       14
origin            4
car_name        312
dtype: int64
```

With few distinct numbers, cylinders and origin features can be treated as categorical variables. Hence, they could be both embedded, a procedure that transforms them into continuous numerical features, or transformed into binaries for each value by one-hot encoding. Domain knowledge can help us classify cylinders as an ordinal feature since cylinders may have different volumes in different car models, and, generally, having more cylinders proportionally corresponds to more engine power. Similarly, the feature relative to years may also be dealt with as an ordinal representing time progress.

Another quick explorative check, based on the examination of the standard deviation of each of your numeric features, could help you identify your data further and even select it:

```
data[numeric_feats].std()
```

The returned results are

```
mpg               7.815984
displacement    105.207362
horsepower       38.522063
weight          849.827166
acceleration      2.820984
dtype: float64
```

By doing so, you can be aware of constant or quasi-constant features in your data. Excluding missing values, if a feature is set to zero or too low in variance, it can be safely excluded from your data because it probably won't bring any tangible advantage to process it further. However, suppose missing values are present in good quantity. In that case, you may want to create an indicator variable to keep track of the missing patterns in that feature, as they could be predictive. Consider checking with a command the number of missing cases:

```
(data.isna()
     .sum(axis=0)
)
```

The `.isna()` method will return a boolean telling us if any feature sample is missing. We can count how many missing samples there are by summing the number of missing samples in a feature. A True value equates 1 and a False 0. The obtained results are

```
mpg              8
cylinders        0
displacement     0
horsepower       6
weight           0
acceleration     0
model_year       0
origin           0
car_name         0
dtype: int64
```

The `.isna` method will help you keep track of the NaN values in your features. As discussed, features with a large number of missing numbers may conceal some interesting predictive pattern and may be turned into missing binary indicator variables, You can use the MissingIndicator in Scikit-learn for this purpose: https://mng.bz/dXoO. Additionally, depending on your predictive algorithm, you always have to deal with missing values, whether there are many or just a few handfuls. If you use a deep learning solution, you must impute the missing values with a numeric value. Usually, you take the mean, median, or mode as a replacement for missing values. Still, more sophisticated treatments are also based on iterative estimations of the best value to use as a substitute. An example is the IterativeImputer in Scikit-learn: https://mng.bz/rKaD.

It is helpful to remember that imputing the missing values with the zero value is a good strategy for neural networks and generalized linear models when your numeric features are standardized when you remove the mean and divide by the standard deviation: in such a case, the zero value corresponds to the mean for all the numeric features. The same goes for most machine learning algorithms but the approach is different for the most advanced gradient boosting implementations, such as XGBoost and LightGBM. Such algorithms can appropriately treat missing data without any further intervention on your side.

Sometimes conventional numbers (such as –999) are used in tabular datasets. If you know that a certain value points out to a missing value, you have to modify your command to consider such information:

```
(data[numeric_feats]==-999).sum(axis=0)
```

In the previous code snippet, you check all the numeric features against the value –999, which is a marker for missing data. Basically, any number could be used as a marker, and you have to know in advance what is used in your data to set a missing value. Though a number, it won't cause any error when training your model, but it will seriously mislead its learning. Hence, the missing marker should always be addressed as a NaN missing value to prevent potential misinterpretation by deep learning models and certain machine learning algorithms. Tree-based models, like gradient boosting or random forest models, are better equipped to handle such situations, especially when the marker is positioned at an extreme end of the feature's data distribution.

Having checked about missing data and standard deviations, you now start checking the distribution of your features to spot other useful information that can guide your treatment of the dataset:

```
data.describe()
```

Figure 2.6 shows the outputs of the describe method.

	mpg	cylinders	displacement	horsepower	weight	acceleration	model_year
count	398.000000	406.000000	406.000000	400.000000	406.000000	406.000000	406.000000
mean	23.514573	5.475369	194.040640	104.832500	2969.561576	15.495074	75.748768
std	7.815984	1.712160	105.207362	38.522063	849.827166	2.820984	5.307431
min	9.000000	3.000000	4.000000	46.000000	732.000000	8.000000	0.000000
25%	17.500000	4.000000	104.250000	75.750000	2223.750000	13.625000	73.000000
50%	23.000000	4.000000	148.500000	95.000000	2811.000000	15.500000	76.000000
75%	29.000000	8.000000	293.250000	129.250000	3612.000000	17.075000	79.000000
max	46.600000	8.000000	455.000000	230.000000	5140.000000	24.800000	82.000000

Figure 2.6 Results from the `data.describe()` command

The pandas describe method allows you to represent basic descriptive statistics for all your numeric features. Note that missing data is ignored. After checking the missing values and the variance or the standard deviation, your attention should focus on the minimum and maximum values with respect to the mean. Too large or too small values should draw your attention to outliers (extreme values in a data distribution) or too skewed distributions. Outliers and skewed distributions are not uncommon in data analysis, and sometimes they have to be removed. Sometimes, they should be taken at face value without any corrective action, depending on the motivation of your analysis. In this phase, outliers and skewed distributions may hint at problems in collecting and assembling your data, and corrective actions imply removing or correcting them. For instance, an outlying value is due to errors in the data. Also, stacked data recorded with different methodologies may have generated a skewed distribution. For instance, in a table, your measures are in meters, and they are instead expressed in centimeters in another one.

The reasons behind all such errors in data vary widely, and it is advised to check your data closely with descriptive statistics and charts and then figure out a corrective action to remove the errors. Such errors are not limited to numeric features but can be easily found in categorical ones. Let's now examine the only string feature available, the car_ name one, by splitting its elements:

```
words = (data.car_name
            .apply(lambda x: x.split())
            .explode()
            .value_counts()
        )
words.head(15)
```

The lambda function in the apply function will split the instances of car_name into single words. Since the result will be a series of lists, using the .explore() method, we unroll all the lists into a single feature. By counting the single values in this new feature, we get the frequency results for each word:

```
ford           53
chevrolet      44
plymouth       32
(sw)           32
amc            29
dodge          28
toyota         25
datsun         23
custom         18
buick          17
pontiac        16
volkswagen     16
honda          13
mercury        11
brougham       10
Name: car_name, dtype: int64
```

It looks fine at first sight, with most instances containing a brand name and some information on the type of car. However, among the most frequent labels, you notice some incongruent information, such as "(sw)", which stands for sport wagon, and custom, which refers to the customized accessories in the car. At a closer inspection, you finally notice that, even in this curated dataset, there are problems since many brands are misspelled:

```
(words.index
      .sort_values()
) [-50:]
```

The returned results are

```
Index(['seville', 'sj', 'skyhawk', 'skylark', 'special', 'spirit', 'sport',
'sportabout', 'squire', 'sst', 'st.', 'stanza', 'starfire', 'starlet',
'strada', 'subaru', 'suburb', 'sunbird', 'super', 'supreme', 'sx', 'tc',
'tc3', 'tercel', 'thunderbird', 'torino', 'town', 'toyota', 'toyouta',
'tr7', 'triumph', 'turbo', 'type', 'v6', 'v8', 'valiant', 'vega',
'ventura', 'vista', 'vokswagen', 'volare', 'volkswagen', 'volvo', 'vw',
'wagon', 'woody', 'x1.9', 'xe', 'yorker', 'zephyr'], dtype='object')
```

In this data slice containing the words composing the categorical feature, we notice how some brands are misspelled (e.g., Toyota and Toyouta, Volkswagen and Vokswagen but also VW as a shortening). Misspells will split the examples related to a true category (Volkswagen and Toyota in this case) into multiple categories, putting your model at risk of picking up noisy evidence or discarding weaker signals. The same happens with other categorical and ordinal features that present erroneous additional categories:

```
(data.origin
    .value_counts()
)
```

The returned results for data origin are

```
1.      253
3.       79
2.       73
.        1
Name: origin, dtype: int64
```

Let's operate the same for `model_year`, ordering the results based on the year:

```
(data.model_year
    .value_counts()
    .reset_index()
    .rename(columns={'index':'model_year',
                     'model_year':'counts'})
    .sort_values(by="model_year")
)
```

Figure 2.7 shows how the ordered value results for `model_year` will appear.

Not all these problems with data taken singularly affect the results much. However, their combined presence may affect your model performances in an evident way when your dataset is composed of tens and tens of features with minor problems. Remediation is simple: just remove the cases with the erroneous category labels unless you can reasonably correct them or treat them as missing cases and then impute them. Since they require inspection and reasoning on every feature, such actions may take considerable time and effort. Still, you are doing EDA precisely for this purpose, and later, a model that is more confident and performing in predictions will repay your efforts in full. Tabular data has stronger requirements on the cleanness of data, especially when applying classical machine learning models than generally expected from unstructured data processed by deep learning, where errors are sometimes considered useful noise to help avoid overfitting.

Being on the lookout for more errors in data, it is now time, after checking on the categorical features, to examine closely the numeric ones too. Here, boxplots and histograms replace category counts, and the focus is also widened from single features (the so-called statistical univariate approach) to more features together. Each value in the features of an example may not appear erroneous per se. Still, if all the values are taken together, you may realize that their combination is highly unlikely, if not the result of some error. You start examining the distributions by boxplots. A boxplot, also called a box and whiskers plot, drafts the key characteristics of a distribution using the boundaries of a box: you can see the first quartile (Q1) and the third quartile (Q3) as the top and bottom sides of the box (the median, Q2, is represented inside the box). Its whiskers represent the farthest points in both directions, not exceeding Q3 + 1.5 × IQR and Q1 – 15 × IQR (as a reminder, IQR is the difference between Q3 and Q1). Outlying observations beyond such boundaries are plotted as separate points, and you can immediately spot if there are any present and how many there are. Since a boxplot scales to the unit measures of the feature you represent, if you are to compare multiple boxplots with the numeric features for their distributions, you need first to standardize them by subtracting the mean and divide by their standard deviation:

	model_year	counts
13	0.0	1
2	70.0	34
7	71.0	29
10	72.0	28
0	73.0	40
12	74.0	27
5	75.0	30
3	76.0	34
11	77.0	28
1	78.0	36
8	79.0	29
9	80.0	29
6	81.0	30
4	82.0	31

Figure 2.7   Ordered value counts

```
standardized = ((data[numeric_feats] - data[numeric_feats].mean())
                / data[numeric_feats].std())
standardized.boxplot(column=numeric_feats, figsize= (12, 4))
```

Figure 2.8 shows the chart output.

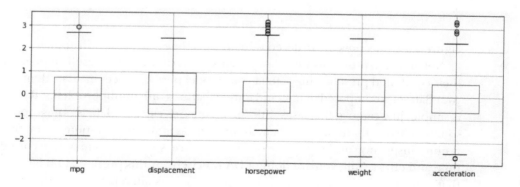

Figure 2.8   Boxplots of numeric features from the Auto MPG Data Set

The purpose is to determine if the data is wrong because of your collection or aggregation procedure. Features with outliers such as mpg, horsepower, and acceleration require a closer inspection through a histogram to exclude the absence of extraneous or erroneous values:

```
data.horsepower.round().hist(bins=64)
```

Figure 2.9 shows the resulting 64-bin histogram.

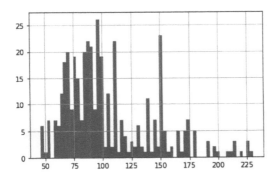

Figure 2.9 Histogram of horsepower feature

As for the horsepower feature, there does not seem to be anything relevant except a peculiar peak at around value 150: a concentration of examples due to fiscal reasons. In fact, since you have to pay more taxes if you own a car exceeding a certain horsepower threshold, designers of many cars' engines just stayed below that threshold to make their cars more marketable.

As for the acceleration feature, everything is okay. There are just long tails on both sides:

```
data.acceleration.hist(bins=24)
```

Figure 2.10 shows the resulting 24-bin histogram.

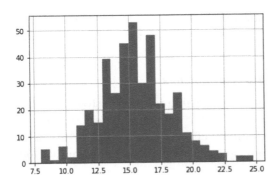

Figure 2.10 Histogram of acceleration feature

Histograms, which are bar charts of frequencies of values bins, work for numeric variables. For ordinal and categorical variables, a simple bar chart on value counts obtains the same information:

```
(data.cylinders
     .value_counts()
     .reset_index()
     .rename(columns={'index':'counts'})
     .sort_values(by="counts")
     .plot.bar(x="counts")
)
```

Figure 2.11 shows the resulting bar plot.

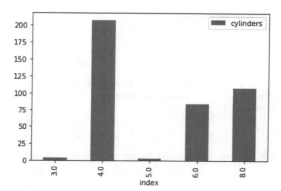

Figure 2.11   Bar plot of cylinders feature

Here, you should look for rarer classes because they can have an error or an outlying rare observation that you must decide whether to keep. Domain knowledge should help you make these decisions. In our example regarding cylinders, we actually should keep both the three-cylinder and five-cylinder classes, even if they are rare, because a quick check can reveal that we have few three-cylinder cars—cars installing this type of engine are smaller and tend to have much less market share than the more common four-cylinder vehicles. In addition, car designers underuse the five-cylinder layout, similar to other odd layouts, because it presents costs similar to the six-cylinder layouts but implies more complexity in many engineering aspects and many more shortcomings in terms of performance.

2.4.3   *Exploring bivariate and multivariate relationships*

Spending time examining how values are distributed using histograms and bar plots will provide information for catching errors that may later affect your work. Even if the errors on every feature may have a minimal effect, the sum of all errors on all the features you will be using may affect your predictive algorithm significantly. Once you are done spotting the problems with single features, it is time to check how they relate to each other. How features relate to your target and how you can exclude part of them, leaving your results unmodified or even improving them, is a topic we will discuss later when discussing feature selection. Your priority at this point is avoiding redundant features in your dataset. For redundant features, we intend duplicated features or features that are extremely similar:

- Duplicated features with different names.
- Highly collinear numeric features.
- Similar categorical features, apparently different because of level aggregations or because of used labels that are different.
- Similar numeric and categorical features that are both derived from the same source. An example is in finance when you have a probability of default and a corresponding default rating, which are usually expressed with alphabetic labels like AAA or BB.

We start figuring out how to spot duplications and high collinearity among numeric features. Our favored tool for this investigation is the bivariate correlation: the correlation between the features, one by another. When the numeric features' bivariate correlations are arranged in a symmetrical matrix, we have a correlation matrix, which can be immediately visualized as a chart for spotting collinearity if there are not too many features:

```
import seaborn as sns
corr = data[numeric_feats].corr()
sns.heatmap(corr, cmap="Blues",annot=True)
```

The resulting plot is shown in figure 2.12.

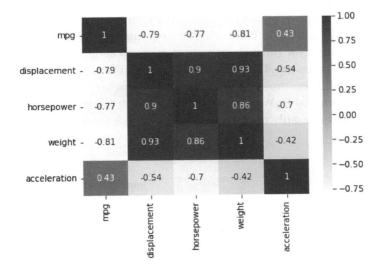

Figure 2.12   Correlation
plot with values heatmap

In our example, we only have a few features involved, and the readability of the matrix is high. When the number of features is high, it is better to list only the bivariate correlations that exceed a certain threshold. In both cases, you must pay attention to correlations that exceed the absolute value of 0.98 to 0.99. Also, correlations may be negative, and a negative correlation approaching minus one is another case of collinearity. When you have such high correlations between features, you must try to understand why and then decide which one to drop. Dropping some of the collinear features will reduce your dataset and avoid problems later, depending on the feature selection method used or the learning algorithm. In fact, with collinearity or multicollinearity, if it involves more than two features at once, you may experience problems in your dataset in both the convergence of the learning algorithm, resulting in suboptimal results and interpretability of the solution.

Collinearity, though associated with correlations, also affects categorical features and sometimes has to be found even among categorical and numeric ones. In this case, you cannot use correlation. Even if correlation for this purpose is quite robust, and even if you are comparing ordinal and binary features, when working with categorical features, you have to transform them into numbers using a procedure called label encoding that implies assigning arbitrary numbers to categories. Since label encoding is based on arbitrary value assignment, you cannot even establish the identity of the same encoded categorical feature using correlation if your encoding is applied differently to the same feature.

In similar situations, we can recur to associative measures based on chi-square statistics or Cramer's V measure when correlation is not applicable. Cramer's V is a statistic based on the chi-square value divided by the number of labels in the features being compared. This operation normalizes the value recorded on a feature, making it comparable across all dataset features. The square root of the result ranges from 0 to 1, providing a measure of intensity but not directionality of the relationship. Regarding intensity, Cramer's V values close to 0 indicate unrelated features, while those near 1 indicate a high association and collinearity among the features.

Cramer's V can also be applied by comparing a categorical feature and a numeric one if you previously discretized the numeric one into a categorical one using a transformation based on deciles, for instance. Listing 2.8 is a comparison between two features from our example dataset. In the example, we first create a function to compute `cramerV` from the chi-square score from a table. We apply it to a comparison between a categorical and a numeric feature after having discretized the numeric feature using deciles.

Listing 2.8 Using Cramer's V to detect association

```
from scipy.stats import chi2_contingency

def cramerV(chi2, table):
```

Imports from Scipy the function for computing the chi-square test of independence

Prepares a function for calculating Cramer's V having as input the score chi-square test of independence and the table it has been derived from

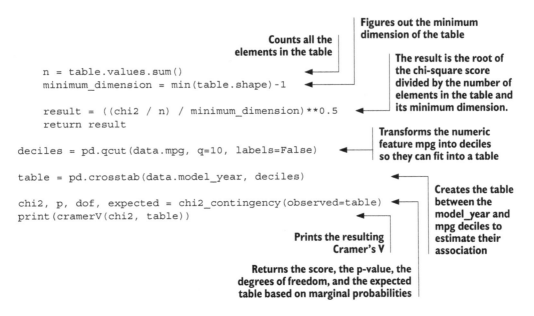

In the code, by providing the chi-square score and the table itself, we call the Cramer-V function to get a 0.855 value for Cramer's V comparing MPGs and the year of the model. Cramer's V is a reciprocal measure used to identify features with a similar role in prediction. Unlike directional measures, Cramer's V is insensitive to feature swapping. This property allows for identifying highly correlated features that can be removed from the analysis. A very high positive or negative correlation between features may indicate redundancy, and one of the two features can be dropped.

As a last step after your EDA has dealt with univariate and bivariate explorations, as we pointed out, you need to examine your dataset from a multivariate point of view: this will help you detect the presence of any chunk of data that doesn't fit in the data. Again, you are performing such an examination not to find better ways to fit your model precisely but as a preliminary operation to validate your tabular data as fit for the problem you want to represent. Multivariate approaches require all features to be numeric, as previously seen for Cramer's V; you can discretize numeric features for this purpose and operate projecting all your data to lower dimensionality, no matter how complex it is, and thus you can visualize it and easily spot anomalies.

The process consists of reducing your data to a few comprehensive summary features of dimensions and plotting them on a chart to visually spot patterns and isolated clusters of points that could be anomalies. Common multivariate approaches for obtaining a lower dimensionality projection are

- Principal component analysis (PCA) and singular value decomposition (SVD): https://mng.bz/VVl0
- T-distributed stochastic neighbor embedding (t-SNE): https://lvdmaaten.github .io/tsne/

- Uniform manifold approximation and projection (UMAP): https://github
  .com/lmcinnes/umap

PCA and SVD have their roots in statistical analysis, and PCA has a long history of being applied for EDA purposes. Both are, however, approaches based on linear combinations of features (your reduced summary dimensions are a weighted summation of your data) and, thus, are only sometimes suitable to catch nonlinear patterns that are frequently found in real-world data. The more recent t-SNE and UMAP are methods that can reduce the dimensionality of data exceptionally well, allowing you to chart a reliable representation of your data where original data characteristics are maintained. There are some caveats, though, since tweaking the hyper-parameters of both methods may lead to entirely different projections from the same data. This is due to the loss of information in the data when passing from multiple features to a few ones that may result in different resulting plots—some more, some less representative of the data itself. In addition, the resulting plots may only sometimes be easily interpretable, especially if there are many data points or if the data is highly clustered. That said, t-SNE and UMAP are valuable tools for data exploration and visualization, as they can help identify patterns and clusters within complex datasets that may not be readily visible through other methods. Of course, a core principle of EDA does not uniquely rely solely on them but compares their outputs with other multivariate, bivariate, and univariate methods, as shown.

Before starting working with these methods, read articles such as "How to t-SNE Effectively" (https://distill.pub/2016/misread-tsne/) or "Understanding UMAP" (https://mng.bz/AQxK), which will provide you with additional confidence on using the methods with the appropriate precautions. Another caveat is that both approaches are computationally intensive, and it may take quite a long time to obtain a reduction from a large and complex dataset. Recently, however, NVIDIA has furthermore developed its RAPIDS suite based on CUDA and GPU technology (https://developer.nvidia.com/rapids), which can dramatically cut the time necessary before getting results from both UMAP and t-SNE, making them even more effective for intensive EDA explorations. Listing 2.9 shows the code to analyze our example dataset using the t-SNE implementation in the Scikit-learn package. We will present the NVIDIA RAPIDS implementations, as well as their other tools for processing tabular data, later in the book.

Listing 2.9   Plotting a t-SNE low-dimensional projection of a dataset

```python
from sklearn.manifold import TSNE
import matplotlib.pyplot as plt

tsne = TSNE(n_components=2,
            perplexity=30.,
            init="random",
            learning_rate="auto",
            random_state=42)

X = data[numeric_feats + ordinal_feats].fillna(
```

Imports the t-SNE class available in Scikit-learn

Imports pyplot from matplotlib for chart plotting

t-SNE is set to project results in two dimensions; the other parameters are kept at their default settings.

Only numeric and ordinal features are used; missing
values are replaced with the mean because the t-SNE
class requires a complete input data matrix.

```
              data[numeric_feats + ordinal_feats].mean())
projection_2D = tsne.fit_transform(X)

plt.figure(figsize=(15, 15))
plt.scatter(projection_2D[:, 0], projection_2D[:, 1],
            edgecolor='none',
            alpha=0.80,
            s=10)
plt.show()
```

By fit_transform, the
projection is created based
on the provided data and
applied to the data itself.

The t-SNE transformed data is plotted
as a bidimensional scatterplot.

Figure 2.13 shows the resulting plot of the t-SNE transformed data.

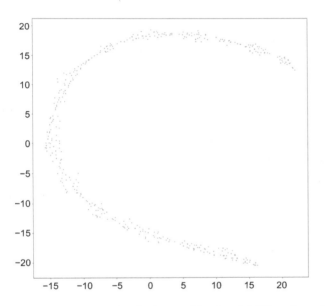

Figure 2.13 Points distribution resulting from t-SNE two-dimensional transformation

The code snippet works only on the numeric features that, after having all the missing values replaced by the mean (neither t-SNE nor UMAP can work with missing data), squeeze the data into a two-dimensional representation that a scatter plot can plot. In this dataset, the results appear to be very regular and do not present much of a surprise if we think this is a selection of curated examples collected for a purpose: all the data points have ended up being aligned in a curvilinear cloud, offering an overall impression of examples chosen progressively and regularly based on specific criteria.

This concludes our exploration of the Auto MPG Data Set. The next chapter will discuss machine learning algorithms and explore fundamental classical models routinely applied to tabular datasets. By proceeding with examples, we will point out each algorithm's strengths and weaknesses regarding the data and features you may encounter in a project.

Summary

- Despite wild differences in domains and organizations, common characteristics in tabular datasets make it possible to outline the best data handling and modeling practices.
- Rows in a tabular dataset relate the units represented, and there are limitations and opportunities to be noticed when they are non-IID. Non-IID data can affect commonly used procedures in data science, such as bootstrapping, subsampling, and cross-validation.
- There are different types of data to be found in columns: numeric (both floating and integer), ordinal (integer), categorical (both low and high cardinality, i.e., with a low or high number of distinct labels), and dates: each one requires a different approach for data processing and analysis. We suggest mastering the pandas package (and its DataFrame data structure) to handle all such different kinds of features found in tabular data.
- Different data pathologies are connected to the type of data you have in columns: constant or quasi-constant features, duplicated or highly collinear features, irrelevant features, rare categories and other incongruencies, missing data, and information leakage. Also, for each one of these, there are specific remedies.
- Finding and obtaining tabular data is relatively easy if you look for open repositories (such as the UCI Machine Learning Repository or Kaggle Datasets) or consult the Google Dataset search engine.
- EDA plays an important role in helping you clean the data you have gathered internally in your organization or from the web. You can use value counts and descriptions, histograms, box plots, correlation matrices, and low-dimensionality projections such as t-SNE to reveal the structure and the problems in data.

3

Machine learning vs. deep learning

This chapter covers

- A comparison of machine learning and deep learning as methods to tackle tabular data problems
- A comparison of machine learning and deep learning in terms of simplicity
- A comparison of machine learning and deep learning in terms of transparency
- A comparison of machine learning and deep learning in terms of efficacy

There's an open debate in the data science community about the best machine learning approach for tabular data. Some assert that classic machine learning techniques, such as gradient boosting using tools like XGBoost or LightGBM, are superior for most tabular data problems. Others advocate for including deep learning in your analysis toolkit. In this chapter, we'll examine these two approaches using two concrete examples:

- Predict the price of Airbnb New York City listings. In this example, we use a real-world dataset of Airbnb listings to train models that predict whether a new listing will have a price above or below the average listing price. We'll use this example to examine simplicity, transparency, and efficacy.
- Predict the length of time a property in a local real estate market is on the market before it is sold. In this example, we use a contrived real estate listing dataset to illustrate the explainability aspect of transparency.

We will focus on three criteria that are of particular value in interpreting scientific and business data:

- *Simplicity*—The simpler the solution in terms of the code for the application and the core API of the framework, the better.
- *Transparency*—A solution that is interpretable and that can be explained easily to a business stakeholder is best.
- *Efficacy*—The solution that provides the best results and takes less time to train and implement is preferable. Also, research interest can lead to more effective results as new approaches are discovered.

3.1 Predicting Airbnb prices in New York City

To compare the simplicity of machine learning and deep learning, we will contrast two solutions to a particular tabular data classification problem: predicting whether a New York City Airbnb listing will have a price that is greater than or less than the average price for Airbnb listings in that market. The two solutions we will compare are

- *Machine learning*—Represented by a solution that uses XGBoost, a popular gradient-based approach.
- *Deep learning*—Represented by a solution that uses the Keras functional API.

We will compare the code complexity of these solutions and review what these two solutions tell us about the overall question of the relative simplicity of machine learning and deep learning approaches.

3.1.1 The Airbnb NYC dataset

To solve the problem of predicting whether a New York City Airbnb listing will have a price that is greater than or less than the average price, we use a tabular dataset with details about Airbnb listings in New York City. Figure 3.1 includes descriptions of the columns of the NYC Airbnb dataset along with the type of data in each column, and the dataset, which you can see a sample of in figure 3.2, has been shared in Kaggle: https://mng.bz/avJ7.

Each row in this dataset has the information for a single listing, and each column in the dataset has the values for all listings for a given characteristic.

Column	Description	Type
id	unique identifier for the listing	numeric ID
name	name of the listing	free-form text
host_id	unique identifier for the person who is the host for the listing	numeric ID
host_name	name of the listing host	free-form text
neighbourhood_group	borough of New York City where the listing is located	categorical
neighbourhood	neighbourhood where the listing is located (a subdivision of the neighbourhood_group)	categorical
latitude	latitude of the listing	continuous - geospatial
longitude	longitude of the listing	continuous - geospatial
room_type	the accomodation provided by the listing	categorical
price	cost of the listing in US dollars	continuous - floating point
minimum_nights	minimum number of nights that the listing can be booked for	continuous - integer
number_of_reviews	number of reviews that have been published for the listing	continuous - integer
last_review	date that the last review was published	date
reviews_per_month	average number of reviews per month that have been published for the listing	continuous - floating point
calculated_host_listings_count	total number of listings that have the same host as this listing	continuous - integer
availability_365	number of days that the listing is available to be booked	continuous - integer

Figure 3.1   Details about the columns in the Airbnb NYC dataset

id	name	host_id	host_name	neighbourhood_group	neighbourhood	latitude	longitude
2539	Clean & quiet apt h	2787	John	Brooklyn	Kensington	40.64749	-73.97237
2595	Skylit Midtown Cast	2845	Jennifer	Manhattan	Midtown	40.75362	-73.98377
3647	THE VILLAGE OF HA	4632	Elisabeth	Manhattan	Harlem	40.80902	-73.9419
3831	Cozy Entire Floor of	4869	LisaRoxanne	Brooklyn	Clinton Hill	40.68514	-73.95976
5022	Entire Apt: Spacious	7192	Laura	Manhattan	East Harlem	40.79851	-73.94399
5099	Large Cozy 1 BR Apa	7322	Chris	Manhattan	Murray Hill	40.74767	-73.975
5121	BlissArtsSpace!	7356	Garon	Brooklyn	Bedford-Stuyvesa	40.68688	-73.95596
5178	Large Furnished Roc	8967	Shunichi	Manhattan	Hell's Kitchen	40.76489	-73.98493
5203	Cozy Clean Guest Rc	7490	MaryEllen	Manhattan	Upper West Side	40.80178	-73.96723
5238	Cute & Cozy Lower	7549	Ben	Manhattan	Chinatown	40.71344	-73.99037
5295	Beautiful 1br on Up	7702	Lena	Manhattan	Upper West Side	40.80316	-73.96545
5441	Central Manhattan/	7989	Kate	Manhattan	Hell's Kitchen	40.76076	-73.98867
5803	Lovely Room 1, Gari	9744	Laurie	Brooklyn	South Slope	40.66829	-73.98779
6021	Wonderful Guest Be	11528	Claudio	Manhattan	Upper West Side	40.79826	-73.96113
6090	West Village Nest - !	11975	Alina	Manhattan	West Village	40.7353	-74.00525
6848	Only 2 stops to Mar	15991	Allen & Irina	Brooklyn	Williamsburg	40.70837	-73.95352
7097	Perfect for Your Par	17571	Jane	Brooklyn	Fort Greene	40.69169	-73.97185
7322	Chelsea Perfect	18946	Doti	Manhattan	Chelsea	40.74192	-73.99501
7726	Hip Historic Browns	20950	Adam And Cl	Brooklyn	Crown Heights	40.67592	-73.94694
7750	Huge 2 BR Upper Ea	17985	Sing	Manhattan	East Harlem	40.79685	-73.94872

room_type	price	minimum_nights	number_of_reviews	last_review	reviews_per_month	calculated_host_listings_count	availability_365
Private room	149	1	9	10/19/2018	0.21	6	365
Entire home/apt	225	1	45	5/21/2019	0.38	2	355
Private room	150	3	0			1	365
Entire home/apt	89	1	270	7/5/2019	4.64	1	194
Entire home/apt	80	10	9	11/19/2018	0.1	1	0
Entire home/apt	200	3	74	6/22/2019	0.59	1	129
Private room	60	45	49	10/5/2017	0.4	1	0
Private room	79	2	430	6/24/2019	3.47	1	220
Private room	79	2	118	7/21/2017	0.99	1	0
Entire home/apt	150	1	160	6/9/2019	1.33	4	188
Entire home/apt	135	5	53	6/22/2019	0.43	1	6
Private room	85	2	188	6/23/2019	1.5	1	39
Private room	89	4	167	6/24/2019	1.34	3	314
Private room	85	2	113	7/5/2019	0.91	1	333
Entire home/apt	120	90	27	10/31/2018	0.22	1	0
Entire home/apt	140	2	148	6/29/2019	1.2	1	46
Entire home/apt	215	2	198	6/28/2019	1.72	1	321
Private room	140	1	260	7/1/2019	2.12	1	12
Entire home/apt	99	3	53	6/22/2019	4.44	1	21
Entire home/apt	190	7	0			2	249

Figure 3.2   Sample of rows from the Airbnb NYC dataset

The Airbnb NYC dataset has characteristics that make it a good choice for comparing approaches to solving tabular data problems:

- It has a convenient size. With around 49,000 records, it is big enough to be interesting but not so huge that it requires special "big data" tools such as Spark to handle it.

- It has a good number of columns for a comparison between machine learning and deep learning. As we will find out in subsequent chapters, a dataset with only three or four columns would immediately favor a classic machine learning approach. A dataset with hundreds of columns would be difficult to examine. The Airbnb NYC dataset has a "just right" number of columns—enough to give deep learning a chance to shine but not so many columns that the dataset is difficult for a human to comprehend.

- Because the dataset has a reasonable number of rows and columns, it is easy to take a quick look at it in a spreadsheet, which means we don't have to write Python code every time we want to answer a question about the dataset. With a spreadsheet, you can sort, filter, and count aspects of the dataset quickly and take advantage of scripting for Excel or Google Sheets to do a more detailed investigation. The Airbnb NYC dataset is amenable to being examined in a spreadsheet, which means it can be examined with minimal effort.

- The dataset includes an interesting range of column types, including several kinds of continuous columns (`minimum_nights` is integer values, `price` and `reviews_per_month` are floating point values, and `latitude` and `longitude` are geospatial values), categorical columns (`neighbourhood_group`, `neighbourhood`, and `room_type`), and free-form text columns (`name` and `host_name`).

- The dataset has some warts—for example, there are missing values in some of the columns—but it is not so messy that it requires massive cleanup before it can be used to train a model. This makes it convenient to build an application around this dataset without getting too distracted by cleanup.

- It is both open sourced and based on real data from a real business. As we will see in subsequent chapters of this book, one of the challenges of exploring machine learning and deep learning with tabular data is the scarcity of substantial open source tabular datasets that represent real business problems. The Airbnb dataset is a rare example of a nontrivial tabular dataset that contains information from a working business.

- With this dataset, the target for the model is evident: `price`. In our case, we are deriving a target based on `price`—namely whether a given listing will have a price that is above or below the median price for the listings in the dataset.

In this subsection we have taken a first look at the Airbnb NYC dataset. In the next subsection we will look at the code that ingests this dataset to train a model.

3.1.2 Introduction to the code

Now that we have introduced the Airbnb NYC dataset, let's take a look at the code for the solutions. We won't go into all the details of the code in this section, but it's important to have an overview of how the pieces fit together.

Figure 3.3 summarizes the files that make up the two solutions.

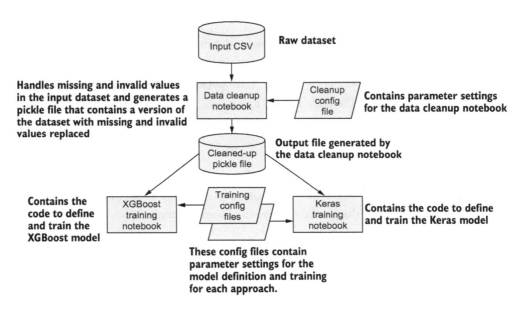

Figure 3.3 Files that make up the Airbnb NYC solution

The following are more details on the files that make up the solutions:

- *Input CSV* (https://mng.bz/avJ7).
- *Data cleanup notebook* (https://mng.bz/gawV). Note that while the XGBoost and Keras versions of the code use the same cleanup notebook, XGBoost has built-in capabilities, such as handling missing values, which means an XGBoost-only version of the cleanup notebook could be simpler than the common version.
- *Cleanup config file* (https://mng.bz/ey7Q).
- *Training config file* for XGBoost (https://mng.bz/pKOz).
- *Training config file* for Keras (https://mng.bz/vKpr).
- *XGBoost training notebook* (https://mng.bz/YDGA). Among the gradient boosting solutions we chose XGBoost because it is very popular and there is plenty of guidance online about XGBoost if we happen to run into any problems.
- *Keras training notebook* (https://mng.bz/JYwP). We chose Keras as a representative deep learning approach because, unlike alternatives like PyTorch or fastai

on top of PyTorch, Keras is, along with raw TensorFlow, most commonly used in business applications. We chose Keras over one of the tabular deep learning libraries introduced in the section "Comparing the research success of gradient boosted approaches with deep learning" because Keras is more widely used than any of those libraries and its APIs can be compared to the APIs of XGBoost in a way that is more "apples to apples" than a comparison between a deep learning library specifically designed for tabular data and the general capabilities of XGBoost.

For your convenience, the XGBoost and Keras solutions are shared in two separate folders, but most of the code is common between the two solutions:

- You can find the code for the XGBoost solution at https://mng.bz/GeEO.
- You can find the code for the Keras solution at https://mng.bz/zZ4Q.

The differences between these two repos are limited to the training notebooks and the training config files.

3.1.3   *A deep learning solution using Keras*

Before digging deeper into the details of the Airbnb dataset and the code used in the solutions, let's put the Keras solution into context of its software stack. Figure 3.4 shows the stack for the Keras solution to the Airbnb price prediction problem.

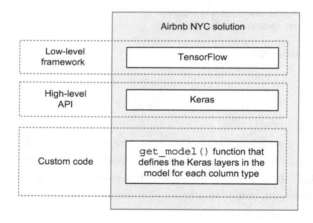

Figure 3.4   The stack for the Airbnb NYC Keras solution

In chapter 8 we will go into more detail about the stack layers shown in figure 3.4. For now, we can observe that Keras is the high-level deep learning API that we use to implement the deep learning solution to the Airbnb problem that we will examine in this chapter. There are two low-level deep learning frameworks, and the deep learning solution we will examine in this chapter depends on the TensorFlow low-level framework because that is the framework on which Keras is built.

3.1.4   *Training features*

The goal of both solutions is to predict whether a given Airbnb listing will have a price that is above or below the average price in the input dataset. To achieve this goal, both models are trained on the same set of features. The subset of features that we will use to train the model is defined in the config file for model training: https://mng.bz/ OBoE. The following is the portion of the config file that specifies the features used to train the models:

```
categorical: # categorical columns
      - 'neighbourhood_group'
      - 'neighbourhood'
      - 'room_type'
continuous: # continuous columns
      - 'minimum_nights'
      - 'number_of_reviews'
      - 'reviews_per_month'
      - 'calculated_host_listings_count'
```

The config file also includes a list of features that are explicitly excluded from the training process:

```
excluded: # columns that are not used as input features for training
      - 'price'
      - 'id'
      - 'latitude'
      - 'longitude'
      - 'host_id'
      - 'last_review'
      - 'name'
      - 'host_name'
      - 'availability_365'
```

The reasons why these columns are not used as features to train the model are as follows:

- `price` is not included as a feature for training the model because it defines the target for the model, whether or not a listing has a price above or below the average price.
- The two ID columns are not included as features because they don't carry any signal about the price of a listing because they are just numeric IDs assigned to listings and hosts.
- We don't use `latitude` or `longitude` as features because the geographic location of listings is already encoded in the `neighbourhood_group` and `neighbourhood` features that are used to train the model. If we didn't have these features to use for the geographic location of the listings, we could use the `latitude` and `longitude` values (or polar coordinates derived from them: https://mng.bz/ 0Q66) to cluster listings according to their locations or convert them into polar

coordinates. Using the raw latitude and longitude for each listing as features could lead to overfitting because each listing would have a unique value for the pair (`latitude`, `longitude`).

- The `name` and `host_name` columns are not included as features because they are somewhat arbitrary sets of tokens that allow human readers to identify the listings. An interesting exercise would be to include `host_name` as a feature to see if it provides some kind of signal related to the price of listings that have the same host.

- We decided to not include `availabiltiy_365` in the feature set because the column is challenging to interpret.

We have examined the features that we will use to train the model to predict whether an Airbnb listing will have a price above or below the average price. In the next section, we will compare the simplicity of the code for the gradient boosting and deep learning models trained on this dataset.

3.1.5   *Comparing gradient boosting and deep learning solutions*

As we mentioned previously, the two solutions for the Airbnb NYC problem only differ in a few places. Figure 3.5 shows the file structure of the solution again with the files that contain differences between the two approaches highlighted.

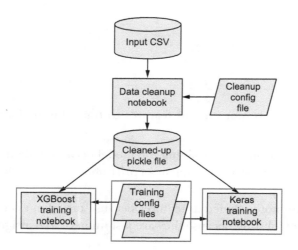

Figure 3.5   Airbnb solution files that differ between the XGBoost and Keras solutions

If the solutions only differ in these four files, how can we use this example to contrast the simplicity of XGBoost vs Keras deep learning? Table 3.1 compares the code complexity across several aspects of the application.

Table 3.1 Comparing the code complexity of XGBoost and Keras in three areas

Aspect of code complexity	XGBoost	Keras deep learning model
Data preparation	Code block required to transform the list of numpy arrays into a numpy array of lists	NA—the data preparation was designed with the Keras deep learning solution in mind
Model definition	Single statement, consistent with the Scikit-learn pattern	Block of code required to define the layers of the model, with unique sets of layers for each column type: continuous, categorical, text
Model training	Single statement, consistent with the Scikit-learn pattern	Block of code required to allow for call-back control of the training process to avoid training iterations that provide no benefit and to ensure the training process outputs the trained model with the best performance Block of code to define the callback objects required to have an efficient Keras training cycle
Model saving	Single statement, consistent with the Scikit-learn pattern	Included as part of model saving callback
Model loading	Block of code—requires installing the latest version of XGBoost or loaded model will fail with error: `AttributeError: 'XGBClassifier' object has no attribute '_le'`	Single statement

Let's look at the code in the Airbnb NYC solution for each of these aspects of code complexity.

The XGBoost solution has some additional data preparation code. The Airbnb NYC solution was originally coded using Keras deep learning and then the XGBoost solution was created using the Keras solution as a starting point. The original Keras model required training input in the form of a list of numpy arrays. XGBoost requires input in the form of a numpy array of lists. The following listing contains the code in the XGBoost training notebook that converts the original data format into the format required by XGBoost.

Listing 3.1 Data preparation code for XGBoost

```
list_of_lists_train = []
list_of_lists_test = []
for i in range(0,7):
    list_of_lists_train.append(X_train_list[i].tolist())
```

Defines lists of lists for the training and test datasets (one list for each feature)

```
        list_of_lists_test.append(X_test_list[i].tolist())
    # convert lists of lists to numpy arrays of lists
    xgb_X_train = np.array(list_of_lists_train).T
    xgb_X_test = np.array(list_of_lists_test).T
```

← **Converts the train list of lists into a numpy array of lists**

← **Converts the test list of lists into a numpy array of lists**

Note that while this is a genuine example of the XGBoost code having some additional complexity compared to the Keras code, this additional code is not intrinsically required by XGBoost but rather is needed because of the way that the XGBoost solution was adapted from the Keras solution.

To get additional confirmation of what the XGBoost data preparation code does, go to Gemini (https://gemini.google.com) and paste the code into the entry field along with the prompt "what does this code do?" and click the Submit button, as shown in figure 3.6.

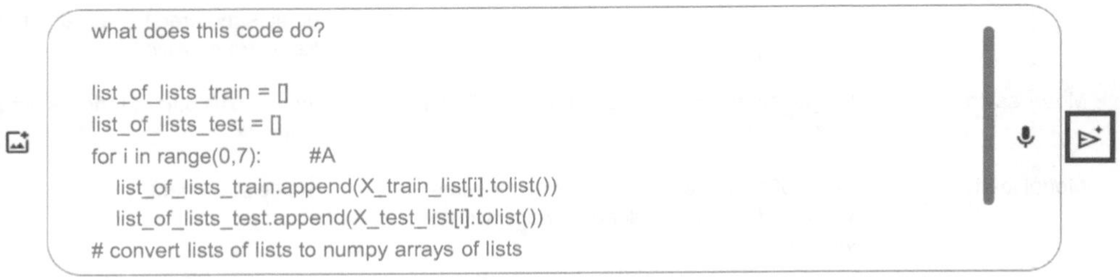

```
what does this code do?

list_of_lists_train = []
list_of_lists_test = []
for i in range(0,7):        #A
    list_of_lists_train.append(X_train_list[i].tolist())
    list_of_lists_test.append(X_test_list[i].tolist())
# convert lists of lists to numpy arrays of lists
```

Figure 3.6   Entering a request to interpret code in Gemini

You will get a response that explains what the code does along with this summary:

```
In essence, the code does the following:
It extracts specific elements from
two input lists (X_train_list and X_test_list).
It arranges those elements into a specific format (lists of lists).
It converts those lists into NumPy arrays,
preparing the data for further processing
or model training.
```

Now that we have looked at the difference between XGBoost and Keras in terms of data preparation, let's compare the model definition code for the two solutions.

The following is the XGBoost model definition for the Airbnb NYC problem—one line of code that follows the pattern of Scikit-learn:

```
model = XGBClassifier()
```

Let's look at what the model definition code looks like for the Keras solution. Figure 3.7 shows the initial part of the function that defines the deep learning model for the Airbnb NYC problem.

```
def get_model():
    ''' define Keras model by specifying layers by column type

    Returns:
        model: Keras model with the layers specified by the structure of the dataset

    '''
    catinputs = {} # list of categorical inputs
    textinputs = {} # list of text inputs
    continputs = {} # list of continuous inputs          Lists for input features
    embeddings = {}                                      and embeddings
    textembeddings = {}
    catemb = 10 # size of categorical embeddings
    textemb = 50 # size of text embeddings

    collistfix = []
    textlayerlist = []
    inputlayerlist = []
    i = 0
    print("textmax is",textmax)
    # define layers for categorical columns
    for col in collist:
        catinputs[col] = Input(shape=[1],name=col)
        inputlayerlist.append(catinputs[col])             Build layers
        #print("inputname",inputname)                     for categorical
        embeddings[col] = (Embedding(max_dict[col],catemb) (catinputs[col]))  features
        # batchnorm all
        embeddings[col] = (BatchNormalization() (embeddings[col]))
        collistfix.append(embeddings[col])
    # define layers for text columns
    if includetext:
        for col in textcols:
            print("col",col)
            textinputs[col] = Input(shape=[X_train[col].shape[1]], name=col)
            print("text input shape",X_train[col].shape[1])
            inputlayerlist.append(textinputs[col])                              Build
            textembeddings[col] = (Embedding(textmax,textemb) (textinputs[col]))  layers
            textembeddings[col] = (BatchNormalization() (textembeddings[col]))  for text
            textembeddings[col] = Dropout(dropout_rate) ( GRU(16,kernel_regularizer=l2(l2_lambda))  features
(textembeddings[col]))
            collistfix.append(textembeddings[col])
            print("max in the midst",np.max([np.max(train[col].max()), np.max(test[col].max())])+10)
        print("through loops for cols")
```

Figure 3.7   Model definition for the Keras deep learning solution for the Airbnb NYC problem (part 1)

Figure 3.8 shows the rest of the function that defines the deep learning model for the Airbnb NYC problem.

Figure 3.9 shows the visualization for the model for the Airbnb problem.

This is a bit of an extreme contrast—the deep learning model could have been defined more simply. This model definition specifies a different set of Keras layers for each column type (continuous, categorical, and text). This is not the minimal layer definition possible for a tabular data model, but it is very flexible. It will be able to deal with tabular datasets with various combinations of continuous, categorical, and text columns. Also, this model definition includes code that specifies the layers for text

```
# define layers for continuous columns
for col in continuouscols:
    continputs[col] = Input(shape=[1],name=col)
    inputlayerlist.append(continputs[col])

# build up layers

main_l = concatenate([Dropout(dropout_rate) (Flatten() (embeddings[collist[0]])
),Dropout(dropout_rate) (Flatten() (embeddings[collist[1]]) )])
for cols in collist:
    if (cols != collist[0]) & (cols != collist[1]):
        main_l = concatenate([main_l,Dropout(dropout_rate) (Flatten() (embeddings[cols]) )])

    if includetext:
        for col in textcols:
            main_l = concatenate([main_l,textembeddings[col]])

    for col in continuouscols:
        main_l = concatenate([main_l,continputs[col]])

# define output layer
output = Dense(1, activation=output_activation) (main_l)

# define model
model = Model(inputlayerlist, output)

# define optimizer
 optimizer = SGD(lr=learning_rate)

# compile model
model.compile(loss=loss_func, optimizer=optimizer, metrics=["accuracy"],
weighted_metrics=["accuracy"])
    return model
```

Build layers for continuous features

Define output layer

Compile model

Figure 3.8 Model definition for the Keras deep learning solution for the Airbnb NYC problem (part 2)

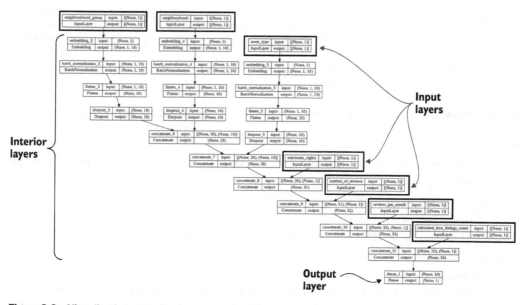

Figure 3.9 Visualization of the Keras model for the Airbnb problem

columns, and we did not choose any text columns to train the Airbnb model, so this code could have been omitted without affecting the Keras version of the Airbnb NYC solution. Nevertheless, the difference between the simplicity of the XGBoost model definition and the complexity of the Keras model definition underlines an advantage of XGBoost: model definition code is simpler in XGBoost than it is in Keras.

We have compared the data preparation code and the model definition code. Next, let's compare the model training code for the XGBoost and Keras solutions. In the XGBoost solution, training is accomplished with a single line of code with defaults accepted for all parameters that have default values:

```
model.fit(xgb_X_train, dtrain.target)
```

The following listing shows that for the Keras solution there are two different versions of the fit statement and several additional parameters (including the batch size and the default number of epochs that will be run in the training process) need to be set.

Listing 3.2 Fit statements for Keras

```
if early_stop:
        modelfit = model.fit(X_train_list, dtrain.target,     ← Fit statement including
epochs=epochs, batch_size=batch_size                             a parameter that lists
            , validation_data=(X_valid_list, dvalid.target),     callbacks for early stopping
verbose=1,callbacks=callback_list)                               and model saving
else:
    modelfit = model.fit(X_train_list,
dtrain.target, epochs=epochs, batch_size=batch_size
            , validation_data=(X_valid_list,          ← Fit statement
dvalid.target), verbose=1)                              without callbacks
```

There isn't a huge difference in the complexity of the training code between XGBoost and Keras. However, to make the Keras training process efficient, we need to use callbacks to avoid wasted training cycles and ending up with a suboptimal trained model at the end of the training process. See chapter 6 of *Deep Learning with Structured Data* (https://mng.bz/KGx0) for details on using Keras callbacks to optimize the training process.

Before taking a look at the callback statements for the Keras solution, let's see what Gemini can tell us about the fit statements. Again, let's submit this code to Gemini preceded with the prompt "what does this code do?" If you don't get a satisfactory answer the first time, click Regenerate draft to get another answer. On the second try with Gemini, we got a detailed description of the code that included the following description of the parameters for the fit statement:

```
In both cases, it trains the model using model.fit(),
which is a common method for training models in
machine learning libraries like TensorFlow or Keras.
Key arguments passed to model.fit():
```

```
X_train_list: Training data features.
dtrain.target: Training data targets (labels).
epochs: Number of training iterations.
batch_size: Number of samples per training step.
validation_data: Validation data for monitoring performance (optional).
verbose: Level of output during training (1 for progress bars).
callbacks: List of callbacks to be executed during
training (only in the early_stop case)
```

Gemini also provides the following summary:

```
The code conditionally trains a model with or without early stopping.
Early stopping is a technique to prevent overfitting
and improve model generalization.
The specific implementation of early stopping depends
on the contents of callback_list.
To fully understand its purpose, more context about the
model, training process, and early stopping criteria
is needed.
```

Note how in the last line Gemini qualifies the limitations of its analysis by correctly noting that given only the training snippet, it cannot infer all the details about the complete solution.

Listing 3.3 shows the code that defines the callbacks that are used in the model training step for Keras. This code adds additional complexity in the Keras version of the Airbnb NYC solution.

Listing 3.3   Callback statements for Keras

```
callback_list = []
    es = EarlyStopping(monitor=es_monitor,
mode=es_mode, verbose=1,
patience = patience_threshold)
    callback_list.append(es)
    model_path = get_model_path()
    save_model_path =
os.path.join(model_path,'scmodel'+modifier+"_"+str(experiment_number)+'.h5')
    mc = ModelCheckpoint(save_model_path,
monitor=es_monitor, mode=es_mode,
verbose=1, save_best_only=True)
    callback_list.append(mc)
```

Defines an early stopping callback object to specify that the training process should stop once the performance stops improving

Adds the first callback to the list of callbacks to be used in the training process

Defines a model-saving callback object to ensure that the trained model that has the optimal performance in the whole training run is the model that is saved at the end of the training run

Adds the second callback to the list of callbacks to be used in the training process

Once we have trained the model, we want to save it to a file so that we can load it and exercise it in another session or as part of the model's deployment. In our simple example, we save and reload the model in the same notebook as the one we use to train the model. The statement to save the model for XGBoost is

```
model.save_model(xgb_save_model_path)
```

For Keras, we don't need an explicit statement to save the model because the model is saved automatically with the model-saving callback.

The following listing shows the code to load the model in XGBoost.

Listing 3.4 Model-loading statements for XGBoost

```
loaded_saved_model =  xgb.XGBClassifier()          ◄──────  Defines a new XGBoost
loaded_saved_model.load_model(xgb_save_model_path)  ◄────┐   classifier object
```

**Loads the new XGBoost classifier
object with the model you saved
with the save_model statement**

The statement to load a model for Keras is

```
saved_model = load_model(save_model_path)
```

One additional difference between XGBoost and Keras is that if you try to load a saved XGBoost classifier model (like the one we trained for the Airbnb NYC problem) and run a prediction, you will get an error if you are not on a very current version of XGBoost. To get around this, the XGBoost model training notebook includes the following statement to ensure that the XGBoost is at the latest version:

```
!pip install --upgrade XGBoost
```

In this section, we have compared the simplicity of the XGBoost and Keras code for data preparation, model definition, model training, and model saving. Next, we will discuss the conclusions that we can draw from this comparison.

3.1.6 Conclusions

One of the best pieces of advice for data science projects is to take the simplest approach possible. Apply Occam's razor to a data science project to make the task easier. If there is more than one way to solve a problem, pick the simplest approach. If linear regression will solve the problem, then why use support vector machines? If a conventional coding approach will solve the problem, then why use machine learning at all? If you take the simplest approach, you will likely get initial results faster, complete development of the whole solution faster, and have an easier time maintaining the system once it has been deployed.

To answer the question of how classic machine learning and deep learning compare in terms of simplicity, we compared solutions using each approach to a concrete problem: the Airbnb NYC price prediction problem. By answering this question, we can apply the dictum "keep it simple" to tabular data problems.

In the previous subsection we reviewed the Airbnb NYC tabular dataset and compared the complexity of two solutions trained with this dataset—one that uses a gradient boosting approach (XGBoost) and one that uses deep learning (Keras). The XGBoost solution required some additional data preparation code, but this additional code is an artifact of the XGBoost solution being adapted from the deep learning solution, not a direct requirement of XGBoost. For the XGBoost solution, only one line of code was needed for model definition and one line of code for model training. For Keras, on the other hand, model definition required many lines of code, and model training required more lines of code than XGBoost, in particular to take advantage of Keras callbacks to ensure an efficient training process. The complexity of the code to save and load the model was about the same in the XGBoost solution and the Keras solution. While the Airbnb NYC problem is not representative of all tabular data problems, it does give us the opportunity to make an apples to apples comparison between a gradient boosting approach and a deep learning approach, and the conclusion of this comparison is that the XGBoost code is simpler. The XGBoost solution has fewer lines of code, and the statements for model definition and model training are simpler and require fewer nondefault parameter values in XGBoost than they do in Keras.

Before closing our conclusion on the comparative simplicity of gradient boosting and deep learning, we need to note that Keras isn't the only deep learning approach available. There are other deep learning approaches that deal with tabular data, and some of these approaches have code for defining and training models that is simpler than the Keras code that we examined for the Airbnb NYC problem. For example, with the fastai framework (https://docs.fast.ai/), which we will review in more detail in chapter 9, you can define a model to work with tabular data, train it, and use it to get predictions in less than 10 lines of code. Tensorflow canned estimators (https://mng .bz/9Y51) are another simple approach to deep learning with tabular data. With these canned estimators, you can train a model on a tabular dataset and get predictions from the model with an API that is as simple as the XGBoost API. These are just two examples of deep learning approaches with code that is simpler than Keras. The benefit of Keras is that it is very flexible, and its flexibility is one of the reasons that businesses frequently use Keras for production systems while simpler approaches, such as fastai, are rarely seen in production deployments.

Now that we have compared machine learning and deep learning in terms of simplicity, in the next section we will compare the two approaches in terms of transparency.

3.2   *Transparency*

There are two aspects of transparency that are relevant when comparing gradient boosting techniques with deep learning: explainability (that is, how easy it is to explain how the model works) and feature importance (that is, how easy it is to determine which feature has the biggest effect). In this section, we'll compare gradient boosting with deep learning according to these two aspects of transparency.

To compare the explainability of gradient boosting and deep learning, we will consider a simple, contrived dataset and how a model trained on this dataset could be explained.

The dataset that we will use contains information about houses in a particular real estate market, as shown table 3.2.

Table 3.2 House time on the market dataset

Time on market (weeks)	City	Asking price (thousand $)	Distance to transit station (km)
6	Kitchener	600	10
5	Waterloo	700	5
12	Kitchener	900	20
6	Waterloo	700	15
1	Waterloo	500	5
4	Waterloo	600	5
8	Waterloo	750	5
2	Kitchener	500	5
9	Kitchener	1000	5
4	Waterloo	750	10

We will return to the Airbnb dataset in the next section. For now, this real estate dataset is simple enough to easily illustrate explainability.

The dataset includes the city the house is located in, the asking price for the house, and the distance from the house to the closest transit station, along with the number of weeks the house was on the market before it was sold. We want to train a model using this dataset that will predict whether a house that is a fresh listing will be on the market for more or less than a month.

3.2.1 Explainability

Suppose that we wanted to give a nonspecialist, business audience an idea of how a decision tree model could be used to solve the "time in the market" problem for this dataset. We could create an illustration like the one in figure 3.10 to give a rough idea of how such a decision tree works.

Figure 3.10   Decision tree illustration

Note that the illustration doesn't contain any jargon or assume that the reader has any background in machine learning. The point of the decision tree is evident. Note this decision tree is a gross simplification, and there are important technical differences between a simple decision tree like this and a model that uses gradient boosting. XGBoost, for example, uses multiple decision trees, so this illustration by itself would not be sufficient to explain an XGBoost model. Nevertheless, it shows that, for some classic machine learning algorithms, it's possible to give nonspecialists an intuition about how the algorithms work without forcing the nonspecialists to learn technical details about them.

What if we wanted to give the same nonspecialist audience a general sense of how a deep learning model would be trained to solve the same "time on the market" problem? We could start with a generic neural network schematic like the one shown in figure 3.11.

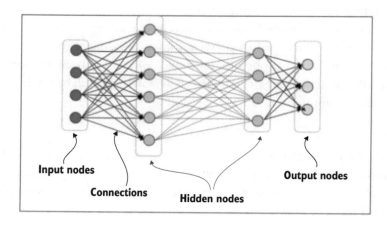

Figure 3.11   Neural network illustration

Such an illustration may help to explain the "deep" in "deep learning," but it provides no insight about how the model is actually trained. Would it help if we zoomed in to show how an individual node in the network works, as shown in figure 3.12?

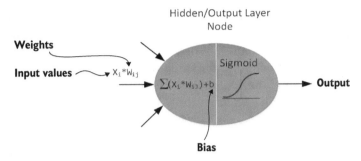

Figure 3.12   Simple illustration of a node in a neural network

Most nonspecialists would find it hard to interpret figure 3.12. If zooming into details of the neural network doesn't yield better explainability, what if we take a different approach and lean on the analogy between neural networks and biological neurons, as shown in figure 3.13? This illustration attempts to relate the overall neural network to the working of an individual node in the network (a "neuron") and then relate that node to a biological neuron.

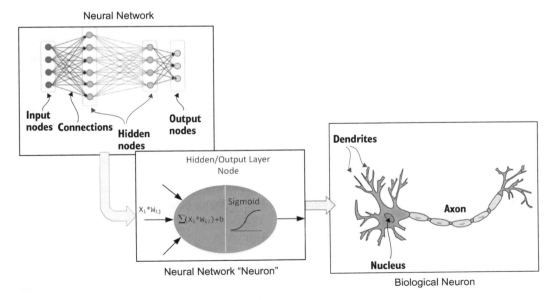

Figure 3.13   Relating a neural network to a biological neuron

Appealing to the biological analogy raises two problems. First, the analogy itself is controversial. Some experts in the industry think that neural networks work nothing like biological neurons (e.g., https://mng.bz/jp2P). Even if you accept that the analogy between neural networks and biological neurons is valid, using this analogy to explain a deep learning system can contribute to serious misunderstanding if nonspecialists infer from the analogy that simple deep learning systems have brain-like capabilities. Second, the analogy doesn't really clarify how a deep learning model is trained. Most people know what a biological neuron is, but they don't know how biological neurons actually work. An analogy is not helpful if the thing that is the source of your analogy is a bit of a mystery itself. In sum, the analogy between nodes of a neural network and biological neurons is, at best, an isolated curiosity that doesn't help a nonspecialist understand how deep learning actually works.

What can we conclude from this example? While millions of people have learned enough about deep learning to appreciate what it can and can't do, deep learning still presents some formidable obstacles when you try to explain it to a business audience. Unlike decision trees, the basics of which can be explained in an easily understood illustration, deep learning does not lend itself to being explained in one easy picture. Even today, with accessible deep learning frameworks like fastai and hundreds of free online resources about deep learning, people with a decent background in linear algebra, calculus, and programming still need several months of study to get a solid intuition of how deep learning works. We assert that it's not possible to pass on this intuition to a nonspecialist audience in one simple illustration, let alone create an instantly accessible explanation of how deep learning will work with a specific dataset.

3.2.2 *Feature Importance*

In the previous section we compared machine learning approaches and deep learning according to one aspect of transparency: how easy it is to explain the approach to a nonspecialist audience. In this section we'll look at the other aspect of transparency: how easy it is to determine the importance of a given feature to the performance of the model as a whole.

Returning to the Airbnb NYC example, we can see that the XGBoost solution uses XGBoost's built-in API for determining feature importance:

```
model.feature_importances_
```

XGBoost offers several different options for calculating feature importance. The default is gain, which is the average gain across all splits the feature is used in, where gain means the degree to which a feature separates the input examples (in our case, Airbnb listings) according to the target (in our case, whether the price of the listing is above or below the median price).

In the Airbnb NYC example, the output for this API shows the gain value for each of the features. The third feature used to train the model (room_type) has the biggest effect, followed by the first feature (neighbourhood_group):

```
array([0.10064548, 0.0438753 , 0.7586573 , 0.01957352, 0.02225152,
       0.01597736, 0.03901952], dtype=float32)
```

We can show the feature importance values in chart form using the following statement:

```
plt.barh(np.array(final_features), model.feature_importances_)
```

The output of this statement is a chart that shows the relative importance of each of the features, as shown in figure 3.14.

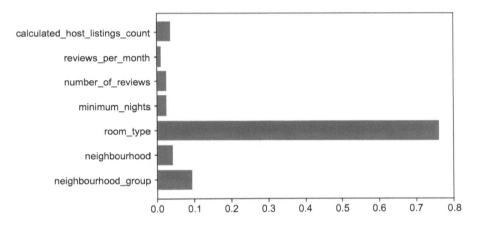

Figure 3.14   Feature importance for the Airbnb NYC problem according to XGBoost

This chart makes it clear that, according to XGBoost built-in feature importance, `room_type` is the most important feature, with `neighbourhood_group` a distant second and all the other features being relatively unimportant to the behavior of the model.

The values for the `room_type` feature are

- Entire home/apartment
- Private room
- Shared room

It intuitively makes sense that `room_type` would have a significant effect on the price of a listing. We would expect a large difference in price between a listing for an entire home and a listing for a shared room.

Now that we have looked at how we can get feature importance for the XGBoost model, let's consider how we can get feature importance for the Keras solution for the Airbnb NYC problem. Unlike XGBoost, Keras (and deep learning frameworks in general) does not have a built-in way to determine feature importance. However, you can apply external methods to get feature importance for Keras similar to the built-in feature importance in XGBoost. For example, you can use a utility like lime (https://github.com/marcotcr/lime) or shap (https://github.com/slundberg/shap) to get feature importance for a Keras deep learning model. Examining these approaches to feature importance analysis is beyond the scope of this chapter. For now, we'll note that with XGBoost you can get a basic idea of feature importance with a couple of lines of code while such a simple approach is not available for deep learning frameworks like Keras.

3.2.3   *Conclusions*

In this section we have compared machine learning and deep learning according to the following two aspects of transparency:

- *Explainability*—How easy is it to explain how the model works, particularly to business stakeholders or other people who are not data science specialists? Business stakeholders will have greater faith in a model that they can grasp in some intuitive way compared to a model that seems like a black box. More critically, for regulated industries like auto insurance, transparency isn't just a question of reassuring business stakeholders with accessible abstractions of how the model works. Regulators in such industries expect to get detailed and comprehensible explanations of how models work and how the model's behavior changes as new versions of the model are deployed externally.
- *Feature importance*—How easy is it to determine which features have the biggest effect on the behavior of the model?

We have seen that machine learning is more explainable than deep learning and that XGBoost provides a built-in feature importance API while Keras does not have a built-in facility for determining feature importance. Now that we have compared machine learning and deep learning in terms of transparency, in the next section we will compare the two approaches in terms of their efficacy.

3.3   *Efficacy*

We have compared machine learning with deep learning in terms of simplicity and transparency. Now let's look at how the two approaches compare to each other in terms of efficacy. We'll look at two aspects of efficacy:

- *Performance*—We will return to the Airbnb NYC example to compare the relative performance of the XGBoost version of the application with the Keras version of the application. In the Airbnb NYC problem, we train a model to predict whether a new listing will have a price above or below the average price. We will compare the accuracy of the predictions produced by each approach and the time required to run the code for each approach.
- *Research*—We will compare the amount of research that argues for and against the idea of applying deep learning to tabular data.

3.3.1 *Evaluating performance*

First, we'll look at the performance of the XGBoost and Keras versions of the Airbnb NYC application. We'll compare the results we get "out of the box" for each approach.

Once we have trained the XGBoost model, we can get the accuracy of the trained model on the test dataset with the following statements:

```
y_pred = model.predict(xgb_X_test)
xgb_predictions = [round(value) for value in y_pred]
xgb_accuracy = accuracy_score(test.target, xgb_predictions)
print("Accuracy: %.2f%%" % (xgb_accuracy * 100.0))
```

For a given run of the training notebook, we get the following result:

```
Accuracy: 79.24%
```

Running the code repeatedly, we get accuracy between 79% and 81% with the original parameter settings in the training configuration file (https://mng.bz/pKOz). Elapsed time to run the notebook is between 3 and 4 seconds in a vanilla Colab environment.

For the Keras model, with the original parameter settings from the training configuration file (https://mng.bz/vKpr) running in a vanilla Colab environment, the model has the following key performance characteristics:

- *Accuracy*—Test accuracy between 80 % and 81%
- *Elapsed time to run the notebook*—Between 10 and 15 seconds. This is without using a GPU on Colab. As an exercise, you can try to run the Keras training notebook with and without a GPU on Colab and compare the time it takes to run the notebook.

If we compare the performance of XGBoost and Keras for the Airbnb NYC problem, XGBoost comes out ahead in terms of speed of training. This one example doesn't tell the whole story, and we shall see in later chapters that, with some patience and tuning, a deep learning solution can rival or, in some cases, exceed the performance of XGBoost. The point of this simple performance comparison is to demonstrate that XGBoost provides good performance "out of the box" without having to do a lot of tweaking and tuning.

3.4 *Digging Deeper*

It's beyond the scope of this book to provide a detailed survey of all the recent research advocating for and against deep learning with tabular data, but in this section we will take a closer look at the research and try to get some idea of which side of the argument is "winning" the research game.

The article "A Short Chronology of Deep Learning for Tabular Data" (https://mng .bz/W2x1) is a great summary of recent academic work, and it's a good place to start a deeper look into research about deep learning and tabular data.

Following is a list of some current research that supports the use of deep learning with tabular data. Compared to the thousands of research papers published on deep learning with nontabular data, including text and images, only a tiny number of papers have been published on deep learning with tabular data.

In addition to making an argument for deep learning with tabular data, the following papers introduce libraries for deep learning with tabular data. These libraries offer convenient ways to apply deep learning to tabular datasets. We will be using some of these libraries in chapter 8 when we go through additional examples of applying deep learning to tabular data and examine alternatives to the Keras-based approach that we used in this chapter for the Airbnb NYC problem.

- SAINT: Improved Neural Networks for Tabular Data via Row Attention and Contrastive Pre-Training (https://arxiv.org/abs/2106.01342). We will examine this framework in more detail in a later chapter.
- TabNet: Attentive Interpretable Tabular Learning (https://arxiv.org/abs/1908.07442). This paper introduces another framework for deep learning with tabular data that we will explore in more detail in a later chapter.
- PyTorch Tabular: A Framework for Deep Learning with Tabular Data (https://arxiv.org/abs/2104.13638). This paper introduces a library based on PyTorch, and it is another library that we will revisit in a later chapter.
- fastai: A Layered API for Deep Learning (https://arxiv.org/abs/2002.04688). This paper introduces fastai, a high-level framework built on top of PyTorch. This framework includes explicit support for tabular data.
- Deep Tables (https://deeptables.readthedocs.io/en/latest/).
- DANets: Deep Abstract Networks for Tabular Data Classification and Regression (https://arxiv.org/abs/2112.02962).

Each of these papers features code that we can exercise to validate the research results and, more importantly, determine the robustness of the libraries. If we want to use any of these libraries to solve real-world tabular data problems with deep learning, we need to assess whether the libraries are easy to use and work with current deep learning frameworks. Figure 3.15 shows the relative popularity of some of these libraries based on the number of citations their papers received along with the number of stars received by their repos.

The popularity of libraries matters. If a library is widely used, it is more likely to work in a variety of environments. We cannot take it for granted that a library will work in every environment. As we shall see in chapter 8, some libraries don't work in Colab, for example, which means it is difficult to assess them. Also, if you use a library that hundreds or thousands of other machine learning practitioners are using, you are more likely to find answers to questions and resolutions to problems. If you are one of a handful of people using a library, you could end up being the first person who has

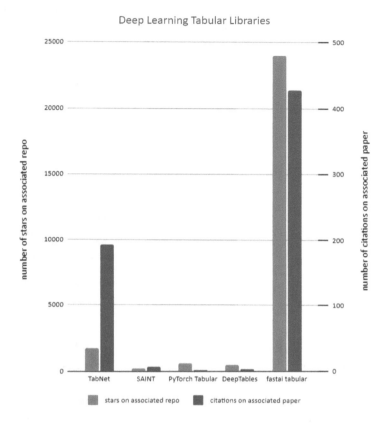

Figure 3.15   Popularity of libraries for deep learning with tabular data

encountered a given problem, and you will need to spend your time resolving it rather than simply finding an existing resolution on Stack Overflow.

The critics of deep learning with tabular data have contributed research to make their case, including the following papers:

- Why Do Tree-Based Models Still Outperform Deep Learning on Tabular Data? (https://arxiv.org/abs/2207.08815)
- Tabular Data: Deep Learning Is Not All You Need (https://arxiv.org/abs/2106.03253)
- Deep Neural Networks and Tabular Data: A Survey (https://arxiv.org/abs/2110.01889)

This list, and the preceding list of pro deep learning papers, is by no means exhaustive. However, it is fair to say that more research is published that advocates for deep learning with tabular data than research published to argue against deep learning with tabular data.

Of all the research papers published on deep learning, what proportion deals with tabular data? It's hard to get an exact ratio, but consider figure 3.16, which shows the number of papers published on deep learning for the decade and a half preceding 2018.

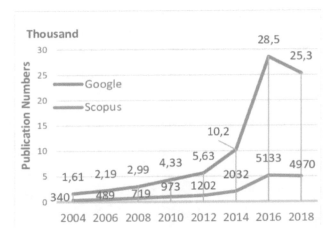

Figure 3.16   Number of published deep learning articles by year. The numbers of articles were obtained from the search results on Scopus and Google Scholar with the query "deep learning."

This figure shows that recently tens of thousands of papers are published every year on the subject of deep learning. In the last few years, less than 100 papers have been published each year on deep learning with tabular data.

One way of getting an idea of what proportion of deep learning research deals with tabular data is to do some searches on Google Scholar (https://scholar.google.com/). Consider the number of search hits on Google Scholar that match the following search criteria:

- "deep learning": ~1.6 million
- "deep learning" along with "tabular data" or "structured data" and excluding "graph-structured": ~34,500
- "deep neural networks": ~530,000
- "deep neural networks" along with "tabular data" or "structured data" and excluding "graph-structured" and "deep learning": ~1,500

Another way of determining what proportion of deep learning research deals with tabular data is to do some searches on arXiv (https://arxiv.org/). Consider the number of papers on arXiv that match the following search criteria:

- "deep learning" in the title: ~32,000
- "deep learning" along with "tabular data" or "structured data": ~200
- "deep neural networks" in the title: ~17,500
- "deep neural networks" along with "tabular data" or "structured data": ~11

From the searches on Google Scholar and arXiv, it's clear that only a tiny proportion of the research published in deep learning deals with tabular data.

To summarize, we can conclude the following points about research on deep learning with tabular data:

- There are more publications that support deep learning with tabular data than there are publications that argue against deep learning with tabular data.
- Several research papers on deep learning with tabular data include libraries that implement the approach described in the paper. So far, none of these libraries has emerged as a clear favorite for data scientists who are interested in deep learning with tabular data.
- Of all the research done on deep learning, research dealing with deep learning and tabular data makes up only a tiny fraction.

With these conclusions, it's clear that neither machine learning nor deep learning is the unambiguous winner in the area of research. In the argument for and against deep learning with tabular data, when it comes to research, the jury is still out.

We've compared machine learning with deep learning across three criteria: simplicity, transparency, and efficacy. Figure 3.17 figure summarizes how the two approaches compare with each other in each of these three criteria.

Criteria	Machine Learning	Deep Learning
Simplicity	Simpler code to: • Define a model • Train the model on a tabular dataset • Use the trained model to make predictions	Simpler code to save a trained model and load it again
Transparency	• Easier to explain to nonspecialists • Built-in reporting of feature importance	
Efficacy	• Better model performance "out of the box"	• Better flexibility • More attention from researchers
	For research dealing with tabular data, neither machine learning nor deep learning has the upper hand.	

Figure 3.17 Summary of the comparison of machine learning and deep learning with tabular data

That wraps up our comparison of machine learning and deep learning. In the next chapter we will go beyond the simple Airbnb NYC example using XGBoost and dig into the details of machine learning with tabular data.

Summary

- There are three characteristics that we can use to compare machine learning with deep learning: simplicity, transparency, and efficacy.
- The comparative simplicity of the code gives us an idea of which solution will be easier to build in the first place and easier to maintain in the long term.
- The transparency of the solution includes how easy it is to explain the model to a nonspecialist audience and how easy it is to assess the relative importance of the features used to train the model.
- Efficacy includes the success of each approach in commercial applications and in research.
- When comparing machine learning and deep learning in terms of code simplicity, machine learning comes out ahead.
- When comparing machine learning and deep learning in terms of transparency, machine learning comes out ahead.
- When comparing machine learning and deep learning in terms of efficacy, the two approaches are too close to call "out of the box," though additional tuning could expose more differences between the results of the two approaches.
- The jury is still out for other measures of success, including success in Kaggle competitions, success in business, and research focus.

Part 2

Machine learning and gradient boosting for tabular data

Chapters 4, 5, and 6 give a complete overview of classical machine learning algorithms and helps you master the most advanced gradient boosting techniques, such as XGBoost and LightGBM. You will learn how to use each algorithm and apply it to suitable tabular data. Chapter 7 helps you consolidate what you learned with a practical example to demonstrate the complete analytical process when tabular data is involved.

Specifically, chapter 4 introduces Scikit-learn and various classical machine learning methods such as linear regression, logistic regression, and generalized linear models. You will grasp how a data pipeline works from a practical point of view and learn to validate results and compare across different models. We then proceed to chapter 5 and explore decision trees and their ensembles, including bagging, random forests, and gradient boosting decision trees. Then we share a detailed explanation of how the gradient boosting algorithm operates and excels with tabular data. Finally, chapter 5 wraps up with an overview of the different implementations, from Scikit-learn to XGBoost and LightGBM.

Chapter 6 is devoted to helping you use the best practices for tabular data in machine learning, with a strong emphasis on gradient boosting methods. We touch on many advanced techniques to select an optimal set of features, optimize the hyperparameters of a model, and obtain improved performance. We also discuss how to deal with missing data from a practical point of view and how to transform categorical data properly. Part 2 concludes with chapter 7, an illustrative chapter where you learn about an end-to-end example using gradient boosting on real-world data. Guided through multiple passages, you grasp how to apply the best practices and methodologies we previously discussed. Afterward, you are ready to compare all these classical and advanced methods against deep learning approaches, which are the focus of the following conclusive part.

Classical algorithms for tabular data

This chapter covers

- An introduction to Scikit-learn
- Exploring and processing features of the Airbnb NYC dataset
- Some classic machine learning techniques

Depending on the problem, classic machine learning algorithms are often the most practical approach to working with tabular data. With decades of research and practice behind these tools and algorithms, there is a rich palette of solutions to choose from.

In this chapter, we'll cover essential algorithms in classical machine learning for making predictions using tabular data. We have focused on the linear models because they are still the most common solutions for both a challenging baseline and a solid and robust model in production. In addition, discussing linear models helps us build concepts and ideas that we can find in deep learning architectures and in more advanced machine learning algorithms, such as gradient-boosting decision trees (which will be one of the topics of the next chapter).

We'll also give you a quick introduction to Scikit-learn, a powerful and versatile machine learning library that we'll use to continue exploring the Airbnb NYC dataset. We'll stay away from lengthy mathematical definitions and textbook details in favor of examples and practical recommendations for applying these models to tabular data problems.

4.1   *Introducing Scikit-learn*

Scikit-learn is an open-source library for classic machine learning. It started in 2007 as a Google Summer of Code project by David Cournapeau, and it later became part of the SciKits (short for Scipy Toolkits: https://projects.scipy.org/scikits.html) until the INRIA (Institut National de Recherche en Informatique et en Automatique) and its foundation took the leadership of the project and of its development. We provide a short example of how Scikit-learn can quickly solve most machine learning problems. In our starting example,

1 We create a synthetic dataset for a classification problem with a binary balanced target with half labels positive and half negative.
2 We set up a pipeline standardizing the features and passing them to a logistic regression model, one of the simplest and most effective statistical-based machine learning algorithms for classification problems.
3 We evaluate its performance using cross-validation.
4 Finally, assured by the cross-validation results that our work with the problem is fine, we train a model on all the available data.

Listing 4.1 shows the complete listing and most of the features offered by Scikit-learn applied in a simple classification problem based on synthetically generated data. After creating the data, we define a pipeline, putting together statistical standardization with a basic model, logistic regression, for classification. Everything is first sent into a function that automatically estimates its performance on an evaluation metric, the accuracy, and the time its predictions are correct. Finally, figuring that its evaluated performances are suitable, we refit the same machine learning algorithm with all the data.

Listing 4.1   Example using Scikit-learn for a classification problem

```
import numpy as np
from sklearn.datasets import make_classification
from sklearn.preprocessing import StandardScaler
from sklearn.linear_model import LogisticRegression
from sklearn.model_selection import cross_validate
from sklearn.pipeline import Pipeline

X, y = make_classification(n_features=32,
                           n_redundant=0,
                           n_informative=24,
                           random_state=1,
```

```
                    n_clusters_per_class=1        ◄──┐ Generates a synthetic dataset
                    )                                │ with specified characteristics

model = LogisticRegression()          ◄──┐ Creates an instance of the
                                         │ LogisticRegression model
pipeline = Pipeline(
    [('processing', StandardScaler()),            ┌ Creates a pipeline that sequentially
     ('modeling', model)])            ◄──┘        │ applies standard scaling and the
                                                  │ logistic regression model
cv_scores = cross_validate(estimator=pipeline,
                           X=X,
                           y=y,                      ┌ Performs a five-fold cross-validation
                           scoring="accuracy",      │ using the defined pipeline,
                           cv=5)        ◄──┘         │ calculating accuracy scores

mean_cv = np.mean(cv_scores['test_score'])       ┌ Prints the mean and standard
std_cv = np.std(cv_scores['test_score'])         │ deviation of the test accuracy
print(f"accuracy: {mean_cv:0.3f} ({std_cv:0.3f})") ◄──┘ scores from cross-validation

model.fit(X, y)          ◄──┐ Fits the logistic regression model to the entire
                            │ dataset X with corresponding labels y
```

The resulting output reports the obtained cross-validation accuracy on the classification:

```
accuracy 0.900 (0.032)
```

The key point here is not the model but the procedure of doing things, which is standard for all tabular problems, whether you work with classical machine learning models or cutting-edge deep learning algorithms. Scikit-learn perfectly embeds such a procedure in its API, thus demonstrating a versatile and indispensable tool for tabular data problems. In the following sections, we will explore its characteristics and workings since we will reuse its procedures multiple times in our examples in the book.

4.1.1 Common features of Scikit-learn packages

The key characteristics of the Scikit-learn package are

- It offers a wide range of models for classification and regression, as well as functions for clustering, dimensionality reduction, preprocessing, and model selection. Most models will work in-memory when data is processed in the computer memory and out-of-core when data cannot fit into memory and is accessed from disk, allowing learning from data that exceeds your available computer memory.

- Across its range of models, it presents a consistent API (class methods such as `fit`, `partial_fit`, `predict`, `predict_proba`, `transform`) that can be quickly learned and reused and that focuses exclusively on the transformations and processes necessary for a model to learn from data and predict from it. Scikit-learn's API also offers automatic segregation of train and test data, the ability to chain and reuse its elements in a data pipeline, and accessibility of its parameters by simply inspecting the used class's public attributes.

- Initially working on NumPy arrays and sparse matrices, Scikit-learn later extended to pandas DataFrames, enabling the practitioner to use them as inputs. In later versions (since version 1.1.3), you can retain key DataFrame characteristics, such as the name of columns and the transformations operated by Scikit-learn functions and classes. The support recently provided by Scikit-learn for pandas DataFrames has been long yearned for and is indeed essential for the topic of our book, tabular data.

- To define the working parameters of each Scikit-learn class, you just use standard Python types and classes (strings, floats, lists). In addition, the default values of all such parameters are already set to a proper value for you to create a baseline to start with and improve.

- Thanks to a core group of top contributors (such as Andreas Mueller, Oliver Grisel, Fabian Pedregosa, Gael Varoquaux, and Gilles Loupe), Scikit-learn is in continuous development. There is constant debugging, and new functionalities and new models are added every time or old ones are excluded based on their robustness and scalability.

- The package also presents extensive and easily accessible documentation with examples you can consult online (https://scikit-learn.org/stable/user_guide .html) or offline using the `help()` command.

Depending on your operating system and installation preferences, if you want to install Scikit-learn, you just need to follow the instructions at https://scikit-learn.org/stable/ install.html. Together with pandas (https://pandas.pydata.org/), Scikit-learn is the core library for tabular data analysis and modeling. It offers a vast range of machine learning and statistical algorithms exclusively for structured data; in fact, the input has to be a pandas Dataframe, a NumPy array, or a sparse matrix to choose from. These algorithms are all well-established because the Scikit-learn team decided to include any algorithm in the package based on "at least three years since publication, 200+ citations, and wide use and usefulness" criteria. For more details on the algorithm inclusion requirements in Scikit-learn, see https://mng.bz/8OMw.

4.1.2   *Common Scikit-learn interface*

The other key aspect of Scikit-learn that makes it so apt for tabular data problems is its current estimator API, the *fit, predict/transform* interface. Such an estimator API is not just limited to Scikit-learn, and it is widely recognized as the most effective approach to handling training and test data. Many other projects have adopted it (see https:// mng.bz/EaWO). In fact, following Scikit-learn API, you automatically incorporate all the best practices in your data science project. In particular, you strictly separate training from validation and test data, an indispensable step for the success of any tabular data modeling, as we will demonstrate in the next section by reprising the Airbnb NYC dataset.

Before delving into more practical examples, we provide some basics about Scikit-learn estimators. First, we distinguish four kinds of objects in Scikit-learn, each with a different interface. One class can implement multiple objects at the same time. Estimators are just one of them, though they are the most important ones because most of the Scikit-learn classes are estimators. In the following example, we define a machine learning estimator, a logistic regression (to be later discussed in this same chapter) for classification using the LogisticRegression class offered by Scikit-learn:

```
from sklearn.linear_model import LogisticRegression
model = LogisticRegression(C=1.0)
```

An *estimator* is an object focused on learning from data using the .fit method. It can be applied to supervised learning, relating data to a target, or to unsupervised learning where only data is involved:

- For supervised learning: `estimator = estimator.fit(data, targets)`
- For unsupervised learning: `estimator = estimator.fit(data)`

Under the hood, an estimator uses data to estimate some parameters that serve for later mapping back data to predictions or transforming it. The parameters and other information collected in the process are made available as object attributes.

Other typical Scikit-learn objects include the following:

- *Transformer* is an object focused on mapping a transformation on data:

  ```
  transformed_data = transformer.transform(data)
  ```

- *Predictor* is an object focussed on mapping a predicted response given some data by the methods `.predict` (predicting a general outcome) and `.predict_proba` (predicting a probability):

  ```
  prediction = predictor.predict(data)
  probability = predictor.predict_proba(data)
  ```

- *Model* is an object focused on providing the goodness of fit in respect of some data, typical of many statistical methods, by the method `.score`:

  ```
  score = model.score(data)
  ```

Whether you need an estimator or a transformer, each class is always instantiated by assigning it to a variable and specifying its parameters.

Under the hood, all these classes store parameters for their task. Some parameters are learned directly from the data and are commonly referred to as the weights or parameters of the models. You can think of these as the coefficients in a mathematical formulation: unknown values to be determined by data and computations. Others are given by the user at instantiation and can be configuration or initialization settings or parameters that influence how the algorithm learns from data. We usually refer to the latter ones as *hyperparameters*. They tend to differ depending on the machine learning model; hence, we will discuss the most important ones when explaining each algorithm.

Configuration and setting parameters are similar for all the algorithms. For instance, the `random_state` setting helps to define a random seed for replicating the exact behavior of the model when using the same data. The results won't change in different runs thanks to setting a random seed. The configuration parameter `n_jobs` will allow you to set how many CPU processors you want to be used in the computations, thus speeding up the time necessary for the model to complete its work but preventing you from doing other computer operations simultaneously. Depending on the algorithm, other available settings of the same kind may define the tolerance or the memory cache used by the model.

As we mentioned, some of these hyperparameters affect how the model operates and others how it learns from data. Let's reprise our previous example:

```
from sklearn.linear_model import LogisticRegression
model = LogisticRegression(C=1.0)
```

Among the hyperparameters that affect how the model learns from data, in our example, we can quote the C parameter, which, by taking different values, instructs the machine learning algorithm to apply some constraints in elaborating patterns from the data. We will address all the parameters to be fixed for each machine learning algorithm as we present them. It is important to notice that you usually set the hyperparameters at the time when the class is instantiated.

After the class instantiation, you usually provide the data to learn from and some limited instruction on how to deal with it—for instance, by giving different weights to each data example. At this stage, we say you train or fit the class on data. This phase is commonly mentioned as "fitting an estimator," and it is done by providing data as a NumPy array, a sparse matrix, or a pandas DataFrame to the `.fit` method:

```
X = [[-1, -1], [-2, -1], [1, 1], [2, 1]]
y = [1, 1, 0, 0]
model.fit(X, y)
```

Since training a model requires mapping an answer to some data, the `.fit` method inputs the data matrix and the answer vector. Such behavior is more than typical to models because some other Scikit-learn classes input data. The `.fit` method is also common to all transformative classes in Scikit-learn. For instance, fitting just data is typical of all the classes dealing with preprocessing, as you can check at https://mng .bz/N161, because transformations also require learning some information from features. For example, if you need to standardize data, you must first learn the standard deviation and the mean of each numeric feature in the data. The Scikit-learn's StandardScaler (https://mng.bz/DMgw) does exactly this:

```
from sklearn.preprocessing import StandardScaler
processing = StandardScaler().fit(X)
```

In our example, we instantiate the class necessary for standardizing the data (Standard-Scaler), and we immediately afterward fit the data itself. Since the `.fit` method returns the instantiated class we used for the fitting procedure, you can safely get in return the class with all the learned parameters by combining these two steps. Such an approach will be helpful when building data pipelines and training models because it helps you separate the activities that learn something from data from the actions that apply what they learned to new data. This way, you won't mistake mixing information from training and validation or test data.

Depending on the complexity of the underlying operations and the quantity of provided data, fitting a model or a function processing data may take some time. After the fitting has been completed, many more attributes will become available for you to use afterward, depending on the algorithm you used.

For a trained model, you will obtain a vector of responses of predictions based on any new data by applying the `.predict` method. This will work both for a classification or a regression problem:

```
X_test = [[-1, 1], [2, -1]]
model.predict(X_test)
```

Suppose you are working on a classification; instead, you must get the probability that a certain class is a correct prediction for a new sample. In that case, you need to use the `.predict_proba` method, which is available only to certain models:

```
model.predict_proba(X_test)
```

Classes that process data, instead, do not have a `.predict` method. Still, they use the `.transform` one, which returns transformed data if the class has been previously instantiated and fitted with some training data for learning the key parameters necessary for the transformation:

```
processing.transform(X)
```

Since the transformation is often applied on the very same data that provided the key parameters, the `.fit_transform` method, which concatenates the two fit and transform phases, will result in a handy shortcut:

```
processing.fit_transform(X)
```

4.1.3   *Introduction to Scikit-learn pipelines*

You can also wrap a sequence of transformations and then predictions, selectively deciding what to transform and joining different sequences of transformations by using utility functions offered by Scikit-learn, such as

- *Pipeline* (https://mng.bz/lYx8)
- *ColumnTransformer* (https://mng.bz/BXM8)
- *FeatureUnion* (https://mng.bz/dX2O)

The Pipeline command allows you to create a sequence of Scikit-learn classes that results in a series of transformations of the data, and it can end up with a model and its predictions. In this way, you can integrate any model with the transformations it requires for the data and deal with all the involved parameters at once—those of the transformations and those of the model itself. The Pipeline command is the core command to move tabular data from source to predictions in the Scikit-learn package. To set it, at instantiation time, you just need to provide a list of tuples, each containing the name of the step in the pipeline and the Scikit-learn class or model to be executed. Once instantiated, you can use it following the common API specifications of Scikit-learn (fit, transform/predict). The pipeline will execute all the predefined steps in sequence, returning the final result. Naturally, you can access, inspect, and tune the single steps of the pipeline sequence for better results and performance, but you can handle the pipeline as a single macro command.

However, tabular columns may have different types and require quite different transformation sequences, or you may have devised two different ways to process your data that you would like to combine. ColumnTrasformer and FeatureUnion are Scikit-learn commands that can help you in such occurrences. ColumnTrasformer allows you to apply a certain transformation or pipeline of transformations only on certain columns (which you can define by their name or position index in the columns' sequence). The command takes a list of tuples, as the Pipeline command, but it requires a name for the transformation, a Scikit-learn class for executing it, and a list of column names or indexes to which the transformation should be applied. Since it is just a transformative command, its ideal usage is inside a pipeline, where its transformations can be part of the data feeding of a model. FeatureUnion, instead, is just an easy way to concatenate the results of two distinct pipelines. You may achieve the same result with a simple NumPy command such as `np.hstack` (https://mng.bz/rKJD). However, when using FeatureUnion you have the advantage that the command can fit into a Scikit-learn pipeline and hence automatically be used as part of the data feeding to the model.

The modularity of operations and API consistency offered by Scikit-learn and its Pipeline, ColumnTrasformer, and FeatureUnion will allow you to easily create complex data transformations to be handled as a single command, thus making your code highly readable, compact, and easily maintainable. In the next section, we will return to the Airbnb NYC dataset we used. We will create a series of transforming sequences in Scikit-learn that will allow us to demonstrate how Scikit-learn and its pipeline functions are the right choices for tackling your tabular data problems. We will also point out how easily you can switch between the different options for machine learning with tabular data thanks to a well-defined pipeline.

4.2   *Exploring and processing features of the Airbnb NYC dataset*

The previously introduced Airbnb NYC dataset is a perfect example for demonstrative purposes because it is a dataset representative of a real-world problem and because of its various types of columns. We will have to create and combine different pipelines to handle the different features, and the following chapters will give us a chance to present even more advanced processing techniques than the ones you can find in this chapter.

For the moment, we will place the features we will deal with into a list named `excluding_list`. They are features, such as the latitude and longitude degrees or the data of the last review (`last_review`), which need special ad hoc processing. Also, the dataset presents a few possible columns that may act as targets: the price, the availability of the listed properties (`availability_365`), and the number of reviews (`number_of_reviews`). For our purposes, we prefer to use the price. Because it is a continuous set of values above zero, we can immediately use it as a regression target. In addition, by applying a split on the mean or the median, or binning the values into deciles, we can quickly turn the price variable into a binary or multiclass classification target. Apart from price, we use all the other features as predictive ones or for more advanced feature engineering.

In the following subsection, we will demonstrate a step-by-step approach to exploring the dataset, filtering the dataset based on the useful columns, and setting up our target variables. In principle, we will follow the hints and examples provided in chapter 2 when discussing *exploratory data analysis* (EDA). In the next section, we will take advantage of our discoveries and prepare suitable data pipelines that will be reused in the following paragraphs when revising the different options for machine learning for tabular data.

4.2.1   *Dataset exploration*

As a first step in exploring the dataset, we import the relevant packages (NumPy and pandas), define the list of excluded features as well as separate lists for categorical and continuous features based on our prior knowledge built in the previous chapter, and load the data from our current working directory. The code to be executed is

```
import numpy as np
import pandas as pd
excluding_list = ['price', 'id', 'latitude',
                  'longitude', 'host_id',
                  'last_review', 'name',          ◀─── List of column names to be
                  'host_name']                         excluded from the analysis
categorical = ['neighbourhood_group',
               'neighbourhood',                   ◀─── List of names of columns that likely represent
               'room_type']                            categorical variables in the dataset
continuous = ['minimum_nights',
              'number_of_reviews',                      List of names of columns that
              'reviews_per_month',                      represent continuous numerical
              'Calculated_host_listings_count']  ◀───   variables in the dataset
data = pd.read_csv("./AB_NYC_2019.csv")
```

Once the code snippet has completed the loading of the data, we first check how many rows and columns have been returned in the data frame:

```
data.shape
```

We will get 48,895 rows available—a fair number for a tabular problem, allowing us to use any available learning algorithm—and 16 columns. Since we are interested only in some of the columns—the ones we defined in the variables named categorical and continuous—we start by refining the classification of categorical features into low cardinality and high cardinality ones based on the number of unique values they have:

```
data[categorical].nunique()
```

The command results in the following output:

```
neighbourhood_group        5
neighbourhood            221
room_type                  3
```

Our standard approach when dealing with categorical features is to apply *one-hot encoding*, creating one binary variable for each unique value in the original feature. However, by using one-hot encoding, features presenting over 20 unique values will result in an excessive number of columns in the dataset and data sparsity. You have sparsity in your data when your data is predominantly of zero values, which is a problem, especially for neural networks and generally for online algorithms because learning becomes more difficult. In chapter 6, we will present techniques, such as target encoding, to deal with features with too many unique values, called *high cardinality categorical features*. For the examples in this chapter, we will separate the low from the high cardinality categorical features and process only the low cardinality ones:

```
low_card_categorical = ['neighbourhood_group', 'room_type']
high_card_categorical = ['neighbourhood']
```

Next, having defined that (for the moment, we will be working only with numeric and low cardinality categorical features), we need to figure out if there are any missing cases in our data. The following command asks to flag true missing values and then computes a count of them across features:

```
data[low_card_categorical + continuous].isna().sum()
```

We obtain the following result that points out a problem only with the `reviews_per_month` feature:

```
neighbourhood_group          0
room_type                    0
minimum_nights               0
number_of_reviews            0
reviews_per_month        10052
```

```
calculated_host_listings_count          0
availability_365                        0
```

As we mentioned in chapter 2, dealing with missing values shouldn't be an automated procedure; rather, it requires some reflection on the data scientist's part to determine if there is some reason for them to be missing. In this case, it becomes evident that there is a processing problem with the data at the source because if you check the minimum value, this will result in a value above zero:

```
data.reviews_per_month.min()
```

The minimum reported is 0.01. Here we have a missing value when there are not enough reviews to make statistics. Hence, we could replace the missing value on this feature with a zero value. Having filtered our features to be used for predictions and having checked missing values because most machine learning algorithms won't work in the presence of missing input data, apart from a few such as the gradient boosting implementations XGBoost or LightGBM (discussed in the next chapter), we can proceed to check about our target. This part of EDA, *target analysis*, is often overlooked, yet it is quite important because, in tabular problems, not all machine learning algorithms can handle the same kind of targets. For example, targets with many zeros, fat tails, and multiple mode values are difficult for certain models and result in your model underfitting. Let's start by checking the distribution of the price feature. A histogram, plotting the frequency of values falling into ranges of values (called bins), is particularly helpful in figuring out how your data distributes. For instance, a histogram can tell you if your data resembles a known distribution, such as the normal distribution, or highlight at around what values there are peaks and where the data is denser (see figure 4.1). If you are working with a pandas DataFrame, the plot can be made just by calling the `hist` method that depicts data distribution by plotting the frequency of values falling into ranges of values (bins):

```
data[["price"]].hist(bins=10)
```

Figure 4.1 **A histogram describing how the Price feature is distributed**

The distribution shown in figure 4.1 is extremely skewed to the right, with many out-lying values because the plotted values range to 10,000. However, just before 2,000, it is hard to distinguish any bar depicting frequencies. This becomes even more evident by plotting a boxplot, which is a very useful tool when one wants to visualize where the core part of the distribution of a variable lies. A *boxplot* for a variable is a plot where the key measurements of the distribution are depicted as a box with "whiskers": two lines outside the box that stretch to the expected limits of the variables' distribution. The box is delimited by the interquartile range (IQR), determined by the 25th and 75th percentiles, and split into two by the line of the median. The whiskers stretch up and down to values 1.5 times the IQR. Everything above or below the whiskers' edges is con-sidered an *outlier*: an unusual or unexpected value. Let's plot a boxplot for the price variable, again using a built-in method in pandas DataFrame, the boxplot method (see figure 4.2):

```
data[["price"]].boxplot()
```

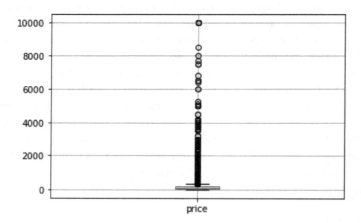

Figure 4.2   A boxplot highlighting the distribution of the Price feature and its right heavy tail on large price values

Not surprisingly, the box and whiskers are squeezed in the lower part of the chart and are almost indistinguishable from each other. A long queue of outliers elongates from the upper limit of the upper extremity of the boxplot. This is an evident case of a right-skewed distribution. In such cases, a standard solution to remediate the variable is to transform the target using a logarithm transformation. It is common practice to add a constant to offset the values into the positive number field for handling values of zero and below. In our case, it is unnecessary, since all the values are positive and above zero. In the following code snippet, we represent the transformed price feature by application of a logarithmic transformation (see figures 4.3 and 4.4):

```
np.log1p(data["price"]).hist(bins=20)
data[["price"]].apply(lambda x: np.log1p(x)).boxplot()
```

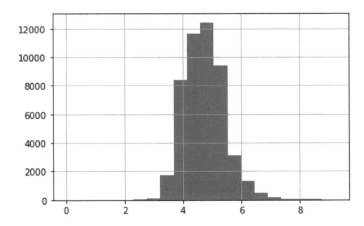

Figure 4.3   A histogram of the Price feature being more symmetrical after log transformation

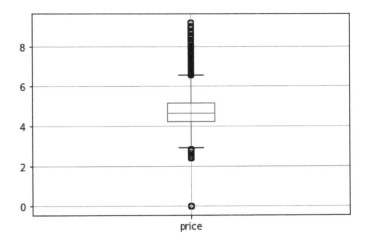

Figure 4.4   A boxplot of the Price feature after log transformation signaling the persistence of extreme values at both the tails of the distribution

Now the distribution, represented both by the new histogram and the boxplot, is more symmetric, though it is evident that there are outlying observations on both sides of the distribution. Since our aim is illustrative, we can ignore the original distribution and focus on a meaningful target representation. For instance, we can keep only the price values below 1,000 (see figure 4.5). In the following code snippet, we produce a histogram focused only on price values below 1,000:

```
data[["price"]][data.price <= 1000].hist(bins=20)
```

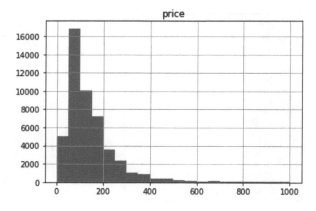

Figure 4.5   A histogram of the Price feature for values under 1,000 still showing a right-skewed long tail

Here the represented distribution is still right-skewed, but it resembles more common distributions found in e-commerce or other sales with long-tail products. In addition, if we focus on the range between 50 and 200, the distribution will appear more uniform (see figure 4.6). In the following code snippet, we restrict our focus further only to prices between 50 and 200 and plot the relative histogram:

```
data[["price"]][(data.price >= 50) & (data.price <= 200)].hist(bins=20)
```

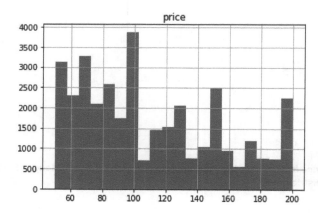

Figure 4.6   A histogram of the Price feature for values between 50 and 200, showing distributed values across the range

Therefore, we can create two masking variables, made of booleans, that can help us filter the target according to the type of algorithm we would like to test. The `price_capped` variable will be instrumental when demonstrating how certain machine learning algorithms can handle long tails easily:

```
price_capped = data.price <= 1000
price_window = (data.price >= 50) & (data.price <= 200)
```

Figure 4.7 shows the boxplot relative to the capped price, which presents right-sided outliers, but at least the boxplot is visible.

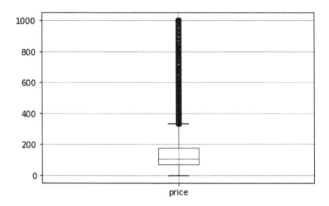

Figure 4.7 A boxplot of the Price feature for values under 1,000 showing a long tail of extreme values in its right tail

Figure 4.8 shows the boxplot relative to the windowed price, showing no sign of outliers:

```
data[["price"]][price_window].boxplot()
```

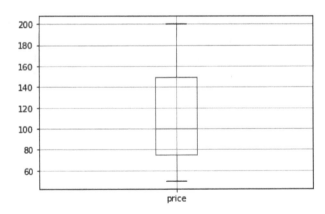

Figure 4.8 A boxplot of the Price feature for values between 50 and 200 showing a slightly right-skewed distribution with no extreme values

After completing our exploration of the predictors and the target, we are ready to prepare four different targets that will be used along with our examples:

```
target_mean = (data["price"] > data["price"].mean()).astype(int)
target_median = (data["price"] > data["price"].median()).astype(int)
target_multiclass = pd.qcut(data["price"], q=5, labels=False)
target_regression = data["price"]
```

We prepared two binary targets, `target_mean` and `target_median`, and a multiclass target with five distinct classes based on percentiles for classification purposes.

In particular, it is important to notice that our `target_median` is a binary balanced target. Hence, we can safely use accuracy as a good performance measurement. As a test, you get an almost equal number of cases for the positive and negative classes if you try to count the values:

```
target_median.value_counts()
```

You get the result

```
0    24472
1    24423
```

Instead, if you try doing the same on the `target_mean` target variable, you get

```
target_mean.value_counts()
```

You will obtain a distribution that is imbalanced toward the negative cases; that is, there are more cases below the mean because of the skewed distribution we previously observed:

```
0    34016
1    14879
```

In such a case, when evaluating the results of a machine learning classifier, we prefer to use metrics such as the Receiver Operating Characteristic Area Under the Curve (ROC-AUC) or Average Precision—both quite sensible for ordering. Finally, as for the multiclass target, counting the cases for each one of the five classes reveals that they are also balanced in distribution:

```
target_multiclass.value_counts()
```

This command returns the result of

```
0    10063
1     9835
2     9804
3    10809
4     8384
```

As for the regression target, `target_regression` is the original target without transformations. However, we will use subsets of it and accordingly transform them based on the machine learning algorithm we will demonstrate.

Having completed our exploration of the data, the target, and some basic feature selection in the next paragraph, using a building blocks approach, we will prepare a few pipelines to accompany our discovery of different machine learning options for tabular data problems.

4.2.2 Pipelines preparation

We will use the previously seen Pipeline and ColumnTransformer classes from Scikit-learn to prepare the pipelines. In a building blocks approach, we first create the different operations to be applied to the other data types that characterize features in a tabular dataset.

The following code defines three core procedures that will be reused multiple times in this chapter:

- *Categorical one-hot encoding*—Categorical features are transformed into binary ones. If a value has never been seen before, it will be ignored.
- *Numeric pass-through*—Numeric features are imputed using zero as a value.
- *Numeric standardization*—After imputing missing values, numeric features are rescaled by subtracting their mean and dividing them by their standard deviation

The code defining these procedures is shown in the following listing.

Listing 4.2 Setting up building blocks for tabular learning pipelines

```
from sklearn.pipeline import Pipeline
from sklearn.compose import ColumnTransformer
from sklearn.preprocessing import OneHotEncoder
from sklearn.preprocessing import OrdinalEncoder
from sklearn.impute import SimpleImputer
from sklearn.preprocessing import StandardScaler

categorical_onehot_encoding = OneHotEncoder(
        handle_unknown='ignore')
numeric_passthrough = SimpleImputer(
        strategy="constant", fill_value=0)
numeric_standardization = Pipeline([
        ("imputation", SimpleImputer(strategy="constant", fill_value=0)),
        ("standardizing", StandardScaler())
        ])
```

Converts categorical features into one-hot encoded format

Replaces missing numeric values with zero

Pipeline replaces missing numeric values with zero and standardizes the features

---

At this point, we can compose specific transformation pipelines that handle the data according to our needs for each machine learning algorithm. For instance, in this example, we set a pipeline that will one-hot encode low categorical features and just impute missing values as zero for numeric ones. Such a pipeline is made by the ColumnTransformer function, a glue function that combines operations applied on different sets of features simultaneously. This is an excellent transformative strategy suitable for most machine learning models:

```
column_transform = ColumnTransformer(
                [('categories',
```

```
            categorical_onehot_encoding,          ◀──┐  First step of the pipeline: one-hot
            low_card_categorical),             ◀──┘  encoding categorical features
          ('numeric',
            numeric_passthrough,               ◀──┐  Second step of the pipeline:
            continuous),                          ┘  handling numeric features
        ],
      remainder='drop',                    ◀─────┐  The features not processed
      verbose_feature_names_out=False,     ◀─────┤  by the pipeline are dropped
      sparse_threshold=0.0     ◀────────┐        │  from the result.
    )
                  The result is always a dense      Names of the features are
                  matrix (i.e., a NumPy array).     kept as they originally are.
```

We can immediately run this code snippet and check how this pipeline transforms our Airbnb NYC data:

```
X = column_transform.fit_transform(data)
print(type(X), X.dtype, X.shape)
```

The result is that the output is now a NumPy array made of floats and that the shape has increased to 13 columns. In fact, because of one-hot encoding, each value in the categorical features has turned into a separate feature:

```
<class 'numpy.ndarray'> float64 (48895, 13)
```

The following section will explore the main machine learning techniques for tabular data. Each will be accompanied by its column transforming class, which will be integrated into the pipeline containing the model.

4.3   *Classical machine learning*

To explain the different models from the classic machine learning techniques for tabular data, we will first introduce the core characteristics of the algorithm, and then demonstrate a code snippet, seeing it at work on our reference tabular problem, the Airbnb NYC dataset. The following are some best practices that we will use in our examples to allow reproducibility and comparability of the different approaches:

- We define a pipeline incorporating both data transformation and modeling.
- We set an error measure, such as root mean squared error (RMSE) for regression or accuracy for classification, and measure it using the same cross-validation strategy.
- We report the average and standard deviation—crucial to figure out if the model has a constant performance across different data samples—of the cross-validated estimate of the error.

In the previous section, we introduced the different tools Scikit-learn offers for building data pipelines integrating feature processing and machine learning models. In this section, we will introduce the recommended evaluation measures and how the cross-validation estimate by the Scikit-learn `cross_validate` command works.

Let's review *evaluation metrics* first. We decided to use RMSE, a common measure for regression tasks, and accuracy, another standard measure for balanced binary and multiclass classification problems when the classes have approximately the same sample sizes. In subsequent chapters, we will also use metrics suitable for unbalanced classification problems, such as ROC-AUC and average precision.

Cross-validation is the de facto standard in data science when you intend to estimate the expected performance of a machine learning model on any data different from the training data but drawn from the same data distribution. It is important to note that cross-validation estimates the future performance of your model based on the idea that your data may change in the future but won't be radically different. To work correctly, the model expects that you will use the same features in the future and that they will have the same unique values (if a categorical feature) with similar distributions (both for categorical and numeric features) and, most importantly, that features will be in the same relation with your target variable.

The assumption that data distributions will remain consistent in the future is frequently not true because economic dynamics, consumer markets, and social and political situations change rapidly in the real world. In the real world, your model may experience concept drifting, when the modeled relationships between features and targets no longer represent reality. Hence, your model will underperform when dealing with new data. Cross-validation is the best tool to evaluate your models at the time of their creation because it is based on your available information at that moment and because, if well designed, it is not influenced by the ability of your machine learning model to overfit the training data. Its usefulness stays true even after cross-validated results are disproved compared to future performances, usually because the underlying data distribution has changed. In addition, alternative methods, such as leave-one-out or bootstrapping, offer better estimates with increasing computational costs, whereas more straightforward methods, such as train/test split, are less reliable in their estimates.

In its most uncomplicated flavor, the *k-fold cross-validation* (implemented in Scikit-learn with the KFold function: https://mng.bz/VVM0) is based on the splitting of your available training data into k partitions and the building of k versions of your model fed each time by different sets of k-1 partitions and then tested on the remaining left out partition (the out-of-sample performance). The average and standard deviation of the resulting k scores will provide an estimate and a quantification of its uncertainty level to be used as a model estimate for expected performance on future unseen data. Figure 4.9 illustrates the k-fold validation when k is set to 5: each row represents the data partitioning at each fold. The validation part of a fold is always distinct from the others, and the training part is always differently composed.

Setting the correct value to k is a matter of how much training data you have available, how computationally costly it is to train your model on it, how the sample you received catches all the possible variations of the data distribution you want to model,

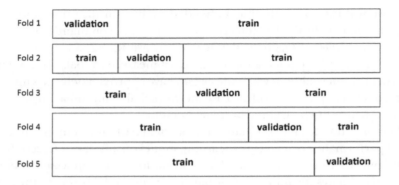

Figure 4.9   How data is distributed between train and validation across the folds of a five-fold cross-validation strategy

and for what purpose you intend to get a performance estimate. As a general rule of thumb, values of k such as 5 or 10 are optimal choices, with k = 10 being more suitable for precise performance evaluation and k = 5 a good value compromising precision and computation costs for activities such as model, features, and hyperparameters evaluation (hence it will be used for our examples).

To get a general performance estimation for your model, you can build the necessary cross-validation iterations using a series of iterations on the KFold function (or its variations, offering sample stratification or control on the time dimension: https://mng.bz/xKne) or rely on the `cross_validate` procedure (https://mng.bz/AQyK) that will handle everything for you and just return the results. For our purposes of testing different algorithms, `cross_validate` is quite handy because, given the proper parameters, it will produce a series of metrics:

- Cross-validation test scores (out-of-sample performance)
- Cross-validation train scores (in-sample performance)
- Fit time and predict time (to evaluate the computational cost)
- The trained estimators on the different cross-validation folds

All we have to do is provide an estimator, which can be any Scikit-learn object with a fit method, predictors and target, a cross-validation strategy, and a single or multiple scoring functions in a list. This estimator should be provided in the form of a callable to be created using the `make_scorer` command (https://mng.bz/ZlAO). In the next section, we will start seeing how we can get cross-validated performance estimates using such inputs, starting with classical machine learning algorithms such as linear regression and logistic regression.

4.3.1   *Linear and logistic regression*

In *linear regression,* a statistical method that models the relationship between a dependent variable and one or more independent variables by fitting a linear equation to observed data, you first have all your features converted to numeric ones and put them into a matrix, including one-hot encoded categorical features. The algorithm's goal is to optimally find the weight values in a column vector (the coefficients) so that, when multiplied against the matrix of features, you get a vector of results best approximating your targets (the predictions). In other words, the algorithm strives to minimize the residual sum of squares between the targets and the predictions obtained by multiplying features with the weight vector. In the process, you can consider using a prediction baseline (the so-called intercept or bias) or placing constraints on the weight values for them to be only positive.

Since the linear regression algorithm is just a weighted summation, you have to take care of three key aspects:

- Ensure there are no missing values since they cannot be used for multiplications or additions unless you have imputed them to some value.
- Ensure you have handled outliers because they can affect the algorithm's work both in training and prediction.
- Validate that the features and the target are linearly related as much as possible (i.e., they have a good Pearson correlation): features weakly related to the target tend just to add noise to the model, and they tend to make it underfit or even, when in high numbers, overfit.

Since a summation of your weighted features gives the prediction, it is easy to determine the most significant effect on the predicted output and how each feature contributes to it. Observing the coefficients relative to each feature gives you insight into how the algorithm behaves. Such understanding can prove valuable when you have to explain how the model works to regulatory authorities or stakeholders and when you want to check if the predictions are justifiable from the point of view of a hypothesis or expert knowledge of the domain.

However, there are also hidden perils in the easy way that a regression model shows how it works under the hood. When two or more features in the data are highly correlated, a condition known as "multicollinearity" in statistics, the interpretation in a regression model can be much more complicated, even if both features effectively contribute to the prediction. Usually, only one of many takes a notable coefficient, whereas the others take small values as if they were unrelated to the target. In reality, the opposite is often true, and the relative ease in understanding the role of a feature in a regression prediction can lead to important conceptual misunderstanding.

Another great advantage of the linear regression algorithm is that, since it is just some multiplications and summations, it is a breeze to implement it on any software platform, even by hand-coding it in a script. Other machine learning algorithms are more complex to replicate, and hence, implementation from scratch of algorithms more complicated than a linear regression may be susceptible to errors and bugs. However, though unfeasible for delivering your projects, we have to note that hand-coding any machine learning model can be a valuable learning experience, allowing you to gain a deeper understanding of the inner workings of the algorithm and making yourself more equipped to troubleshoot and optimize the performance of the similar models in the future. We present some manageable from-scratch implementations of some algorithms for learning purposes in chapter 5.

We will start with an example of a linear regression model applied end to end to our Airbnb NYC data. The example follows the schema proposed in figure 4.10, a schema that we will replicate for every classical machine learning algorithm we will present and that is based on Scikit-learn's pipelines and cross-validation evaluation functions.

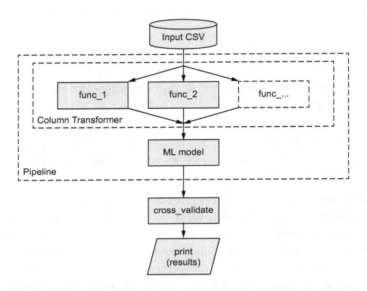

Figure 4.10   Schema of how we will organize the examples for classical machine learning algorithms

The schema is quite linear. The input from a comma-separated values file first goes through a ColumnTransformer, which constitutes the data preparation part, which applies transformation on data, discards data, or lets it pass as it is, based on column names and then a machine learning model. Both are wrapped into a pipeline tested by a `cross_validate` function that executes cross-validation and records computation times, trained models, and performances on a certain number of folds. Finally, the results are selected to demonstrate how the model worked. In addition, we can access, passing by the pipeline, the model coefficients and weights to get more insights into the functionalities of the algorithm we tested.

Applying such a schema, we just use a vanilla linear regression model in listing 4.3 since this algorithm usually does not need to specify any parameter. For special applications related to model interpretability, you could have specified the `fit_intercept` to be false to remove the intercept from the model and derive all the predictions from the features only or the positive parameter to be true to get only positive coefficients.

Listing 4.3 Linear regression

```
from sklearn.linear_model import LinearRegression
from sklearn.metrics import make_scorer, mean_squared_error
from sklearn.model_selection import KFold
from sklearn.model_selection import cross_validate

column_transform = ColumnTransformer(
    [('categories', categorical_onehot_encoding, low_card_categorical),
     ('numeric', numeric_passthrough, continuous)],
    remainder='drop',
    verbose_feature_names_out=False,
    sparse_threshold=0.0)

model = LinearRegression()

model_pipeline = Pipeline(
    [('processing', column_transform),
     ('modeling', model)]
)

cv = KFold(5, shuffle=True, random_state=0)
rmse =  make_scorer(mean_squared_error,
                    squared=False)

cv_scores = cross_validate(estimator=model_pipeline,
                           X=data[price_window],
                           y=target_regression[price_window],
                           scoring=rmse,
                           cv=cv,
                           return_train_score=True,
                           return_estimator=True)

mean_cv = np.mean(cv_scores['test_score'])
std_cv = np.std(cv_scores['test_score'])
fit_time = np.mean(cv_scores['fit_time'])
score_time = np.mean(cv_scores['score_time'])
print(f"{mean_cv:0.3f} ({std_cv:0.3f})",
      f"fit: {fit_time:0.2f}",
      f"secs pred: {score_time:0.2f} secs")
```

ColumnTransformer, transforming data into numeric features and imputing missing data

Vanilla linear regression model

Pipeline assembling ColumnTransformer and model

Cross-validation strategy based on five folds and random sampling

Function for evaluation metric derived from mean squared error

Automated cross-validate procedure

Reports the results in terms of evaluation metric, standard deviation, fitting, and prediction time

Running the listed code will produce the following RMSE results:

```
33.949 (0.274) fit: 0.06 secs pred: 0.01 secs
```

That's a good result, obtained in a minimal time (using a standard Google Colab instance or a Kaggle notebook), and can act as a baseline for more sophisticated attempts. For example, if you try to run the code in listing 4.4, you will realize that you can get similar results with fewer but accurately prepared features. That's called *feature engineering*, and the interesting point of doing it is that you can get better results or the same results but with fewer features meaningful for domain or business experts. For example, we create various new features in the code listing by generating binary features relative to specific values, combining features, and transforming them using a logarithmic function.

Listing 4.4 Customized data preparation for linear regression

A binary column indicating whether the 'neighbourhood_group' is 'Manhattan'

A column containing the natural logarithm of the values in the 'number_of_reviews' column plus 1

Creates an empty DataFrame

A binary column indicating whether the 'room_type' is 'Entire home/apt'

A binary column indicating whether the 'neighbourhood_group' is 'Queens'

A column containing the natural logarithm of the values in the 'minimum_nights' column plus 1

A product of the binary 'neighbourhood_group_Manhattan' and 'room_type_Entire home/apt' columns

A product of 'availability_365' and the binary 'neighbourhood_group_Manhattan' column

A product of 'availability_365' and the binary 'room_type_Entire home/apt' column

```python
data_2 = data[[]].copy()
data_2['neighbourhood_group_Manhattan'] = (
    (data['neighbourhood_group']=='Manhattan')
    .astype(int))
data_2['neighbourhood_group_Queens'] = (

(data['neighbourhood_group']=='Queens').astype(int))
data_2['room_type_Entire home/apt'] = (
                            (data['room_type']=='Entire
home/apt').astype(int))
data_2['minimum_nights_log'] = np.log1p(
                    data["minimum_nights"])
data_2['number_of_reviews_log'] = np.log1p(
                    data["number_of_reviews"])
label1 = 'neighbourhood_group_Manhattan*room_type_Entire home/apt'
data_2[label1] = (
    data_2['neighbourhood_group_Manhattan'] *
    data_2['room_type_Entire home/apt'])
label2 = 'availability_365*neighbourhood_group_Manhattan'
data_2[label2] = (data['availability_365'] *
    data_2['neighbourhood_group_Manhattan'])
label3 = 'availability_365*room_type_Entire home/apt'
data_2[label3] = (data['availability_365'] *
    data_2['room_type_Entire home/apt'])

rmse = make_scorer(mean_squared_error, squared=False)
cv = KFold(5, shuffle=True, random_state=0)

cv_scores = cross_validate(estimator=LinearRegression(),
                    X=data_2[price_window],
                    y=target_regression[price_window],
                    scoring=rmse,
                    cv=cv,
                    return_train_score=True,
                    return_estimator=True)

mean_cv = np.mean(cv_scores['test_score'])
std_cv = np.std(cv_scores['test_score'])
print(f"{mean_cv:0.5f}, {std_cv:0.5f}")
```

The resulting RMSE is

```
33.937 (0.240)
```

Though the result is comparable to the previous experiment, this time you are using a dataset with fewer features that have been created by specific transformations, such as the one-hot encoding of categorical features, the transformations applied to numeric ones by specific functions (i.e., cubed, squared, logarithm, or square root transformation) and by multiplying features together. In our experience, a model presenting fewer, more meaningful features generated by reasoned feature engineering and domain expertise is usually more accepted by business users, even if it has comparable or even less predictive performance than a purely data-driven one.

Multiplying features together is an operation that you find only when working with linear regression models; the obtained result is called interactions between features. Interactions work by multiplying two or more features to get a new one. All such transformations on the features are intended to render the relationship between each feature and the target as linear as possible. Good results can be obtained automatically or based on your knowledge of the data and the problem. Applying such transformations to the features is typical of the family of linear regression models. They have little or no effect on the more complex algorithms we will explore later in this chapter and subsequent chapters. Investing time in defining how the features should be expressed is both an advantage and a disadvantage of linear regression models. However, there are ways to automatically perform it using regularization, as we will propose in the next section.

The next section will discuss regularization in linear models (linear regression and logistic regression). Regularization is the best solution to implement when you have many features and their reciprocal multicollinearity (you have multicollinearity when two predictors are highly correlated with one another) doesn't allow the linear regression model to find the best coefficients for the prediction because they are unstable and unreliable—for instance, showing a coefficient you didn't expect in terms of sign and size.

4.3.2 *Regularized methods*

Linear regression models are usually simple enough for humans to understand directly as formulas of coefficients applied to features. This means that, when applied to a real-world problem, they can turn out to be a rough approximation of complex dynamics and thus systematically miss correct predictions. Technically, they are models with a high bias. A remedy for this is to make their formulations more complex by adding more and more features and their transformations (logarithmic, squared, root transformations, and so on) and by making features interact with many others (through multiplication). In this way, a linear regression model can diminish its bias and become a better predictor. At the same time, however, the variance of the model will also increase, and it can start overfitting.

Occam's razor principle, which states that among competing hypotheses, the one with the fewest assumptions should be selected (https://mng.bz/RV40), works perfectly for linear models, whereas it doesn't matter for neural networks applied to tabular data where the more complex, the better. Hence, linear models should be as simple as possible to meet the needs of the problem. Here is where regularization enters the scene, helping you reduce the complexity of a linear model until it fits the problem. Regularization is a technique used to reduce overfitting in machine learning by limiting the complexity of the model, thus effectively improving its generalization performance. Regularization works because the linear regression model is penalized as it looks for the best coefficients for its predictions. The used penalization is based on the summation of the coefficients. Therefore, the regression model is incentivized to keep them as small as possible, if not to set them to zero. Constraining regression coefficients to limit their magnitude has two significant effects:

- It avoids any form of data memorization and overfitting (i.e., certain specific coefficient values to be taken when there is a large number of features compared to the available examples).
- As coefficient shrinking happens, estimates are stabilized because multicollinear features will have the values of their coefficients resized or concentrated on only one of the features.

In the optimization process, coefficients are updated multiple times, and these steps are called iterations. At each step, each regression coefficient incorporates a correction toward its optimal value. The optimal value is determined by the gradient, which can be intended as a number representing the direction that greatly improves the coefficient at that step. A more detailed explanation closes this chapter. Penalization is a form of constraint that forces the weights deriving from the optimization of the model to have specific characteristics. We have two variants of regularization:

- The first variant is where the penalization is computed by summing the absolute values of the coefficients: this is called L1 regularization. It makes the coefficients sparse because it can push some coefficients to zero, making their related features irrelevant.
- The second option is where the penalization is computed by summing the squared coefficients: this is called L2 regularization, and its effect is generally to reduce the size of the coefficients (it is also relatively fast to compute).

L1 regularization (or Lasso regression) pushes many coefficients to zero values, thus operating an implicit selection of the useful features (setting a coefficient to zero means that a feature doesn't play any role in prediction). In addition, coefficients are always pushed toward zero with the same strength (technically, the gradients toward the solution are always +1 or −1). Hence, through the optimization steps, the features less associated with the target tend quickly to be assigned a zero coefficient and become totally irrelevant regarding the predictions. In short, if two or more features are multicollinear and all quite predictive, by applying L1 regularization, you will have only one of them with a coefficient different from zero.

Instead, in L2 regularization (or Ridge regression), the fact that coefficients are squared prevents negative and positive values from canceling each other in the penalization and puts more weight on larger coefficients. The result is a set of generally smaller coefficients, and multicollinear features tend to have similar coefficient values. All the features involved are included in the summation. You can notice better important features because, contrary to what happens with standard regression, the role of a feature in the prediction is not hidden by its correlation with other features. L2 regularization tends to attenuate the coefficients. It does so proportionally during the optimization steps; technically, the gradients toward the solution tend to be smaller and smaller. Hence, coefficients can reach the zero value or be near it. Still, even if the feature must be completely irrelevant to the prediction, it takes many optimization iterations and is quite time-consuming. Consequently, reprising the previous example of two or more multicollinear features in L2 regularization, instead of L1 regression that keeps only one non-zero coefficient, all the features would have a non-zero, similar size coefficient.

In our example, we first try to create new features through systematic interactions between our available features and then perform an L2 and L1 penalized regression to compare their results and resulting coefficients. PolynomialFeatures is a Scikit-learn function (https://mng.bz/2ynd) that automatically creates multiplications between features by multiplying them many times with other features and by themselves. The process is reminiscent of the mathematical *polynomial expansion* where a power of sums is expressed into its single terms:

$$(a + b)^2 = a^2 + 2ab + b^2$$

Scikit-learn makes it easier because when you state a degree, the function automatically creates the polynomial expansions up to that degree. You can decide whether to keep only the interactions. Such a process is interesting for a regression model because

- *Interactions* help the regression model to better take into account the conjoint values of more features since features usually do not relate to the target in isolation but in synergy with others.
- The set of *powers* of a feature helps to model it as a curve. For instance, $a + a^2$ is a curve in the shape of a parabola.

Though using polynomial expansion can avoid the heavy task of creating specific features for your problem, it has a downside because it dramatically increases the number of features your model uses. More features usually provide more predictive power, but they also mean more noise, more multicollinearity, and more chances that the model has just to memorize examples and overfit the problem. Applying penalties can help us fix this problem with the L2 penalty and select only the features to be kept with the L1 penalty.

In the code in listing 4.5, we test applying L2 and, successively in listing 4.6, L1 regularization to the same polynomial expansion. It is important to note the effect of each kind of regularization. In this first example, we apply L2 regularization (Ridge). Since regularization makes sense if you have plenty of features for your prediction, we create new features from the old ones using a polynomial expansion. Our ridge model is then set to a high alpha value to handle the increased number of collinear features.

Listing 4.5   L2 regularized linear regression

```
from sklearn.preprocessing import PolynomialFeatures
from sklearn.linear_model import Ridge, Lasso

column_transform = ColumnTransformer(
    [('categories', categorical_onehot_encoding, low_card_categorical),
     ('numeric', numeric_passthrough, continuous)],
    remainder='drop',
    verbose_feature_names_out=False,
    sparse_threshold=0.0)

polynomial_expansion = PolynomialFeatures(degree=2)

model = Ridge(alpha=2500.0)

model_pipeline = Pipeline(
    [('processing', column_transform),
     ('polynomial_expansion', polynomial_expansion),
     ('standardizing', numeric_standardization),
     ('modeling', model)]
)

cv = KFold(5, shuffle=True, random_state=0)
rmse = make_scorer(mean_squared_error, squared=False)

cv_scores = cross_validate(estimator=model_pipeline,
                           X=data[price_window],
                           y=target_regression[price_window],
                           scoring=rmse,
                           cv=cv,
                           return_train_score=True,
                           return_estimator=True)

mean_cv = np.mean(cv_scores['test_score'])
std_cv = np.std(cv_scores['test_score'])
fit_time = np.mean(cv_scores['fit_time'])
score_time = np.mean(cv_scores['score_time'])
print(f"{mean_cv:0.3f} ({std_cv:0.3f})",
      f"fit: {fit_time:0.2f} secs pred: {score_time:0.2f} secs")
```

PolynomialFeatures instance performing second-degree polynomial expansion on the features

A Ridge regression model instance with a regularization strength (alpha) of 2,500

Pipeline for column transformation, polynomial expansion, standardization, and Ridge regression modeling

Five-fold cross-validation using the defined pipeline and calculating RMSE scores

Prints the mean and standard deviation of the test RMSE scores from cross-validation

The script results in the following output:

```
33.738 (0.275) fit: 0.13 secs pred: 0.03 secs
```

If we count the number of non-zero coefficients (after rounding to five decimals to exclude extremely small values), we get

```
(cv_scores['estimator'][0]['modeling'].coef_.round(5)!=0).sum()
```

Ninety-one coefficients out of 105 have non-zero values.

In the next example, we apply an L1 regularization and compare the results with the previous example. The procedure is the same as the last code listing, though we resort to a lasso model this time.

Listing 4.6   L1 regularized linear regression

```
model = Lasso(alpha=0.1)

model_pipeline = Pipeline(
    [('processing', column_transform),
     ('polynomial_expansion', polynomial_expansion),
     ('standardizing', numeric_standardization),
     ('modeling', model)]
)

cv = KFold(5, shuffle=True, random_state=0)
rmse =  make_scorer(mean_squared_error, squared=False)

cv_scores = cross_validate(estimator=model_pipeline,
                           X=data[price_window],
                           y=target_regression[price_window],
                           scoring=rmse,
                           cv=cv,
                           return_train_score=True,
                           return_estimator=True)

mean_cv = np.mean(cv_scores['test_score'])
std_cv = np.std(cv_scores['test_score'])
fit_time = np.mean(cv_scores['fit_time'])
score_time = np.mean(cv_scores['score_time'])
print(f"{mean_cv:0.3f} ({std_cv:0.3f})",
      f"fit: {fit_time:0.2f} secs pred: {score_time:0.2f} secs")
```

A Lasso regression model instance with a regularization strength (alpha) of 0.1

Pipeline applying column transformation, polynomial expansion, standardization, and Lasso regression modeling

Five-fold cross-validation using the defined pipeline and calculating RMSE scores

Prints the mean and standard deviation of the test RMSE scores from cross-validation

The resulting output is

```
33.718 (0.269) fit: 0.64 secs pred: 0.03 secs
```

If we check how many coefficients have non-zero-values by taking the first model built by the cross-validation cycle, this time we have fewer:

```
(cv_scores['estimator'][0]['modeling'].coef_.round(5) !=0).sum()
```

With 53 non-zero coefficients, the number of working coefficients has been halved. By increasing the alpha parameter of the Lasso call, we can obtain an even sharper reduction of used coefficients, albeit at the price of a higher computation time. There's a sweet spot after which applying a higher L1 penalty doesn't improve the prediction results. For prediction purposes, you have to find the correct alpha by trial and error or using convenient automatic functions such as LassoCV (https://mng.bz/1XoV) or RidgeCV (https://mng.bz/Pdn9) that will do the experimentation for you.

Interestingly, regularization is also used in neural networks. Neural networks use sequential matrix multiplications based on matrices of coefficients to transit from features to predictions, which is an extension of the working of linear regression. Neural networks have more complexities, though; yet in such an aspect of matrix multiplication, they resemble a regression model. Based on similar workings, you may find it beneficial for your tabular data problem to fit a deep learning architecture and, in doing so, to apply an L2 penalty, so the coefficients of the network are attenuated and distributed, and/or an L1 penalty, so coefficients are instead sparse with many of them set to zeros. In the next section, we will continue our discussion of linear models by discovering how to solve a classification problem.

4.3.3   *Logistic regression*

The linear regression model can be effectively extended to classification. In a binary classification problem, where you have two classes (a positive one and a negative one), you use the same approach as in a regression (feature matrix, vector of coefficients, bias). Still, you transform the target using the logit function (for details about this statistical distribution, see https://mng.bz/JY20). The transformative function is called the *link function*. On the optimization side, the algorithm uses as a reference the Bernoulli conditional distribution (for revising this distribution, see https://mng.bz/wJoq) instead of the normal distribution. As a result, you get output values ranging from 0 to 1, representing the probability that the sample belongs to the positive class. This is called logistic regression. Logistic regression is quite an intuitive and practical approach to solving binary classification problems and multiclass and multilabel ones.

In listing 4.7, we replicate the same approach as seen with linear regression—this time trying to build a model to guess if an example has a target value above the median. Please note that transformations are the same, though we use a logistic regression model this time. Our target is a class that tells if the target value is above the median. Such a target is a binary balanced outcome, where half of the labels are positive and half are negative.

Listing 4.7   Logistic regression

```
from sklearn.linear_model import LogisticRegression
from sklearn.metrics import make_scorer, accuracy_scorehttps://mng.bz/JY20

accuracy = make_scorer(accuracy_score)
cv = KFold(5, shuffle=True, random_state=0)
model = LogisticRegression(solver="saga",
                           penalty=None,
                           max_iter=1_000)

column_transform = ColumnTransformer(
    [('categories', categorical_onehot_encoding, low_card_categorical),
     ('numeric', numeric_standardization, continuous)],
    remainder='drop',
    verbose_feature_names_out=False,
```

A logistic regression model instance with the "saga" solver, no penalty, and a maximum of 1,000 iterations

```
        sparse_threshold=0.0)

model_pipeline = Pipeline(
    [('processing', column_transform),
     ('modeling', model)])

cv_scores = cross_validate(estimator=model_pipeline,
                           X=data,
                           y=target_median,
                           scoring=accuracy,
                           cv=cv,
                           return_train_score=True,
                           return_estimator=True)

mean_cv = np.mean(cv_scores['test_score'])
std_cv = np.std(cv_scores['test_score'])
fit_time = np.mean(cv_scores['fit_time'])
score_time = np.mean(cv_scores['score_time'])
print(f"{mean_cv:0.3f} ({std_cv:0.3f})",
      f"fit: {fit_time:0.2f} secs pred: {score_time:0.2f} secs")
```

A column transformer applying one-hot encoding to categorical features and standardization to numeric features

A pipeline that sequentially applies column transformation and logistic regression modeling

Five-fold cross-validation using the defined pipeline and calculating accuracy scores

Prints the mean and standard deviation of the test accuracy scores from cross-validation

The script results in the following scores:

```
0.821 (0.004) fit: 3.00 secs pred: 0.02 secs
```

As the feature processing is the same, we just focus on noticing how the logistic regression has some specific parameters with respect to linear regression. In particular, you can set the penalty directly without changing the algorithm and decide what optimizer will be used (using the parameter solver). Each optimizer allows specific penalties, and it can be more or less efficient based on the characteristics of your data:

- lbfgs for L2 or no penalty.
- liblinear for L1 and L2 penalties—better for smaller datasets, limited to one-versus-rest schemes for multiclass problems.
- newton-cg for L2 or no penalty.
- newton-cholesky for L2 or no penalty.
- sag for L2 or no penalty—ideal for large datasets. It requires standardized features (or features all with similar scale/standard deviation).
- saga for no penalty, L1, L2, elasticnet (a mix of L1 and L2) penalties—ideal for large datasets, it requires standardized features (or features all with similar scale/standard deviation).

In listing 4.8, we use an L2 penalty on the multiclass target to test how multiple targets are easily dealt with using the multi_class parameter set to "ovr" (one-versus-rest), a solution that takes a multiclass problem and builds a binary model for each of the classes to be predicted. At prediction time, prediction probabilities across all the classes are normalized to sum 1.0, and the class corresponding to the highest probability is taken and the predicted class. Such an approach is analogous to the softmax function approach used in neural networks where a vector of arbitrary real values is turned into a probability distribution, where the sum of all elements is 1 (for a more detailed explanation of softmax, see https://mng.bz/qxYw). The alternative to the one-versus-rest approach is the multinomial option, where a single regression model directly models the probability distribution across all classes simultaneously.

The multinomial approach is preferred when inter-class relationships are important (e.g., for ranking or confidence-based decisions) or when a compact, single-model solution is desired.

Listing 4.8 L2 regularized multiclass linear regression

Logistic regression model instance with L2 penalty, regularization C=0.1, "sag" solver, "ovr" multiclass strategy

```python
from sklearn.linear_model import LogisticRegression
from sklearn.metrics import make_scorer, accuracy_score

accuracy = make_scorer(accuracy_score)
cv = KFold(5, shuffle=True, random_state=0)
model = LogisticRegression(penalty="l2", C=0.1, solver="sag",
multi_class="ovr", max_iter=1_000)

column_transform = ColumnTransformer(
    [('categories', categorical_onehot_encoding, low_card_categorical),
     ('numeric', numeric_standardization, continuous)],
    remainder='drop',
    verbose_feature_names_out=False,
    sparse_threshold=0.0)
```

Column transformer that applies one-hot encoding to categorical features and standardization to numeric features

```python
model_pipeline = Pipeline(
    [('processing', column_transform),
     ('modeling', model)])
```

Pipeline that sequentially applies column transformation and logistic regression modeling

```python
cv_scores = cross_validate(estimator=model_pipeline,
                           X=data,
                           y=target_multiclass,
                           scoring=accuracy,
                           cv=cv,
                           return_train_score=True,
                           return_estimator=True)
```

Cross-validation using the defined pipeline and calculating accuracy scores

```python
mean_cv = np.mean(cv_scores['test_score'])
std_cv = np.std(cv_scores['test_score'])
fit_time = np.mean(cv_scores['fit_time'])
score_time = np.mean(cv_scores['score_time'])
print(f"{mean_cv:0.3f} ({std_cv:0.3f})",
      f"fit: {fit_time:0.2f}",
      f"secs pred: {score_time:0.2f} secs")
```

Prints the mean and standard deviation of the test accuracy scores from cross-validation

---

Predicting the target as a class is certainly more complicated than guessing if the target price is over a threshold value or not:

```
0.435 (0.002) fit: 31.08 secs pred: 0.02 secs
```

From this output, it is important to notice how the training time for a cross-validation fold has skyrocketed 10 times more. The reason is that applying a penalty to the coefficients involves more iterations of the algorithm's optimization processes before reaching a stable result and because now a model for each class is being built. As a general rule, consider that penalization requires longer computations for the L2 penalty and even longer for the L1 penalty. By setting the `max_iter` parameter, you can impose a limit to the algorithm's iterations, but be aware that the result you obtain by cutting off the time required for the algorithm to converge won't be assured to be the best.

4.3.4 Generalized linear methods

The idea of extending linear regression to binary classification by logit transformation can be applied to distributions other than Bernoulli conditional distribution. This is dictated by the target that may represent categorical data, count data, or other data whose distribution is known not to be from a normal distribution. As we have seen in the previous paragraph, multiclass problems can be modeled using the Bernoulli distribution (the one-versus-rest strategy of fitting multiple logistic regressions) and the multinomial one. Other problems, more typical of domains such as finance or insurance, require different approaches. For instance, the Scikit-learn package mentions a few real-world applications and their best-fitting distributions (for reference, see https://mng.bz/7py9):

- *Climate modeling*—Number of rain events per year (Poisson distribution for count data and discrete events). The Poisson distribution is used for modeling events such as the number of calls to a call center or the number of customers visiting a restaurant), amount of rainfall per event (using Gamma distribution, a theoretical distribution useful for modeling because of its skewness and long tail), or total rain precipitation per year (Tweedie distribution, a distribution which is a compound of Poisson and Gamma distributions).

- *Risk modeling or insurance policy pricing*—Number of claim events or policyholder per year (Poisson), cost per event (Gamma), the total cost per policyholder per year (Tweedie).

- *Predictive maintenance*—Number of production interruption events per year (Poisson), the duration of interruption (Gamma), and the total interruption time per year (Tweedie).

Figure 4.11 shows the three distributions—Poisson, Tweedie, and Gamma—for different averages. The Tweedie distribution is calculated for power equal to 1.5, a blend between the Poisson and Gamma distributions.

Of course, you may try any distribution you want—even a plain regression model—for any such situation. However, approaching each of them using the appropriate generalized linear model that optimizes that specific distribution assures the best result in most cases.

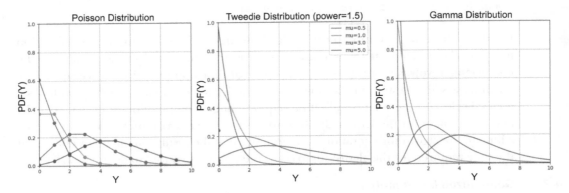

Figure 4.11   Comparing Poisson, Tweedie, and Gamma distributions at different mean values (mu) of the distribution

We don't enter into the specifics of each distribution; you just need to know that the Swiss Army Knife of general linear models is the TweedieRegressor (https://mng .bz/mGOr). This Scikit-learn implementation, depending on the power parameter, can allow you to quickly test normal distribution (a regular regression), Poisson distribution (https://mng.bz/4a4w), Gamma distribution (https://mng.bz/QDvG), Inverse Gaussian distribution (for nonnegative positively skewed data), and a blend of Gamma and Poisson (the Tweedie distribution) (see table 4.1).

Table 4.1   Power values and their corresponding statistical distributions

Power	Distribution
0	Normal
1	Poisson
(1,2)	Compound Poisson Gamma
2	Gamma
3	Inverse Gaussian

In listing 4.9, we test the different distributions offered by the TweedieRegressor on the entire distribution of prices of the Airbnb NYC dataset, a model fitting that we previously avoided because of the heavy distribution tails revealed by the EDA. We do so by testing each of these distributions one by one on the full range of price values since we are confident that using such specialized distribution will solve our problem of a target with heavy tails. It is important to remember that such distributions have limitations due to their formulations:

- *Normal*—Any kind of value
- *Poisson*—Zero or positive values
- *Tweedie, Gamma, Inverse Gaussian*—Only non-zero positive values

This implies that you must adapt your data if you have negative or zero values by adding an offset value. Hence, depending on the modeled distribution, we clip the target values to a lower bound based on the aforementioned limitations.

Listing 4.9 Tweedie regression

```
from sklearn.linear_model import TweedieRegressor
from sklearn.metrics import make_scorer, mean_squared_error
from sklearn.model_selection import KFold
from sklearn.model_selection import cross_validate

experiments = [
    ['normal', 0, float('-inf')],
    ['poisson', 1, 0.0],
    ['tweedie', 1.5, 0.1],
    ['gamma', 2, 0.1],
    ['inverse gaussian', 3, 0.1]]

for experiment, power, min_val in experiments:

    column_transform = ColumnTransformer(
        [('categories', categorical_onehot_encoding, low_card_categorical),
         ('numeric', numeric_standardization, continuous)],
        remainder='drop',
        verbose_feature_names_out=False,
        sparse_threshold=0.0)

    model = TweedieRegressor(power=power,
                    max_iter=1_000)

    model_pipeline = Pipeline(
        [('processing', column_transform),
         ('modeling', model)])

    cv = KFold(5, shuffle=True, random_state=0)
    rmse =  make_scorer(mean_squared_error, squared=False)

    cv_scores = cross_validate(estimator=model_pipeline,
                X=data,
                    y=target_regression.clip(
                        lower=min_val),
                    scoring=rmse,
                    cv=cv,
                    return_train_score=True,
                    return_estimator=True)

    mean_cv = np.mean(cv_scores['test_score'])
    std_cv = np.std(cv_scores['test_score'])
    fit_time = np.mean(cv_scores['fit_time'])
    score_time = np.mean(cv_scores['score_time'])
    print(f"{experiment:18}: {mean_cv:0.3f} ({std_cv:0.3f})",
        f"fit: {fit_time:0.2f}",
        f"secs pred: {score_time:0.2f} secs")
```

A list of experiments, made of a distribution name, power parameter, and minimum target value

Loops through the experiments list with distribution names and power parameters

Instance of the TweedieRegressor model with the specified power parameter for the current experiment

Clips the target regression data to a minimum value, according to the used distribution

Prints the experiment name along with the results from cross-validation

The resulting best-fitting are the Poisson and Tweedie with power 1.5 distributions:

```
normal           : 233.858 (15.826) fit: 0.13 secs pred: 0.03 secs
poisson          : 229.189 (16.075) fit: 0.66 secs pred: 0.03 secs
tweedie          : 229.607 (16.047) fit: 0.46 secs pred: 0.03 secs
gamma            : 233.991 (15.828) fit: 0.22 secs pred: 0.03 secs
inverse gaussian : 239.577 (15.453) fit: 0.18 secs pred: 0.03 secs
```

It is crucial to remember that the secret of the performances of the generalized linear models lies in the specific distribution they strive to model during the optimization phase. When faced with similar problems, we could resort to similar distributions on some more advanced algorithms than generalized linear models, particularly on gradient boosting implementations such as XGBoost or LightGBM, which will be discussed in the next chapter. In the next section, we will deal with a different approach related to large datasets.

4.3.5   *Handling large datasets with stochastic gradient descent*

When your tabular dataset cannot fit into your system's memory, whether it is a cloud instance or your desktop computer, your options in modeling shrink. Apart from deep learning solutions, which will be discussed in the third part of this book, one other option, using classical machine learning, is to resort to out-of-core learning. In out-of-core learning, you keep your data in its storage (for instance, your data warehouse), and you have your model learn from it bit by bit, using small samples extracted from your data, called *batches*. This is practically feasible because modern data storage allows for the picking of specific data samples at a certain cost in terms of latency: the time interval between the initiation of a data-related operation and its completion or response. In addition, there are also tools for handling and processing data on the fly (for instance, Apache Kafka or Amazon Kinetics) that can redirect the data to out-of-core learning algorithms.

It is also algorithmically feasible because of linear/logistic regression models. Both models are made up of additions of coefficients relative to the features you use for learning. Out-of-core learning involves first estimating these coefficients using some small samples from the data and then updating such coefficients using more and more batches extracted from your data. In the end, though the process is particularly long, your final estimated coefficient would not be much different from the ones you would have obtained if you could have fit all the data into the memory.

How many such batches you have to use for your out-of-core modeling, and if you have to reuse them multiple times, is a matter of empirical experimentation: it depends on the problem and the data you are using. Though providing new batches of unseen data may simply prolong your training phase, having the algorithm see the same batches again may cause it to overfit. Unfortunately, in most situations, you need to reiterate the same batches multiple times because out-of-core learning is not as straightforward as when optimizing; it takes a long time, and you may need more passes on the same data, even if we are talking about massive amounts of it. Fortunately, you can rely on regularization techniques, such as L1 and L2 regularization, to avoid overfitting.

In listing 4.10, we reprise our logistic regression example and make it out-of-core. First, we split our data into a training set and a test set since it is complicated to create a cross-validation procedure when using out-of-core learning strategies. In real out-of-core learning settings, cross-validation is not just complicated but often infeasible because, in such settings, you often handle examples a single time. After all, they are streamed from sources and often discarded. The usual validation strategy is to collect a list of examples for testing purposes or to use a batch of every n-one as an out-of-sample testing batch. In our example, we prefer reserving a test set.

Listing 4.10 Out-of-core logistic regression with L2 regularization

```
from sklearn.linear_model import SGDClassifier
from sklearn.model_selection import train_test_split
from sklearn.utils import gen_batches
from sklearn.metrics import accuracy_score

def generate_batches(X,
                     y,
                     batch_size,            Defines a function to generate
                     random_state):         batches of data for training
    """split dataset into batches """
    examples = len(X)
    batches = gen_batches(n=examples,       Generates batches of data
                   batch_size=batch_size)   indices for processing
    sequence = np.arange(examples)
    if random_state:                        Shuffles the sequence of examples
        np.random.seed(random_state)        if a random state is provided
        np.random.shuffle(sequence)

    for batch in batches:
        items = sequence[batch]             Yields batches of input features
        yield(X.iloc[items], y.iloc[items]) and corresponding labels

model = SGDClassifier(loss="log_loss",
                      average=True,         Creates an instance of the SGDClassifier
                      penalty='l2',         model with logistic loss, averaging, L2
                      alpha=0.001)          penalty, and alpha regularization

column_transform = ColumnTransformer(
    [('categories', categorical_onehot_encoding, low_card_categorical),
     ('numeric', numeric_standardization, continuous)],
    remainder='drop',
    verbose_feature_names_out=False,
    sparse_threshold=0.0)                   Splits the data and target into training
                                            and testing sets using an 80-20 ratio

X_train, X_test, y_train, y_test = train_test_split(data, target_median,
                                        test_size=0.20,
                                        random_state=0)

iterations = 10
```

Iterates through training data
batches, fitting the column
transformer on the first batch

```
for j in range(iterations):
    generator = generate_batches(X_train, y_train, batch_size=256,
random_state=j)
    for k, (Xt, yt) in enumerate(generator):
        if k == 0:
            column_transform.fit(Xt)
                Xt = column_transform.transform(Xt)
        if k == 0:
            model.partial_fit(Xt, yt, classes=(0, 1))
        else:
            model.partial_fit(Xt, yt)

predictions = model.predict(column_transform.transform(X_test))
score = accuracy_score(y_true=y_test, y_pred=predictions)
print(f"Accuracy on test set: {score:0.3f}")
```

Uses partial fitting to
train the model on
the first batch,
specifying the classes

Uses partial
fitting to further
train the model
on subsequent
batches

Prints accuracy score of
test data predictions

The train data is then split into multiple batches, and each batch is proposed for learning to the *stochastic gradient descent* (SGD) algorithm. SGD is not a stand-alone algorithm but an optimization procedure for linear models, optimizing the model weights by iteratively learning them from small batches of the data or even just single examples taken alone. It is based on the *gradient descent* optimization procedure and is also used in deep learning. Gradient descent starts with an initial guess for the model weights and computes the error. The next step involves computing the gradient of the error, which is obtained by taking the negative of the vector that contains the partial derivatives of the error with respect to the model weights. Since the gradient can be interpreted as taking the steepest descent on an error surface, a common example for gradient descent is always to figure it as descending from highs in the mountains to the lowest valley by taking the steepest path downward. The "mountains" in this analogy represent the error surface, and the "lowest valley" represents the minimum of the error function. Figure 4.12 visually represents this process by the progressive descent from a random high place to the lowest point in a bowl-shaped error curve.

Besides the analogy, it is important to remember that the gradient determines how the weights should be adjusted to reduce the error at that step. Through repeated iterations, the error can be minimized by adjusting the model's weights. However, how the weights are updated can significantly affect the outcome. If the updates are too large and decisive, the algorithm may take overly wide steps, potentially causing the model to overshoot the target and climb the error curve. In the worst-case scenario, this can result in a continuous worsening of the error, with no possibility of recovery. Conversely, taking smaller steps is generally safer but may be computationally burdensome. The size of such steps is decided by the learning rate, a parameter that regulates how the updates are done.

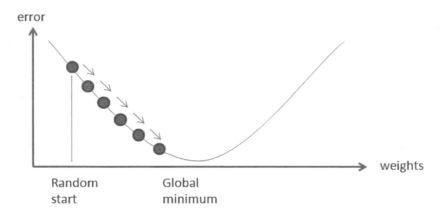

Figure 4.12 Gradient descent optimization in action in a simple optimization landscape

Linear models can be optimized easily using gradient descent because their error surface is simple and bowl-shaped. However, more complex models like gradient boosting (which will be discussed in the next chapter) and deep learning architectures may encounter challenges in optimization due to their higher complexity, with interrelated parameters and a more complex error landscape. Depending on the starting point, as illustrated in figure 4.13, these models may become stuck in a local minimum or plateau during optimization, leading to suboptimal results.

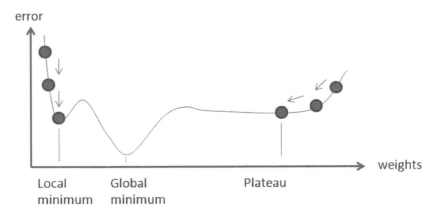

Figure 4.13 Gradient descent in a complex error landscape showing how local minima and plateaus can lead to less-than-optimal solutions

Learning a linear model by SGD is made possible using Scikit-learn's method `partial_fit`, which, after an informed start (the algorithm needs to know the target labels), can learn by partially fitting one batch after the other. The same procedure is repeated multiple times, called iterations or epochs, to consolidate and improve the learning, though repeating the same examples too often may also cause overfitting. The algorithm will see, though in a different order, the same examples multiple times and update its coefficients every time. To avoid abrupt changes in the coefficients, which frequently occur when an outlier is present in the batch, the updated coefficients are not substituted for the existing ones. Instead, they are averaged together, allowing a more gradual transition.

After all the learning process is completed, you will get the following result:

```
Accuracy on test set: 0.818
```

The result is quite comparable with in-core learning logistic regression. Out-of-core learning, though limited to only the simplest machine learning algorithms such as linear or logistic regression, is an effective way to train on your tabular data when too many samples cannot fit into memory. All deep learning solutions also use the idea of a stream of batches, and it will be discussed again in the chapters devoted to deep neural network methods for tabular data, together with strategies such as *early stopping*, a technique interrupting the iterations over data when necessary to avoid overfitting the data because of an excessive exposition of the algorithm to examples seen in previous iterations.

We can now anticipate that a fundamental recipe of such learning strategies is the randomization of the order of the examples. Since the optimization is progressive, if your data is ordered in a specific way, it will cause a biased optimization, which may result in suboptimal learning. Repeating the same batches in the same order can negatively influence your results. Hence, randomizing the order is critical for a better-trained algorithm. Another important point with SGD, however, is the data preparation phase. In such a phase, you should include all feature rescaling operations, because the optimization process is sensible to the scale of features and all the feature engineering and feature interaction computations, and set it in a way as deterministic as possible since it could be difficult to use global parameters, such as the maximum/minimum or average and the standard deviation of a feature, when your data is split into multiple batches.

4.3.6   *Choosing your algorithm*

As a general rule of thumb, you should first consider that machine learning algorithms scale differently based on how many rows and columns you have. Starting from the number of available rows, you must strictly resort to simple rule-based or statistical-based algorithms when operating with about or fewer than 10^2 rows of data. For up to 10^3 rows, models based on linear combinations, such as linear and logistic regression, are best suited because they tend not to overfit the little data available. You usually cannot tell what algorithm will work better from about 10^3 to $10^4 - 10^5$ rows. Hence, it is all a matter of testing and experimenting. Here, deep learning solutions may outrun other choices only if there is some structure to exploit, such as an ordered series of information or a hierarchical structure. Up to 10^9 rows, solutions from the gradient boosting family are likely the most effective. Again, you may find that something like out-of-core learning is a much better solution for specific problems, such as in the advertisement industry, where you have many fixed interactions that you need to estimate—for instance, between display devices, websites, and advertisements.

Out-of-core learning refers to a learning strategy that certain machine learning algorithms can adopt when learning from data: instead of learning all at once from the data, they learn bit by bit from smaller samples of the data, the batches, or even from single examples, one by one, which is also mentioned as online learning. Finally, in our experience, in situations with datasets above 10^9 rows, deep learning solutions, and some out-of-core learning algorithms tend to perform better because they can effectively deal with such an amount of data, whereas other machine learning algorithms may be forced to learn from subsamples from the data or find other suboptimal solutions.

Regarding columns, we find that some algorithms need to scale better with datasets characterized by multiple columns, especially if they present sparse information—that is, many binary features. The sparser the datasets, which can be measured by the percentage of zeros values in relation to the total numeric values in the dataset, the earlier you may need to apply online learning algorithms or deep learning.

However, apart from scalability reasons, which relate to memory and computational complexity, each machine learning solution also suits different needs in terms of model control, openness, and understandability of the solution. In such a way, the variety of needs in tabular problems and of models in machine learning defies the notion of one best algorithm that is all you need for your work. In other words, it is not just that you need to try more machine learning models because "there's no free lunch," as stated in the well-known theorem by David Wolpert and William Macready (see http://www.no-free-lunch.org for more details). More often than expected, there are cases where the underdog algorithm surprisingly beats the best-in-class algorithm. The necessity of more algorithms is mostly dictated because, as you change perspective on your problem as an artisan/artist creating their work from different angles, you may need different tools for the task.

In the next chapter, we will present a more powerful class of machine learning algorithms, the ensembles, and finally, the gradient boosting family and its successful and popular implementations, such as XGBoost and LightGBM.

Summary

- Determining what machine learning algorithm involves several factors: the number of examples and features, the expected performances, speed at prediction time, and interpretability. As a general rule of thumb,
  - Statistical machine learning is suitable for datasets with few cases.
  - Classical machine learning is suitable for datasets with a moderate number of cases.

- – Gradient boosting algorithms are particularly effective for datasets with a moderate to large number of cases.
- – Deep learning solutions are the most feasible and effective for datasets with massive amounts of data.
- Scikit-learn is an open-source library for machine learning that offers a wide range of models for classification and regression, as well as functions for clustering, dimensionality reduction, preprocessing, and model selection. We can summarize its core advantages as follows:
  - – Consistent API across models
  - – Supports in-memory and out-of-core learning
  - – Supports working with pandas DataFrames
  - – Ideal for tabular problems
  - – Easy to install
  - – Extensive documentation
- Linear regression is the summation of weighted features that have been converted to numeric values (one-hot encoding for categorical features):
  - – The algorithm finds optimal weight values (coefficients) to minimize the residual sum of squares between targets and predictions.
  - – Linear regression is easy to explain and understand how each feature contributes to the final result.
  - – A high correlation between features (multicollinearity) can cause conceptual misunderstanding.
  - – Linear regression is computationally simple and easy to implement.
  - – Linear regression is limited in its ability to fit complex problems with nonlinear data unless features are carefully prepared beforehand with feature engineering, such as creating polynomial features, which can help linear regression capture nonlinear relationships.
- Regularization is used to prevent overfitting by reducing the complexity of a regression model and improving its generalization performance. There are two types of regularization:
  - – L1 regularization (or Lasso regression) pushes many coefficients to zero values, thus making some features irrelevant in the model.
  - – L2 regularization generally reduces the size of coefficients.
  - – L1 regularization can be helpful for feature selection, while L2 regularization reduces overfitting when using many features while being faster to compute.
- Linear regression can be extended to classification problems using the logit function to transform the target and the Bernoulli conditional distribution to optimize the algorithm. This results in a logistic regression model that can be used for binary classification, multiclass, and multilabel problems. Logistic

regression is easy to implement and understand but has the same limitations as linear regression.

- The same approach of transforming the target can be applied to other distributions as well, such as Poisson and Gamma, depending on the nature of the data. The resulting generalized linear models can be used for various real-world applications, such as climate modeling, risk modeling, and predictive maintenance. However, it's important to note that the results may not be optimal without a proper understanding of the specific distribution applied to each situation.

Decision trees and gradient boosting

This chapter covers

- Decision trees and their ensembles
- Gradient boosting decision trees
- Scikit-learn's gradient boosting decision trees options
- XGBoost algorithm and its innovations
- How LightGBM algorithm works

So far, we have explored machine learning algorithms based on linear models because they can handle tabular problems from datasets consisting of a few rows and columns and find a way to scale to problems of millions of rows and many columns. In addition, linear models are fast to train and get predictions from. Moreover, they are relatively easy to understand, explain, and tweak. Linear models are also helpful because they present many concepts we will keep building on in the book, such as L1 and L2 regularization and gradient descent.

This chapter will discuss a different classical machine learning algorithm: decision trees. Decision trees are the foundations of ensemble models such as random forests and boosting. We will especially focus on a machine learning ensemble algorithm, gradient boosting, and its implementations eXtreme Gradient Boosting (XGBoost) and Light Gradient Boosted Machines (LightGBM), which are considered state-of-the-art solutions for tabular data.

5.1 Introduction to tree-based methods

Tree-based models are a family of ensemble algorithms of different kinds and the favored methods for handling tabular data because of their performance and low requirements in data preprocessing. Ensemble algorithms are sets of machine learning models that contribute together toward a single prediction. All tree-based ensemble models are based on decision trees, a popular algorithm dating to the 1960s. The basic idea behind decision trees, no matter whether they are used for classification or regression, is that you can split your training set to have subsets where your prediction is more favorable because there is a predominant output class (in a classification problem) or there is a decreased variability of the target values (i.e., they are all very near; this refers to a regression problem instead).

Figure 5.1 shows a scheme of the key elements that make up a decision tree. The problem the decision tree is trying to solve is classifying an animal based on the number of legs and eyes. You start from the root of the tree, which corresponds to the entire dataset you have available, and set a condition for split. The condition is usually true/false—a so-called binary split. Still, some variants of decision trees allow for multiple conditions applied at the same node, resulting in multiple splits, each decided based on a different value or label from the feature. Each branch leads to another node, where a new condition may be applied, or to a terminal node, which is used for predictions based on the instances that terminate there.

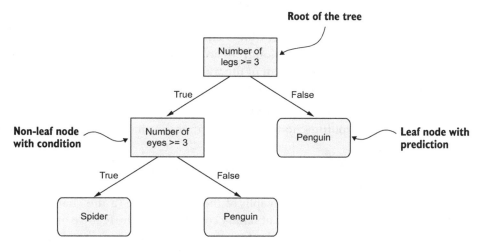

Figure 5.1 The key elements, such as roots, branches, and leaves, constituting a decision tree classifying animals based on the number of legs and eyes

A split happens based on a deliberate search of the algorithm among features and, inside the feature, its observed values. As a splitting criterion in a classification problem, the decision trees algorithm searches for the best feature and feature value combination that splits the data into subsets with a homogeneous target. The homogeneity of a target in a subset is typically measured in a classification problem using criteria such as entropy, information gain, or Gini impurity:

- *Entropy* measures the degree of disorder or randomness in the distribution of labels in the subset.
- *Information gain,* derived from entropy, measures the reduction in uncertainty about the class labels of the data, which is achieved by splitting the data based on a particular feature.
- *Gini impurity* measures the probability of misclassifying a randomly chosen element in the subset if labeled randomly according to the distribution of labels in the subset.

If the decision tree is being used for regression, it resorts to different splitting criteria than classification. In regression, the goal is to split the data into subsets to minimize the resulting mean squared error, the mean absolute error, or simply the variance of the target variable within each subset. In the training process, there's an automatic selection of the best features, and most of the computations for a decision tree are to determine the best feature splits. However, once the tree is constructed, predicting the class label or target value for new data is relatively fast and straightforward, involving traversing the tree starting from the root and ending at the leaf based on the values of a limited set of features.

Decision trees are simple to compute and are also relatively easy to visualize. They don't require scaling or modeling nonlinearities or otherwise transforming your features or output target because they can approximate any nonlinear relationship between target and predictors since they can consider separately single parts of their distribution. Basically, they are cutting a curve into parts so that each part looks like a line. On the other hand, decision trees are prone to overfitting and end up with an excessive number of splits that can fit the training data you are working on. Over time, different strategies have been devised to avoid overfitting:

- Limiting the number of splits in the tree
- Pruning the splitting nodes backward after they have been built to reduce their overfitting

Figure 5.2 shows a different perspective on a decision tree. Figure 5.1 visualizes a tree as a graph based on two features, while figure 5.2 visualizes a decision tree in terms of partitions of the data itself. Each split of the tree is a line in the chart, and there are seven vertical lines (thus a result of binary conditions on the feature on the x-axis) and three horizontal ones (thus on the feature on the y-axis) for a total of 10 splits. You can consider the decision tree a success because each class is well separated into its partitions (each partition is a terminal node in the end). However, by observation, it also becomes evident that specific partitions have been carved out just to fit examples in a certain position in the space. There are a few partitions containing only one single case. Any new example risks being incorrectly classified if it doesn't perfectly fit the training distribution (an overfitting situation).

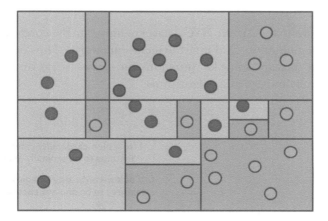

Figure 5.2 How a fully grown decision tree branching can also be interpreted as a series of dataset splits

Figure 5.3 shows the same problem visualized with fewer splits—two for every feature. You can achieve this by pruning the previous tree splits backward, removing the ones enclosing too few training examples, or you accomplish that simply by limiting in the first place the tree's growth—for instance, by imposing a maximum number of splits to be created. If you use fewer partitions, the tree may not fit the training data as perfectly as before. However, a simpler approach provides more confidence that new instances will likely be classified correctly, as the solution depends explicitly on single points in the training set.

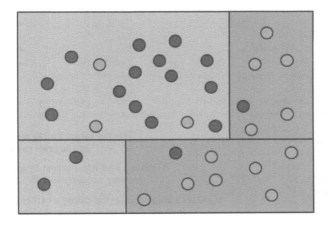

Figure 5.3 The problem handled by a simpler decision tree, obtained by pruning or by limiting its growth

Thinking of this algorithm in terms of underfitting and overfitting, it is a high-variance algorithm because its complexity always tends to exceed what should be given the problem and the data. It is not easy to find its sweet spot by tuning. In truth, the best way to use decision trees to achieve more accurate predictions is not as single models but as part of an ensemble of models. In subsequent subsections, we will explore ensemble methods such as bagging, random forests, and gradient boosting, an advanced method based on decision trees.

In this chapter, we'll return to the Airbnb NYC dataset to illustrate the core gradient-boosted decision tree implementations and how the technique works. The code in the following listing reprises the data and some key functions and classes we previously used to illustrate other classical machine learning algorithms.

Listing 5.1   Reprising the Airbnb NYC dataset

```
import numpy as np
import pandas as pd
from sklearn.preprocessing import OneHotEncoder, OrdinalEncoder
from sklearn.compose import ColumnTransformer
from sklearn.impute import SimpleImputer

data = pd.read_csv("./AB_NYC_2019.csv")
excluding_list = ['price', 'id', 'latitude', 'longitude', 'host_id',
                  'last_review', 'name', 'host_name']
low_card_categorical = ['neighbourhood_group',
                        'room_type']
high_card_categorical = ['neighbourhood']
continuous = ['minimum_nights', 'number_of_reviews', 'reviews_per_month',
              'calculated_host_listings_count', 'availability_365']
target_mean = (
    (data["price"] > data["price"].mean())
    .astype(int))
target_median = (
    (data["price"] > data["price"].median())
    .astype(int))
target_multiclass = pd.qcut(
    data["price"], q=5, labels=False)
target_regression = data["price"]
categorical_onehot_encoding = OneHotEncoder(handle_unknown='ignore')
categorical_ord_encoding =
OrdinalEncoder(handle_unknown="use_encoded_value", unknown_value=np.nan)
numeric_passthrough = SimpleImputer(strategy="constant", fill_value=0)

column_transform = ColumnTransformer(
    [('low_card_categories',
      categorical_onehot_encoding,
      low_card_categorical),
     ('high_card_categories',
      categorical_ord_encoding,
```

List of high-cardinality categorical features to be ordinally encoded

List of low-cardinality categorical features to be one-hot encoded

List of features to be excluded from data processing

Creates a binary target indicating whether the price is above the mean (unbalanced binary target)

Sets the target for regression as the price column

Creates a multiclass target by quantile binning the price into five classes

Creates a binary target indicating whether the price is above the median (balanced binary target)

```
    high_card_categorical),
  ('numeric',
   numeric_passthrough,
   continuous),
  ],
  remainder='drop',
  verbose_feature_names_out=False,
  sparse_threshold=0.0)
```

> **Creates a column transformer that applies different transformations to different groups of features**

The code reads a CSV file containing data related to Airbnb listings in New York City in 2019 using the pandas library. It then defines several lists that categorize the features of the data into different types:

- `excluding_list`—A list of features that should be excluded from the analysis, such as unique identifiers and text features
- `low_card_categorical`—A subset of categorical features that have a low cardinality (few unique values) and will be one-hot encoded
- `high_card_categorical`—A subset of categorical features that have a high cardinality (many unique values) and will be encoded using an ordinal encoding
- `continuous`—A list of continuous numerical features that will be standardized for analysis

The code then creates several target variables based on the Price feature of the data:

- `target_mean`—A binary variable indicating whether the price is higher than the mean price of all listings
- `target_median`—A binary variable indicating whether the price is higher than the median price of all listings
- `target_multiclass`—A variable with five classes based on the quantiles of the price distribution
- `target_regression`—The actual price values, which will be used for regression analysis

All these targets allow us to deal with different regression and classification problems and thus test machine learning algorithms. In this chapter, we will always use `target_median`, but you can experiment with all the other targets by making small changes in the code.

Next, the code sets up several transformers to preprocess the data for the analysis in this chapter:

- `categorical_onehot_encoding`—A one-hot encoding transformer for the low-cardinality categorical features
- `categorical_ord_encoding`—An ordinal encoding transformer for the high-cardinality categorical features
- `numeric_passthrough`—A transformer that simply passes through the continuous numerical features

Finally, the code sets up a `ColumnTransformer` object that will apply the appropriate transformers to each subset of features based on their type. It applies one-hot encoding to the low-cardinality categorical features and passes through the continuous numerical features. The transformer is set to drop any features not explicitly included in the transformation steps and output concise feature names. The `sparse_threshold` parameter is set to zero to ensure that the transformer always returns dense arrays.

Listing 5.2 shows how a standard decision trees model is applied to our example problem. As in the examples seen in the previous chapter, we import the necessary modules from the Scikit-learn library, define a custom scoring metric based on accuracy, and set up a five-fold cross-validation strategy. Then we define a ColumnTransformer named `column_transform`, which orchestrates data preprocessing. It involves

- Transforming categorical variables using a function `categorical_onehot_encoding` for specific low-cardinality categorical columns
- Passing through numeric features with a function `numeric_passthrough` for continuous variables
- Dropping any remaining unprocessed columns (`remainder='drop'`)
- Setting some options like suppressing verbose feature names and not applying sparse matrix representation

At this point, a pipeline combining the ColumnTransformer with a decision tree classifier model is tested using cross-validation, which returns accuracy scores along with the average fit time and score time.

Under the hood of the cross-validation procedure and the data pipelining, the dataset is separated multiple times by the decision tree classifier during the training based on a splitting value from a feature. The procedure can be algorithmically explained as "greedy" because the decision tree picks the feature with the best split at each step without questioning whether alternatives could lead to a better result. Despite such a simple approach, decision trees are effective machine learning algorithms. The process goes on until there are no more splits that improve the training, as shown in the following listing.

Listing 5.2   A decision tree classifier

```
from sklearn.tree import DecisionTreeClassifier
from sklearn.pipeline import Pipeline
from sklearn.metrics import make_scorer, accuracy_score
from sklearn.model_selection import KFold, cross_validate

accuracy = make_scorer(accuracy_score)
cv = KFold(5, shuffle=True, random_state=0)

column_transform = ColumnTransformer(
    [('categories', categorical_onehot_encoding, low_card_categorical),
     ('numeric', numeric_passthrough, continuous)],
    remainder='drop',
    verbose_feature_names_out=False,
```

Creates a column transformer that applies different transformations to categorical and numeric features

```
        sparse_threshold=0.0)

model = DecisionTreeClassifier(random_state=0)
```

An instance of a
decision tree classifier

```
model_pipeline = Pipeline(
    [('processing', column_transform),
     ('modeling', model)])
```

A pipeline that sequentially
applies column transformation
and the decision tree model

```
cv_scores = cross_validate(estimator=model_pipeline,
                    X=data,
                    y=target_median,
                    scoring=accuracy,
                    cv=cv,
                    return_train_score=True,
                    return_estimator=True)
```

A five-fold cross-validation
using the defined pipeline,
calculating accuracy
scores, and returning
additional information

```
mean_cv = np.mean(cv_scores['test_score'])
std_cv = np.std(cv_scores['test_score'])
fit_time = np.mean(cv_scores['fit_time'])
score_time = np.mean(cv_scores['score_time'])
print(f"{mean_cv:0.3f} ({std_cv:0.3f})",
      f"fit: {fit_time:0.2f}",
      f"secs pred: {score_time:0.2f} secs")
```

Prints the mean and standard
deviation of the accuracy
scores from cross-validation

The result we obtain in terms of accuracy is

```
0.761 (0.005) fit: 0.22 secs pred: 0.01 secs
```

The result could be better after comparing the results of our previous experiments with other machine learning algorithms. We can determine this because the decision tree has overfitted, and it ended up building too many ramifications. We can get better performance by limiting its growth by trial and error (you have to state the max_depth parameter to do so). However, there are even better ways to obtain improved results from this algorithm. In the next subsection, we will examine the first of such methods, which is based on multiple decision trees based on variations of the examples and the employed features.

5.1.1   *Bagging and sampling*

We have examined all the single learning algorithms with decision trees. Ensembling algorithms of the same type is the next step that can help you achieve more predictive power on your problem. The idea is intuitive: if a single algorithm can perform at a certain level, using the insights of multiple models or chaining them together (so that one can learn from the results and errors of the other) should render even better results. There are two core ensemble strategies:

- *Averaging*—Predictions are obtained by averaging the predictions of multiple models. Differences in how the models are built, for instance by pasting, bagging, random subspaces, and random patches as we will see in this section, lead to different results. The best example of ensemble models of this kind is the random forests algorithm, which is built on an approach similar to random patches.

- *Boosting*—Predictions are built as a weighted average of chained models, which are models sequentially built on the results of previous ones. The best example of a boosting algorithm is gradient boosting machines such as XGBoost and LightGBM.

In the following subsection, we will look at random forests. Before delving into the random forests algorithm, it is necessary to spend some time on the other averaging approaches, not only because the random patches approach is built upon them but also because they point out solutions that are always worth applying to tabular data when you need to reduce the variance of the estimates, hence obtaining more reliable predictions, of any machine learning model you may want to use on your data.

Pasting is the first approach to consider. Leo Breiman, the creator of the random forests algorithm, suggests that pasting consists of creating a set of different models trained on subsamples, obtained by sampling without replacement, of your training data. The models' predictions are pooled together by averaging in the case of a regression problem or by majority voting in the case of a classification task.

The pros of pasting are

- Improvement of the results by reducing the variance of the predictions by only partially increasing their bias, which is a measure of how far the predictions of a model are from the true values
- Predictions that are more robust and less affected by outliers
- Reduction of the amount of data to learn at training time, thus reducing memory requirements

The cons are

- Reduction of the amount of data available, which increases the bias because there is the chance of excluding important parts of the data distribution by sampling
- Very computationally intensive with complex algorithms

The last con depends on your time constraints or available resources. Historically, averaging methods have been suggested to be applied using weak models (i.e., machine learning models that are very fast to be trained because of their simplicity, such as a linear regression or a k-nearest neighbors model). Practitioners observed that combining multiple weak models could beat the results of a single, more complex algorithm. However, weak models usually have a high bias problem, and by subsampling, you induce only some variance in their estimates, but their bias problem remains mostly untouched. Using an averaging approach has the main advantage in that it reduces the variance of the estimates by trading it with a bit more bias. Since weak models inherently carry a substantial bias, they might not achieve comparable results to the same approach applied to more complex models. In situations where more significant improvements are needed by reducing the variance of the estimates, employing an averaging strategy can be more effective with more complex models.

Bagging, also suggested by Leo Breimar as a better solution, differs from pasting because you switch from subsampling to bootstrapping. Bootstrapping consists of sampling with replacement multiple times from a data sample to approximate the population distribution of a statistic. Bootstrapping is a frequently employed statistical technique that allows us to estimate the variability and uncertainty of statistics relative to the underlying data population from which our sample has been drawn. By using the information from the available sample through multiple resamples that mimic the original population's behavior, bootstrapping emulates the population's behavior without requiring explicit knowledge about its statistical distribution.

The reason for using bootstrapping in machine learning is to estimate the uncertainty of a model's performance or to assess the distribution of a statistic. In addition, bootstrapping helps create more diverse variations of the original dataset for training and ensembling purposes. This is based on the observation that averaging multiple models reduces variance more if the predictions of the models being used are less correlated (i.e., more diverse). Subsampling creates diverse datasets to train. However, it has limitations because if you subsample aggressively—for instance, picking up less than 50% of the original data—you tend to introduce bias.

In contrast, if you subsample in a more limited way, such as using 90% of the data, the resulting subsamples will tend to be correlated. Instead, bootstrapping is more efficient because, on average, you use about 63.2% of the original data at each bootstrap. For a detailed statistical explanation of such calculated proportions, see the detailed cross-validated answer at https://mng.bz/zZ0w. Moreover, sampling with replacement tends to give results that mimic the original distribution of the data. Bootstrapping creates a set of more different datasets to learn from and, consequently, a set of more different predictions that can ensemble, reducing variance.

In fact, since in averaging we are building a distribution of predictions and getting the center of the distribution as our prediction, the more the averaged predictions resemble a random distribution, the less the center of the distribution will be biased by problems in the data picked up by the model (such as overfitting).

By contrast, with *random subspaces*, introduced by T. Ho ["The Random Subspace Method for Constructing Decision Forests," *Pattern Analysis and Machine Intelligence*, 20(8), 832-844, 1998], the sampling is limited only to features. This works because the model used for the ensemble is the decision tree, a model whose high variance of the estimates is greatly reduced in the ensemble by using only a part of the features for every model that is a part of it. The improved result is because the models trained on a subsample of the features tend to produce uncorrelated predictions—all the decision trees overfit the data but in a different way with respect to each other.

Finally, with *random patches* [G. Louppe and P. Geurts, "Ensembles on Random Patches," in *Machine Learning and Knowledge Discovery in Databases* (2012): 346–361], sampling of both samples and features are used together to achieve even more uncorrelated predictions that can be averaged even more profitably.

Pasting, bagging, random subspaces, and random patches can all be implemented using Scikit-learn functions for bagging. The behavior of `BaggingClassifier` for classification tasks and `BaggingRegressor` for regression tasks can be controlled in regards to training data thanks to the following parameters:

- `bootstrap`
- `max_sample`
- `max_features`

By combining them according to each averaging method's specifications, you can obtain all four of the averaging strategies we have described (see table 5.1).

Table 5.1   Bagging and sampling strategies

Averaging strategy	What happens to data	Parameters for BaggingClassifier/ BaggingRegressor

Pasting	Training examples are sampled without replacement	`bootstrap = False`
		`max_samples < 1.0`
		`max_features = 1.0`

Bagging	Training examples are sampled with replacement (bootstrapping)	`bootstrap = True`
		`max_samples = 1.0`
		`max_features  = 1.0`

Random subspaces	Features are sampled (without replacement)	`bootstrap = False`
		`max_samples = 1.0`
		`max_features < 1.0`

Random patches	Training examples and features are sampled without replacement	`bootstrap = False`
		`max_samples < 1.0`
		`max_features < 1.0`

By inputting the desired Scikit-learn model class in the parameter estimator, you can instead decide what algorithm to use for building the ensemble. A decision tree is the default, but you can decide what weak or strong models you prefer. In the following example, we apply a bagged classifier, setting the number of decision tree models to 300. The following listing shows all the models contributing together to improve the low performances that, as we have seen from listing 5.2, a decision tree tends to produce in this problem.

Listing 5.3   Bagged tree-based classifier

```
from sklearn.ensemble import BaggingClassifier
from sklearn.tree import DecisionTreeClassifier
from sklearn.metrics import accuracy_score

accuracy = make_scorer(accuracy_score)
```

```
cv = KFold(5, shuffle=True, random_state=0)
model = BaggingClassifier(
    estimator=DecisionTreeClassifier(),
    n_estimators=300,
    bootstrap=True,
    max_samples=1.0,
    max_features=1.0,
    random_state=0)

column_transform = ColumnTransformer(
    [('categories', categorical_onehot_encoding, low_card_categorical),
     ('numeric', numeric_passthrough, continuous)],
    remainder='drop',
    verbose_feature_names_out=False,
    sparse_threshold=0.0)

model_pipeline = Pipeline(
    [('processing', column_transform),
     ('modeling', model)])

cv_scores = cross_validate(estimator=model_pipeline,
                           X=data,
                           y=target_median,
                           scoring=accuracy,
                           cv=cv,
                           return_train_score=True,
                           return_estimator=True)

mean_cv = np.mean(cv_scores['test_score'])
std_cv = np.std(cv_scores['test_score'])
fit_time = np.mean(cv_scores['fit_time'])
score_time = np.mean(cv_scores['score_time'])
print(f"{mean_cv:0.3f} ({std_cv:0.3f})",
      f"fit: {fit_time:0.2f}",
      f"secs pred: {score_time:0.2f} secs")
```

Creates a BaggingClassifier ensemble model based on decision trees

Sets bootstrap sampling for the BaggingClassifier

Sets no sampling of features for the BaggingClassifier

Sets no sampling of data for the BaggingClassifier

A column transformer that applies different transformations to categorical and numeric features

A pipeline that sequentially applies column transformation and the bagging classifier model

Five-fold cross-validation using the defined pipeline and calculating accuracy scores

Prints the mean and standard deviation of the accuracy scores from cross-validation

The results take a little while more and look promising, but they are still not enough to compete with our previous solutions based on support vector machines and logistic regression:

```
0.809 (0.004) fit: 37.93 secs pred: 0.83 secs
```

In the next subsection, we take the next step in ensembling by revisiting random forests, which make use of the random patches in bagging for a good reason.

5.1.2 Predicting with random forests

Random forests work similarly to bagging. Still, it also simultaneously applies random patches (training examples and features are sampled without replacement): it bootstraps the samples before each model is trained and subsamples the features during modeling. Since the basic algorithm used in a random forests ensemble is a decision tree built by binary splits, the feature sampling happens at every tree split when a set of features is sampled as potential candidates for the split itself.

Allowing each decision tree in the ensemble to grow to its extremities may lead to overfitting the data and high variance in the estimates; employing bootstrapping and feature sampling might mitigate these problems. Bootstrapping ensures that the models are trained on slightly different data samples from the same distribution, while feature sampling at each split guarantees diverse tree structures. This combination helps generate a set of models that are quite distinct from one another. Different models produce very different predictions (hence, we can say that their predictions are quite uncorrelated), and that's a great advantage for the averaging technique because, when ensembling to a single prediction vector, the result is more reliable and accurate predictions.

Figure 5.4 shows how random forests work. The figure illustrates a binary classification problem with a dataset of two classes. The dataset is modeled using multiple decision trees, employing bootstrapping and feature sampling techniques. These techniques result in different partitions of the dataset, represented in the top-most part of the figure by three example results. The trees partition the dataset space in diverse ways, showcasing the variability in their splitting strategies. To simplify the representation, only two features are shown, providing a clearer understanding of the process.

Finally, when all the results are put together by majority voting, where you pick the more frequent classification as a predicted class, the random forests will provide better predictions derived from the results of all the trees. This is shown in the bottom part of the figure, where different shades indicate the prevalence of one or another class in a specific partition. The definitive boundary between classes is shown as a black polygonal line in the majority voting. The line can be even smoother when using multiple trees, resembling a curve. Ensemble methods can approximately resemble any curve if given enough models to the ensemble.

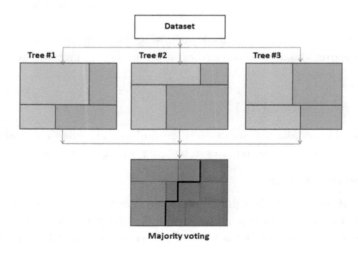

Figure 5.4   How random forests arrives at its results by combining the different data partitioning due to its decision trees thanks to majority voting

Originally devised by Leo Breiman and Adele Cutler (https://mng.bz/0Qlp), though commercially protected, the algorithm has been open-sourced—hence the many different names of its implementations. Random forests open up even more interesting possibilities, apart from better predictions, because you can use the algorithm to determine feature importance and measure the degree of similarity of the cases in a dataset.

In the example in listing 5.4, we test how random forests would work on our classification problem with the Airbnb NYC dataset. Apart from the algorithm, there are no differences from our standard data processing when applying decision trees. One-hot encoding turns low-categorical features into binaries, and numeric features are left as they are.

Listing 5.4 Random forests classifier

```
from sklearn.ensemble import RandomForestClassifier
from sklearn.metrics import accuracy_score

accuracy = make_scorer(accuracy_score)
cv = KFold(5, shuffle=True, random_state=0)
model = RandomForestClassifier(n_estimators=300,
                               min_samples_leaf=3,
                               random_state=0)
```
A RandomForestClassifier with 300 estimators and a minimum number of samples at a leaf node set to 3

```
column_transform = ColumnTransformer(
    [('categories', categorical_onehot_encoding, low_card_categorical),
     ('numeric', numeric_passthrough, continuous)],
    remainder='drop',
    verbose_feature_names_out=False,
    sparse_threshold=0.0)
```
A column transformer that applies different transformations to categorical and numeric features

```
model_pipeline = Pipeline(
    [('processing', column_transform),
     ('modeling', model)])
```
A pipeline that sequentially applies column transformation and the random forests classifier model

```
cv_scores = cross_validate(estimator=model_pipeline,
                           X=data,
                           y=target_median,
                           scoring=accuracy,
                           cv=cv,
                           return_train_score=True,
                           return_estimator=True)
```
A five-fold cross-validation using the defined pipeline and calculating accuracy scores

```
mean_cv = np.mean(cv_scores['test_score'])
std_cv = np.std(cv_scores['test_score'])
fit_time = np.mean(cv_scores['fit_time'])
score_time = np.mean(cv_scores['score_time'])
print(f"{mean_cv:0.3f} ({std_cv:0.3f})",
      f"fit: {fit_time:0.2f}",
      f"secs pred: {score_time:0.2f} secs")
```
Prints the mean and standard deviation of the accuracy scores from cross-validation

After running the script, you will obtain the following results, which are actually the best performance you will find in this chapter for this problem:

```
0.826 (0.004) fit: 12.29 secs pred: 0.68 secs
```

The secret to obtaining a good result with random forests is to choose its few hyper-parameters wisely. Though the random forests algorithm is a no-brainer since it works fine with default parameters, fine-tuning it will bring better results. First, the purpose of the algorithm is to reduce the variance of the estimates, and that's done by setting a high enough number of n_estimators. The principle is that if you have many trees, you have a distribution of results, and if the results are randomly drawn, you have an effect similar to the regression to the mean (the best prediction) due to the law of large numbers. The bootstrapping of examples and sampling of the features to be considered for splitting is usually enough to make the resulting trees of the forests different enough to be considered "random draws." However, you need enough draws to have a proper regression to the mean.

You need some tests to fine-tune how many trees you build since there's always a sweet spot: after a certain number of trees, you won't obtain any more improvements, and sometimes some decrements in performance will result instead. Also, setting a too-high number of trees to be built by the algorithm will increase its computational costs, and more time will be needed in training and inference. However, no matter how many trees you train for, if your variance starts high using the default settings of a random forests model, you can do little to reduce it. Here the tradeoff between variance and bias comes into play; that is, you can trade some variance, implying you are overfitting the data, for some higher bias.

You can set a proper bias for random forests by making the following adjustments:

- Setting a lower number of features to consider when looking for the best split by setting the max_features parameter
- Setting a max number of splits per tree, which will limit its growth to a certain predefined extent, by setting the max_depth parameter
- Setting a minimum number of examples in the terminal leaves of the tree, which will limit its growth, by setting the min_samples_leaf parameter with a number higher than 1

In the next section, we explore extremely randomized trees (ERT), a variant of random forests that can be quite handy when data is larger and noisy.

5.1.3   *Resorting to extremely randomized trees*

ERT (also known as extra-trees in Scikit-learn) is a more randomized kind of random forests algorithm. The reason is the choice of candidates for splits in the ensemble's single trees. In random forests, the algorithm samples its candidates for each split and then decides on the best feature to use among the candidates. Instead, the feature to be split in ERT is not evaluated among the possible candidates but randomly chosen. Afterward, the algorithm evaluates the best split point in the randomly chosen feature. This has some consequences. First, since the resulting trees are even more uncorrelated, there is even less variance in predictions from ERT—but at the price of a higher bias. Randomly split features have an effect on the accuracy of the predictions.

Second, ERT is more computationally efficient because it doesn't test sets of features but a single feature each time for the best split. All these characteristics make ERT best suited for handling

- *High-dimensional data* because it will split features faster than any other decision-tree ensemble algorithm
- *Noisy data* because the random feature and sample selection process can help reduce the influence of noisy data points, making the model more robust to extreme values
- *Imbalanced data* because, due to the random feature selection, the signals from the minority subset of the data won't be systematically excluded in favor of the majority subset of the data

The following listing tests ERT by replacing the random forests in listing 5.4, where you built a model with the Airbnb NYC dataset to figure out if the price of a listing is above or below the median value.

Listing 5.5   ERTs classifier

```python
from sklearn.ensemble import ExtraTreesClassifier

accuracy = make_scorer(accuracy_score)
cv = KFold(5, shuffle=True, random_state=0)
model = ExtraTreesClassifier(n_estimators=300,
                             min_samples_leaf=3,
                             random_state=0)
```
> An ExtraTreesClassifier with 300 estimators and a minimum number of samples at a leaf node set to 3

```python
column_transform = ColumnTransformer(
    [('categories', categorical_onehot_encoding, low_card_categorical),
     ('numeric', numeric_passthrough, continuous)],
    remainder='drop',
    verbose_feature_names_out=False,
    sparse_threshold=0.0)
```
> A column transformer that applies different transformations to categorical and numeric features

```python
model_pipeline = Pipeline(
    [('processing', column_transform),
     ('modeling', model)])
```
> A pipeline that sequentially applies column transformation and the random forests classifier model

```python
cv_scores = cross_validate(estimator=model_pipeline,
                           X=data,
                           y=target_median,
                           scoring=accuracy,
                           cv=cv,
                           return_train_score=True,
                           return_estimator=True)
```
> A five-fold cross-validation using the defined pipeline and calculating accuracy scores

```python
mean_cv = np.mean(cv_scores['test_score'])
std_cv = np.std(cv_scores['test_score'])
fit_time = np.mean(cv_scores['fit_time'])
score_time = np.mean(cv_scores['score_time'])
print(f"{mean_cv:0.3f} ({std_cv:0.3f})",
```

```
        f"fit: {fit_time:0.2f}",
        f"secs pred: {score_time:0.2f} secs")
```
◄─── **Prints the mean and standard deviation of the accuracy scores from cross-validation**

You obtain a bit better result than using random forests:

```
0.823 (0.004) fit: 4.99 secs pred: 0.42 secs
```

If you run this example, you will see that training by ETR is much faster than by random forests, given that you use the same dataset and build the same number of trees. ETR becomes an interesting alternative when your dataset is larger (more cases) and even more when it is wider (more features) because it saves a lot of time picking the feature to split since it is randomly decided. By contrast, the random forests algorithm has to look for the best feature among a selection.

The fact that splits are decided randomly is a great advantage when many collinear and noisy features are related to the target. The algorithm avoids picking the same signals as an algorithm driven by searching for the feature that best fits the target. In addition, you can see the working dynamics in feature splitting of an ETR as another way to trade variance with bias. Splitting randomly is a limitation for the algorithm and reduces the variance because the resulting set of trees will be very uncorrelated.

In the next section, we complete our overview of tree-based ensembles by examining gradient boosting. This slightly different ensembling approach is often more effective for tabular data problems than bagging or random patches.

5.2   *Gradient boosting*

In recent years, *gradient boosting decision trees* (GBDT) has firmly established itself as a cutting-edge method for tabular data problems. GBDT is generally considered a state-of-the-art machine learning method across a wide range of problems across multiple domains, including multiclass classification, advertising click prediction, and search engine ranking. When applied to standard tabular problems, you can expect GBDT to perform better than neural networks, support vector machines, random forests, and bagging ensembles.

Above all, GBDT's ability to handle heterogeneous features and its flexibility in the choice of the loss function and evaluation metrics make the algorithm most suitable for tabular data predictive modeling tasks. In sum, GBDT offers the following benefits for tabular data problems:

- With the proper hyperparameter tuning, it can achieve the best performance among all other techniques.
- There is no need for scaling or other monotone transformations of the features.
- It automatically captures nonlinear relationships in the data.
- It is robust to outliers and noisy data.
- It automatically handles missing data.
- It automatically selects the best features and can report their importance.

All these characteristics depend on how the algorithm works, combining sequences of decision trees in a gradient descent optimization. In fact, in gradient boosting, starting from a constant value, you add tree models to an ensemble sequentially, each one correcting the errors of the previous models in a fashion similar to gradient descent optimization. Gradient boosting represents an evolution of the original boosting approach. Used in models such as Adaboost, in the original boosting, you just average models built on the residuals of the previous model.

In Adaboost, the algorithm fits a sequence of weak learners, any machine learning algorithm that consistently beats random guessing, to the data (for an explanation about how to choose weak learners, see https://mng.bz/KG9P). It then attributes more weight to incorrect predictions and less to correct ones. Weighting helps the algorithm to focus more on the observations that are harder to predict. The process is concluded after multiple corrections by a majority vote in classification or an average of the predictions in regression.

By contrast, in gradient boosting, you rely on a double optimization: first that of the single trees that strive to reduce the error based on their optimization function and then the general one, involving calculating the error from the summation of the boosted model, in a form that mimics gradient descent, where you gradually correct the model's predictions. Since you have an optimization also based on a second level, the optimization based on the error of the entire ensemble procedure, gradient boosting is more versatile than the previously seen tree ensembles because it allows arbitrary loss functions to be used when calculating how much the summation of the predictions of models diverges from the expected results.

Figure 5.5 visually represents how the training error decreases after adding a new tree. Each tree takes part in a gradient descent style optimization, contributing to predicting the correction of the residual errors from the previous trees.

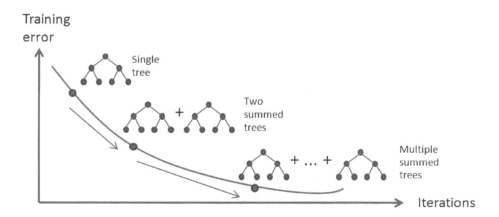

Figure 5.5 How gradient descent works with boosted trees

If gradient descent provides optimal results and flexibility in the optimization, having decision trees as base learning (ensembles, as seen, are not limited to decision trees) offers various advantages. This is because it automatically selects the features it needs. It doesn't need to specify a functional form (a formula as in regression), scaling, or linear relationships between features and the target.

In the next section, before seeing specific implementations in action (Scikit-learn, XGBoost, LightGBM), we will try building our simple implementation of gradient boosting to understand how to use this powerful algorithm.

5.2.1   *How gradient boosting works*

All implementations of GBDT offer a variety of hyperparameters that need to be set to get the best results on the data problem you are trying to solve. Figuring out what each setting does is a challenge, and being agnostic and leaving the task to an automatic tuning procedure doesn't help too much since you will have challenges telling the tuning algorithm what to tune and how to tune.

In our experience, writing down a simple implementation is the best way to understand how an algorithm works and to figure out how hyperparameters relate to predictive performances and results. Listing 5.6 shows a `GradientBoosting` class capable of addressing any binary classification problem, such as the Airbnb NYC dataset we are tackling as an example, using two parameters for the gradient descent procedure and the parameters from the decision tree model offered by Scikit-learn.

The code creates a GradientBoosting class that comprises methods for fitting, predicting probabilities, and predicting class. Internally, it stores the sequence of fitted decision trees in a list, from where they can be accessed sequentially to reconstruct the following summation formula:

$$H(X) = \sum_{m=1}^{M} v \cdot h_m(X, w_m)$$

In the formula,

- $H(X)$ is the gradient boosting model applied to predictors X
- M corresponds to the number of tree estimators used
- v represents the learning rate
- w^m instead represents the corrections from previous trees that have to be predicted
- The h^m symbol refers to the mth decision tree used

Interestingly, gradient boosting trees are always regression trees (even for classification problems)—hence our choice of using Scikit-learn's DecisionTreeRegressor. This also explains why GBDT is better at predicting probabilities than other tree-based ensemble models: gradient boosting trees regress directly on the logit of class probability, thus optimizing in a fashion not too different from logistic regression. On the other hand, algorithms such as random forests are optimized for purity metrics, and they estimate probabilities by counting the fraction of a class in a terminal node, which is not truly a probability estimate. Generally, probabilities outputted by GBDTs are correct, and they rarely require subsequent probabilistic calibration, which is a post-processing step used to adjust predicted probabilities to improve their accuracy and reliability in applications where probability estimates are paramount, such as medical diagnosis (e.g., disease detection), fraud detection, or credit risk assessment.

In our code implementation, we allow passing any parameter for the DecisionTree-Regressor (see https://mng.bz/9YQx), though the most useful are the ones related to the complexity of the tree development, such as `max_depth`, fixing the maximum depth of the tree, or `min_samples_split` and `min_samples_leaf`, the minimum number of samples needed to split an internal node or to be at a leaf node, respectively.

The role of each tree regressor is to provide a w vector containing the learned corrections to be summed together with the previous estimates after being weighted by the learning rate. Each w vector depends on the previous one because it is produced by a tree regressor trained on the gradients necessary to correct the estimates to match the true classification labels. The chained vectors w resemble a sequence of gradient corrections—at first large, then finer and finer, converging toward an optimal output prediction. Such gradient descent is perfectly similar to the gradient descent optimization procedure we introduced in chapter 4. In addition, by changing the cost function on which you base your gradients' computation, you can ask the GBDT to optimize for different loss functions.

Listing 5.6 Building a gradient boosting classifier

```
from sklearn.tree import DecisionTreeRegressor
import numpy as np

class GradientBoosting():
    def __init__(self, learning_rate=0.1, n_estimators=10, **params):
        self.learning_rate = learning_rate
        self.n_estimators = n_estimators
        self.params = params
        self.trees = list()

    def sigmoid(self, x):
        x = np.clip(x, -100, 100)
        return 1 / (1 + np.exp(-x))

    def logit(self, x, eps=1e-6):
        xp = np.clip(x, eps, 1-eps)
        return np.log(xp / (1 - xp))

    def gradient(self, y_true, y_pred):
        gradient =  y_pred - y_true
        return gradient

    def fit(self, X, y):
```

Sigmoid function implementation used for probability transformation that converts logits back into probabilities

Logit function implementation used to transform probabilities into logits

Calculates the gradient of the loss function (negative log-likelihood) with respect to the predictions

```
        self.init = self.logit(np.mean(y))
        y_pred = self.init * np.ones((X.shape[0],))
        for k in range(self.n_estimators):
            gradient = self.gradient(self.logit(y), y_pred)
            tree = DecisionTreeRegressor(**self.params)
            tree.fit(X, -gradient)
            self.trees.append(tree)
            y_pred += (
                self.learning_rate * tree.predict(X)
            )

    def predict_proba(self, X):
        y_pred = self.init * np.ones((X.shape[0],))
        for tree in self.trees:
            y_pred += (
                self.learning_rate * tree.predict(X)
            )
        return self.sigmoid(y_pred)

    def predict(self, X, threshold=0.5):
        proba = self.predict_proba(X)
        return np.where(proba >= threshold, 1, 0)
```

Initializes the model with the logit-transformed mean of the target values

Fits a decision tree regressor to the negative gradient of the log-odds transformed target

Updates the predicted values using the output of the fitted tree with a learning rate factor

Predicting back requires cumulating predictions from all the trees.

As in the gradient descent we have seen applied to linear models, you rely on making the process stochastic to avoid the optimization being struck on a suboptimal solution, which is achieved by sampling rows or columns before the training of each decision tree. In addition, you use early stopping to prevent the GBDT from using too many decision trees in sequence and adapting too much to the training data. We will demonstrate early stopping in the next chapter.

Now that we have explained the inner workings of our GradientBoosting class, we can now experiment with it. We'll use the Airbnb NYC dataset and begin by dividing it into a training set and a testing set. This will involve creating two lists of row indexes—one for the training set and one for the testing set—employing the Scikit-learn function train_test_split (https://mng.bz/jp1z). We instantiate our GradientBoosting class, which requires a learning rate of 0.1 and 300 decision trees, with a maximum depth of four branches and terminal leaves with at least three examples. After transforming the training data, by treating numeric and categorical features, we fit the model, predict the test set, and evaluate the results.

Listing 5.7   Testing our gradient boosting class

```
from sklearn.model_selection import train_test_split

train, test = train_test_split(range(len(data)), test_size=0.2,
random_state=0)

cls = GradientBoosting(n_estimators=300,
                       learning_rate=0.1,
                       max_depth=4,
                       min_samples_leaf=3,
```

Splits the dataset indices into training and test sets using a fixed random seed

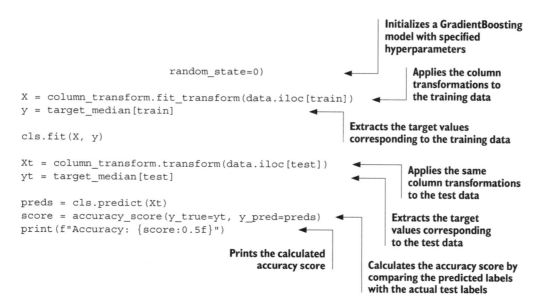

```
                              random_state=0)
X = column_transform.fit_transform(data.iloc[train])
y = target_median[train]

cls.fit(X, y)

Xt = column_transform.transform(data.iloc[test])
yt = target_median[test]

preds = cls.predict(Xt)
score = accuracy_score(y_true=yt, y_pred=preds)
print(f"Accuracy: {score:0.5f}")
```

Initializes a GradientBoosting model with specified hyperparameters

Applies the column transformations to the training data

Extracts the target values corresponding to the training data

Applies the same column transformations to the test data

Extracts the target values corresponding to the test data

Calculates the accuracy score by comparing the predicted labels with the actual test labels

Prints the calculated accuracy score

The evaluated accuracy on our test set is

```
Accuracy: 0.82503
```

This is a very good result, pointing out that even our basic implementation is able to do a very good job on the data we are working with. In the next section, we will investigate the results obtained and observe a key characteristic of GBDT models that distinguishes them from other decision tree ensembles.

5.2.2 Extrapolating with gradient boosting

In our implementation from scratch of a GBDT, we can visualize how the model fits the data by predicting the same training set. The visualization shown in figure 5.6, created by the small code snippet in listing 5.8, is a normalized density histogram. In a normalized density histogram, the height of each bar represents the relative frequency of data points falling within a specific bin, and the total area under the histogram becomes equal to 1. The result depicts a distribution of values predominantly polarized to the extremities of 0-1 boundaries, showing a model quite decisive in classifying the examples.

> **Listing 5.8 Plotting gradient boosting predicted probabilities**

```
import matplotlib.pyplot as plt

proba = cls.predict_proba(Xt)
plt.figure(figsize=(8, 6))
plt.hist(proba,
         bins=30,
```

Generates predicted probabilities for the test data using the trained model

```
        density=True,
        color='blue',
        alpha=0.7)
plt.xlabel('Predicted Probabilities')
plt.ylabel('Density')
plt.title('Histogram of Predicted Probabilities')
plt.grid(True)
plt.show()
```

Creates a histogram of the predicted probabilities with specified bins and normalized density

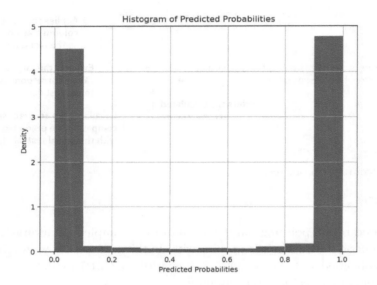

Figure 5.6   **A histogram describing the fitted probabilities for a gradient boosting classification, showing how the model has strongly decided for most cases if they are positive or negative**

Our implementation, under the hood, uses a regression loss, the squared loss, whose gradient is equal to the residual of the probabilities transformed into logits. For a definition of logits, see https://mng.bz/W214.

The logits for a probability p are calculated as

$$\text{logit}(p) = \log\left(\frac{p}{1-p}\right)$$

The advantage of this definition is that the logit function maps the probabilities to a log odds scale, which is an unbounded scale that ranges from negative infinity to positive infinity, allowing us to treat our problem as a regression problem.

This means that at each iteration, the gradient boosting algorithm fits a regression model to the gradient of the loss function with respect to the logit values, which corresponds to the difference between the logit of the true target values and the current predictions expressed in logits. This approach allows the algorithm to iteratively improve the predictions by adjusting them in the direction of the steepest descent of the loss function and to finally have a logit prediction that is bounded in the range between 0 and 1, thanks to the inverse function of the logit, the sigmoid. A sigmoid is a mathematical function that maps its input to a value between zero and one, providing a smooth and continuous curve.

The formula for the sigmoid is

$$\sigma(x) = \frac{1}{1 + \exp(-x)}$$

where

- $\sigma(x)$ represents the sigmoid function applied to the input value x.
- $\exp(-x)$ is the exponential function, where exp denotes Euler's number (approximately 2.71828) raised to the power of $-x$.
- $1 + \exp(-x)$ is the denominator, which ensures that the output of the sigmoid function is always positive.
- $1 / (1 + \exp(-x))$ represents the division of 1 by the denominator, resulting in the output value of the sigmoid function.

It is commonly used in machine learning and statistical models to convert logit predictions into probabilities.

What if, instead, we treat the problem as a regression one? In listing 5.9, we define a `GradientBoostingRegression` class by building on our `GradientBoosting` class and overwriting the fit and predict methods by removing logit and sigmoid transformations.

Listing 5.9 Testing a gradient boosting regression class

```
class GradientBoostingRegression(GradientBoosting):

    def fit(self, X, y):
        self.init = np.mean(y)                           Initializes predictions
        y_pred = self.init * np.ones((X.shape[0],))      with mean of y

        for k in range(self.n_estimators):
            gradient = self.gradient(y, y_pred)
            tree = DecisionTreeRegressor(**self.params)  Fits the tree to the
            tree.fit(X, -gradient)                       negative gradient
            self.trees.append(tree)
            y_pred += (
                self.learning_rate * tree.predict(X)
            )
                                                         Updates predictions
    def predict(self, X):                                with tree's predictions
        y_pred = self.init * np.ones((X.shape[0],))      scaled by learning rate
        for tree in self.trees:
            y_pred += (
                self.learning_rate * tree.predict(X)
```

```
            )
        return y_pred
```

> Predicting back requires cumulating predictions from all the trees.

```
reg = GradientBoostingRegression(n_estimators=300,
                                 learning_rate=0.1,
                                 max_depth=4,
                                 min_samples_leaf=3,
                                 random_state=0)

reg.fit(X, y)

proba = reg.predict(Xt)
plt.figure(figsize=(8, 6))
plt.hist(proba,
         bins=10,
         density=True,
         color='blue',
         alpha=0.7)
plt.xlabel('Predicted Probabilities')
plt.ylabel('Density')
plt.title('Histogram of Predicted Probabilities')
plt.grid(True)
plt.show()
```

> Plots a histogram of regression predicted probabilities

When the code in listing 5.9 is run, it will produce a histogram of the fit predictions, as shown in figure 5.7. Figure 5.7 shows how fit probabilities exceed the 0-1 boundaries. As with linear regression, which is a weighted combination based on the features, gradient boosting, a weighted combination based on the results of a chained sequence of models, can extrapolate beyond the limits of the learned target. Such extrapolations are impossible with other ensembles based on decision trees, such as random forests. Decision trees in regression cannot predict anything exceeding the values seen in training since predictions are based on means of training subsamples. The extrapolative potentiality of GBDT, based on the fact that they are an additive ensemble, is the basis for their success with time series, where you extrapolate future results that may be very different from past ones.

As a caveat, however, always consider that the extrapolative capabilities of GBDTs cannot be extended as far as could be achieved using a linear model. In time series predictive situations where the value to be predicted is way too far from the targets you provided for training, for instance in case of an outlier, the extrapolation will be limited, missing a correct estimation. A linear model, which directly associates a linear relationship between the input data and the predictions, could prove more suitable in such situations. Linear models are capable of handling extreme predictions for completely unseen outlying data points. To offer an alternative to decision trees as base learners in such situations, many GBDT implementations offer linear boosting by simply ensembling linear models (such as in the XGBoost implementation) or applying a piecewise linear gradient boosting tree, where linear models are built on the terminal nodes of a decisions trees (such as in LightGBM implementation).

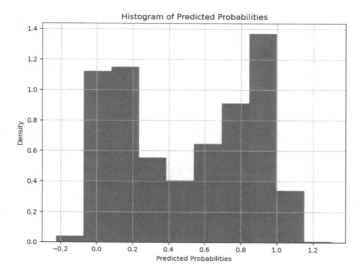

Figure 5.7
A histogram describing
fitted probabilities with
a gradient boosting
regression model where
some probabilities
exceed the 0-1 boundary

Also, the strength of GBDTs in time series problems relies on their being automatic in choosing the information for the predictions, with very few hyperparameters to set. All you need to do is to have enough examples, at least in the range of thousands of data points, and to have some careful engineering of time series features such as lagged values and moving averages at different time horizons. For shorter series, classical time series methods such as ARIMA or exponential smoothing are still the recommended choice. For complex problems such as hierarchically structured series, GBDTs can outperform even the most sophisticated deep learning architectures explicitly designed for time series data. For example, GBDTs excel in solving problems found in supermarket networks where both slow- and fast-moving goods are sold.

A clear example of the advantage of GBDTs in time series analysis has been demonstrated during the M5 forecasting competition recently held on Kaggle (https://github .com/Mcompetitions/M5-methods), where solutions made by a LightGBM algorithm proved superior to deep learning architectures designed for the task of predicting in hierarchical structured series, such as DeepAR (https://arxiv.org/abs/1704.04110) or NBEATS (https://arxiv.org/abs/1905.10437). A lucid and insightful analysis of the competition and the success and ubiquity of tree-based methods in the practice of time series analysis can be found in the paper "Forecasting with Trees" by Tim Januschowski et al. [*International Journal of Forecasting* 38.4 (2022): 1473–1481: https://mng .bz/8O4Z].

5.2.3 *Explaining gradient boosting effectiveness*

Today, despite the remarkable results in image and text recognition and generation, neural networks do not match the performance on tabular data of gradient boosting solutions such as XGBoost and LightGBM. Both practitioners and participants in data science competitions favor these solutions. For instance, see the "State of Competitive Machine Learning" regarding tabular competitions at https://mlcontests.com/tabular-data/. But where exactly does the advantage that GBDTs have over deep neural networks (DNNs) come from? From our experience building a gradient boosting classifier, we could appreciate how the algorithm combines gradient descent with the flexibility of decision trees with heterogeneous data. Is this enough to explain why GBDTs are so effective with tabular data?

"Why Do Tree-Based Models Still Outperform Deep Learning on Typical Tabular Data?" by Leo Grinsztajn, Edouard Oyallon, and Gael Varoquaux (Thirty-sixth Conference on Neural Information Processing Systems Datasets and Benchmarks Track, 2022: https://hal.science/hal-03723551v2/document) is a recent study that tries to shed some light on the different performances of deep learning architectures and gradient-boosting decision trees. The study shows that tree-based methods outperform deep learning methods (even modern architectures) in achieving good predictions on tabular data. The authors explicitly focus on the heterogeneity of columns that distinguishes tabular data from datasets with exclusively continuous features (we could refer to them as homogenous tabular datasets) and define a standard benchmark using 45 open datasets. They considered only data from about 10,000 samples, consisting of columns of different types, including numerical features with different units and categorical features, because that's considered the typical situation with tabular datasets.

Various deep learning models, including multilayer perceptrons (MLPs), ResNets, SAINT, and FTtransformer, were tried, but tree-based methods were found to have better performance with less hyperparameter tuning. Even when considering only numerical features, tree-based methods outperformed deep learning methods. This advantage became more pronounced when considering fitting time, although the hardware used (including GPUs) also influenced the results. The gap between the two methods was narrower on large datasets, which are not typical for tabular data.

The authors also investigated the features of tabular data that explain the performance difference between tree-based and deep learning methods. They found that smoothing the outcome in feature space narrowed the gap since deep architectures struggle with irregular patterns, whereas smoothness does not affect tree models. Removing uninformative features narrowed the gap for MLP-like neural architectures more. However, it was only after applying random rotations to the data that deep architectures outperformed tree models.

Random rotations refer to applying a random rotation matrix to the input features of a dataset before feeding them into a machine learning model. This rotation matrix is a square matrix that preserves the length of vectors and the angles between them, ensuring that the rotated data remains equivalent to the original data. Random rotations are used in machine learning for various purposes, including enhancing the diversity of ensembles, improving the robustness of models, and addressing rotation invariance in tasks such as computer vision and machine learning for quantum chemistry. Such a technique, perfectly reversible, however, tends to obscure the relationship between predictors and the target for tree-based algorithms, whereas deep learning models are unaffected thanks to their representative learning capacity to learn also the applied rotation.

This result doesn't necessarily indicate an advantage of DNNs but rather a limitation of GBDTs. Deep architectures are rotationally invariant, which means they can detect rotated signals, as in image recognition, where certain images can be recognized regardless of their orientation. In contrast, GBDTs are not rotationally invariant and can only detect signals that are always oriented in the same fashion, since they operate based on splitting rules. Therefore, using any kind of rotation on data, such as a principal component analysis or a singular value decomposition, can be detrimental to GBDTs. DNNs, unaffected by rotation, can catch up in these situations.

Currently, this study reinforces our experience with GBDTs and their perceived strengths:

- Can perform well even on datasets of moderate size (1,000–5,000 cases) but outshines other algorithms from 10,000 to 100,000 samples (based on our experience)
- Tend to excel with datasets that are heterogeneous in nature
- Robust against noise and irregularities in the target data
- Filter out noisy or irrelevant features due to their automatic feature selection process

In addition to the strengths mentioned here, it should also be noted that GBDTs are often preferred over DNNs in certain scenarios. One reason is that GBDTs require less data preprocessing, making them more efficient and straightforward to implement. Moreover, GBDTs are as flexible as DNNs in terms of objective functions. In both cases, there are many to choose from, which can be especially useful in domains with complex optimization goals. Another benefit of GBDTs is that they offer more control over how their decision tree rules are built, providing users with some transparency and interpretability. Finally, GBDTs can train faster than DNNs in most cases, and they can also predict in a reasonable inference time, depending on their complexity, which can be a critical factor in real-time applications or time-sensitive tasks.

Now that you've gained an understanding of the fundamental concepts behind gradient boosting and its effectiveness in solving tabular data problems compared to deep learning, the next section will explore some of its implementations, starting with the one provided by Scikit-learn.

5.3   *Boosting in Scikit-learn*

Scikit-learn offers gradient boosting algorithms for both regression and classification tasks. These algorithms can be accessed through the GradientBoostingClassifier (https://mng.bz/Ea9o) and GradientBoostingRegressor (https://mng.bz/N1VN) classes, respectively.

The Scikit-learn implementation of gradient boosting was one of the earliest options available to Python users in data science. This implementation closely resembles the original proposal of the algorithm by Jerome Friedman in 1999 ["Greedy Function Approximation: A Gradient Boosting Machine," *Annals of Statistics* (2001): 1189–1232]. Let's see the implementation in action in the next code listing, where we cross-validate the classifier performance on the Airbnb NY dataset to predict if a listing is above or below the median value.

Listing 5.10 Scikit-learn gradient boosting classifier

```
from sklearn.ensemble import GradientBoostingClassifier
from sklearn.metrics import accuracy_score
accuracy = make_scorer(accuracy_score)
cv = KFold(5, shuffle=True, random_state=0)
model = GradientBoostingClassifier(
    n_estimators=300,
    learning_rate=0.1,
    max_depth=4,
    min_samples_leaf=3,               A GradientBoostingClassifier
    random_state=0                    model with specified
)                                     hyperparameters

model_pipeline = Pipeline(
    [('processing', column_transform),
     ('modeling', model)])            A pipeline that first applies data
                                      processing with column_transform
                                      and then fits the model
cv_scores = cross_validate(
    estimator=model_pipeline,
    X=data,
    y=target_median,
    scoring=accuracy,
    cv=cv,                            A five-fold cross-validation using
    return_train_score=True,          the defined pipeline, calculating
    return_estimator=True             accuracy scores, and returning
)                                     additional information

mean_cv = np.mean(cv_scores['test_score'])
std_cv = np.std(cv_scores['test_score'])
fit_time = np.mean(cv_scores['fit_time'])
score_time = np.mean(cv_scores['score_time'])
print(f"{mean_cv:0.3f} ({std_cv:0.3f})",      Prints the mean and standard
      f"fit: {fit_time:0.2f}",                deviation of the accuracy scores
      f"secs pred: {score_time:0.2f} secs")   from cross-validation
```

Using the same set of parameters previously used, the performances we obtain are a bit better than those we obtained in our implementation:

```
0.826 (0.004) fit: 16.48 secs pred: 0.07 secs
```

One notable aspect of this Scikit-learn implementation is that the training process can take a considerable amount of time, and the bottleneck can be attributed to the decision trees, the only supported model for building the sequential ensemble utilized by Scikit-learn itself. In exchange, you have some flexibility in parameters and control over how the GBDT uses single decision trees. For instance, Scikit-learn's gradient boosting allows you to

- Define the `init` function. We used an average as the first estimator in our implementation. Here you can use whatever estimator you want as a starting point. Since gradient boosting is based on gradient descent and the gradient descent optimization process is sensitive to the starting point, this can prove an advantage when solving more complicated data problems.
- Revert the algorithm to Adaboost, the original algorithm that inspired sequential ensembles, by training a `GradientBoostingClassifier` with the exponential loss (`loss="exponential"`).
- Control in detail the complexity of the decision trees used, implying that you can model more complex data at risk of overfitting by means of parameters such as
  - `min_samples_split` for the minimum number of samples required to split an internal node
  - `min_sample_leaf` for the minimum number of samples needed to be at a leaf node
  - `min_weight_fraction_leaf` for the minimum weighted fraction of the total of weights of all the input samples required at a leaf node
  - `max_depth` for the max depth of the tree
  - `min_impurity_decrease` as the threshold in impurity decrease, used to decide whether to split or stop the growth of the tree
  - `max_leaf_nodes` as the maximum reachable number of final nodes before stopping growing the tree
- If controlling the growth of the decision trees is not enough, once they are grown, you can reduce their complexity using the `ccp_alpha` parameter. This parameter reduces the trees backward from the final nodes by removing the nodes that do not pass a complexity test (see https://mng.bz/DM9n for details).
- Subsample both rows (`subsample`) and columns (`max_features`), a particularly effective way to reduce overfitting and increase the training model's generalizability.

In addition, the implementation also offers support for sparse data and early stopping, a procedure to prevent overfitting in GBDT and neural networks that will be discussed in detail in the next chapter.

Also, on the side of the provided outputs, the support offered by this version is quite impressive, making it a perfect tool for understanding and explaining why your GBDT model came to certain predictions. For instance, you can access all the decision trees used and require the raw values predicted from the trees of the ensemble, both as a total (`decision_function` method) or as a sequence of steps (`staged_decision_function` method).

Recently, this implementation has been less used by practitioners because of the faster, more performing solutions offered by XGBoost, LightGBM, and Scikit-learn, with its HistGradientBoosting. However, it remains an interesting choice for smaller datasets if you want to control certain aspects of the gradient boosting procedure. In the next section, we will explore XGBoost and determine how it can be a more powerful choice for solving your tabular data problems.

5.3.1 *Applying early stopping to avoid overfitting*

The presentation of the original Scikit-learn classes for gradient boosting offers a chance to introduce a procedure that can help control overfitting. The procedure is early stopping, a method originally used in gradient descent to restrict the number of iterations when further adjustments to the coefficients under optimization would lead to no enhancements or a poor generalization of the solution. The method has also been used to train neural networks. In gradient boosting, which takes gradient descent as part of its optimization process, the method can help solve the same problem: limiting the number of added decision tree models to reduce the computational burden and avoid possible overfitting.

Early stopping works in a few simple steps:

1 A fraction of the training dataset is set aside to form a validation set.
2 During each iteration of the training process, the resulting partial model is evaluated using the validation set.
3 The performance of the partial model on the validation set is recorded and compared with previous results.
4 If the model's performance does not improve, the algorithm increases its counting (commonly called *patience*) of how many iterations since its last improvement. Otherwise, it resets the counting.
5 The training process is stopped if there has been no improvement over a certain number of iterations.
6 Otherwise, the training process continues for another iteration unless all the designated decision trees to be boosted have been completed. At this point, the training process is halted.

Figure 5.8 shows this process in a process flow chart.

Figure 5.9 shows the very same process from the point of view of the validation metric, which can be the loss or any other metric for which you want to get the best result. As the iterations progress, it is customary to observe training errors decrease. Validation error, on the other hand, tends to have a sweet point before the algorithm starts overfitting. Early stopping helps to catch this increase in validation error, and monitoring the validation error dynamics allows you to retrace to the iteration before any overfitting happens.

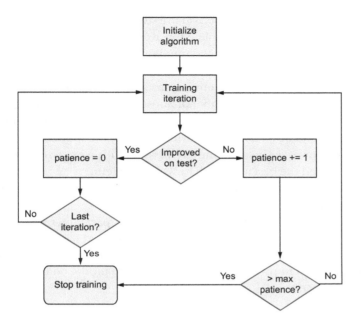

Figure 5.8 **A process flow chart describing how early stopping works in GBDTs**

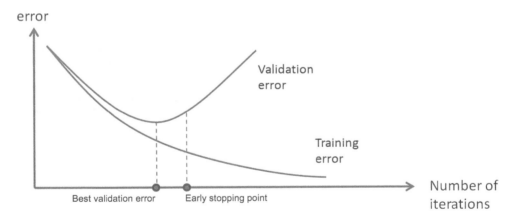

Figure 5.9 **How validation error and training error generally behave when using GBDTs through multiple iterations**

Different stopping points may be found for each model trained on different folds in a cross-validation process with early stopping. When training on the entire dataset, you can still rely on using early stopping based on a validation sample. Hence, you just need to set a high number of iterations and see when the training stops. Otherwise, you can use a fixed number of iterations based on the stopping iterations you observed in cross-validation. In this case, you can calculate the average or median of all stopping points seen in cross-validation to determine the number of boosting trees to use. However, there's no fixed rule, and you may choose to use the second maximum value for an aggressive stopping policy or the second minimum value for a conservative one.

Additionally, consider increasing the number of boosting trees since training is done on more data than during cross-validation. As a general guideline, increase the number of boosting trees by a percentage equivalent to dividing one by the number of folds you used in cross-validation. However, since no one-size-fits-all solution exists, experimentation may be necessary to find the best approach for your problem.

As an example, we run the previous code again, this time setting a higher number of base estimators to be used and two parameters, `validation_fraction` and `n_iter_no_change`, that activate the early stopping procedure. The parameter `validation_fraction` determines the fraction of the training data to be used for validation, and it is effective only when `n_iter_no_change` is set to an integer indicating how many iterations should pass without improvements when testing the model on the validation set before stopping the process.

Listing 5.11   Applying early stopping with GradientBoostingClassifier

```
model = GradientBoostingClassifier(
    n_estimators=1000,
    learning_rate=0.1,
    validation_fraction=0.2,
    n_iter_no_change=10,
    max_depth=4,
    min_samples_leaf=3,
    random_state=0
)

model_pipeline = Pipeline(
    [('processing', column_transform),
     ('modeling', model)])

cv_scores = cross_validate(estimator=model_pipeline,
                           X=data,
                           y=target_median,
                           scoring=accuracy,
                           cv=cv,
                           return_train_score=True,
                           return_estimator=True)

mean_cv = np.mean(cv_scores['test_score'])
std_cv = np.std(cv_scores['test_score'])
fit_time = np.mean(cv_scores['fit_time'])
score_time = np.mean(cv_scores['score_time'])
print(f"{mean_cv:0.3f} ({std_cv:0.3f})",
      f"fit: {fit_time:0.2f} secs pred: {score_time:0.2f} secs")
iters = [cv_scores["estimator"][i].named_steps["modeling"].n_estimators_
         for i in range(5)]
```

A GradientBoostingClassifier model whose iterations are raised to 1,000 from the previous 300

As a validation fraction, the GradientBoostingClassifier uses 20% of the training data for validation.

The training of the GradientBoostingClassifier will stop after 10 iterations without improvements on the validation.

Extracts the number of estimators used during training for each fold's estimator

```
print(iters)
```

← Prints the list of the number of
estimators for each fold's estimator

The output is

```
0.826 (0.005) fit: 6.24 secs pred: 0.04 secs
[145, 109, 115, 163, 159]
```

Since the mean number of iterations for cross-validation folds is 268 iterations, based on a rule of thumb, when using all the available data during the training phase, we suggest increasing the number of iterations by 20%, fixing it at 322 iterations.

In the following sections, we will introduce new implementations of gradient boosting, such as XGBoost and LightGBM. We will also present how to use early stopping with them.

5.4 Using XGBoost

XGBoost gained traction after being successful in a Kaggle competition, the Higgs Boson Machine Learning Challenge (https://www.kaggle.com/c/higgs-boson), where XGBoost has been proposed in the competition forums as a fast and accurate solution in comparison to Scikit-learn's gradient boosting. XGBoost has since been adopted and successfully used in many other data science competitions, proving its effectiveness and the usefulness of Kaggle competitions as a good place to introduce innovations that disrupt performance benchmarks. Keras is another example of an innovation that was widely adopted after success in Kaggle competitions. At the time of writing, the XGBoost package had been updated and reached the milestone of version 2.0.3, which is the version we have used in this book.

Initially conceived as a research project by Tianqi Chen, later further developed with the contribution of Carlos Guestrin, XGBoost, is a gradient boosting framework available as open-source software. It is noticeable that, contrary to other initiatives, such as LightGBM, sponsored by Microsoft, and Yggdrasil Decision Forests (see https://mng .bz/lYV6) that Google sponsors, XGBoost remained completely independent, maintained by the Distributed (Deep) Machine Learning Common community (dmlc .github.io).

Over time, the framework has undergone significant enhancements and now provides advanced capabilities for distributed processing and parallelization, which enables it to operate on large-scale datasets. Meanwhile, XGBoost has also gained wide adoption, and it is currently accessible in several programming languages, including C/C++, Python, and R. Moreover, this framework is supported on multiple data-science platforms, such as H2O.ai and Apache Spark.

As a data science user, you will immediately notice several key characteristics of this framework, including

- The ability to handle various input data types
- Support for customized objective and evaluation functions
- Automatic handling of missing values

- Easy support for GPU training
- Accommodation of monotonicity and feature interaction constraints
- Optimization of multiple cores and cache on standalone computers

From a system performance perspective, notable features include

- Networked parallel training, which allows for distributed computing across a cluster of machines
- Utilization of all available CPU cores during tree construction for parallelization
- Out-of-core computing when working with large datasets that don't fit into memory

However, what sets the "extreme" XGBoost algorithm apart is its innovative algorithmic details for optimization, including a variant of gradient descent known as Newton Descent and regularization terms, as well as its unique approach to feature splitting and sparse data handling. The following section briefly summarizes these groundbreaking techniques that power XGBoost's performance.

Now let's try the algorithm with our classification task on the Airbnb NYC dataset. In this case, use the XGBClassifier from XGBoost. For regression problems, you can use the XGBRegressor class. First, however, you need to have XGBoost installed on your system. To install XGBoost, you can just pip install it:

```
pip install XGBoost
```

Or use conda for the job:

```
conda install -c conda-forge py-XGBoost
```

The installation commands should do all the necessary steps for you; also install both CPU and GPU variants of the algorithm, if possible, on your system. See instructions and details on the installation process at https://mng.bz/BXd0.

In the following listing, we replicate the same approach we previously used with Scikit-learn's GradientBoostingClassifier: we boost 300 trees, limit the depth of decision trees to four levels, and accept nodes of at least three examples.

Listing 5.12 XGBoost classifier

```
from XGBoost import XGBClassifier

accuracy = make_scorer(accuracy_score)
cv = KFold(5, shuffle=True, random_state=0)
xgb = XGBClassifier(booster='gbtree',          ◀──  Creates an XGBClassifier model
                    objective='reg:logistic',  ◀──  with specified hyperparameters,
                    n_estimators=300,               including the booster type
                    max_depth=4,
                    min_child_weight=3)        ◀──  The learning objective,
                                                    equivalent to Scikit-learn's loss

model_pipeline = Pipeline(                          min_child_weight is equivalent to
    [('processing', column_transform),              Scikit-learn's min_samples_leaf.
```

```
        ('XGBoost', xgb)])

cv_scores = cross_validate(estimator=model_pipeline,
                           X=data,
                           y=target_median,
                           scoring=accuracy,
                           cv=cv,
                           return_train_score=True,
                           return_estimator=True)

mean_cv = np.mean(cv_scores['test_score'])
std_cv = np.std(cv_scores['test_score'])
fit_time = np.mean(cv_scores['fit_time'])
score_time = np.mean(cv_scores['score_time'])
print(f"{mean_cv:0.3f} ({std_cv:0.3f})",
      f"fit: {fit_time:0.2f}",
      f"secs pred: {score_time:0.2f} secs")
```

> **Prints the mean and standard deviation of cross-validated test scores**

The obtained result is the best obtained so far, and it is impressive that the training fit is just a fraction of what previously the Scikit-learn implementation took:

```
0.826 (0.004) fit: 0.84 secs pred: 0.05 secs
```

In the next subsection, we explore the key parameters we used for running this example and discuss what parameters, of the many offered by the algorithm (see https://mng.bz/dX6N for a complete list) you need for running successfully any tabular data project using XGBoost.

5.4.1 XGBoost's key parameters

Let's review the specific options we decided on in our previous example shown in listing 5.12, beginning with the n_estimators parameter, which specifies the number of decision trees involved in building the ensemble and is part of the gradient descent process that we discussed previously in this chapter.

The n_estimators parameter in XGBoost determines the number of decision trees used to produce the output. In standard tabular problems, the usual values for this parameter range between 10 to 10,000. While increasing this value can improve prediction performance by involving more weak learners, it can also slow down the training time. It's worth noting that there is an ideal number of trees that maximizes performance on prediction tasks with unseen data, and finding this sweet spot depends on other XGBoost parameters, such as the learning rate. To achieve a high-performing XGBoost model, it's important to choose the appropriate number of trees based on the problem at hand while setting the other parameters correctly, including the learning rate.

Whereas Scikit-learn is limited to just decision trees, XGBoost proposes more choices using its booster parameter:

- gbtree—Decision trees, as you would expect in gradient boosting
- gblinear—Linear regression models

- `dart`—Decision trees, but the optimization process is more regularized

The `gblinear` booster produces a sum of chained linear models. Since a sum of linear combinations is linear, you end up with a coefficient for each feature you have used, similar to a linear model. You can access the coefficients using the `.coef` method. It is a different way to fit a GBDT model with an emphasis on interpretability since the model can be reduced to a linear combination, different from the one you could directly fit because of using a different approach for complexity penalization and optimization. The most notable difference is that you cannot interpret the coefficients as you would if a linear regression or a generalized linear model produced them. Furthermore, the interpretation of the intercept generated by the `gblinear` booster differs from classical linear models as it is influenced by both the learning rate and the initial estimate employed by the booster.

The `dart` booster is different because it combines the optimization based on gradient descent with an approach similar to dropout, a technique used in deep learning. Presented by a UC Berkeley researcher and a Microsoft researcher in the paper "DART: Dropouts Meet Multiple Additive Regression Trees" by Rashmi Korlakai Vinayak and Ran Gilad-Bachrach (Artificial Intelligence and Statistics. PMLR, 2015), DART focuses on overfitting due to the dependence of each decision tree's estimates on the previous ones. The researchers then take the idea of dropout from deep learning, where a dropout mask randomly and partially blanked a neural network layer. The neural network cannot always rely on certain signals in a particular layer to determine the next layer's weights. In DART, the gradients are not calculated compared to the sum of the residuals from all previously built trees. Still, instead, the algorithm at each iteration randomly selects a subset of the previous trees and scales their leaves by a factor of $1/k$, where k is the number of trees that were dropped.

The `gblinear` and the `dart` are the only alternative boosters available. For instance, there is no booster to mimic random forests (as there is for another GBDT implementation, LightGBM). However, though a random forests booster is not supported yet by `XGBClassifier` and `XGBRegression`, you can obtain a similar result by playing with XGBoost parameters and functions:

- Use the `num_parallel_tree` parameter and set it to a number above 1. At each step of the optimization, the gradients are estimated not from a single decision tree but from a bagged ensemble of decision trees, thus creating a boosted random forests model. In some instances, this approach may provide better results than the gradient boosting approach because it will reduce the variance of the estimates at the expense of an increased computational cost.

- Use the `XGBRFClassifier` or `XGBRFRegressor`, two classes from XGBoost that implement a random forests approach. The classes are still experimental. For more details see https://mng.bz/rKVB with the caveat that there are some differences with the random forests algorithm offered by Scikit-learn because XGBoost computes a matrix made up of second derivatives and called the Hessian (see https://brilliant.org/wiki/hessian-matrix/ for a mathematical definition) to weight the gradients and it has no bootstrap capability. Hence, your results will be different.

As for the loss function, controlled by the parameter `objective`, we chose `reg:logistic`, but we could have also chosen `binary:logistic`, both comparable to log-loss for binary classification. In XGBoost, you have loss functions organized into six classes:

- `reg` for regression problems (but you also have the logistic regression among its options).
- `binary` for binary classification problems.
- `multi` for multiclass classification.
- `count` for count data—that is, discrete events.
- `survival` for survival analysis, which is a statistical technique to analyze data on the time it occurs for an event of interest to occur, such as the failure of a part in a machinery. It considers censoring, where the event of interest has not yet happened for some individuals in the study.
- `rank` for ranking problems, such as estimating what rank a site should have in the results.

Apart from Poisson distribution, useful for modeling the frequency of events, XGBoost also offers `reg:gamma` and `reg:tweedie`, optimizing for two distributions used in insurance for claim amount modeling as mentioned in chapter 4 when discussing generalized linear models.

The availability of various objective functions demonstrates the multiple possible applications that XGBoost may have in different domains. For a full overview of the loss functions see https://mng.bz/dX6N. Loss functions are essential in gradient boosting, as they define the optimization objective. By contrast, the evaluation metrics are not used to optimize the gradient descent in gradient boosting. However, they play a crucial role in monitoring the training process, optimizing for feature selection, hyperparameter optimization, and even enabling early stopping to halt the training once it is no longer providing benefit. The equivalent of Scikit-learn's `min_samples_leaf` in XGBoost is `min_child_weight`. Both parameters control the minimum number of samples needed to be at a leaf node of the decision tree. Thus, they regularize the decision tree by limiting the depth of the resulting tree. There are differences, however, since `min_child_weight` refers to the minimum sum of Hessian weight needed in a child node, while `min_samples_leaf` refers to the minimum number of samples required in a leaf. Hence, the two parameters are not completely comparable since their values are used differently in XGBoost and Scikit-learn.

As a general rule of thumb, `min_child_weight` affects how single decision trees are built, and the larger the value of this parameter, the more conservative the resulting tree will be. The usual values to be tested range from 0 (implying no limit to the size of the leaf nodes) to 10. In his 2015 talk at the NYC Data Science Academy, titled "Winning Data Science Competitions," Owen Zhang, a former top Kaggle competitor, suggested computing the optimal value of this parameter by dividing 3 by the percentage of the rarest events in the data to be predicted. For instance, following this rule of thumb, since our classes are split 50%/50%, the ideal value should be 3/0.5, resulting in 6.

Other important XGBoost parameters we didn't use in our example are as follows:

- The `learning_rate`, also called `eta`, is a parameter in XGBoost that determines the rate at which the model learns. A lower learning rate allows the model to converge more slowly yet more precisely, potentially leading to better predictive accuracy. However, this will result in a greater number of iterations and a longer training time. On the other hand, setting the value too high can speed up the process but result in worse model performance because, as it happens in gradient descent when your learning parameter is too high, the optimization overshoots its target.

- `alpha` and `lambda` are the L1 and L2 regularizers, respectively. They both contribute to avoiding overfitting in the gradient descent optimization part of XGBoost.

- The `max_depth` parameter in XGBoost controls the algorithm's complexity. If this value is set too low, the model may not be able to identify many patterns (known as underfitting). However, if it is set too high, the model may become overly complex and identify patterns that do not generalize well to new data (known as overfitting). Ideally, it is a value between 1 and 16.

- The `gamma`, or `min_split_loss`, parameter in XGBoost is a regularization parameter ranging from 0 to infinity, and setting this value higher increases the strength of regularization, reducing the risk of overfitting but potentially leading to underfitting if the value is too large. Also, this parameter controls the resulting complexity of the decision trees. We suggest starting with this value at 0 or a low value and then testing increasing it after all the other parameters are set.

- The `colsample_bytree` parameter in XGBoost controls the fraction of the total number of features or predictors to be used for a given tree during training. Setting this value to less than 1 means that each tree may use a different subset of features for prediction, potentially reducing the risk of overfitting or being too much influenced by single features in data. It also improves training speed by not using all features in every tree. The allowable range of values for this parameter is between 0 and 1.

- The `subsample` parameter in XGBoost controls the fraction of the number of instances used for a given tree during training. Like `colsample_bytree`, this parameter can help reduce overfitting and improve training time. By using a fraction of the cases for each tree, the model can identify more generalizable patterns in the data. The default value for `subsample` is 1.0, which means that all instances are used in each tree.

In many cases, you will only require some of the parameters provided by XGBoost or discussed here for your projects. Simply adjusting the `learning_rate`, setting the optimization steps, and `min_child_weight` to prevent overfitting individual decision trees in the gradient boosting process will be sufficient most of the time. Additionally, you may derive benefits from setting the `objective`, `max_depth`, `colsample_bytree`, and `subsample` parameters, but it is unlikely that tweaking the numerous other available parameters will yield significant improvements. This holds not only for XGBoost but also for different implementations of gradient boosting.

Next we explain what makes the XGBoost implementation perform better in computations and predictions.

5.4.2 How XGBoost works

As explained in the paper "Xgboost: A Scalable Tree Boosting System" by Tianqi Chen and Carlos Guestrin (*Proceedings of the 22nd ACM SIGKDD International Conference on Knowledge Discovery and Data Mining*, 2016), the great performance of XGBoost boils down to a few innovations that weren't present in other implementations:

- Column block for parallel learning
- Second-order approximation for quicker optimization
- Improved split-finding algorithms
- Sparsity-aware split finding

Column Block is a technique used in parallel learning that involves dividing a dataset into blocks of columns or subsets of features. This allows for parallel training across multiple processors, significantly reducing the overall training time. You can see it in action when you train an XGBoost model and look for CPU utilization pointing to multiple usages of different cores. XGBoost cannot use multiple cores to train multiple models simultaneously, as it happens in other ensemble models such as random forests. That's because gradient boosting is a serial model, where each model is trained after the results of another one. Instead, the XGBoost training process of every single model is divided among multiple cores to increase efficiency and speed.

Currently, XGBoost can be utilized in Python through two distinct APIs: the Native API and the Scikit-learn API. In this book, we will exclusively use the Scikit-learn API due to its benefits in terms of best modeling practices and the added benefit of being able to easily utilize various tools available in the Scikit-learn library, such as model selection and pipelines, as explained in chapter 4.

When using the Native API, the user is required to convert their data into a DMatrix, which is an internal XGBoost data structure optimized for both memory efficiency and training speed (https://mng.bz/VVxP). The use of the DMatrix format makes the column block technique possible. However, when using the Scikit-learn API, users can input their data as pandas DataFrames or Numpy arrays without requiring explicit conversion into the DMatrix format. This is because XGBoost performs the conversion under the hood, making the process more streamlined. Therefore, it is safe to choose the API that best suits your preferences, as both APIs offer the same performance and differ only in some of the parameters, default values, and options they provide.

The second-order approximation for speeding up the optimization incorporating the second derivative (the gradient derived from the first derivative) is based on a more comprehensive root-finding technique, Newton's method. In the context of minimization, we often refer to Newton's method as Newton descent instead of gradient descent. Listing 5.13 shows it implemented as a new class, the NewtonianGradientBoosting class, that inherits the original GradientBoosting class with some additions and modifications to its existing methods and attributes. In particular, we add the Hessian calculations to balance the gradient steps in regard to the convergence acceleration and a regularization term to prevent overfitting.

Listing 5.13   How XGBoost works

**Defines a new class NewtonianGradientBoosting
as a subclass of GradientBoosting**

```
class NewtonianGradientBoosting(GradientBoosting):     ◄───
    """the Newton-Raphson method is used to update the predictions"""

    reg_lambda = 0.25                        ◄─────    Sets a regularization
                                                       parameter reg_lambda
    def hessian(self, y_true, y_pred):
        hessian = np.ones_like(y_true)       ◄─────    Initializes a constant
        return hessian                                 Hessian matrix with ones

    def fit(self, X, y):
        self.init = self.logit(np.mean(y))
        y_pred = self.init * np.ones((X.shape[0],))

        for k in range(self.n_estimators):
            gradient = self.gradient(self.logit(y), y_pred)
            hessian = self.hessian(self.logit(y), y_pred)
            tree = DecisionTreeRegressor(**self.params)
            tree.fit(
                X,
                -gradient / (                      Fits the decision tree by dividing
                    hessian + self.reg_lambda      the negative gradient by the
                )                                  sum of the Hessian and the
            )                               ◄───   regularization parameter
            self.trees.append(tree)
            y_pred += self.learning_rate * tree.predict(X)

cls = NewtonianGradientBoosting(n_estimators=300,
                                learning_rate=0.1,        Creates an instance of the
                                max_depth=4,              NewtonianGradientBoosting
                                min_samples_leaf=3,       class with specified
                                random_state=0)    ◄───   hyperparameters

cls.fit(X, y)                                ◄───┐   Fits the NewtonianGradientBoosting
preds = cls.predict(Xt)                          │   model to the training data
score = accuracy_score(y_true=yt, y_pred=preds)
print(f"Accuracy: {score:0.5f}")             ◄───   Predicts target values using the
                                                    fitted model and calculating the
                                                    accuracy score for evaluation
```

The resulting accuracy is a little better than what we obtained from the original GradientBoosting class:

```
Accuracy: 0.82514
```

In our case, the Hessian is probably not particularly helpful because it is the same for all due to the kind of objective function we use: the squared error. However, in the context of optimization with other objective functions, the Hessian matrix provides information about the curvature of a function, which can be used to determine the direction and rate of change of the function. Intuitively, you can figure out that, with larger curvatures, you have larger Hessian values, which reduce the effect of the gradient, acting as a brake for the learning rate. On the contrary, smaller curvatures lead to an acceleration of the learning rate. Using the information of the Hessian, you get an adaptive learning rate for each of your training examples. However, as a side effect, computing the second derivative can often be complicated or intractable, necessitating significant computation. Analytical expressions and numerical methods for determining the second derivative require substantial computational effort. In the next chapter, devoted to more advanced topics, we will provide further information on how to build your customized objective functions by computing gradients and Hessians analytically and numerically.

A role in the Newton optimization used by XGBoost is also played by the regularization term that is summed up in Hessian and reduces the target further—that is, the adjustment to be estimated by the base learners. Another idea taken from gradient descent that XGBoost uses is regularization in the form of L2 regularization, as implemented in our example, and L1 regularization. The additional regularization terms help to smooth the final learned weights and avoid overfitting by directly modifying the Newtonian descent step. Consequently, it is important to consider how to tune both L1 and L2 values, referred to as lambda and alpha in the XGBoost and LightGBM implementations, as significant hyperparameters for improving optimization results and reducing overfitting. These regularization values ensure that the Newton descent takes smaller steps during optimization.

In the next section, we will continue to explore the new capabilities introduced by XGBoost by examining the contribution of split-finding algorithms to the increased speed performance offered by the algorithm.

5.4.3 *Accelerating with histogram splitting*

Gradient boosting is based on binary trees, which work by partitioning the data to have a better-optimized objective metric in the resulting splits than in the original set. Since gradient boosting treats all the features as numeric, it has a unique way of deciding how to partition. To find the feature to use for the split and the rule for the split, a binary tree decision should iterate through all the features, sort each feature, and evaluate every split point. Ultimately, the decision tree should pick the feature and its split point that led to better improvement relative to the objective.

With the emergence of larger datasets, the splitting procedure in decision trees poses serious scalability and computational problems for the original GBDT architecture based on serial models that continuously scan through data. From a computational point of view, the main cost in GBDT lies in learning the decision trees, and the most time-consuming part of learning a decision tree is finding the best split points.

Continuously looking for the best splitting point takes quite some time, rendering the algorithm quite demanding when training on a large number of features and instances. Histogram splitting helps reduce the time by replacing each feature's value with the histogram's split points to summarize its values. Listing 5.14 simulates a split search on our data problem. In doing so, we define an objective function and a splitting function that can operate both as the original decision tree splitting algorithm or by the faster histogram-based splitting.

Listing 5.14   The histogram split

```python
import numpy as np

def gini_impurity(y):
    _, counts = np.unique(y, return_counts=True)    # Function calculating and
    probs = counts / len(y)                         # returning the Gini impurity
    return 1 - np.sum(probs**2)                      # of a set of labels y

def histogram_split(x, y, use_histogram, n_bins=256):    # If use_histogram is true,
    if use_histogram:                                    # computes the histogram
        hist, thresholds = np.histogram(                 # for the selected feature
            x, bins=n_bins, density=False
        )
    else:                                                # If use_histogram is false,
        thresholds = np.unique(x)                        # just enumerates all the
                                                         # unique values in the feature
    best_score = -1
    best_threshold = None                                # Initializes the best score
    for threshold in thresholds:                         # and threshold
        left_mask = x <= threshold
        right_mask = x > threshold                       # Iterates over all possible
        left_y = y[left_mask]                            # thresholds
        right_y = y[right_mask]
        score = (                                        # Splits y based into left and
            gini_impurity(left_y) * len(left_y)          # right subsets based on the
            + gini_impurity(right_y) * len(right_y)      # selected threshold
        )
        if score > best_score:                           # Calculates the Gini
            best_threshold = threshold                   # impurity score for the
            best_score = score                           # left and right subsets
    return best_threshold, best_score
```

Returns the best threshold and its corresponding Gini impurity score

Calculates the Gini impurity score for the left and right subsets

Updates the best score and threshold if the current split has a higher Gini impurity score than the previous best split

In the code in listing 5.14, after defining a scoring function, the Gini impurity, we define a function that picks a feature and enumerates the values of its potential splits to be evaluated. If we use the basic approach, all its unique values are taken into account. Using the histogram approach instead, a 256-bin histogram is computed, and we use the bins delimiting values to be explored as potential split candidates. If our feature has more than 256 unique values, using the histogram will save us a lot of time when we just iterate through all split candidates and evaluate them by the scoring function.

Now that we have explained the workings of the example functions, we are ready for a test. We decided to optimally split the latitude in the classification task of predicting if the host is in the upper or lower price range. Since the latitude feature has many unique values to be considered as splitting candidates because Manhattan is a long, thin north-south island where property values vary by latitude, it should result in a difficult task because we expect many different latitudes to be evaluated against the target.

In our first test, we try to find the best split just by evaluating all the unique values that the feature presents:

```
%%time
histogram_split(x=data.latitude, y=target_median, use_histogram=False)

CPU times: user 46.9 s, sys: 10.1 ms, total: 46.9 s
Wall time: 46.9 s
(40.91306, 24447.475447387256)
```

In our second test, we rely on evaluating the splitting points found out by a histogram with 256 bins built on the feature:

```
%%time
histogram_split(
    x=data.latitude,
    y=target_median,
    use_histogram=True,
    n_bins=256
)

CPU times: user 563 ms, sys: 0 ns, total: 563 ms
Wall time: 562 ms
(40.91306, 24447.475447387256)
```

Looking under the hood of histogram splitting, we find binning, where values for a variable are grouped into discrete bins, and each bin is assigned a unique integer to preserve the order between the bins. Binning is also commonly referred to as k-bins, where the k in the name refers to the number of groups into which a numeric variable is rearranged, and it is used in histogram plotting, where you can declare a value for k or automatically have it set to summarize and represent your data distribution.

The speed-up is due not only to a minor number of split points to evaluate, which can be tested in parallel, thus using multicore architectures, but also to the fact that histograms are integer-based data structures that are much faster to handle than continuous values vectors.

XGBoost uses an algorithm to compute the best split based on presorting the values and usage of histograms. The presorting splitting works as follows:

- For each node, enumerating the features
- For every feature, sorting instances by their values

- Using a linear scan and histograms, determining the best split for the feature and computing the information gain
- Picking the best solution among all the features and their best split

XGBoost has other concept improvements: the traditional split finding algorithm is denoted by `exact` specified as the value of the `tree_method` parameter. The Weighted Quantile Sketch, referred to as `approx` in the XGBoost API, is an exclusive feature unique to XGBoost. This split-finding technique utilizes approximations and harnesses information derived from gradient statistics. By employing quantiles, the method defines potential split points among candidates. Notably, the quantiles are weighted to prioritize selecting candidates capable of mitigating high gradients, reducing significant prediction errors.

Weighted Quantile Sketch using histograms is now available as `tree_method="hist"`, which, since the 2.0.0 release, is the default method. In contrast, the `approx` tree method generates a new set of bins for each iteration, whereas the `hist` method reuses the bins over multiple iterations.

Another feature of the algorithm is related to data storage in DMatrices. The most time-consuming part of tree learning is sorting the data. To reduce the sorting cost, we propose storing the data in in-memory units: a block. This allows linearly scanning over the presorted entries and parallelizing, giving us an efficient parallel algorithm for split finding.

After the successful histogram aggregation implementation in LightGBM, XGBoost adopted it. Histogram aggregation is also the main feature of `HistGradientBoosting`, the Scikit-learn histogram-based gradient boosting we will present after LightGBM.

5.4.4   *Applying early stopping to XGBoost*

Section 5.3.1 illustrates how early stopping works with Scikit-learn's gradient boosting. XGBoost also supports early stopping. You can specify early stopping by adding a few arguments when instantiating an XGBClassifier or XGBRegressor model:

- `early_stopping_rounds`—This is the number of rounds to wait patiently without improvement in the validation score before stopping the training. If you set it to a positive integer, the training will stop when the performance on the validation set hasn't improved in that many rounds.
- `eval_metric`—This is the evaluation metric to use for early stopping. By default, XGBoost uses `rmse` for regression's root mean squared error and `error` for accuracy in classification. Still, you can specify any other from a long list (available at https://mng.bz/xK2W) as well as specify your own metric (which will be discussed in the next chapter on advanced machine learning topics).

In addition to setting these parameters, you also have to specify, at fitting time, a sample with its target where to monitor the evaluation metric. This is done by the `parameter eval_set`, which contains a list of tuples containing all the validation samples and their responses. In our example, we use only a validation set. Still, if there are multiple samples to monitor, XGboost will consider only the last tuple of data and response for stopping purposes.

In listing 5.15, we replicate the same approach we experimented with earlier by splitting our data into a train and a test set. However, to properly monitor the evaluation metric, we further split the train set to extract a validation set from it.

Listing 5.15 Applying early stopping to XGBoost

```
train, test = train_test_split(
    range(len(data)),
    test_size=0.2,
    random_state=0
)
train, validation = train_test_split(
    train,
    test_size=0.2,
    random_state=0
)

xgb = XGBClassifier(booster='gbtree',
                    objective='reg:logistic',
                    n_estimators=1000,
                    max_depth=4,
                    min_child_weight=3,
                    early_stopping_rounds=100,
                    eval_metric='error')

X = column_transform.fit_transform(data.iloc[train])
y = target_median[train]

Xv = column_transform.transform(data.iloc[validation])
yv = target_median[validation]

xgb.fit(X, y, eval_set=[(Xv, yv)], verbose=False)

Xt = column_transform.transform(data.iloc[test])
yt = target_median[test]

preds = xgb.predict(Xt)
score = accuracy_score(y_true=yt, y_pred=preds)
print(f"Accuracy: {score:0.5f}")
```

Splits the indices of the data into training and test sets using a fixed random seed

Further splits the training set into training and validation sets using the same random seed

Initializes an XGBoost classifier with an early stopping patience for 100 rounds

Uses the 'error' parameter, equivalent to accuracy, as an evaluation metric

Fits the XGBoost classifier to the training data X and labels y and performance on the validation data Xv and yv

Prints the accuracy score after comparing the predicted labels with the true labels

After completing the training, we managed to get this accuracy measure, which is slightly underperforming in respect of our previous cross-validation results because it is obtained by training on fewer examples—that is, 64% of available data since we reserved 20% for test and 16% for validation:

```
Accuracy: 0.82657
```

During the training, the evaluation metric is constantly checked, and the fit procedure is halted if it doesn't improve from more iterations than those specified by early_stopping_rounds. The best iteration is automatically recorded and used at prediction time. Thus, you have nothing more to do with the model. If you need to verify how many iterations it took before stopping, you can obtain it by inquiring about the model using the best_iteration attribute. In our example, xgb.best_iteration returns 200.

5.5 *Introduction to LightGBM*

LightGBM was first introduced in a 2017 paper titled "LightGBM: A Highly Efficient Gradient Boosting Decision Tree" by Guolin Ke and his team at Microsoft (https://mng.bz/AQdz). Recently, the package reached the 4.3.0 version, which is the version we tested in this book. According to the authors, the term "light" in LightGBM highlights the algorithm's faster training and lower memory usage than traditional gradient boosting decision trees. The paper demonstrated, through experiments on multiple public datasets, the algorithm's effectiveness and its ability to speed up the training process of conventional gradient boosting decision trees by over 20 times while maintaining almost the same accuracy. LightGBM was made available as open-source software on GitHub (https://github.com/microsoft/LightGBM/), quickly gaining popularity among data scientists and machine learning practitioners.

On paper, LightGBM shares many characteristics similar to those of XGBoost, such as support for missing values, native handling of categorical variables, GPU training, networked parallel training, and monotonicity constraints. We will tell you more about all that in the next chapter. In addition, LightGBM also supports sparse data. However, its major advantage lies in its speed, as it is significantly faster than XGBoost on various tasks, which has made it popular in both Kaggle competitions and real-world applications. The Kaggle community quickly took notice of LightGBM and began incorporating it into their competition entries alongside the already-popular XGBoost. In fact, mlcontests.com, a website that tracks the data science competition scene, reported in 2022 that LightGBM had become the preferred tool among competition winners, surpassing XGBoost in popularity. An impressive 25% of reported solutions for tabular problems were based on LightGBM. While LightGBM has seen comparable success among data science practitioners, XGBoost remains more popular overall. For example, the XGBoost repository has many more GitHub stars than the LightGBM repository.

LightGBM is a cross-platform machine learning library available for Windows, Linux, and MacOS. It can be installed using various tools, such as pip or conda, or built from source code (see the complete installation guide at https://mng.bz/ZlEP). Its usage syntax is similar to Scikit-learn's, making it easy for users who are familiar with Scikit-learn to transition to LightGBM. When optimizing gradient descent, LightGBM follows in the footsteps of XGBoost by utilizing the Newton-Raphson update, which involves dividing the gradient by the Hessian matrix. Guolin Ke's answer on GitHub confirms that (see https://github.com/microsoft/LightGBM/issues/5233).

Let's put the algorithm to the test on the same problem we previously examined with ScikitLearn's GradientBoosting and XGBoost.

Listing 5.16   LightGBM classifier

```
from lightgbm import LGBMClassifier

accuracy = make_scorer(accuracy_score)
cv = KFold(5, shuffle=True, random_state=0)
lgbm = LGBMClassifier(boosting_type='gbdt',
                      n_estimators=300,
                      max_depth=-1,
                      min_child_samples=3,
                      force_col_wise=True,
                      verbosity=0)

model_pipeline = Pipeline(
    [('processing', column_transform),
     ('lightgbm', lgbm)])

cv_scores = cross_validate(estimator=model_pipeline,
                           X=data,
                           y=target_median,
                           scoring=accuracy,
                           cv=cv,
                           return_train_score=True,
                           return_estimator=True)

mean_cv = np.mean(cv_scores['test_score'])
std_cv = np.std(cv_scores['test_score'])
fit_time = np.mean(cv_scores['fit_time'])
score_time = np.mean(cv_scores['score_time'])
print(f"CV Accuracy {mean_cv:0.3f} ({std_cv:0.3f})",
      f"fit: {fit_time:0.2f}",
      f"secs pred: {score_time:0.2f} secs")
```

Initializes an LGBMClassifier with a number of estimators, maximum tree depth, and minimum number of child samples

Forces column-wise histogram building

Creates a model pipeline that includes a column transformation step and an LGBMClassifier step

Performs five-fold cross-validation using the model pipeline using accuracy scoring

Prints the mean test score and standard deviation of the test scores obtained during cross-validation

The following are the impressive results in terms of accuracy, training, and prediction times:

```
0.826 (0.004) fit: 1.16 secs pred: 0.16 secs
```

Like XGBoost, LightGBM controls gradient descent with parameters such as n_estimators, learning_rate, lambda_l1, and lambda_l2 (L1 and L2 regularization, respectively). The most important parameters of LightGBM that help control its complexity are as follows:

- max_depth—This parameter controls the maximum depth of each tree in the ensemble. A higher value increases the complexity of the model, making it more prone to overfitting. If it is set to −1 it means that no limit is set to the growth of the trees.

- num_leaves—This parameter specifies the maximum number of leaves in a tree and, therefore, the complexity of the model. To avoid overfitting, it should be set to less than 2**(max_depth).

- `min_data_in_leaf`—This parameter controls the minimum number of samples required to be present in each leaf node. A higher value can prevent the tree from growing too deep and overfitting but can also lead to underfitting if set too high. The default value is 20. We suggest trying lower values, such as 10, and then testing, increasing the value to 300.

The parameters `feature_fraction` and `bagging_fraction` control how LightGBM samples from features and examples:

- `feature_fraction`—This parameter controls the fraction of features to be considered at each split. Similar to the `colsample_bytree` parameter in XGBoost, it can help reduce overfitting by preventing the model from relying too heavily on any feature.

- `bagging_fraction`—This parameter controls the fraction of data to be used for each tree. Similar to the subsample parameter in XGBoost, it can help reduce overfitting and improve training speed by randomly sampling from the data.

- `bagging_freq`—This parameter, which is not present in XGBoost, determines how frequently bagging should be applied. It turns off bagging examples when set to 0, even if `bagging_fraction` is specified. A value of n means bagging at every n iteration. For instance, a value of 2 means you have a bagged iteration every two (half of the time).

Related to the way LightGBM executes during the training, `verbosity` controls the amount of output information during training, while `force_col_wise` indicates histograms for feature splits during tree construction to be built based on columns. LightGBM can build histograms either column-wise or row-wise. Column-wise histogram building is generally faster, but it can require more memory, especially for datasets with a large number of columns. Row-wise histogram building is slower, but it can be more memory-efficient when dealing with datasets with a large number of columns. LightGBM will automatically choose the best method for building histograms for the dataset. However, you can also force LightGBM to use a specific method by setting the `force_col_wise` or `force_row_wise` parameters.

As for XGBoost, LightGBM can also use different base learners by specifying the `boosting` parameter:

- `gbdt`—The default option, using decision trees as base learners
- `rf`—Implements the random forests algorithm
- `dart`—Implements the "Dropouts meet Multiple Additive Regression Trees" algorithm

In addition, setting the parameter `linear_tree` to true, as you are using the default `boosting=gbdt`, will fit a piecewise linear gradient boosting tree—that is, decision trees having linear models as their terminal nodes. This is a compromise solution that uses both the nonlinear learning capabilities of decision trees and the extrapolative capabilities of linear models with unseen, outlying cases.

In the following section, we will examine closely all the innovations that distinguish LightGBM from XGBoost.

5.5.1 How LightGBM grows trees

Let's examine each characteristic that distinguishes LightGBM from XGBoost, starting with how LightGBM grows decision trees. Instead of increasing the tree level-wise (also known as *depth-first*) like XGBoost, LightGBM grows the tree leaf-wise (also known as *best first*). This means that the algorithm chooses the leaf node that provides the maximum gain and then splits it further until it is no longer advantageous. In contrast, the level-wise approach simultaneously splits all the nodes at the same depth.

To sum up, in XGBoost's level-wise growth approach, the algorithm grows all tree leaves to the same level. Then it splits them simultaneously, which may result in many insignificant leaves that don't contribute much to the final prediction. In contrast, LightGBM's leaf-wise growth approach splits the leaf with the maximum loss reduction at each step, resulting in fewer leaves but with higher accuracy. The leaf-wise approach allows LightGBM to focus only on the important features with the most significant effect on the target variable. This means that the algorithm can quickly converge to the optimal solution with fewer splits and a smaller number of trees.

Figure 5.10 shows a representation of the two approaches: on the left, the level-wise approach and, on the right, the leaf-wise approach, both constrained to have, at the most, four terminal nodes. The two approaches take completely different paths in terms of the rules they decide to apply and how they segment the data.

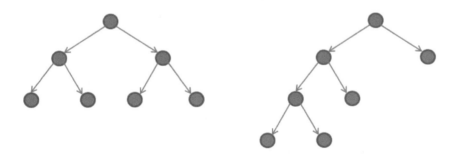

Figure 5.10   How level-wise (on the left) and leaf-wise (on the right) tree growth differ

It is important to point out that if you allow two trees to grow using the same data, one using a leaf-wise approach and one using a level-wise approach fully, they will define the same terminal leaves and predictions. The distinction lies in how they are built, with the leaf-wise approach being more aggressive in splitting nodes that provide the most information gain first.

This implies that the leaf-wise and level-wise approaches differ when a stopping rule is applied based on reaching a certain number of terminal nodes or a specific depth in tree splitting. In this case, the leaf-wise approach can result in smaller trees, faster training times, and higher accuracy, but it also carries an increased risk of overfitting. To control the depth of the tree leaf-wise growth and address overfitting, you can control the max-depth parameter in LightGBM.

5.5.2   Gaining speed with exclusive feature bundling and gradient-based one-side sampling

To further reduce the training time, a basic strategy in gradient boosting and many other machine learning algorithms is reducing the number of examples processed. The simplest way to reduce the number of processed values is using stochastic sampling (i.e., row reduction) and/or dimensionality reduction techniques such as column sampling or principal component analysis (i.e., column reduction). Although sampling can improve accuracy in the presence of noise in data, excessive sampling can harm the training process and decrease predictive performance. In LightGBM, the *Gradient-Based One-Side Sampling* algorithm (GOSS) determines the manner and extent of sampling. Dimensionality reduction techniques rely on identifying redundancies in the data and combining them using a linear combination, typically a weighted sum. However, linear combinations can destroy nonlinear relationships in the data. Dimensionality reduction by discarding rare signals may lead to a decrease in model accuracy if the successful resolution of the data problem depends on those weak signals. In LightGBM, dimensionality reduction is handled by *Exclusive Feature Bundling* (EFB), which is a way to reduce the column dimension without losing information.

Let's start by explaining the two major speed improvements in LightGBM, starting with how EFB works. EFB is a technique that efficiently decreases the number of features without compromising data integrity. When using extensively one-hot encoded and binary features, many features become sparse, with few values and an abundance of zeros. You can retain all non-zero values without loss by summing these features and encoding some values. LightGBM optimizes computations and data dimensionality by grouping these features into *Exclusive Feature Bundles*, ensuring that predictive accuracy is maintained.

Figure 5.11 shows how effectively two features can be bundled together. The solution involves adding feature B to feature A only for non-zero values, using the maximum value present in feature A. This combined feature will preserve the original features' order because the values from feature A are separate from the values from feature B and will be located in different sections of the value distribution.

Finding the optimal way to bundle exclusive features is a complex problem, classified as NP-hard. However, according to the LightGBM paper by Guolin Ke and his team, a greedy algorithm can provide a good approximation by automatically bundling many features. The feature bundling algorithm works sequentially, selecting the features with the least number of overlapping values and bundling them together. If it finds another feature with minimal overlap, it continues to bundle. Otherwise, it starts a new bundle until no more bundles can be found. The stopping rule is provided by the degree of conflicts two features have. If they have more conflicts than a certain gamma threshold,

Future A	Feature B		Bundle
1	0		1
2	0		2
1	0		1
2	0		2
0	0		0
0	1		3
0	2		4
0	3		5
0	4		6

Figure 5.11   Demonstrating how EFB works when combining two features

the bundle cannot be made, and the entire process may stop if there aren't better candidates. Although the resulting bundles from this greedy process are not guaranteed to be optimal, the algorithm provides an acceptable solution in a reasonable time.

The other performance improvement presented in the paper is GOSS. As we mentioned, if EFB is aimed at reducing column dimensionality, GOSS works on the rows by sampling them effectively without bias.

GOSS is based on the observation that certain data instances are unlikely to provide useful information for finding a split point. Searching a carefully selected subset of the training set can save computation time without affecting predictive accuracy. Additionally, in gradient boosted decision trees, the algorithm implicitly specifies a weight for data instances when optimizing for the gradient for each data instance. Determining weights is crucial to compute a correction of the previous estimates, but that could also be used for sampling the data instances that could be more interesting to learn.

GOSS estimates data examples with larger gradients to contribute more toward information gain. Focusing on examples with larger gradients and ignoring part of those with smaller ones should reduce the number of processed data instances while still optimizing the algorithm for predictions. The procedure for GOSS results in the following:

- GOSS first sorts the data examples according to the absolute value of their gradients.
- It selects the top a × 100% data examples.
- It randomly samples b × 100% data examples from the rest of the data.
- It trains the decision tree on the combined samples using a weight of 1 for the top data examples and a weight of $(1 - a) / b$ for the randomly sampled data examples.

The final weighting is necessary to maintain the original data distribution of the dataset and avoid any unwanted shift in its representation.

GOSS can accelerate the training of gradient boosted decision trees, especially when dealing with larger datasets and complex trees. The original paper's authors demonstrate that the error incurred by GOSS's sampling approximation becomes negligible for larger datasets compared to the traditional method. In our experience using GOSS, at best, you get similar results compared to standard LightGBM training. Still, the speed-up is significant, making GOSS a good choice for faster experimentation when looking for the correct hyperparameters or selecting the most relevant features for your problem.

Contrary to the other speed-ups we presented, GOSS is not used by default: you must specify that you want to use it.

5.5.3   *Applying early stopping to LightGBM*

LightGBM supports early stopping, and the parameters to control it are similar to those used in the XGBoost implementation. In the example in listing 5.17, we use LightGBM for training and have the algorithm assess its performance during the training phase using a test set. If there is no improvement in performance on the test set for 100 iterations, the algorithm halts the training process. It selects the round of iterations that achieved the highest performance on the test set so far.

Listing 5.17   Applying early stopping to LightGBM

```
from lightgbm import LGBMClassifier, log_evaluation

train, test = train_test_split(range(len(data)), test_size=0.2,
random_state=0)
train, validation = train_test_split(
    train,
    test_size=0.2,
    random_state=0
)

lgbm = LGBMClassifier(boosting_type='gbdt',
                      early_stopping_round=150,
                      n_estimators=1000,
                      max_depth=-1,
                      min_child_samples=3,
                      force_col_wise=True,
                      verbosity=0)

X = column_transform.fit_transform(data.iloc[train])
y = target_median[train]

Xv = column_transform.transform(data.iloc[validation])
yv = target_median[validation]

lgbm.fit(X, y, eval_set=[(Xv, yv)],
    eval_metric='accuracy',
    callbacks=[log_evaluation(period=0)])

Xt = column_transform.transform(data.iloc[test])
yt = target_median[test]
```

Splits the indices of the data into training and test sets using a fixed random seed

Further splits the training set into training and validation sets using the same random seed

Initializes a LightGBM classifier with a number of estimators, max depth, and minimum number of child samples

Fits the LightGBM classifier to the training data X and labels y and performance on the validation data Xv and yv

Sets accuracy as an evaluation metric

Sets a callback to suppress the evaluation (period=0)

```
preds = lgbm.predict(Xt)
score = accuracy_score(y_true=yt, y_pred=preds)
print(f"Test accuracy: {score:0.5f}")
```

Prints the accuracy score after comparing the predicted labels with the true labels

Even in this case, the result is penalized by the fact that we are training only on 64% of the available data:

```
Accuracy: 0.82585
```

However, there are some minor differences from the XGBoost implementation that you can notice from the code. The `eval_metric` takes different names (that you can check at https://mng.bz/RVZK) and, to suppress the printing of the evaluations during the training, you don't use the verbose parameters as in XGBoost; rather, you have to specify a callback function (`log_evaluation`) that has to be declared at the fitting time in the list of callbacks.

Recently, early stopping has been implemented as a callback function too (see https://mng.bz/2yK0). Keeping the declaration of early stopping rounds during model instantiation stayed just for maintaining API compatibility with XGBoost. In case you use early stopping as a callback, you have more control over the way the LightGBM stops its training:

- `first_metric_only` allows you to indicate whether to use only the first metric for early stopping or any metric you pointed out using.
- `min_delta` signals the minimum improvement in the metric to keep on training, which usually is set to zero (any improvement), but it could be raised to impose more strict control over the growth of the ensemble.

In the previous example, you just need to remove the `early_stopping_rounds` from the LGBMClassifier instantiation and add the proper call back to the callback list in the fit method to obtain the same result:

```
early_stopping(
    stopping_rounds=150,
    first_metric_only=True,
    verbose=False,
    min_delta=0.0
)
```

Whatever method you use, the iteration index, resulting in the best validation score, will be stored in the `best_iteration` attribute of a model, and that iteration will be automatically used when predicting.

5.5.4 *Making XGBoost imitate LightGBM*

Since the introduction of LightGBM and its impressive usage of unbalanced decision trees, XGBoost also started supporting the leaf-wise strategy in addition to its original level-wise strategy. In XGBoost, the original level-wise approach is called `depthwise`, and the leaf-wise strategy is called `lossguide`. By setting one or another using the `grow_policy` parameter, you can have your XGBoost behave as a LightGBM. In addition, XGBoost authors suggested, when using the lossguide grow policy, to set the following parameters to avoid overfitting:

- `max_leaves`—Sets the maximum number of nodes to be added and is only relevant for the lossguide policy.
- `max_depth`—Sets the maximum depth of the tree. If `grow_policy` is set to `depthwise`, `max_depth` behaves as usual. However, if `grow_policy` is set to `lossguide`, `max_depth` can be set to zero, indicating no depth limit.

Incidentally, you also have the same parameters in LightGBM to be used for the same purpose (`max_leaves` is an alias—i.e., another working name of the parameter `num_leaves`).

5.5.5   *How LightGBM inspired Scikit-learn*

In version 0.21 of Scikit-learn, two novel implementations of gradient boosting trees were added: `HistGradientBoostingClassifier` and `HistGradientBoosting-Regressor`, inspired by LightGBM. You may wonder why you would bother with this new implementation if the current LightGBM and XGBoost versions can offer you everything you need to develop the best-performing tabular solutions based on gradient boosting. They also ensure full compatibility with Scikit-learn API. It is worth the time to look at it because the histogram-based implementation, though now a work in progress, is expected to take over the original, offering the same control over the learning process and building of decision trees. Moreover, it has shown even better predictive performances than XGBoost and LightGBM in some specific applications. Hence, it may be worth testing for your specific problems.

In comparison with the original Scikit-learn implementation for gradient boosting, the new histogram-based ones present new characteristics:

- Binning
- Multicore (the initial implementation was single-core)
- No sparse data support
- Built-in support for missing values
- Monotonicity and interaction constraints
- Native categorical variables

At the moment, talking about differences, there is no support for sparse data in the new histogram-based implementation. Consequently, if your data is in a sparse matrix, you should first densify the data matrix. Also, some other features typical of `Gradient-BoostingClassifier` and `GradientBoostingRegressor` still need to be supported—for instance, some loss functions.

On the API side, most parameters are unchanged from `GradientBoosting-Classifier` and `GradientBoostingRegressor`. One exception is the `max_iter` parameter that replaces n_estimators. The following listing shows an example of the HistGradientBoostingClassifier applied to our classification problem with the Airbnb NYC dataset classifying listings above the median market value.

Listing 5.18 The new Scikit-learn's histogram gradient boosting

```
from sklearn.ensemble import HistGradientBoostingClassifier
from sklearn.metrics import accuracy_score

accuracy = make_scorer(accuracy_score)
cv = KFold(5, shuffle=True, random_state=0)

model = HistGradientBoostingClassifier(learning_rate=0.1,
                                       max_iter=300,
                                       max_depth=4,
                                       min_samples_leaf=3,
                                       random_state=0)

model_pipeline = Pipeline(
    [('processing', column_transform),
     ('modeling', model)])

cv_scores = cross_validate(estimator=model_pipeline,
                           X=data,
                           y=target_median,
                           scoring=accuracy,
                           cv=cv,
                           return_train_score=True,
                           return_estimator=True)

mean_cv = np.mean(cv_scores['test_score'])
std_cv = np.std(cv_scores['test_score'])
fit_time = np.mean(cv_scores['fit_time'])
score_time = np.mean(cv_scores['score_time'])
print(f"{mean_cv:0.3f} ({std_cv:0.3f})",
      f"fit: {fit_time:0.2f}",
      f"secs pred: {score_time:0.2f} secs")
```

Initializes a HistGradientBoostingClassifier with specific hyperparameters for the boosting algorithm

Creates a model pipeline combining data preprocessing (column_ transform) and the model

Executes five-fold cross-validation on the model pipeline returning scores and trained estimators

Prints the mean and standard deviation of the accuracy scores from cross-validation

The results are

```
0.827 (0.005) fit: 1.71 secs pred: 0.13 secs
```

Compared to our previous examples with XGBoost and LightGBM, this one differs from the used command and the max_iter parameter in exchange for the usual n_estimators. Also, the Scikit-learn new boosting algorithm is a histogram one. You just set the max_bins argument to change the initial default value of 255 (it is 256 bins because 1 is reserved for missing cases).

The algorithm is still under development and lacks support for sparse data. This implies that it cannot perform as fast as XGBoost or LightGBM in the presence of many one-hot encoded features, no matter how you prepare your data.

Summary

- Ensemble algorithms are used to improve the predictive power of a single model by using multiple models or chaining them together:
  - Ensemble algorithms are often based on decision trees.
  - There are two core ensemble strategies: averaging and boosting.
  - Averaging strategies, such as random forests, tend to reduce the variance of predictions while only slightly increasing the bias.
  - Pasting is a type of averaging approach that involves creating a set of different models trained on subsamples of the data and pooling the predictions together.
  - Bagging is similar to averaging but with bootstrapping instead of subsampling.
  - Averaging methods can be computationally intensive and increase bias by excluding important parts of the data distribution through sampling.
- Random forests is an ensemble learning algorithm that combines decision trees by bootstrapping samples and subsampling features during modeling (random patches):
  - It creates a set of models that are different from each other and produces more reliable and accurate predictions.
  - It can be used to determine feature importance and measure cases' similarity in a dataset.
  - The algorithm requires fine-tuning its few hyperparameters, like the number of employed trees, and adjusting bias-variance tradeoffs by setting the maximum number of features used for splits, the maximum depth of trees, and the minimum size of the terminal branches.
  - It can be computationally costly if the number of trees is set too high.
- ERT, Extremely Randomized Trees, is a variation of the random forests algorithm:
  - It randomly selects the feature for the split at each decision tree node, leading to less variance (because trees are more diverse) but more bias (randomization sacrifices some of the decision trees' predictive accuracy, resulting in a higher bias).
  - It is more computationally efficient and useful for large datasets with many collinear and noisy features.
  - It reduces variance by making the resulting set of trees less correlated.
- GBDT is a highly effective machine learning method for tabular data problems. It has become a leading approach in various domains, including multiclass classification, advertising click prediction, and search engine ranking. Compared to other methods, such as neural networks, support vector machines, random forests, and bagging ensembles, GBDT generally performs better in standard tabular problems.

- Gradient boosting is effective because it combines gradient descent, an optimization procedure typical of linear models and neural networks, and decision trees trained on the gradients derived from the sum of the previous decision trees.

- Scikit-learn offers one of the earliest options for gradient boosting algorithms for regression and classification tasks. Recently, the original algorithm was replaced by a speedier histogram-based one, which is still under development.

- XGBoost, an algorithm for gradient boosting decision trees, gained popularity after its successful use in the Higgs Boson Machine Learning Challenge on Kaggle. It is based on a more complex optimization based on Newton's Descent, and it offers the following advantages:
  - The Ability to handle various input data types
  - Support for customized objective and evaluation functions
  - Automatic handling of missing values
  - Easy support for GPU training
  - Accommodation of monotonicity and feature interaction constraints
  - Optimization of multiple cores and cache on standalone computers

- LightGBM is a highly efficient gradient boosting decision tree algorithm, introduced in a 2017 paper by Guolin Ke and his team at Microsoft. The algorithm was designed to be faster and use less memory than traditional gradient boosting decision trees, as demonstrated in experiments on multiple public datasets. The LightGBM algorithm achieves this thanks to its leaf-wise splitting policy and EFB.

Advanced feature processing methods

This chapter covers

- Processing features with more advanced methods
- Selecting useful features for lighter, more understandable models
- Optimizing hyperparameters to make your models shine in performance
- Mastering the specific characteristics and options from gradient boosting decision trees

We've now discussed decision trees, their characteristics, their limitations, and all their ensemble models, both those based on random resamplings, such as random forests, and those based on boosting, such as gradient boosting. Since boosting solutions are considered the state of the art in tabular data modeling, we have explained how it works and optimized its predictions at length. In particular, we have presented a couple of solid gradient boosting implementations, XGBoost and LightGBM, that are proving the best solutions available to a data scientist dealing with tabular data.

This chapter will deal with more general topics regarding classical machine learning. However, we will focus on gradient boosting decision trees (GBDTs), especially XGBoost. In the chapter, we discuss more advanced methods for feature processing, such as multivariate imputation of missing values, target encoding for reducing high categorical features to simple numeric ones, and a general way to figure out how to transform or elaborate your features based on how they relate to the target. We will propose a few ways to reduce the number of your features to the essential and optimize your hyperparameters depending on the computational resources available and the model you have chosen. The chapter will then close with a section on only advanced methods and options related to GBDTs.

6.1   *Processing features*

There are any number of problems you may face when dealing with real-world tabular datasets, and all the methods we've discussed so far will produce substandard results if you aren't adjusting your techniques to address the realities of your data. Here, we'll consider a few such problems, such as dealing with missing values in the smartest way possible, transforming categorical features with a large number of unique values, and finding a way to reprocess your features after you have trained your model to squeeze out even more performance. This isn't an exhaustive list, of course, but it should give you some practice in spotting problems and planning an appropriate approach.

As in the previous chapter, for our explanations and examples, we will rely again on the Airbnb NYC dataset to present practical examples to tackle the most challenging task in tabular data problems. The following listing reprises the data and some key functions and classes we will use again in this chapter.

> **Listing 6.1   Reprising the Airbnb NYC dataset**

```
import numpy as np
import pandas as pd
from sklearn.preprocessing import (
    StandardScaler,
    OneHotEncoder,
    OrdinalEncoder
)
from sklearn.impute import SimpleImputer
from sklearn.compose import ColumnTransformer
from sklearn.pipeline import Pipeline                    List of excluded columns
                                                         for feature processing
data = pd.read_csv("./AB_NYC_2019.csv")
excluding_list = ['price', 'id', 'latitude', 'longitude', 'host_id',
                  'last_review', 'name', 'host_name']
low_card_categorical = [
    'neighbourhood_group',
    'room_type'                                    List of categorical columns with low
]                                                  cardinality to be one-hot encoded
high_card_categorical = ['neighbourhood']
continuous = [                                      List of categorical columns with high
    'minimum_nights',                              cardinality to be ordinally encoded
```

```
        'number_of_reviews',
        'reviews_per_month',
        'calculated_host_listings_count',
        'availability_365'
]                                 ◄──────┤ List of continuous feature columns
target_mean = (
        (data["price"] > data["price"].mean())    Creates a binary target indicating
        .astype(int)                              whether the price is above the
)                                          ◄──────┤ mean (unbalanced binary target)
target_median = (
        (data["price"] > data["price"].median())    Creates a binary target indicating
        .astype(int)                                whether the price is above the
)                                            ◄──────┤ median (balanced binary target)
target_multiclass = pd.qcut(
        data["price"], q=5, labels=False    Creates a multiclass target by quantile
)                                    ◄──────┤ binning the price into five classes
target_regression = data["price"]
categorical_onehot_encoding = OneHotEncoder(handle_unknown='ignore')
categorical_ord_encoding =
OrdinalEncoder(handle_unknown="use_encoded_value", unknown_value=np.nan)
numeric_standardization = Pipeline([('StandardScaler', StandardScaler()),
                                    ('Imputer',
SimpleImputer(strategy="constant", fill_value=0))])

                                               Sets the target for regression
                                                     as the price column
column_transform = ColumnTransformer(
    [
        ('low_card_categories',
         categorical_onehot_encoding,
         low_card_categorical),
        ('high_card_categories',
         categorical_ord_encoding,
         high_card_categorical),
        ('numeric',
         numeric_standardization,
         continuous)
    ],
    remainder='drop',                Creates a column transformer that
    verbose_feature_names_out=True,  applies different transformations
    sparse_threshold=0.0)       ◄────┤ to different groups of features

lm_column_transform = ColumnTransformer(
    [
        ('low_card_categories',
         categorical_onehot_encoding,
         low_card_categorical),
        ('numeric',
         numeric_standardization,
         continuous)
    ],
    remainder='drop',
    verbose_feature_names_out=True,  Creates a column transformer
    sparse_threshold=0.0)       ◄────┤ suitable for linear models
```

We refer to the explanations presented in the previous chapter for all the details about what the code does. The only addition is a column transformer designed explicitly for linear models. This transformer handles just low cardinality categorical features by performing one-hot encoding, leaving high cardinality categorical ones apart.

6.1.1 *Multivariate missing data imputation*

Having missing data in your tabular dataset is a blocking problem because, apart from GBDTs solutions such as XGBoost, LightGBM, and Scikit-learn's HistGradientBoosting, classical machine learning algorithms do not have any native support for missing values. In addition, even if your GBDTs algorithm of choice can handle missingness, as explained in the next section, you may still find directly imputing the missing values more effective because you can check beforehand how each feature or specific case is handled.

In chapter 2, we discussed simple imputation methods, such as using the mean or the median, and the usefulness of building missing indicators, thus enabling algorithms to spot missing patterns that are present more easily. This section will provide more details about these techniques and multivariate imputation.

First, unless missing cases depend on unobserved variables such as features you don't have access to, missing data can be categorized as

- *Missing completely at random* (MCAR)—In this scenario, data missingness is unrelated to observed and unobserved variables. The missingness occurs randomly across the dataset.
- *Missing at random* (MAR)—MAR assumes that observed variables, not the unobserved ones, can explain the missingness. In other words, the probability of missingness solely depends on the observed data.

When the missing cases depend on the unobserved values of the missing data itself, you fall into the case of missing not at random (MNAR), which requires quite a specialized treatment that is not a topic of this book. However, suppose you understand the mechanism behind some missing not at random missing data, such as when you don't get information in the census about people who are too rich (because of privacy) or too poor (because of a general lack of access). In that case, you can try to gather new features that hint at their wealth to add to your dataset and fall back to the MAR case.

Generally, you often have cases where missing data is MCAR or MAR. In both cases, apart from simple imputation using an expected value that works perfectly with MCAR, you can better reconstruct your missing data through multivariate imputation. *Multivariate imputation* is a method that uses the correlations among predictors in a dataset to impute missing values. It involves building a series of models to estimate the missing values based on the relationships between variables. In this approach, each model treats a feature with missing values as the target variable (by modeling only its known values) and uses the remaining features as predictors. The resulting model is then used to determine what values to replace the missing values in the target. You may set how the algorithm cycles through the features to impute. You usually use the default setting, starting from the features with less missing data and progressing to those with more missing values, which is preferred and most effective.

To handle missing values in the predictors, an initial imputation step is performed using a simple mean or another basic imputation method. Then, through multiple iterations, the imputation process refines the initial estimates by incorporating the results from the imputing models. This iterative process continues until the imputed values reach a state of stability, where further iterations do not lead to significant changes. Multivariate imputation is implemented in Scikit-learn by `IterativeImputer` (https://mng.bz/MDZQ). Inspired by the R MICE package (Multivariate Imputation by Chained Equations: https://mng.bz/avEj), it allows both for multivariate imputation and multiple imputations, a common approach in statistics and social sciences where, instead of a single imputed value, you get a distribution of plausible replacements. Multiple imputations are possible with `IterativeImputer` by running it multiple times with the `sample_posterior` parameter set to True, using a different random seed each time.

However, multivariate imputation is the favored choice in data science tabular data applications because it allows building models based on single but precise estimations. In our example, we take the Airbnb NYC dataset's continuous features and randomly remove 5% of the data, thus mimicking an MCAR situation. Afterward, we run a `SimpleImputer`, replacing missing values with a mean and an `IterativeImputer`. Finally, we compare, using the mean absolute error (MAE), the features reconstructed by each method against the original values.

Listing 6.2   Multivariate imputation

```
from sklearn.experimental import (
    enable_iterative_imputer
)
from sklearn.impute import SimpleImputer, IterativeImputer
from sklearn.ensemble import RandomForestRegressor

Xm = data[continuous].copy()
missing_percentage = 0.05
np.random.seed(0)
mask = np.random.rand(*Xm.shape) < missing_percentage
Xm[mask] = np.nan

simple_imputer = SimpleImputer()
Xm_si = simple_imputer.fit_transform(Xm)

rf = RandomForestRegressor(random_state=0, n_jobs=-1)
multivariate_imputer = IterativeImputer(
    estimator=rf,
    max_iter=1,
    tol=0.01
)
Xm_mi = multivariate_imputer.fit_transform(Xm)

mae = pd.DataFrame(
    {
        "simple": np.mean(
```

Imports IterativeImputer, which is still experimental and under improvement in Scikit-learn

Creates a copy of continuous feature data

Creates a mask to randomly mark missing values

Uses a SimpleImputer instance with mean imputation strategy

Instantiates a RandomForestRegressor for iterative imputation

Creates an IterativeImputer instance with max_iter and tol are the stopping criteria

Imputes missing data using iterative imputation

```
            np.abs(data[continuous] - Xm_si), axis=0
        ),
        "multivariate": np.mean(
            np.abs(data[continuous] - Xm_mi), axis=0
        )
    },
    index = continuous          │ Calculates MAE for imputed
)                          ◄────┘ data and original data
print(mae)
```

The result provided by the command `print(mae)` is a table that compares the simple imputation with the multivariate imputation method:

	Simple	Multivariate
minimum_nights	0.347355	0.260156
number_of_reviews	1.327776	0.858506
reviews_per_month	0.057980	0.036876
calculated_host_listings_count	0.579423	0.368567
availability_365	6.025748	4.62264

The comparison results demonstrate that the multivariate method, specifically the `IterativeImputer`, consistently yields lower MAE values than the simple imputation method, even after a single iteration. This indicates that `IterativeImputer` is more effective at replacing missing values with fewer errors. To obtain even better estimations, you can increase the `max_iter` to a higher number and leave the algorithm to decide if to stop earlier based on the tol values, a tolerance threshold used to check if the results are stable. Increasing the `max_iter` will lead to longer imputation times because, as an imputing model, we are using a random forests algorithm. Random forests are usually the most effective way to handle multivariate estimations (a method known in the R community as *MissForest*: https://rpubs.com/lmorgan95/MissForest). However, you can choose faster methods based on linear models or k-nearest neighbors by simply replacing the `estimator` in the `IterativeImputer`:

- BayesianRidge—Regularized linear regression simply using `BayesianRidge()`
- RandomForestRegressor—For forests of randomized trees regression, you can set `n_estimators`, `max_depth`, and `max_features` to create shallower trees and thus accelerate the imputation process such as `RandomForestRegressor (n_estimators=30, max_depth=6, max_samples=0.5)`
- Nystroem + Ridge—A pipeline with the expansion of a degree 2 polynomial kernel and regularized linear regression by combining different Scikit-learn commands: `make_pipeline(Nystroem(kernel="polynomial", degree=2, random _state=0), Ridge(alpha=1e3))`
- KNeighborsRegressor—A k-nearest neighbors imputation approach where you decide the number of neighbors to consider, such as `KNeighbors- Regressor(n_neighbors=5)`

The estimator you use will affect the quality of the results you obtain and the computation time. As a start, `BayesianRidge` is the default choice and also the fastest. If you have more time, `RandomForestRegressor` will provide you with better estimates. By jointly inputting multiple variables, `IterativeImputer` captures the dependencies between variables more accurately at the price of more computations and written code. For a straightforward, out-of-the-box solution, some GBDT implementations provide native support for handling missing values, which we will discover in the next section.

6.1.2 *Handling missing data with GBDTs*

Both XGBoost and LightGBM algorithms (and Scikit-learn's HistGradientBoosting) handle missing values similarly by assigning them to the side that minimizes the loss function the most in each split. XGBoost introduced this technique with its sparsity-aware split finding algorithm, which provides a default direction to use when data is missing, either because it is missing or stored in a sparse matrix where only non-zero values are kept.

Consequently, don't forget that XGBoost will treat the zeros in a sparse matrix as missing and apply its specific algorithm to handle missing data. Hence, on the one hand, you may find it convenient when analyzing one-hot encoded matrices of categorical variables with high cardinality to create them as sparse matrices because that will save you a lot of memory and computations. On the other hand, you may notice that XGBoost returns completely different models if you analyze some data represented as a dense matrix or as a sparse matrix.

The difference is in what happens when XGBoost encounters a missing example. During training, the algorithm learns at each split point whether samples with missing values should go to the left or right branching based on the resulting gain. When making predictions, samples with missing values are assigned to the appropriate child accordingly. This allows the algorithm to split on the feature value's missingness pattern if it is predictive. If there are no missing values for a given feature during training, then samples with missing values are assigned to whichever child has the most samples.

You can use the missing parameter to specify what value XGBoost will have to consider as missing. This parameter is set to NaN by default, but you can decide on any value you want.

Another critical thing to remember about XGBoost is that the `gblinear` booster, using linear models as base learners, treats missing values as zeros. Suppose you standardize your numeric features, as is often used with linear models. In that case, the `gblinear` booster will treat missing values as the average value for that feature because the average takes the zero value in a standardized variable.

LightGBM employs a similar approach (see https://github.com/microsoft/LightGBM/issues/2921), using specific parameters:

- LightGBM enables the missing value to be handled by default. Turn it off by setting `use_missing=false`.
- LightGBM uses NA (NaN) to represent missing values by default. Change it to use zero by setting `zero_as_missing=true`.

- When `zero_as_missing=false` (default), the unrecorded values in sparse matrices (and LightSVM) are treated as zeros.
- When `zero_as_missing=true`, NA and zeros (including unrecorded values in sparse matrices [and LightSVM]) are treated as missing.

This strategy for handling missing data works well on average, especially if your data is MCAR. This means the pattern of missing instances is completely random and unrelated to any other feature or hidden underlying process. The situation is different with MAR when missingness is related to other features' values but not to the values of the feature itself and NMAR, where there is a systematic pattern of missing values related to the feature itself and other features. In MAR and NMAR cases, the best solution is to try to impute these values by other means because the XGBoost and LightGBM strategy for missing data may reveal itself as underperforming.

There are alternatives to imputing missing data, however. For instance, you can create missing data indicators, which are binary features valued in correspondence to missing instances in a variable. Missing data indicators can prove quite valuable if your data is not completely missing at random, and they can work with any classical machine learning algorithm. Another popular solution with decision trees is to assign missing values to an extreme value (usually a negative extreme value) not used by any variable in the dataset. If you use exact splits, not histogram-based ones, where values are reduced into bins, missing data replaced by extreme values can prove an efficient and easy solution.

6.1.3 Target encoding

Categorical features, usually represented in a dataset as strings, can be efficiently dealt with through different strategies. We already mentioned one-hot-encoding in chapter 2 and chapter 4. As one-hot-encoding, all the other strategies for categorical features, whether presenting low or high cardinality, require *encoding*, a procedure to transform data numerically into a suitable format for machine learning algorithms. Although there are some similarities, encoding is not to be confused with *embeddings*, which is a procedure to reduce high-dimensional data, such as text or images, into a lower-dimensional space while preserving certain characteristics or relationships of the original data. Embeddings are typically learned through neural network-based models and are briefly touched on in our book.

The Scikit learn package offers a couple of encoding solutions:

- `OneHotEncoder`—For one-hot encoding (i.e., transforming each unique string value into a binary feature), which is the solution we have up so far used
- `OrdinalEncoder`—For ordinal encoding (i.e., transforming the string values in a feature into ordered numeric ones; there is also `LabelEncoder`, but it works the same, and it is mainly for transforming categorical targets)

Generally, one-hot encoding works fine both for linear models and tree-based models, and ordinal encoding works fine for more complex tree-based models, such as random forests and GBDTs, because trees can recursively split on the categorical feature and finally find a set of partitions useful for predictions. However, problems arise with high cardinality categoricals when using one-hot or ordinal encoding. High cardinality is a weak point for both linear and tree-based models. When one-hot encoded, high cardinality categoricals produce sparse matrices that cannot easily be turned into dense ones because of memory limitations. In addition, decision trees with many branching levels may need help splitting ordinally encoded high cardinality categorical features into meaningful partitions for prediction.

There is no commonly fixed standard to declare when a categorical is high cardinality because that also depends on how many rows your dataset has and how large one-hot encoded features your computer memory could handle. However, high cardinality categorical features generally include IDs, zip codes, and product or geographical names with many unique values. For instance, a reasonable threshold could be over 512, but it may be lower depending on the dataset. Using the rule of thumb that the number of classes in a feature should not exceed 5%–10% of the total rows in the dataset, 512 may be too high for smaller datasets. In such circumstances, standard practice, especially from data science competitions such as Kaggle's, suggests resorting to *target encoding* (also known as *mean encoding*).

First presented in the paper by Micci-Barreca, "A Preprocessing Scheme for High-Cardinality Attributes in Classification and Prediction Problems" (ACM SIGKDD Explorations Newsletter 3.1, 2001), target encoding is simply a way to transform the values in a categorical feature into their corresponding expected target values. If your problem is a regression, target encoding will use the average target value corresponding to that value in the dataset, with a classification problem: conditional probability or odds ratio. Such a process, bringing about the risk of overfitting for the model when the category has few examples in the dataset, is mitigated by using a weighted average between the expected value for that category (posterior probability of the target) and the average expected value of all the dataset (the prior probability of the target over all the training data).

Target encoding is available in the category-encoders package (https://mng.bz/gave), a Scikit-learn compatible project as the target TargetEncoder class (https://mng.bz/5glq), and you can install it by a `pip install category_encoders` command in the shell. In the TargetEncoder class, you have to specify a smoothing parameter (to be fixed at a value above zero) to balance between the posterior probability of the target and the prior probability all over the training data. The best smoothing parameter for your data has to be found by experimentation, or you can rely on another similar encoder, the James Steiner encoder, which guesses the best way to smooth your expected target values based on the variance conditioned by the category you want to encode (https://mng.bz/5glq). The James Stenier encoder makes stronger assumptions about your data. You have to decide among different ways to estimate conditional variance by the model parameter (for regression problems, it is advisable to use "independent" and for classification ones, "binary"). Still, it lifts you from experimenting with different blending thresholds as if it were a hyperparameter.

In our example, we use the `neighborhood` feature, which has over 200 unique values, and the latitude and longitude coordinates after mapping them into a 100 x 100 grid space. The mapping returns a feature presenting over 2,000 distinct values, which makes it a high cardinality categorical feature without any doubt. In listing 6.3, we first bin latitude and longitude and then combine them by summing them in a way that results in a distinct code for every bin combination of latitude and longitude. Binning is obtained by dividing the range between the feature's minimum and maximum value into equal parts. Also, the code snippet performs binning on two separate features, resulting in sets of integer values for each feature. The values of one feature are multiplied by a power of 10, which is larger than the maximum value of the other feature. This ensures that a unique value is always obtained when the two sets of values are summed, regardless of the specific values being summed.

Listing 6.3 Creating a high cardinality categorical feature

```
def bin_2_cat(feature, bins=100):
    min_value = feature.min()
    bin_size = (feature.max() - min_value) / bins      Function to convert
    bin_values = (feature - min_value) / bin_size      numerical data into
    return bin_values.astype(int)                      categorical bins

data['coordinates'] = (                        Converts latitude and
    bin_2_cat(data['latitude']) * 1000         longitude to categorical
    + bin_2_cat(data['longitude']              coordinates
)
high_card_categorical += ['coordinates']
                                               Prints the number of unique
                                               values in the high-cardinality
print(data[high_card_categorical].nunique())  categorical features
```

The code snippet closes by checking the number of unique values for each feature among the high cardinality ones:

```
neighbourhood    221
coordinates      2259
```

With two categorical features considered high cardinality, we can add to our preprocessing pipeline the TargetEncoder from category-encoders.

Listing 6.4 Using target encoding in the pipeline

```
from category_encoders.target_encoder import TargetEncoder
from XGBoost import XGBClassifier                               Initializes
from sklearn.model_selection import KFold, cross_validate       TargetEncoder for
from sklearn.metrics import accuracy_score, make_scorer         high cardinality
                                                                categorical
                                                                features
target_encoder = TargetEncoder(cols=high_card_categorical,
                               smoothing=0.5)
accuracy = make_scorer(accuracy_score)                   Smoothes value to
cv = KFold(5, shuffle=True, random_state=0)              blend prior and
xgb = XGBClassifier(booster='gbtree',                    posterior probabilities
                    objective='reg:logistic',
                    n_estimators=300,
```

```
                    max_depth=4,
                    min_child_weight=3)          ◄———  Initializes XGBoost classifier
                                                        with specific hyperparameters
column_transform = ColumnTransformer(
    [
        ('low_card_categories',
         categorical_onehot_encoding,
         low_card_categorical),
        ('high_card_categories',
         target_encoder,
         high_card_categorical),
        ('numeric',
         numeric_standardization,
         continuous)                             Defines ColumnTransformer for
    ],                                           preprocessing features with
    remainder='drop',                            TargetEncoder for high cardinality
    verbose_feature_names_out=True,              categorical features
    sparse_threshold=0.0)               ◄———

model_pipeline = Pipeline(
    [('processing', column_transform),           Creates a pipeline that combines
     ('model', xgb)])                  ◄———      preprocessing and modeling

cv_scores = cross_validate(estimator=model_pipeline,
                           X=data,
                           y=target_median,
                           scoring=accuracy,          Performs five-fold
                           cv=cv,                     cross-validation
                           return_train_score=True,   and obtaining
                           return_estimator=True)  ◄— evaluation metrics

mean_cv = np.mean(cv_scores['test_score'])
std_cv = np.std(cv_scores['test_score'])
fit_time = np.mean(cv_scores['fit_time'])
score_time = np.mean(cv_scores['score_time'])
print(f"{mean_cv:0.3f} ({std_cv:0.3f})",       Prints mean accuracy, fit time,
      f"fit: {fit_time:0.2f}",                  and prediction time from
      f"secs pred: {score_time:0.2f} secs") ◄—  cross-validation
```

When executed, the code procedures the results for running XGBoost on the problem with the extra help of the high cardinality categorical features. The results point to a slight improvement in the accuracy. Later in this chapter, we will investigate the weight of the contribution by target encoding when examining the explainability:

```
0.840 (0.004) fit: 4.52 secs pred: 0.06 secs
```

Although target encoding is a convenient procedure because it may quickly transform any categorical into a numeric feature, in doing so, you have to pay attention to keeping all important information from your data. Target encoding renders further modeling of any interaction between features impossible. Let's say, for instance, that you are working on an advertising response dataset with click results for many websites and advertising formats. If you encode both features, having transformed two high cardinality categoricals with potentially thousands and thousands of values, you may easily create any kind of classical model. However, after encoding, your model, whether linear or tree-based, won't be able to grasp any possible interaction between the encoded features. In this case, the solution is to create a new feature beforehand, combining the two high cardinality categorical features and then target encode their combination.

Hence, as for other tools, we should consider the pros and cons of this advanced encoding technicality. In our experience, depending on the situation, before resorting to target encoding, there are a few options for classic machine learning algorithms and for gradient boosting for dealing with high cardinality categorical features:

- Just dropping problematic categorical features
- Using a OneHotEncoder
- Using an OrdinalEncoder and treating categories as ordered equidistant quantities
- Using an OrdinalEncoder and relying on the native category support of gradient boosting histogram-based algorithms
- Using target encoding as a last resort

Dropping features is only sometimes considered. However, we already mentioned in chapter 2 how you can evaluate how a nominal feature can contribute to predicting a target utilizing Cramer's V measure of association.

When confronted with a high cardinality categorical feature, opting for one-hot encoding is almost necessary for linear models. When dealing with other models, such as decision trees and their ensembles, there might be a more suitable approach. This is because one-hot encoding creates an additional feature for each category value of the categorical feature. This leads to an increased number of split points that the tree-based model must consider during fitting. Consequently, using one-hot encoded data requires more depth in a decision tree to achieve an equivalent split that could be achieved with a single split point using a different way of handling the categorical feature.

For an ordinal encoder, the categories are encoded as 0, 1, 2, and so on, treating them as continuous features. While this approach can be misleading for linear models, it works effectively for decision trees. Decision trees can accurately split the data based on ordinal encoding, separating the categories according to their relationship with the target variable. This happens with XGBoost, which treats all the features as numerical, continuous features.

If we decide to use the native support for categorical features, this option is available in LightGBM and in the version of XGBoost provided by the H2O.ai library (https://mng.bz/6e75). Native categorical support allows these models to handle categorical features more effectively, without converting them into numerical values. In that case, since native handling requires sorting categories, we expect the algorithm to be slightly slower when using native handling of categorical features with respect to treating categories as ordinal numbers. In the native category support, the sorting of the categories of a feature is based on the associated target variance for each category. Once the sorting has happened, the feature can be used as a continuous numerical attribute.

6.1.4   *Transforming numerical data*

Decision trees can automatically handle nonlinearities and interactions in data. This is because they can split a variable at any point into two parts and then further split them repeatedly. This property comes in particularly handy for handling subtle and deep interactions in the data, with a caveat, because decision trees are quite rough approximators. Under the aspect of precisely modeling complex relationships in data, neural networks with enough examples are better approximators.

Figure 6.1 shows how a bagged ensemble of decision trees can approximate a nonlinear function. The result is an approximation constructed by a set of if-then-else decision rules that recursively divide the space. However, noise in the data can result in inaccuracies in certain parts of the space. In contrast, a neural network with the same number of nodes as the trees used in the bagged decision trees can provide a smoother and more accurate curve estimation.

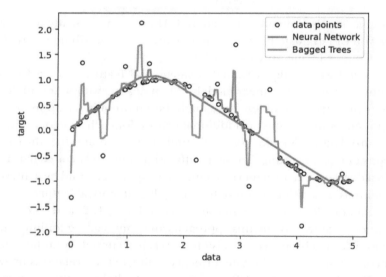

Figure 6.1   Comparison of predictions between a neural network and a bagged trees ensemble for a random dataset with a noisy sine function

Since GBDT is also based on decision trees, it may similarly struggle in shaping nonlinear functions using binary splits. Consequently, when using GBDT, and you know specific nonlinearities or interactions, it benefits you to explicitly define them by using transformations toward linear forms, binning or discretization, and precomputed interactions between features. For nonlinearities, transformations help reduce the number of splits. In addition, computing specific interactions beforehand also reduces the number of splits, which occur at better split points.

However, before applying such transformations, you need to understand your data. Linearities and nonlinearities, even if there is no relationship with the target, can be easily spotted after you complete fitting your training data by a partial dependence plot (PDP). This model-agnostic chart technique explains how features and targets are related through the model you have trained.

PDPs display how the target output changes based on specific input features while ignoring the effects of other input features. In other words, it shows us the average expected prediction if we set a certain value on all the data points of the specific input feature we are examining. The assumption underlying the analysis is that the input we represent by a PDP is independent of other features. Under such conditions, the PDP represents how the input feature directly affects the target. However, this assumption is often violated in practice, meaning that the input feature we are examining is usually not completely independent of the other features. As a result, the plot typically shows how the target value changes as we vary the value of the input feature, while also reflecting the average effects of the other features in the model.

In listing 6.5, we explore PDPs' possible usage and limitations. Given an XGBoost model trained on our Airbnb NYC dataset, we demonstrate how our target changes regarding our numeric features, trying to spot any nonlinearities or other characteristics of the modeled data. The four resulting charts are plotted using matplotlib axes and are to be analyzed.

> **Listing 6.5 Partial dependence plot**

```
from XGBoost import XGBClassifier
import matplotlib.pyplot as plt
from sklearn.inspection import PartialDependenceDisplay

xgb = XGBClassifier(booster='gbtree',
                    objective='reg:logistic',
                    n_estimators=300,
                    max_depth=4,
                    min_child_weight=3)

model_pipeline = Pipeline(               ⟵  Creates a model pipeline
    [('processing', column_transform),      combining data processing
     ('XGBoost', xgb)])                      and XGBoost classifier

model_pipeline.fit(X=data, y=target_median)

fig, axes = plt.subplots(
    nrows=2,
    ncols=2,
    figsize=(8, 4)                       ⟵  Creates a 2 × 2 subplot layout
)
fig.subplots_adjust(hspace=0.4, wspace=0.2)

PartialDependenceDisplay.from_estimator(
```

```
    model_pipeline,
    X=data,
    kind='average',                          ◄────  Creates a partial dependence
                                                    plot of the average effect
    features=[
        'minimum_nights',
        'number_of_reviews',
        'calculated_host_listings_count',
        'availability_365'
    ],                                       ◄────  A list specifying
    ax=axes                                         features for the plot
)                                                                         Adds a red dashed line
for ax in axes.flatten():                                                 at y=0.5 on each
    ax.axhline(y=0.5, color='red', linestyle='--')  ◄───────             subplot, a reference
                                                                          line for interpretation

plt.show()
```

Figure 6.2 shows the four charts. The dashed line marks the classification threshold for one (above or equal to 0.5) and zero (below 0.5). The solid line describes the relationship between the feature value on the x-axis and the target probability on the y-axis. The tick marks on the x-axes point out the distribution deciles of the feature, hinting at ranges denser (where the ticks are next to each other) with values and at those sparser (where the ticks are farther from each other). Ranges sparser with values are less reliable in their estimates. For instance, `minimum_nights` and `calculated_host_listings_count` display a nonlinear pattern, whereas `number_of_reviews` and `availability_365` oscillate stationary.

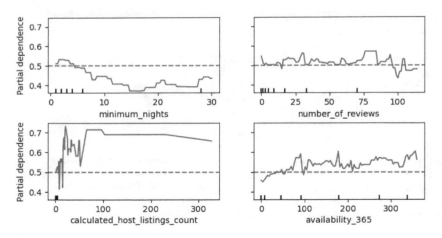

Figure 6.2   A panel of PDPs for numeric features

Given such results, you may evaluate to try to transform `minimum_nights` and `calculated_host_listings_count` using transformative functions by trial and error, such as

- Square or cubic transformations
- Square root or cube root
- Log or exponent transformations
- Tangent, sine, and cosine transformations
- Inverse, squared inverse, cubed inverse, square root inverse, cube root inverse
- Log inverse, exponent inverse, tangent inverse, sine inverse, cosine inverse

However, before rushing to test transformation, it is important to verify if the obtained PDP average curve represents that feature's behavior under all circumstances. You can verify that using individual conditional expectation (ICE) plots. ICE plots are the single components of the PDP curve. You can obtain ICE plots with a slight change in the previous code.

Listing 6.6   ICE plots

```
import matplotlib.pyplot as plt
from sklearn.inspection import PartialDependenceDisplay

fig, axes = plt.subplots(nrows=2, ncols=2, figsize=(8, 4))
fig.subplots_adjust(hspace=0.4, wspace=0.2)

PartialDependenceDisplay.from_estimator(model_pipeline,
                                        X=data,
                                        kind='both',
                                        subsample=30,
                                        features=['minimum_nights',
                                                  'number_of_reviews',

                                                  'calculated_host_listings_
count',

                                                  'availability_365'],
                                        ax=axes)

for ax in axes.flatten():
    ax.axhline(y=0.5, color='red', linestyle='--')
    ax.legend().set_visible(False)

plt.show()
```

Creates a partial dependence plot showing both individual and average effects

Uses a random subset of 30% of data for plotting efficiency

After running the code, you may examine the results, as seen in figure 6.3. You can see the same PDP average curve as before, represented with a dashed lighter line, and a sample of 30 curves taken randomly from the sample. Suppose you can verify that the sampled curves are being clustered together, approximately reproducing the shape of the average curve. In that case, you have a confirmation that the average PDP curve is representative of the behavior of the feature with respect to the target. Otherwise, as in our example, if the single curve appears different and dispersed, the other features somehow mediate the feature's relationship because of collinearity or interactions, and you cannot benefit much from transforming the feature.

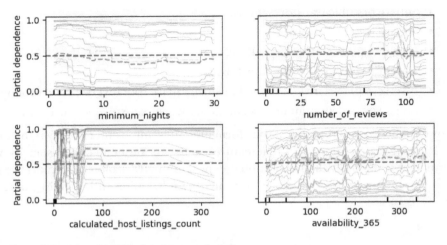

Figure 6.3   A panel of ICE plots for numeric features

Up to now, we have just used PDP for numeric features. Still, you can also apply them to binary and categorical features after encoding them by one-hot encoding. In this case, you have first to compute the curve value by the stand-alone function `partial_dependence` and afterward represent the obtained values as bars (for PDP average curves) or boxplots (for PDP and ICE curves together). In the following listing, we extract the necessary values and create a box plot representation for the single levels of the `neighbourhood_group`.

Listing 6.7   Partial dependence plot for binary features

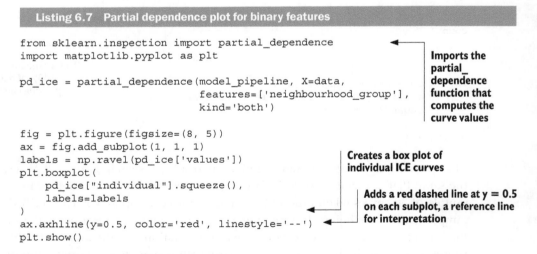

Figure 6.4 shows the result, providing insights on how a flat's location in Manhattan is usually associated with higher prices. The other locations are associated with lower prices, according to the model. However, Brooklyn shows the largest variability, with

sometimes higher prices similar to Manhattan, clearly depending on other factors related to the exact position or characteristics of the flat.

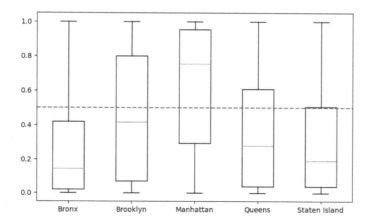

Figure 6.4 For each binary feature, the boxplot associated target values obtained by PDP

As with numeric features, PDP curves also provide useful insight on how to power up your model. For instance, they can be used to aggregate the levels of a categorical feature that behave the same—in our example, Bronx, Staten Island, and probably also Queens.

PDPs show us what we can expect from the target output based on the input features we're interested in. They also help us understand the relationship between the target response and the input feature of interest, whether linear or nonlinear. By observing the shape of the curve drawn by the analysis, we can also figure out what transformation could linearize it. When providing the `features` parameter of the `PartialDependence-Display` function with tuples of features, the function will output a contour map showing the conjoint effects of two specific features. Discovering interactions this way is long and tedious, especially if you have many features to explore. A solution would be to automatically discover the potential interactions and then test them with the PDP conjoint chart. Detecting interactions automatically using XGBoost is straightforward by using a project such as XGBoost Feature Interactions Reshaped (XGBFIR; https://github.com/limexp/xgbfir). The following listing shows an example you can run after installing the package by `pip install xgbfir` on a command shell.

Listing 6.8 Discovering interactions by XGBFIR

```
import xgbfir
xgbfir.saveXgbFI(
    model_pipeline['XGBoost'],
    feature_names=(
```

```
            model_pipeline['processing']
            .get_feature_names_out()
        ),
        OutputXlsxFile='fir.xlsx')
fir = pd.read_excel('fir.xlsx', sheet_name='Interaction Depth 1')
result = fir[["Interaction", "Gain"]].sort_values(by="Gain",

ascending=False).head(10).round(2)
for index, row in result.iterrows():
    print(f"{row['Interaction']}")

PartialDependenceDisplay.from_estimator(
    model_pipeline,
    X=data,
    kind='average',
    features=[(
        'minimum_nights',
        'calculated_host_listings_count')])
```

Generates a report with xgbfir and saves it to an Excel file

Reads the Excel file created in the previous steps

Extracts and sorts based on split gain the "Interaction" and "Gain" columns from the feature interaction report

Generates a partial dependence plot for the features "minimum_nights" and "calculated_host_listings_count"

The code will print a series of interactions. If you work with a linear model, each interaction returned by XGBFIR should be tested because they could enhance your model's performance. If you work with decision trees, you can ignore the ones that involve a binary feature and concentrate on only numeric ones. An example is the interaction between minimum_nights and calculated_host_listings_count. Figure 6.5 shows how combining them with specific values is strongly associated with a positive target response.

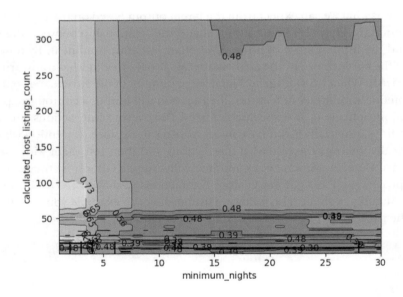

Figure 6.5   Conjoint PDP for two numeric features

In such cases, combining the numeric features by multiplying them will optimize your GDBT model much faster and more effectively.

6.2 *Selecting features*

Feature selection is not always necessary. Still, when it is, it plays a vital role in identifying the most valuable features for training among the existing set of features, whether they derive directly from the data extraction or are the product of your feature engineering work. By employing effective feature selection techniques, you can pinpoint and retain the most relevant features that contribute significantly to the machine learning process.

In chapter 2, section 2.2.3, we discussed avoiding collecting irrelevant and redundant features for the tasks based on your knowledge of the problem and exploratory data analysis. In the subsequent chapters, we discussed machine learning algorithms that handle irrelevant and redundant features.

In classic machine learning, we have a large set of algorithms, including the family of linear models, that are particularly susceptible to irrelevant and redundant features, reducing performance and accuracy. Uninformative and noisy features, deemed irrelevant because they lack a meaningful association with the target of the learning task, can pose significant challenges for linear models. This is due to the possibility of random alignment between the feature values and the target, which can mislead the algorithm and assign undue importance to these features. Linear models utilize all the features provided, making them particularly vulnerable since the more noisy features there are, the more the results will be degraded. Ensembles based on decision trees are instead less affected by irrelevant and redundant features because they automatically select what features to use and ignore. This also happens with deep learning. However, deep learning may not be as robust as decision tree ensemble methods when dealing with noisy or irrelevant features on tabular data. For optimal performance under such conditions, large amounts of data are required, as well as careful choice of architecture, such as using dropout, regularization, or batch normalization layers, and tuning of learning rates.

Feature selection benefits classic machine learning algorithms such as linear models. However, it is also valuable in the case of decision tree-based ensembles and deep learning architectures, and it should not be ignored that it makes a machine learning process faster because of fewer columns to handle. By selecting the features before training, these complex algorithms can achieve improved clarity and ease of explanation by distilling the most relevant and informative features and enabling a clearer understanding of the underlying patterns and relationships captured by the models. This simplification enhances interpretability and facilitates the communication of the algorithm's decision-making process.

In the following sections, we discuss and test a few solutions that can work well, standalone or sequentially, to select only essential features for solving your tabular data problem with the best results. We discuss algorithms for figuring out both relevant features (the all-relevant set), which may lead to redundant but useful sets of features, from algorithms to select minimal subsets of features (the nonredundant set) that produce models comparable to the set of relevant features but with the added advantage of increased interpretability due to a fewer number of features.

6.2.1   *Stability selection for linear models*

Stability selection is based on the idea that if you use a variable selection procedure, you won't always get the same results if you subsample or bootstrap your data because of variability in the process itself. For instance, if you use L1 regularization for feature selection in a linear model, you may find that different samples may return different non-zero coefficients, especially for highly correlated features.

As we have discussed, the L1 regularization penalty results in sparsity in the coefficient estimates. It works by adding a penalty term to the loss function, the sum of the absolute values of the coefficients. Such a penalty term imposes a constraint on the sum of the absolute magnitudes of the coefficients, promoting some coefficients to become exactly zero. Consequently, the L1 regularization can effectively select features by shrinking some coefficients to zero and excluding the corresponding features from the model. In the presence of highly correlated features, the L1 regularization may face difficulty selecting a unique set of features due to their similarity in their contributions to the target variable. Here, chance plays a role in the fact that certain features get non-zero coefficients depending on what data you have in your sample. However, this can be used to our advantage.

By introducing randomness through data sampling, stability selection aims to identify features that consistently appear important across multiple subsets, indicating their robustness and reducing the likelihood of selecting features by chance or noise. Stability selection will provide a useful set of features, not a minimal one. By ruling out unimportant features, stability selection ensures that all the relevant features are identified, thus making it a perfect algorithm for the first step in reducing the number of your features.

Presented in the paper by Meinshausen and Büehlmann (https://arxiv.org/abs/0809.2932), for some time, stability selection has been offered as part of Scikit-learn and then maintained among the Scikit-learn compatible projects. We can easily replicate its procedures using Scikit-learn's `BaggingClassifier` with `LogisticRegression` with L1 regularization for a classification problem. You can also adopt the same code for regression problems, using `BaggingRegressor` with the L1 regression class, `Lasso`.

In our implementation, we test a series of C values for the L1 logistic regression against bootstrap resamples. The procedure creates a series of logistic regression coefficients that we can sum, average, or count how many times they differ from zero. Given that we are using a mix of binary and continuous features, we find it more useful to count the times the coefficient associated with a variable has an absolute value above a threshold. Thus, we can finally deem all the features that, most of the time, tend to have a relevant coefficient as relevant, which can affect the resulting prediction.

Listing 6.9   Stability selection

```
import numpy as np
from sklearn.pipeline import Pipeline
from sklearn.preprocessing import StandardScaler
from sklearn.linear_model import LogisticRegression
from sklearn.ensemble import BaggingClassifier

lambda_grid=np.logspace(-4, -1, 10)
sparse_coef = list()

for modeling_c in lambda_grid:
    estimator = LogisticRegression(
        solver='liblinear',
        penalty='l1',
        C=modeling_c
    )
    model = BaggingClassifier(
        estimator,
        n_estimators=100,
        bootstrap=True
    )
    model_pipeline = Pipeline(
        [('processing', lm_column_transform),
         ('standardize', StandardScaler()),
         ('modeling', model)])
    model_pipeline.fit(data, target_median)
    sparse_coef += [estimator.coef_.ravel() for estimator in
model_pipeline["modeling"].estimators_]

epsilon = 1e-2
threshold = 0.5

non_zero = (np.abs(sparse_coef) > epsilon).mean(axis=0)
feature_names = model_pipeline["processing"].get_feature_names_out()
print(non_zero)
print(feature_names[non_zero > threshold])
```

Generates a grid of lambda values using a logarithmic scale for use in LI regularization

Creates a Logistic Regression estimator with LI (Lasso) penalty

Creates a BaggingClassifier that uses the Logistic Regression estimator as its base model

Standardizes after data processing renders all the coefficients comparable, no matter the scale

Sets a small value as epsilon for a threshold

Sets a threshold value for selecting significant coefficients

The output highlights both the distributions of relevant coefficients and the selected features:

```
[0.635 0.    0.9   0.7  0.592 1.    0.    0.6   0.593 0.444 0.6   0.506 0.7  ]
['low_card_categories__neighbourhood_group_Bronx'
 'low_card_categories__neighbourhood_group_Manhattan'
 'low_card_categories__neighbourhood_group_Queens'
 'low_card_categories__neighbourhood_group_Staten Island'
 'low_card_categories__room_type_Entire home/apt'
 'low_card_categories__room_type_Shared room' 'numeric__minimum_nights'
 'numeric__reviews_per_month' 'numeric__calculated_host_listings_count'
 'Numeric__availability_365']
```

Stability selection offers several advantages. It can handle high-dimensional data, avoid overfitting by incorporating randomness, and provide a measure of feature importance that considers the selection process's stability. It is commonly used in applications with large features, such as genomics, text mining, or image analysis. On the other hand, the selection algorithm is limited to classic machine learning algorithms that use L1 regularization and return a set of coefficients, which are among the ones we discussed before: logistic regression and lasso regression. You can extend the concept proposed by stability selection by using feature importance (many ensemble models estimate feature importance), such as done in Scikit-learn by the command `SelectFromModel` (https://mng.bz/oKej), but things will get trickier because you'll have to figure how what makes an importance estimate relevant and what selection threshold to use. In the next section, we reprise how feature importance works, and we present Boruta. Using a solid automatic feature selection procedure, this algorithm can figure out the relevant features for a decision-tree ensemble, such as random forests or gradient boosting.

6.2.2   *Shadow features and Boruta*

Boruta is a smart procedure for determining whether a feature is relevant in a machine learning problem by relying on the internal parameters of the model, such as coefficients in linear models or importance values based on gain, such as in decision trees and their ensembles. It was first published in "Feature Selection with the Boruta Package" by Miron B. Kursa and Witold R. Rudnicki [*Journal of Statistical Software* 36 (2010): 1-13]; for a copy of the article, see https://www.jstatsoft.org/article/view/v036i11.

Boruta, although innovative, presents quite a few analogies with stability selection. It can be used only with decision tree-based ensembles. To measure the relevance of a feature, as in stability selection, we look for non-zero coefficients. In Boruta, we count the times when the importance of a feature exceeds the highest importance obtained by shadow features. We call them hits. Shadow features are random versions of the feature themselves (basically shuffled features), which, given that they are random, should attain any importance just by chance. If any feature cannot exceed the same importance of a shadow feature, it cannot be considered more predictive than any random sequence of values.

A threshold for selection, usually a minimum number of occurrences of non-zero coefficients in stability selection, is given in Boruta by how the number of hits translates into a binomial distribution. A significance threshold for retaining or dropping a feature test according to the distribution if the number of hits can prove that the feature is consistently better than any random construct.

Listing 6.10 shows an example using Boruta to select all the relevant features for an XGBoost classification on the Airbnb NYC dataset. Boruta in the BorutaPy implementation (https://github.com/scikit-learn-contrib/boruta_py) has some limitations because, apart from working only with tree-based models, such as random forests or gradient boosting (no matter what the implementation is), it cannot work with pipelines. Hence, we first had to transform the data and then run Boruta on the transformed features as we were training the final model. Boruta takes as key parameters the estimator—that is, the model you want to use, the number of decision trees in the ensemble, and the n_estimators hyperparameter, which can be left empty, set to an integer, or set to "auto" where the number of trees is decided upon the size of the dataset. Other important parameters in Boruta are max_iter, the number of rounds of testing, usually set to 100, and the alpha threshold for the binomial test, which can be increased from 0.05 to allow for more features to be retained or decreased for more features to be discarded.

Listing 6.10 Boruta selection

```
from XGBoost import XGBClassifier
from boruta import BorutaPy

xgb = XGBClassifier(booster='gbtree',
                    objective='reg:logistic',
                    n_estimators=300,
                    max_depth=4,
                    min_child_weight=3)

X = column_transform.fit_transform(data, target_median)
boruta_selector = BorutaPy(estimator=xgb, n_estimators='auto', verbose=2)
boruta_selector.fit(X, target_median)
selected_features = boruta_selector.support_
selected_data = column_transform.get_feature_names_out()[selected_features]
print(selected_data)
```

Initializes a BorutaPy feature selection object using an XGBoost classifier

Transforms the input data, performing any necessary preprocessing steps

Retrieves a Boolean mask of selected features determined by the Boruta feature selector

Fits the Boruta feature selector

After a few iterations, you should get the results of only a single feature discarded as not relevant to the problem:

```
Iteration:    50 / 100
Confirmed:    13
Tentative:    0
Rejected:     1
['low_card_categories__neighbourhood_group_Bronx'
 'low_card_categories__neighbourhood_group_Brooklyn'
 'low_card_categories__neighbourhood_group_Manhattan'
 'low_card_categories__neighbourhood_group_Queens'
 'low_card_categories__room_type_Entire home/apt'
 'low_card_categories__room_type_Private room'
 'low_card_categories__room_type_Shared room'
 'high_card_categories__neighbourhood' 'numeric__minimum_nights'
 'numeric__number_of_reviews' 'numeric__reviews_per_month'
 'numeric__calculated_host_listings_count' 'numeric__availability_365']
```

The same procedure can be executed using LightGBM as predictor, instead of XGBoost:

```
from lightgbm import LGBMClassifier

lgbm = LGBMClassifier(boosting_type='gbdt',
```

```
                        n_estimators=300,
                        max_depth=4,
                        min_child_samples=3)
```
Initializes a BorutaPy feature selection object using the provided LightGBM classifier

```
boruta_selector = BorutaPy(estimator=lgbm, n_estimators='auto', verbose=2)
boruta_selector.fit(X, target_median)
selected_features = boruta_selector.support_
selected_data = column_transform.get_feature_names_out()[selected_features]
print(selected_data)
```

The result is reached after only 9 iterations, and this time, we have an increased number of rejected features:

```
Iteration:      9 / 100
Confirmed:      8
Tentative:      0
Rejected:       6
['low_card_categories__neighbourhood_group_Manhattan'
 'low_card_categories__room_type_Entire home/apt'
 'high_card_categories__neighbourhood' 'numeric__minimum_nights'
 'numeric__number_of_reviews' 'numeric__reviews_per_month'
 'numeric__calculated_host_listings_count' 'numeric__availability_365']
```

LightGBM not only converges more quickly, but the way it splits allows, in this problem, the creation of a performing model with many fewer features than XGBoost.

In our example, we have trained on all the available data. Still, you can use Boruta even in a cross-validation loop, where you can consolidate a result for the dataset by using all the selected features in all the folds or by only those selected at least a minimum number of times across the folds.

6.2.3 *Forward and backward selection*

One limitation of Boruta is that it selects all the relevant features for your problem but not the essential ones. This means you may end up with a list with redundant and highly correlated features that can be cut to a shorter selection. After applying Boruta, we suggest resorting to a sequential feature selection procedure, as implemented in the Scikit-learn function `SequentialFeatureSelector`. This procedure adds by forward selection or removes by backward elimination features from your selection based on their performance on the prediction in a greedy fashion—that is, always picking up the best-performing choice, based on the cross-validation score, in terms of addition or discard. The technique relies on the learning algorithm and its objective function. Hence, its selection will always be among the best possible. Since it is a greedy procedure, there is always the risk of choosing a local optimum set.

Sequential selection is a very effective procedure in reducing the number of features you have to deal with. Still, it is quite time-consuming because the algorithm has to evaluate all the candidates at each round. In the forward procedure, this will turn slower and slower as you proceed because, despite having fewer candidates to evaluate at each round, the increasing number of features used will slow down the training. However, in the backward procedure, you start slow and tend to accelerate after discarding a number of features. The backward procedure may be impractical if you start from many features to evaluate and the training is very slow.

As a stopping rule for the procedure, you may set a certain number of features, or you can leave the selection algorithm to find out the point at which adding or removing a feature bears no more improvements to the predictions. A tolerance threshold helps give the algorithm a certain freedom to proceed or not: the larger the tolerance, the more likely the algorithm will proceed in its operations, even if adding or removing a feature somehow deteriorates the performance.

In listing 6.11, we apply a forward selection to an XGBoost model trained on the Airbnb NYC dataset. The selection algorithm is set free to determine the correct number of features to add, and the low tolerance (set to 0.0001 on accuracy measures ranging from 0 to 1) should stop it at the first signs of deterioration of the predictive performances.

Listing 6.11 Forward selection

```
from sklearn.feature_selection import SequentialFeatureSelector
from sklearn.metrics import accuracy_score, make_scorer
from XGBoost import XGBClassifier

xgb = XGBClassifier(booster='gbtree',
                    objective='reg:logistic',
                    n_estimators=300,
                    max_depth=4,
                    min_child_weight=3)

cv = KFold(5, shuffle=True, random_state=0)
accuracy = make_scorer(accuracy_score)
X = column_transform.fit_transform(data, target_median)
selector = SequentialFeatureSelector(
    estimator=xgb,
    n_features_to_select="auto",
    tol=0.0001,
    direction="forward",
    scoring=accuracy,
    cv=cv
)
selector.fit(X, target_median)
selected_features = selector.support_
selected_data = column_transform.get_feature_names_out()[selected_features]
print(selected_data)
```

Annotations:
- Initializes a KFold cross-validation splitter object with five folds
- Creates a scoring function for use in the feature selection process
- Sets a tolerance value used by the sequential feature selector to determine convergence during the search
- Specifies the direction of feature selection (which is "forward" in this case)
- Retrieves a boolean mask of selected features

The obtained results point out to six features to be used: three binary ones, a high cardinality categorical, and two numeric ones:

```
['low_card_categories__neighbourhood_group_Bronx'
 'low_card_categories__room_type_Entire home/apt'
 'low_card_categories__room_type_Shared room'
 'high_card_categories__neighbourhood' 'numeric__minimum_nights'
```

```
'numeric__number_of_reviews' 'numeric__reviews_per_month'
'numeric__calculated_host_listings_count' 'numeric__availability_365']
```

We can replicate the experiment in a backward fashion by running the following commands:

```
selector = SequentialFeatureSelector(
    estimator=xgb,
    n_features_to_select="auto",
    tol=0.0001,
    direction="backward",          ◄───  Specifies the direction of
    scoring=accuracy,                    feature selection (which is
    cv=cv                                "backward" in this case)
)
selector.fit(X, target_median)
selected_features = selector.support_
selected_data = column_transform.get_feature_names_out()[selected_features]
print(selected_data)
```

The resulting selection is made of nine features, many of those already seen in the set resulting from the forward selection:

```
['low_card_categories__neighbourhood_group_Bronx'
 'low_card_categories__neighbourhood_group_Manhattan'
 'low_card_categories__neighbourhood_group_Queens'
 'low_card_categories__neighbourhood_group_Staten Island'
 'low_card_categories__room_type_Entire home/apt'
 'low_card_categories__room_type_Shared room'
 'high_card_categories__neighbourhood' 'numeric__minimum_nights'
 'numeric__number_of_reviews' 'numeric__reviews_per_month'
 'numeric__calculated_host_listings_count' 'numeric__availability_365']
```

In our own experience, choosing a forward or backward selection depends on the need you may have to risk leaving out some slightly important feature from your chosen set. With forward addition, you are sure to keep only the essential features but risk leaving something marginally relevant out. With the backward elimination, you are assured that all the key features are in the set, allowing for some redundancy.

Besides choosing a forward or backward procedure, sequential selection will help you build models faster in training and prediction and will be much easier to interpret and maintain because of the limited number of features involved.

6.3   *Optimizing hyperparameters*

Feature engineering can improve the results you obtain from your classical machine learning models. Creating new features can reveal the underlying patterns and relationships in data that the models cannot grasp because of their limitations. Feature selection can improve your models' results by removing unuseful and redundant features for the problem, thus reducing the noise and spurious signals in data. Finally, by optimizing hyperparameters, you can gain another performance boost and have your classical machine learning model shine on the tabular data problem you are dealing with.

As discussed in chapter 4, hyperparameters are those settings that work under the hood of all machine learning algorithms and determine how specifically they can work. From an abstract point of view, each machine learning algorithm potentially offers a limited, yet still wide, range of functional forms—that is, the mathematical ways you can relate your predictor variables to your outcome. Straight out of the box, a machine learning algorithm may less or more match the functional form required by your specific machine learning problem.

For instance, if you are using a gradient boosting algorithm to solve a classification problem, it may be that the default number of iterations or how its trees are grown do not match the requirements of the problem. You may need fewer or more iterations and tree growth than specified by the default values. By opportunely setting its hyperparameters, you can find the best settings that work better with your problem.

However, it is not just a matter of twiddling all the many knobs that an algorithm presents until it gets the results you expect. Sometimes the knobs are too many to be tested together, and even if you manage to test enough of them, if not done properly, it will result in overfitting your data and, on the contrary, obtaining worse results. You need a systematic approach after defining one or more evaluation metrics:

- Defining a search space containing the hyperparameters whose effects you want to explore and the boundaries of the values to test
- Building a proper cross-validation scheme to ensure that you are discovering a solution that generalizes beyond the data you have
- Choosing a search algorithm that, by a proper strategy, will find out in less time and with less cost—for instance, in terms of computations—the solution you need

In the following subsections, under the light of different search strategies, we discuss the way you can accomplish tuning some of the classical machine learning algorithms we have seen so far.

6.3.1 *Searching systematically*

Grid search works through all the possible combinations of hyperparameters' values. For every hyperparameter you want to test, you pick a sequence of values and iterate through all their combinations exhaustively. In the end, you pick the combination that returns the best results.

In listing 6.12, we apply it to a logistic regression model, helping to choose the kind of regularization and the settings of L1 and L2 regularization values. The most important part of the code is the search grid, which is a list containing one or multiple dictionaries. Instead, each dictionary is a search space, a sequence of hyperparameters (the keys of the dictionary) associated with a list of a generator of values, which are the possible values you want to test (the values of the dictionary). Structuring one or more search spaces is a common practice across all the optimization methods, whether they are from Scikit-learn or not. Just notice how the name of the hyperparameters are for-mulated in the form `model__name_of_the_hyperparameter` because we are optimizing a pipeline and addressing parameters that are first internal to the pipeline and then of the model. We will come back to this in the next subsection with more explanations.

Listing 6.12   Grid search

```
from sklearn.linear_model import LogisticRegression
from sklearn.metrics import accuracy_score
from sklearn.model_selection import KFold, GridSearchCV
from sklearn.metrics import make_scorer

accuracy = make_scorer(accuracy_score)
cv = KFold(5, shuffle=True, random_state=0)
model = LogisticRegression(solver="saga", max_iter=5_000)

model_pipeline = Pipeline(
    [('processing', lm_column_transform),
     ('model', model)])

search_grid = [
    {"model__penalty": [None]},
    {"model__penalty": ["l1", "l2"], "model__C": np.logspace(-4, 4, 10)},
    {"model__penalty": ["elasticnet"], "model__C": np.logspace(-4, 4, 10),
     "model__l1_ratio": [.1, .3, .5, .7, .9, .95, .99]},
]

search_func = GridSearchCV(estimator=model_pipeline,
                           param_grid=search_grid,
                           scoring=accuracy,
                           n_jobs=-1,
                           cv=cv)
search_func.fit(X=data, y=target_median)
print (search_func.best_params_)
print (search_func.best_score_)
```

> **A list of dictionaries specifying a search grid of hyperparameters for the logistic regression model**

> **Initializes a GridSearchCV object using the defined search grid**

> **Prints the best hyperparameters found by the grid search**

> **Prints the best score achieved by the model using the best hyperparameters found during the grid search**

After testing all the combinations, the grid search procedure returns that the best set of hyperparameters is just not to use any penalty at all. It returns the best cross-validated score in support of its report:

```
{'model__penalty': None}
0.8210860006135597
```

Grid search is effective when your hyperparameters are few; they take discrete values, and you can parallelize in memory the testing operations because your dataset is not too large.

First, the more combinations, the more tests you have to take and the longer and more computations you'll have to spend. It could be a serious problem if you need to test many hyperparameters and suspect some of them are irrelevant for properly tuning your algorithm. When you add a hyperparameter to the grid search, you must make all the other hyperparameters cycle through it, which can turn into a waste of energy if the hyperparameter you are testing is irrelevant.

In addition, if a parameter takes continuous values, you must decide how to turn its continuous search space into a discrete one. Usually, this is done by uniformly dividing the continuum of values into discrete values, but by doing so without any knowledge of the way the algorithm behaves with respect to that hyperparameter and its values may again turn into wasting multiple computations on testing values that cannot improve the algorithm performances.

The last aspect to consider is using multiple cores and parallelizing their operations. Grid search is completely unaware of the results each test obtains. The results are only ranked at the end, and you are offered the best result. Hence, grid search is fine if your algorithm naturally works on a single core. However, suppose your algorithm uses multiple threads and cores, such as a random forest or an XGBoost. In that case, you have to trade off between having the algorithm running at full speed or having the optimization procedure go parallel and speedier. Usually, the best choice is to push the algorithm to run faster by using parallel running. Regardless of whether you decide to take advantage of the parallelization capabilities of the algorithm or those of the search procedure, grid search is not the best-performing option when working with a multi-core algorithm.

Based on our experience and the limits of the grid search strategy, we deem it the best fit for testing linear models since they are easily parallelizable and have few limited parameters, often characterized by taking Boolean or discrete values.

6.3.2 *Using random trials*

Important limitations when using grid search are that

- You need to discretize continuous hyperparameters.
- If a hyperparameter is irrelevant to the problem, you are going to have many trials wasted as they test the space of the irrelevant feature.

For these reasons, the idea of sampling the search space randomly is rooted in the machine learning community. As described in the paper "Random Search for Hyper-Parameter Optimization" by James Bergstra and Yoshua Bengio (*Journal of Machine Learning Research;* https://mng.bz/nRg8), random search optimization becomes the standard optimization when you have many hyperparameters and you don't know exactly how they affect the results or how they work together.

In our example, we reprise our classification problem using an XGBoost classifier. XGBoost, as with other gradient boosting implementations, features several hyperparameters that can be deemed important, and you should try to test them to check if your model's performance can be improved. In the example, we also make things a bit more sophisticated because we operate by the XGBoost model wrapped into a pipeline, thus requiring a specific way to address hyperparameters. Since each element in the pipeline has a name, you must address each parameter in a part of the pipeline by the name of the element in the pipeline, two underlines, and then the name of the hyperparameter. For instance, in our example, XGBoost is in a part of the pipeline named "xgb." To address the hyperparameter n_estimators of XGBoost, just use the label xgb__n_estimators in your search space. The idea is to demonstrate how to optimize a model and its pipeline without testing all the possible choices influencing a model's predictive performance.

Listing 6.13   Random search

```
from sklearn.utils.fixes import loguniform
from sklearn.model_selection import KFold, RandomizedSearchCV
from sklearn.metrics import accuracy_score
from sklearn.metrics import make_scorer
from XGBoost import XGBClassifier

accuracy = make_scorer(accuracy_score)
cv = KFold(5, shuffle=True, random_state=0)

xgb = XGBClassifier(booster='gbtree', objective='reg:logistic')
model_pipeline = Pipeline(
    [('processing', column_transform), ('xgb', xgb)]           ◄─── Creates a pipeline that
)                                                                    combines data processing
                                                                     and the XGBoost classifier
search_dict = {                                               ◄───
    'xgb__n_estimators': np.arange(100, 2000, 100),             A dictionary containing
    'xgb__learning_rate': loguniform(0.01, 1),                  various hyperparameters
    'xgb__max_depth': np.arange(1, 8),                          with their search spaces for
    'xgb__subsample': np.arange(0.1, 0.9, 0.05),               the RandomizedSearchCV
    'xgb__colsample_bytree': np.arange(0.1, 0.9, 0.05),
    'xgb__reg_lambda': loguniform(1e-9, 100),                   Specifies the number of
    'xgb__reg_alpha': loguniform(1e-9, 100)                     iterations for the
}                                                               random search process

search_func = RandomizedSearchCV(estimator=model_pipeline,
                                 param_distributions=search_dict,
                                 n_iter=60,                     ◄───
                                 scoring=accuracy,
                                 n_jobs=1,           ◄─── Specifies the number
                                 cv=cv,                   of parallel jobs to run
                                 random_state=0)          for the search

search_func.fit(X=data, y=target_median)      ◄─── Prints the best
print (search_func.best_params_)                   hyperparameters found by
print (search_func.best_score_)   ◄───             the RandomizedSearchCV
```

Prints the best score achieved using the best hyperparameters found during the random search

After a while (the code runs in about one hour in a Google Colab instance), we get the set of the best parameters and the cross-validated score obtained:

```
{'xgb__colsample_bytree': 0.3500000000000001,
 'xgb__learning_rate': 0.020045491299569684,
 'xgb__max_depth': 6,
 'xgb__n_estimators': 1800,
 'xgb__reg_alpha': 3.437821898520205e-08,
 'xgb__reg_lambda': 0.021708909914764426,
 'xgb__subsample': 0.1}
0.8399836384088353
```

Random search optimization, in spite of its simplicity and the fact it relies on randomness, really works, and it provides the best optimization in many situations. Many AutoML systems rely on this optimization strategy when there are many hyperparameters to tune (see, for instance, "Google Vizier: A Service for Black-Box Optimization," by D. Golovinb et al., 2017 at https://mng.bz/8OrZ). Compared to grid search, which works well when you have a limited set of hyperparameters that you expect to be impactful and a limited set of values to test, random search works the best when you have too many values to tune, without prior knowledge of how they work.

All you have to do is rely on enough random tests to have a good combination emerge, which may not take long. In our experience, 30 to 60 random draws usually suffice for good optimization. One strong point of random search optimization is that it works well for complex problems and is not affected by irrelevant hyperparameters. The number of relevant ones determines how fast you can find a good solution. The algorithm is also suited for parallel search on different computers or instances (you pick the best result among all). Still, this positive point comes with the limitation that since tests are independent, they do not inform each other about their results.

6.3.3   *Reducing the computational burden*

Both grid search and random search do not utilize the outcomes from previous experiments. Grid search strictly adheres to a predefined procedure, while random search conducts a set of independent tests. In both cases, the prior results are not considered or used in any way during the search process. *Successive halving*, a wrapper of both strategies, can instead take advantage of knowing the prior results. The idea is like that of a tournament where you first hold many rounds and put forth few resources to test different hyperparameters' values. Then, as you progress and drop the values that underperform, you invest more resources to test the remaining values thoroughly. Usually, the resource you initially dilute and then later concentrate on is the number of training examples. More examples imply certain results from a hyperparameter test, but it costs more computational power.

Available as `HalvingGridSearchCV` and `HalvingRandomSearchCV` in Scikit-learn, in listing 6.14, we test the random search variant to verify if we can obtain similar optimization results at a fraction of the time. As stated, we use the number of samples as a scarce resource to optimize, using just the 30% available at the start. In addition, we instruct the algorithm to start from 20 initial candidates and to decrease the number of candidates by three times at each round (from 20 to 6 to 2).

Listing 6.14   Halving random search

```
from sklearn.experimental import (
    enable_halving_search_cv
)
from sklearn.model_selection import HalvingRandomSearchCV

search_func = HalvingRandomSearchCV(
    estimator=model_pipeline,
    param_distributions=search_dict,
    resource='n_samples',
    n_candidates=20,
    factor=3,
    min_resources=int(len(data) * 0.3),
    max_resources=len(data),
    scoring=accuracy,
    n_jobs=1,
    cv=cv,
    random_state=0
)
search_func.fit(X=data, y=target_median)
print (search_func.best_params_)
print (search_func.best_score_)
```

Enables the experimental
HalvingRandomSearchCV module

Specifies that the resource being used
for halving is the number of samples

Sets the number of candidates
that will be sampled and
evaluated at the first iteration

Determines the factor by which
the number of candidates will be
reduced in each iteration

Sets the minimum number of
resources (samples) that will be
used in the halving process

Sets the maximum number of
resources (samples) that will be
used in the halving process

The following are the results you obtain, at a fraction of the time previously required
(in Google Colab the procedure runs in about 10 minutes):

```
{'xgb__colsample_bytree': 0.6500000000000001,
 'xgb__learning_rate': 0.02714215181104359,
 'xgb__max_depth': 7,
 'xgb__n_estimators': 400,
 'xgb__reg_alpha': 3.281921389446602,
 'xgb__reg_lambda': 0.00039687940902191534,
 'xgb__subsample': 0.8000000000000002}
0.8398409090909091
```

In our experience with this optimization strategy, the strategy is to set the initial
round in a way that it can catch some good hyperparameters. Hence it is important to
have the highest possible number of candidates running at a minimum of resources,
although not so low to compromise the results of optimization. Setting as little as 1,000
starting samples should work sufficiently well if the factor parameter is reduced. This
determines the proportion of candidates selected for each subsequent iteration to two
instead of three, thus going to a longer number of rounds.

6.3.4   *Extending your search by Bayesian methods*

Another optimization strategy that makes informed choices is Bayesian optimization.
Introduced in the paper "Practical Bayesian Optimization of Machine Learning Algorithms" by Snoek, Larochelle, and Adams (https://arxiv.org/abs/1206.2944), the

idea behind this optimization strategy is to understand how the hyperparameters of a model work, by building a model of themselves. The algorithm optimizes a proxy function, called the surrogate function, to increase the algorithm's performance. Of course, the surrogate function is updated by the feedback from the objective function of the machine learning model under optimization. However, the Bayesian optimization algorithm's decisions are solely based on the surrogate function.

In particular, it is another that alternates exploration with exploitation: the acquisition function. The acquisition function reports how much exploring a certain combination of parameters is promising and how much is uncertain, based on the surrogate function. Exploration implies trying combinations of the parameters that have never been tried before, and this happens when there is much uncertainty, and thus consequently hope, in certain areas of the search space that need at least to be tried to improve the surrogate function. On the contrary, exploitation happens when the acquisition function ensures that the algorithm can improve performance when trying a certain set of hyperparameters.

As the "Bayesian" in the name implies, and from our brief description of how the Bayesian optimization works under the hood, the process is influenced by prior expectations and subsequently corrected by posterior observations in a fine-tuning cycle. The surrogate function in all of this is nothing more than a model of our model. Usually, Gaussian processes are chosen as a model for the surrogate function. Still, there are alternatives, such as using tree algorithms such as random forests or tree-structured Parzen estimators, which are a multivariate distribution capable of describing the behavior of the hyperparameters in our model. Packages such as Scikit-optimize (https://scikit-optimize.github.io/stable/) or KerasTuner (https://keras.io/keras_tuner/) use Gaussian processes, with Scikit-optimize also capable of using tree ensembles and KerasTuner using multiarmed bandits, as well. Optuna, an optimization framework developed by Preferred Networks, a Japanese AI research and development company, instead uses tree-structured Parzen estimators. Initially released in May 2019 as an open-source project, Optuna is particularly popular in the Python machine learning community due to its simplicity, versatility, and integration with popular machine learning libraries such as TensorFlow, PyTorch, and Scikit-learn.

In our example, we use Optuna to improve our XGBoost classifier. When using Optuna, you just set up a study and provide its running parameters, such as the number of trials, `n_trials`, and the direction parameter if you want to minimize or maximize your objective function. Behind the scenes, all the heavy lifting is done by the objective function, which you define and returns an evaluation. The objective function expects just an input parameter, trial, which Optuna provides. By the trial parameter, you define the values of the hyperparameters to test. Then, you just test them as you like because it is up to you inside the objective function to decide if to apply a cross-validation, a simple test on a sample, or anything else. This flexibility also allows you to run complex optimizations where certain hyperparameters are used or depend on others and their values. It is up to you to code the procedure you want.

Listing 6.15 Bayesian search with Optuna

```python
import optuna
from XGBoost import XGBClassifier
from sklearn.model_selection import cross_validate

def objective(trial):

    params = {
        'n_estimators': trial.suggest_int('n_estimators', 100, 2000),
        'learning_rate': trial.suggest_float(
            'learning_rate', 0.01, 1.0, log=True
        ),
        'subsample': trial.suggest_float('subsample', 0.1, 1.0),
        'colsample_bytree': trial.suggest_float(
            'colsample_bytree', 0.1, 1.0
        ),
        'max_depth': trial.suggest_int('max_depth', 1, 7),
        'min_child_weight': trial.suggest_int('min_child_weight', 1, 7),
        'reg_lambda': trial.suggest_float(
            'reg_lambda', 1e-9, 100.0, log=True
        ),
        'reg_alpha': trial.suggest_float(
            'reg_alpha', 1e-9, 100.0, log=True
        ),
    }

    xgb = XGBClassifier(
        booster='gbtree',
        objective='reg:logistic',
        **params
    )
    model_pipeline = Pipeline(
        [('processing', column_transform), ('xgb', xgb)]
    )
    accuracy = make_scorer(accuracy_score)
    cv = KFold(5, shuffle=True, random_state=0)

    cv_scores = cross_validate(estimator=model_pipeline,
                               X=data,
                               y=target_median,
                               scoring=accuracy,
                               cv=cv)

    cv_accuracy = np.mean(cv_scores['test_score'])
    return cv_accuracy

study = optuna.create_study(direction="maximize")
study.optimize(objective, n_trials=60)
print(study.best_value)
print(study.best_params)
```

A dictionary defining the search space for hyperparameters for Optuna

Creates an XGBoost classifier with hyperparameters suggested by Optuna

Performs cross-validation to evaluate the model's performance using the hyperparameters

A function acting as the objective value for optimization by returning the mean accuracy score from cross-validation

Creates an Optuna study object with the goal of maximizing the objective function

Starts the optimization process using the defined objective function and a maximum of 60 trials

Prints the best hyperparameters found by Optuna

Prints the best-achieved value of the objective function

On a Google Colab instance, the process can take up to two hours, but the results are by far the best in class you can obtain from hyperparameter optimization:

```
{'n_estimators': 1434,
 'learning_rate': 0.013268588739778429,
 'subsample': 0.782534239551612,
 'colsample_bytree': 0.9427647573058971,
 'max_depth': 7,
 'min_child_weight': 2,
 'reg_lambda': 2.3123673571345327e-06,
 'reg_alpha': 1.8176941971395193e-05}
0.8419879333265161
```

As an extra feature offered by Optuna, with a few simple additions to the previous code, you can store your study in a project database and restart optimization at any time. Optuna can integrate its optimization procedures with SQLite if, at the time of the creation of the study, you declare the name of the study and a target database:

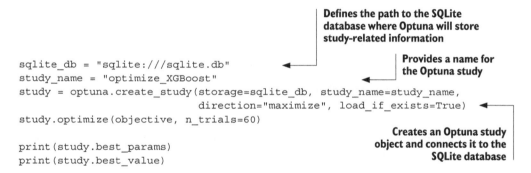

Defines the path to the SQLite database where Optuna will store study-related information

Provides a name for the Optuna study

```
sqlite_db = "sqlite:///sqlite.db"
study_name = "optimize_XGBoost"
study = optuna.create_study(storage=sqlite_db, study_name=study_name,
                            direction="maximize", load_if_exists=True)
study.optimize(objective, n_trials=60)

print(study.best_params)
print(study.best_value)
```

Creates an Optuna study object and connects it to the SQLite database

Regarding the specification of the SQLite storage database, `sqlite://` is a Uniform Resource Identifier (URI) scheme used to specify the protocol or mechanism for connecting to an SQLite database. In the context of the URI scheme, `sqlite://` indicates that the database connection will be established using the SQLite database engine. When using this URI scheme, the `sqlite://+` portion is followed by the path to the SQLite database file. In your example, `sqlite:///sqlite.db` specifies that the SQLite database file is named `sqlite.db` and is located in the current directory. The three slashes (`///`) after `sqlite:` are optional and indicate that the path is relative to the current directory.

Once the study has been completed, you can also obtain useful visualization regarding the results of the iterations and gain insights useful on successive runs of the same search. For instance, you can explore the optimization history and check if you have reached a plateau in the optimization or if going on with more iterations is advisable:

```
fig = optuna.visualization.plot_optimization_history(study)
fig.show()
```

Figure 6.6 shows how our optimization proceeded. After a few iterations, the optimization reached a good result, but then it struggled to progress through the rest of the available iterations. Under such conditions, further progress in optimization is improbable because any gains cannot be but tiny at this point.

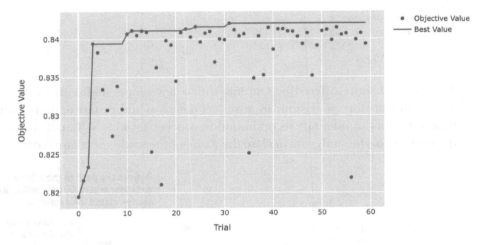

Figure 6.6   History of optimization results across the trials

Another useful plot depicts how the hyperparameters have been determinant in the resulting optimum settings:

```
fig = optuna.visualization.plot_param_importances(study)
fig.show()
```

Figure 6.7 shows the estimated importance of our optimization of the XGBoost algorithm. The results appear dominated by the max_depth hyperparameter and somehow by the subsample values. Such an outcome suggests that the algorithm is susceptible to the depth of the trees and that increasing the depth significantly affects the optimization results. This could indicate that the data contains complex patterns that require deeper trees to capture, and the sweet point of seven found by the optimization marks a point after which the algorithm starts overfitting.

Understanding why your XGBoost (or LightGBM) behaves better under certain conditions differs from problem to problem. However, being able to understand why, explain the reasons to others (such as the stakeholders), and take steps to adjust your data or optimization settings is indeed an invaluable feature offered by Optuna in comparison to other optimization methods.

After completing the panoramic illustration on optimization techniques, we are left dealing with the case when you don't want to set up anything complicated to make your

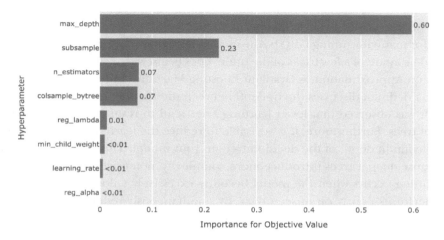

Figure 6.7   A plot chart of hyperparameter estimated importance during the Optuna optimization process

machine learning algorithms work but you need some direction on how to make fast adjustments by trial and error.

6.3.5   *Manually setting hyperparameters*

Despite the efficiency of the previously described optimization strategies, you may not be surprised to read that we know that many practitioners still tune the settings of their models by intuition and trial and error. Such a procedure seems particularly well-grounded during the experimentation phase when you try to make everything work reasonably as you look for ways to improve your solution in various iterations. A thorough optimization is, therefore, left after the processing and experimentation iterations have been completed.

The book's appendices provide a comprehensive guide to the key parameters of the machine learning algorithms covered thus far. We begin with linear models, such as linear or logistic regressions, which can be effectively tuned using a grid search due to their limited number of parameters and ease of discretization. A table covers random forests and extremely randomized trees, as they share similar hyperparameters, being based on the same bootstrapped ensemble approach.

Regarding GBDTs, we have different sets of hyperparameters depending on the specific implementation. For your convenience, we have selected the most essential ones. Feel free to use them along with the proposed ranges for manual or automatic optimization. The guide starts with HistGradientBoosting and then covers XGBoost and LightGBM. It's important to note that XGBoost has a larger set of relevant hyperparameters (you can find the complete list at https://mng.bz/6e7e). Lastly, we include the list of hyperparameters for LightGBM, which differs slightly from XGBoost (you can find the complete list at https://mng.bz/vK8q). This comprehensive guide will aid you in effectively tuning the machine learning algorithms and optimizing their performance based on the specific hyperparameter settings.

As for manually tuning GBDTs, the models tend to work worst out of the box, so you should be aware of a few tricks of the trade. Let's begin with a 1999 paper titled "Greedy Function Approximation: A Gradient Boosting Machine" by Jerome Friedman. In this paper, Friedman discusses the tradeoff between the number of trees and the learning rate. It was observed that lower learning rates tend to result in higher optimal numbers of trees. Furthermore, it is advisable to reduce the learning rate when increasing the maximum depth of the decision trees in your model. This precautionary measure is because deeper trees introduce more complexity, potentially leading to overfitting. Overfitting occurs when the model becomes excessively tailored to the training data and performs poorly on unseen data. By simultaneously reducing the learning rate, you can mitigate this risk. This is because a lower learning rate translates to smaller and more cautious updates to the model. This gradual learning process allows for finer adjustments, helping the model strike a better balance between capturing complex relationships and avoiding overfitting.

Another great resource for hints on manually adjusting parameters in a GBDT is Owen Zhang's talk to the NYC Data Science Academy in 2015 titled "Winning Data Science Competitions." Owen, previously a top competitor on Kaggle, provided a few interesting tips:

- Decide the number of trees to use based on the dataset size (usually in the range of 100 to 1,000) and keep it fixed during the optimization. Prefer fewer trees to more.
- Test the learning rate in the range from 2 to 10 divided by the number of trees. Hence, for 1,000 trees, test learning rates in the interval from 0.002 to 0.01.
- Test row sampling on 0.5, 0.75, 1.0 values.
- Test column sampling on 0.4, 0.6, 0.8, 1.0 values.
- Test max tree depth on 4, 6, 8, 10 values.
- Tune the minimum leaf weight/count as an approximate ratio of 3 over the square root of the percentage of the rarest class you have to predict. Therefore, if the class you need to predict has a 10% coverage in the data, you should set the minimum leaf weight/count to about 9. This figure is calculated by dividing 3 by the square root of 0.1 (since 10% coverage is 0.1 as a decimal).

In the concluding section, we keep exploring some ideas and tricks to master even better GBDTs when solving tabular data problems.

6.4   *Mastering gradient boosting*

Having discussed how gradient boosting works and its implementations, we close this chapter with suggestions about how to use gradient boosting at its best, understand how it works under the hood, and speed it up to cut time at training and prediction.

6.4.1 Deciding between XGBoost and LightGBM

When considering using gradient boosting for your data problem, XGBoost and LightGBM (along with HistGradientBoosting) are among the most popular and high-performing implementations of histogram gradient boosted machines. Despite their being so powerful, in our experience, you never can a priori go for XGBoost or LightGBM or just generally favor GBDTs in regards to other classical or deep learning solutions because of the no free lunch theorem in machine learning: there is no universal learning algorithm that performs best for all possible problems. Hence, stating that "XGBoost is all you need" for tabular data problems is surely a catchy phrase, but it may not always fit your specific problem or situation with data. GDBTs often tend to overperform other solutions for tabular data. Thus, starting with them, but not limited to them, is a good choice. Returning to specific implementations, while it is always advisable to test any algorithm on your data and make your own decisions, there are also a few other criteria to consider when deciding whether to try one implementation first or the other. We have validated them based on our own experience. They are summarized in table 6.1.

Table 6.1 Criteria to consider when using GBDTs

Type	Description
Amount of data	XGBoost works fine for all tabular problems; LightGBM, because of its leaf-wise splitting method that can create deeper trees, tends to overfit more often with smaller datasets.
Scalability	XGBoost is more scalable and GPU ready; LightGBM struggles more.
Speed of experimentation	On CPUs, LightGBM is undoubtedly faster than XGBoost.

The availability of large amounts of data is the first criterion to consider. LightGBM uses leaf-wise (vertical) growth, which can result in overfitting. The tendency to overfit the data available explains well the algorithm's success in Kaggle competitions. Hence, LightGBM works better when you have a lot of data available. In contrast, XGBoost builds more robust models than LightGBM on smaller data samples.

Another criterion to consider is whether you have access to multiple GPUs and strong CPUs or more limited access to computational resources. If you have plenty of resources, XGBoost is more scalable, making it a better option for use in institutional or business settings. However, if you prefer to focus on experimentation and feature engineering and cannot access GPUs, LightGBM makes more sense because of its faster training time. You can use the saved training time to improve the robustness of your final model. If you have limited resources, such as a stand-alone computer, you should consider that the training time for XGBoost increases linearly with the sample size, while LightGBM requires a much smaller fraction of training time.

6.4.2   *Exploring tree structures*

As previously discussed, GBDTs are complicated algorithms, not inexplicable or unreplicable ones. You just need to reproduce the various decision trees they are made of in a more performing way and combine them to obtain your fast predictions. Both XGboost and LightGBM allow for exploring and extracting their model's structure. In listing 6.16, we take a few steps to demonstrate that. After dumping an XGBoost simple solution on a JSON file, we navigate inside its structure like a graph, using a depth-first search strategy. In depth-first search, the algorithm explores each branch as far as possible before backtracking.

Taking a closer look at the code in listing 6.16, you can notice that in the `traverse_xgb_tree` function, the code recursively explores the tree by first traversing the left subtree (`tree['children'][0]`) and then the right subtree (`tree['children'][1]`). This is evident from the recursive calls `traverse_xgb_tree(tree['children'][0])` and `traverse_xgb_tree(tree['children'][1])`.

Listing 6.16   Extracting XGBoost tree structure

```
import json
import matplotlib.pyplot as plt
from XGBoost import XGBClassifier, plot_tree
from collections import namedtuple

xgb = XGBClassifier(booster='gbtree',
                    objective='reg:logistic',        ◀── Creates an XGBoost classifier
                    n_estimators=10,                      limited to 10 estimators and
                    max_depth=3)                          trees of three levels

model_pipeline = Pipeline(
    [('processing', column_transform),               ◀── Extracts the XGBoost
     ('XGBoost', xgb)])                                   model from the pipeline

model_pipeline.fit(X=data, y=target_median)
model = model_pipeline["XGBoost"]
tree_info = model.get_booster().dump_model(
    "xgb_model.json",
    with_stats=True,                      Dumps the XGBoost
    dump_format="json"                    model's information (the
)                                    ◀──  booster) into a JSON file

fig, ax = plt.subplots(figsize=(12, 15), dpi=300)
ax = plot_tree(
    model, num_trees=0, ax=ax, rankdir='LR    ◀── Creates a plot of the first
)                                                 tree in the ensemble
plt.show()

with open("xgb_model.json", "r") as f:      Retrieves the JSON structure from
    json_model = json.loads(f.read())  ◀──  disk with the model's information

print(f"Number of trees: {len(json_model)}")    Prints the number of trees in
tree_structure = json_model[0]          ◀──      the model and extracts the
                                                 structure of the first tree
```

```
Split = namedtuple("SplitNode", "feature origin gain count threshold")
Leaf = namedtuple("LeafNode", "index origin count")

def extract_xgb_node_info(tree):
    return [tree['split'], tree['origin'], tree['gain'],
            tree['cover'], tree['split_condition']]

def extract_xgb_leaf_info(tree):
    return (
        [tree['nodeid'],
         tree['origin'],
         tree['cover']
        ]
)

def traverse_xgb_tree(tree):
    if not 'origin' in tree:
        tree['origin'] = "="
    if not 'children' in tree:
        return [[Leaf(*extract_xgb_leaf_info(tree))]]
    left_branch = tree['children'][0]
    right_branch = tree['children'][1]
    left_branch['origin'] = '<'
    right_branch['origin'] = '>='
    left_paths = traverse_xgb_tree(left_branch)
    right_paths = traverse_xgb_tree(right_branch)
    node_info = [Split(*extract_xgb_node_info(tree))]
    return [node_info + path for path in left_paths + right_paths]

paths = traverse_xgb_tree(tree_structure)

print(f"Number of paths on tree: {len(paths)}")
print("Path 0:", paths[0])
```

Function extracting various information from a split node in the tree structure

Function extracting information from a leaf node in the tree structure

Function traversing the tree structure recursively to extract paths

The code trains a XGBoost model, saves its tree structure, processes the structure into a readable way, and presents the results to the user:

```
Number of trees: 10
Number of paths on tree: 8
Path 0: [SplitNode(
            feature='f5',
            origin='=',
            gain=19998.9316,
            count=12223.75,
            threshold=0.5),
         SplitNode(
            feature='f2',
            origin='<',
            gain=965.524414,
            count=5871.5,
            threshold=0.5
         ),
         SplitNode(
            feature='f13',
```

```
            origin='<',
            gain=66.1962891,
            count=3756,
            threshold=1.88965869
        ),
        LeafNode(
            index=7,
            origin='<',
            count=3528)
    ]
```

Figure 6.8 compares the obtained outputs with the graphical representation of the complete tree, as provided by the `plot_tree` from the XGBoost package itself.

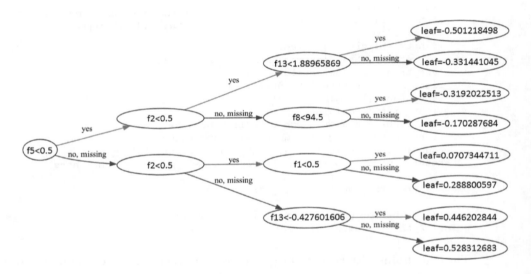

Figure 6.8   XGBoost's `plot_tree` **output**

From the 10 trees built in the model, the code presents the first tree and, among the 8 different paths available from the sample to the prediction leaf, it represents the first path. Visually, this path is the leftmost one. The path is made up of different nodes in sequence. The code reports the name of the used feature, the split branch origin from the previous node (in XGBoost, minor always stands for the left branch, and major is equal to the right branch), the cut threshold, the gain with respect to the objective function, and the resulting reduction in the sample given the split of the dataset. All this information allows you to perfectly replicate the results of every tree of an XGBoost model.

We can also extract the same tree structure from LightGBM, though the approach is a bit different because the LightGBM package follows a few slightly different conventions. For instance, XGBoost always splits the minus than the threshold on the left; LightGBM instead, for each node, defines a rule using minus or major-equal and threshold and splits on the left if the rule is true and on the right if it is false.

Listing 6.17 Extracting LightGBM tree structure

```python
from lightgbm import LGBMClassifier, plot_tree

lgbm = LGBMClassifier(boosting_type='gbdt',
                      n_estimators=10,
                      max_depth=3)

model_pipeline = Pipeline(
    [('processing', column_transform),
     ('lightgbm', lgbm)])

model_pipeline.fit(X=data, y=target_median)
model = model_pipeline["lightgbm"]

tree_info = model._Booster.dump_model()["tree_info"]
tree_structure = tree_info[0]['tree_structure']
plot_tree(
    booster=model._Booster,
    tree_index=0,
    dpi=600
)

Split = namedtuple(
    "SplitNode",
    "feature origin decision_type threshold gain count"
)
Leaf = namedtuple("LeafNode", "index origin count value")

def extract_lgbm_node_info(tree):
    return [tree['split_feature'], tree['origin'], tree['decision_type'],
            tree['threshold'], tree['split_gain'], tree['internal_count']]

def extract_lgbm_leaf_info(tree):
    return [
        tree['leaf_index'],
        tree['origin'],
        tree['leaf_count'],
        tree['leaf_value']
    ]

def traverse_lgbm_tree(tree):
    if not 'origin' in tree:
        tree['origin'] = ""
    if not 'left_child' in tree and not 'right_child' in tree:
        return [[Leaf(*extract_lgbm_leaf_info(tree))]]
    left_branch = tree['left_child']
    right_branch = tree['right_child']
    left_branch['origin'] = 'yes'
    right_branch['origin'] = 'no'
    left_paths = traverse_lgbm_tree(left_branch)
```

Extracts the tree information from the LightGBM model booster

Extracts the structure of the first tree from the tree information

Plots the first tree in the ensemble using the plot_tree function

Function extracting various information from a split node in the LightGBM tree structure

Function extracting information from a leaf node in the LightGBM tree structure

Function recursively traversing the LightGBM tree structure to extract paths

```
        right_paths = traverse_lgbm_tree(right_branch)
        node_info = [Split(*extract_lgbm_node_info(tree))]
        return [node_info + path for path in left_paths + right_paths]

paths = traverse_lgbm_tree(tree_structure)
print(paths[0])
```

The results from this exploration report a path from the structure of the first decision tree in the ensemble:

```
[SplitNode(
    feature=5,
    origin='',
    decision_type='<=',
    threshold=1.0000000180025095e-35,
    gain=20002.19921875,
    count=48895),
 SplitNode(
    feature=2,
    origin='yes',
    decision_type='<=',
    threshold=1.0000000180025095e-35,
    gain=967.0560302734375,
    count=23486),
 SplitNode(
    feature=13,
    origin='yes',
    decision_type='<=',
    threshold=1.8896587976897459,
    gain=67.53350067138672,
    count=15024),
 LeafNode(
    index=0,
    origin='yes',
    count=14112,
    value=-0.16892421857257725)
]
```

Figure 6.9 shows the entire tree plotted by the `plot_tree` function, this time from the LightGBM package.

The tree is plotted horizontally from left to right. We can check that the path returned by the code is the uppermost one, ending in leaf 0.

6.4.3   *Speeding up by GBDTs and compiling*

When the number of cases or the available features are many, even the faster LightGBM may take a long time to train a model on such data. At training time, you can overcome long waits by reducing the cases and features handled by smaller values of the parameter `subsample` for limiting the cases involved in building each decision tree and the parameter `colsample_bytree` for limiting the number of features considered at tree splitting time. However, reducing cases or features may not be optimal for getting the best results from your model. An alternative is using GPUs, which are widespread

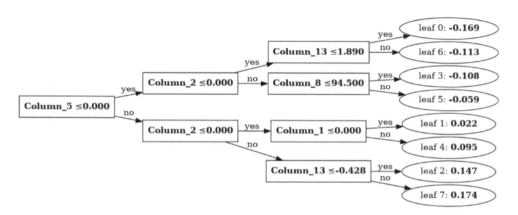

Figure 6.9   LightGBM's `plot_tree` **output**

because they utilize deep learning models. GPUs can speed up training operations, especially with XGBoost, and, in a lesser but significant way, with LightGBM models.

With XGBoost, from a modeling point of view, using your GPU is quite straightforward: you just need to specify `"gpu_hist"` as a value for the `tree_method` parameter. With the new 2.0.0 version, such a method is, however, deprecated, and users can now instead specify the used device by the parameter `device`. You can set it to `"cpu"` for XGBoost to execute on CPU or `device="cuda"` as well as `device="gpu"` to have it run on a CUDA-powered GPU, which is the only option at the moment, but in the future, more GPU types will be supported. If you have multiple GPUs, you can specify their ordinal to choose a particular one; for instance, `device="cuda:1"` will execute on your second GPU device.

For XGBoost to perform, you need at least CUDA 11.00 installed and a GPU with a compute capability 5.0. If you have more GPUs available, you can specify which to use by the `gpu_id` parameter, which represents the GPU device ordinal reported by CUDA runtime (usually set to zero if you have a single GPU). In this way, XGBoost moves the growth of decision trees to the GPU memory and processors, thus obtaining a relevant speed of operations, especially feature histograms, as described in the paper "Accelerating the XGBoost Algorithm Using GPU Computing" by Mitchell and Frank (https://peerj.com/articles/cs-127/).

Once GPU trains a model, it can be used for prediction on a machine with a GPU. All you have to set is the `predictor` parameter to `gpu_predictor` or to `cpu_predictor` if you want to use your CPU. Selecting the predictor parameter to GPU can also speed up things when you have to compute SHAP values and SHAP interaction values for model interpretability:

```
model.set_param({"predictor": "gpu_predictor"})
shap_values = model.predict(X, pred_contribs=True)
shap_interaction_values = model.predict(X, pred_interactions=True)
```

Although using a GPU with XGBoost is easy, it becomes a little bit trickier with LightGBM. LightGBM doesn't have an option for GPU running but rather requires a special version of itself to be compiled for the purpose. Depending on your operating system (Windows, Linux/Ubuntu, MacOS), the compilation may be less or more challenging. Instructions are available at https://mng.bz/nRg5 for POSIX systems and at https://mng.bz/vK8p for Windows systems. However, if you have all the prerequisites ready on your system as stated by the instructions at https://mng.bz/4aJg, you can just require to directly install it using the pip install instruction on your shell or command prompt:

```
pip install lightgbm --install-option=--gpu
```

Once everything has been installed, you need to set the parameter `device` to `gpu` Don't expect astonishing performance improvements, however. As stated by LightGBM authors (see https://mng.bz/vK8p), the best results are obtained on large-scale and dense datasets because of the inefficient data turnover that causes latencies when working on smaller datasets. In addition, setting a lower number of bins for the histogram algorithm will make the GPU work more efficiently with the LightGBM. The suggestion is to set `max_bin=15` and single precision, `gpu_use_dp=false`, for the best performances.

GPUs are quite useful for speeding up training, but there are more options at prediction time. With tree structures so readily available, as we have seen in the previous section, it has been possible for specific projects to use such information for rebuilding prediction trees using more performing programming languages such as C, JAVA, or LLVM that can turn your model into pure assembly code. Such tree-compiling projects aim for fast prediction and easier deployment. Examples are Treelite (https://github.com/dmlc/treelite), which can read models produced by XGBoost, LightGBM, and even Scikit-learn, and lleaves (https://github.com/siboehm/lleaves), which is a project for LightGBM only.

Starting from Treelite, this project strives to be a universal model exchange and serialization format for decision tree forests. It compiles your GBDT into C or Java with the least possible dependencies, so you can easily deploy it into any system. To have it tested, you must install a few packages at the command line: `pip install t12cgen treelite treelite_runtime`.

Listing 6.18   XGBoost prediction speedup by Treelite

```
import treelite
import treelite_runtime
import t12cgen

xgb = XGBClassifier(booster='gbtree',
                    objective='reg:logistic',
                    n_estimators=10,
                    max_depth=3)
```

```
model_pipeline = Pipeline(
    [('processing', column_transform),
     ('XGBoost', xgb)])

model_pipeline.fit(X=data, y=target_median)
model = model_pipeline["XGBoost"]

model.save_model("./xgb_model.json")
treelite_model = treelite.Model.load("./xgb_model.json",
model_format="XGBoost_json")
tl2cgen.generate_c_code(treelite_model, dirpath="./",
params={"parallel_comp": 4})
tl2cgen.export_lib(treelite_model, toolchain="gcc",
libpath="./xgb_model.so",
                    params={"parallel_comp": 4})

predictor = tl2cgen.Predictor("./xgb_model.so")
X = model_pipeline["processing"].transform(data)
dmat = tl2cgen.DMatrix(X)
predictor.predict(dmat)
```

Saves the XGBoost model to a JSON file

Loads the XGBoost model in Treelite format from the JSON file

Generates C code from the Treelite model and exports it as a shared library

Transforms the input data using the preprocessing steps defined in the pipeline

Creates a Treelite DMatrix from the transformed data, compatible with the exported Treelite model

The result is a compiled model that, inside a Python script, can return predictions in a much faster fashion. Predictors must always be transformed beforehand since the pipeline is not part of the compiling. Only the model is. In addition, you also have to convert the data in DMatrix format, the native XGBoost data format, before it is sent to the compiled model.

Developed by Simon Boehm, lleaves promises x10 speed up by LLVM compiling into assembly based on the text tree structure that can be outputted from a LightGBM model. After having installed the package by a `pip install leaves` instruction on the command line, you can obtain a speed up by following these steps.

Listing 6.19 LightGBM prediction speedup by `lleaves`

```
import lleaves

lgbm = LGBMClassifier(boosting_type='gbdt',
                      n_estimators=10,
                      max_depth=3)

model_pipeline = Pipeline(
    [('processing', column_transform),
     ('lightgbm', lgbm)])

model_pipeline.fit(X=data, y=target_median)
model = model_pipeline["lightgbm"]

model.booster_.save_model('lgb_model.txt')

llvm_model = lleaves.Model(model_file="lgb_model.txt")
```

Saves the LightGBM model to a text file

Loads the LightGBM model using the lleaves library

```
llvm_model.compile()
X = model_pipeline["processing"].transform(data)
llvm_model.predict(X)
```

Compiles the loaded
LightGBM model into
LLVM representation

Transforms the input data
using the preprocessing steps
defined in the pipeline

Also, in this case, the model is compiled and can predict in a faster way inside a Python script. From a general point of view, lleaves, though limited only to LightGBM, is a compiling solution that requires many fewer settings and specifications from the user, resulting in a much simpler and straightforward usage.

Summary

- Among processing problems, missing data is one of the most problematic. If your data is MCR or is just MAR because missing patterns are related to the other features, multivariate imputation can use the correlations among predictors in a dataset to impute missing values.
- Both XGBoost and LightGBM algorithms automatically handle missing data by assigning them to the side that minimizes the loss function the most in each split.
- When a categorical presents high cardinality because of its many labels, you can use target encoding, which gained popularity in Kaggle competitions. Target encoding is a way to transform the values in a categorical feature into their corresponding expected target values.
- PDP is a model-agnostic chart technique that explains how features and the target are related by means of the model you have trained. It is beneficial because it helps you better model the relationship between the predictive feature and the target if you notice it is nonlinear and complex.
- XGBoost, thanks to packages such as XGBFIR, can inform you about the most important interactions between predictive features.
- By employing effective feature selection techniques, you can pinpoint and retain the most relevant features that contribute significantly to the machine learning process. Standard techniques to handle feature selection are stability selection based on L1 regularization for linear models, iterative selection, and Boruta for tree ensembles:
  - Based on L1 regularization, stability selection aims to identify features that consistently appear as important across multiple subsets, indicating their robustness and reducing the likelihood of selecting features by chance or noise.
  - Boruta is a procedure to determine if a feature is relevant in a machine learning problem by relying on the internal parameters of the model, such as coefficients in linear models or importance values based on gain, such as in decision trees and their ensembles.

- Iterative selection additions by forward selection, or removes by backward elimination, features from your selection based on their performance on the prediction in a greedy fashion, leaving only the essential features for your prediction.

- By optimizing hyperparameters, you can gain another performance boost to your classical machine learning model. Apart from manually setting the hyperparameters, depending on the model you are working on, grid search, random search, successive halving, and Bayesian optimization are popular optimization methods within the data science community:

  - Grid search simply works by searching through all the possible combinations of hyperparameters' values. For every hyperparameter you want to test, you pick a sequence of values and iterate through all their combinations exhaustively.

  - Random search optimization decides what values to test by randomly drawing them from the search space. The technique is particularly effective if you know little about your hyperparameters, if there are many of them, and if some are irrelevant but you don't know which ones.

  - Successive halving is a wrapper of the previously discussed strategies. It works as a tournament between sets of hyperparameters, where first, they are tested using a few computational resources. Then, only a fraction of the best is further tested using more resources. In the end, there will be only one surviving set of hyperparameters.

  - Bayesian optimization uses informed search to find the best set of hyperparameters. It builds a model of the hyperparameter's behavior based on prior knowledge of how it works on the data problem. Then it sets a series of experiments to explore further and refine its own internal model, exploit the previous trials, and validate the actual performances of a solution.

- Both XGBoost and LightGBM have specific settings and options that are not commonly found in other machine learning algorithms, such as the possibility of extracting and representing their internal structure and speeding up their execution by GPU use and compiling.

7
An end-to-end example using XGBoost

This chapter covers

- Gathering and preparing data from the internet, using generative AI to help
- Drafting a baseline and first tentative model to be optimized
- Figuring out how the model works and inspecting it

This chapter concludes our overview of classical machine learning for tabular data. To wrap things up, we'll work through a complete example from the field of data journalism. Along the way, we'll summarize all the concepts and techniques we've used so far. We will also use a generative AI tool, ChatGPT, to help you get the job done and demonstrate a few use cases where having a large language model (LLM) can improve your work with tabular data.

We will finally build a model to predict prices, this time using a regression-based approach. Doing this will help us understand how the model works and why it performs in a particular manner to gain further insights into the pricing dynamics for Airbnb listings and challenge our initial hypothesis regarding how pricing happens for short-term rentals.

7.1   *Preparing and exploring your data*

To get started, we'll focus on a different dataset as we continue our analysis of short-term and long-term Airbnb rental listings in New York City. This dataset comes directly from the Inside Airbnb Network initiative (http://insideairbnb.com/), "a mission-driven project that provides data and advocacy about Airbnb's effect on residential communities." We will also be using public data from other online services, such as Foursquare (https://foursquare.com), the social network and geolocation technology company.

Following the data acquisition phase, we will organize and conduct comprehensive feature engineering based on relevant business hypotheses to extract valuable insights for our modeling stage. During this process, we will also perform basic exploratory analysis on our predictors and target variables, making necessary adjustments or exclusions of examples and features to ensure we get the optimal data for our project.

7.1.1   *Using generative AI to help prepare data*

ChatGPT is an advanced language model developed by OpenAI. To create and train a generative pretrained transformer (GPT) model like ChatGPT, OpenAI applied vast amounts of diverse internet text to help the model learn to understand and generate human-like text by predicting the next word in a sequence of words based on its contextual understanding. This pretraining allows ChatGPT to capture grammar, context, and even nuanced information, but it is not enough to make it a helpful assistant in every circumstance. In fact, these models have the potential to produce outputs that are inaccurate or harmful or contain toxic content. The reason for this is that the training dataset—that is, the internet—contains text that is varied and, at times, unreliable. To enhance the safety, utility, and alignment of ChatGPT models, a method known as reinforcement learning from human feedback is employed. In the reinforcement learning from human feedback process, human labelers provide feedback illustrating the preferred model behavior, and they evaluate multiple outputs produced by the model through ranking. This data is subsequently utilized to fine-tune GPT-3.5 further, refining its responses based on the human feedback.

To use the free version of ChatGPT (at the moment, that is ChatGPT 3.5, which is updated with information up to January 2022), you must first create an account at https://chat.openai.com. Once you have an account, you can start using ChatGPT by simply entering a prompt. A prompt, in the context of an LLM like ChatGPT, is a written instruction or input provided to the model to generate a specific output. It serves as a query or request that guides the model in producing a relevant response. Prompts can vary in complexity, ranging from simple commands to more detailed descriptions or inquiries, and they play a crucial role in shaping the nature of the language model's output. The prompt's quality and clarity significantly influence the generated content's accuracy and relevance, but selecting the right prompt is not always straightforward.

The effectiveness of different prompts can vary depending on the specific language model they are designed for. Each language model has its own strengths, weaknesses, and nuances, making it essential to tailor prompts accordingly. When working with ChatGPT, for instance, we obtained the best results starting with simple prompts, evaluating their results, and then proceeding by adding more specifications to the prompt to refine the results toward our expectations. ChatGPT tend to work better when you tell it to "write," "create," "show me how to," or "summarize." Sometimes showing examples and how you expect ChatGPT to elaborate them is quite helpful. Also, let ChatGPT know your expectations in terms of the answer, like how long the response should be, what information it should include, if you want just code as a result or just text, and how the answer should be structured in return; for instance, you could ask using the JSON format or a Python style list.

LLMs such as ChatGPT, and the related Copilot feature in GitHub, have proven to be useful assistants for a variety of programming tasks. This usefulness applies to tabular data applications. You can ask these models various questions or request assistance in coding tasks, and they can assist by providing code snippets, explanations about how code works, or guidance in using specific commands or algorithms. However, although LLMs such as ChatGPT can assist users by generating code snippets for data manipulation, cleaning, and transformation tasks, as well as provide explanations and guidance on various statistical and machine learning techniques applicable to tabular datasets, our intention in this chapter is to show a few select and less obvious LLM capabilities that you can use for your tabular data analysis and modeling.

7.1.2 Getting and preparing your data

As a starting point, we will navigate the Inside Airbnb Network website (http://insideairbnb.com/) and find the data we need. Our goal is to explore the situation in a completely different city: Tokyo. First, you have to manually download the data and store it in a working directory on your computer or cloud instance. To do so, on the home page of the Inside Airbnb Network initiative, as shown in figure 7.1, in the Data menu, choose Get the Data.

Figure 7.1   Choosing from the Data menu

Once you choose the menu item, you will be moved to a new page containing Data Downloads, presenting various cities and their data file to be downloaded. Scroll the page until you find the city of Tokyo.

Figure 7.2 shows the portion of the page containing the data files for Tokyo as they were at the time of writing this book.

Tokyo, Kantō, Japan

29 June, 2023 (Explore)

Country/City	File Name	Description
Tokyo	listings.csv.gz	Detailed Listings data
Tokyo	calendar.csv.gz	Detailed Calendar Data
Tokyo	reviews.csv.gz	Detailed Review Data
Tokyo	listings.csv	Summary information and metrics for listings in Tokyo (good for visualisations).
Tokyo	reviews.csv	Summary Review data and Listing ID (to facilitate time based analytics and visualisations linked to a listing).
Tokyo	neighbourhoods.csv	Neighbourhood list for geo filter. Sourced from city or open source GIS files.
Tokyo	neighbourhoods.geojson	GeoJSON file of neighbourhoods of the city.

show archived data
(generally quarterly data for the last 12 months. For additional data, make an archived data request.)

Figure 7.2   The Tokyo Data Downloads section

For our analysis, we need two files from the page: `listings.csv`, which contains the summary listings and other information about the Airbnb accommodations in Tokyo, and `calendar.csv.gz`, a zipped file containing `calendar.csv`, a dataset containing occupancy and price information for a given year for each listing. Hover over the links, right-click, and select to save them to disk in your working directory. For example, in Google Chrome, you need to select "Save link as," and in Mozilla Firefox, you have to select "Save target as." At this point, you will just need to extract the files into your working directory. Once the files we need are unzipped in our local directory, we can ingest them into a pandas DataFrame using the `read_csv` command:

```
import pandas as pd
summary_listings = pd.read_csv("listings.csv")
```

With the list and type of columns, we can get an idea of the kind of data we will be dealing with:

```
summary_listings.dtypes
```

The list comprises 18 columns, largely the same as the Airbnb NYC dataset introduced in chapter 3. Here we describe each of them:

- `id`—A unique identifier for each listing on Airbnb. It is an `int64` data type, meaning it is a numerical ID representation. In other tables, it can be referred to as `listing_id`.
- `name`—The description of the Airbnb listing. It is of the `object` data type, which typically represents a string or text.
- `host_id`—A unique identifier for each host on Airbnb. It is an `int64` data type.
- `host_name`—The name of the host who owns the listing. It is of the `object` data type.
- `neighbourhood_group`—Represents the broader area or region the neighborhood belongs to. It is stored as a `float64` data type, but it is important to note that using a float data type to represent groups or categories is uncommon. In this case, the presence of float values indicates that the data for this field is entirely made up of missing values.
- `neighbourhood`—The specific neighborhood where the listing is located. It is of the `object` data type.
- `latitude`—The latitude coordinates of the listing's location. It is of the `float64` data type.
- `longitude`—The longitude coordinates of the listing's location. It is of the `float64` data type.
- `room_type`—The type of room or accommodation offered in the listing (e.g., entire home/apartment, private room, shared room). It is of the `object` data type.
- `price`—The price per night to rent the listing. It is of the `int64` data type, representing an integer price value.
- `minimum_nights`—The minimum number of nights that is required for booking the listing. It is of the `int64` data type.
- `number_of_reviews`—The total number of reviews received by the listing. It is of the `int64` data type.
- `last_review`—The date of the last review received by the listing. It is of the `object` data type, which could represent date and time information, but it might require further parsing to be used effectively.
- `reviews_per_month`—The average number of reviews per month for the listing. It is of the `float64` data type.
- `calculated_host_listings_count`—The total number of listings the host has on Airbnb. It is of the `int64` data type.
- `availability_365`—The number of days the listing is available for booking in a year (out of 365 days). It is of the `int64` data type.
- `number_of_reviews_ltm`—The number of reviews received in the last 12 months. It is of the `int64` data type.

- `license`—The license number or information related to the listing. It is of the `object` data type, which typically represents a string or text.

We can safely ignore features such as `host_id`, `host_name`, `neighbourhood_group` (because they are completely missing), or `license` (which is a kind of identifier based on the host's license).

As for the other features, whereas most of them are numeric, the `name` feature is a string containing various pieces of information to be extracted based on how the data has been organized. By visualizing a single example from it, we can have an idea of its organization:

```
summary_listings['name'].iloc[0]
```

The string is arranged into five distinct parts separated by conventional signs and with some kind of partially structured and repeated content:

```
'Rental unit in Sumida · ★4.78 · 1 bedroom · 2 beds · 1 bath'
```

The first portion of the string is a description of the unit type and location. The second portion is the average score received from guests. The third portion is the number of bedrooms, the fourth portion is the number of beds, and the last is the number of bathrooms.

Apart from the numeric values, we can also extract some specific information related to the kind of accommodation or services offered—for instance, if the apartment is a studio, if the bath is shared, and if it is a half-bath (a room with a toilet and washbasin but no bath or shower). We can deal with such information by creating simple string correspondence checks and obtaining a binary feature pointing out the presence or absence of the characteristic or using regex commands. Regex (short for regular expressions) commands are a sequence of characters constituting a search pattern. They are used for pattern matching within strings. Table 7.1 shows the transformations we apply to the description field and highlights what strings we strive to match, what regex command we use, and what resulting feature we obtain.

Table 7.1 Regex commands for feature engineering

Matched description	Regex	Resulting feature
Text that starts with "in," followed by a space, then captures any characters until another space, and ends with a dot	`r'in\s(.*?)\s·'`	Area of Tokyo of the listing
Text that starts with the character "★" (a star), followed by one or more digits, a dot, and one or more additional digits (e.g., ★4.5)	`r'★(\d+\.\d+)'`	Star ratings

Table 7.1   Regex commands for feature engineering (*continued*)

Matched description	Regex	Resulting feature
Text containing a numerical value followed by zero or more whitespace characters and the words "bedroom" or "bedrooms" (with or without the "s" at the end)	`r'(\d+)\s*(?:bedroom` `|bedrooms)'`	Number of bedrooms
Text containing a numerical value followed by one or more whitespace characters and the word "bed" or "beds" as a whole word (with or without the "s" at the end)	`r'(\d+)\s+(?:beds?\b)'`	Number of beds
Text containing a numerical value representing the number of baths	`r'(?P<baths>\d+)\s*(shared\` `s+)?(?:half-)?baths?\b'`	Number of baths

Working with regex commands is a bit complicated. Hence this is the first application where generative AI could help. Most LLMs, such as ChatGPT, have a good knowledge of different programming languages (in particular, most of them are quite strong in Python) because they have been trained on text and information extracted from the internet, where there is plenty of information about how to code even very specific problems. In our case, showing an example of the strings in the prompt and asking for the desired information to be extracted should do the trick:

```
I have a series of strings in this format: 'Rental unit in Sumida · ★4.78
· 1 bedroom · 2 beds · 1 bath' Show me a series of regex commands in
order to extract the following information: 1) the area of Tokyo of the
listing 2) the star ratings expressed as floats 3) the number of bedrooms
4) the number of beds 5) the number of baths.
```

The output should be something already suitable for usage, arranged in blocks of code snippets with some explanation about the extraction rule, such as shown in figure 7.3.

Without being asked, the language model should simply decide to propose a Python-based solution, and you just click on the "Copy code" icon on top of the code listing to copy the snippet on the clipboard and then paste it into your notebook or IDE editor.

Usually, the solutions provided may vary from query to query and can differ from the solution we provided in the table. This is because LLMs are, in the end, probabilistic machines. Temperature is the parameter usually set to influence the randomness of the model's output. It is used during text generation to control the generated content's creativity. In simple terms, temperature affects the likelihood of the model choosing the next word in a sequence. Low-temperature values result in more deterministic and expected output. In contrast, high-temperature values introduce more randomness

ChatGPT

Certainly! You can use regular expressions to extract information from strings with a consistent format. Here are examples of regex commands for each of the requested pieces of information:

1. **Area of Tokyo:**

```python
import re

text = 'Rental unit in Sumida · *4.78 · 1 bedroom · 2 beds · 1 bath'

# Assuming the area name is before '.'
area_match = re.search(r'in\s(.*?)\s·', text)
area_of_tokyo = area_match.group(1) if area_match else None

print("Area of Tokyo:", area_of_tokyo)
```

Figure 7.3   Results from a prompt on regex processing on ChatGPT 3.5

and creativity in the generated output because the model tends to choose less probable words.

After getting an apparently useful answer, one important step prior to using the solutions proposed by an LLM is to test them on more examples than the one or two shown in the prompt. Such a step may reveal that the code is not working well, and you may also need to tell the model that the example doesn't work or signal the problem you are experiencing by more detailed instructions to the model. For instance, we found that sometimes the commands didn't work properly if there were upper-case letters in some parts of the input string. Hence, we had to find a supplemental solution. All these regex commands operate lowercase, thanks to the re.IGNORECASE flag, which makes the match operating case insensitive. In the following listing, we proceed to extract information from the text descriptions using the regex commands we found using ChatGPT.

Listing 7.1   Extracting information from text descriptions

```python
import pandas as pd
import re

classification_list = [
    'aparthotel', 'barn', 'bed and breakfast', 'boutique hotel',
    'bungalow', 'cabin', 'camper/rv', 'chalet', 'condo', 'cottage',
    'earthen home', 'farm stay', 'guest suite', 'guesthouse', 'home',
    'hostel', 'hotel', 'houseboat', 'hut', 'loft', 'place to stay',
    'rental unit', 'resort', 'ryokan', 'serviced apartment',
    'tiny home', 'townhouse', 'treehouse', 'vacation home', 'villa']
```

```
summary_listings = summary_listings.assign(
    type_of_accommodation=(
        summary_listings['name']
        .str.extract(
            f"({'|'.join(classification_list)})",
            flags=re.IGNORECASE)),
    area_of_tokyo=(
        summary_listings['name']
        .str.extract(
            r'in\s(.*?)\s·',
            flags=re.IGNORECASE)),
    score=(
        summary_listings['name']
        .str.extract(
            r'★(\d+\.\d+)',
            flags=re.IGNORECASE)
        .astype(float)),
    number_of_bedrooms=(
        summary_listings['name']
        .str.extract(
            r'(\d+)\s*(?:bedroom|bedrooms)',
            flags=re.IGNORECASE)
        .fillna(0)
        .astype(int)),
    number_of_beds=(
        summary_listings['name']
        .str.extract(
            r'(\d+)\s+(?:beds?\b)',
            flags=re.IGNORECASE)
        .fillna(0)
        .astype(int)),
    number_of_baths=(
        summary_listings['name']
        .str.extract(
            r'(?P<baths>\d+)\s*(shared\s+)?' +
            r'(?:half-)?baths?\b',
            flags=re.IGNORECASE)["baths"]
        .fillna(0)
        .astype(int)),
)
```

◄── Extracts the type of accommodation from a list of options

◄── Extracts the area of Tokyo mentioned in the listing name

◄── Extracts the rating score from a star symbol followed by a numerical value

◄── Extracts the number of bedrooms from the listing name

◄── Extracts the number of beds from the listing name

◄── Extracts the number of baths from the listing name

Listing 7.2 completes the feature extraction work by creating additional Boolean columns based on specific keywords in the name column. It computes two calculated features based on a difference telling us the number of days between today's date and the last_review date and a ratio expressing how the number of reviews in the last year relates to the total number of reviews. Such a ratio can reveal if the bulk of reviews is recent or if the listing has been successful mainly in the past.

Listing 7.2 **Extracting binary flags and time information**

```
import numpy as np
import pandas as pd
from datetime import datetime
```

```
summary_listings = summary_listings.assign(
    is_new=(summary_listings['name']
            .str.contains('new', case=False)
            .astype(int)),
    is_studio=(summary_listings['name']
            .str.contains('studio', case=False)
            .astype(int)),
    has_shared_bath=(summary_listings['name']
                .str.contains('shared', case=False)
                .astype(int)),
    has_half_bath=(summary_listings['name']
            .str.contains('half', case=False)
            .astype(int)),
)

summary_listings['days_since_last_review'] = (
    datetime.today() -
    pd.to_datetime(
        summary_listings['last_review'])
).dt.days
summary_listings['days_since_last_review'] = (
    summary_listings['days_since_last_review'] -
    summary_listings['days_since_last_review'].min()
)

zero_reviews = summary_listings['number_of_reviews'] == 0
ratio = summary_listings['number_of_reviews_ltm'] /
summary_listings['number_of_reviews']
summary_listings['number_of_reviews_ltm_ratio'] = (
    np.where(zero_reviews, 0, ratio)
)
```

Checks if the word "new" is present in the name (case-insensitive)

Checks if the word "studio" is present in the name (case-insensitive)

Checks if the word "shared" is present in the name (case-insensitive)

Checks if the word "half" is present in the name (case-insensitive)

Calculates the number of days between today's date and the last_review date

Calculates the ratio of number_ of_reviews_ltm to number_of_ reviews for each listing

The summary_listings data also has a price feature that we could use as a target. Still, we prefer to create it by aggregating the calendar.csv data to decide whether to pick an average of all the prices, the minimum, or the maximum. The calendar .csv contains information for each day about the availability of the accommodation, its price (also adjusted for discounts), and the minimum and maximum number of nights allowed for booking at that time. We are interested in processing the adjusted price as a target, representing the effective market price of the accommodation.

Listing 7.3 Creating the target from daily listings

```
calendar = pd.read_csv("calendar.csv")

calendar["adjusted_price"] = (
    calendar["adjusted_price"]
    .apply(lambda x: float(
        x.replace('$', '')
         .replace(',', '')))
    )
)
```

Removes the dollar sign ($) and commas (,) from the values and then converts them to float

```
price_stats = (
    calendar.groupby('listing_id')['adjusted_price']   ◄── A group by operation
    .agg(['mean', 'min', 'max'])                            on the calendar
)                                                           DataFrame based on
            ◄── Calculates three statistics for the         the listing_id column
                adjusted_price column: the mean,
                minimum, and maximum values
```

After completing the aggregation, we can check the result by requiring the first five rows of this newly created dataset:

```
price_stats.head()
```

Figure 7.4 verifies how we now have both a mean price per listing available together with the maximum and minimum prices.

listing_id	mean	min	max
197677	11000.000000	11000.0	11000.0
776070	7208.000000	7208.0	7208.0
905944	24184.243836	23066.0	28833.0
1016831	19383.561644	15000.0	22000.0
1196177	29081.934247	10000.0	33106.0

Figure 7.4   Price statistics for Airbnb listings

We will save this `price_stats` DataFrame and concentrate in the next section on improving the number and effectiveness of our features.

7.1.3   Engineering more complex features

Real estate assets have a pretty peculiar behavior, distinguishable from other products or services you find on the market. An adage in the real estate business mentions that all that matters when dealing with buildings and facilities is "location, location, location." The position of an apartment in a city or a road can make a difference to the value of a property. We will adopt this adage for Airbnb listings and develop some feature engineering based on location.

As a first step, we will reprise the example from the previous chapter, where we created small geographic subdivisions that we later target encoded. By this approach, you should be able to capture the specific characteristics of an area, though it will be difficult to explain why renting in one particular location costs more than in others. We should prepare more specific features to provide some explainability to listings in Tokyo. Here is another point where generative AI can come to the aid of the tabular data practitioner by providing help in the form of suggestions and idea generation.

LLMs have sifted through more data than you can imagine, and if queried with enough details (and some role-playing, i.e., asking them to personify an expert proficient in a specific field), they can return hints and reflections that could have cost you multiple hours of research and readings on the web.

Our prompt for ChatGPT is

> You are an expert data scientist and you have downloaded a dataset containing summarized Airbnb listings. This is the structure of the dataset: id (int64), name (object), neighbourhood (object), latitude (float64), longitude (float64), room_type (object), price (int64), minimum_nights (int64), number_of_reviews (int64), last_review (object), reviews_per_month (float64), calculated_host_listings_count (int64), availability_365 (int64), number_of_reviews_ltm (int64). You are training a machine learning model to predict the price of listings. Which features should you engineer to improve the performance of the model?

Our strategy is to set a persona ("you are an expert data scientist") and to provide some further information about the features available (removing the features that we actually already decided not to use) and the target variable. Here we also used the fact that we expected ChatGPT to already know something about the dataset we were using ("a dataset containing summarized Airbnb listings"), but you can also propose less known problems to the LLM by briefly describing the dataset, including the types of features and their relationships to each other. In addition, if you have any domain expertise relevant to the dataset, for instance, any hypotheses about how the features in the dataset might be related to the target variable, share them with the LLM. This information can help it identify features that may be important for the task. Moreover, providing a list of the existing features in the dataset, as we did, may not be enough for more challenging tasks. Providing an explanation or description of each variable and clearly stating the objective of your machine learning model, such as predicting customer churn, estimating real estate values, or forecasting sales, will help the LLM identify gaps or opportunities for creating new well-engineered features.

The following are the suggested features, or feature types, to strive to generate to obtain the best results in our dataset and type of problem, as stated by ChatGPT:

- *Distance from key locations*—Calculate the distance of each listing from key locations or landmarks in the city. This can be done using the latitude and longitude information.

- *Neighborhood statistics*—Aggregate statistics for each neighborhood, such as the average price, minimum and maximum prices, and the number of listings in each neighborhood.

- *Room type encoding*—Convert the categorical variable `room_type` into numerical values using one-hot encoding or label encoding.

- *Temporal features*—Extract relevant features from the `last_review` column, such as the month or season of the last review or the time since the last review.

- *Host experience*—Combine information from `calculated_host_listings_count` and `number_of_reviews_ltm` to create a feature representing the host's experience or popularity.
- *Booking density*—Calculate the ratio of `number_of_reviews` to `availability_365` to represent how frequently a listing is booked relative to its availability.
- *Review sentiment*—If you have access to the actual review texts, you can use natural language processing techniques to analyze sentiment and extract sentiment-based features.
- *Interaction terms*—Create interaction terms between relevant features, such as the product of `minimum_nights` and `availability_365` to capture the overall availability for longer stays.
- *Price binning*—Convert the continuous `price` variable into bins or categories, creating a new categorical feature representing different price ranges.
- *Geographical clustering*—Use clustering algorithms to group listings based on geographical proximity. This can capture spatial patterns in pricing.

Of the proposed points, a few do resonate with our experience, such as computing distance from key locations and neighborhood statistics or creating geographical clustering. Also, we already provided room-type encoding with our previous work on text fields and regex commands. Leaving aside review sentiment and price binning (price is actually our target), what is left is a set of ideas that can guide or inspire you to improve your work. Use the outputs of LLMs to your advantage, but don't forget that your previous knowledge, experience, sensibility, and critical thinking can play an even more important role in the task of a tabular data analysis and that LLMs are just facilitators in your work.

Keeping in mind the proposed features suggested by ChatGPT, we proceed to create some of them. Regarding geographical clustering, you can find all you need in listing 7.4 to create a high cardinality geographical feature from coordinates. Later, in the data pipeline, we will target encode the high cardinality categorical feature we are going to generate with the code.

Listing 7.4   Creating a high cardinality geographical feature

```
def bin_2_cat(feature, bins=32):
    min_value = feature.min()
    bin_size = (feature.max() - min_value) / bins
    return ((feature - min_value) / bin_size).astype(int)
```
Discretizes the latitude and longitude by bin size

```
summary_listings['coordinates'] = (
    bin_2_cat(summary_listings['latitude']) *
    1000 +
    bin_2_cat(summary_listings['longitude'])
)
```
Composes the new coordinates feature by summing the discretized latitude and longitude

```
print(summary_listings['coordinates'].nunique())
```

This code generates a feature with 317 unique values. We covered all the Tokyo municipalities in a 32 × 32 grid, which means potentially 1,024 values. Only 317 of these coordinates contain a listing, meaning that in the future, our model can effectively predict based on this feature only if a new listing falls in one of the 317 slots previously defined. In case a new area appears, thanks to the target encoder novelty dealing capabilities (see the description of the `handle_unknown` parameter at https://mng.bz/oK1p), we can simply impute unknown values to the target means using the setting `handle_unknown=“value”`.

A critical aspect of the Tokyo real estate market is that there is an important geographical center for cultural and historical reasons, which is the Imperial Palace. Locations near this site tend to have higher real estate valuations, and some of Japan's most expensive flats are located close to the Imperial Palace. We try to reflect this reality by creating a feature comparing the location of our Airbnb accommodation with the area of the Imperial Palace (which can be taken from sites such as latlong.net: https://mng.bz/nRW2). For distances, we convert the value into meters using a formula that involves the cosine of the radiants multiplied by a conversion factor for the measure to be intelligible to a human examination. We also adopt the Manhattan distance for better-representing distances in a city, which is the summed difference in absolute values between the latitudes and longitudes.

Listing 7.5   Computing a distance metric from the city center

```
imperial_palace_lat = 35.6841822633
imperial_palace_lon = 139.751471994

def degrees_to_meters(distance_degrees, latitude):
    conversion_factor = 111000
    distance_meters = (distance_degrees * conversion_factor
                        * np.cos(np.radians(latitude)))
    return distance_meters

distance_degrees = (
    np.abs(
        summary_listings['latitude']
        imperial_palace_lat) +
    np.abs(
        summary_listings['longitude']
        imperial_palace_lon)
)

summary_listings['imperial_palace_distance'] = (
    degrees_to_meters(distance_degrees,
    summary_listings['latitude']
)
```

Conversion factor representing the approximate number of meters per degree of latitude

Calculates the distance in meters by multiplying the degree-based distance by the conversion factor and adjusting for the latitude's cosine

Calculates the absolute distance in degrees by subtracting the Imperial Palace's latitude and longitude from the values in the dataset

When dealing with coordinates inside a city, the choice between Euclidean distance and Manhattan distance as a feature for machine learning depends on the specific context and the problem you are trying to solve:

- *Euclidean distance* is based on the straight-line distance between two points in an Euclidean space. It assumes a direct path between the points and can be more suitable when considering physical distances. You may also hear it referred to as the *L2 norm*, which instead is a mathematical concept referring to the distance between the vector and the origin of the vector space. Since the L2 norm is based on the Euclidean distance formula, it is used interchangeably because it is a closely related mathematical concept.

- *Manhattan distance*, also known as city block distance or taxicab distance, measures the distance between two points by adding up the absolute differences between their coordinates. It considers only horizontal and vertical movements and disregards diagonal paths. Similarly to the Euclidean distance, you may hear the Manhattan distance referred to as the *L1 norm* when operating with vectors and vector spaces.

Manhattan distance can be more appropriate when considering the actual movement or navigation within a city, where travel often occurs along streets and road networks. Considering that coordinates are inside a city, where the road network structure and navigation along streets matter, Manhattan distance might be more suitable for capturing the movement and accessibility between locations. It aligns with the concept of following the roads and making right-angle turns.

After calculating the `imperial_palace_distance` feature, we can examine its average value, expressed in meters, using the following code:

```
summary_listings.imperial_palace_distance.mean()
```

The result shows that the average distance to the Imperial Palace is around 7.9 kilometers.

Next, we can identify the listing that is located nearest to the Imperial Palace. To achieve this, we can use the `idxmin()` function to find the index of the listing with the minimum distance and then access its corresponding details:

```
(summary_listings[
    ['id', 'name', 'neighbourhood', 'imperial_palace_distance']
].iloc[np.argmin(summary_listings['imperial_palace_distance'])])
```

The result is as follows, which is a bit surprising:

```
id                                              874407512426725982
name                      Home in Shibuya City · ★New · 3 bedrooms · ...
neighbourhood                                          Chiyoda Ku
imperial_palace_distance                               137.394271
Name: 10255, dtype: object
```

Indeed, the listing is not situated close to the Imperial Palace, which emphasizes the presence of potentially misleading errors in the geolocation of listings. It is not uncommon to encounter similar problems in datasets, no matter how carefully they are curated. As discussed in chapter 2, from a general point of view, after some data quality checks where you look for consistency among features and marking likely inexact values, you have a few viable options, listed here in descending order of effort from more demanding to less demanding:

- *Geocoding* (from address to coordinate) and *reverse geocoding* (from coordinates to address)—To figure out if location information matches with the provided latitude and longitude coordinates and decide whether to trust the provided address or coordinates
- *Data imputation*—Imputing the dubious values as they were missing, using the coordinates of a default location
- *Listwise deletion*—Removing all rows that have some dubious values
- *Leave it to XGBoost*—Tree-based methods tend to be less affected by erroneous and dubious values being robust to outliers and noise in the data

In our example, we decided to leave the situation to XGBoost because our model is not so critical as to require a thorough data quality check. It could be different with your own project, and you may evaluate a solution requiring more data-cleaning efforts.

Distances from landmarks and services work well as features in real estate modeling. Hence we do not limit ourselves to computing the distance from the Imperial Palace, the center of Tokyo. In the paper "Modeling User Activity Preference by Leveraging User Spatial Temporal Characteristics in LBSNs" by Dingqi Yang, Daqing Zhang, Vincent W. Zheng, Zhiyong Yu (*IEEE Transactions. on Systems, Man, and Cybernetics: Systems*, 45(1), 129-142, 2015), the authors collected datasets from Foursquare check-ins in New York City and Tokyo with their geographical coordinates and the type of location they refer to; we can access the data from Kaggle Datasets (https://mng.bz/4aDj).

Foursquare is a social network based on geopositioning. Thanks to its mobile app, it allows users to discover nearby venues to visit, such as restaurants and shops, and means of transportation and to share information about the places they visit. Another characteristic of the app is check-ins, which happen when using the platform at a venue. Check-ins refer to the presence of a user at a specific location. When a user checks into a place, they share their positioning with their Foursquare friends, and they may also have the option to post about their visit to other social media platforms like Facebook and X. To map the value of a listing in terms of convenience, we have available airports, bus, train, and subway stations among commonly checked-in venues. Together with convenience stores, a type of retail store that mainly sells a wide selection of everyday items and products to customers for their convenience, the proximity of such venues can add value to an accommodation.

Hence, to enrich our dataset, we first extracted the GPS coordinates of these Tokyo locations directly from Kaggle. The code and the extracted dataset are available at https://mng.bz/QDPv, and you can download the processed file into your working directory from the page https://mng.bz/XxNa where you can get the file `relevant_spots_Tokyo.csv`. The file contains information about 3,560 convenience store locations, 1,878 bus stations and stops, 439 subway stations, and 264 locations associated with airports. Then, using listing 7.6, we can compare the location of our Airbnb Tokyo listings with each of these venues and report the nearest distance of each one. Our idea is that the closer a listing is to a convenience store and means of transportation, the higher the expected price.

In listing 7.6 we do not compare each accommodation with all the possible venues we have gathered because that would take too much time and computation. Instead, we utilize the k-dimensional tree (KDTree) data structure from Scikit-learn, an optimized algorithm designed to efficiently find the nearest point among many points for a given location. Scikit-learn is used for algorithms such as K-nearest neighbors in situations when you have to find the most similar examples to a test sample in the training set. In our case, the training set is the set of venues, and the algorithm is trained to find the nearest venue to a given location based on Manhattan distance.

Listing 7.6   Finding the nearest facilities and transportation

```python
from sklearn.neighbors import KDTree

relevant_spots = pd.read_csv("relevant_spots_Tokyo.csv")

venue_categories = ['Convenience Store', 'Train Station',
                    'Airport', 'Bus Station', 'Subway']      # Stores the minimum distances in a dictionary
min_distances = {'listing_id': summary_listings['id']}

for venue in venue_categories:
    venue_filter = relevant_spots['venueCategory'] == venue
    venues = relevant_spots[
        ['latitude', 'longitude']
    ][venue_filter]                                          # Filters the relevant venue locations
    tree = KDTree(venues, metric='manhattan')               # Creates a KDTree using the filtered venue locations with the Manhattan metric for fast nearest-neighbor searches
    distance, index = tree.query(
        summary_listings[['latitude', 'longitude']],
        k=1
    )                                                        # Queries the KDTree to find the nearest point and its distance to each Airbnb listing (k=1 returns the nearest one)
    min_distances[
        'nearest_' +
        venue.lower().replace(" ", "_")
    ] = degrees_to_meters(
            np.ravel(distance),
            summary_listings['latitude']
    )                                                        # The dictionary of the minimum distances for each type of venue is converted into a DataFrame.
min_distances = pd.DataFrame(min_distances)
```

The code will run quite quickly by iterating over each type of venue, training on the locations of selected venues, and finding, using the KDTree, the nearest location to each accommodation and automatically calculating the distance. Ultimately, we just have to wrap up the results into a pandas DataFrame after converting the distances (Manhattan distances in degrees) to meters by the previously seen function degrees_to_meters. We can verify the results by inspecting the first five rows of the resulting dataset:

```
min_distances.head()
```

Figure 7.5 shows the results, representing the contents from the created `min_distances` DataFrame.

	listing_id	nearest_convenience_store	nearest_train_station	nearest_airport	nearest_bus_station
0	197677	475.837692	666.488917	8326.122756	829.211343
1	776070	114.974697	384.929313	5430.623850	453.968550
2	3427384	410.735809	367.589007	6343.224540	417.734902
3	905944	155.409734	268.125319	2929.393383	783.601883
4	3514008	160.799573	836.908222	5532.347474	619.141342

Figure 7.5   The first five rows of the `min_distances` DataFrame

Having the minimum distance to our selection of venues for each listing of our dataset, we now proceed with putting together all these new features into a final dataset of predictors and extracting a target series or vector to be used for modeling.

7.1.4   Finalizing your data

After creating some additional features, we can finalize our predictive features and their target. In listing 7.7, we join the `summary_listing` dataset to the minimum distance to our selected landmarks (airports, subway, train, bus stations, convenience stores). Then, we rearrange the joined data with respect to our target: the mean price we computed in the `price_stats_ordered` dataset.

Listing 7.7   Assembling data

```
summary_listings_features = [
    'neighbourhood',
    'coordinates',
    'room_type',
    'minimum_nights', 'number_of_reviews', 'days_since_last_review',
    'reviews_per_month', 'calculated_host_listings_count',
    'availability_365', 'number_of_reviews_ltm',
'number_of_reviews_ltm_ratio',
    'number_of_bedrooms', 'number_of_beds', 'number_of_baths',
    'type_of_accommodation', 'score', 'is_new',
    'is_studio', 'has_shared_bath', 'has_half_bath',
    'imperial_palace_distance'
]

summarized = summary_listings[['id'] +
```

```
summary_listings_features].rename({'id': 'listing_id'}, axis=1)

X = summarized.merge(min_distances, on='listing_id').set_index('listing_id')

X = X.reindex(price_stats.index)
price_stats_ordered = price_stats.reindex(X.index)
y = price_stats_ordered['mean'].copy()
```

Reindexes X to match the index of price_stats

Reindexes price_stats to match the index of X, ensuring the reindexed price statistics align with the listings in X

Copies the "mean" price column as the target variable

Once we have completed the script, we can visualize our dataset:

```
X.head()
```

As index, we have our `listing_id`, and among the columns, there are all the features we have prepared for the problem, as shown in figure 7.6.

listing_id	neighbourhood	coordinates	room_type	minimum_nights	number_of_reviews	days_sin
197677	Sumida Ku	20028	Entire home/apt	3	173	30.0
776070	Kita Ku	22026	Private room	3	243	9.0
905944	Shibuya Ku	16022	Entire home/apt	3	186	3.0
1016831	Setagaya Ku	14022	Private room	1	244	28.0
1196177	Adachi Ku	23027	Private room	2	95	1199.0

Figure 7.6   Top rows of the predictors' dataset

At this point, we can start examining the data in detail and figure out if there are any additional problems to be fixed or other insights to be discovered that could play an essential role in how we develop our XGBoost model.

7.1.5   *Exploring and fixing your data*

The next step after having assembled all the predictors into a single dataset is to explore it to detect any problems, such as missing data or extreme values, that may affect the performance of a machine learning algorithm. Therefore, our first action is to check for any missing data with the following command:

```
X.isna().sum()
```

The resulting list points out that there are three features with some missing data:

```
days_since_last_review          1252
reviews_per_month               1252
score                           2381
```

As we discussed in chapter 2 and then again in the previous chapter, it is crucial in the presence of missing data to investigate why there are missing values and if that could be deemed a missing completely at random, missing at random, or missing not at random situation. In this specific case, missing values are not at all at random, but they depend on the fact that there are no reviews or there are not enough reviews to compute a score. In fact, by inspecting how many accommodations are there without reviews, you will notice how the figure matches the number of missing cases on two features with missing values:

```
(X.number_of_reviews==0).sum()
```

As anticipated, the result is 1,252, matching the number of missing values. In this case, it is better to refrain from using the capabilities of XGBoost and other GBDT implementations to deal with missing data because its behavior will mimic an average situation. Missing reviews is an extreme yet legitimate case when an accommodation has just entered the market or is seldom chosen. Here, you need to directly input a number that may help any machine learning algorithm figure out that there are no reviews, hence the missing values. A common strategy is to use a value at the boundaries of the existing distribution, usually a negative number if we are representing counts or positive values. A quick check can assure us if there are the prerequisites for such a missing values strategy:

```
X[["days_since_last_review", "reviews_per_month", "score"]].describe()
```

As a result, we confirmed that the minimum value is always greater than zero for all three considered features. It means we can simply replace the missing values using the −1 value (we cannot use zero because the minimum value is zero for `days_since_last_review`), which will work as a solution both for a linear model (it is at the lower extreme of the existing distributions) and for tree-based ensembles (they will just split on that negative figure):

```
X.fillna(-1, inplace=True)
```

As a next step, we will be on the lookout for extreme values among our numeric features. As discussed in chapter 2, a straightforward approach to looking for outliers and extreme values is to chart a boxplot for each numeric feature arranged in a panel of subplots or a single plot if they have comparable scales. In our case, in the following listing, we have prepared a panel of boxplots to be inspected for extreme values.

Listing 7.8   Plotting boxplots for numeric features

```python
import matplotlib.pyplot as plt

numeric = ['minimum_nights', 'number_of_reviews',
           'days_since_last_review', 'reviews_per_month',
           'calculated_host_listings_count',
           'availability_365', 'score',
           'number_of_reviews_ltm',
           'number_of_reviews_ltm_ratio',
           'number_of_bedrooms', 'number_of_beds',
           'number_of_baths', 'imperial_palace_distance',
           'nearest_convenience_store',
           'nearest_train_station', 'nearest_airport',
           'nearest_bus_station', 'nearest_subway']

num_plots = len(numeric)
num_rows = (num_plots + 2) // 3          ← Estimates the number of rows
num_cols = min(num_plots, 3)             needed to arrange subplots
                                         ← Calculates the number of columns
                                         needed to arrange subplots
fig, axes = plt.subplots(
    num_rows,
    num_cols,
    figsize=(8, 12)      ← Creates a figure with subplots
)
axes = axes.flatten()    ← Flattens the axes array to a ID array
                         so that it can be iterated through

for i, feat in enumerate(numeric):
    X[[feat]].boxplot(ax=axes[i])

fig.tight_layout()
plt.show()
```

Figure 7.7 shows the charted results. By inspecting the values outside the whiskers of the plots, represented as empty points, we immediately notice that almost all the distributions have heavy tails on the right, with values decisively much larger than the mean value. If, for distance-based features, such extreme values may sound reasonable because of the extension of Tokyo's metropolitan area, as for features such as minimum_ night and number_of_reviews, such extreme values may represent outliers quite far from the core of the distribution. We could use winsorizing to solve such a problem, using a solution we proposed in chapter 2. This data transformation technique replaces extreme values in a dataset with less extreme values to reduce the influence of outliers on statistical analyses and modeling.

In listing 7.9, using the winsorize function from the Scipy package, we winsorize the 0.1% of the upper part of the distribution of the minimum_nights feature. All values above the 0.999 percentile will be changed to the value of the 0.999 percentile, thus removing any extreme values.

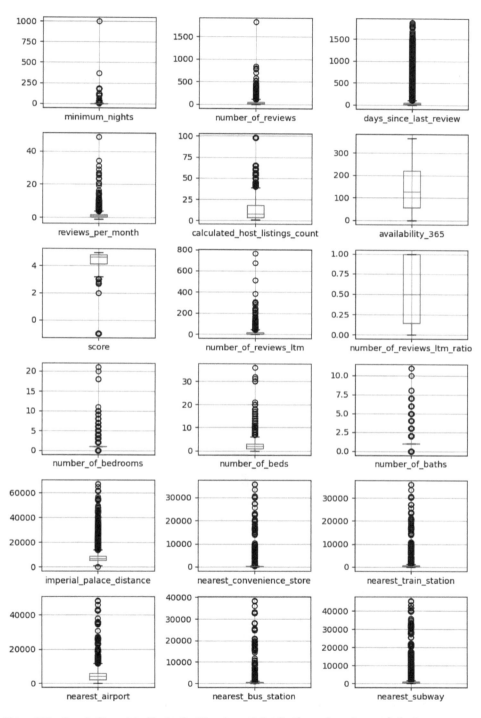

Figure 7.7 **Panel of boxplots illustrating the skewed distributions of most numeric features**

Listing 7.9   Winsorizing extreme values

```
from scipy.stats.mstats import winsorize

lower_cut_percentile = 0.00
upper_cut_percentile = 0.001

X['minimum_nights'] = winsorize(X['minimum_nights'].values,
                                limits=(lower_cut_percentile,
upper_cut_percentile))

X[['minimum_nights']].boxplot()
```

Indicates the lower percentile below which values will not be changed during winsorization

Indicates the upper percentile above which values will not be changed during winsorization

Figure 7.8 shows the highest value is now 120, not over 1,000 as before.

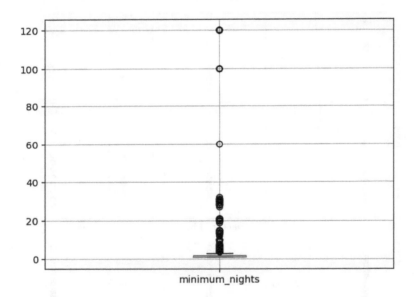

Figure 7.8   Boxplot of winsorized `minimum_nights` **feature**

We replicate the same also for the `number_of_reviews` feature:

```
X['number_of_reviews'] = winsorize(X['number_of_reviews'].values,
                                   limits=(lower_cut_percentile,
upper_cut_percentile))

X[['number_of_reviews']].boxplot()
```

Figure 7.9 shows that now the feature still has a heavy right tail. However, the extreme values have been compressed to below the 500 value.

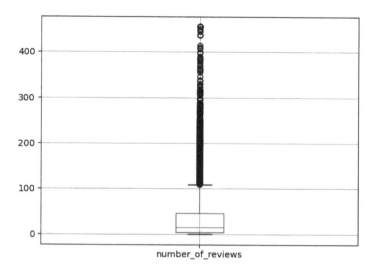

number_of_reviews

Figure 7.9 Boxplot of winsorized `number_of_reviews` **feature**

Having completed checking and remediating for missing values and extreme values in our dataset of predictors, we can proceed in the next subsection to look at the target itself.

7.1.6   Exploring your target

When dealing with exploratory data analysis (EDA), it is critical to examine the predictors and the target, and sometimes both predictors and target together and how they relate to each other. For our example, being a regression problem, we simply start by figuring out the mean and the range of the target:

```
print(f»minimum: {y.min()}»)
print(f"average: {y.mean().round(2)}")
print(f"maximum: {y.max()}")
```

These commands will print the minimum, the average, and the maximum values in the target variable y:

```
minimum: 1450.0
average: 36573.1
maximum: 1306500.0
```

We immediately notice that the maximum is on a quite different scale than the average and the minimum. Estimating percentiles can be helpful to understand better if there is a problem with extreme values or skewed distribution in the target. The presence of extreme values can be better understood by requiring a range of percentiles focusing on the extremities of the distribution:

```
perc = [1, 5, 10, 25, 50, 75, 90, 95, 99]
for p in perc:
    print(f"percentile {p:2}: {np.percentile(y, p).round(2)}")
```

The following are the output percentiles, and we have confirmation of the presence of extreme values at the right of the distribution since even the 99th percentile is quite far from the maximum we had previously reported:

```
percentile  1: 3000.0
percentile  5: 5198.02
percentile 10: 7315.67
percentile 25: 11870.07
percentile 50: 19830.78
percentile 75: 37741.64
percentile 90: 83936.03
percentile 95: 84857.11
percentile 99: 304531.4
```

Not only is the maximum value quite far from the 99th percentile, but there also appears to be a significant gap between the 95th and 99th percentiles. Our decision is to focus on the core of the distribution by dropping 10% of the distribution: 5% on the lower and 5% on the upper part. We manage this by selection using a Boolean selection variable:

```
valid_samples = (y >= 5200) & (y <=84857)
```

Before definitely applying the selection, we plot the resulting distribution.

Listing 7.10 Plotting the target distribution

```
import matplotlib.pyplot as plt
import seaborn as sns

valid_y = y[valid_samples]          # Selects only the part of the target
sns.kdeplot(valid_y, fill=True)     #   distribution we consider to model

median = np.median(valid_y)          # Represents the median
plt.axvline(median, color='r', linestyle='--', linewidth=2, label='Median')   #   value of the distribution

plt.xlabel('Values')
plt.ylabel('Density')
plt.title('Distribution Curve with Median')
plt.legend()
plt.show()
```

The previous code snippet will output a density plot, revealing the distribution and the median value for the selection of the target based on the selection variable we have just defined. Figure 7.10 shows the resulting plot.

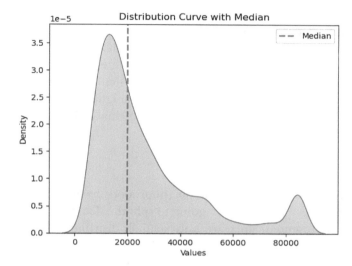

Figure 7.10 Density distribution of the target variable

The resulting distribution shown in figure 7.10 is definitely skewed to the right, a condition also called a positive skew. In particular, you can observe a lump of data at the start and a long decreasing tail following to the right, although, by the end, we can notice another small lump closing the distribution, probably a separate cluster of high-end accommodations. However, the range and distribution of the target are fine now. Therefore, we will select both the target and data using the previously defined Boolean selection variable:

```
X = X[valid_samples]
y = y[valid_samples]
```

In the next section, we will proceed to define both aspects of the validation process and the data pipeline necessary for modeling. Afterward, we will try a baseline model using classical machine learning linear models and a first tentative XGBoost model and optimize it before training our definitive model for the Tokyo Airbnb dataset problem.

7.2 Building and optimizing your model

In this section, we will use the data we have prepared to build a model. Before getting a complete final model, we will address various challenges related to defining the cross-validation strategy, preparing the data pipeline, and building first a baseline model and then a tentative first XGBoost model.

7.2.1 Preparing a cross-validation strategy

Generally, a K-fold cross-validation strategy works quite well in most cases, but in our specific situation, we are dealing with real estate units whose value is strongly influenced by their location. In our case, Stratified K-fold cross-validation is more appropriate, controlling for the effect of location. Although similar to K-fold cross-validation, there is a key difference in stratified K-fold cross-validation: the class distribution of a feature of our choice in the dataset is preserved in each fold. Such stratified sampling will allow folds to have a similar mix of territories as the complete dataset. However, it is important to check beforehand if some territories are difficult to split among folds because of their low numerosity. If we count the different neighborhoods represented in the data, we get a long list with many locations, some showcasing a considerable number of listings and others only a limited few:

```
X['neighbourhood'].value_counts()
```

Clearly you cannot accept considering all the neighborhoods having less than a certain number of examples because, if you are going to split the data into folds, you will hardly have them well represented. Since areas are spatially distributed, just gathering them into an extra class won't do because you will mix very different situations of areas quite far from each other. In listing 7.11, we solve this problem by aggregating areas with less than 30 examples (implying about 6 examples for each fold if we use a five-fold validation split) with their nearest larger neighborhood. To achieve that, we use a KDTree data structure again. Thus we can match each area with less than 30 accommodations with its nearest area with more than 30.

Listing 7.11   Aggregating nearby neighborhood areas

```
neighbourhoods = (
    summary_listings[
        ['neighbourhood', 'latitude', 'longitude']
    ]
    .groupby('neighbourhood')
    .agg({'latitude': 'mean',            Calculates the mean latitude,
          'longitude': 'mean',           mean longitude, and the count
          'neighbourhood': 'count'})     of listings in each neighborhood
)

less_than_30 = (
    neighbourhoods[neighbourhoods['neighbourhood'] < 30]
)                                        Separates the
more_than_30 = (                         neighborhoods into
    neighbourhoods[neighbourhoods['neighbourhood'] > 30]   two groups based on
)                                        the number of listings

kdtree = KDTree(                         Creates a KDTree using the mean latitude
    more_than_30[['latitude', 'longitude']]   and longitude values of neighborhoods
)                                        with counts greater than 30
change_list = {}

for i in range(len(less_than_30)):       Initializes an empty dictionary
    row = less_than_30.iloc[[i]]         to store the mappings of the
    _, idx = kdtree.query(              neighborhoods
        row[['latitude', 'longitude']]
```

```
    )
    change_list[row.index[0]] = more_than_30.index[idx[0, 0]]

X["neighbourhood_more_than_30"] = (
    X["neighbourhood"].replace(change_list)
)
```

Iterates through each neighborhood with counts less than 30 and queries the KDTree to find the nearest neighborhood with a count greater than 30

Replaces the original neighborhood values with the new neighborhood values based on the mapping in change_list

After having run the code, you can check how the mapping has been performed and if the resulting aggregation has neighborhood areas with less than 30 listings by issuing the following commands:

```
print(change_list)
print(X["neighbourhood_more_than_30"].value_counts())
```

Having elaborated a suitable area subdivision, we can now proceed to define our stratified cross-validation strategy in the following listing.

Listing 7.12 Defining a stratified strategy

```
from sklearn.model_selection import StratifiedKFold

cv = StratifiedKFold(5, shuffle=True, random_state=0)
cv_splits = cv.split(
    X, y=X["neighbourhood_more_than_30"]
)
```

Defines a five-fold stratified random splitting

Generates the cross-validation splits while maintaining the same distribution of neighborhoods with more than 30 listings in each fold

The resulting `cv_splits` is a generator, and you can examine it using the following command:

```
print(cv_splits)
```

The output is the type of object:

```
<generator object _BaseKFold.split at 0x78356223c660>
```

Since `cv_splits` is a generator, it can be used a single time, but you can reinstantiate an identical one by simply re-executing the commands in listing 7.12. In the next subsection, we will deal with the data pipeline and determine which transformations to apply to our data.

7.2.2 Preparing your pipeline

A second preparatory step is to define a pipeline for transforming our predictors in the most appropriate way for running generally with all classical machine learning algorithms, not just gradient boosting. Ideally, it would be better to have multiple pipelines based on how each model deals with the different features. For instance, in our pipeline, we are going to ordinally encode a couple of categorical features, and such encoding, though fit for tree-based models, doesn't always work properly with linear models. However, while having unique pipelines can lead to better performance, it can also become a maintenance nightmare. The human effort required to create and manage multiple pipelines may outweigh the marginal performance gains achieved by customizing each pipeline for specific models. Therefore it is better to decide on multiple pipelines if you have evidence that it is worth it.

Let's start by classifying the different kinds of features that we will be using into categorical features, numeric, and binary features:

```
categorical = [
    'room_type',
    'neighbourhood_more_than_30',
    'type_of_accommodation',
    'coordinates'
]
numeric = [
    'minimum_nights',
    'number_of_reviews',
    'days_since_last_review',
    'reviews_per_month',
    'calculated_host_listings_count',
    'availability_365',
    'score',
    'number_of_reviews_ltm',
    'number_of_reviews_ltm_ratio',
    'number_of_bedrooms',
    'number_of_beds',
    'number_of_baths',
    'imperial_palace_distance',
    'nearest_convenience_store',
    'nearest_train_station',
    'nearest_airport',
    'nearest_bus_station',
    'nearest_subway'
]
binary = [
    'is_new',
    'is_studio',
    'has_shared_bath',
    'has_half_bath'
]
```

A further inspection of the categorical features is necessary because we need to understand whether to treat them as high cardinality features or not. We can understand better what to do after having counted how many unique values each categorical feature has:

```
for feat in categorical:
    print(f"{feat} has {X[feat].nunique()} unique values")
```

From the results, we can determine that probably the only feature that could be considered as a high cardinality categorical is the `coordinates` feature, which has almost 300 unique values. As for `neighbourhood_more_than_30` and `type_of_accomodation`, we could apply ordinal encoding to them for tree-based modeling, whereas for linear models, it would be better to apply one-hot-encoding to these features (thus producing about 50 new binary features) or target encoded:

```
room_type has 4 unique values
neighbourhood_more_than_30 has 24 unique values
type_of_accommodation has 29 unique values
coordinates has 296 unique values
```

Since our example revolves around XGBoost and demonstrating how it can work with similar problems, we decide to one-hot encode only the `room_type`, ordinal encoding `neighbourhood_more_than_30` and `type_of_accomodation`, and target encoding `coordinates`:

```
onehot_encoding = ['room_type']
ordinal_encoding = ['neighbourhood_more_than_30', 'type_of_accommodation']
target_encoding = ['coordinates']
```

Our choice of working with XGBoost, a tree-based model, also justifies leaving all the numeric features as-is. Using linear models, statistical standardization, for better convergence when using regularization or generalized linear models, and feature transformation, for better fitting nonlinearities, are usually the standard.

In listing 7.13, we define all the necessary feature transformations and ensemble them in a Scikit-learn's Column Transformer, which will be part of the pipeline that also contains the machine learning model of our choice. It is also important to note that we take steps in defining the column transformers to handle unknown categories and missing values that may unexpectedly appear at test time. Our strategy for one-hot encoding is to ignore new unknown categories. For ordinal encoding, the value assigned to the parameter `unknown_value`, which is by default `np.nan`, will be used to encode unknown categories. This means an XGBoost model will deal with such situations as missing cases using the most frequent split. Other machine learning algorithms may instead break into similar occurrences, which is an advantage of XGBoost. As for the target encoder, the target mean is substituted for unknown categories. Don't forget to install the `category_encoders` package. If it is unavailable on your system, use the `pip install category_encoders` command.

Listing 7.13 Defining column transformations

```
from sklearn.preprocessing import OneHotEncoder, OrdinalEncoder
from sklearn.compose import ColumnTransformer
from sklearn.pipeline import Pipeline

from category_encoders.target_encoder import TargetEncoder
```

Creates an Ordinal Encoder object with handling of unknown categories and the unknown value replaced by np.nan

Creates a One-Hot Encoder object with the option to handle unknown categories by ignoring them during encoding

```
onehot_encoder = OneHotEncoder(handle_unknown='ignore')
ordinal_enconder = OrdinalEncoder(handle_unknown="use_encoded_value",
                                  unknown_value=np.nan)
target_encoder = TargetEncoder(
    cols=target_encoding,
    handle_unknown="value",
    smoothing=0.5
)
```

Creates a TargetEncoder object, handling unknown values by encoding them using the mean target value and applying smoothing with a parameter of 0.5

```
column_transform = ColumnTransformer(
    [('onehot_encoding', onehot_encoder, onehot_encoding),
     ('ordinal_encoding', ordinal_enconder, ordinal_encoding),
     ('target_encoding', target_encoder, target_encoding),
     ('numeric', 'passthrough', numeric),
     ('binary', 'passthrough', binary)],
    remainder='drop',
    verbose_feature_names_out=True,
    sparse_threshold=0.0)
```

A Column Transformer object applying the specified encoders to the respective columns

Drops remaining columns that are not specified in the transformer

Ensures that the transformed data is kept as dense arrays

Keeps verbose feature names for transformed columns

After having run the code listing, we can immediately test transforming the data we have and checking the transformed column names:

```
Xt = column_transform.fit_transform(X, y)
column_transform.get_feature_names_out()
```

The output shows that now the features are preceded by a prefix pointing out what transformation they underwent. Binary features created by one-hot encoding are also followed by the category they represent:

```
array(['onehot_encoding__room_type_Entire home/apt',
       'onehot_encoding__room_type_Hotel room',
       'onehot_encoding__room_type_Private room',
       'onehot_encoding__room_type_Shared room',
       'ordinal_encoding__neighbourhood_more_than_30',
       'ordinal_encoding__type_of_accommodation',
       'target_encoding__coordinates', 'numeric__minimum_nights',
       'numeric__number_of_reviews', 'numeric__days_since_last_review',
       'numeric__reviews_per_month',
       'numeric__calculated_host_listings_count',
       'numeric__availability_365', 'numeric__score',
       'numeric__number_of_reviews_ltm',
```

```
'numeric__number_of_reviews_ltm_ratio',
'numeric__number_of_bedrooms', 'numeric__number_of_beds',
'numeric__number_of_baths', 'numeric__imperial_palace_distance',
'numeric__nearest_convenience_store',
'numeric__nearest_train_station', 'numeric__nearest_airport',
'numeric__nearest_bus_station', 'numeric__nearest_subway',
'binary__is_new', 'binary__is_studio', 'binary__has_shared_bath',
'binary__has_half_bath'], dtype=object)
```

As a final step, we just store away into a single CSV file both the processed features and the target. We will use such data again later, in chapter 12, when we test a deep learning solution and compare its performance with the XGBoost model we train in this chapter.

```
data = pd.DataFrame(
    Xt,
    columns=column_transform.get_feature_names_out(),
    index=y.index
)
data = data.assign(target=y).reset_index()
data.to_csv("airbnb_tokyo.csv", index=False)
```

Now that we have the data processing part of our pipeline, we can proceed to define a baseline model and then, finally, an XGBoost regressor.

7.2.3 Building a baseline model

Having a baseline model in machine learning is important for several reasons:

- *Comparing performance*—The baseline model serves as a benchmark to compare the performance of more complex models, helping you to understand whether more complexity really adds value.

- *Detecting overfitting*—By comparing the performance of your advanced model against the baseline on unseen data, you can identify if the advanced model is overfitting because the baseline model will perform much better.

- *Understanding the problem*—Creating a simple baseline model, especially if it is a linear model, forces you to understand the data and the problem better.

- *Debugging and validation*—A baseline model can help you validate that your data preprocessing pipeline is correct because the effects of the variables on the model won't be hidden by its complexity.

- *Providing a minimum viable model*—A baseline model provides a minimum viable solution to the problem at hand.

For all these reasons, we won't immediately jump into training our model using a gradient boosting model, which we expect will perform well on the problem, but we take a step back and test a simple linear model. In addition, at this time, we will try to get predictions from a type of model we can easily evaluate and compare. Instead of just evaluating metrics through cross-validation, we'll employ cross-validation prediction. This method provides unbiased predictions for all training cases by making predictions on validation folds within cross-validation.

During cross-validation, evaluation metrics are calculated separately for each fold. These metrics represent the performance of the model on each fold individually. The final evaluation metric reported from cross-validation is usually an average (mean or median) of the individual fold metrics. This aggregated metric provides an estimate of the model's generalization performance on unseen data. However, if we are using cross-validation predictions, we concentrate on the ability of the model to perform on the data at hand. In fact, the primary use of cross-validation predictions is to analyze the predictions made by the model on different parts of the data used as validation. Using such predictions helps us understand how well the model performs across different subsets of the data and identifies if the model is overfitting or underfitting because we can compare the predictions with the expected target values.

Listing 7.14 Linear regression baseline model with diagnostic plots

```python
import matplotlib.pyplot as plt
from sklearn.linear_model import LinearRegression
from sklearn.model_selection import cross_val_predict
from sklearn.metrics import r2_score, mean_squared_error, mean_absolute_error

lm = LinearRegression(fit_intercept=False)      # Initializes a LinearRegression model without intercept
lm.fit(Xt, y)                                   # Fits the LinearRegression model to the transformed training data

cv_splits = cv.split(
    X,
    y = X["neighbourhood_more_than_30"]
)                                               # Creates stratified cross-validation splits based on the neighborhoods with more than 30 counts
y_pred_cv = cross_val_predict(
    lm, Xt, y, cv=cv_splits
)                                               # Performs cross-validated predictions
prediction_range = y_pred_cv.min()} - {y_pred_cv.max()
print(f"prediction range: {prediction_range}")  # Prints the range of cross-validated predictions

r2 = r2_score(y, y_pred_cv)
rmse = np.sqrt(mean_squared_error(y, y_pred_cv))
mae = mean_absolute_error(y, y_pred_cv)         # Calculates R-squared, root mean squared error, and mean absolute error evaluation metrics to assess the model's performance

print(f'R-squared: {r2:.3f}')
print(f'RMSE: {rmse:.3f}')
print(f'MAE: {mae:.3f}')

plt.scatter(y, y_pred_cv)                        # Creates a scatter plot of actual vs. predicted values
plt.plot([y.min(), y.max()], [y.min(), y.max()], 'r--', label='Ideal Fit')
plt.axhline(
    0, color='orange', linestyle='--', label='Zero Line'
)                                               # Plots a dashed orange zero line to the plot as a reference for the ideal fit
plt.xlabel('Actual')
plt.ylabel('Predicted')
plt.title('Linear Regression - Fitted Results')
plt.legend()
plt.show()
```

After running the code, we obtain the evaluation results, and we can immediately notice how some predictions are negative. Since a linear regression model is not bounded in its predictions, the mean absolute error (MAE) is quite high (over 12,000 Yen), and the R squared, a typical measure of fit measuring how much of the variance of the target is captured by the model, is just a modest 0.32:

```
prediction range: -34929.50241836217 - 136479.60736257263
R-squared: 0.320
RMSE: 17197.323
MAE: 12568.371
```

Clearly, the fitting of the model is not particularly impressive, and we can get a confirmation as shown in figure 7.11, where we represent the scatterplot of the cross-validation predictions on the y-axis against the expected target values on the x-axis. Apart from a few negative predictions at the start of the target distribution, we can also notice how the predictions depart from the ideal fit dashed line, showing a flat trend, a clear sign of underfitting, and how there are a few outlying predictions.

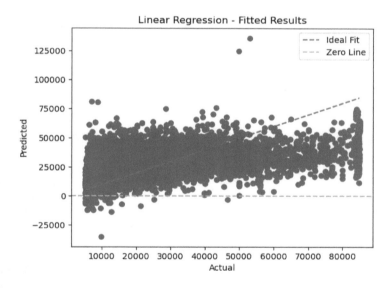

Figure 7.11 Plot of the fitted results from the baseline linear regression against their ideal value

As a first step in examining the results, we ask for the percentage of predictions that are below or equal to zero, an unfeasible prediction because listings should be positive:

```
(y_pred_cv <= 0).sum() / len(y_pred_cv)
```

The result is a minimal percentage, about 0.5%:

```
0.005178767055074196
```

Ideally, our predictions should be greater than zero, and in a linear model that could be achieved by a target transformation—for instance, a logarithmic transformation. However, the role of a baseline model is not to be a perfect model but just a model to highlight challenges in the data and be a helpful comparison for more sophisticated models.

Now we proceed to locate the rows that are positive outliers:

```
print(np.where(y_pred_cv > 100_000))
```

We received two cases: 5509 and 8307:

```
(array([5509, 8307]),)
```

We also inquiry about the negative outliers:

```
print(np.where(y_pred_cv < -25_000))
```

Here we get a single case, 182:

```
(array([182]),)
```

In listing 7.15, we define a function that can help us check for outliers. For each predictor feature, this function prints the coefficient and the resulting multiplication of the coefficient with the value of the feature for that case, thus making explicit the contributions of each feature to the prediction.

Listing 7.15   Inspection of the coefficients

```
def report_case(model, data, feature_names, case_no):
    case_values = data[case_no]
    coef_values = case_values * model.coef_
    for feature_name, value, coef_value in zip(
            feature_names, case_values, coef_values):
        print(f"{feature_name:50s}" +
              f"({value:10.2f}) : " +
              f"{coef_value:+0.2f}")
    print("-" * 80)
    print(" "*66 + f"{np.sum(coef_values):+0.2f}")
```

Extracts the feature values for the specified case number from the data array

Calculates the coefficient values for each feature by multiplying its value with the corresponding coefficient from the model

Loops and prints through the feature names, their values, and corresponding coefficient values

Prints the sum of the calculated coefficient values for the case

---

Having our inspection function ready, we can start examining case 8307, which represents a case of too positively large outlier in the predictions:

```
report_case(model=lm,
            data=Xt,
            feature_names=column_transform.get_feature_names_out(),
            case_no=8307)
```

The following are the results for case 8307, where it is evident that the extra contribution that made the prediction an outlier is because of the number of bedrooms (hinting that this property is probably a hostel). This high value pushed the final predicted listing upwards:

```
onehot_encoding__room_type_Entire home/apt     (        1.00) : -8295.89
onehot_encoding__room_type_Hotel room          (        0.00) : -0.00
onehot_encoding__room_type_Private room        (        0.00) : -0.00
onehot_encoding__room_type_Shared room         (        0.00) : -0.00
ordinal_encoding__neighbourhood_more_than_30   (       12.00) : +576.48
ordinal_encoding__type_of_accommodation        (       20.00) : +2377.99
target_encoding__coordinates                   (    29649.71) : +26556.25
numeric__minimum_nights                        (        1.00) : -268.05
numeric__number_of_reviews                     (        0.00) : -0.00
numeric__days_since_last_review                (       -1.00) : -0.66
numeric__reviews_per_month                     (       -1.00) : -172.50
numeric__calculated_host_listings_count        (       15.00) : +1470.92
numeric__availability_365                      (      354.00) : +16503.11
numeric__score                                 (       -1.00) : +524.08
numeric__number_of_reviews_ltm                 (        0.00) : -0.00
numeric__number_of_reviews_ltm_ratio           (        0.00) : +0.00
numeric__number_of_bedrooms                    (       18.00) : +64407.67
numeric__number_of_beds                        (       18.00) : +31283.70
numeric__number_of_baths                       (        2.00) : -1787.41
numeric__imperial_palace_distance              (     2279.80) : -859.33
numeric__nearest_convenience_store             (      149.84) : +549.07
numeric__nearest_train_station                 (      545.08) : -1043.20
numeric__nearest_airport                       (      389.85) : -137.44
numeric__nearest_bus_station                   (      322.04) : -266.55
numeric__nearest_subway                        (      221.93) : -17.29
binary__is_new                                 (        0.00) : -0.00
binary__is_studio                              (        0.00) : +0.00
binary__has_shared_bath                        (        0.00) : -0.00
binary__has_half_bath                          (        0.00) : -0.00
-------------------------------------------------------------------------
                                                               +131400.95
```

Similar problems are due to the fact that each feature is modeled in a linear way. Thus the prediction contribution of a feature is unbounded, having no maximum or minimum but decreasing and increasing in accordance with the feature value. Typically, introducing nonlinearities and interactions into the model nonlinearities and interactions can mitigate such problems. Let's now check the only negative outlier:

```
report_case(model=lm,
            data=Xt,
            feature_names=column_transform.get_feature_names_out(),
            case_no=182)
```

Here the problem is represented by the value of the minimum of nights, which is again too high and drags down the estimated value. In fact, some listings act as seasonal accommodation, typically for workers or students, not just for short stays. The model is indeed too simple to catch such nuances, and again, having introduced nonlinearities and interactions could have helped:

```
onehot_encoding__room_type_Entire home/apt    (       0.00) : -0.00
onehot_encoding__room_type_Hotel room         (       0.00) : -0.00
onehot_encoding__room_type_Private room       (       1.00) : -11573.69
onehot_encoding__room_type_Shared room        (       0.00) : -0.00
ordinal_encoding__neighbourhood_more_than_30  (       6.00) : +288.24
ordinal_encoding__type_of_accommodation       (      14.00) : +1664.59
target_encoding__coordinates                  (   27178.66) : +24343.02
numeric__minimum_nights                       (     120.00) : -32166.38
numeric__number_of_reviews                    (     122.00) : -1241.88
numeric__days_since_last_review               (     132.00) : +87.20
numeric__reviews_per_month                    (       1.33) : +229.43
numeric__calculated_host_listings_count       (       4.00) : +392.25
numeric__availability_365                     (       0.00) : +0.00
numeric__score                                (       4.98) : -2609.92
numeric__number_of_reviews_ltm                (       4.00) : -18.33
numeric__number_of_reviews_ltm_ratio          (       0.03) : +54.17
numeric__number_of_bedrooms                   (       1.00) : +3578.20
numeric__number_of_beds                       (       0.00) : +0.00
numeric__number_of_baths                      (       0.00) : -0.00
numeric__imperial_palace_distance             (   32506.70) : -12252.79
numeric__nearest_convenience_store            (    5020.81) : +18397.51
numeric__nearest_train_station                (    5689.32) : -10888.48
numeric__nearest_airport                      (   11438.81) : -4032.76
numeric__nearest_bus_station                  (    4999.17) : -4137.76
numeric__nearest_subway                       (   16976.69) : -1322.52
binary__is_new                                (       0.00) : -0.00
binary__is_studio                             (       0.00) : +0.00
binary__has_shared_bath                       (       0.00) : -0.00
binary__has_half_bath                         (       0.00) : -0.00
-------------------------------------------------------------------------
                                                             -31209.90
```

In conclusion, our baseline model has signaled us that successfully solving the problem presented by the Tokyo Airbnb dataset requires a better fitting mode that can handle positive predictions (they should be necessarily positive) and can represent nonlinear relationships and interactions between a particular characteristic of the accommodation (a large number of bedrooms indicate a hostel, a high number of minimum stay nights indicates an accommodation for seasonal tenants). In the next subsection, we will solve all these problems at once by using an XGBoost model, which should be able to deal with this data in a more sophisticated and smart way.

7.2.4   *Building a first tentative model*

First, we chose an XGBoost regressor, trying to incorporate some of the insights we gained from our previous EDA and baseline model inspections. We decided to use a gamma objective function, commonly used in regression problems, for modeling positive continuous variables that are positive and right-skewed. Gamma is particularly useful when the target variable is always positive, and it includes many small values and a few larger values, as it handles such distribution characteristics quite well.

In addition, since our baseline model has shown signs of underfitting and not handling interactions or linearities properly, we decide on a max depth of at most six for the decision trees composing the boosted ensemble, thus allowing for an adequate number of splits to handle most common similar data characteristics.

In the following listing, arranged similarly as the previous listing training the linear regression baseline, we train an XGBoost regressor, and we test its out-of-fold cross-validation predictions.

Listing 7.16   First XGBoost model

```
from sklearn.model_selection import cross_validate
from sklearn.metrics import r2_score, mean_squared_error, mean_absolute_error
from XGBoost import XGBRegressor

xgb = XGBRegressor(booster='gbtree',
                   objective='reg:gamma',
                   n_estimators=300,
                   max_depth=6)

cv_splits = cv.split(
    X, y=X["neighbourhood_more_than_30"]
)
y_pred_cv = cross_val_predict(
    xgb, Xt, y, cv=cv_splits
)
prediction_range = y_pred_cv.min()} - {y_pred_cv.max()
print(f"prediction range: {prediction_range}")

r2 = r2_score(y, y_pred_cv)
rmse = np.sqrt(mean_squared_error(y, y_pred_cv))
mae = mean_absolute_error(y, y_pred_cv)

print(f'R-squared: {r2:.3f}')
print(f'RMSE: {rmse:.3f}')
print(f'MAE: {mae:.3f}')

plt.scatter(y, y_pred_cv)
plt.plot([y.min(), y.max()], [y.min(), y.max()], 'r--', label='Ideal Fit')
plt.axhline(0, color='orange', linestyle='--', label='Zero Line')
plt.xlabel('Actual')
plt.ylabel('Predicted')
plt.title('XGBoost - Fitted Results')
plt.legend()
plt.show()
```

- Sets up an XGBoost regressor with specific hyperparameters
- Defines 'reg:gamma' as the objective function
- Generates cross-validation splits based on the neighbourhood_more_than_30 feature
- Performs cross-validated predictions
- Prints the range of predicted values
- Calculates R-squared, root mean squared error, and MAE evaluation metrics to assess the model's performance
- Creates a scatter plot of actual vs. predicted values
- Adds reference lines to the plot for an ideal fit and a zero line

---

This time, the prediction range is strictly in the positive range, as we expected. The MAE is almost half of those of the baseline linear model and the R-squared scores almost 0.7, which is a reasonably good result showing how the model is now able to intercept most of the variance present in the target:

```
prediction range: 3291.401123046875 - 123069.8828125
R-squared: 0.693
RMSE: 11562.836
MAE: 7227.435
```

A further inspection of the fitted results, represented in figure 7.12 as a scatterplot between the cross-validation predictions (on the y-axis) and the expected target values (on the x-axis), shows that the points are now slightly more in line with our ideal fit. In addition, it is important to notice how the XGBoost model tends to extrapolate the predictions: the column of predictions at the rightmost part of the chart indicates that our model predicted values sometimes higher than the observed maximum in the target, whereas, on the leftmost part of the chart, there are no nonpositive estimations.

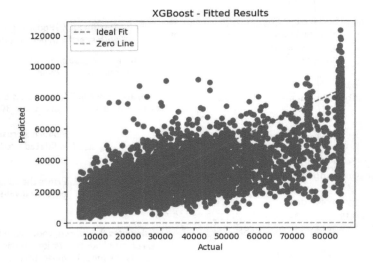

Figure 7.12   Plot of the fitted results for the XGBoost model against their ideal value

Typically, you shouldn't limit yourself to a single model in a data science project, as in our example. Because of space constraints, we just focus on an XGBoost model. Still, it is advisable in a working project to try even more diverse classical machine learning algorithms, such as other gradient boosting implementations, as well as more tree ensembles, generalized linear models, and even more unusual, nowadays, classical machine learning models (such as k-nearest neighbors or support vector machines). There is no free lunch in machine learning, and you may find reasonable solutions to this problem even with different algorithms that may better suit your necessities in terms of performance, speed of inference, memory occupancy, and portability onto other systems.

In the following subsection, we optimize our XGBoost solution using Bayesian optimization to strive to perform as best as possible on our problem.

7.2.5 *Optimizing your model*

Since XGBoost works quite well for the problem, we'll take some time to refine its parameters and test different boosting approaches and objectives. We are going to use Optuna, a Bayesian optimizer presented in the previous chapter, because it can efficiently explore a GBDT hyperparameter search space, adaptively choosing in a short set of rounds, based on the outcomes of the previous experiments, the next set of hyperparameters to be evaluated.

If you don't have Optuna available on your system, you can install it by issuing the command `pip install optuna` in a shell or a notebook cell.

Listing 7.17 performs hyperparameter optimization using Optuna for our previously tested XGBoost Regressor model to find the best hyperparameters that minimize the MAE of the model on the Tokyo Airbnb dataset. The core of the listing is the objective function that suggests to Optuna different hyperparameter values using `trial.suggest_...` methods. In particular, it tests the classic `gbtree` booster (gradient boosting) and also the `gblinear`. This booster utilizes a linear model as its base learner, incorporating both L1 and L2 regularization instead of employing a decision tree. Regarding the objective function, it tests the classical squared error, the gamma objective, and the Tweedie, blending aspects of the gamma and Poisson distributions. When selecting the gblinear boosting or the Tweedie objective, the code overrides the chosen parameters. It makes modifications and additions to them to fit the requirements of the gblinear booster or the Tweedie objective. Finally, it then creates an XGBoost Regressor with the suggested hyperparameters at each test and performs cross-validation to evaluate the MAE. The process is repeated for a specified number of trials (60 in this case). After optimization, the best achieved MAE and corresponding best hyperparameters are printed.

Listing 7.17 Optimizing the XGBoost regressor

```
import optuna

def objective(trial):          ◄──── Defines an optimization objective
                                     function using the Optuna library

    params = {                               ◄── Dictionary containing
        'booster': trial.suggest_categorical(     hyperparameters for
            'booster',                            optimization, including booster
            ['gbtree', 'gblinear']               type, objectives, and others
        ),
        'objective': trial.suggest_categorical(
            'objective',
            ['reg:squarederror', 'reg:gamma', 'reg:tweedie']
        ),
        'n_estimators': trial.suggest_int(
            'n_estimators', 100, 1000
        ),
```

```
            'learning_rate': trial.suggest_float(
                'learning_rate', 0.01, 1.0, log=True
            ),
            'subsample': trial.suggest_float(
                'subsample', 0.3, 1.0
            ),
            'colsample_bytree': trial.suggest_float(
                'colsample_bytree', 0.3, 1.0
            ),
            'max_depth': trial.suggest_int('max_depth', 1, 7),
            'min_child_weight': trial.suggest_int('min_child_weight', 1, 7),
            'reg_lambda': trial.suggest_float(
                'reg_lambda', 1e-9, 100.0, log=True
            ),
            'reg_alpha': trial.suggest_float(
                'reg_alpha', 1e-9, 100.0, log=True
            ),
        }
```
◄── **Adjusts hyperparameters based on the chosen booster type**

```
    if params['booster'] == 'gblinear':
        keys_to_remove = [
            "colsample_bytree", "max_depth",
            "min_child_weight", "subsample"
        ]
        params = {
            key:value for key, value in params.items()
            if key not in keys_to_remove
        }
```
◄── **Suggests the additional parameter 'tweedie_variance_power' for a tweedie objective**

```
    if params['objective'] == 'reg:tweedie':
        # Must be between in range [1, 2) : 1=poisson 2=gamma
        params['tweedie_variance_power'] = trial.suggest_float(
            'tweedie_variance_power', 1.01, 1.99
        )

    xgb = XGBRegressor(**params)
    model_pipeline = Pipeline(
        [('processing', column_transform),
         ('xgb', xgb)]
    )
```
◄── **Initializes an XGBoost Regressor with the suggested hyperparameters**

```
    cv_splits = cv.split(X, y=X["neighbourhood_more_than_30"])

    cv_scores = cross_validate(
        estimator=model_pipeline,
        X=X,
        y=y,
        scoring='neg_mean_absolute_error',
        cv=cv_splits
    )
```
◄── **Performs cross-validation using the defined pipeline and optimizing for MAE**

```
    cv_evaluation = np.mean(
        np.abs(cv_scores['test_score'])
    )
```
◄── **Calculates the MAE from the negative MAE scores**

```
    return cv_evaluation
```
◄── **Returns the calculated evaluation metric value to be minimized**

```
sqlite_db = "sqlite:///sqlite.db"
```

```
study_name = "optimize_XGBoost_tokyo_airbnb"
study = optuna.create_study(
    storage=sqlite_db,
    study_name=study_name,
    direction="minimize",
    load_if_exists=True
)

study.optimize(objective, n_trials=100)
print(study.best_value)
print(study.best_params)
```

Creates an Optuna study with storage in a SQLite database for optimization

Performs optimization for a specified number of trials

Prints the best evaluation metric value achieved during optimization

Prints the best hyperparameters found during optimization

After having the optimization run for a while, we obtain a reduced MAE in respect of our first attempt and a set of suitable hyperparameters, showing a max depth of seven levels, about 900 estimators, and a Tweedie objective function with a variance power of 1.5, indicating a mixed distribution between Poisson and gamma:

```
6616.859370931483
{'booster': 'gbtree',
 'colsample_bytree': 0.946407058507176,
 'learning_rate': 0.06867015067874482,
 'max_depth': 7,
 'min_child_weight': 5,
 'n_estimators': 901,
 'objective': 'reg:tweedie',
 'reg_alpha': 0.0006368936493084075,
 'reg_lambda': 3.8302865696045996,
 'subsample': 0.8956307610431394,
 'tweedie_variance_power': 1.560801988491813
}
```

At this point, we can also plot some diagnostic charts to understand better how the optimization went. For instance, we can first plot how the optimization proceeds across the 60 trials that we initially set:

```
fig = optuna.visualization.plot_optimization_history(study)
fig.show()
```

Figure 7.13 shows how the best value was achieved quite early, before 20 trials, and it didn't improve after that. This is important information because if the best optimization could have been achieved later, you may have suspected further improvements lying ahead in some more rounds of hyperparameter exploration by Optuna. Actually, you may have achieved that anytime by rerunning the command `study.optimize (objective, n_trials=100)`, setting your intended number of extra trials instead of the initial 100. Since we set to store trials on an SQLite database, you may reprise the optimization any time from the point it stopped (which is a strong point for using Optuna instead of other optimization options). Another important fact to gather from the chart is that there is quite a crowd of hyperparameter sets that are optimal or almost optimal. That means that there is no single optimization possible for this problem. That allows you to explore the different settings and decide on the solution that suits your needs. For instance, you may decide on a near-optimal solution that samples more features or requires fewer estimators since they are faster at inference time.

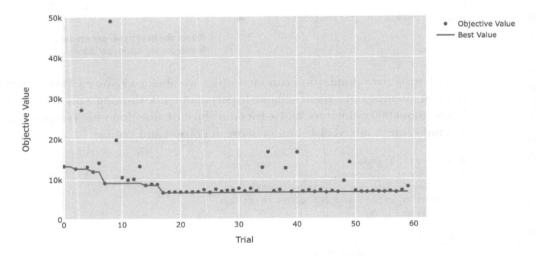

Figure 7.13   How tests by Optuna progressively performed during the optimization

After observing how the optimization proceeded, another important piece of information is provided by charting the importance of the hyperparameters because it could hint at expanding the search space for such hyperparameters if they proved so important for the optimization process:

```
fig = optuna.visualization.plot_param_importances(study)
fig.show()
```

In our case, the most critical factors proved to be `colsample_bytree` and `min_child_weight`, hyperparameters that caused the most variance in results, as seen in figure 7.14.

Now we have a good set of hyperparameters. In the next subsection, we will complete our training phase by testing the model with cross-validation, an evaluation for generalization purposes, and training the final model using all the available data.

7.2.6   *Training the final model*

Having completed the optimization, we can conclude our work by testing the results directly by cross-validation and then training the model on all available data. The

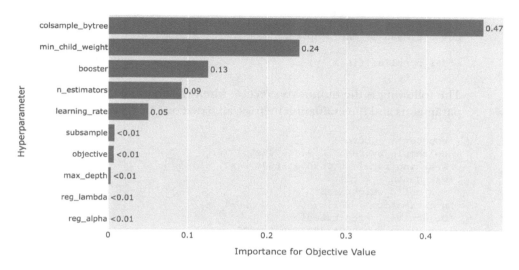

Figure 7.14 Importance of hyperparameters in the tuning process

code presented in listing 7.18 doesn't change much from the code we previously used. Notice that now, for our estimation, we are using a cross-validation procedure, not cross-validation predictions, because we are more interested in understanding the generalization capabilities of our model and not how it fits precisely the data at hand.

Listing 7.18 Training the model with full data

```
best_params = study.best_params
print(best_params)

xgb = XGBRegressor(**best_params)
model_pipeline = Pipeline([('processing', column_transform), ('xgb', xgb)])

cv_splits = cv.split(X, y=X["neighbourhood_more_than_30"])

r2_scores = []
rmse_scores = []
mae_scores = []

for train_index, test_index in cv_splits:
    X_train, X_test = X.iloc[train_index], X.iloc[test_index]
    y_train, y_test = y.iloc[train_index], y.iloc[test_index]

    model_pipeline.fit(X_train, y_train)
    y_pred = model_pipeline.predict(X_test)

    r2_scores.append(r2_score(y_test, y_pred))
    rmse_scores.append(np.sqrt(mean_squared_error(y_test, y_pred)))
    mae_scores.append(mean_absolute_error(y_test, y_pred))
```

Initializes an XGBoost Regressor using the best hyperparameters obtained from the Optuna study

Splits the data using the specified StratifiedKFold strategy

Iterates through the cross-validation folds to test the model

```
print(f"Mean cv R-squared: {np.mean(r2_scores):.3f}")
print(f"Mean cv RMSE: {np.mean(rmse_scores):.3f}")
print(f"Mean cv MAE: {np.mean(mae_scores):.3f}")

model_pipeline.fit(X, y)                              ◄─── Trains the final model
                                                          on the entire dataset
```

The following is the output you receive when running the code, containing the used parameters and the evaluation metrics, all based on our cross-validation strategy:

```
{'booster': 'gbtree',
 'colsample_bytree': 0.946407058507176,
 'learning_rate': 0.06867015067874482,
 'max_depth': 7,
 'min_child_weight': 5,
 'n_estimators': 901,
 'objective': 'reg:tweedie',
 'reg_alpha': 0.0006368936493084075,
 'reg_lambda': 3.8302865696045996,
 'subsample': 0.8956307610431394,
 'tweedie_variance_power': 1.560801988491813
}

Mean cv R-squared: 0.727
Mean cv RMSE: 10886.568
Mean cv MAE: 6667.187
```

We can also visualize, as shown in figure 7.15, the complete pipeline comprising the column transformer, accepting the different features for its distinct transformation operations, and the XGBoost model receiving all the assembled data from the column transformer.

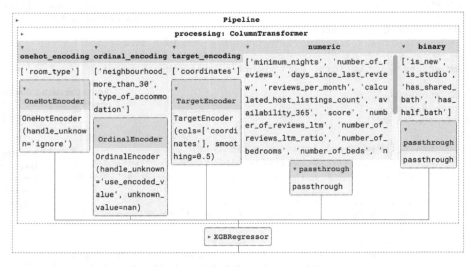

Figure 7.15   Pipeline comprising column transformations and XGBoost model

Having thoroughly trained our model, we could say that we are done. Actually, this could be just the first cycle of multiple iterations because models have to be retrained often to escape what is called concept drift, as we explained in chapter 2, where the relationships between the predictors and the target change over time, rendering past models ineffective after a while.

In addition, often, the work of a machine learning engineer and of a data scientist doesn't end with a working model because it is crucial to be able to figure out how it works and how the predictors actually relate with the target, providing insights into how a model arrives at its predictions. Explaining how a model works helps build trust, facilitates debugging, aids regulatory compliance, and enables humans to understand, validate, and improve the decision-making process of AI systems, which is the topic of the concluding section of this chapter.

7.3 *Explaining your model with SHAP*

To conclude, we spend some time trying to understand how our XGBoost model works because, as EDA helps you understand how your model can use data, explainability techniques such as SHAP (SHapley Additive exPlanations) or partial dependence plots (described in the previous chapter) can help you know how your model uses the data to come to its predictions. Explainability can provide valuable insights that help you better prepare your data, revise previous assumptions, and discard unuseful or detrimental features.

In addition, explainability plays other softer roles in a data science project than providing insights into how the model uses its features and generates predictions:

- *Human-AI collaboration*—When working with tabular data, data scientists collaborate with domain experts or business stakeholders who may not be well-versed in complex models. Explainability allows data scientists to communicate model insights effectively to nontechnical audiences.
- *Building trust*—In certain domains, such as healthcare or finance, model explainability is essential to build trust with stakeholders and regulatory bodies.
- *Compliance and regulations*—In some geographical areas and industries, there are regulatory requirements for model transparency and explainability, such as in the European Union, where the General Data Protection Regulation emphasizes the "right to explanation" for automated decision-making systems.
- *Bias detection and mitigation*—Explainability can help identify biases in the data and the model's decision-making process, highlighting if the model's decision-making process could disadvantage any sensible group.

Given all these reasons, we decided to produce SHAP values, which can be generated by the SHAP package (https://github.com/shap/shap; install with `pip install shap`) and its TreeSHAP algorithm for tree-based models but also natively and more efficiently by XGBoost, as well as LightGBM, using a simple procedure.

SHAP values are a method that can explain the way predictions of machine learning models are built. They are based on Shapley values, a cooperative game theory concept that fairly distributes each feature's "credit" or "importance" in a model's prediction for a specific data instance. In other words, SHAP values allocate the contribution of each feature to the model's output using a simple additive formula.

Shapley values consider the contribution of a feature across all possible combinations of features, which can be thought of as "games" in the model. These "games" involve training the model on different feature subsets. SHAP values approximate Shapley values using a resampling strategy to avoid computing all possible games for the model and feature sets. By using SHAP values, we gain insights into how each feature influences the model's predictions on specific instances. This information is valuable for model debugging, feature engineering, and enhancing machine learning models' overall interpretability and trustworthiness.

We implemented SHAP values in listing 7.19 to gain insights into our previously built XGBoost model. In the code, we first retrieve the trained XGBoost model from a pipeline. In particular, we get its booster, the core component of the XGBoost model responsible for implementing the gradient boosting algorithm. Then we transformed the training data two times: first because we could not use the pipeline to feed the data into the booster directly. Hence, we preprocess it by hand and extract its feature names for reference. Second, we transform the data into a DMatrix data structure (see the XGBoost documentation at https://mng.bz/yWQd), a specific XGBoost data structure for efficient processing that is required for feeding the booster directly. At this point, we compute the SHAP values by a predict command with the parameter `pred_contribs` set to true. Another simple predict command just provides us with the predictions from the model to be used for comparison.

Listing 7.19   SHAP values as an XGBoost output

```
from XGBoost import DMatrix

booster = model_pipeline['xgb'].get_booster()          ◄── Retrieves the trained XGBoost
                                                            booster object from the pipeline's
                                                            trained XGBoost model
Xt = model_pipeline['processing'].transform(X)         ◄── Transforms the input data X
feature_names = (                                           using the processing pipeline
    model_pipeline['processing']
    .get_feature_names_out()                           ◄── Gets the names of the transformed
)                                                           features after the processing
Xd = DMatrix(Xt)                                            pipeline's transformations

shap_values = booster.predict(Xd, pred_contribs=True)  ◄── Creates a
preds = booster.predict(Xd)                            ◄── DMatrix from
                                                            the transformed
                                                            input data
```

Gets the raw predicted values for the input data

Calculates SHAP values using the booster's predict function with the pred_contribs=True argument

Just for comparison, we have to note that LightGBM is also capable of the same, using the same prediction method with the `pred_contribs` parameter set to true. The only difference is that you do not need to extract any booster from the trained LightGBM model. You just use the model itself directly.

Note that whether you are doing a classification or a regression, the resulting SHAP values obtained by this method are log transformations of a multiplicative model. It means that if you want to recreate the original prediction, you first have to exponentiate the values and then multiply them by themselves, as demonstrated by the following code snippet, reconstructing for the first example the prediction from the SHAP values and comparing it to the effective prediction:

```
np.prod(np.exp(shap_values[0])), preds[0]

(10627.659, 10627.469)
```

As you can see, there are slight discrepancies in the reconstruction, which can be attributed to approximations and small errors. However, in general, the SHAP values provide a good approximation of the predictions themselves. When applying the same approach to the entire training set and assessing its adherence to the original predictions using Pearson's correlation, it demonstrates a strong fit of the SHAP values to the predictions:

```
np.corrcoef(preds, np.prod(np.exp(shap_values), axis=1))

array([[1., 1.],
       [1., 1.]])
```

As an alternative to directly outputting the SHAP values as an XGBoost prediction, you can use the `TreeExplainer` function from the SHAP package (https://mng.bz/pKXR). The function, though being declared built with fast C++ implementations, is way slower than the direct predictions from XGBoost. However, using the `TreeExplainer`, you can specify more output options, particularly the output type and the calculation method, which can allow you to reconstruct the original prediction as seen previously (using the parameter `feature_perturbation="tree_path_dependent"`) or using a method that "breaks the dependencies between features according to the rules dictated by casual inference," thus providing more reliable insights when there is strong collinearity among the features (using the parameter `feature_perturbation="interventional"`). You can obtain the interventional SHAP values using the following code snippet:

```
from shap import TreeExplainer

explainer = TreeExplainer(model_pipeline['xgb'], data=Xt, model_output='raw',
    feature_perturbation='interventional')
interventional_shap_values = explainer.shap_values(Xt)
```

The resulting SHAP values matrix is less truthful to the original data and cannot reconstruct the predictions as seen before. Still, such an approach could provide more reliable contribution estimates "true to the model" as explained in technical terms in the following GitHub problem: https://github.com/shap/shap/issues/1098. Based on our experience, we suggest using `TreeExplainer` and the interventional approach, although it may require longer computation times when dealing with data presenting highly multicollinear features.

Up to now, we have used the SHAP values as a method for explaining individual samples. We investigated, by the inspection of feature contributions, the reasons why a certain prediction is made. However, we can consider all the SHAP values together and reason about them to figure out a general explanation for the entire model. In this case, as for other methods, we can plot some summary and diagnostic charts to figure this out better. The first listing we propose quantifies the relative importance of the features by an average of the SHAP values. Here, we use plotting facilities from the `shap` package. You install the package by running the command `pip install shap` in a shell or a cell of your notebook.

Listing 7.20 SHAP importance plot

```
import shap

shap.summary_plot(
    shap_values[:,:-1],
    Xt,
    plot_type="bar",
    feature_names=feature_names,
    max_display=10,               Generates a summary plot of
    show=False                    SHAP feature importance for the
)                              ◄── top 10 most important features
plt.xticks(fontsize=8)
plt.yticks(fontsize=8)
plt.xlabel("SHAP Importance", fontsize=10)
plt.show()
```

Figure 7.16 shows the resulting plot, and you can immediately determine that four features tend to dominate the predictions, which are the availability, which is also a proxy for the market offer-demand dynamic for a certain accommodation (less availability may imply a shared use or less demand for that accommodation); target encoded coordinates (i.e., the position of the accommodation in the city); the number of bedrooms, a proxy of how large the accommodation is; and the number of beds, which helps together with the previous figure to distinguish the hostel-like listings, which are usually less pricey. All the other features play a lesser role, which can be seen from the scale of the plot: the importance of the last of the 10 most important features is a fifth of the top important features.

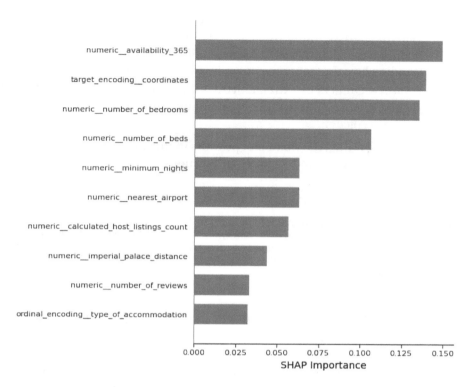

Figure 7.16   SHAP importance

Importance, however, tells just a part of the story. We also need directionality. Hence, the violin chart can provide even more information on the model's behavior. In a violin plot produced by the `shap` package, you can get hints from these details:

- *Feature importance*—The width of the violin plot indicates the density of SHAP values. Wider sections represent more instances with similar SHAP values for that feature. Thus, features with broader violin plots are generally more important in the model's predictions.

- *Shape of the violin*—The violin's shape indicates the distribution of SHAP values for the corresponding feature. If the violin is symmetric, it suggests that SHAP values are evenly distributed around the median, signifying a balanced effect on predictions. Asymmetry indicates skewness and suggests that certain feature values have more significant effects than others.

- *Positive and negative contributions*—The violin plot's center line (median) is usually zero. The left and right halves of the violin represent their respective contributions for features with positive and negative SHAP values. Positive SHAP values push predictions higher, while negative SHAP values push them lower.

- *Association with the feature value*—The color of the violin plot can help you associate blue areas, where the feature has lower values, and red areas, where the feature has higher values, with specific SHAP contributions. This helps in understanding how the feature is generally related to the outcome.

- *Outliers*—Outliers or extreme SHAP values outside the range of the violin plot suggest instances where the corresponding feature has an unusually strong effect on the prediction.

In the following listing, the violin plot provides useful insights into the distribution and the role of each feature on the model's predictions.

Listing 7.21   SHAP violin plot

```
shap.summary_plot(shap_values[:,:-1], Xt,
                  plot_type="violin",
                  feature_names=feature_names,
                  show=False)
plt.yticks(fontsize=8)
plt.show()
```

Creates a SHAP summary plot using violin plots to visualize the distribution of SHAP values for each feature

Figure 7.17 shows the resulting violin plot. As for our top important features, we can figure out the following:

- `Numeric__availability_365`—Higher availability corresponds to a positive effect on price. Listings with lower availability are usually penalized.

- `Target_encoding__coordinates`—It is difficult to interpret since its values are unrelated to a specific directionality. We can observe that there are long tails on both sides with a prevalence of a negative contribution to the pricing of the accommodation.

- `Numeric__number_of_bedrooms`—A higher number of bedrooms implies a higher price, with a long skewed tail to the right.

- `Numeric__number_of_beds`—Similarly, a higher number of beds implies a higher price, with a long skewed tail to the right.

A glance at other features provides an idea of how the model behaves intuitively. For instance, the nearer the accommodation is to the Imperial Palace or the airports, the higher the price.

This concludes our end-to-end example using gradient boosting. In the next chapter, we are going to get back to the Airbnb NYC problem and will review a set of deep learning stacks (low-level framework, high-level API, and deep learning for tabular data library) and use three of these stacks (fastai, PyTorch with TabNet, and Lightning Flash) to solve it and compare the different solutions.

In this phase, a generative AI tool such as ChatGPT could be useful for creating narratives explaining the SHAP values assigned to each example. Being able to create an easy explanation for each prediction could prove to be a strong point when demonstrating the potentialities of your model or trying to persuade clients and stakeholders.

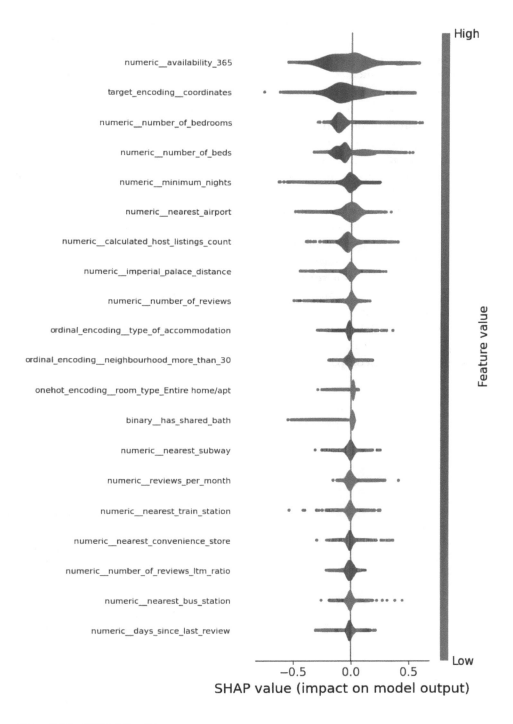

Figure 7.17 SHAP violin plot

In addition, the need for a narration explaining the model's predictions of the dataset is crucial under regulations such as those in the European Union. Transparency and interpretability are essential components of regulations striving at data protection and preserving privacy, such as the General Data Protection Regulation in the EU. According to these regulations, individuals have the right to make sense of the logic behind automated decision-making processes that significantly affect their lives. Providing a clear and comprehensible explanation for why a specific prediction has been made ensures transparency and accountability and promotes fairness: it gives individuals the power to seek clarification, challenge unfair decisions, and ultimately safeguard their rights.

You can actually generate each of these narratives by single prompts to create explanations on the fly or by using the ChatGPT API and have the model process batches of explanations that you can later recall when questioned about the reason for a specific prediction. The recipe is, however, the same in both on-the-fly or batch processing approaches: you have to tell the LLM to explain by providing the list of the features (detailed with their description or meaning, if necessary), the original value in the dataset, and the SHAP value relative to the feature. Of course, it is necessary to mention the resulting prediction. Gluing together all such information for the LLM to process using JSON (a dictionary of dictionaries) could be ideal. In listing 7.22, we offer a solution for preparing a JSON structure to facilitate the prompt request to ChatGPT to explain a specific example in the dataset, identified by its row index. The code generates a data structure that encompasses all the information required to construct a coherent narrative explanation.

Listing 7.22   Building a JSON of SHAP explanations as part of a prompt

```
def generate_prediction_explanation(
    index,
    X,
    feature_names,
    shapley_values,
    predictions
):                                                         Instantiates the JSON data
    explanation = {}                                       structure as a Python dictionary
    explanation["prediction"] = predictions[index]         Includes the
    for feature, original_value, shap_value in zip(        predicted value to
        feature_names,                                     explain in the JSON
        X[index],
        shapley_values[index, :]
    ):                                                     Iterates over the features,
        explanation[feature] = {                           original value, and SHAP
            "original_value": original_value,              values of the examined row
            "shap_value": shap_value
        }
    return explanation
                                                           Index of the prediction
index_to_explain = 5                                       to explain
explanation_json = generate_prediction_explanation(
    index_to_explain,
```

```
    feature_names,
    Xt,
    shap_values,
    preds
)
print(explanation_json)
```

In our example, we require a description of why the model predicted a particular value for row 5 of the dataset. The printed JSON can then be enclosed in a prompt such as

```
You are an expert data scientist, and you need to interpret the predictions
 of a regression model based on the shape values provided in a JSON file.
 You build the explanations as a narration of how the most important
variables contribute to the prediction. Here is the JSON file:
{'prediction': 55225.176, 'onehot_encoding__room_type_Entire home/apt':
{'original_value': 1.0, 'shap_value': 0.03404991},
'onehot_encoding__room_type_Hotel room': {'original_value': 0.0,
'shap_value': 0.00020163489}, … }
```

When you submit this prompt to ChatGPT, you will receive a text organized in bullet points categorized by types of variables. This text describes the influence of each individual variable or group of variables on the outcome. The following is an excerpt of the insights we derived for the specific instance represented by row 5:

- *Room type*—The "Entire home/apt" room type has a positive effect on the predicted price, contributing a SHAP value of 0.034. This suggests that listings with the entire home/apartment as the room type tend to have higher prices.
- *The other room types* ("Hotel room," "Private room," and "Shared room")—These have smaller positive or negligible contributions, indicating that their effect on the price is not as significant.
- *Neighborhood*—The feature `neighbourhood_more_than_30` has a positive SHAP value of 0.083, suggesting that being in a neighborhood with more than 30 listings positively influences the price.
- *Type of accommodation*—The `type_of_accommodation` feature has a small negative effect with a SHAP value of −0.008. This implies that certain types of accommodation might have a slightly lower price.

The complete text actually touches on all the features, and you can prompt the LLM to reduce the results to only the top 5 or 10 impactful features, if you prefer. Certainly, using a language model for this job makes a difficult task simple and automates it in a breeze.

Summary

- Getting and preparing your data requires downloading, restructuring, and assembling it all together. It is often a long and laborious part of the work in an end-to-end project, but it is an indispensable one, building the foundations for the success of your following work.

- Feature engineering is not just magic or randomly combining features; most often, it is embedding prior knowledge about a problem and how to solve it in the features you will be using to train your model. Exploring the set of domain knowledge related to a problem is the first step to model your data effectively.

- Exploring your predictions and target in the EDA phase is an essential part of your schedule for modeling a tabular problem. Look for outliers and extreme values, missing data, and any other peculiarity from the data. Feel free to drop examples if you are unsure they can provide real value to your model.

- Before delving into modeling, check for your validation strategy, which may require extra work, EDA, and your data pipeline. Both can make a difference in the modeling phase. Ideally, prepare a pipeline for each type of model you want to test because each model has different ways of dealing with the various types of data you find in tabular datasets. In our example, as a simplification, we tried a one-size-fits-all approach. Please remember that such examples work well in books, but there are better ways to do it in real-world projects.

- Building a baseline model is an often-neglected phase in modeling tabular data problems. Still, it can provide valuable insights by inspecting how the model underfits or overfits the data and its internal coefficients. A baseline model should necessarily be simple, meaning that linear and logistic regression are the best candidates for regression and classification problems.

- After you get insights from your baseline model, you can proceed to more complex models such as XGBoost. Cues about underfitting, nonlinearities, interactions, targets, and the predictors' characteristics should be considered when setting up the first tentative values for key hyperparameters.

- Optimizing your model using Optuna can save you a lot of time if you set your search space to incorporate insights and hypotheses you have developed so far regarding how your model should handle the data and the problem. Once the optimization has been completed, further insights can be gained from observing hyperparameter importance and optimization path charts.

- Explaining your trained model can be easily done with XGBoost and LightGBM using the predict method with the parameter `pred_contribs` set to true. Once the SHAP values, which are effectively multipliers with respect to the prediction, are obtained, you can use standard charts from the `shap` package, such as the importance plot or the violin plot.

Part 3

Deep learning for tabular data

Part 3 is your guide to the know-how and practical insights needed to apply deep learning to tabular data problems. As a stand-alone solution or integrated with gradient boosting, deep learning can get good results with tabular data when you know how to use its unique way of finding solutions to predictive tasks.

Chapter 8 explores various deep learning stacks and frameworks for working with tabular data, including low-level frameworks like TensorFlow and PyTorch and high-level APIs like fastai and Lightning Flash. It introduces several libraries specifically designed for tabular deep learning tasks, such as TabNet, PyTorch Tabular, SAINT, and DeepTables. We compare the different stacks and discuss each one's strengths and weaknesses. Chapter 9 extends the discussion to best practices. We use the Kuala Lumpur real estate dataset to illustrate these best practices for deep learning with tabular data, including data preparation, model architecture design, and model training. A Keras-based project, the example emphasizes easy, understandable, and effective data pipelines, along with a modular approach that promotes code reuse.

Chapter 10 explores how to make a trained deep learning model available for use in a real-world environment using Flask, a Python framework that excels in web interfaces and API serving. Chapter 11 extends the discussion by guiding you through the steps to define a pipeline for training and deploying a model using the Vertex AI environment in Google Cloud, including creating Docker containers to encapsulate the model code and dependencies, defining pipeline steps, and running the pipeline on Vertex AI. We then proceed to discuss Gemini's capabilities for Google Cloud, such as answering questions about Google Cloud, generating code from text, interpreting code, and summarizing log entries. All these capabilities can be applied to your workflow to create your own machine learning pipeline.

The book concludes with chapter 12, where you will learn how to combine deep learning with machine learning to achieve state-of-the-art results in predictive tasks. After you read this book, model design, training, deployment, and interpretability will no longer hold any secrets for you!

Getting started with deep learning with tabular data

8

Up to this point, we have focused on classical machine learning tools and algorithms to analyze tabular data. Ranging from traditional regression algorithms to more sophisticated gradient boosting techniques, these approaches offer advantages in simplicity, transparency, and efficacy. That said, deep learning tools have become much easier to access and use, and they also provide a powerful alternative for handling tabular data.

In this chapter, we will review a set of deep learning stacks (low-level framework, high-level API, and deep learning for tabular data library) and use three of these stacks—fastai, PyTorch with TabNet, and Lightning Flash—to solve the Airbnb NYC problem. We'll work the same problem three times, once with each stack. The goal is to illustrate both the general form of the deep learning approach and to highlight the unique characteristics of the three tools we've selected.

8.1   *The deep learning with tabular data stack*

Before we examine the stacks that are available for deep learning with tabular data in general, let's look at a specific example: the Keras-based deep learning solution for the Airbnb NYC price prediction problem from chapter 3.

> ### The Keras solution vs. the XGBoost solution
>
> The code that is distinct for the Keras solution is contained in the training notebook. In particular, the key differences between the Keras solution and the XGBoost solution described in chapter 3 include
>
> - *Model definition*—The Keras model has a large function to define the layers that make up the model, with each class of column (continuous, categorical, and text) getting a specific set of layers.
> - *Model training*—The Keras model includes additional code to define the callbacks required to make the training process efficient, including a callback to stop the training process early if the training is no longer making the model better and a callback to ensure that the optimal model is saved during the training process.
>
> The Keras solution that we examined in chapter 3 gives us a concrete baseline with which to compare the other stacks we will examine in this chapter. In this chapter, we will exercise a set of other stacks so you can see the pros and cons of each choice.
>
> We will also discuss an additional set of stacks that we weren't able to exercise and explain what this experience tells us about these choices. It is important to understand the stack choices and the pros and cons of the choices so that you can select a deep learning with tabular data stack that works best for your requirements.

Let's briefly review the Keras solution from chapter 3. Figure 8.1 shows the files that make up the Keras solution, with the training notebook highlighted.

The training notebook contains the code that varies between the Keras solution and the other solutions that we will explore in this chapter. The other files stay consistent across all the deep learning solutions, with the exception of some settings in the training config file.

Figure 8.2 shows the components that make up the stack for this solution. These components are used in the training notebook.

In this stack the underlying, low-level deep learning framework is TensorFlow. Since Keras is delivered as part of the TensorFlow distribution and is the recommended

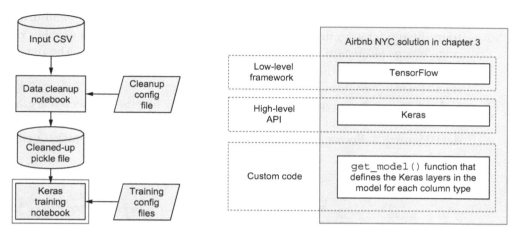

Figure 8.1   Files that make up the Keras solution to the Airbnb problem

Figure 8.2   The stack for the Airbnb NYC solution in chapter 3

high-level API for TensorFlow, it may sound a bit redundant to talk about TensorFlow and Keras separately, but keeping them distinct will make the description of the general stack choices clearer. In the deep learning solution from chapter 3, we used custom-written code to define the model itself. For example, listing 8.1 shows the custom code that defines layers for categorical columns in the deep learning solution from chapter 3. The listing also shows the statements in the get_model() function that define the layers for categorical columns.

Listing 8.1   Statement in the get_model() function for categorical column layers

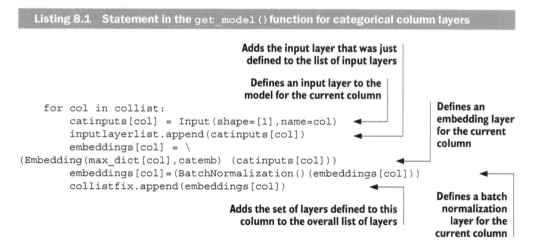

The get_model() function specifies the Keras layers in the model for three types of input columns: categorical, continuous, and text. The get_model() function shown in listing 8.1 also contains statements that define the model layers for continuous layers and text layers. Note that this model has multiple inputs (each column selected to train the model is an input) and a single output: a prediction of whether or not the price of a given Airbnb listing will be above or below the median. The details of how the layers for each of the input columns are defined is beyond the scope of this chapter, so we won't go through those now.

Now that we have reviewed what the stack looks like for the deep learning Airbnb NYC solution in chapter 3, let's generalize to other deep learning approaches to tabular data. Figure 8.3 shows a selection of choices for the deep learning stack for tabular data problems.

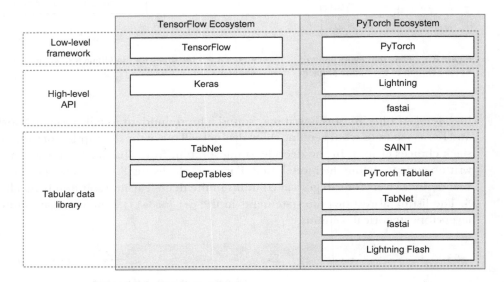

Figure 8.3   Deep learning stacks for tabular data

Let's examine each layer of the stacks in more detail:

- *Low-level framework*—There are two predominant low-level deep learning frameworks. TensorFlow is used most frequently in industry. PyTorch is the most popular choice for researchers.
- *High-level API*—To make it easier for beginners to create deep learning applications and to abstract some of the complexity for experienced developers, in the mid-2010s the need was identified for a high-level API for deep learning. Initially, you could use Keras as a front end for several low-level frameworks. In 2019, Keras was integrated into the TensorFlow ecosystem and identified as the recommended high-level framework for TensorFlow. There isn't an exact analogy for Keras in the PyTorch world. The overall design of PyTorch is supposed to make it more accessible than TensorFlow and reduce the need for a high-level

API. Nevertheless, there are two high-level APIs that abstract different aspects of PyTorch. fastai is intended specifically for people coming from other disciplines who want to use deep learning to solve problems in their discipline and has as its central ethic being able to define, train, and exercise a deep learning model with just a handful of lines of code. Lightning, by contrast, abstracts a single aspect of PyTorch, the training loop. Lightning Flash, which is built on top of Lightning, is, according to its documentation, "a high-level deep learning framework for fast prototyping, baselining, fine-tuning and solving deep learning problems." While both fastai and Lightning have devoted communities of users, neither has attracted the popularity in the PyTorch world that Keras has in the TensorFlow world.

- *Tabular data library*—The low-level framework and high-level API provide an environment for deep learning in general. The deep learning libraries provide capabilities specifically for dealing with tabular data. As we demonstrated with the deep learning solution for the Airbnb NYC price prediction problem in chapter 3, you don't need to use a tabular data library to do deep learning with tabular data.

Two details to note about the tabular data libraries are

- Tabular data libraries may be supported for both TensorFlow and PyTorch. TabNet is an example of a library that is supported for both low-level deep learning frameworks.

- fastai is a general-purpose, high-level API as well as a tabular data library. fastai fits into both categories because it abstracts some of the complexity of PyTorch to make it easier to build and train models on a variety of data types (including image and text) and also has facilities aimed specifically at tabular data (for example, automatically handling basic operations required for categorical features in tabular datasets).

Now that we have examined the deep learning with tabular data stack, let's look at the stacks that we will examine in this chapter by applying them to solve the Airbnb NYC price prediction problem:

- *PyTorch with fastai*—This is the most "traditional" approach since fastai is an established framework with tens of thousands of developers using it. fastai is the most popular framework that explicitly supports tabular data, according to repo stars. fastai is particularly popular with people who are learning about deep learning and hobbyists.

- *PyTorch with TabNet*—TabNet is the next most popular tabular data library after fastai according to repo stars. TabNet is a library for tabular data highlighted by Google in its documentation (https://mng.bz/av1m). This stack demonstrates how a dedicated tabular data library can be used to create a model trained on tabular data.

- *Lightning Flash*—PyTorch Lightning is a popular framework that abstracts some of the complexity of PyTorch. Lightning Flash is built on top of PyTorch Lightning and offers an easily accessible way to create deep learning applications. It also includes explicit support for tabular data and thus is an interesting comparison point for the other stacks we review in this chapter.

The next three sections in this chapter describe the solution to the Airbnb NYC price prediction problem using each of these three stacks. In each section we will review the code for a solution and compare the pros and cons of the solution with those of our baseline, the Keras solution from chapter 3.

8.2 *PyTorch with fastai*

Now let's take a look at one of the toolkits: PyTorch/fastai. Because we're considering the same dataset and problem we just discussed, we won't rehash it here. Much of the solution is quite similar among the different toolkits. Here, we'll concentrate on the distinctive portions of the PyTorch code. You can find the complete solution in the code repository for the book: https://mng.bz/gaBv.

8.2.1 *Reviewing the key code aspects of the fastai solution*

Now let's dive into the fastai solution to our Airbnb NYC listing price prediction problem. To start with, fastai has a unique set of imports, as shown in listing 8.2, that get the libraries required to use fastai in a Jupyter notebook.

Listing 8.2   Import statements for the fastai solution

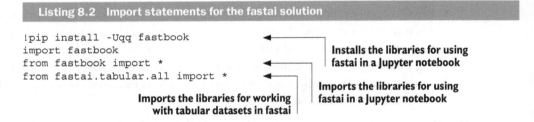

```
!pip install -Uqq fastbook
import fastbook
from fastbook import *
from fastai.tabular.all import *
```

Installs the libraries for using fastai in a Jupyter notebook

Imports the libraries for using fastai in a Jupyter notebook

Imports the libraries for working with tabular datasets in fastai

With these libraries imported as shown in listing 8.2, you have the libraries required to run a fastai tabular data application in a Jupyter notebook.

Next, fastai needs to have the characteristics of the tabular dataset defined, including the column that contains the target for the model (called the *dependent variable* in fastai) and the lists for the categorical and continuous columns, as shown in the following listing.

Listing 8.3   Dataset definition statements for the fastai solution

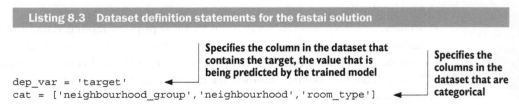

Specifies the column in the dataset that contains the target, the value that is being predicted by the trained model

Specifies the columns in the dataset that are categorical

```
dep_var = 'target'
cat = ['neighbourhood_group','neighbourhood','room_type']
```

```
cont = \
['minimum_nights','number_of_reviews',\
'reviews_per_month','calculated_host_listings_count']
```
◄─── Specifies the columns
in the dataset that are
continuous

We'll use the values defined in listing 8.3 when we define the `TabularDataloaders` (https://mng.bz/5gwO) object for this model. The `TabularDatalloaders` object encapsulates the samples from the dataset, including the labels, to make it easy to work with the dataset.

Next, we need to ensure that the target column contains string values:

```
merged_data['target'] =merged_data.target.astype(str)
```

If we don't do this, we will encounter a subtle problem. To try it for yourself, comment out this statement and run the fastai training notebook. You will see that the training produces some strange results, as shown in figure 8.4.

epoch	train_loss	valid_loss	accuracy	time
0	0.140194	0.135970	0.645500	00:20
1	0.137121	0.140755	0.645500	00:11
2	0.127553	0.137144	0.645500	00:11

Figure 8.4 fastai training results when the target column is not explicitly converted to string values

Figure 8.4 shows the results for each epoch of the training process, including the training loss, the validation loss, and the accuracy. The accuracy values shown in figure 8.4 are significantly lower than the accuracy we saw in chapter 3 for the XGBoost and Keras deep learning solutions (between 79% and 81%), and accuracy does not improve from one epoch to another. Training for a larger number of epochs doesn't help; the accuracy stays the same. Why does fastai produce such disappointing results? There's a clue in the output of the `learn.loss_func` statement, as shown in the following listing.

> **Listing 8.4 Statement to show the loss function used in model training**

```
learn.loss_func
FlattenedLoss of MSELoss()
```
◄─── Statement that returns the loss function
used in training the fastai model

Statement output showing the loss
function used in training the fastai model

The output shown in listing 8.4 shows the loss function being used for the model. If you don't specify a loss function for the fastai model, fastai selects a loss function based on the values in the target column. We want to train a classification model, so the loss function should be cross-entropy. However, it looks like fastai selected a loss function for a regression problem rather than a classification problem. That's why the training results shown in listing 8.4 are bad—fastai is trying to solve a classification problem (predicting a continuous value) rather than the classification problem we intended (predicting a 0 or a 1 to indicate whether the listing has a price above or below the median price).

The output of `dls.valid.show_batch()`, as shown in figure 8.5, gives us another clue because the values in the `target` column are floating point when they should be "0" or "1."

	neighbourhood_group	neighbourhood
0	Manhattan	Hell's Kitchen
1	Manhattan	Hell's Kitchen
2	Manhattan	Hell's Kitchen
3	Brooklyn	Bushwick
4	Brooklyn	Williamsburg

Categorical features

minimum_nights	number_of_reviews	reviews_per_month	calculated_host_listings_count	target
1.000000	18.000000	2.490000e+00	30.000001	1.0
1.000000	16.000000	2.220000e+00	30.000001	1.0
1.000000	13.000000	1.820000e+00	30.000001	1.0
15.000000	0.000001	1.455204e-08	2.000000	0.0
19.999999	1.999999	4.200000e-01	1.000000	0.0

Continuous features   **Target**

Figure 8.5   Sample batch values when the target column is not explicitly converted to string values

If we go back and look at the dataset using `merged_data.head()`, as shown in figure 8.6, the values in the `target` column all look like 0 or 1.

These values in the `target` column are, in fact, numeric values, which means that if we don't explicitly convert them to strings, then by default fastai will assume that if we use this dataset to train a model, the model desired is a regression model.

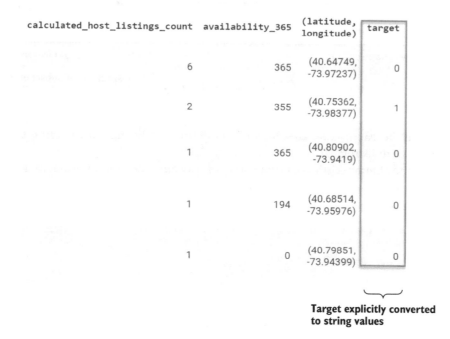

calculated_host_listings_count	availability_365	(latitude, longitude)	target
6	365	(40.64749, -73.97237)	0
2	355	(40.75362, -73.98377)	1
1	365	(40.80902, -73.9419)	0
1	194	(40.68514, -73.95976)	0
1	0	(40.79851, -73.94399)	0

Target explicitly converted to string values

Figure 8.6 Sample batch values when the target column is explicitly converted to string values

Now that we have examined why it's critical to convert the values in the target column to string values, let's review the rest of the code to create a trained fastai model. Listing 8.5 shows the block of code that defines the `TabularDataLoaders` object. This object is a tabular-data specific wrapper around the PyTorch `DataLoader` (https://mng.bz/6eDe) object, which is an iterable encapsulation of the samples and labels in a dataset.

Listing 8.5   Defining the `TabularDataLoaders` object

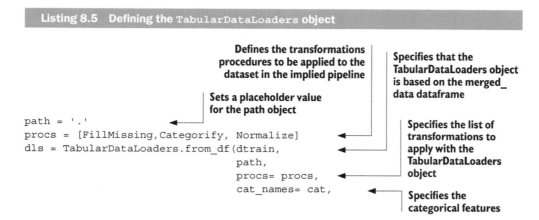

Defines the transformations procedures to be applied to the dataset in the implied pipeline

Specifies that the TabularDataLoaders object is based on the merged_data dataframe

Sets a placeholder value for the path object

```
path = '.'
procs = [FillMissing,Categorify, Normalize]
dls = TabularDataLoaders.from_df(dtrain,
                    path,
                    procs= procs,
                    cat_names= cat,
```

Specifies the list of transformations to apply with the TabularDataLoaders object

Specifies the categorical features

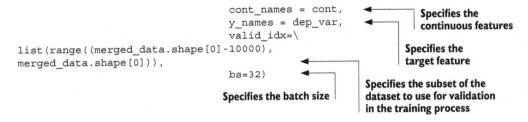

We will use the `TabularDataLoaders` object defined in listing 8.5 to define the fastai model shown in listing 8.7.

One of the characteristics of fastai is a set of convenience functions that makes it easy to examine the dataset through the stages of training. The `show_batch()` statement shown in the following listing is an example of such a convenience function.

Listing 8.6   Statement to show a batch of the training data

```
dls.valid.show_batch()
```

The statement shown in listing 8.6 makes it easy to see what the data that is training the model looks like after the transformations specified in the `procs` parameter of the `TabularDataLoaders` definition. Figure 8.7 shows the output of this statement.

neighbourhood_group	neighbourhood	room_type
Manhattan	Hell's Kitchen	Private room
Manhattan	Hell's Kitchen	Private room
Manhattan	Hell's Kitchen	Private room
Brooklyn	Bushwick	Private room
Brooklyn	Williamsburg	Private room

minimum_nights	number_of_reviews	reviews_per_month	calculated_host_listings_count	target
1.000000	18.000000	2.490000e+00	30.000001	1
1.000000	16.000000	2.220000e+00	30.000001	1
1.000000	13.000000	1.820000e+00	30.000001	1
15.000000	0.000001	1.455204e-08	2.000000	0
19.999999	1.999999	4.200000e-01	1.000000	0

Figure 8.7   Output of the `show_batch()` statement

Now that we have specified the data that will be used to train the model, it's time to define and train the model.

Listing 8.7   Defining and fitting the fastai model

Defines the model as a tabular_learner object using
the TabularDataLoaders object dls and using accuracy
as the performance measurement for training

```
learn = tabular_learner(dls, metrics=accuracy)        ◄──┐  Trains the model
learn.fit_one_cycle(3)                                 ◄──┘  with three epochs
```

Note that the statements in listing 8.7 that define and fit the model are much simpler than the model definition and fit statements that we saw for the Keras model in chapter 3. In this sense, the code for the fastai solution resembles the code for the XGBoost solution that we saw in chapter 3.

Figure 8.8 shows the output of the fit statement. For each epoch, the training loss, validation loss, and accuracy are listed. If we compare the training results shown in figure 8.4 (when the target column was not explicitly converted to string values) with the training results shown in figure 8.8 (when the target column was converted to string values), it's clear that we get better results when fastai treats the problem as a classification problem rather than a regression problem.

epoch	train_loss	valid_loss	accuracy	time
0	0.434672	0.407458	0.817900	00:17
1	0.424458	0.406396	0.814900	00:11
2	0.385092	0.405317	0.817100	00:10

Epoch number	Training loss	Validation loss	Accuracy	Elapsed time for epoch

Figure 8.8   Output of the fit statement

Before continuing with the rest of the fastai solution, let's take a moment to discuss the relationship between training loss, validation loss, and test loss. Figure 8.8 shows the training and validation loss at each epoch. Training loss that is lower than validation loss indicates that the model could be underfit or that regularization techniques that only apply to training (such as dropout) are having an outsize effect. Figure 8.8 shows the validation loss as being lower than the training loss in the first epoch. For the subsequent epochs, the training loss drops faster than the validation loss until it is lower than the validation loss by the final epoch.

The following listing confirms that fastai is treating the problem as a classification problem because the loss function is CrossEntropyLoss(), a loss function that is appropriate for a classification problem.

Listing 8.8   Statement to show the loss function used in model training

```
learn.loss_func
FlattenedLoss of CrossEntropyLoss()
```

Statement that returns the loss function used in training the fastai model

Statement output showing the loss function used in training the fastai model

The output shown in listing 8.8 establishes that we now get the desired loss function after setting the target column to contain string values. Now let's look at what layers fastai defines for the model. The following listing shows the `summary()` statement, which lets us see the layers that make up the fastai model.

Listing 8.9   Statement to get a summary of the fastai model

```
learn.summary()
```

The output of the statement in listing 8.9 is shown in figure 8.9, which shows the output of the `summary()` statement, including the layers that make up the model along with the number of parameters in the model and callbacks used.

```
TabularModel (Input shape: 32 x 3)
========================================================================
Layer (type)         Output Shape          Param #    Trainable
========================================================================
                     32 x 4
Embedding                                  24         True
_____
                     32 x 33
Embedding                                  7326       True
_____
                     32 x 3
Embedding                                  12         True
Dropout
BatchNorm1d                                8          True
_____
                     32 x 200
Linear                                     8800       True
ReLU
BatchNorm1d                                400        True
_____
                     32 x 100
Linear                                     20000      True
ReLU
BatchNorm1d                                200        True
_____
                     32 x 2
Linear                                     202        True
_____

Total params: 36,972
Total trainable params: 36,972
Total non-trainable params: 0

Optimizer used: <function Adam at 0x7fdb00a86cb0>
Loss function: FlattenedLoss of CrossEntropyLoss()

Model unfrozen

Callbacks:
  - TrainEvalCallback
  - CastToTensor
  - Recorder
  - ProgressCallback
```

Figure 8.9   Output of the `summary()` statement

Now that we have examined the key code areas in the fastai solution, let's revisit the stack diagram to see where the fastai stack fits. Figure 8.10 shows the deep learning with tabular data stack from the example in this section. Note that the figure shows fastai as both a high-level API and a tabular data library since fastai plays both roles in the stack.

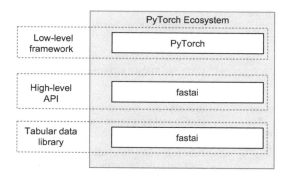

Figure 8.10   The stack for PyTorch with fastai

Now that we have reviewed the code in the fastai solution, in the next section we'll compare this solution to the Keras solution that we saw in chapter 3.

8.2.2   *Comparing the fastai solution with the Keras solution*

We have now seen two deep learning solutions to the Airbnb NYC listing price prediction problem: the Keras solution and the fastai solution. In this section, we'll compare the two solutions and review the pros and cons of each.

The fastai and Keras solutions make interesting comparison points because they are very different. The Keras solution contains a lot of custom code, and all the details are evident. The fastai framework infers details about the model from the dataset and makes assumptions about the defaults to use so that there aren't many parameters that we need to specify to get a working model. The benefit of this is that the fastai code is much more compact than the Keras code. In particular, the Keras solution has multiple lines of code to specify the pipeline and the details of the layers that make up the model. In the fastai solution, we get the pipeline for free by simply specifying the transformations that we want applied to the input data (as shown in listing 8.6), and we don't need to specify the layers that make up the model. The downside of the compactness of the fastai solution is that subtle problems can get introduced if we're not careful. In the previous section, we saw that if we don't explicitly convert the target column to string values, then fastai will interpret the values in the target column as continuous values and assume we want to train a regression model rather than a classification model.

Table 8.1 shows a summary of the pros and cons of the Keras and fastai solutions to the Airbnb NYC problem. If we compare the performance of the two solutions, the Keras model gets between 70% and 74% accuracy, while the fastai model consistently gets around 81% accuracy.

Table 8.1   Summary of the pros and cons of the Keras and fastai solutions

	Keras	**fastai**
Pro	Model details are transparent. Large community using the framework means that it's easy to find solutions to common problems	Framework includes explicit support for tabular data models, which means the code is much more compact. Framework automatically defines pipeline. Framework includes convenience functions that make it easy to examine the dataset.
Con	No built-in support for tabular data, which means we need to define custom code to define the pipeline and layers for the model.	Assumptions made by the framework can lead to tricky problems that are hard to debug. User community is smaller and less involved in deploying production applications than the Keras community, which means it can be harder to find solutions to problems.

Let's cover one more point of comparison between the Keras solution and the fastai solution: the underlying low-level deep learning framework. For Keras, the underlying framework is TensorFlow, while fastai is built on top of PyTorch. This means we have now reviewed deep learning solutions for tabular data problems with both of the major deep learning frameworks.

One of the similarities between Keras and fastai is that they are both general-purpose high-level deep learning APIs. We have seen they can both be used for tabular data problems, but they are also designed to deal with a range of data types, not just tabular data. In the next section, we look at a deep learning library that is specifically designed for tabular data problems: TabNet. We examine a solution for the Airbnb NYC problem that uses TabNet and then contrast it with the Keras solution.

8.3   *PyTorch with TabNet*

The two tools we've considered so far are designed as general deep learning libraries. Now, we will try out a purpose-built tabular data library: TabNet. Again, we'll skip the introduction to the problem and concentrate our discussion only on the parts of the solution that differ from the previous examples. You can find the code for this solution at https://mng.bz/oK1Z.

8.3.1   *Key code aspects of the TabNet solution*

In this section, we'll go through the key parts of the code that make up the TabNet solution to the Airbnb NYC listing price prediction problem.

The TabNet solution requires a set of imports, as shown in the following listing.

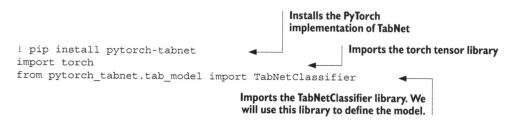

Listing 8.10 Import statements for TabNet

Installs the PyTorch implementation of TabNet

Imports the torch tensor library

```
! pip install pytorch-tabnet
import torch
from pytorch_tabnet.tab_model import TabNetClassifier
```

Imports the TabNetClassifier library. We will use this library to define the model.

Note that, unlike the fastai import statements, the import statements for TabNet in listing 8.10 include an explicit statement to import the PyTorch library `torch`.

Unlike the fastai solution, which does not have any explicit code to define the pipeline and has unique code to define the dataset, the TabNet solution uses the same code as the Keras and XGBoost solutions up to and including the definition of the pipelines. After the pipeline definitions, the TabNet solutions use code similar to XGBoost to convert the list of NumPy arrays that comes out of the pipeline into a NumPy array of lists, as shown in the following listing.

Listing 8.11 Statements to generate NumPy arrays of lists

```
list_of_lists_train = []
list_of_lists_test = []
list_of_lists_valid = []
for i in range(0,7):
    list_of_lists_train.append(X_train_list[i].tolist())
    list_of_lists_valid.append(X_valid_list[i].tolist())
    list_of_lists_test.append(X_test_list[i].tolist())
X_train = np.array(list_of_lists_train).T
X_valid = np.array(list_of_lists_valid).T
X_test = np.array(list_of_lists_test).T
y_train = dtrain.target
y_valid = dvalid.target
y_test = test.target
```

Defines lists of lists for the training, validation, and test datasets (one list for each feature)

Converts the train list of lists into a NumPy array of lists

Converts the validation list of lists into a NumPy array of lists

Defines variables for the training, validation, and test target sets

Converts the validation list of lists into a NumPy array of lists

The transformations shown in listing 8.11 are needed because the TabNet solution expects the input to the model to be in the form of a NumPy array of lists. Next, the TabNet solution includes code to define the model.

Listing 8.12 Statements to define the TabNet model

Defines a TabNetClassifier object as the model for the solution and specify an adam optimizer

Sets the learning rate for the model

```
tb_cls = TabNetClassifier(optimizer_fn=torch.optim.Adam,
                optimizer_params=dict(lr=1e-3),
```

```
                    scheduler_params={"step_size":10,"gamma":0.9},   ◄──────┐
                    scheduler_fn=torch.optim.lr_scheduler.StepLR,          │
                    mask_type='entmax' # "sparsemax"          ┌────────────┘
                    )                                         Sets parameters for the
                                                              learning rate scheduler
```

The model definition shown in listing 8.12 specifies a set of hyperparameters, including the optimizer and learning rate. Next, the TabNet solution includes code to train the model.

Listing 8.13 Statements to train the TabNet model

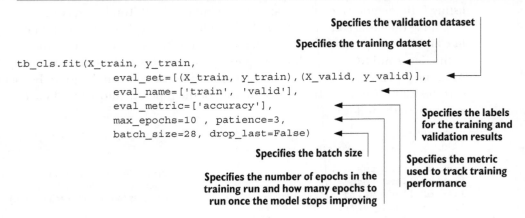

The statement in listing 8.13 that specifies the training for the TabNet model includes early stopping setting, including the `patience` parameter that indicates how many epochs the training will continue once the model stops improving.

The output of the training statement shows the results of each epoch, including loss, training accuracy, and validation accuracy, as well as the effect of early stopping, as shown in figure 8.11.

```
/usr/local/lib/python3.7/dist-packages/pytorch_tabnet/abstract_model.py:75: UserWarning: Device used :
  warnings.warn(f"Device used : {self.device}")
epoch 0  | loss: 0.51915 | train_accuracy: 0.77486 | valid_accuracy: 0.76751 |  0:00:40s
epoch 1  | loss: 0.46227 | train_accuracy: 0.78681 | valid_accuracy: 0.78093 |  0:01:13s
epoch 2  | loss: 0.45386 | train_accuracy: 0.78547 | valid_accuracy: 0.78055 |  0:01:47s
epoch 3  | loss: 0.45003 | train_accuracy: 0.78848 | valid_accuracy: 0.78387 |  0:02:20s
epoch 4  | loss: 0.44799 | train_accuracy: 0.78995 | valid_accuracy: 0.78515 |  0:03:02s
epoch 5  | loss: 0.44571 | train_accuracy: 0.79084 | valid_accuracy: 0.78694 |  0:03:36s
epoch 6  | loss: 0.44432 | train_accuracy: 0.79065 | valid_accuracy: 0.78566 |  0:04:09s
epoch 7  | loss: 0.44506 | train_accuracy: 0.79052 | valid_accuracy: 0.78655 |  0:04:43s
epoch 8  | loss: 0.44116 | train_accuracy: 0.79225 | valid_accuracy: 0.78783 |  0:05:16s
epoch 9  | loss: 0.43959 | train_accuracy: 0.79174 | valid_accuracy: 0.78732 |  0:05:50s
Stop training because you reached max_epochs = 10 with best_epoch = 8 and best_valid_accuracy = 0.78783
```

Figure 8.11 Output of the TabNet fit statement

In the training run output shown in figure 8.11, the maximum number of epochs (10) are run because the validation accuracy does not stop improving for more than 2 epochs until the maximum number of epochs is reached. This means that the `patience` threshold of 3 set in the `fit` statement is never crossed, so the training run goes for the max-

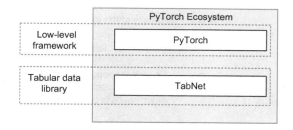

Figure 8.12   The stack for PyTorch with TabNet

imum number of epochs. Figure 8.12 shows the deep learning with tabular data stack from the example in this section.

Now that we have reviewed the code in the TabNet solution, in the next section we'll compare this solution to the Keras solution that we saw in chapter 3.

8.3.2 *Comparing the TabNet solution with the Keras solution*

We have now seen three deep learning solutions to the Airbnb NYC listing price pre-diction problem: the Keras solution, the fastai solution, and the TabNet solution. In this section we'll compare the Keras solution with the TabNet solution and review the pros and cons of each.

The Keras solution and the TabNet solution are interesting to compare because they demonstrate some of the strengths and weaknesses of their underlying frameworks, TensorFlow and PyTorch. The Keras solution benefits from the simple `summary()` state-ment that gives a compact list of the layers that make up the model. PyTorch lacks this elegant feature, so the TabNet solution is also missing that benefit. Keras, on the other hand, does not provide built-in control for the training process, so you have to define callbacks to ensure that you end up with the optimal model from the training run at the end of the run and that you don't waste resources running epochs when the model has stopped improving. PyTorch, on the other hand, incorporates early stopping and saving of the optimal model by default, so the TabNet solution doesn't need to include code to explicitly define callbacks to optimize the training process. Table 8.2 shows a summary of the pros and cons of the Keras and TabNet with PyTorch solutions to the Airbnb NYC problem.

Table 8.2   Summary of the pros and cons of the Keras and TabNet solutions

	Keras	**TabNet**
Pro	Large community using the frame-work means that it's easy to find solutions to common problems Simple summary statement to show the layers in the model	Simple statements to define and train the model Don't need an explicitly defined callback to get the benefit of early stopping

Table 8.2 Summary of the pros and cons of the Keras and TabNet solutions (*continued*)

	Keras	TabNet
Con	No built-in support for tabular data, which means the model definition needs to be hand-coded.	Training process is much slower. The Keras model training notebook took ~20 seconds to run. The TabNet training notebook took over 4 minutes. No one-stop summary statement to see the structure of the model

In this section we reviewed the Airbnb NYC pricing prediction solution for PyTorch TabNet. In the next section we will review our final approach to the Airbnb problem: PyTorch with Lightning Flash.

8.4   *PyTorch with Lightning Flash*

So far, we've considered Keras, fastai, and TabNet PyTorch solutions for the Airbnb NYC price prediction problem. Now let's turn to our final stack: Lightning Flash. As a platform designed for fast prototyping, baselining, and fine-tuning, along with a clear API and outstanding documentation, Lightning Flash potentially offers advantages over the stacks we have explored so far.

You can find the code for this solution at https://mng.bz/vKnp. Figure 8.13 shows the fastai and Tabnet on PyTorch stacks.

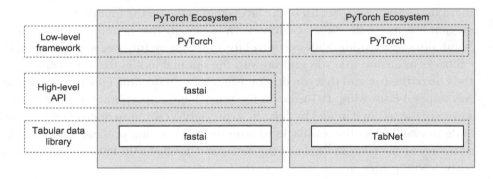

Figure 8.13   The fastai and Tabnet on PyTorch stacks

8.4.1   *The key code aspects of the Lightning Flash solution*

The code for the Lightning Flash solution has many aspects that are different from the solutions we have seen so far. In this section, we go through the model training notebook (https://mng.bz/4aDR) to highlight the most interesting points about this solution.

To work in Colab, the Lightning Flash solution requires a set of installs done in a particular order, as shown in listing 8.14. The source for this list is https://mng.bz/QDP6.

Listing 8.14   Installs required to get Lightning Flash to work in Colab

```
!pip install torch==1.8.1+cu102 -f
https://download.pytorch.org/whl/torch_stable.html
!pip install icevision #==0.9.0a1
!pip install effdet
!pip install lightning-flash[image]
!pip install git+https://github.com/PyTorchLightning/lightning-flash.git
!pip install torchtext==0.9.1
!pip uninstall fastai -y
!curl https://raw.githubusercontent.com/airctic/ \
icevision/944b47c5694243ba3f3c8c11a6ef56f05fb111eb/ \
icevision/core/record_components.py -output \
   /usr/local/lib/python3.7/dist- \
packages/icevision/core/record_components.py
```

Series of pip installs to get the required levels of PyTorch Lightning

To eliminate potential conflicts between fastai and Lightning Flash, fastai needs to be uninstalled.

Manually applies a fix for a bug in the current release of icevision

Listing 8.14 includes a long list of installs (and one uninstall) to get Lightning Flash to work in Colab. From experience, we know that this very specific list of installs is required or there will be conflicts between the levels of libraries that Lightning Flash requires and the default library levels for Colab.

Next, the libraries required by Lightning Flash need to be imported.

Listing 8.15   Library imports required by Lightning Flash

Imports the torch tensor library

Imports the flash library

```
import torch
import flash
from flash.tabular import TabularClassificationData,
from flash.tabular import TabularClassifier
```

Imports the objects needed for a tabular classification model

Note that the torch import statement in listing 8.15 is the same statement that you saw to import torch in listing 8.11 for TabNet.

Next, we define the parameters for the dataset that we will use to train the model.

Listing 8.16   Setting dataset parameters

Sets the target field as the value that the trained model will predict

Defines the list of categorical features

```
dep_var = 'target'
cat=['neighbourhood_group','neighbourhood','room_type']
cont = ['minimum_nights','number_of_reviews',
'reviews_per_month','calculated_host_listings_count']
```

Defines the list of continuous features

The definitions in listing 8.16 should remind you of a similar block of code in the fastai solution (listing 8.3), where we defined the target feature along with lists for the categorical and continuous features.

Next we use the values we just defined to define a `TabularClassificationData` object. This object specifies the minimum characteristics of the dataset that we will use to train the model.

Listing 8.17   Defining a `TabularClassificationData`

```
datamodule = TabularClassificationData.from_csv(
    categorical_fields=cat,                    ← Defines the categorical features
    numerical_fields=cont,                     ← Defines the continuous features
    target_fields="target",                    ← Defines the target feature
    train_file='../data/train.csv',            ← Defines the training dataset
    val_file='../data/valid.csv',              ← Defines the validation dataset
    predict_file='../data/test.csv',           ← Defines the test dataset
    batch_size=64
)
```

We should explain why the definition of the `TabularClassificationData` object shown in listing 8.17 uses separate CSV files for the train, validation, and test datasets. For all the other solutions, the dataset is loaded from a pickle file that is the output of the data cleanup notebook (https://mng.bz/XxN9), which is then split into train, validation, and test datasets in the model training notebook. The Lightning Flash solution is different because it has distinct CSV files for each segment of the dataset. The reason for this is that the very specific installation requirements shown in listing 8.14 were incompatible with loading the pickle file that contains the output dataframe from the data cleanup notebook. As a workaround, we loaded that pickle file in a separate notebook into a pandas DataFrame and saved the separate CSV files for the training, validation, and test that you see in the definition of the `TabularClassificationData` object in listing 8.17. As an exercise, you could update the data cleanup notebook for the Lightning Flash solution so that it saves the cleaned-up dataset as three separate CSV files rather than as a single pickle file.

Now that we have specified the details about the dataset, we are ready to define and train the model, as shown in the following listing.

Listing 8.18   Setting dataset parameters

```
model = TabularClassifier.from_data(datamodule,
learning_rate=0.1)                              ← Defines the model using the
trainer = flash.Trainer(max_epochs=3,            TabularClassifierData object
gpus=torch.cuda.device_count())                  defined in listing 8.18
trainer.fit(model, datamodule=datamodule)       ← Defines a Trainer object
                                                ← Fits the model
```

The training code in listing 8.18 generates the output shown in figure 8.14.

```
INFO:pytorch_lightning.accelerators.cuda:LOCAL_RANK: 0 - CUDA_VISIBLE_DEVICES: [0]
INFO:pytorch_lightning.callbacks.model_summary:
  | Name          | Type                | Params
---------------------------------------------------------
0 | train_metrics | ModuleDict          | 0
1 | val_metrics   | ModuleDict          | 0
2 | test_metrics  | ModuleDict          | 0
3 | adapter       | PytorchTabularAdapter | 12.7 K
---------------------------------------------------------
12.7 K    Trainable params
0         Non-trainable params
12.7 K    Total params
0.051     Total estimated model params size (MB)
Epoch 2: 100% ████████████████████████████████████

   611/611 [00:19<00:00, 31.67it/s, loss=0.481, v_num=3, train_loss=0.456, valid_loss=0.461, valid_accuracy=0.710, train_accuracy=0.698]

INFO:pytorch_lightning.utilities.rank_zero:`Trainer.fit` stopped: `max_epochs=3` reached.
```

Figure 8.14   Output of the Lightning Flash training process

Note the output includes the validation accuracy and training accuracy for the model. Figure 8.15 shows the deep learning with tabular data stack from the example in this section.

The code for the Lightning Flash solution incorporates some very elegant ideas, such as being able to specify the training, validation, and test datasets in the same object where you define the overall characteristics of the dataset. Overall, the API for Light-

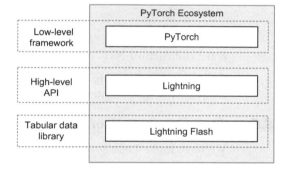

Figure 8.15   The PyTorch with Lightning Flash stack

ning Flash is easy to understand. Unfortunately, these benefits are undermined because Lightning Flash requires such specific requirements to run in Colab. Otherwise, Lightning Flash could have been a favorite, combining the simplicity of fastai with the intuitiveness of Keras.

8.4.2   *Comparing the Lightning Flash solution with the Keras solution*

We have now seen four deep learning solutions to the Airbnb NYC listing price prediction problem: the Keras solution, the fastai solution, the TabNet solution, and, finally, the Lightning Flash solution. In this section we'll compare the Keras solution with the Lightning Flash solution and review the pros and cons of each.

We've seen that Lightning Flash has some real advantages for rolling out a fast, simple solution. However, the lack of a beaten path to using Lightning Flash in Colab is concerning, and one has to wonder how long the elaborate set of installs shown in listing 8.15 will continue to make it possible to run Lightning Flash experiments in Colab. Table 8.3 shows a summary of the pros and cons of the Keras and Lightning Flash solutions to the Airbnb NYC problem.

Table 8.3   Summary of the pros and cons of the Keras and TabNet solutions

	Keras	Lightning Flash
Pro	Large community using the framework means that it's easy to find solutions to common problems. Simple summary statement to show the layers in the model	Simple statements to define and train the model Don't need to explicitly define a pipeline—just need to identify the categorical and continuous columns.
Con	No built-in support for tabular data, which means the model definition needs to be hand-coded.	To get working in Colab, you need a very specific order and level of installs. Does not seem to be widely used, at least not with Colab. Out of the box, test accuracy was worse than other solutions.

So far in this chapter we have applied three deep learning with tabular data stacks to solve the Airbnb NYC price prediction problem and compared the pros and cons of each solution. In the next section, we review an overall comparison of all the stacks we exercised in this chapter.

8.5   *Overall comparison of the stacks*

We have looked at a total of four deep learning for tabular data stacks. Table 8.4 summarizes the performance of all of these stacks on a default Colab setup, with a standard GPU Colab runtime option selected for the deep learning solutions.

Table 8.4   Summary of accuracy and running time of the deep learning with tabular data stacks (plus XGBoost) for the Airbnb NYC listing price prediction problem

	Test Accuracy	Notebook running time
TensorFlow with Keras	81%	16 seconds
fastai with PyTorch	83%	69 seconds
TabNet with PyTorch	81%	568 seconds
Lightning Flash with PyTorch	TBD	14 seconds
XGBoost	79%	14 seconds

It is important to note here that for the purposes of this comparison we didn't do any tuning of any of the approaches. We wanted to have a genuine "apples-to-apples" comparison of how the approaches compare to the Keras baseline without additional tuning. In subsequent chapters, we will discuss some of the tuning that can be done to get optimal results from a deep learning solution.

For accuracy, fastai is slightly better than the other stacks. For execution time, Lightning Flash is best, and TabNet is the slowest. So what is the best stack to use for tabular data? First, if we compare XGBoost with any of the deep learning solutions, which is best? We will answer this question in more detail in chapter 9, but we can say now that if it's a straight-up comparison between deep learning and gradient boosting, for the sake of simplicity and overall performance "out of the box," gradient boosting approaches like XGBoost are currently better than any of the deep learning solutions for most datasets. There are use cases where it is worthwhile to explore one of the deep learning solutions, and we will review these use cases in chapter 9.

If you do decide to use a deep learning solution for a tabular data problem, of the four we explored so far, which one should you use? Here is our overall advice:

- If you are new to deep learning and are primarily interested in exploring a solution without needing to immediately implement the solution in production, fastai is the best choice. It is the simplest stack to use, and it has a big enough user community that you are not likely to be stuck with a problem that nobody has seen before. Fastai includes many convenience features to make it easy to work with tabular data, so you can rapidly prototype your solution. However, if you need to move your solution rapidly to production, fastai is probably not your best choice because it is not commonly used in production.

- If you are already comfortable with deep learning and you need to get an application into production, we recommend the Keras stack. First, TensorFlow, the low-level component of the stack, is the deep learning framework that is used most commonly in industry. Second, Keras has a huge user community. While Keras does not yet have native support for tabular data the same way that fastai does, Keras is high-level enough to lend itself to tabular data problems.

This advice may change as more people use deep learning with tabular data. One of the other stacks, such as TabNet on PyTorch, could mature and become the default choice for deep learning with tabular data. However, looking at the current state of the art, we recommend fastai for beginners and explorers and Keras for people who are more experienced and need to proceed to production rapidly.

In the next section we will discuss the stacks that we didn't explore in this chapter.

8.6 The stacks we didn't explore

You may have asked why we chose three particular stacks (fastai, PyTorch TabNet, and Lightning Flash) to solve the Airbnb NYC problem and didn't explore the other options, such as TabNet on TensorFlow, SAINT, or PyTorch Tabular. In this section, we'll look at this question and see what the answer tells us about the options that we have for deep learning with tabular data stacks. Figure 8.16 shows the deep learning with tabular data stacks that we didn't explore.

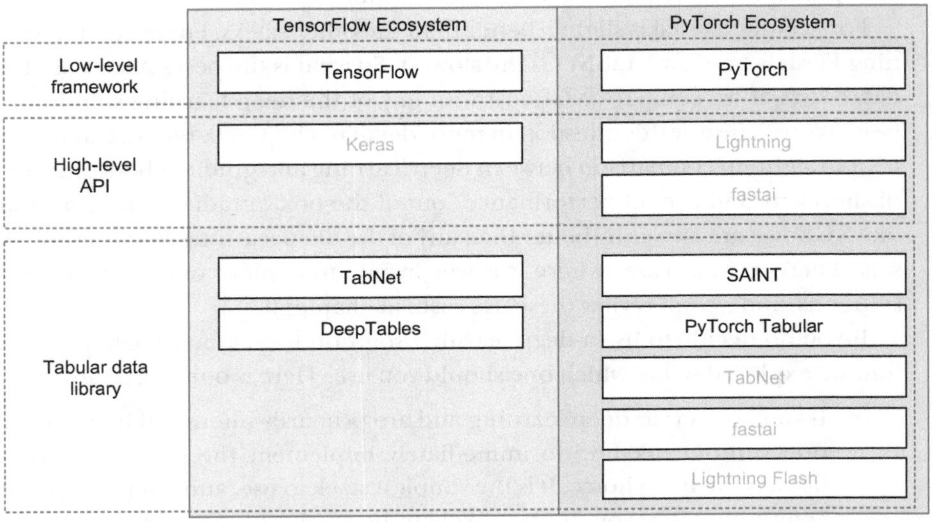

	TensorFlow Ecosystem	PyTorch Ecosystem
Low-level framework	TensorFlow	PyTorch
High-level API	Keras	Lightning
		fastai
Tabular data library	TabNet	SAINT
	DeepTables	PyTorch Tabular
		TabNet
		fastai
		Lightning Flash

Figure 8.16   The stacks we didn't explore

There are a couple of characteristics that the unexplored stacks have in common:

- All of the unexplored stacks involve dedicated tabular data libraries.
- We were not able to get any of the unexplored stacks to work in Colab, the environment that we used to exercise the code examples in this book.

Our inability to get the unexplored stacks to work in Colab could be due to a number of reasons. There could theoretically be some limitations with Colab. However, Colab is a very common environment for exploration, so it's not a good sign if a library cannot be coaxed to life in Colab. All of the stacks featured "hello world" examples for exercising the stack, and for all the unexplored stacks these examples generated errors, mostly to do with contradictory Python library prerequisites. It's possible that if we had been more patient, or looked a little harder, we would have been able to work through the errors to get the basic examples to work in Colab. Of the stacks that we did explore, Keras, fastai, and PyTorch TabNet all worked "out of the box" in Colab. Lighting Flash, on the other hand, did require some tweaking before it worked in Colab.

The difference between Lightning Flash and the unexplored stacks is that it was clear that other people had tried to get Lightning Flash to work in Colab, and we could find informal documentation that showed exactly what we needed to do to get it to work in Colab. If your goal is to solve a tabular data problem with deep learning, you want to focus on the problem, not on fiddling with conda and pip installing boutique levels of libraries to avoid incompatibilities. By that criteria, Keras, fastai, PyTorch TabNet, and, to a lesser extent, Lightning Flash are viable choices for deep learning with tabular data in Colab. SAINT, DeepTables, PyTorch Tabular, and TabNet on TensorFlow are not viable choices for exploration in Colab because they don't work right away, and the recipes to get them to work either don't exist or are not easy to find.

While it is disappointing that we weren't able to exercise the Airbnb NYC price prediction problem with more of the dedicated deep learning with tabular data libraries, we were still able to accomplish the goal of this chapter by exploring three deep learning with tabular data stacks. Figure 8.17 shows all the stacks that we were able to explore.

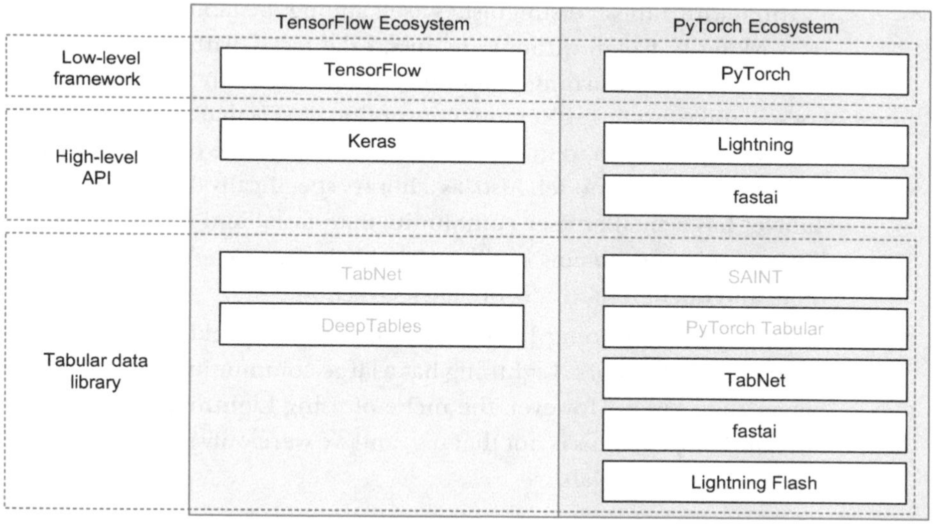

Figure 8.17 The stacks we explored

The stacks we explored in this chapter, plus TensorFlow with Keras, present a well-rounded set of options:

- TensorFlow with Keras is a rock-solid stack with a huge community of users. For just about any problem that you encounter with this stack, you can bet that somebody else has hit the problem and posted a solution. The stack works flawlessly in Colab, so doing initial investigation is easy. TensorFlow with Keras is commonly used in production for all kinds of applications. On the downside, Keras does not have built-in support for tabular data, so you need to be prepared to write some custom code to tackle tabular data problems.

- PyTorch with fastai is designed to be easy to get started with, and it works flawlessly in Colab, so you can expect to prototype deep learning with tabular data problems with this stack with minimal hassle. fastai treats tabular data as a first-class citizen, so you get built-in support for dealing with categorical and continuous features and you don't need to worry about hand-coding a pipeline to ensure that when you feed data to the trained model to get a prediction, the data goes through the same transformations as the data used to train the model. On the downside, you can pay a price for the simplicity of fastai code. The automated steps that fastai takes can lead to some hard-to-debug problems (such as the problem we described in this chapter where the wrong kind of model gets trained if the target column isn't explicitly converted to a string type), and you need to be prepared to dig deep into the fastai API if you want to go off the beaten path provided by fastai's tabular data structures.

- PyTorch with TabNet distinguishes itself among the tabular-data-specific libraries by working in Colab without any fuss. Like fastai, with TabNet you can define and train a deep learning model on tabular data with just a handful of lines of code. Unlike fastai, TabNet uses conventional APIs that are easy for anybody who has used Scikit-learn to understand. Compared to the other stacks, TabNet took longer to train the model. Also, as a library specifically designed for tabular data, TabNet has a smaller user community than fastai and Keras, which means that if you run into problems it will be less likely that somebody else has already hit them and documented a fix on Stack Overflow.

- PyTorch with Lightning Flash trains the model quickly and has a simple API, once you get it to work. Lightning has a large community—not as big as Keras but bigger than fastai. However, the niche of using Lightning Flash on Colab to do tabular data problems is not that big, and we were only just able to get Lightning Flash to work on Colab.

In this chapter we have explored a set of deep learning with tabular data stacks, compared the pros and cons of each approach, and discussed why we left some other stacks unexplored. In the next chapter we are going to review the best practices for deep learning with tabular data.

Summary

- There are two low-level deep learning frameworks: TensorFlow and PyTorch.
- TensorFlow is used more frequently in industry.
- PyTorch is the predominant deep learning framework for research.
- Keras is a high-level API for TensorFlow.
- fastai is both a general-purpose, high-level API for PyTorch and a tabular data library.
- PyTorch Lightning is a high-level API that abstracts some of the details of PyTorch. Lightning Flash is a tabular data library based on Lightning.

- Lightning Flash and fastai each provide some of the same benefits for PyTorch that Keras does for TensorFlow by abstracting aspects of the underlying PyTorch framework.
- TabNet is a tabular data library that is available for both TensorFlow and PyTorch.
- SAINT is a tabular data library for TensorFlow.
- PyTorch Tabular is a tabular data library for PyTorch.
- Of all the choices available, TensorFlow with Keras, PyTorch with fastai, PyTorch with TabNet, and PyTorch with Lightning Flash are all valid options for deep learning with tabular data on Colab.

Deep learning best practices

In chapter 8 we examined a set of stacks for doing deep learning with tabular data. In this chapter, we use one of these stacks, Keras, to explore some best practices for deep learning with tabular data, including how to prepare the data, how to design the model, and how to train the model. We introduce a new problem to demonstrate all these best practices: predicting whether real estate properties in Kuala Lumpur will have a price above or below the median price for the market. We selected this dataset because it is messier and more challenging to prepare than the Airbnb NYC dataset we have used so far. Consequently, we'll be able to demonstrate a wider range of techniques for applying deep learning to tabular datasets.

If you are new to training deep learning models, the examples in this chapter will help you learn some best practices. If you already have extensive experience with defining and training deep learning architectures, this chapter could be beneficial for you as a review of principles.

9.1　*Introduction to the Kuala Lumpur real estate dataset*

In this chapter, we will use the Kuala Lumpur real estate dataset to explain the best practices for deep learning with tabular data. This dataset consists of records that describe properties sold in Kuala Lumpur, the capital of Malaysia. Figure 9.1 presents a sample of the records in this dataset from the output of df.head(). The code illustrated in this chapter is at https://mng.bz/yWQp.

	Location	Price	Rooms	Bathrooms
0	KLCC, Kuala Lumpur	RM 1,250,000	2+1	3.0
1	Damansara Heights, Kuala Lumpur	RM 6,800,000	6	7.0
2	Dutamas, Kuala Lumpur	RM 1,030,000	3	4.0
3	Cheras, Kuala Lumpur	NaN	NaN	NaN
4	Bukit Jalil, Kuala Lumpur	RM 900,000	4+1	3.0

Car Parks	Property Type	Size	Furnishing
2.0	Serviced Residence	Built-up : 1,335 sq. ft.	Fully Furnished
NaN	Bungalow	Land area : 6900 sq. ft.	Partly Furnished
2.0	Condominium (Corner)	Built-up : 1,875 sq. ft.	Partly Furnished
NaN	NaN	NaN	NaN
2.0	Condominium (Corner)	Built-up : 1,513 sq. ft.	Partly Furnished

Figure 9.1　Sample of the Kuala Lumpur real estate dataset

In the next section, we'll go through the steps we need to take to clean up each of the columns in this dataset. To prepare for those descriptions, let's first review what's in each column of the dataset:

- Location—The neighborhood in which the property is located.
- Price—The listed price for the property in Ringgit, including RM, the conventional symbol for Malaysian currency.
- Rooms—The number of rooms in the property. Values like "2 + 1" in this column mean the property has two bedrooms and one room that cannot be classified as a bedroom.
- Bathrooms—The number of washrooms in the property.
- Car Parks—The number of parking spaces on the property.

- `Property Type`—The category of property, such as "Condominium," "Serviced Residence," etc.
- `Size`—The dimensions of the property. There are several aspects of the property that values in this column could refer to, including the overall land area or the built-up area within the property.
- `Furnishing`—Whether the property is furnished or not.

One of the basic questions we need to answer about this dataset is what columns are continuous or categorical. By looking at figure 9.1, we can spot a subset of columns that contain numeric values. Let's take a closer look at this subset of the dataset to see if we can determine which columns are continuous. Figure 9.2 shows values from the subset of columns in the dataset that appear to contain numeric data.

Price	Rooms	Bathrooms	Car Parks	Size
RM 1,250,000	2+1	3.0	2.0	Built-up : 1,335 sq. ft.
RM 6,800,000	6	7.0	NaN	Land area : 6900 sq. ft.
RM 1,030,000	3	4.0	2.0	Built-up : 1,875 sq. ft.
NaN	NaN	NaN	NaN	NaN
RM 900,000	4+1	3.0	2.0	Built-up : 1,513 sq. ft.

Figure 9.2   Subset of columns that look like they contain numeric data

We can validate which of these columns have numeric data by using the following command:

```
df.describe()
```

This command returns descriptive statistics for all numeric columns in the DataFrame, providing insights into the data distribution, central tendency, and spread within each numeric column. By examining the output of this command, you can identify which columns indeed contain numerical values. The output of this command is shown in figure 9.3.

Figure 9.3 indicates that only `Bathrooms` and `Car Parks` are numeric columns and that `Price`, `Rooms`, and `Size` are not numeric columns even though they contain some data that looks numeric. In the next section, as part of processing the dataset, we will describe the steps to extract the numeric data from the `Price`, `Rooms`, and `Size` features and make it available to train a model.

Another way of evaluating which columns are categorical or continuous is to count the number of unique

	Bathrooms	Car Parks
count	51870.000000	36285.000000
mean	3.073434	2.006973
std	1.631079	1.306358
min	1.000000	1.000000
25%	2.000000	1.000000
50%	2.000000	2.000000
75%	4.000000	2.000000
max	20.000000	30.000000

Figure 9.3   Output of `describe()` for this dataset

values in each column. If a column contains a large number of unique values, that may be an indication that we should treat it as continuous, and if it contains a relatively small number of values, that may be an indication that we should treat it as categorical. In fact, features presenting few unique values are often considered categorical because they typically represent discrete categories or groups rather than continuous numerical measurements. This is not a hard and fast rule, as we shall see. The output of the `df.unique()` command gives the number of unique values in each column in the dataset.

Listing 9.1 Getting the count of unique values in each column

```
counts = df.nunique()
print("unique value counts:\n",counts)
```
Returns the number of unique values in each column of the dataframe df

The output of the command in listing 9.1 looks like the following:

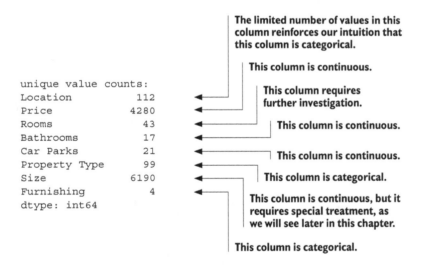

The limited number of values in this column reinforces our intuition that this column is categorical.

This column is continuous.

This column requires further investigation.

This column is continuous.

This column is continuous.

This column is categorical.

This column is continuous, but it requires special treatment, as we will see later in this chapter.

This column is categorical.

```
unique value counts:
Location         112
Price           4280
Rooms             43
Bathrooms         17
Car Parks         21
Property Type     99
Size            6190
Furnishing         4
dtype: int64
```

To summarize what the output of the command in listing 9.1 tells us about the dataset:

- *Columns that appear to be categorical*—`Location`, `Property Type`, `Furnishing`.
- *Columns that appear to be continuous*—`Price`, `Bathrooms`, `Car Parks`, `Size`. Of these columns, `Size` also requires further investigation.
- *Columns that need further investigation to determine whether they should be treated as continuous or categorical*—`Rooms`.

Two of these columns require further investigation: `Rooms` and `Size`. In the following section on processing the dataset, we will dig deeper into these two columns to determine how to deal with them.

Now that we have a sense of the columns in the dataset and what kind of information they offer, let's explore some more aspects of the dataset. First, let's check the dimensions of the dataset, as shown in the following listing.

Listing 9.2   Code to check the dimensions of the dataset

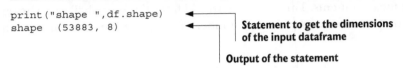

```
print("shape ",df.shape)
shape  (53883, 8)
```
Statement to get the dimensions of the input dataframe

Output of the statement

Listing 9.2 shows that this dataset has over 53,000 rows and eight columns. In chapter 12, we will examine the relationship between the number of rows in a dataset, the nature of the columns in a dataset, and the applicability of a deep learning model to the data. For now, it is safe to say that while this dataset is on the small side, it is big enough for us to have a decent chance of training a deep learning model with it.

The following listing contains the statements that list the number of missing values in each column of the dataset.

Listing 9.3   Statements to list missing values in each column

```
missing_values_count = df.isnull().sum()
print("missing values before cleanup:\n",missing_values_count)
```
The output of this statement is a count of the number of missing values by column.

The following is the output of the commands in listing 9.3:

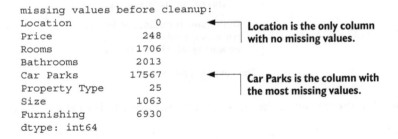

```
missing values before cleanup:
Location           0
Price            248
Rooms           1706
Bathrooms       2013
Car Parks      17567
Property Type     25
Size            1063
Furnishing      6930
dtype: int64
```
Location is the only column with no missing values.

Car Parks is the column with the most missing values.

From the output of the command in listing 9.3, we can see that all but one of the columns in this dataset have missing values. This is an early sign of some of the problems we will need to correct to get this dataset ready to train with a deep learning model. In comparison, the Airbnb NYC dataset only had missing values in four columns:

```
Missing values:
id                 0
name              16
```
Missing values in the name column

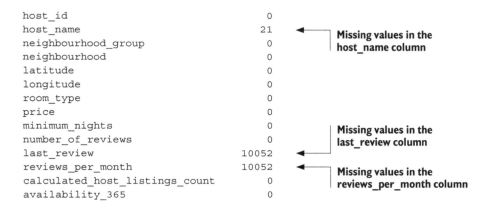

As shown here, almost every column in the Kuala Lumpur dataset is missing values, which warns us that, as often happens with real-world data, we will have to perform a lot of work to clean up this dataset before we can start using it with a model.

In this section, we have taken a first look at the Kuala Lumpur real estate dataset. In the next section, we will review the process of preparing this dataset to train a deep learning model.

9.2   *Processing the dataset*

Now that we've looked at the Kuala Lumpur real estate dataset and seen that it has a large number of missing values, we have some idea that it will require a good deal of processing before we can use it to train a model. In this section, we will look at the features of the dataset one by one to describe the cleanup required.

At this point, we haven't decided yet if we are going to use a subset or the full set of columns. Initially, our approach defaults to utilizing all available features. As we progress and examine the model's performance and behavior, we may decide to exclude some features, for example, because these features have undetected invalid values that effect the model's performance. It is not just because we cannot anticipate what features will work and what won't that we strive to obtain the full set of clean features available to the model for training. It is also a way to get the most out of data, as we will learn more about the dataset through processing it entirely and rendering it reusable for other projects as well. This comprehensive approach ensures better results than we would have obtained if we only cleaned up the features that we ultimately use to train the model.

The code highlighted in this section is available at https://mng.bz/MDBQ and the config file is at https://mng.bz/av1j.

We will begin by addressing columns that only involve handling missing values: `Bathrooms`, `Car Parks`, `Furnishing`, `Property Type`, `Location`. Next, we will describe the process for the columns that require more cleanup than simply dealing with missing information: `Price`, `Rooms`, and `Size`.

9.2.1 Processing Bathrooms, Car Parks, Furnishing, Property Type, and Location columns

For a subset of the columns in the dataset (Bathrooms, Car Parks, Furnishing, Property Type, Location), we can accomplish an effective cleanup by simply dealing with missing values. The config file contains default values to replace missing values for these columns that we determined based on their characteristics and domain knowledge.

Listing 9.4 Defining the default replacement values for missing values

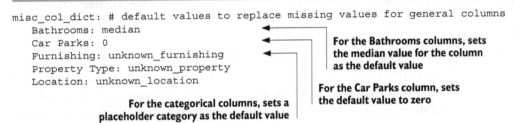

```
misc_col_dict: # default values to replace missing values for general columns
    Bathrooms: median
    Car Parks: 0
    Furnishing: unknown_furnishing
    Property Type: unknown_property
    Location: unknown_location
```

> For the Bathrooms columns, sets the median value for the column as the default value

> For the Car Parks column, sets the default value to zero

> For the categorical columns, sets a placeholder category as the default value

---

Listing 9.4 shows that we set missing values for the Bathrooms column in this dictionary to the median value for the column. For the Car Parks column, we set missing values to zero. The reason for the difference between these is due to the specific use case of real estate listings. Residential properties will rarely have no washrooms, so picking the median value as the default for Bathrooms makes sense. On the other hand, many properties will have no parking spaces. If a property does have a parking space, it is in the best interests of the seller and the seller's agent to include this in the listing to ensure they get the best selling price for the property. Thus, when Car Parks is missing a value, it makes sense to assume that this property does not have any parking spaces, so we set missing values in this column to zero.

In this dictionary, we also have distinct placeholder category values for the categorical columns. The code for obtaining this simple cleanup is placed in the data cleanup notebook's function clean_up_misc_cols().

Listing 9.5 Function to replace general missing values

> Iterates through the columns that have simple data cleanup

```
def clean_up_misc_cols(df,misc_col_dict):
  for col in misc_col_dict:
    if misc_col_dict[col] == 'median':
      df[col] = df[col].fillna(df[col].median())
    else:
      df[col] = df[col].fillna(misc_col_dict[col])
  return(df)
```

> Replaces missing values with the median for the column where specified

> For the other columns, replaces missing values in the column with the default value for that column

In the `clean_up_misc_cols()` function shown in listing 9.5, the dictionary defined in the config file, as shown in listing 9.4, is used to replace missing values in the columns that require a simple cleanup.

Now that we have described how the cleanup is done for the columns that only require missing values to be dealt with, the subsequent subsections in this section will describe the more intensive data operations that are required for the remaining three columns: `Price`, `Rooms`, and `Size`.

9.2.2 Processing the Price column

Before we get into what needs to be cleaned up in the `Price` column, let's review some examples of values in this column, as shown in figure 9.4.

The values in figure 9.4 show a few items that need to be dealt with in the `Price` column:

- Values including the symbol "RM", representing Ringgit, the Malaysian currency
- Missing values
- Values needing to be converted to float

Price
RM 1,250,000
RM 6,800,000
RM 1,030,000
NaN
RM 900,000

Figure 9.4 Examples of values in the Price column

Listing 9.6 presents the `clean_up_price_col()` function, which contains a code snippet to effectively clean up the `Price` column.

Listing 9.6   Function to clean up the `Price` column

```
def clean_up_price_col(df):
    df.dropna(subset=['Price'], inplace=True)        ◄─── Drops rows in the dataframe
    df['Price'] = \                                        that are missing a value in
df['Price'].apply(lambda x:\                               the Price column
remove_currency_symbol("RM ",x))       ◄─── Removes the currency symbol
    df['Price'] = \
pd.to_numeric(df['Price'].\
str.replace(',',''), errors='coerce')   ◄─── Removes commas and
    return(df)                                   convert the values to float
```

As shown in listing 9.6, the `clean_up_price_col()` function removes rows with missing `Price` values. The rationale for removing these rows (as opposed to replacing missing `Price` values with some placeholder) is that `Price` is the target for our model; hence it won't work to keep rows where such a value is missing. The output of the `clean_up_price_col()` function is a dataframe with valid numeric values in all rows for the `Price` column.

9.2.3 Processing the Rooms column

Before we get into what needs to be cleaned up in the `Rooms` column, let's review what some of the values in this column look like, as shown in figure 9.5.

The values in figure 9.5 present some examples of the problems that need to be dealt with in the `Price` column:

- Missing values.
- Double-barrelled values that contain more than one constituent value. In the Kuala Lumpur real estate dataset, some such values include string expressions such as "4 + 1." These values require parsing to extract usable values for the model training.
- As for the missing values, we can opt to replace the `NaN` values with zero.

At this point, we have the urge to make a choice about how to deal with the `Rooms` column overall: should we treat it as a categorical column or a continuous column? To help us decide, let's review the count of unique values in the `Rooms` column:

```
Rooms              43
```

With around 40 values in the `Rooms` column, which is a not-too-large number of categories, we could convert it into a categorical column if we wished. Suppose we opt to treat it as a numeric column; let's check the necessary steps to take. To begin with, let's look at the first few unique values and their counts.

Rooms
2+1
6
3
NaN
4+1

Figure 9.5 Examples of values in the Rooms column

Listing 9.7   Count of the most common values in the Rooms column

```
3            14249  ◀───   Example of a value that is
3+1           8070  ◀───   immediately convertible
2             5407         to a numeric value
4             5018
4+1           4404         Example of a value that can be
5+1           2340         turned into a numeric value by
1             2322         treating it as an equation
5             2065
2+1           1938
1+1           1191
6              937
Studio         874  ◀───   Example of a value that is a
6+1            807         string that is not convertible
4+2            479         to a numeric value
3+2            477
5+2            410
7              358
7+1            237
2+2            132         Example of a value that could be
8              125         converted to a numeric value
6+             86   ◀───   with some extrapolation
```

If we want to treat `Rooms` as a continuous column, we can deal with the representative examples shown in listing 9.7 in the following ways:

- Values like 3 that can be converted directly to numeric: convert to numeric.
- Values like 3 + 1 that we can use the built-in eval() Python function to evaluate the string value as if it were an equation.
- Values like Studio: replace them with a reasonable numeric value, such as 1.
- Values like 6+ should be treated as if they were 6+1. This is not a perfect approach—the dataset does not clarify whether 6+ is a short form of 6+1 or if it means "6 plus an unspecified number of additional rooms."

Note that the treat_rooms_as_numeric setting in the config file for data preparation controls whether Rooms is prepared as a continuous column or a categorical column. If you set this value to True, Rooms is prepared as a continuous column, and if you set it to False then Rooms is prepared as a categorical column. In addition to updating the data preparation config file, you also need to ensure that Rooms is in the appropriate list in the model training config file so that the model training notebook knows whether to treat Rooms as categorical or continuous, as shown in the following:

```
categorical: # categorical columns
        - 'Location'
#       - 'Rooms'
        - 'Property Type'
        - 'Furnishing'
        - 'Size_type_bin'
continuous: # continuous columns
        - 'Bathrooms'
        - 'Car Parks'
        - 'Rooms'
        - 'Size'
```

Now that we have looked at the transformations we would make to treat Rooms as a numeric column, we can look at the clean_up_rooms_col() function.

Listing 9.8 Count of the most common values in the Rooms column

Checks the parameter to determine whether Rooms will be treated as a continuous column

Deals with values like "6+"

If a value ends with +, adds 1 to the end of the string.

```
def clean_up_rooms_col(df,treat_rooms_as_numeric):
  if treat_rooms_as_numeric:
    print("Rooms treated as numeric")
    df['Rooms'] = df['Rooms'].fillna("0")
    df['Rooms'] = \
df['Rooms'].apply(lambda x: x+"1" \
if x.endswith('+') else x)
    df['Rooms'] = df['Rooms'].replace("Studio", "1")
    df['Rooms']= \
df['Rooms'].replace("20 Above", "21")
    df['Rooms']=\
df['Rooms'].apply(lambda x:eval(str(x)))
    df['Rooms'] = pd.to_numeric(df['Rooms'],
```

If the value is Studio, replaces it with 1.

Example of a value that could be converted to a numeric value with some extrapolation

Replaces strings that are valid equations with the numeric result of the equation

```
errors='coerce')
    # replace missing values with 0
    df['Rooms'] = df['Rooms'].fillna(0)
else:
    print("Rooms treated as non-numeric")
    df['Rooms'] = df['Rooms'].fillna("unknown_rooms")
return(df)
```

⟵ **Converts all values in the column to numeric**

If any NaNs have been introduced in these transformations, replaces them with 0.

If the column is being treated as categorical, replaces missing values with a placeholder value.

Listing 9.8 shows that we need to perform many transformations if we want to treat the `Rooms` column as a continuous column. In particular, we need to replace one-off non-numeric values (`Studio`, `20 Above`) with our best guess of the corresponding numeric value, and we need to replace values that include + with the evaluation of the string as if it were an equation. For values that end with +, we assume it's valid for the string to end with +1 so that the value can be treated as an equation by the `eval()` function. We've made some assumptions about what values like `6+`, `Studio`, and `20 Above` mean.

In a real-world scenario, we might have access to a subject matter expert, or we may have to make similar guesses to see whether we can get a signal out of these values. Given the expected importance of the `Rooms` column (more rooms typically mean more surface area, which can often contribute to higher property values), the acid test will be when we train the model and compare the resulting performance based on treating this column differently, either as categorical or continuous. When we get to train the model later in the chapter, we will try it using both variations of the `Rooms` column to determine which one produces the best results.

9.2.4 *Processing the Size column*

Among all the potential features for the Kuala Lumpur real estate price prediction problem, the `Size` column is the most problematic. Before going into the details of how to clean up this specific column, let's review some samples of values in the `Size` column, as shown in figure 9.6.

Along with some missing values, this column contains as a string the classification of the size type (`Built-up` or `Land area`) as well as the area of the property and the area metric ("sq. ft"). But that's not all. As you can see in figure 9.7, there are entries in the `Size` column that express the area as length by width.

There is still more to be done with the `Size` column. Figure 9.8 shows examples of values in the `Size` column where the area of the property is expressed in various equations.

So it appears that the `Size` column combines three or more different pieces of information for each entry:

- Size type (`Land area` or `Built up`).
- Area, which can be formatted as a numeric value (e.g., `6900`), length by width (e.g., `20 × 80`), or length by width with an equation in one or both dimensions

Size
Built-up : 1,335 sq. ft.
Land area : 6900 sq. ft.
Built-up : 1,875 sq. ft.
NaN
Built-up : 1,513 sq. ft.

Figure 9.6 Examples of values in the Size **column**

Size
Land area : 25x75 sq. ft.
Land area : 22 x 80 sq. ft.
Land area : 20x75 sq. ft.
Land area : 16x55 sq. ft.
Land area : 20 X 80 sq. ft.

Figure 9.7   Examples of values in the Size **column with area expressed in length by width**

Size
Land area : 10+24 x 80 sq. ft.
Land area : 40+30 X 80 sq. ft.
Land area : 20+26 x 80 sq. ft.
Land area : 22+5x80 sq. ft.
Land area : 25X85+17X85 sq. ft.

Figure 9.8 Examples of values in the Size **column with area expressed in complex equations**

(e.g., `10 + 24 x 80`). We are assuming that the property is rectangular. Note that this assumption needs to be validated by a real estate professional, and this is an essential point. To conduct a thorough analysis of a dataset, it's crucial to have access to a subject matter expert who can verify assumptions. For instance, an expert could suggest using missing value replacements such as the median number of bathrooms, which is a good default value to replace missing values in the `Bathrooms` column, or 0, which is a good replacement for missing values in the `Car Parks` column. We have set up config files for the data preparation and model training notebooks to make it easy to make changes if our assumptions don't match what the subject matter expert says. By putting parameters like this in config files, we can update the behavior of the system without touching the Python code and run experiments methodically.

- Area metric (e.g., `sq. ft.`).

You may be asking now how we were able to identify that the `Size` column contained all these anomalies and find a remedy. The answer is through trial and error. First, we separated the size type from the area and area metric. Next, we removed the area metric (since it is always the same). Then, we iterated through the remaining area values, removing or replacing characters until every area value could be applied to `eval()`.

This meticulous iterative process is not uncommon for real-world datasets. We chose the Kuala Lumpur real estate dataset for this section of the book because it presents these kinds of real-world challenges, and working through them illustrates the approaches that need to be taken, some systematic and some tactical, to squeeze as much useful signal as possible out of a dataset.

We need to separate the three kinds of values in the `Size` column. We will discard the area metric because it is always a variation of "square feet" and create a new categorical column that combines the size type value with an identifier for the bin that the area value falls into. To do this, we will need to

- Convert the area values to numeric values by discarding extraneous characters and using the eval() function to convert the string representation of equations into the numeric result of evaluating the equation. That is, 20 × 80 is replaced with 160.
- Get bins for the resulting numeric area values and add a new column to the dataset with the bin value for each row.
- Create a new categorical column that combines size type and bin number.

The following listing shows the clean_up_size_col() function, which implements the changes we have described so far in this section.

Listing 9.9   Code to clean up the Size column

```
def clean_up_size_col(df,clean_up_list,size_bin_count):
    df.dropna(subset=['Size'], inplace=True)
    df['Size'] = df['Size'].str.lower()
    df[['Size_type','Size']] = \
    df['Size'].str.split(':',expand=True)
    df['Size'] = df['Size'].fillna("0")
    df = df[df.Size.str.contains(r'\d')]

    for string in clean_up_list:
        df = df[~df.Size.str.contains(string,na=False)]

    df['Size'] = (df['Size'].str.replace(',','')
                            .str.replace('`','')
                            .str.replace('@','x')
                            .str.replace('\+ sq. ft.','')
                  )
    df['Size'] = (df['Size'].str.replace(' sq. ft.','')
                            .str.replace('sf sq.ft.','')
                            .str.replace('ft','')
                            .str.replace('sq','')
                            .str.replace("xx","*")
                            .str.replace("x ","*")
                            .str.replace(" x","*")
                            .str.replace("x","*")
                            .str.replace("X","*")
                            .replace('\'','')
                  )
    df['Size'] = \
    df['Size'].apply(lambda x: remove_after_space(x))
    df['Size'] = \
df['Size'].apply(lambda x: eval(str(x)))
    df['Size'] = df['Size'].fillna(0.0)
    print("min is: ",df['Size'].min())
    print("max is: ",df['Size'].max())
    bins = np.linspace(df['Size'].min(),
    df['Size'].max(), size_bin_count)
```

Annotations:
- Removes rows that are missing Size values
- Changes all values in the Size column to lowercase
- Splits the Size column by moving the size type values into a new column"
- Replaces any remaining missing values with 0
- Removes any rows where the size column contains no digits
- Removes any rows where the size column cannot be converted to a numeric value
- Replaces characters that will cause problems treating multiplications correctly
- Removes remaining characters that will cause problems treating the remaining Size values as numeric
- Removes extraneous characters following spaces
- Evaluates the remaining Size values as equations
- Defines bins for the Size values

```
print("bins is: ",bins)
bin_labels = range(1,size_bin_count+1)                    ◄────┘ Defines bin names
print("bin_labels is: ",bin_labels)
df['Size_bin'] = pd.qcut(df['Size'],                           Creates a new column that contains the
size_bin_count, labels=bin_labels)               ◄────┘      bin value for the Size value in that row
df['Size_type_bin'] = \
df['Size_type']+df['Size_bin'].astype(str)       ◄────┐     Creates a new categorical column
return(df)                                                 │  that combines the Size type value
                                                           │  and the Size_bin value
```

The `clean_up_size_col()` function shown in listing 9.9 comprises a series of transformations that allow the evaluation of the area information from the `Size` column as a numeric value. To do this, we need to remove the rows where the area cannot be interpreted. The area of the property is so fundamental to determining its pricing value that it does not make sense to train a model using examples from listings where it is impossible to extract the area information; hence, we simply drop those rows. Next, we need to clean up the remaining area values so that they can be evaluated as numeric values, either because they can be directly converted to numeric values or because they can be interpreted as equations that can be applied to the `eval()` function.

Given the significant influence of a listing's area on its price, it's worthwhile to invest a lot of effort into extracting the area information in any way we can. For this purpose, we create new categorical columns containing the bin number corresponding to the size of the listing. Utilizing this bin value makes it possible to evaluate the area portion of the `Size` column as a numeric value. In doing this, we need to remove rows where the area cannot be interpreted. The area of the property is so fundamental to its value that it does not make sense to train the model with the data from listings where it is impossible to extract the area information because it is concatenated with the size type (`built-up` or `land area`).

Figure 9.9 displays examples of values in the revised `Size` column along with the new columns (`Size_type`, `Size_bin`, and `Size_type_bin`) created by the function in listing 9.9.

Size	Size_type	Size_bin	Size_type_bin
1335.0	built-up	5	built-up 5
6900.0	land area	10	land area 10
1875.0	built-up	7	built-up 7
1513.0	built-up	6	built-up 6
7200.0	land area	10	land area 10

Figure 9.9 Examples of values in the new columns generated from the `Size` column

Let's look at each column in figure 9.9:

- `Size`—Replacing the original values in the `Size` column are single continuous values that correspond to the land area from the original `Size` column.
- `Size_type`—This new column contains the size type (`built-up` or `land area`) portion of the original `Size` column value.
- `Size_bin`—This new column contains the bin number that the `Size` column value belongs to. Notice that for the examples in figure 9.9, the row with the smallest `Size` value has the smallest bin number, and the rows with the largest `Size` values have the largest bin number.
- `Size_type_bin`—This new column contains a combination of the values in the other two new columns.

Consider a specific value from the original `Size` column and how it gets processed to create the values in the new `Size`, `Size_type`, `Size_bin`, and `Size_type_bin` columns, as shown in figure 9.10.

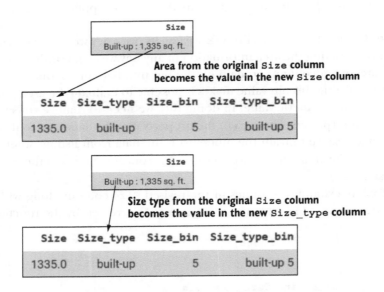

Figure 9.10   Original `Size` column and values in the new columns

We started with a `Size` column that contained a jumble of two kinds of critical information jammed into a single column and that had numeric data (the area of the property), sometimes as a number and sometimes as an equation. After applying the cleanup steps, we have split the `Size` column into four columns: one continuous (`Size`) and three categorical (`Size_type`, `Size_bin`, and `Size_type_bin`) that we can choose from to train the model.

9.3 Defining the deep learning model

In this section, we will go through the code that defines the deep learning model for the Kuala Lumpur real estate price prediction model. First, we'll compare the approach for defining the model used in this chapter, with Keras preprocessing layers, to the approach that we saw in chapter 3, which used custom layers. Then we'll review in detail the code that makes up the model definition. Finally, we'll wrap up this section by discussing the rationale for using Keras preprocessing layers as a best practice for deep learning with tabular data.

The code in this section is available at https://mng.bz/gaBe, and the config file is at https://mng.bz/ey19.

9.3.1 Contrasting the custom layer and Keras preprocessing layer approaches

Starting in chapter 3, we have examined the Keras-based solution for the Airbnb NYC price prediction problem. In that solution, we created a deep learning model and the associated pipelines "from scratch." That is, we didn't use any functions from TensorFlow or Keras specifically designed for tabular data. In the solution we propose for the Kuala Lumpur real estate problem, we are going to switch gears and take advantage of Keras preprocessing layers to make it easier to handle the tabular dataset. To provide some context on the differences between the two approaches, let's compare:

- *Using custom layers*—This is the approach we used for the Airbnb NYC price prediction problem in chapter 3 and the baseline for comparison with other deep learning approaches in chapter 8.
- *Using Keras preprocessing layers*—This is the approach we will use for this chapter and the subsequent chapters in this book.

See table 9.1.

Table 9.1 Comparison of the Kuala Lumpur real solutions using custom classes and using Keras preprocessing layers

	Using custom layers	Using Keras preprocessing layers
Pipeline	Custom pipeline classes based on Scikit-learn Pipeline class (https://mng.bz/pKP5); requires classes to be defined in a separate file so they can be used at training and inference (https://mng.bz/OBxK); complex code to define, train, invoke, and save the pipelines.	The standard, off-the-shelf Keras preprocessing layers, available at https://mng.bz/YD1o. The code to define, train, and invoke the pipeline is much simpler and more robust.
Model definition	A complex set of layers, specified to work with categorical, continuous, and text inputs	A simple set of layers, capable of working with generic categorical and continuous inputs

Figure 9.11 shows the layers that make up the Kuala Lumpur real estate price prediction model using Keras preprocessing layers.

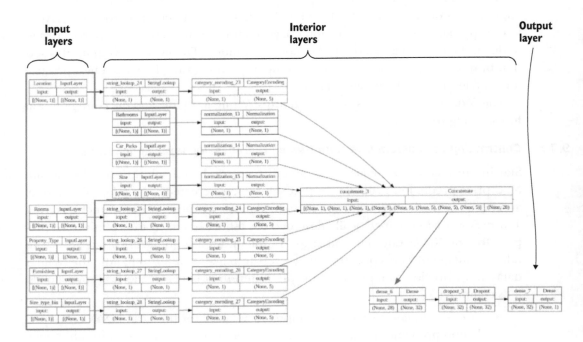

Figure 9.11   Kuala Lumpur real estate price prediction model with Keras preprocessing layers

Figure 9.12 shows the layers that make up the Kuala Lumpur real estate price prediction model using custom layers; the code is available at https://mng.bz/KGeP.

The overall structure for the Keras model with custom layers in figure 9.12 looks more complex than the structure in figure 9.11 for the model with Keras preprocessing layers, but there is a lot going on, so it's not easy to see the details. Let's zoom into the layers that just process the Size column to get a more specific idea of how these two architectures differ. Figure 9.13 shows the layers for the Size column in the model with Keras preprocessing layers.

We can see that there are four layers between the input layer for Size and the final output layer. Compare this to the layers for the Size column for the Keras model with custom layers, as shown in figure 9.14.

For the Keras model defined with custom layers, there are seven layers between the input layer for Size and the final output layer, compared to four layers for the model that uses Keras preprocessing layers. Because of the way that the layers are chained together in the model with customer layers, there is a series of individual concatenation operations layer by layer. In contrast, the model with Keras preprocessing layers has a

Input layers

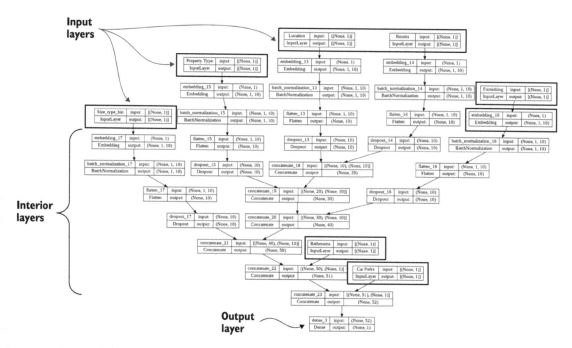

Figure 9.12   Kuala Lumpur real estate price prediction model with custom layers

Interior layers

Output layer

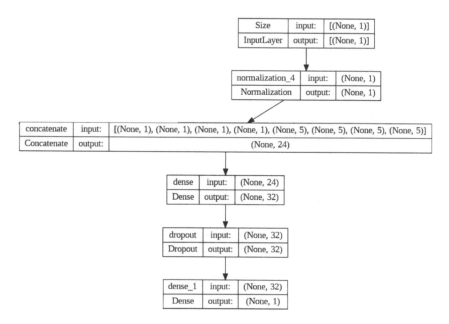

Figure 9.13   Layers for the `Size` column with Keras preprocessing layers

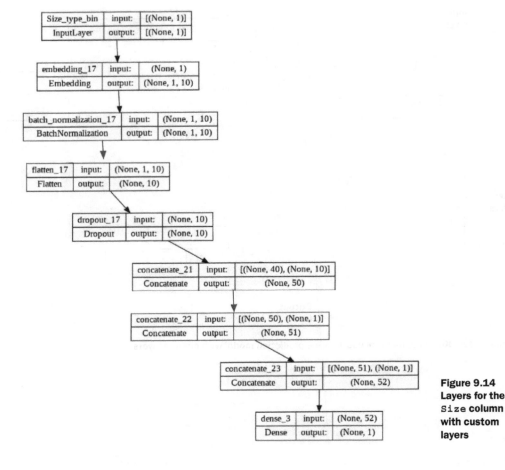

**Figure 9.14
Layers for the
Size column
with custom
layers**

single concatenation layer that pulls together all layers coming in from each input. This difference in the number of intermediate layers between the input of the Size column and the final layer reflects the overall additional complexity of the Keras model with custom layers compared to the model with Keras preprocessing layers.

9.3.2 *Examining the code for model definition using Keras preprocessing layers*

In general, the code for defining and training the model using Keras preprocessing is simpler and more streamlined than the deep learning code you read about in previous chapters that used custom layers and Scikit-learn based pipelines. However, a small price is to be paid in exchange for the increased simplicity of a model based on Keras preprocessing layers. To avoid getting an error when saving the model using model. save() and in the model saving callback, we need to ensure that all column names are lowercase and contain no spaces (this can be achieved using the snake_case naming convention instead) for the model using Keras preprocessing layers. The code in the following listing automatically does this.

Listing 9.10 Lowercase column names and replacing spaces

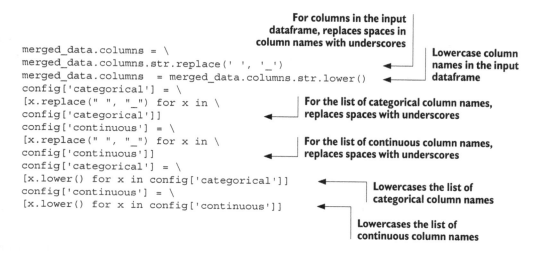

```
merged_data.columns = \
merged_data.columns.str.replace(' ', '_')
merged_data.columns  = merged_data.columns.str.lower()
config['categorical'] = \
[x.replace(" ", "_") for x in \
config['categorical']]
config['continuous'] = \
[x.replace(" ", "_") for x in \
config['continuous']]
config['categorical'] = \
[x.lower() for x in config['categorical']]
config['continuous'] = \
[x.lower() for x in config['continuous']]
```

For columns in the input dataframe, replaces spaces in column names with underscores

Lowercase column names in the input dataframe

For the list of categorical column names, replaces spaces with underscores

For the list of continuous column names, replaces spaces with underscores

Lowercases the list of categorical column names

Lowercases the list of continuous column names

The code shown in listing 9.10 replaces spaces in the column names in the input Data-Frame and the lists of categorical and continuous column names. For example, the variable name Car Parks becomes Car_Parks.

The following listing presents the definition of the df_to_dataset function, which creates an input pipeline for the model that uses Keras preprocessing layers.

Listing 9.11 Function to create an input pipeline

```
# function from https:
//www.tensorflow.org/tutorials/structured_data/preprocessing_layers
def df_to_dataset(dataframe, shuffle=True, batch_size=32):
  df = dataframe.copy()
  labels = df.pop('target')
  df = {key: value[:,tf.newaxis] for key,
    value in dataframe.items()}
  ds = tf.data.Dataset.from_tensor_slices((dict(df),
    labels))
  if shuffle:
    ds = ds.shuffle(buffer_size=len(dataframe))
  ds = ds.batch(batch_size)
  ds = ds.prefetch(batch_size)
  return ds
```

Gets the target column from the local copy of the dataframe

Creates a new dictionary df with the same keys and values but with a new axis added to it

Creates a TensorFlow Dataset ds using the from_tensor_slices method

Shuffles the elements of the dataset to avoid overfitting if the data has some intrinsic sorting

Applies prefetch() to the dataset

Groups the elements of the dataset into batches of size batch_size

The df_to_dataset function shown in listing 9.11, which is taken directly from https://www.tensorflow.org/tutorials/structured_data/preprocessing_layers, will be applied to the training, validation, and test datasets to convert them into `tf.data` `.Dataset` objects, then shuffle and batch the datasets. Note that the definition of the dataset `ds` takes two arguments: `dict(df)`, a dictionary version of the input dataframe, and `labels`, the target values from the input dataframe. Also, note that applying `prefetch()` to the dataset allows the dataset to be processed more efficiently by overlaying the preprocessing and model execution of one batch while the next batch is being loaded.

The following listing defines the `get_normalization_layer()` function, which defines a normalization layer for a given feature.

Listing 9.12   Creating normalization layers for continuous columns

```
# function from
https://www.tensorflow.org/tutorials/structured_data/preprocessing_layers
def get_normalization_layer(name, dataset):
    normalizer = layers.Normalization(axis=None)
    feature_ds = dataset.map(lambda x, y: x[name])
    normalizer.adapt(feature_ds)
    return normalizer
```

Defines a normalization object

Creates a dataset from the input dataset with only the input feature

Trains the normalizer using the specified input feature

The `get_normalization_layer()` function defined in listing 9.12, which is taken directly from https://www.tensorflow.org/tutorials/structured_data/preprocessing_layers, will be applied to all the continuous columns that we want to use to train the model. This function scales input values with a distribution centered around 0 with a standard deviation of 1. For details about the normalization object defined in this function, see https://mng.bz/9YDx. Note that for gradient boosting solutions, normalization would not be needed.

The following listing presents the definition of the `get_category_encoding_layer()` function, which specifies an encoding layer for a given categorical column.

Listing 9.13   Creating encoding layers for categorical columns

Creates layers for the column depending on whether or not it's a string column

```
# function from
https://www.tensorflow.org/tutorials/structured_data/preprocessing_layers
def get_category_encoding_layer(name, dataset, dtype, max_tokens=None):
    if dtype == 'string':
        index = layers.StringLookup(max_tokens=max_tokens)
    else:
        index = layers.IntegerLookup(max_tokens=max_tokens)
    feature_ds = dataset.map(lambda x, y: x[name])
    index.adapt(feature_ds)
    encoder = \
layers.CategoryEncoding(num_tokens= \
```

Creates a dataset from the input dataset with only the input feature

Learns the set of possible values for the column and assigns them a fixed numeric index

```
index.vocabulary_size())
    return lambda feature: encoder(index(feature))
```

← Encodes the numeric indices

← Applies multi-hot encoding to the indices

The `get_category_encoding_layer()` function defined in listing 9.13, which is taken directly from https://www.tensorflow.org/tutorials/structured_data/preprocessing_layers, will be applied to all the categorical columns that we want to use to train the model. In this function, if a column is a string column, a layer is generated that turns strings into numeric indices; otherwise, a layer is created that turns integer values into numeric indices.

The following listing shows the code to apply the `df_to_dataset()` function to the training, validation, and testing datasets.

Listing 9.14 Applying `df_to_dataset()` to train, validate, and test datasets

```
# function from
# https://www.tensorflow.org/tutorials/structured_data/preprocessing_layers
train_ds = df_to_dataset(train, batch_size=batch_size)
val_ds = df_to_dataset(val, shuffle=False,
    batch_size=batch_size)
test_ds = df_to_dataset(test, shuffle=False,
    batch_size=batch_size)
```

← Generates training dataset

← Generates validation dataset

← Generates test dataset

Once the code in listing 9.14 is applied, we will obtain the datasets and be ready to start the training process.

The following listing shows the code to apply the `df_to_dataset()` function to the training, validation, and testing datasets.

Listing 9.15 Defining layers for continuous and categorical columns

```
all_inputs = []
encoded_features = []

for header in config['continuous']:
  numeric_col = tf.keras.Input(shape=(1,), name=header)
  normalization_layer = get_normalization_layer(header, train_ds)
  encoded_numeric_col = normalization_layer(numeric_col)
  all_inputs.append(numeric_col)
  encoded_features.append(encoded_numeric_col)

for header in config['categorical']:
  categorical_col = tf.keras.Input(shape=(1,), name=header, dtype='string')
  encoding_layer = get_category_encoding_layer(name=header,
                                    dataset=train_ds,
                                    dtype='string',
                                    max_tokens=5)
```

← List for input features

← List for encoded features

← Creates a normalization layer for each continuous column

← Creates an encoding layer for each categorical column

```
encoded_categorical_col = encoding_layer(categorical_col)
all_inputs.append(categorical_col)
encoded_features.append(encoded_categorical_col)
```

In the code in listing 9.15, for each continuous column, `get_normalization_layer()` defines a normalization layer for the column. The new layer is added to the `encoded_features` list, and the column name is appended to the `all_inputs` list. For each categorical column, `get_category_encoding_layer()` defines an encoding layer for the column. The new layer is added to the `encoded_features` list, and the column name is appended to the `all_inputs` list. Once the code in listing 9.15 is run, the `all_features` list contains the following values:

```
[<KerasTensor: shape=(None, 1) dtype=float32 (created by layer 'Bathrooms')>,
 <KerasTensor: shape=(None, 1) dtype=float32 (created by layer 'Car_Parks')>,
 <KerasTensor: shape=(None, 1) dtype=float32 (created by layer 'Rooms')>,
 <KerasTensor: shape=(None, 1) dtype=float32 (created by layer 'Size')>,
 <KerasTensor: shape=(None, 1) dtype=string (created by layer 'Location')>,
 <KerasTensor: shape=\
(None, 1) dtype=string \
(created by layer 'Property_Type')>,
 <KerasTensor: shape=(None, 1) dtype=string (created by layer 'Furnishing')>,
 <KerasTensor: shape=\
(None, 1) dtype=string \
(created by layer 'Size_type_bin')>]
```

If we look at the settings in the config file that specify the continuous and categorical columns used to train the model, we see that they match the layers specified in the `all_features` list:

```
categorical: # categorical columns
        - 'Location'
        - 'Property Type'
        - 'Furnishing'
        - 'Size_type_bin'
continuous: # continuous columns
        - 'Bathrooms'
        - 'Car Parks'
        - 'Rooms'
        - 'Size'
```

Now that we have defined the layers that correspond with the columns of the input dataset, we can define the model. The following listing shows the code that defines the model.

Listing 9.16   Code to define the model

```
all_features = \
tf.keras.layers.concatenate(encoded_features)     ◄─── Concatenates the features from
x = \                                                  the encoded_features list created
tf.keras.layers.Dense(32,                              in the code in listing 9.15
```

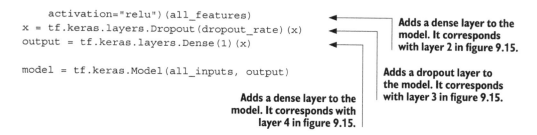

```
                   activation="relu")(all_features)
x = tf.keras.layers.Dropout(dropout_rate)(x)
output = tf.keras.layers.Dense(1)(x)

model = tf.keras.Model(all_inputs, output)
```

Adds a dense layer to the model. It corresponds with layer 2 in figure 9.15.

Adds a dropout layer to the model. It corresponds with layer 3 in figure 9.15.

Adds a dense layer to the model. It corresponds with layer 4 in figure 9.15.

Listing 9.16 includes concatenating the features from the encoded_features list with the concatenate() function. It corresponds with layer 1 in figure 9.15.

Once the code in listing 9.16 is applied, the set of layers for the model is defined. As shown in figure 9.15, every categorical column has an input layer, a StringLookup layer, and a CategoryEncoding layer, and every continuous column has an input layer and a normalization layer.

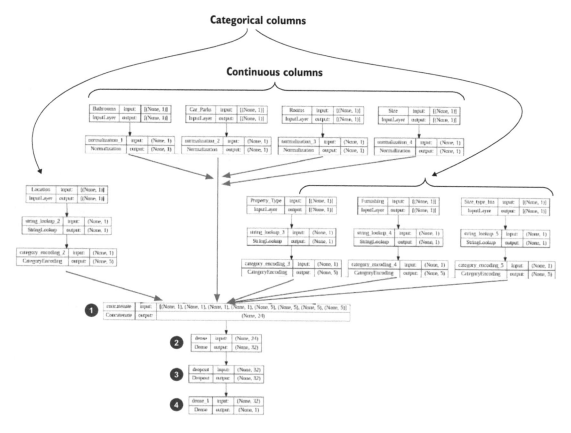

Figure 9.15 Diagram of the layers in the model

Figure 9.15 shows the layers rendered in the default vertical arrangement. To get a horizontal arrangement, we can use the `rankdir='LR'` parameter in the `plot_model` function:

```
tf.keras.utils.plot_model(model, show_shapes=True, rankdir="LR")
```

In addition, note that the architecture shown in figure 9.15 is simple enough for the modest number of features in the Kuala Lumpur dataset. The architecture will get complicated if you are working with a dataset with a large number of features. In addition, the approach described in this chapter for categorical columns depends on one-hot encoding. This approach works out for the Kuala Lumpur real estate dataset since the maximum number of unique values in any categorical column is just a bit over 100:

```
Rooms             18
Location         108
Property Type     97
Furnishing         5
Size_type_bin     20
```

However, if we had a dataset with hundreds or thousands of values in some of its categorical columns, using one-hot encoding could cause memory problems. In that case, we may have to consider using embeddings for categorical columns, as we did for the categorical columns in the Keras model with custom layers.

In this section, we have reviewed the code to define the model. In the next section, we will go over the code to train the model.

9.4   *Training the deep learning model*

In the previous section, we examined the code to define the model and examined how the layers in the model were built up based on the input columns. In this section, we'll describe the process of training the model that we defined in the previous section.

The code in this section is available at https://mng.bz/gaBe and the config file at https://mng.bz/ey19. The following listing shows the code necessary to compile and train the model.

Listing 9.17   Code to compile and train the model

Compiles the model defined in listing 9.16 using the hyperparameters from the config file

```
model.compile(optimizer=config['hyperparameters']['optimizer'],
              loss=tf.keras.losses.BinaryCrossentropy(from_logits=True),
              metrics=config['metrics'])
if config['general']['early_stop']:
    callback_list, save_model_path = set_early_stop(es_monitor, es_mode)
    model.fit(train_ds,
              epochs=config['hyperparameters']['epochs'],
              validation_data=val_ds,
```

```
                    callbacks=callback_list)
else:
    model.fit(train_ds,
            epochs=config['hyperparameters']['epochs'],
            validation_data=val_ds)
```

Creates the list of callbacks and uses it in the call to fit to train the model

Calls fit to train the model without the callback list

Listing 9.17 shows that the hyperparameter values are from the config file. By defining the hyperparameters in the config file, we can adjust them and rerun the model training notebook without touching the Python code. Maintaining the config values in a file separate from the Python code reduces the chance of regressions caused by touching the code and makes it easier to track the results of experiments.

Note also that we can call `fit()` to train the model with callbacks. The code in listing 9.17 shows that we can call `fit()` using a set of callbacks if we want to control the training process or without callbacks to let the training process run through all the specified epochs without interruption. Using callbacks to control the training process is a best practice for deep learning models with Keras because it allows us to use the resources to train the model more efficiently. Instead of running through all the specified epochs and getting the performance of the model from whatever it happened to be in the last epoch, we can use callbacks to stop the training process if it stops improving for a given number of epochs. We can ensure that the outcome of the training process is optimal for the whole training process.

Now that the model has been trained, the following listing presents how to perform a quick evaluation of the trained model.

Listing 9.18 Code to get a quick evaluation of the trained model

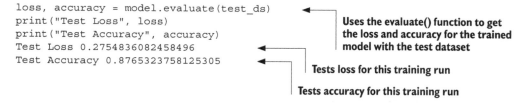

```
loss, accuracy = model.evaluate(test_ds)
print("Test Loss", loss)
print("Test Accuracy", accuracy)
Test Loss 0.2754836082458496
Test Accuracy 0.8765323758125305
```

Uses the evaluate() function to get the loss and accuracy for the trained model with the test dataset

Tests loss for this training run

Tests accuracy for this training run

The output from running listing 9.18 presents decent results on the test set using the trained model.

9.4.1   *Cross-validation in the training process*

In chapter 4 we highlighted cross-validation (that is, segmenting the dataset and repeatedly training the model on different subsets of the data with different holdouts to validate the model) as a best practice for classic machine learning approaches. Do we need to worry about cross-validation for deep learning with tabular data? The short answer is "no." In Keras, by default, when we do repeated training runs with proportions of the dataset specified to use for training, validation, and testing, the subsets of the dataset that get put in each category are randomized, so we will get the benefits of cross-validation with Keras naturally if we do repeated training runs (https://mng.bz/jpPz).

9.4.2 *Regularization in the training process*

Another technique we highlighted in chapter 4 was regularization (that is, preventing overfitting by reducing the complexity of the model to improve its generalization performance). Do we need to be concerned the same about overfitting using deep learning as we do with classic machine learning? The answer is "absolutely," and you can see in figure 9.16 a subset of the diagram for the model that highlights the part of the model that is specifically concerned with avoiding overfitting, the dropout layer. The dropout layer randomly sets inputs to 0 to reduce overfitting (https://mng.bz/W2z4).

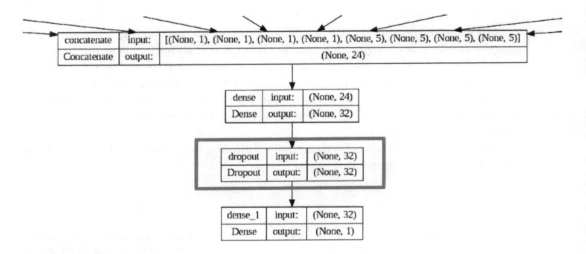

Figure 9.16   Regularization in the deep learning model

9.4.3 *Normalization in the training process*

Normalization refers to adjusting continuous values across features so that their values fall into a consistent range. In chapter 4, we covered using this technique (also known as standardization) in classic machine learning. In listing 9.12, we showed the Kuala Lumpur solution code that uses normalization layers.

There are examples of continuous columns in the Kuala Lumpur dataset whose values have significantly different ranges. For example, in the Kuala Lumpur dataset, the Bathrooms feature ranges between 0 and 20 while Size ranges from 0 to 11 million. Leaving the continuous columns with such disparate ranges can make the training process less efficient. Figure 9.17 shows the normalization layers that make the ranges of values for the continuous features fall within more consistent ranges.

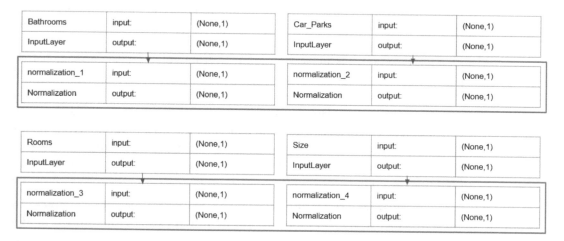

Figure 9.17   Normalization in the deep learning model

The normalization layers adjust the values in each of the continuous columns into a distribution centered around 0 with a standard deviation of 1 (https://mng.bz/0QKp).

In this section, we have reviewed the code for training the Kuala Lumpur real estate price prediction model, along with a set of best practices demonstrated in the model: regularization to avoid overfitting, and normalization to bring the values of continuous columns into consistent ranges. In the next section, we will put all our work together by exercising the trained deep learning model with brand-new data points.

9.5   *Exercising the deep learning model*

So far in this chapter, we have prepared the Kuala Lumpur real estate dataset, defined a deep learning model using Keras preprocessing layers, and trained the model. In this section, we'll exercise the trained model.

The code in this section is available at https://mng.bz/gaBe and the config file at https://mng.bz/ey19.

9.5.1   *Rationale for exercising the trained model on some new data points*

The process of deploying a model is complex, and we will examine it in more depth in chapters 10 and 11. It can be a big investment to complete the initial deployment, so we want to ensure that deployment goes smoothly and we don't have to backtrack to earlier points in the process if we don't have to. If we exercise the trained model on a few real-world data points as soon as possible, we can save more problems from appearing later in the process. There are two key benefits to exercising the trained model on new data points as soon as possible:

- It's an easy way of detecting data leakage (see https://mng.bz/zZXw). It can take months between the start of a data science project and the deployment of the trained model, particularly if you are dealing with the demands of deep learning. During that time, it's possible to lose track of exactly what data will be available to the trained model once it has been deployed. Exercising the trained model with a few data points is an easy way of uncovering potential data leakage before the project has gone too far. The reason for this is that exercising the model will force you to think about what a new data point looks like.

- It provides a way to validate the performance of the model on the test dataset. For example, if you exercise the trained model with some brand-new data points from the Kuala Lumpur real estate market, you get a sense of whether the performance of the model on the test dataset is consistent with its performance with brand-new data points.

To illustrate how exercising the trained model on a few new, real-world examples can help to prevent data leakage, let's look at how we would exercise the trained model to predict whether a brand-new listing would have a selling price above or below the median for Kuala Lumpur. For the Kuala Lumpur real estate dataset, suppose there was a column called Weeks on the market that had the number of weeks the property had been on the market before it was sold. If we included such a column in the training of the model, what would happen when we tried to exercise the trained model with a handful of new data points? Figure 9.18 illustrates the problem we would run into.

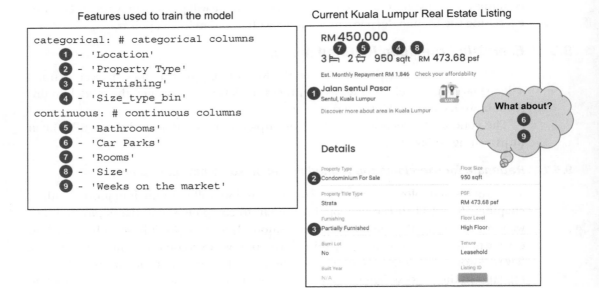

Figure 9.18   Validating the features used to train the model with a new data point

On the left side of figure 9.18, we have the list of features used to train the model as they would be specified in the config file, including the `Weeks on the market` feature. On the right is an extract from a real Kuala Lumpur real estate listing. If we want to be able to use the trained model to get a price prediction for actual real estate listings, then we should be able to find values for all the features on the left in the listing on the right.

As shown by the numbers in figure 9.18, for most of the features we will use to train the model, there is a value in the real Kuala Lumpur real estate listing. However, there are two features where we can't get the values from the real estate listing:

- `Car Parks`—This particular listing mentions covered parking for the building overall but doesn't include any information about parking spaces for this particular unit. For the sake of a quick test, we can assume that the value of `Car Parks` for this listing should be 0.

- `Weeks on the market`—The listing does not include the number of weeks it was on the market before it was sold because we won't know this value until after the listing has sold. We cannot include `Weeks on the market` in the training process.

Now that we have explained why it's important to exercise the trained model on a handful of real data points, we will review the code for exercising the model in the next subsection.

9.5.2 *Exercising the trained model on some new data points*

Now that we have established the benefits of exercising the trained model on new data points, let's review the code for doing this.

The following listing shows the code to save the model to the file system, define a new data point by specifying values for all the features used to train and exercise the model on the new data point.

Listing 9.19 Code to exercise the trained model on a new data point

```
model_file_name = \
os.path.join(get_model_path(),config['file_names']['saved_model'])     Saves the trained model
model.save(model_file_name)                                            to the file system
reloaded_model = \
tf.keras.models.load_model(model_file_name)     ◄── Reloads the saved model
sample = {
    'location': 'Dutamas, Kuala Lumpur',            Defines a new data
    'rooms': 7.0,                                    point point
    'property_type': 'Serviced Residence (Intermediate)',
    'furnishing': 'Partly Furnished',
    'size_type_bin': 'built-up 1',
    'bathrooms': 1.0,
    'car_parks': 1.0,
    'size': 16805.0,
}
input_dict = \
```

```
{name: tf.convert_to_tensor([value]) for name,
value in sample.items()}
predictions = reloaded_model.predict(input_dict)
prob = tf.nn.sigmoid(predictions[0])

print(
    "This property has a %.1f percent probability of "
    "having a price over the median." % (100 * prob)
)
```

Puts the new data point into the format expected by the model

Gets a prediction for the new data point

If we run the code shown in listing 9.19, we get an output like the following:

```
This property has a 99.4 percent probability
of having a price over the median.
```

The model seems certain that this listing will be over the median price. Can you think of a reason why? It could be because the size shown in this property is huge—over 16,000 square feet. Suppose we rerun this code with a size value of 1,500 and leave all the other values the same. We get output as follows:

```
This property has a 47.5 percent probability
of having a price over the median.
```

This seems roughly in line with our expectations. When we reduce the size to a more reasonable value and leave all the other feature values the same, we get a prediction that is roughly what we expect. With the code shown in listing 9.19, we can exercise a wide variety of data points. For example, a data point for the real Kuala Lumpur listing shown in figure 9.18 would look something like the following:

```
sample = {
    'location': 'Sentul, Kuala Lumpur',
    'rooms': 3.0,
    'property_type': 'Condominium For Sale',
    'furnishing': 'Partly Furnished',
    'size_type_bin': 'built-up 1',
    'bathrooms': 2.0,
    'car_parks': 0.0,
    'size': 950.0,
}
```

And if we get a prediction for this data point, the output looks like the following:

```
This property has a 12.6 percent probability
of having a price over the median.
```

This prediction seems to be on the low side. We can check the median price value from the input dataset to see how it compares with the prediction:

```
merged_data['price'].median()
980000.0
```

So, the median price from the input dataset is RM 980,000, and the list price for the brand-new property is RM 450,000. This one data point does not prove that the model is good—the dataset was collected four years prior to this new listing, and the list price for this new listing could be well below what the listing actually sells for. However, by trying out several data points, including some with extremes in an important feature (i.e., size, along with a brand-new real-world data point), we can get some assurance that the model's performance on the test set is not a fluke. By exercising a real-world example of a real estate listing, we have proved that the pipeline in the model is capable of handling real-world data and that the model has not been trained on features that are not available at the point when we want to get a prediction.

There is one complication with getting the prediction for the brand-new listing that goes back to the way that we created the `size_type_bin` column when we prepared the data. Recall that the values in this column are a combination of the `size_type` value (`built-up` or `land area`) and the bin value for the area. We reasonably guess the `size_type` value for the new listing, but getting the `bin` value requires some work. Now that we have seen a real-world value, one thing to consider is whether we need this combined feature. Perhaps we could refactor this feature so that it is only the `size_type` value without the `bin` value for the area. After all, a signal for the area of the listing is already in the `size` column. In the next chapter, we will revisit this problem when we go through the end-to-end process for a deep learning solution to a tabular data problem.

Summary

- To train a model effectively, it is necessary to clean up the dataset. In this chapter, we examined a range of processes used to clean up the dataset.
- Deep learning algorithms cannot deal with missing values, so we must fill in values (such as the mean value for a continuous column) or eliminate records.
- Strings that express numeric values (such as 24 x 12) can be converted into numeric values using the built-in Python `eval()` function. By converting such strings into numeric values, we can extract useful information that can improve the performance of the model.
- Columns that contain multiple types of data (such as the original `size` column) can be separated into columns with distinct categories of data. By separating such columns into distinct columns with just one kind of data, we can use each of the new columns as a feature to train the model.
- By taking advantage of the postprocessing layers that are built into Keras, we can define a deep learning model that is simpler and easier to maintain than a Keras model, where the tabular data characteristics are coded from scratch.
- Keras callbacks allow us to control the training process and ensure that we don't waste resources on training iterations when the model is no longer improving. Callbacks also ensure that the model we get at the end of the training run is the peak performance achieved during training.

- Many of the best practices from classic machine learning also apply to deep learning, including regularization to avoid overfitting and normalization to adjust values in continuous columns to fall within consistent ranges.
- Exercising the trained model on a handful of real-world examples helps avoid data leakage and validate the model's performance on the test dataset.

Model deployment

This chapter covers

- Deploying a deep learning model in a simple web application on our local system
- An introduction to key Google Cloud concepts
- An introduction to Vertex AI, the machine learning environment in Google Cloud
- Deploying a deep learning model with a Vertex AI endpoint
- Adapting the web application to use a Vertex AI endpoint
- Getting generative AI assistance with Gemini for Google Cloud

In chapter 9, we reviewed a set of best practices for training a deep learning model with tabular data and introduced the Kuala Lumpur real estate price prediction problem as a challenging tabular problem because of its mixed-type features. In this chapter, we will take the model we trained in chapter 9 and deploy it in a simple web application. First, we will deploy it locally—that is, having both the web server

359

and the trained model on our local system. Next, we will introduce Google Cloud as an alternative way to deploy our model. In fact, we will take the trained model and deploy it with an endpoint in Vertex AI, the machine learning environment in Google Cloud. Finally, we will examine how to use Google's generative AI assistant Gemini on Google Cloud. The code described in this chapter is available at https://mng.bz/6e1A.

10.1   A simple web deployment

Once we have trained a deep learning model, having followed the best practices described in chapter 9, we have only just scratched the surface of the process of getting value out of the model. Take the example of the Kuala Lumpur real estate price prediction model we trained in chapter 9. This model could be useful for real estate agents who want to provide advice to their clients about the price they should set for new real estate listings. This model could also be useful for property owners who want to put their properties on the market to get an idea of what value they could expect to get from their properties. Finally, the model could also be useful for buyers who are interested in purchasing properties in Kuala Lumpur so they can get an idea of what kind of property they could buy in a particular location given a certain budget.

It's evident that the model that we trained in chapter 9 has the potential to be useful to a variety of audiences. The dilemma we face is how to make the model available to all these audiences who have different business goals and potentially different computer proficiency. Later in this chapter, we will learn how to put a model into production on a public cloud environment, but what if we want to do an initial experiment to learn the characteristics of the model and run some tests with some beta clients? Do we need to implement the whole process of deploying a model in a public cloud? No, because we can take advantage of Flask, a Python web application library and set up a self-contained web deployment of the model. Flask was first released in 2010 by Armin Ronacher and has since become one of the most popular web frameworks for Python. It may sound a bit outdated, given the more recent packages such as Streamlit (https://streamlit .io/) or Gradio (https://www.gradio.app/). However, despite its age, Flask remains a relevant choice for web development due to its lightweight and flexible nature, especially for small personal projects. We are not going to explore all the details of Flask in this book; we just provide the nuts and bolts to set up a demonstration for a model, but if you want to learn more about Flask, check out the documentation: https://flask .palletsprojects.com/en/2.3.x/.

Now that we have introduced the idea of a simple web deployment, we can get started. In this section, we will go over how to create a simple yet complete deployment of the model in a pair of web pages served by Flask.

10.1.1   Overview of web deployment

So far in this book, we have examined a variety of libraries and frameworks for machine learning and deep learning. With the exception of configuration files defined in YAML, all of the code that we have looked at so far in this book has been Python. Like the examples we have seen so far, the web deployment of a machine learning or deep learning model does include Python, but it also requires handling HTML, JavaScript, and CSS scripts. Figure 10.1 shows an overview of the web deployment we have in mind.

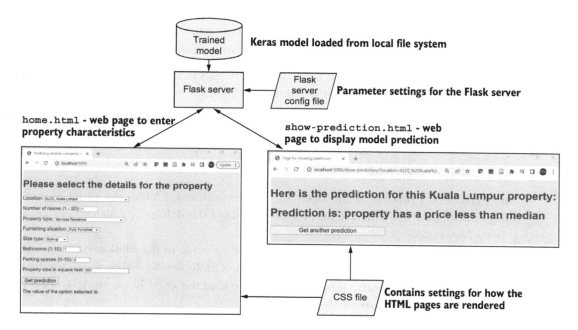

Figure 10.1 Overview of the web deployment

Let's review the components that make up the web deployment depicted in figure 10.1:

- *Trained model*—This is the model that we saved in the Keras with the preprocessing layers notebook. The model is actually saved as a directory structure (https://mng.bz/oKJp). In the Flask server module, the model is loaded using a reference to this directory.

- *Flask server module*—This is a Python module that loads the trained model and contains view functions for each of the solution's HTML pages. The view functions specify the actions that the Flask server module takes when these HTML pages are loaded.

- *Flask server config file*—YAML file where you can specify parameters for the Flask server, such as the directory containing the trained model.

- home.html—One of the HTML pages served by the Flask server. This page contains fields in which the user can specify the characteristics (such as location, number of rooms, and number of parking spaces) of the property for which they want to get a price prediction. This page also contains JavaScript functions that load default values into each of the fields on the page, specify the valid values that can be entered into each field, and package the values entered by the user so they can be sent back to the Flask server module.

- `show-prediction.html`—One of the HTML pages served by the Flask server. This page displays the prediction made by the model for the property with the characteristics entered by the user on the `home.html` page.
- *CSS file*—Specifies how the HTML pages in the solution are rendered.

Unlike the other examples in this book, the web deployment runs on your local system by default. When the Flask server is running, it serves `home.html` at `localhost:5000` so you can exercise the system in your browser.

Now that we have introduced the web deployment, we will look at the Flask server module and the HTML pages in more detail in the subsequent subsections.

10.1.2 *The Flask server module*

The Flask server module is the heart of web deployment. Unlike the other Python programs we have examined so far in this book, it is a standalone `.py` file rather than a Jupyter Notebook.

In this subsection, we will review the key pieces of code in the Flask server module and explain how they drive the web deployment. The following listing shows the first key section of the Flask server module: the code to load the saved Keras model from the file system into an object in the Python module.

Listing 10.1 Loading the saved Keras model

```
rawpath = os.getcwd()
model_path = os.path.abspath(os.path.join(rawpath, 'models'))    ◄── Gets the current directory
model_directory_name = \
os.path.join(model_path,config['file_names'] \
['saved_model'])    ◄── Gets the fully qualified model directory
loaded_model = \
tf.keras.models.load_model(model_directory_name)    ◄── Loads the model using the fully qualified model filename
```

In listing 10.1, the fully qualified model directory is built using the model filename loaded from the config file. The model directory is expected to be in a directory called `models`, in the same directory as the Flask server module. The model is loaded by the same `tf.keras.models.load_model` function that was used to load the model in the Keras preprocessing layers training notebook in chapter 9.

The most important parts of the Flask server module are the view functions which specify the actions taken for each of the HTML pages in the application. The following listing shows the view function for `home.html`, the code that gets invoked when `home.html` is the target.

Listing 10.2 `home.html` **view function**

```
@app.route('/'):
def home():
    title_text = "web deployment of Keras model"
    title = {'titlename':title_text}
    return render_template('home.html',title=title)
```

Decorator to indicate that this view function is for home.html

Parameter sent to home.html for its rendering

The view function shown in listing 10.2 simply sends a title to the `home.html` page and renders the page.

Listing 10.3 shows the view function for `show-prediction.html`. The Flask module runs this code when `show_prediction.html` is the target. This view function processes the values that the user entered in `home.html` and invokes the model to get a prediction on these values.

Listing 10.3 `show-prediction.html` **view function**

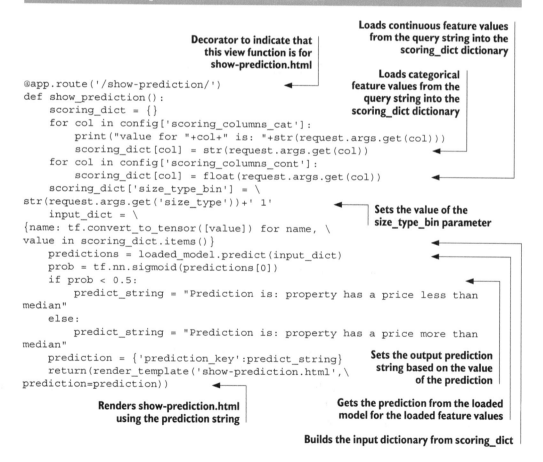

```
@app.route('/show-prediction/'):
def show_prediction():
    scoring_dict = {}
    for col in config['scoring_columns_cat']:
        print("value for "+col+" is: "+str(request.args.get(col)))
        scoring_dict[col] = str(request.args.get(col))
    for col in config['scoring_columns_cont']:
        scoring_dict[col] = float(request.args.get(col))
    scoring_dict['size_type_bin'] = \
str(request.args.get('size_type'))+' 1'
    input_dict = \
{name: tf.convert_to_tensor([value]) for name, \
value in scoring_dict.items()}
    predictions = loaded_model.predict(input_dict)
    prob = tf.nn.sigmoid(predictions[0])
    if prob < 0.5:
        predict_string = "Prediction is: property has a price less than
median"
    else:
        predict_string = "Prediction is: property has a price more than
median"
    prediction = {'prediction_key':predict_string}
    return(render_template('show-prediction.html',\
prediction=prediction))
```

Decorator to indicate that this view function is for show-prediction.html

Loads continuous feature values from the query string into the scoring_dict dictionary

Loads categorical feature values from the query string into the scoring_dict dictionary

Sets the value of the size_type_bin parameter

Sets the output prediction string based on the value of the prediction

Renders show-prediction.html using the prediction string

Gets the prediction from the loaded model for the loaded feature values

Builds the input dictionary from scoring_dict

The view function shown in listing 10.3 takes the query string returned from `home`
`.html`, loads all the values from the query string into the Python dictionary `scoring_`
`dict`, and uses those values to invoke the model loaded by the code in listing 10.1 to
get a prediction. The one exception is `size_type_bin`. For the purposes of this simple
web deployment, we hard-code the bin value. As an exercise, consider how you would
calculate the bin value to avoid this hard coding. The value of the prediction is used to
set a string value that is sent to `show-prediction.html` to be displayed when the page
is rendered.

Figure 10.2 illustrates how the view functions shown in listings 10.2 and 10.3 interact
with the web pages `home.html` and `show-prediction.html`.

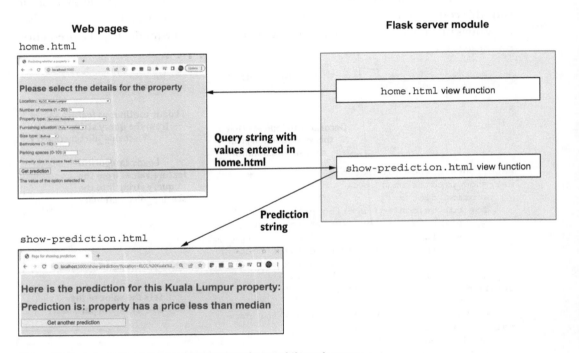

Figure 10.2   Interaction between the view functions and the web pages

Figure 10.2 explains that the view function for `home.html` in the Flask server module renders `home.html`. The JavaScript functions in `home.html` build a query string
containing the user's feature values in `home.html`. This query string is returned to the
`show-prediction` view function in the Flask server module. That view function loads
the feature values from the query string and uses them to get a prediction for the
property from the model. The model prediction is used to create a prediction string,
which is passed to `show-prediction.html` when it is rendered. The prediction string is
displayed in `show-prediction.html`.

Now that we have examined the key parts of the Python code in the Flask server module on the right side of figure 10.2, in the next section, we will move beyond Python to look at the HTML and JavaScript code that drives what's happening on the left side of figure 10.2.

10.1.3 *The home.html page*

There is a lot happening in the `home.html` page:

- Setting up fields where the user can enter values for the eight property characteristics that the prediction is based on
- Setting default values and ranges for each of the fields
- Gathering the input from the fields when the user clicks Get Prediction and sending them to the view function in the Flask server module

Figure 10.3 summarizes the interaction between the JavaScript functions in `home.html` and the user interface elements in `home.html`.

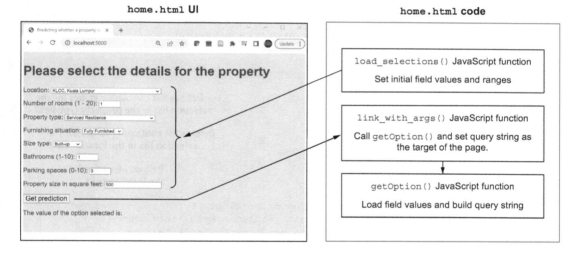

Figure 10.3 Interaction between JavaScript and UI elements in `home.html`

Having introduced what is happening in `home.html`, let's examine the code for this web page. listing 10.4 shows examples of the definitions of the input fields in `home.html`. These are HTML fields where the user can enter input values to specify the details about the property for which they want to get a price prediction.

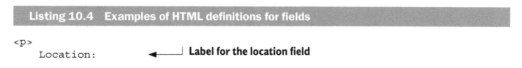

```
<p>
    Location:          ◀─────┘ Label for the location field
```

```
        <select id="location" >
        </select>
    </p>
    <p>
        <label for="rooms">
Number of rooms (1 - 20):</label>
            <input type="number" id="rooms" name="rooms"
            min="1" max="20">
    </p>
```

Defines ID for location field

Defines label for rooms field

Defines ID for rooms field

Defines maximum and minimum values for the rooms field

Listing 10.4 shows examples of HTML definitions for a categorical field (location) and a continuous field (rooms). The HTML definitions for other fields follow the same pattern, with minimums and maximums set for all the continuous fields.

The load-selections() JavaScript function gets run when the page is loaded by the following statement near the beginning of the HTML page:

```
<body onload="load_selections()">
```

The following listing presents the key parts of the load-selections() JavaScript function, the function that sets up the page so it is ready for the user to select the characteristics of the property for which they want to get a prediction.

Listing 10.5 load-selections() **JavaScript function**

Defines list containing values for the selection list in the property type field

Defines list containing values for the selection list in the location field

Defines identifier for the location field

```
function load_selections(){
    // initialize all selections
    var select_location =
document.getElementById("location");
    var select_property_type = document.getElementById("property-type");
    var select_furnishing = document.getElementById("furnishing");
    var select_size_type = document.getElementById("size-type");
    var location_list = ["KLCC, Kuala Lumpur",..
    var property_type_list =
["Serviced Residence","Bungalow",...
    var furnishing_list = ["Fully Furnished","Partly Furnished",...];
    var size_type_list = ["Built-up" ,"Land area" ];
    document.getElementById("rooms").defaultValue
= 1;
    document.getElementById("bathrooms").defaultValue = 1;
    document.getElementById("car-parks").defaultValue = 0;
    document.getElementById("size").defaultValue = 500;
    // Populate location list:
    for(var i = 0; i < location_list.length; i++) {
        var opt = location_list[i];
```

Defines list containing values for the selection list in the size type field

Loops to populate the values in the selection list in the location field

Sets the default value for the rooms field

```
        select_location.innerHTML +=
"<option value=\"" + opt + "\">" + opt + "</option>";
        }
....
    };
```

From listing 10.5 we can see the main actions taken by the `load-selections()` Java-Script function:

- For continuous fields, set the default value. This is the value that appears in the field when the page is initially loaded and is passed along to the Flask server module if the user doesn't change it.

- For categorical fields, define the values from which the user can select and populate the field's selection list with those values. In `home.html`, these values are defined in a hard-coded list. In a more robust web application, these values would be maintained in a control file separate from the code to make it easier to maintain the values and reduce the chance of adding regressions to the code.

When the user has set the values they want for their property and clicks the Get Prediction button, the following code specifies that the `link_with_args()` JavaScript function gets run:

```
<button>
<a onclick=
"link_with_args();" style="font-size : 20px; width: 100%;
height: 100px;">Get prediction</a>
</button>
```

Listing 10.6 shows the `link_with_args()` JavaScript function. This function is called when the user clicks the Get Prediction button in `home.html`. It invokes the rest of the code in `home.html`, which collects the user's input values and packages them into a query string that is passed back to the `show_prediction()` view function in the Flask module.

Listing 10.6 `link_with_args()` **JavaScript function**

```
function link_with_args(){
    getOption();
    console.log("in link_with_args");      Echoes the query
    console.log(window.output);            string to the console
    window.location.href = window.output;  Sets the page target
    }
```

As listing 10.6 shows, the `link_with_args()` JavaScript function simply calls the `get-Option()` function and sets the resulting query string as the target of the page in `window.output`.

Listing 10.7 shows the `getOption()` JavaScript function. This function loads all the values that the user has entered in `home.html` and packages them into a query string that is passed back to the `show_prediction()` view function in the Flask module.

Listing 10.7 `getOption()` **JavaScript function**

```
function getOption() {                          Gets the selected entry in the
  selectElementlocation =                       selection list for the location field
document.querySelector('#location');
  selectElementpropertytype = document.querySelector('#property-type');
  selectElementfurnishing = document.querySelector('#furnishing');
  selectElementsizetype = document.querySelector('#size-type');
  rooms_value = document.getElementById("rooms").value;          Gets the
  bathrooms_value = document.getElementById("bathrooms").value;  value
  car_parks_value = document.getElementById("car-parks").value;  entered
  size_value = document.getElementById("size").value;            into the
  location_string =                                              rooms field
selectElementlocation.options\
[selectElementlocation.selectedIndex].value        Gets the value of the
  property_type_string =                           selected entry in the
selectElementpropertytype.\                        selection list for the
options[selectElementpropertytype.selectedIndex].value  location field
  furnishing_string =
selectElementfurnishing.\
options[selectElementfurnishing.selectedIndex].value
  size_type_string = selectElementsizetype.\
options[selectElementsizetype.selectedIndex].value
  prefix = "/show-prediction/?"
  window.output =
prefix.concat("location=",location_string,"&rooms=",\
rooms_value,"&property_type=",property_type_string,\   Sets the value of
"&furnishing=",furnishing_string,"&size_type=          window.output
\",size_type_string,"&bathrooms=\                       to the query string
",bathrooms_value,"&car_parks=",car_parks_value,\
"&size=",size_value);
  document.querySelector('.output').textContent = window.output;
}
```

The `getOption()` JavaScript function shown in listing 10.7 performs the following actions:

- Loads the values from the continuous fields: `rooms`, `bathrooms`, `car-parks`, and `size`.
- Loads the selected entries in the categorical fields: `location`, `property-type`, `furnishing`, and `size-type`.
- Builds the query string. The query string looks as follows:

```
/show-prediction/?location=KLCC, Kuala Lumpur&rooms=1
&property_type=Serviced Residence&furnishing=Fully Furnished
&size_type=Built-up&bathrooms=1&car_parks=0&size=500
```

The query string consists of

- The URL `/show-prediction/`. Note that this URL matches the decorator that precedes the view function for `show-prediction` view function from the Flask server module shown in listing 10.3:

```
@app.route('/show-prediction/')
```

- ? to indicate the beginning of the query string.
- A set of parameter and value pairs to indicate the values that have been set for each field in home.html, delineated by the separator &. For example, the parameter and value pairs could look as follows:

```
location=KLCC, Kuala Lumpur
rooms=1
property_type=Serviced Residence
furnishing=Fully Furnished
size_type=Built-up
bathrooms=1
car_parks=0
size=500
```

The query string is passed to the show-prediction view function in the Flask server module. As shown in listing 10.3, in that function, the query string is parsed to get the values entered in home.html for each feature, and those values are used to get a prediction from the model.

10.1.4 *The show-prediction.html page*

Now that we have looked at the Flask server module and home.html, there is one more component of the web deployment to examine: show-prediction.html. This page displays the prediction that the model makes for the property that the user entered values for in home.html and has a button that takes the user back to home.html, where they can enter values for another property.

Listing 10.8 `show-prediction.html`

```html
<!DOCTYPE html>
<head>
  <title>
    Page for showing prediction        ◄─── Sets the text that appears in
  </title>                                    the browser tab for this page
  <link rel="stylesheet" href="{{ url_for('static',
filename='css/main2.css') }}">          ◄───
</head>                                        Sets the stylesheet
                                              for the page
<body>
<!-- display the prediction  -->
<div class="home">
    <h1 style="color: green">
        Here is the prediction for \
this Kuala Lumpur property:          ◄─── Introductory text
    </h1>
    <h1 style="color: green">
        {{ prediction.prediction_key }}
    </h1>

<!-- link back to home.html for entering
scoring parameters for another prediction  -->
```

```
<form action="{{ url_for('home') }}">
     <input type="submit"
value="Get another prediction"
style="font-size : 20px; width: 40%; height: 30px;"/>
    </form>

</div>
</body>
```

**Button to return
to home.html**

As shown in listing 10.8, show-prediction.html does not contain any JavaScript functions. The HTML for the page defines the text that appears on the page, and the button Get Another Prediction returns the user to home.html. Figure 10.4 shows how the elements we have discussed in this section appear in show-prediciton.html.

title text   **URL including query string**

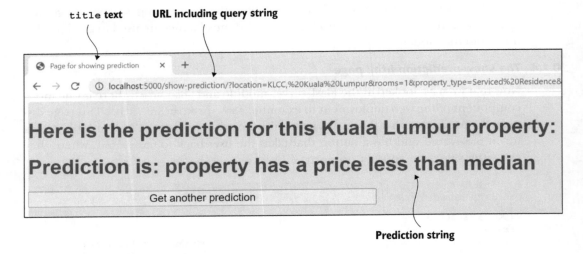

Prediction string

Figure 10.4   Key elements in show-prediction.html

Now that we have examined all the components of web deployment, we will review the rationale for deploying our model simply on the web in the next section.

10.1.5 Exercising the web deployment

Now that we have gone through the components that make up the web deployment, the next step is to see the deployment in action. To exercise the web deployment,

1 Create a new directory on your local system and clone the repo https://github.com/lmassaron/ml_on_tabular_data.

2 Make chapter_10 your current directory and start the Flask server module:

```
python flask_endpoint_deploy.py
```

3 Once the Flask server module is running, go to `localhost:5000` in a browser to exercise the deployment.

Congratulations! You have exercised a deep learning model trained on tabular data in the context of a simple, local web application. This deployment is an efficient way for us to exercise the trained model and see if it behaves as we expect. However, this very basic deployment does not incorporate many of the characteristics we expect to have in a production deployment. For example, we don't want the resources for serving the model to be limited by our local system. In the remainder of this chapter, we will examine how we can use this same web application to exercise the trained model deployed from an endpoint in a cloud environment.

10.2 *Public clouds and machine learning operations*

The simple web deployment that we reviewed in the previous section demonstrates some useful aspects of what it takes to put a trained model into production, but it has some serious limitations. It is running entirely on a local system, so it won't be accessible to anyone who doesn't have access to the local system. This is probably a good thing, because this deployment does not incorporate the characteristics that we want to have in a production deployment, including

- *Scaling capacity to meet demand.* What happens if the interest rate drops and the demand for price predictions doubles?
- *Seamless model updates.* What if we retrain the model on the latest data and need to deploy it quickly, without any interruption to the service?
- *Serving multiple versions of the model at the same time.* What if we want to experiment with a version of the model that is trained on a different dataset by exposing the new model to a subset of the users? How do we serve multiple versions of the model and control what proportion of users see each version?
- *Model monitoring.* How do we track the accuracy of the model as the real estate market develops? How do we catch and correct problems before they impact our users?
- *Resiliency and up-time.* With this application implemented on a local system, what happens when the system needs maintenance or has an unplanned outage? How do we ensure that our users can continue to get access to the application?

We could implement custom code to handle all of these scenarios, but there is a simpler solution. Public clouds provide complete, end-to-end machine learning and machine learning operations (MLOps) environments to address all the challenges listed here. The three most-used public clouds in the world are

- AWS
- Azure
- Google Cloud

Many organizations will use one or more of these public clouds to put their models into production.

The public cloud concepts that we describe in this chapter and chapter 11 are available in all three of these public clouds, but we are going to use Google Cloud for the public cloud examples in this chapter. There are a few reasons for this. One of the authors is a Google employee, but, more importantly, our objective opinion is that Google Cloud provides an easy-to-use environment for deploying models trained with tabular data and exploring the key concepts of MLOps. In the remainder of this chapter, we will go through how to get started with Google Cloud and how to use it to deploy a model. In chapter 11, we will go beyond the simple deployment in this chapter to explore the features in Google Cloud that make it easy to retrain and redeploy the model.

10.3   *Getting started with Google Cloud*

In this section, we will go through the initial steps of getting started with Google Cloud, including accessing Google Cloud for the first time, creating a project, and creating a Google Cloud Storage bucket, a data storage container. In the subsequent section, we will see how to use Vertex AI, the machine learning platform in Google Cloud, to deploy our model.

10.3.1   *Accessing Google Cloud for the first time*

In this section, we will go through signing into Google Cloud for the first time and setting up a Google Cloud *project*. Everything you do in Google Cloud is associated with a project. You can use projects to organize your work and to control the teams and individuals who have access to given Google Cloud resources. To get started, go to https:// cloud.google.com and click Sign In, as shown in figure 10.5.

Build what's next. Better software. Faster.

Figure 10.5   Signing into Google Cloud

Once you have signed in, click Console to open up the Google Cloud console, as shown in figure 10.6.

If you have not used Google Cloud before, you will need to set up your account for billing. You may be eligible for free credit, but you will need to enter credit card details to use the features that are described in this chapter and chapter 11. Once you have signed in and, if necessary, completed setting up your account with billing details, you will be at the console, as shown in figure 10.7.

Build what's next. Better software. Faster.

Figure 10.6   Entering the Google Cloud console

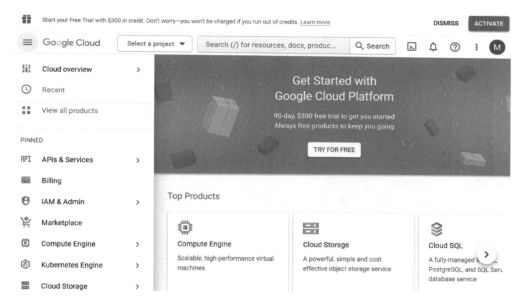

Figure 10.7   Google Cloud console

The console is the user interface for Google Cloud. This is one of the interface choices for working with Google Cloud features, and it is what we will use for most of the actions we will take in Google Cloud in this chapter. In addition to the Cloud console, you can interact with Google Cloud features using

- Command-line interface
- Client libraries

NOTE   See https://cloud.google.com/docs/overview for more details on the interfaces for Google Cloud.

10.3.2 Creating a Google Cloud project

You can create a project once you have successfully logged into Google Cloud and accessed the Google Cloud Console. In this section, we will go through the steps to create a project.

In the Google Cloud console, click the Project Selection field, as shown in figure 10.8. In the Select a Project screen, select New Project, as shown in figure 10.9. Then, enter `first-project-ml-tabular` in the Project Name field and click on Create, as shown in figure 10.10.

Figure 10.8   Selecting a project

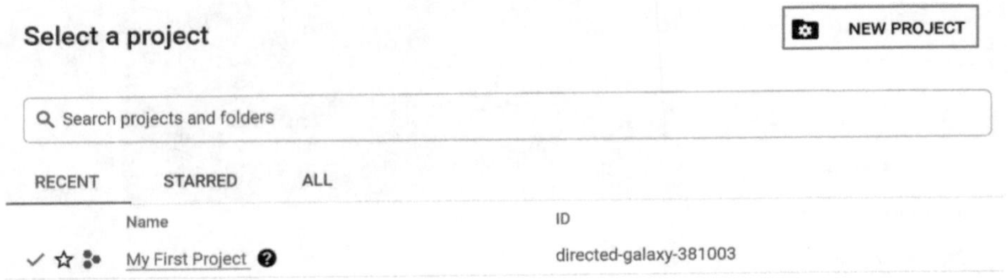

Figure 10.9   Selecting a project screen

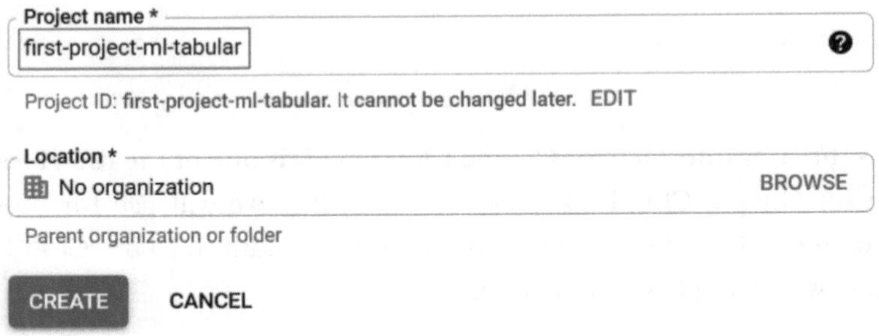

**Figure 10.10
Entering a
project name**

Congratulations! You have created your first Google Cloud project.

Note that the project name needs to be unique for your set of projects. The project ID, which appears below the Project name field, must be universally unique, so if you have a project name that is shared with any other project in Google Cloud, the project ID for that project will be automatically updated to be unique.

10.3.3 Creating a Google Cloud Storage bucket

The primary way to store data in Google Cloud is to use Cloud Storage buckets. In this section, we will go through just what you need to know about Cloud Storage buckets for the purposes of deploying a model. If you are interested in more details on Cloud Storage buckets, see the documentation: https://cloud.google.com/storage/docs/buckets. We will be using a bucket to store the model we trained in chapter 9. To create a Cloud Storage bucket, enter "cloud storage" in the search bar in the Cloud Console and select Cloud Storage, as shown in figure 10.11.

Figure 10.11 Searching for Cloud Storage

The Cloud Storage Buckets page appears. Select Create to create a new Cloud Storage bucket, as shown in figure 10.12.

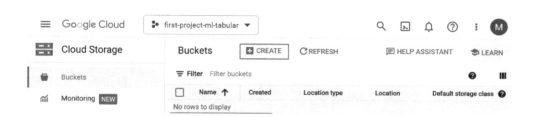

Figure 10.12 Cloud Storage view

In the Create a bucket page, enter a unique name for your bucket (figure 10.13), click Continue, and select Region in Location Type, and select a region, as shown in figure 10.14. To work with the machine learning pipeline script code that we will explore in chapter 11, the bucket needs to be created in a region. For the purposes of this example, you can pick any region that you like. Click Create. Note that your bucket name has to be universally unique.

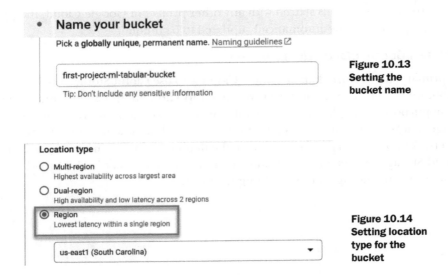

**Figure 10.13
Setting the
bucket name**

**Figure 10.14
Setting location
type for the
bucket**

The Bucket details page appears, showing your new bucket, as shown in figure 10.15.

Figure 10.15   Bucket details showing the new bucket

Congratulations! You have created your first Google Cloud Storage bucket.

10.4   *Deploying a model in Vertex AI*

Earlier in this chapter, we deployed the Kuala Lumpur real estate price prediction model using a simple, Flask-based web application. In this section, we are going to deploy the same model using the Google Cloud Vertex AI environment.

Now that we have created a project in Google Cloud and created a Cloud Storage bucket in the new project, we are ready to deploy a model in Google Cloud. The following are the steps we will follow for this deployment (described in more detail in the Vertex AI documentation at https://mng.bz/nRJ2):

1 Upload the model we trained in chapter 9 to Google Cloud storage.
2 Import the model to the Vertex AI Model Registry.

The following sections describe each of these steps.

10.4.1 Uploading the model to a Cloud Storage bucket

The simplest way to get your trained model into Google Cloud Storage is to upload a folder containing the trained model. If you want to upload a version of the model that has already been trained, clone the repo at https://github.com/lmassaron/ Advanced_Analytics_for_Business. The directory you want to upload is `chapter_10/ models/k1_real_estate_keras_preprocessing_model`.

To upload the model that you created in chapter 9, select the Cloud Storage bucket you created in the Cloud Storage page, as shown in figure 10.16. In the Bucket Details page, select Upload Folder, as shown in figure 10.17.

Figure 10.16　Selecting your bucket in the Cloud Storage page

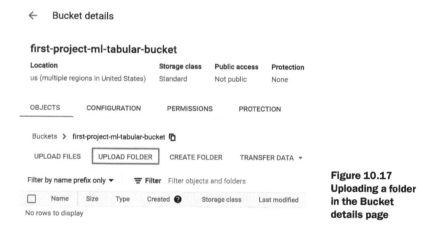

**Figure 10.17
Uploading a folder
in the Bucket
details page**

Select the folder on your local system containing the trained model from chapter 9. When the upload is complete, the folder will appear on the Bucket details page, as shown in figure 10.18.

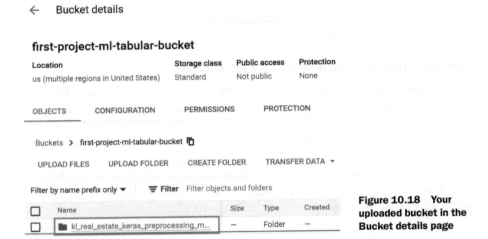

Figure 10.18   Your uploaded bucket in the Bucket details page

Congratulations! You have uploaded your model to Google Cloud.

10.4.2 *Importing the model to Vertex AI*

Now that we have uploaded the model to a Google Cloud Storage bucket, we can import it to the Vertex AI Model Registry. Enter "vertex ai" in the Google Cloud console search bar to get to the Vertex AI page. If this is the first time you have used Vertex AI, you will see Enable All Recommended API. If you see this button, click on it to enable the APIs that are required to use Vertex AI, as shown in figure 10.19.

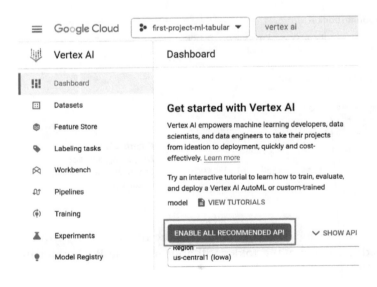

Figure 10.19   Enabling Vertex AI APIs

Then select Model Registry in the left navigation panel, as shown in figure 10.20, and on the Model Registry page, click Import, as shown in figure 10.21.

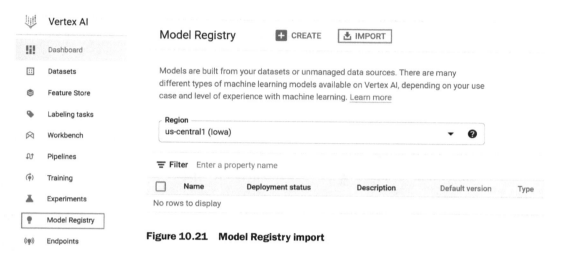

Figure 10.21 **Model Registry import**

**Figure 10.20 Model
Registry in the Vertex AI
page navigation panel**

In the Import model page, select Import as New Model, enter "first-model-ml-tabular" in the Name field, and click Continue, as shown in figure 10.22.

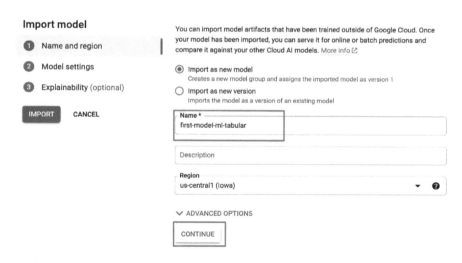

Figure 10.22 **Specifying the name of the imported model in Model Registry**

On the Model settings tab of the Import model page, follow these steps:

1 In Model Framework, select TensorFlow. Recall from chapter 8 TensorFlow is the low-level framework for Keras, the framework we used to train the model.

2 In Model Framework Version, select the TensorFlow level used to train the model. You can find this level from the output of `tf.__version__` in the notebook used to train the model:

```
tf.__version__
2.9.2
```

3 In Model Artifact Location, click Browse and select the folder where you uploaded the model.

4 Click Continue and Import, as shown in figure 10.23.

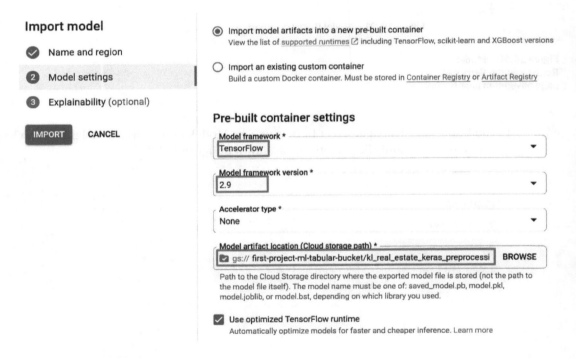

Figure 10.23 Specifying model settings

The model import process may take several minutes to complete. When the import is complete, you will see the new model name on the Model Registry page, as shown in figure 10.24.

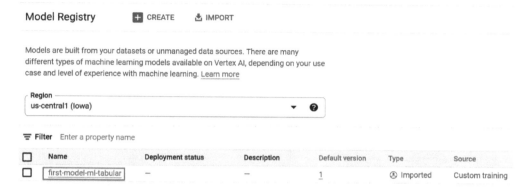

Figure 10.24 Model Registry showing the imported model

Congratulations! You have imported a model into Vertex AI. In the next section, we will go through the steps to make this model available through an endpoint.

10.4.3 Deploying the model to an endpoint

Now that we have imported the trained model into Vertex AI, we can deploy it to an endpoint. By deploying the model to an endpoint, we get a URL that we can use to invoke the model. In effect, the endpoint deployment can take the place of the model file in the local file system that the Flask server loaded in the simple web deployment that we did earlier in this chapter.

To deploy the model to an endpoint, on the Model Registry page, select the model we created in the previous section. In the model details page, select the version of the model (by default, 1), as shown in figure 10.25. In the version page for the model, click Deploy to Endpoint, as shown in figure 10.26. In the Deploy to Endpoint page, enter a name in Endpoint name and click Continue, as shown in figure 10.27.

←   first-model-ml-tabular   ✎ EDIT DETAILS

Model description
—

Region
us-central1 (Iowa)

Versions

≡ Filter   Enter a property name

	Version ID ↓	Alias	Status	Description	Endpoints
☐	1	⊛ default	✔ Ready	—	—

Figure 10.25 Model details page

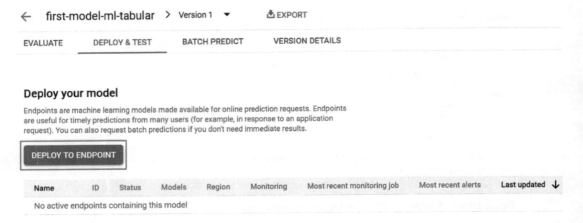

Figure 10.26   Deploying your model

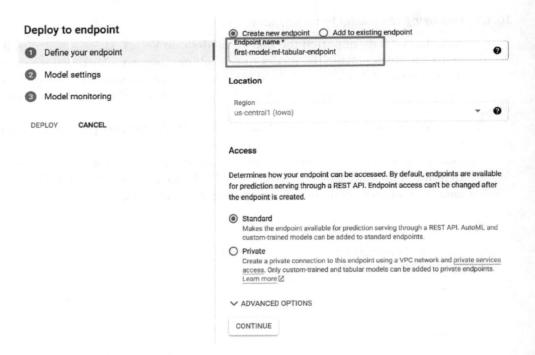

Figure 10.27   Deploying to endpoint page

In the Model Settings tab, under Advanced Scaling Options, select a minimal machine type, such as `n1-standard-2`, as shown in figure 10.28, and click Continue.

Figure 10.28   Setting the machine type for the deployment

Because this is a test deployment of a simple model, we only need a minimal machine type. If we were deploying a more demanding model, or making a production deployment, we could choose a machine type with more memory or compute resources, depending on the requirements of our model. A minimal machine type is good enough for our test deployment, and it will cost us less than a more advanced machine type. When you are using a cloud environment, it's a best practice to use the resources that are sufficient for your application and not more. Doing this will save you money.

> **TIP** For more details about machine types for Vertex AI endpoint deployments, see the documentation at https://mng.bz/vK14.

Click Deploy, as shown in figure 10.29.

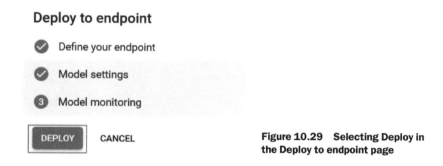

Figure 10.29   Selecting Deploy in the Deploy to endpoint page

Deployment can take several minutes to complete. When deployment is complete, the status of the deployment on the Model version details page changes to Active, as shown in figure 10.30.

Name	ID	Status	Models	Region	Monitoring	Most recent monitoring job	Most recent alerts
first-model-ml-tabular-endpoint	389644930651258880	✔ Active	1	us-central1	Disabled	—	—

Figure 10.30   Confirmation that the model has been deployed

Congratulations! You have completed the deployment of a model in Vertex AI. In the next section, we will go through the steps to quickly test the deployment.

10.4.4 *Initial test of the model deployment*

Now that we have deployed the model, we can do an initial test of the model deployment directly in the Google console.

Recall the test of the trained model that we did in chapter 9 to exercise the model in the context of a Jupyter Notebook. We defined a Python dictionary that contained all the features used to train the model, along with values for each of the features:

```
sample = {
    'location': 'Sentul, Kuala Lumpur',
    'rooms': 3.0,
    'property_type': 'Condominium For Sale',
    'furnishing': 'Partly Furnished',
    'size_type_bin': 'built-up 1',
    'bathrooms': 2.0,
    'car_parks': 0.0,
    'size': 950.0,
}
```

We can reuse this sample to test the model deployment in Vertex AI. In the Model version details page, go to the Test Your Model section, as shown in figure 10.31.

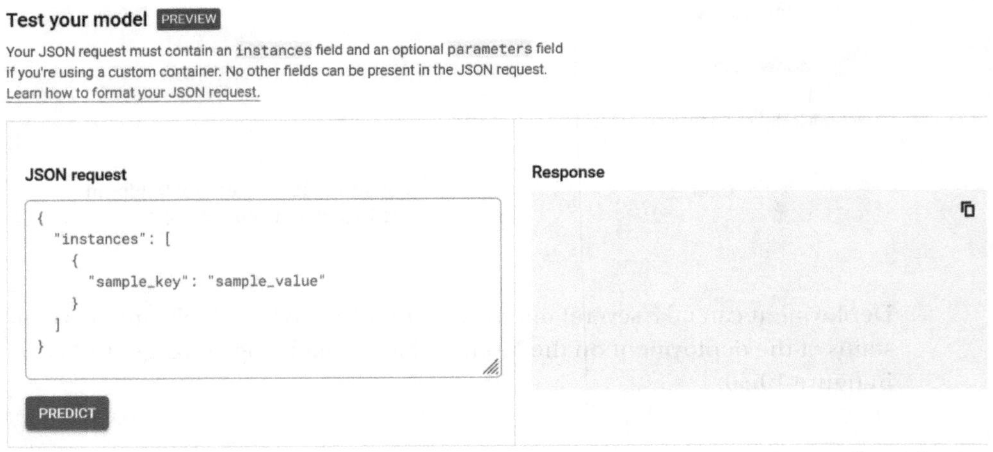

Figure 10.31   Test Your Model section of the Deploy and Test tab

Update the JSON request field to use the values from the sample from chapter 9, with each value being an entry in a list and double quotes being used throughout. When you have completed the update, the JSON request field should look like figure 10.32.

JSON request

```
{
"instances":[
{
    "location": ["Sentul, Kuala Lumpur"],
    "rooms": [3.0],
    "property_type": ["Condominium For Sale"],
    "furnishing": ["Partly Furnished"],
    "size_type_bin": ["built-up 1"],
    "bathrooms": [2.0],
    "car_parks": [0.0],
    "size": [950.0]
}
]
}
```

PREDICT

Figure 10.32 Test sample in JSON format

Note three differences between the format of the sample in the JSON request and the original sample from the chapter 9 Jupyter Notebook:

- Values in the key-value pairs are all arrays rather than single values. You will get an error if you have single values.
- Double quotes (" ") are used throughout rather than single quotes.
- There is no comma after the last key-value pair.

Once the JSON Request field contains valid JSON, the frame turns blue. Click Predict to see the output of the endpoint in the Response field, as shown in figure 10.33.

Response

```
{
  "predictions": [
    [
      -1.52191401
    ]
  ],
  "deployedModelId": "3381917447132020736",
  "model": "projects/1028332300603/locations/us-central1/models/4355669133946
  "modelDisplayName": "first-model-ml-tabular",
  "modelVersionId": "1"
}
```

Figure 10.33 Response from the endpoint for the test sample

Note that the prediction value is not a probability. Recall that when we got a prediction from the model in the model training notebook in chapter 9, and when we got a prediction from the model in the Flask server module, we needed to apply the sigmoid function to the output of the model to get the probability that the property has a price above the median:

```
predictions = loaded_model.predict(input_dict)
prob = tf.nn.sigmoid(predictions[0])
```

We need to apply the sigmoid function to get the probability from the output provided by the endpoint. If we update the statements that we used in the training notebook so that the input to the sigmoid function is the output of the endpoint, then we get the same probability that we got for this property when we used it to exercise the model in chapter 9:

```
prob2 = tf.nn.sigmoid(-1.52191401)
print(
    "This property has a %.1f percent probability of "
    "having a price over the median." % (100 * prob2)
)
This property has a 17.9 percent probability
of having a price over the median.
```

Now, having validated that the endpoint works and that for the same property, we get the same results as when we applied the model directly in a Jupyter Notebook.

10.5   *Using the Vertex AI deployment with Flask*

In the previous section, we deployed the Kuala Lumpur property price prediction model to an endpoint in Vertex AI. In this section, we will adapt the Flask web deployment to use this endpoint. When we are done, we should have the same experience from the web pages `home.html` and `show-prediction.html`, with the model being served from the Vertex AI endpoint rather than from a local system.

To adapt the Flask deployment to work with the Vertex AI endpoint deployment, we will need to take the following steps:

1 Set up the Vertex AI SDK.
2 Update the Flask server module to access the Vertex AI endpoint to get predictions from the model served there.

Figure 10.34 shows the key components of the application that is adapted to use a Vertex AI endpoint deployment of the model.

In the remainder of this section, we will go through the steps required to deploy the model with the Vertex AI endpoint using the web application.

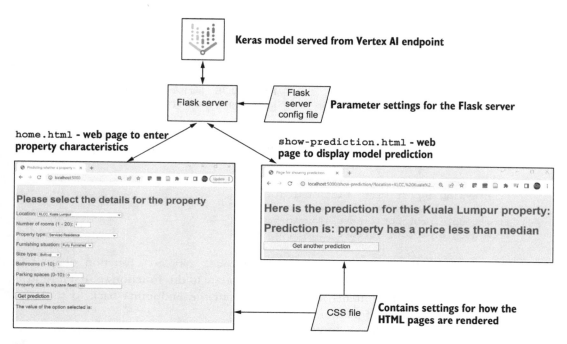

Figure 10.34   **Sample request link in the Deploy and Test tab**

10.5.1 Setting up the Vertex AI SDK

Vertex AI provides client libraries that allow you to access Vertex AI features via an API in Python, Java, and `node.js` applications. The client library for Python is included in the Python SDK for Vertex AI, so we will install the SDK to get the API access required to invoke the model via the endpoint.

> **NOTE**   For full details on the Vertex AI SDK, see the documentation at https://mng.bz/4a1j.

You can use the following command to install the Vertex AI SDK:

```
pip install google-cloud-aiplatform
```

Now that we have the Vertex AI SDK installed, we can proceed to the next step: updating the Flask server module.

10.5.2 Updating the Flask server module to call the endpoint

To get an overview of how to use the Vertex AI API to access the model via the endpoint, click the Sample Request link in the Model version details page, as shown in figure 10.35.

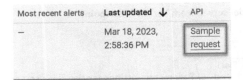

Figure 10.35   Sample request link in the Deploy and Test tab

The first update to the Flask server module is to import the libraries required for Vertex AI:

```
from typing import Dict, List, Union
from google.cloud import aiplatform
from google.protobuf import json_format
from google.protobuf.struct_pb2 import Value
```

Next, we add the `predict_custom_trained_model_sample()` function defined in https://mng.bz/QD8v. We need to make one update to this function so that it returns `predictions` (which contains the response from the endpoint) back to the `show -prediction.html` view function.

Listing 10.9 highlights the updates that we need to make to the `show-prediction .html` view function. These changes package the input values in the format expected by the Vertex AI endpoint deployment and invoke the model at the Vertex AI endpoint via the `predict_custom_trained_model_sample()` function.

Listing 10.9   `show-prediction.html` view function for endpoints

```
def show_prediction():
    scoring_dict = {}                                       # Removes size_type
    for col in config['scoring_columns_cat']:               # from the feature list
        print("value for "+col+" is: "+str(request.args.get(col)))
        scoring_dict[col] = str(request.args.get(col))
    for col in config['scoring_columns_cont']:
        scoring_dict[col] = float(request.args.get(col))
    scoring_dict['size_type_bin'] = str(request.args.get('size_type'))+' 1'
    scoring_dict.pop('size_type')
    input_dict = {name: [value] for name, \
value in scoring_dict.items()}                              # Converts the values
    print("input_dict: ",input_dict)                        # in the scoring_dict
    predictions = predict_custom_trained_model_sample(      # to lists of values
    project = config['endpoint']['project'],
    endpoint_id = config['endpoint']['endpoint_id'],
    location = config['endpoint']['location'],              # Calls predict_custom_
    instances = input_dict)                                 # trained_model_sample
    prob = tf.nn.sigmoid(predictions[0])
```

Listing 10.9 shows the following updates to the `show-prediction.html` view function:

- The call to the endpoint has to have the exact correct list of features and values, with no missing features or extra features. Since we don't use `size_type` directly with the model, we need to explicitly remove it from the dictionary of features and values with the `scoring_dict.pop('size_type')` statement.

- The endpoint expects to get the features and values in a dictionary with the same format as the JSON that we used to exercise the endpoint directly in the console in section 10.4.4. That means the values in the dictionary need to be converted to lists of values, each of which contains exactly one value. This statement converts the dictionary to lists of values:

  input_dict = {name: [value] for name, value in scoring_dict.items()}

- The `predict_custom_trained_model_sample()` function needs to be called with parameters specifying the project, endpoint, and key-value pairs for the features we want a prediction for.

In addition to these updates to the Flask server module, we can also remove the statements that loaded the model from the local file system since we don't use the local model in this solution.

NOTE An updated version of the Flask server module that uses the endpoint is available at https://mng.bz/Xx5a.

To run this version of the Flask server module, follow these steps:

1 Authorize the account you used to access Google Cloud with this application by running the following command on the command line in the local system where you are running the Flask server module:

```
gcloud auth application-default login
```

2 Start the Flask server module:

```
python flask_endpoint_deploy.py
```

If you get an error related to the protobuf (protocol buffer) level, try the following command:

```
pip install protobuf==3.20.*n
```

This command adjusts the protobuf level to exactly what the endpoint requires.

NOTE You don't need to know about the protobufs for the purposes of this application, but if you are curious, you can check out the documentation: https://protobuf.dev/.

3 Once the Flask server module is running, go to `localhost:5000` in a browser to exercise the deployment.

Now we have seen two kinds of deployments of the model: a web deployment run entirely from a local system and a web deployment that uses the model served from a Vertex AI endpoint.

10.5.3 *Benefits of deploying a model to an endpoint*

If we get the same results from the model whether it is deployed in a simple web deployment or deployed to an endpoint, you may ask what the point is of deploying the model to an endpoint. There are a number of benefits that come from deploying to an endpoint:

- You can scale the endpoint instance to handle additional load.
- You can deploy multiple models to the same endpoint. Imagine a situation where you need to replace one model in production with another. If you deploy both models to the same endpoint, you can gradually adjust how much of the traffic goes to the new model without making any changes to the application and without causing jarring changes to the users of the application.
- You can deploy the same model to different endpoints, allowing you to optimize the machine resources. For example, if you have a production and a development environment, you can deploy the same model to two endpoints, with higher-spec machine resources for the production environment and cheaper machine resources for the development environment.
- With an endpoint, you can enable Vertex AI monitoring to detect skew (differences in the distribution between training data and the data seen applying the model in production) and drift (changes in the distribution of data seen by the model in production over time). Model monitoring can help to ensure that the model's performance does not degrade over time and that changes in the data the model is being applied to in production do not occur unexpectedly. For more details on monitoring, see the documentation at https://mng.bz/yWdd.

Figure 10.36 shows examples of multiple models deployed to the same endpoint and one model deployed to multiple endpoints.

In figure 10.36, there are two scenarios:

- *Multiple models are deployed to the same endpoint*—Model A is the version currently in production, and Model B is the next level of the model that we want to introduce to production. By adjusting the values of X and Y, we can control the proportion of traffic that goes to each model, gradually increasing the proportion that goes to the new level of the model.
- *Same model deployed to multiple endpoints*—Endpoint 1 has basic compute resources, and endpoint 2 has sufficient compute resources to handle our current production load. By doing this we can optimize the resource cost for the system to meet the needs of multiple groups of users.

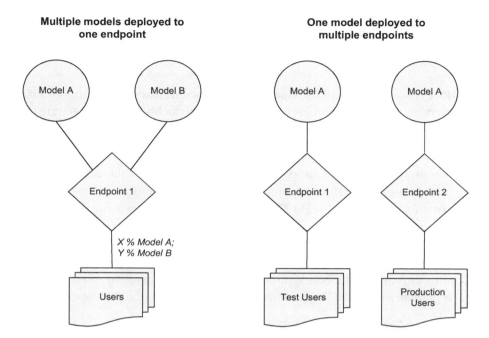

Figure 10.36   Relationship between models and endpoints

NOTE   For more details on model deployment in Vertex AI, see the documentation at https://mng.bz/MDlB.

10.6   *Gemini for Google Cloud: Generative AI assistance in Google Cloud*

As you worked through the steps in this chapter, you may have run into a roadblock or needed to clarify a question. To make progress, you may have referred to the documentation for Google Cloud, searched in Stack Overflow, or asked a colleague for help. In addition to these traditional sources of assistance, Google Cloud also includes an integrated, generative AI-driven source of assistance: Gemini for Google Cloud.

Gemini for Google Cloud is a set of generative AI capabilities for Google Cloud. Gemini for Google Workspace is a companion set of generative AI capabilities for Google Workspace (Google Docs, Sheets, Slides; see https://workspace.google.com/solutions/ai/). In this chapter and chapter 11, we'll show how you can use generative AI via Gemini for Google Cloud to simplify the deployment of tabular data models and to automate some of scripting for machine learning pipelines. Gemini for Google Cloud provides a variety of capabilities, including the following:

- Answering questions about Google Cloud

- Generating code (including SQL and a variety of programming languages such as Python, Java, and JavaScript) from text
- Explaining code

NOTE   See the Gemini for Google Cloud documentation for a more detailed overview of what Gemini for Google Cloud can do: https://cloud.google.com/gemini/docs/overview.

In this section, we'll cover setting up Gemini for Google Cloud and using it to answer questions about Google Cloud. We'll also discuss some of the actions we completed in this chapter to deploy our model in a Vertex AI endpoint. In chapter 11, we'll return to Gemini for Google Cloud to show how you can use it to generate and explain code.

Google Cloud is not the only cloud platform that harnesses generative AI to make it easier to use the platform and to automate some steps in the development workflow. Copilot in Azure and Code Whisperer in AWS are generative AI-based features that each provide a subset of the benefits provided by Gemini for Google Cloud.

10.6.1 *Setting up Gemini for Google Cloud*

The following are instructions for setting up Gemini for Google Cloud:

- Setting up Gemini for Google Cloud for a project: https://cloud.google.com/gemini/docs/quickstart
- Setting up Gemini Code Assist, the part of Gemini for Google Cloud that provides AI assistance for development, to be used in Cloud Shell Editor in Google Cloud: https://mng.bz/avMm

Once you have set up Gemini for Google Cloud for a project, you will see the Gemini for Google Cloud icon in the toolbar (see figure 10.37).

Figure 10.37   Gemini for Google Cloud icon

Now that we have done the basic setup for Gemini for Google Cloud, we'll see how we can use it to get answers to questions about Google Cloud in the next section.

10.6.2 *Using Gemini for Google Cloud to answer questions about Google Cloud*

Gemini for Google Cloud manifests itself in various ways in Google Cloud, including

- *In a chat pane that's available throughout Google Cloud*—Figure 10.38 shows the Gemini for the Google Cloud chat pane.

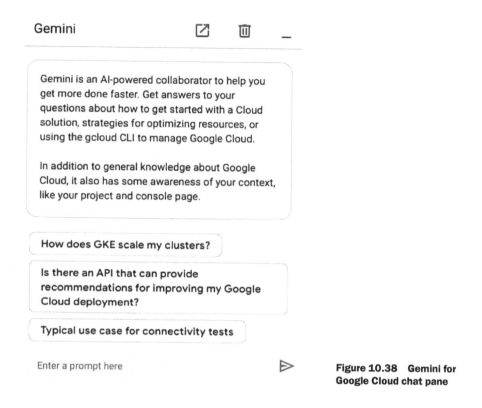

Figure 10.38   Gemini for
Google Cloud chat pane

- *In a range of IDEs supported by Google Cloud, including VS Code, Cloud Workstations, and Cloud Shell Editor*—Figure 10.39 illustrates how Gemini for Google Cloud can generate a simple Python function from a comment in Cloud Shell Editor.

```
 test_example.py  ×

duet_ai_test >   test_example.py > ...
    1    # function to add two integers and return the sum as a string
    2    def add(a, b):
    3        return a + b
    4
    5
```

Figure 10.39   Gemini for Google Cloud generating Python in Cloud Shell Editor

- *In the query editors for Big Query and Spanner*—Figure 10.40 shows how Gemini for Google Cloud can generate SQL from a comment in the Spanner query editor.

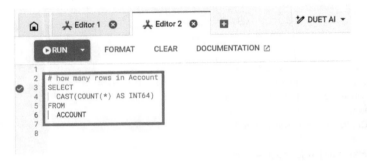

Figure 10.40   Gemini for Google Cloud generating SQL in the query editor in Spanner

Now that we have reviewed examples of where Gemini for Google Cloud can be used, let's examine the Gemini for Google Cloud chat pane more to see how it can be used to get answers to questions about Google Cloud. You can click on the Gemini icon (see figure 10.37) to open the Gemini for Google Cloud chat pane, as shown in figure 10.41.

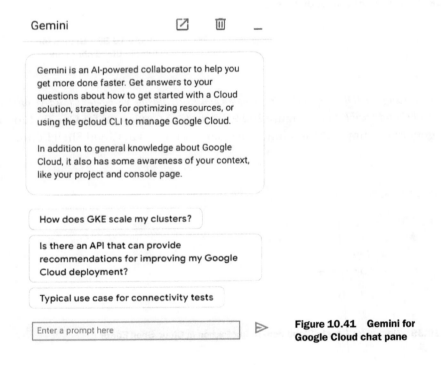

Figure 10.41   Gemini for Google Cloud chat pane

Try out the Gemini for Google Cloud chat pane by entering an instruction prompt in the prompt field and clicking on the Send button, as shown in figure 10.42.

Figure 10.42   Gemini for Google Cloud chat pane Send button

The Gemini for Google Cloud chat pane is available whenever you need it in Google Cloud, and you can use it to ask all kinds of questions about Google Cloud. For example, suppose we want to create a Cloud Storage bucket and we forgot the steps listed earlier in this chapter. Figure 10.43 shows the response given by Gemini for Google Cloud to the prompt "How to create a Google storage bucket."

How to create a Google Cloud storage bucket

To create a Google Cloud storage bucket, you will need to first create a project. Once you have created a project, you can navigate to the Cloud Storage page and click the "Create bucket" button. On the "Create a bucket" page, you will need to enter a name for your bucket and select a location for it. You can also choose to enable versioning for your bucket. Once you have entered all of the required information, click the "Create" button to create your bucket.

Here are the steps on how to create a Google Cloud storage bucket:

1. Go to the Cloud Storage page in the Google Cloud console.
2. Click the "Create bucket" button.
3. Enter a name for your bucket.
4. Select a location for your bucket.
5. (Optional) Enable versioning for your bucket.
6. Click the "Create" button.

Your bucket will be created and you will be able to use it to store your data.

Figure 10.43   Gemini for Google Cloud response to "how to create a Google Cloud storage bucket"

Gemini for Google Cloud has been trained specifically to provide useful answers to questions about using Google Cloud. Try out Gemini for Google Cloud by giving it prompts related to some of the sections in this chapter. For example, try "how to import a custom model into Vertex AI" or "how to deploy a model to a Vertex AI endpoint" and see how the responses from Gemini for Google Cloud compare to the steps listed in the analogous sections in this chapter.

Summary

- Deploying your model in a simple web application can give you a sense of its characteristics in production.

- We can create a simple web application to deploy the model we trained in chapter 9. This application includes a Flask server module and two simple web pages.

- A public cloud environment provides an environment for deploying a model that allows you to scale capacity and control availability.

- To prepare to deploy the model we trained in chapter 9 in Google Cloud, we need to create a Google Cloud project, create a Google Cloud bucket, and upload the model to the bucket.

- Once we have completed the steps to prepare for a Google Cloud model deployment, we can deploy a trained model to a Vertex AI endpoint.

- We can test the Vertex AI endpoint deployment of the model by making a few simple updates to the Flask module from the web application that we created at the beginning of this chapter.

- Deploying a model to an endpoint in Vertex AI makes the deployment more robust. In particular, we can specify the machine resources that are appropriate for our application, provide a mix of model levels, and monitor the model's performance in production.

- Gemini for Google Cloud provides generative AI capabilities that can be helpful for model development and deployment tasks in Google Cloud.

11
Building a machine learning pipeline

This chapter covers

- An overview of machine learning pipelines
- Prerequisites for running a machine learning pipeline in Vertex AI
- Model training and deployment: local implementation vs. machine learning pipeline implementation
- Defining a machine learning pipeline to train and deploy a model
- Updating the model training code to work with a machine learning pipeline
- Using generative AI to help create the machine learning pipeline

In chapter 10, we went through the steps to deploy a deep learning model trained on tabular data. We deployed the model in a web application, first with the model running entirely on our local system and then having the model deployed to a Vertex AI endpoint. In this chapter, we will go through the further steps to automate the training and deployment process by using a machine learning (ML) pipeline in Vertex AI. We will start by going over the setup steps necessary for a ML pipeline, including defining a Vertex AI dataset. Next, we will contrast the local model training and deployment we have seen from chapter 10 with model training and deployment using an ML pipeline. We will proceed to review the code specifically for the ML pipeline itself, along with the updates to the existing code required for the model training code to work in the context of an ML pipeline. Finally, we will examine some of the ways that we can apply generative AI and get useful help from its outputs in the workflow for creating a ML pipeline. The code described in this chapter is available at https://mng.bz/DM4n.

11.1 Introduction to ML pipelines

Consider the steps that we have covered so far in this book to prepare a deep learning model trained on tabular data:

- Process the data to deal with problems such as missing values, columns containing two distinct kinds of data, and numeric data expressed as strings
- Train the model using the processed data
- Deploy the trained model so that it can be used by an application

Suppose we needed to go through this process repeatedly for the Kuala Lumpur real estate problem. This is a reasonable expectation because the real estate market will keep changing as prices develop, interest rates change, and macroeconomic factors affect the demand for real estate. Rather than running the various notebooks and deployment steps manually for each end-to-end cycle from raw data to deployed model, it would be better to have a coded solution that we could run as a unit repeatedly and consistently. An ML pipeline gives us this exactly, and in this section, we will go through an example illustrating how to set up a simple, end-to-end pipeline for the Kuala Lumpur real estate problem.

11.1.1 Three kinds of pipelines

Before getting into the details of an ML pipeline, it is worth noting that the term *pipeline* has been overloaded with different meanings over time. At the moment, there are at least three distinct meanings for the term *pipeline* that are predominant in the world of ML/data science:

- *Training/inference pipeline*—This pipeline ensures that data transformations, such as assigning text to tokens or assigning values in a categorical column to numeric identifiers, are done consistently in the training and inference steps. The preprocessing Keras layers in the Kuala Lumpur model constitute this kind of pipeline because they ensure, for example, that the transformations done on the processed data prior to training exactly match the transformations done on the data points entered in `home.html` in the web deployment.

- *Data pipeline*—This pipeline deals with anomalies in the input training data, such as missing values or schema problems. It can overlap the pipeline described in the previous point, but it performs a distinct task. In the context of Google Cloud, Dataflow and Cloud Data Fusion are examples of products that can perform data pipeline tasks. You don't need to know about Dataflow or Cloud Data Fusion for the purposes of this chapter, but if you are curious, you can check out the documentation: https://cloud.google.com/dataflow/docs and https://cloud.google.com/data-fusion/docs.

- *ML pipeline*—This is a pipeline that automates various steps such as training, deploying, and monitoring the model. TFX and KubeFlow are the two approaches that are available in Vertex AI for implementing ML pipelines.

Figure 11.1 shows how each of these three kinds of pipelines fits into the end-to-end ML workflow.

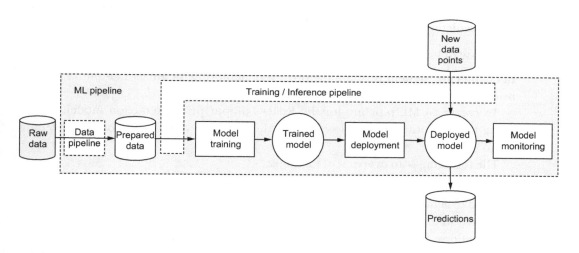

Figure 11.1   **Three kinds of pipelines and how they relate**

Figure 11.1 illustrates the following characteristics of the pipelines:

- The ML pipeline can encompass the entire workflow, from raw data to monitoring the deployed model. The rationale for this is that the ML pipeline is intended to automate the complete process when the model needs to be retrained and redeployed.

- The distinction between a data pipeline and a training/inference pipeline is that the training/inference pipeline handles transformations that need to be applied to new data points to which we want to apply the trained model to get predictions, such as replacing categorical values with numeric identifiers. The same transformations need to be applied to the prepared data prior to training the model.

- As we saw in the Keras custom layers solution to the Airbnb NYC price prediction problem in chapter 3, the training/inference pipeline can be distinct from the model training process. In the Keras customer layers solution, the training/ inference pipeline was implemented using Scikit-learn pipeline structures and custom classes, both of which need to be applied to data prior to model training and prior to applying new data points to the trained model to get predictions. In chapter 9, on the other hand, we saw how the same processing could be incorporated directly into the Keras model.

- Data pipelines can exist outside the context of the ML workflow. The same data pipeline tools, such as Dataflow and Cloud Data Fusion, that can be used in ML workflows in Google Cloud can be part of applications that don't include ML.

Now that we have described three different kinds of pipelines, in the next section, we will start to explore how to create an ML pipeline for the Kuala Lumpur real estate price prediction problem in Google Cloud using Kubeflow.

11.1.2 *Overview of Vertex AI ML pipelines*

In chapter 10, we went through the process of deploying the Kuala Lumpur real estate price prediction model to a Vertex AI endpoint.

To create an ML pipeline for the Kuala Lumpur price prediction model, we are going to start with the steps described in the Vertex AI documentation: https://mng .bz/IYW6.

The following is an overview of the steps:

- Set up a *service account*. A service account is an account used by an application to take actions in Google Cloud. When we imported the Keras model into Google Cloud and deployed it to an endpoint, we used our own ID to perform these actions. Since the ML pipeline will be an automated script, we need a service account to allow the script to perform actions without depending directly on manual intervention from any individual. See the Google Cloud documentation for more details on service accounts: https://mng.bz/BXA0.

- Get a service account key for the service account and provide the service account with the required access to run the ML pipeline.

- Create a pipeline script to invoke the Vertex AI SDK.

- Adapt the model training notebook to be a standalone Python script that can be run in a prebuilt Vertex AI container.

- Run the pipeline script to run the training script inside a container and generate a trained model.

In the subsequent sections, we will go through these steps to create an ML pipeline for the Kuala Lumpur real estate prediction model.

11.2 ML pipeline preparation steps

Before we can run the ML pipeline to train and deploy a model, we need to set up the Google Cloud objects the pipeline needs. In this section, we will set up a service account and introduce the Cloud Shell, an instance that is available directly in Google Cloud that we can use to enter commands. We will also upload our dataset to Google Cloud Storage and use the uploaded dataset to create a Vertex AI dataset.

11.2.1 Creating a service account for the ML pipeline

Since we want to be able to run the ML pipeline automatically without manual intervention, we need to set up a service account to run the pipeline.

To create a service account, follow these steps:

1 Select IAM & Admin -> Service Accounts from the overall Google Cloud Console menu, as shown in figure 11.2.

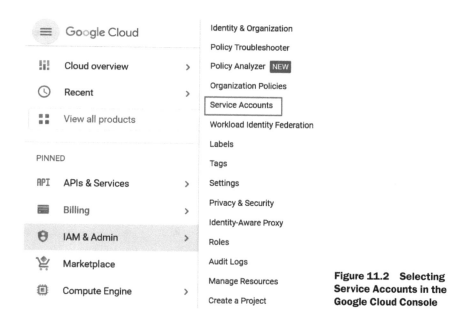

Figure 11.2   Selecting Service Accounts in the Google Cloud Console

2 In the Service Accounts page, select Create Service Account, as shown in figure 11.3.

Figure 11.3   Creating a service account

3   In the Create service account page, enter a name for the service account and click Create and Continue, as shown in figure 11.4. Note that the service account ID gets filled in automatically and that an email ID for the service account is shown in the form `service-account-id@project-id.iam.gserviceaccount` `.com`—in this case: `ml-tabular-pipeline@first-project-ml-tabular.iam` `.gserviceaccount.com`

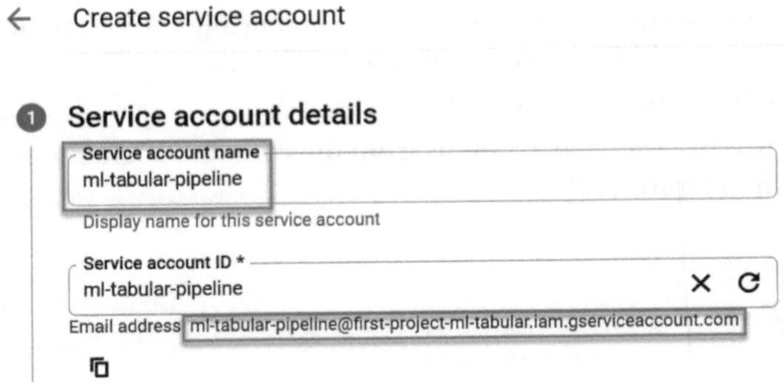

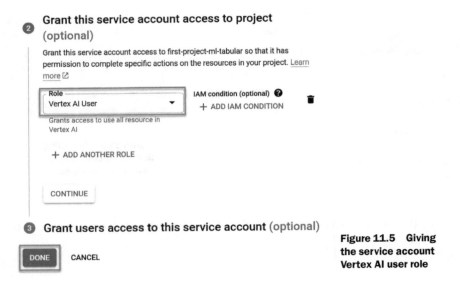

Figure 11.4 Setting a service account name

4   Select Vertex AI User in the Role field and click Done, as shown in figure 11.5.

Figure 11.5   Giving the service account Vertex AI user role

Now that we have created a service account and given it access to Vertex AI, in the next section we can create a service account key.

11.2.2 Creating a service account key

The ML pipeline uses a service account key to authenticate the service account used to run the ML pipeline.

To create a service account key, follow these steps:

1 In the Service accounts page, click on the email address for the service account that you just created, as shown in figure 11.6.

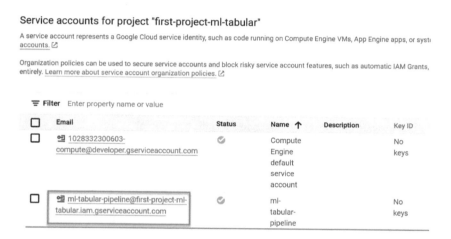

Figure 11.6 Selecting the service account

2 Select the Keys tab and click Add key -> Create new key, as shown in figure 11.7.

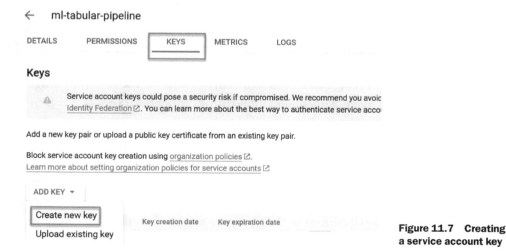

Figure 11.7 Creating a service account key

3 Select JSON and click Create, as shown in figure 11.8.

Create private key for "ml-tabular-pipeline"

Downloads a file that contains the private key. Store the file securely because this key can't be recovered if lost.

Key type

◉ JSON

    Recommended

○ P12

    For backward compatibility with code using the P12 format

CANCEL   CREATE

Figure 11.8   Downloading the service account key

A JSON file containing the service account key is created and downloaded to your local system with a name that looks like: `first-project-ml-tabular-039ff1f820a8.json`.

11.2.3 *Granting the service account access to the Compute Engine default service account*

When you set up your project in Google Cloud, a Compute Engine default service account was created. This account has an email address like `PROJECT_NUMBER-compute@developer.gserviceaccount.com`. For more details on the Compute Engine default service account, see the documentation (https://mng.bz/dXdN).

We need to give the service account that we set up in the preceding sections access to the Compute Engine default service account to run the ML pipeline. Follow these steps to set up this access to the Compute Engine default service account:

1 In the Service accounts page, click the copy icon beside the email address for the service account you just created (you will need this in the next step) and then click the email address of the Compute Engine default service account, as shown in figure 11.9.

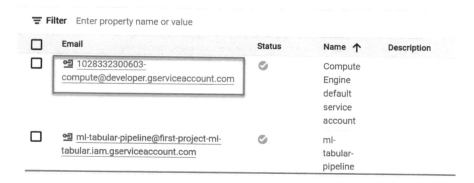

Service accounts for project "first-project-ml-tabular"

A service account represents a Google Cloud service identity, such as code running on Compute Engine VMs, App Eng accounts. ⬀

Organization policies can be used to secure service accounts and block risky service account features, such as autom entirely. Learn more about service account organization policies. ⬀

Figure 11.9 Compute Engine default service account

2 Click the Permissions tab and click Grant Access, as shown in figure 11.10.

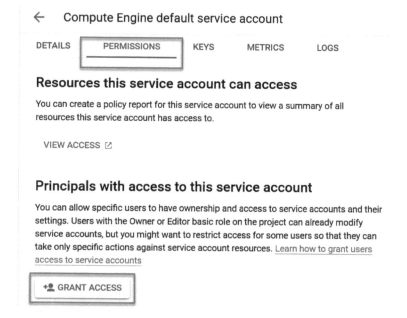

Figure 11.10 Granting access to the Compute Engine default service account

3   In the Grant access page, paste the email ID of the service account that you cre-
    ated in the New Principals field, select Service Account User in the Role field,
    and click Save, as shown in figure 11.11.

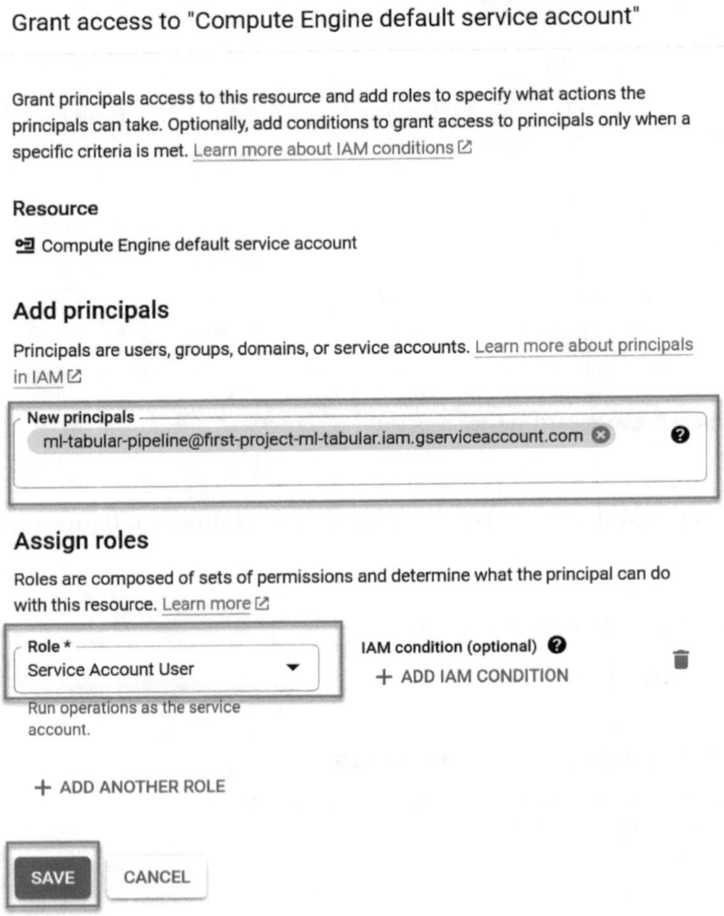

Grant access to "Compute Engine default service account"

Grant principals access to this resource and add roles to specify what actions the
principals can take. Optionally, add conditions to grant access to principals only when a
specific criteria is met. Learn more about IAM conditions ⧉

Resource

⚙ Compute Engine default service account

Add principals

Principals are users, groups, domains, or service accounts. Learn more about principals
in IAM ⧉

┌─ New principals ───┐
│   ml-tabular-pipeline@first-project-ml-tabular.iam.gserviceaccount.com ⊗   ❷ │
│   │
└──┘

Assign roles

Roles are composed of sets of permissions and determine what the principal can do
with this resource. Learn more ⧉

┌─ Role * ─────────────────────────┐   IAM condition (optional) ❷
│   Service Account User   ▼   │   ╋ ADD IAM CONDITION   🗑
└──────────────────────────────────┘
  Run operations as the service
  account.

  ╋ ADD ANOTHER ROLE

┌──────────┐
│   SAVE   │   CANCEL
└──────────┘

Figure 11.11   Specifying access to the Compute Engine default service account

Now that we have completed the steps to set up the service account for the ML pipeline, we can continue with the setup of the pipeline.

11.2.4 *Introduction to Cloud Shell*

So far, all the actions that we have taken in Google Cloud have been in the Console UI.
Google Cloud also includes the Cloud Shell, which is a self-contained instance that lets
you run command line commands to interact with Google Cloud. In addition to the

command line interface, you can use the Cloud Shell Editor to edit files in the Cloud Shell filesystem. With Cloud Shell, you get the function of a local Linux instance combined with the convenience of a web-based environment that is integrated with Google Cloud resources. Cloud Shell is particularly well-suited for prototyping and working through tutorials. We will use the Cloud Shell in the next few steps of setting up the ML pipeline. For additional details about Cloud Shell, see the documentation: https://cloud.google.com/shell.

To start the Cloud Shell, click on the Activate Cloud Shell icon at the top of the Google Cloud Console, as shown in figure 11.12.

Figure 11.12   Activating Cloud Shell icon

When you click on the Activate Cloud Shell icon, the Cloud Shell terminal opens at the bottom of the console with your home directory as the current directory, as shown in figure 11.13.

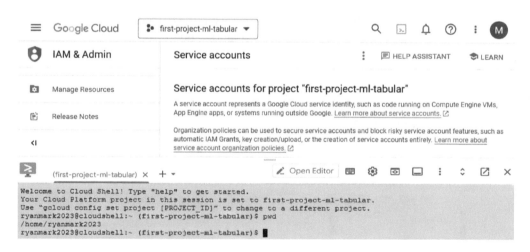

Figure 11.13   Cloud Console with Cloud Shell activated

You can run commands directly in the Cloud Shell Terminal, including standard Linux commands and Google Cloud-specific commands. You can click Open Editor to edit files in the Cloud Shell file system, as shown in figure 11.14. To get back to the Cloud Shell Terminal, click on Open Terminal.

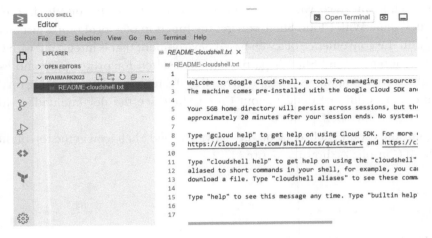

**Figure 11.14
Cloud Shell
Editor**

Now that we have taken a brief tour of the Cloud Shell, we can continue with the next step of setting up the ML pipeline: making the service account key available to the pipeline.

11.2.5 *Uploading the service account key*

In this section, we will use the Cloud Shell to upload the service account key JSON file and then set an environment variable to point to the location of the service account key:

1   In Cloud Shell, set your home directory as the current directory, create a new directory called `ml_pipeline`, and then set that new directory as your current directory:

```
cd ~
mkdir ml_pipeline
cd ml_pipeline
```

2   To upload the service account key, select the three dots in the Cloud Shell toolbar and select Upload, as shown in figure 11.15.

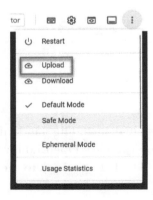

Figure 11.15   Uploading a file in Cloud Shell

3 In the Upload page, update Destination Directory to be the `ml_pipeline` directory in your home directory, click Choose Files, and select the service account key JSON file that you downloaded in section 11.2.2 and click Upload, as shown in figure 11.16.

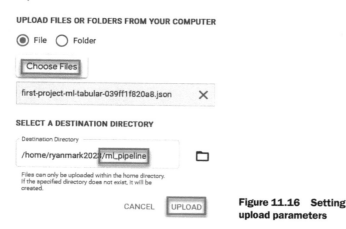

Figure 11.16   Setting upload parameters

4 Validate the upload by making `~/ml_pipeline` your current directory and using the `ls` command to ensure that the JSON service account key is now in this directory:

```
cd ~/ml_pipeline
ls
```

5 Set the environment variable `GOOGLE_APPLICATION_CREDENTIALS` to the fully qualified filename of the service account key JSON file. In the following example, replace the fully qualified filename with that for your own service account key JSON file:

```
export \
GOOGLE_APPLICATION_CREDENTIALS=\
'/home/ryanmark2023/ml_pipeline/\
first-project-ml-tabular-039ff1f820a8.json'
```

6 Confirm the value of the `GOOGLE_APPLICATION_CREDENTIALS` environment variable with the following command and validate that it is set to the fully qualified path of your service account key file:

```
$ echo $GOOGLE_APPLICATION_CREDENTIALS
```

Now that we have uploaded the service account key and set the environment variable to point to the location of the service account key, we are ready to get into the key step of defining the ML pipeline.

11.2.6 *Uploading the cleaned-up dataset to a Google Cloud Storage bucket*

To simplify the pipeline, we will upload the processed dataset generated by the data preparation notebook (https://mng.bz/rKjB) to a Cloud Storage bucket so that it is accessible to the rest of the ML pipeline. In a real-world application, we would incorporate the data cleanup steps into the ML pipeline, but for the sake of simplicity, we will start the pipeline with the data already cleaned up. Follow the steps in this section to upload the cleaned-up dataset to Google Cloud Storage:

1 Upload the CSV version of the cleaned-up dataset to the same bucket that you created to upload the model.

2 From the Google Cloud Console main menu, select Cloud Storage -> Buckets, as shown in figure 11.17.

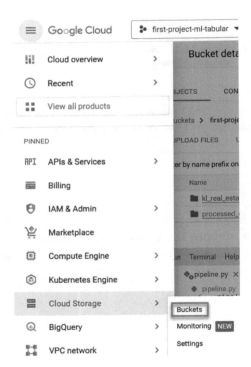

Figure 11.17   Setting upload parameters

3 In the Buckets page, select the bucket you created in chapter 10 to contain the trained model. In the Bucket details page, select Create Folder, as shown in figure 11.18.

Figure 11.18   Creating a folder

4 Enter `processed_dataset` in the name field and click Create.
5 Select the new folder that you just created, as shown in figure 11.19.

Figure 11.19   Selecting the folder

6 Click Upload Files and select the CSV file containing the processed version of the Kuala Lumpur dataset (output of the data preparation notebook).
7 You will see the file in the Bucket details page when the upload is complete. Click the three dots, then Copy gsutil URI, as shown in figure 11.20.

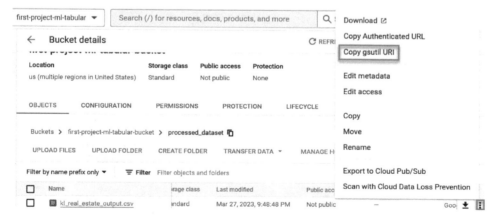

Figure 11.20   Copying gsutil URI

The gsutil Uniform Resource Identifer (URI) value will look like this: `gs://first-project-ml-tabular-bucket/processed_dataset/kl_real_estate_output.csv`

Now that we have uploaded the cleaned-up dataset to a Google Cloud Storage bucket, we can use it to create a Vertex AI dataset.

11.2.7 Creating a Vertex AI managed dataset

The ML pipeline invokes the Vertex AI SDK to train the model; it identifies the dataset used to train the model as a Vertex AI managed dataset. To learn more about Vertex AI managed datasets, see the documentation: https://mng.bz/VVRP.

The Vertex AI SDK automatically does the following to make the managed dataset available to the training script:

- Copies the content of the dataset to Cloud Storage.
- Divides the dataset into training, validation, and testing subsets. The proportion of the dataset for each subset is set in the pipeline config file `pipeline_config.yml`, as shown in figure 11.2.

```
# training specs - these supercede the splits in the model training config
training_fraction_split : 0.8
validation_fraction_split : 0.1
test_fraction_split : 0.1
```

Figure 11.21 Proportions for train, validation, and test in the pipeline configuration

- Divides each of the subsets into multiple CSV files. Figure 11.22 shows an example of what the CSV files for the dataset look like in Cloud Storage.

Name	Size	Type
test-00000-of-00004.csv	155.3 KB	text/plain
test-00001-of-00004.csv	143.4 KB	text/plain
test-00002-of-00004.csv	146.1 KB	text/plain
test-00003-of-00004.csv	141 KB	text/plain
training-00000-of-00004.csv	1.1 MB	text/plain
training-00001-of-00004.csv	1.1 MB	text/plain
training-00002-of-00004.csv	1.1 MB	text/plain
training-00003-of-00004.csv	1.1 MB	text/plain
validation-00000-of-00004.csv	140.8 KB	text/plain
validation-00001-of-00004.csv	139.1 KB	text/plain
validation-00002-of-00004.csv	143.3 KB	text/plain
validation-00003-of-00004.csv	138.6 KB	text/plain

Figure 11.22 Processed dataset in Google Cloud Storage

Now that we have seen how the dataset gets set up in Cloud Storage, let's go through the steps to create a Vertex AI dataset for the training data.

1 In Vertex AI, select Datasets. In the Datasets page, click Create as shown in figure 11.23.

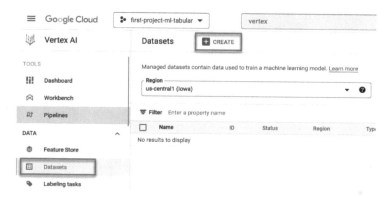

**Figure 11.23
Creating a
dataset**

2 In the Create dataset page, set `kuala-lumpur-real-estate` as the dataset name, select the Tabular tab, select Regression/Classification, and click Create, as shown in figure 11.24.

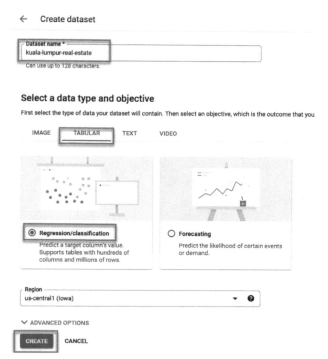

**Figure 11.24   Specifying
dataset details**

3 In the Source tab, select Select CSV file from Cloud Storage. In Import file path, click Browse, select the Cloud Storage bucket location where you uploaded the processed training file in the previous section, and click Continue, as shown in figure 11.25.

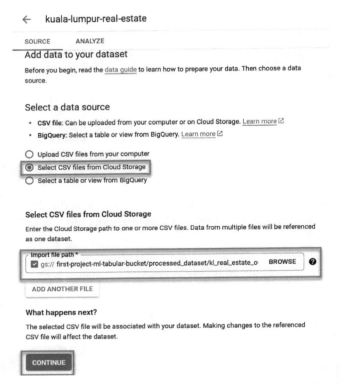

Figure 11.25 **Specifying the source for the dataset**

4 Note the ID value of the dataset that you just created, as shown in figure 11.26.

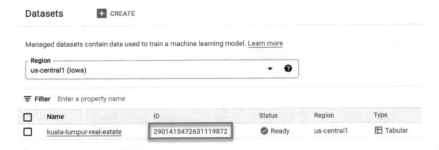

Figure 11.26 **Dataset ID in Google Cloud Console**

This is the value that needs to be set for `dataset_id` in the pipeline config file `pipeline_config.yml`, as shown in figure 11.27.

```
ENDPOINT_NAME : 'klrealestate'
# from https://cloud.google.com/vertex-ai/docs/training/pre-built-containers
train_image : "us-docker.pkg.dev/vertex-ai/training/tf-cpu.2-9:latest"
# from https://cloud.google.com/vertex-ai/docs/predictions/pre-built-containers
deploy_image : "us-docker.pkg.dev/vertex-ai/prediction/tf2-cpu.2-9:latest"
config_file_path : "model_training_config.yml"
# Google Cloud Storage file containing the config settings for the training script

script_path : "model_training_keras_preprocessing.py"
machine_type : 'n1-standard-4'
# project details
project_id : 'first-project-ml-tabular'
region : 'us-central1'
dataset_id : '2901415472631119872'
```

Figure 11.27 `dataset_id` **in the pipeline config file**

Congratulations! You have set up a Vertex AI managed dataset for the dataset that the model training portion of the ML pipeline will use to train the model.

11.3 Defining the ML pipeline

So far in this chapter, we have completed the following preparation steps for the ML pipeline:

1 Created a service account and a service account key
2 Uploaded the service account key to the directory where we will run the pipeline script
3 Uploaded the cleaned-up dataset to Cloud Storage
4 Created a Vertex AI-managed dataset from the cleaned-up dataset

In this section, we will take the elements we prepared in the preceding section and use them to create an ML pipeline that takes in a preprocessed dataset at one end and produces a trained model deployed with a Vertex AI endpoint at the other end.

11.3.1 Local implementation vs. ML pipeline

Before we continue with defining the ML pipeline, let's contrast the ML pipeline with the local setup to train the Kuala Lumpur real estate price prediction model that we implemented in chapter 10. Figure 11.28 shows this contrast and highlights some of the differences between the two implementations.

Training the model on a local system   Training the model with an ML pipeline in Vertex AI

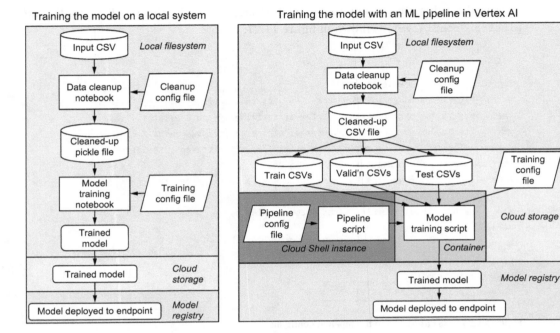

Figure 11.28   Training on a local system vs. training with an ML pipeline

Figure 11.28 contrasts the structure of the training process for an entirely local implementation compared to the training process using an ML pipeline. The key ways that the ML pipeline implementation differs from the local system implementation of the solution are

- The data cleanup process is identical. In a real-world production pipeline, we would move this data processing step into the Vertex AI environment and make it part of the ML pipeline, but to make the ML pipeline as simple as possible, we skip that step for our ML pipeline implementation and start the pipeline with the cleaned-up dataset.

- In the local implementation, the data cleanup process output is a pickle file. To avoid compatibility problems, we switched to a CSV file for the ML pipeline. The ML pipeline takes the contents of this CSV file and splits them into train, validation, and test subsets, each of which is segmented into multiple CSV files in Cloud Storage.

- The training code in the ML pipeline implementation is in a Python .py file (the *model training script*) rather than a notebook. Significant updates to the training code to make it work in a container environment are described in the following section.

- In the ML pipeline implementation, the model training config file is in Cloud Storage so that its location can be shared by the pipeline script as a parameter for the model training script.

- The pipeline script is a new component in the ML pipeline. This script sets up the input necessary for the model training script, uses the Vertex AI SDK to create a container for the model training script, and invokes the script to do the model training.

- The pipeline config file is a new component in the ML pipeline. This config file contains parameters for the pipeline script, including the built-in Vertex AI containers to use for the ML pipeline; the proportion of the cleaned-up dataset for each of the training, validation, and testing subsets; the dataset ID; and the location of the code for the training script.

- The trained model is automatically put in the model registry in the ML pipeline implementation and deployed to a Vertex AI endpoint. In the local system implementation, we manually uploaded the model to Cloud Storage and then deployed it to an endpoint.

The endpoint that is the result of both the local system implementation and the ML pipeline implementation can be plugged into our web deployment simply by updating the endpoint_id parameter in the Flask server config file, as shown in figure 11.29.

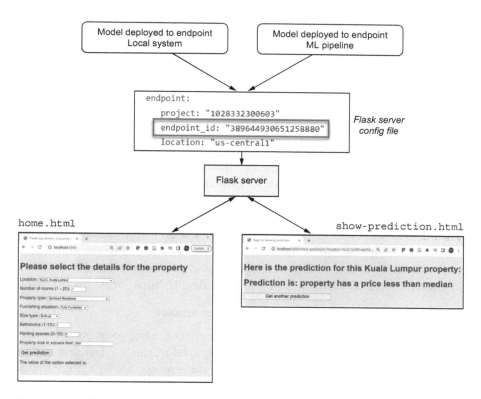

Figure 11.29 Web deployment with endpoint from local or ML pipeline

For more details on the workflow for training a custom model on Vertex AI, see the documentation: https://mng.bz/xKjW.

11.3.2 Introduction to containers

One key point of an ML pipeline in Vertex AI is using containers to make the model training process easy to automate and flexible. In this section, we will briefly introduce containers and their benefits to the ML pipeline. If you are already familiar with the concept of containers and Docker, you can skip this section.

A container is a software construct that allows you to package an application with its dependencies so that you can run the application predictably and efficiently across a range of environments. Google Cloud uses Docker containers. A detailed description of containers is beyond the scope of this book, but we need to spend some time looking at them to understand why they are used for ML pipelines and what constraints they place on our code. For more details on containers, see the Docker site: https://www .docker.com/resources/what-container/.

11.3.3 Benefits of using containers in an ML pipeline

Using containers to package the training code means that we don't have to worry about the Python libraries that are required for the training because the container comes with all the required Python libraries already set up. Also, the code is easy to reproduce anywhere. Vertex AI provides a range of prebuilt container images for the most popular machine learning frameworks, including PyTorch, TensorFlow, and XGBoost. We use TensorFlow prebuilt containers for our ML pipeline. See the Vertex AI documentation for details on prebuilt containers:

- *Prebuilt containers for training custom models*—https://mng.bz/AQ8z
- *Prebuilt containers for prediction*—https://mng.bz/ZlRP

If our training ends up becoming more demanding (either in terms of how quickly a training cycle needs to be completed or the compute resources needed to complete a training cycle of a given duration), we can take advantage of the containerized nature of the training to distribute training across multiple compute engines. For a simple problem like the Kuala Lumpur real estate price prediction problem, a single node is more than sufficient to do the training, but bigger applications can really benefit from distributed training. A detailed explanation of all the options that are available for distributed training with Vertex AI is beyond the scope of this book. Check out the documentation if you are interested in more details: https://mng.bz/RVmK.

11.3.4 Introduction to adapting code to run in a container

Now that we have reviewed some of the benefits of using containers for the training process, we can look at changes that are required to run the training code in a container. To understand the difference between running code in a nonvirtualized environment and in a container, it helps to think of the container as its own self-contained machine where the code runs. In particular, code running in a container will not, by default, have access to the file system of the environment from which the container is managed. Figure 11.30 shows how the model training notebook interacts with files in the filesystem.

When the training code runs in a container, it can't get access to files on an external local filesystem. Instead, the artifacts that the model training script uses are stored in Cloud Storage, and the locations for these artifacts in Cloud Storage are passed to the model training script as URIs. Figure 11.31 gives an example of how to interpret a Google Cloud Storage URI.

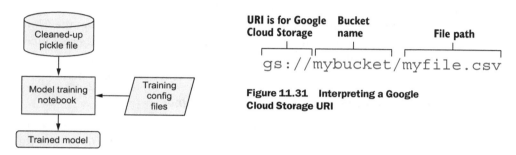

Figure 11.31 Interpreting a Google Cloud Storage URI

Figure 11.30 Training code interactions with external files

In the ML pipeline, we use two methods to pass URIs to the training script running in a container: via the environment variables set in the container by the Vertex AI SDK and via the argument list of the `job.run` call in the pipeline script, as shown in figure 11.32.

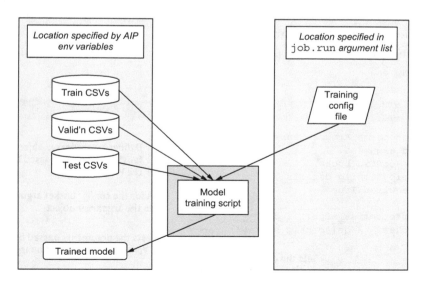

Figure 11.32 Training code interactions with content in Cloud Storage

The location of the training data (split into training, validation, and test subsets) is automatically assigned to environment variables that get set in the container when it is set up by the pipeline script. This is standard for all Vertex AI containers; see the documentation at https://mng.bz/2y70.

The way that the URI for the config file is passed to the model training script is not the default for Vertex AI. If we had a training script that had a small number of arguments, we could create an `argparser` list that contains the argument values and pass that list to the model training script. The config file for our application is too complex for this to be efficient, so instead of passing each argument individually, we pass a single argument: the URI for the Cloud Storage location where we have saved a copy of the config file. With that, all the model training script needs to do is get the Cloud Storage location from the argument list and ingest the YAML file from there. Once the arguments have been pulled into the config dictionary in the model training script, the rest of the code that uses them can work unchanged. This is a major benefit.

11.3.5 *Updating the training code to work in a container*

In this section, we will review how we changed the model training notebook (https://mng.bz/1XJj) that we ran in Colab in chapter 9 to get a model to predict Kuala Lumpur property prices. By making these changes, we convert the model training notebook into a training script that can run in a Vertex AI built-in container.

The following are the key changes we made to the training notebook to create the training script:

- Removed extraneous library imports and associated code. For example, we don't need to generate a diagram of the model when we run the training script, so we removed the code associated with `plot_model`.
- Removed code that splits the dataset into training, validation, and testing subsets. In the ML pipeline, the Vertex AI SDK takes care of splitting the dataset prior to the testing script being started.
- Added code to interpret the `job.run` argument list, as shown in the following listing.

Listing 11.1 Loading the saved Keras model

```
parser = argparse.ArgumentParser()          ◄─── Defines an argparser object
parser.add_argument(                               for the arguments passed by
        '--config_bucket',                  ◄───   the Vertex AI SDK
        help='Config details',
        required=True                             Adds the config_bucket argument
    )                                             to the argparser object
args = parser.parse_args().__dict__         ◄───
config_bucket = args['config_bucket']       ◄─┐  Ingests the arguments passed by
                                               the Vertex AI SDK as a dictionary
              Gets the config file URI from
                 the argument dictionary
```

- Updated the code that ingests the training config file so that it ingests the contents of the config file from the Cloud Storage URI passed by the pipeline script (`config_bucket` from listing 11.1) rather than from the local file system. As shown in the following listing, the URI for the config file in Cloud Storage (`config_bucket`) is used to copy the config file from Cloud Storage to a file in the container, and then the contents of that file are copied into the dictionary `config`.

Listing 11.2   Ingesting the training config file via the URI argument

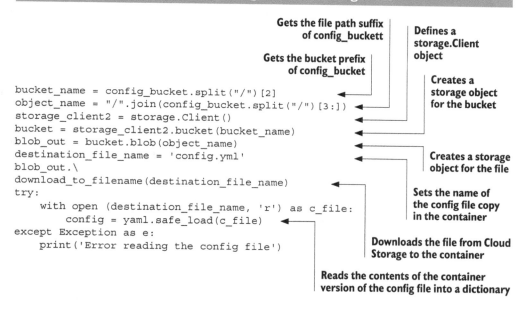

```
bucket_name = config_bucket.split("/")[2]
object_name = "/".join(config_bucket.split("/")[3:])
storage_client2 = storage.Client()
bucket = storage_client2.bucket(bucket_name)
blob_out = bucket.blob(object_name)
destination_file_name = 'config.yml'
blob_out.\
download_to_filename(destination_file_name)
try:
    with open (destination_file_name, 'r') as c_file:
        config = yaml.safe_load(c_file)
except Exception as e:
    print('Error reading the config file')
```

Gets the file path suffix of config_buckett

Gets the bucket prefix of config_bucket

Defines a storage.Client object

Creates a storage object for the bucket

Creates a storage object for the file

Sets the name of the config file copy in the container

Downloads the file from Cloud Storage to the container

Reads the contents of the container version of the config file into a dictionary

- Copied the values of the AIP environment variables that the Vertex AI SDK sets in the container. These environment variables contain URI patterns for the CSV files that the SDK creates in Google Storage that contain the train, validation, and test subsets of the dataset.

Listing 11.3   Copying AIP environment variable values

```
def assign_container_env_variables():
    OUTPUT_MODEL_DIR = os.getenv("AIP_MODEL_DIR")
    TRAIN_DATA_PATTERN = \
os.getenv("AIP_TRAINING_DATA_URI")
    EVAL_DATA_PATTERN = \
os.getenv("AIP_VALIDATION_DATA_URI")
    TEST_DATA_PATTERN = \
os.getenv("AIP_TEST_DATA_URI")
    return OUTPUT_MODEL_DIR, TRAIN_DATA_PATTERN, \
EVAL_DATA_PATTERN, TEST_DATA_PATTERN
```

Gets the URI for the location to save the trained model

Gets the URI for the training dataset CSVs

Gets the URI for the validation dataset CSVs

Gets the URI for the testing dataset CSVs

- Created dataframes for each of the patterns from the AIP environment variables. For each of these environment variables, we parsed the URI, got the list of matching files CSV blobs in Cloud Storage, and reassembled them into a single dataframe.

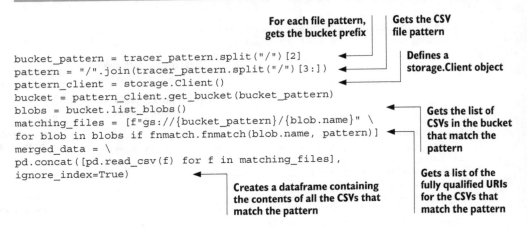

Listing 11.4   Creating a dataframe for subsets of the dataset

- Saved the trained model to a location specified by OUTPUT_MODEL_DIR, the URI set by the Vertex AI SDK as the location for saving the model:

```
tf.saved_model.save(model, OUTPUT_MODEL_DIR)
```

With these changes, the rest of the training code works running in a container. Now that we have gone through the updates required to create the training script, in the next section we will go through the key parts of the pipeline script that sets up the container that the training script runs in.

11.3.6   *The pipeline script*

Now that we have gone through the training script, we can examine the code that makes up the pipeline script. You can see the complete pipeline script code at https://mng.bz/PdRn.

The key parts of the pipeline script are

- Ingest the pipeline config file: https://mng.bz/JYdV.
- Set the arguments for the training script:

```
model_args = ['--config_bucket', config['config_bucket_path']]
```

- Create a CustomTrainingJob object that specifies the location of the training script script_path, the prebuilt image to use for training container_uri, and any additional Python libraries that need to be installed in the training container requirements, as shown in the following listing.

Listing 11.5 Creating a `CustomTrainingJob` object

```
def create_job(config):
    model_display_name = '{}-{}'.format(config['ENDPOINT_NAME'], TIMESTAMP)
    job = aiplatform.CustomTrainingJob(
            display_name='train-{}'.format(model_display_name),
            script_path = config['script_path'],
            container_uri=config['train_image'],                    ◀── Sets the prebuilt Vertex
            staging_bucket = config['staging_path'],                    AI container image to
            requirements=['gcsfs'],                          ◀──        run the training script
            model_serving_container_image_uri= \
config['deploy_image']              ◀──                   Defines the list of any
    )                              Sets the prebuilt Vertex  additional requirements to
    return job                     AI container image to    be installed in the container
                                   use for prediction
```

- Define the path for the managed dataset used for training (using the dataset ID for the managed dataset that you created in section 11.2.7) and create a `Tabular-Dataset` object using that path:

```
dataset_path = \
'projects/'+config['project_id']+\
'/locations/'+config['region']+\
'/datasets/'+config['dataset_id']
 ds = aiplatform.TabularDataset(dataset_path)
```

- Run the job defined previously, specifying the dataset created here; the proportion of the dataset to use for training, validation, and test; and the `machine_type` to use for the training.

Listing 11.6 Running the job

```
def run_job(job, ds, model_args,config):
    model_display_name = \                           Associates the job with
'{}-{}'.format(config['ENDPOINT_NAME'], TIMESTAMP)   the managed dataset
    model = job.run(
        dataset=ds,                        ◀──       Sets proportions of the
        training_fraction_split = \                  dataset to use for training,
config['training_fraction_split'],       ◀──         validation, and testing
        validation_fraction_split = config['validation_fraction_split'],
        test_fraction_split = config['test_fraction_split'],
        model_display_name=model_display_name,
        args=model_args,                             Sets the argument list (which
        machine_type= config['machine_type']  ◀──   contains the URI for the
    )                                                testing script config file)
    return model
```

- Create an endpoint and deploy the model trained in the training script to that endpoint.

Listing 11.7   Deploying the trained model to an endpoint

```
def deploy_model(model,config):                          Sets characteristics of the endpoint
    endpoints = aiplatform.Endpoint.list(    ◄─────────┘
        filter='display_name="{}"'.format(config['ENDPOINT_NAME']),
        order_by='create_time desc',
        project=config['project_id'],
        location=config['region']
    )
    endpoint = aiplatform.Endpoint.create(    ◄─────┘  Creates the endpoint
        display_name=config['ENDPOINT_NAME'],
        project=config['project_id'],
        location=config['region']
    )                                    Deploys the model
    model.deploy(                        to the endpoint
        endpoint=endpoint,    ◄─────────┘
        traffic_split={"0": 100},
        machine_type=config['machine_type_deploy'],
        min_replica_count=1,
        max_replica_count=1,
    )
```

- The following listing is the main function of the pipeline script that invokes the functions to run the pipeline.

Listing 11.8   Main function of the pipeline script

```
    start_time = time.time()
    config = get_pipeline_config('pipeline_config.yml')
    model_args = ['--config_bucket', config['config_bucket_path']]    ◄─────┐
    job = create_job(config)
    dataset_path = \                                        Sets characteristics
'projects/'+config['project_id']+\                          of the endpoint
'/locations/'+config['region']+\
'/datasets/'+config['dataset_id']
    ds = aiplatform.TabularDataset(dataset_path)
    model = run_job(job, ds, model_args,config)    ◄─────┘  Creates the endpoint
    if config['deploy_model']:
        deploy_model(model,config)    ◄─────┐
    print("pipeline completed")             Deploys the model
                                            to the endpoint
```

To run the pipeline script, do the following:

- Clone https://github.com/lmassaron/ml_on_tabular_data in a new directory in Cloud Shell and make `chapter_11` the current directory.
- Update the pipeline config file to ensure that `project_id` and `region` match the settings for your project, `dataset_id` matches the ID for your managed dataset, `staging_path` matches your staging path, and `config_bucket_path` matches the

location in Cloud Storage, where you copied the training script config file, as shown in figure 11.33.

```
project_id : 'first-project-ml-tabular'
region : 'us-central1'
dataset_id : '2901415472631119872'
# bucket locations
staging_path : "gs://second-project-ml-tabular-bucket/staging/"
config_bucket_path : "gs://third-project-ml-tabular-bucket/training_scripts/model_training_config.yml"
```

Figure 11.33   Training code interactions with content in Cloud Storage

■ In the root directory where you cloned the repo, enter the following command:

```
python pipeline_script.py
```

Note that running the entire pipeline script can take 10 minutes or more. If the script fails, you will get a message that includes a link to the log file containing diagnostic messages about the training run. If the script succeeds, the output will end with the pipeline completed and the time taken to run it.

11.3.7   *Testing the model trained in the pipeline*

Once you have run the pipeline script to run the ML pipeline to train and deploy a model, you can use the resulting Vertex AI endpoint to exercise the model in the same web deployment framework that we used in chapter 10. Note that testing the endpoint using this simple web deployment does not match what you would do in a production environment. However, using the same web deployment that we used in chapter 10 simplifies the testing process for this exercise.

The steps to test the model trained in the pipeline are

1   In the Google Cloud Console, go to the Vertex AI Endpoints. Copy the ID for the deployment that was created by the ML pipeline, as shown in figure 11.34.

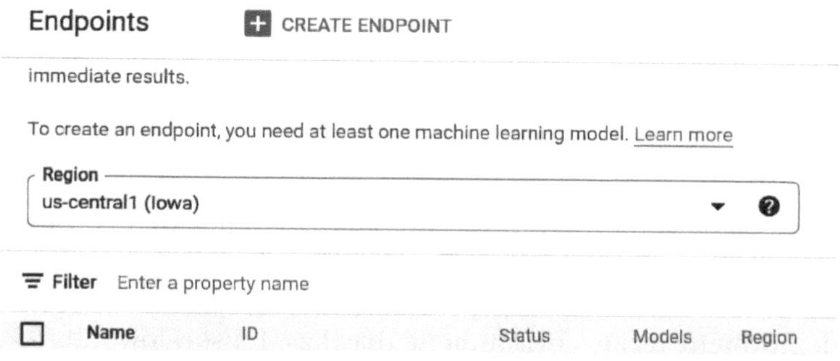

Endpoints   ✚ CREATE ENDPOINT

immediate results.

To create an endpoint, you need at least one machine learning model. Learn more

Region
us-central1 (Iowa)   ▼   ❓

≡ Filter   Enter a property name

☐   **Name**   ID   Status   Models   Region

**Figure 11.34
Endpoint ID for the
model generated by
the pipeline**

2 In the same local system where you tested the initial endpoint deployment with Flask in chapter 10, paste the endpoint ID that you just copied into the value of the `endpoint_id parameter` in the `flask_web_deploy_config.yml` config file and save the file:

```
endpoint:
    project: "1028332300603"
    endpoint_id: "1447850105594970112"
    location: "us-central1"
```

3 On your local system, start the Flask server module:

```
python flask_endpoint_deploy.py
```

4 Once the Flask server module is running, go to `localhost:5000` in a browser. `home.html` will be rendered as shown in figure 11.35. When you click on Get prediction, the model trained and deployed at a Vertex AI endpoint by the ML pipeline will be invoked (see figure 11.35).

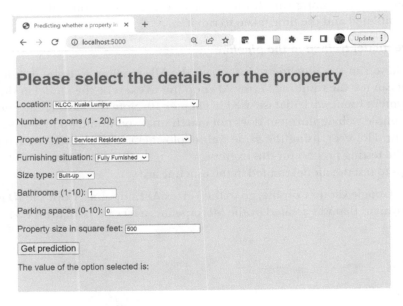

Figure 11.35   Home.html

Note that the TensorFlow level used in the prebuilt container that you used for the model training has to match the TensorFlow level in the environment where you run the web application to test the endpoint. For example, if we want to exercise the endpoint deployment in an environment that has TensorFlow 2.9, then in the pipeline config file, we need to specify a value for `train_image` (the prebuilt training container) that is consistent with that level of TensorFlow level, such as `us-docker` `.pkg.dev/vertex-ai/training/tf-cpu.2-9:latest`.

If you get a protobuf error when you run the pipeline script in Cloud Shell, try running the following command to specify the protobuf level:

```
pip install protobuf==3.20.*
```

If you want to experiment with different training configurations, you can update the training config file, upload it to Cloud Storage (ensuring that the value of `config_bucket_path` in the pipeline config file matches the URI for the training config file), and rerun the pipeline script. You can use the web application to exercise the new model by updating the value of `endpoint_id` in the pipeline config file to match the endpoint ID of the new endpoint and repeating the steps in this section. By encapsulating multiple steps in the ML workflow in an ML pipeline, we make it easy to get repeatable results and experiment with new settings.

11.4 Using generative AI to help create the ML pipeline

So far in this chapter, we have seen how we use a combination of actions in Google Cloud and manual scripting to set up a basic ML pipeline to train and deploy a model trained on tabular data. In this section, we'll explore how we can use the generative AI capabilities in Gemini for Google Cloud, introduced in chapter 10, to simplify or automate some of these actions. As we saw in chapter 10, there are four ways that Gemini for Google Cloud can help us:

- Answer questions about Google Cloud.
- Generate code from text.
- Interpret code. That is, given a piece of code, generate text that explains what the code does. We can use this capability to help us understand the code that we are adapting from other places. We can use this capability to document the code that we are writing ourselves.
- Summarize log entries to help debug problems.

11.4.1 Using Gemini for Google Cloud to answer questions about the ML pipeline

As we saw in chapter 10, we can use the generative AI capabilities in Gemini for Google Cloud to get answers to questions about Google Cloud. The following are some examples of questions about creating an ML pipeline that Gemini for Google Cloud could help us to answer:

- What is an ML pipeline? While Gemini for Google Cloud is trained specifically for Google Cloud, it is able to answer broad questions about technology, such as this one. Note that the answer shown in figure 11.36 is generally applicable and not limited to just Google Cloud. The citations come from a variety of credible sources, including the documentation for TensorFlow and Scikit-learn:

- – What is an ML pipeline? (https://mng.bz/wJjP)
- – Building a data pipeline (https://cs230.stanford.edu/blog/datapipeline/)
- – ML pipelines with Scikit-learn (https://mng.bz/qxjr)

- What is a Vertex AI pipeline? When we take the same question and qualify it, as shown in figure 11.37, Gemini for Google Cloud gives us an answer that is specific to the ML pipeline implementation in Google Cloud.

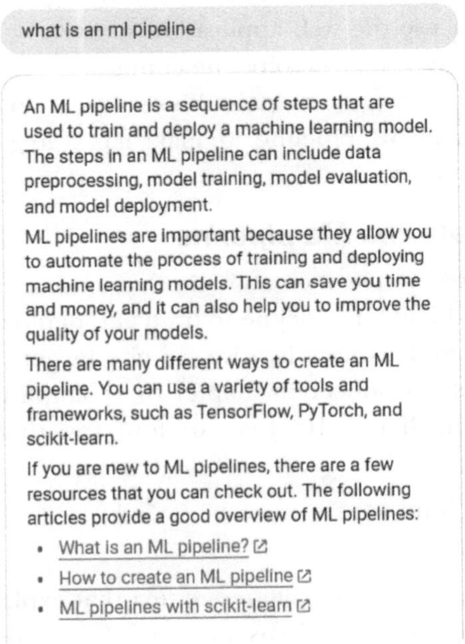

what is an ml pipeline

An ML pipeline is a sequence of steps that are used to train and deploy a machine learning model. The steps in an ML pipeline can include data preprocessing, model training, model evaluation, and model deployment.

ML pipelines are important because they allow you to automate the process of training and deploying machine learning models. This can save you time and money, and it can also help you to improve the quality of your models.

There are many different ways to create an ML pipeline. You can use a variety of tools and frameworks, such as TensorFlow, PyTorch, and scikit-learn.

If you are new to ML pipelines, there are a few resources that you can check out. The following articles provide a good overview of ML pipelines:

- What is an ML pipeline? ⊡
- How to create an ML pipeline ⊡
- ML pipelines with scikit-learn ⊡

Figure 11.36 Gemini for Google Cloud answers the question "what is an ML pipeline?"

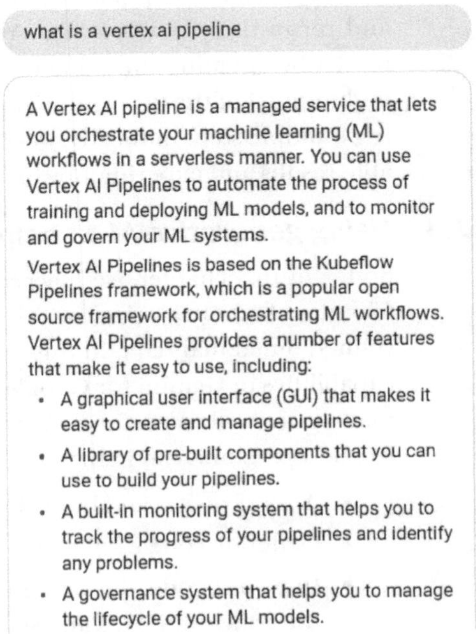

what is a vertex ai pipeline

A Vertex AI pipeline is a managed service that lets you orchestrate your machine learning (ML) workflows in a serverless manner. You can use Vertex AI Pipelines to automate the process of training and deploying ML models, and to monitor and govern your ML systems.

Vertex AI Pipelines is based on the Kubeflow Pipelines framework, which is a popular open source framework for orchestrating ML workflows. Vertex AI Pipelines provides a number of features that make it easy to use, including:

- A graphical user interface (GUI) that makes it easy to create and manage pipelines.
- A library of pre-built components that you can use to build your pipelines.
- A built-in monitoring system that helps you to track the progress of your pipelines and identify any problems.
- A governance system that helps you to manage the lifecycle of your ML models.

Figure 11.37 Gemini for Google Cloud answers the question "what is a Vertex AI pipeline?"

- What are Vertex AI prebuilt containers for training custom models? Finally, let's try asking a question related to a specific task we tackled in this chapter. As you can see in figure 11.38, the answer provided by Gemini for Google Cloud describes both what prebuilt containers for training custom models are as well as the point of using them.

In this section, we have seen how we can use Gemini for Google Cloud to answer questions, both general and specific, about building an ML pipeline. In the next section, we'll look at how we use Gemini for Google Cloud to generate the code required for the ML pipeline.

11.4.2 Using Gemini for Google Cloud to generate code for the ML pipeline

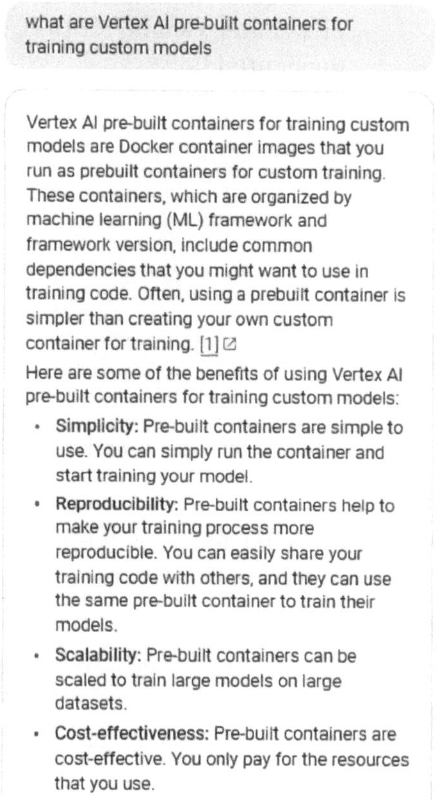

Now that we have seen how Gemini for Google Cloud can answer questions about creating an ML pipeline, let's explore how the generative AI capabilities in Gemini for Google Cloud can help us to create the code related to the ML pipeline.

Gemini for Google Cloud is enabled in several IDEs supported by Google Cloud, including VS Code, Cloud Workstations, and Cloud Shell Editor. In this section, we will use Gemini for Google Cloud in the context of Cloud Shell Editor. If you need a refresher on Cloud Shell Editor, see the overview documentation: https://mng.bz/7pvv.

We will see how Gemini for Google Cloud is able to generate the code for functions in the pipeline script: https://mng.bz/PdRn Using the function signatures and introductory comments from this script, we will see what Gemini for Google Cloud generates.

To begin with, if you have not done so already, follow the documentation to enable Gemini Code Assist in Cloud Shell Editor: https://mng.bz/mGja.

Once you have enabled Gemini Code Assist in Cloud Shell Editor, open a new

what are Vertex AI pre-built containers for training custom models

Vertex AI pre-built containers for training custom models are Docker container images that you run as prebuilt containers for custom training. These containers, which are organized by machine learning (ML) framework and framework version, include common dependencies that you might want to use in training code. Often, using a prebuilt container is simpler than creating your own custom container for training. [1] ☑

Here are some of the benefits of using Vertex AI pre-built containers for training custom models:

- **Simplicity:** Pre-built containers are simple to use. You can simply run the container and start training your model.
- **Reproducibility:** Pre-built containers help to make your training process more reproducible. You can easily share your training code with others, and they can use the same pre-built container to train their models.
- **Scalability:** Pre-built containers can be scaled to train large models on large datasets.
- **Cost-effectiveness:** Pre-built containers are cost-effective. You only pay for the resources that you use.

Figure 11.38 Gemini for Google Cloud answers the question "what are Vertex AI prebuilt containers for training custom models?"

Python file in Cloud Shell Editor and enter the signature and introductory comment for the `get_pipeline_config` function, as shown in the following listing.

Listing 11.9 Signature for `get_pipeline_config`

```
def get_pipeline_config(path_to_yaml):
    '''ingest the config yaml file
    Args:
        path_to_yaml: yaml file containing parameters for the pipeline script

    Returns:
        config: dictionary containing parameters read from the config file
    '''
```

Note that this code snippet does not include the logic of the function.

To get Gemini for Google Cloud to generate code to complete this function, simply press Enter. Gemini for Google Cloud generates provisional code in italics, as shown in the figure 11.39.

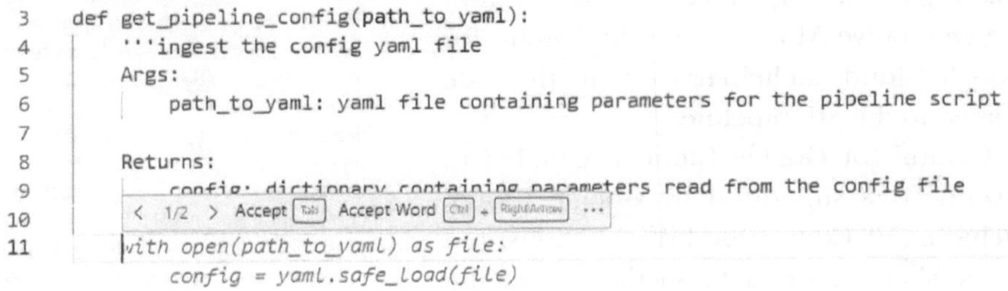

```
3    def get_pipeline_config(path_to_yaml):
4        '''ingest the config yaml file
5        Args:
6            path_to_yaml: yaml file containing parameters for the pipeline script
7
8        Returns:
9            config: dictionary containing parameters read from the config file
10       < 1/2 >  Accept [Tab]  Accept Word [Ctrl] + [RightArrow] ...
11       with open(path_to_yaml) as file:
            config = yaml.safe_load(file)
```

Figure 11.39   First set of provisional code generated by Gemini for Google Cloud

Press Tab to accept this provisional code and then press Enter again to get the next set of code generated, as shown in figure 11.40.

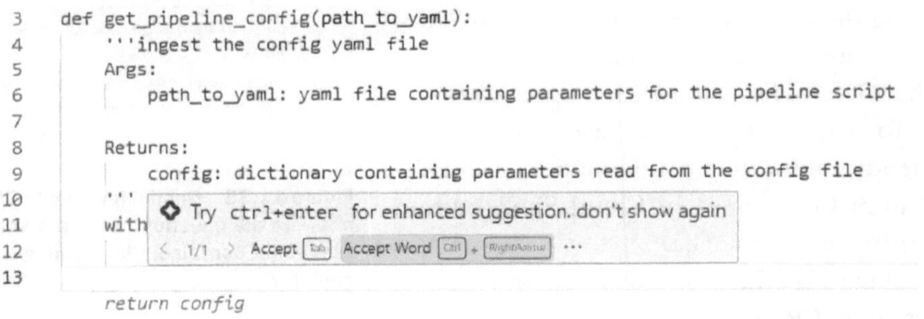

```
3    def get_pipeline_config(path_to_yaml):
4        '''ingest the config yaml file
5        Args:
6            path_to_yaml: yaml file containing parameters for the pipeline script
7
8        Returns:
9            config: dictionary containing parameters read from the config file
10       '''
11       with  ◆ Try ctrl+enter  for enhanced suggestion. don't show again
12           < 1/1 >  Accept [Tab]  Accept Word [Ctrl] + [RightArrow] ...
13
         return config
```

Figure 11.40   Second set of provisional code generated by Gemini for Google Cloud

Press Tab again to accept this second set of provisional code. The resulting function is shown in the following listing.

Listing 11.10 `get_pipeline_config` **function**

```
def get_pipeline_config(path_to_yaml):
    '''ingest the config yaml file
    Args:
        path_to_yaml: yaml file containing parameters for the pipeline script

    Returns:
        config: dictionary containing parameters read from the config file
```

```
    '''
    with open(path_to_yaml) as file:
        config = yaml.safe_load(file)

    return config
```

◄—— **First set of code generated by Gemini for Google Cloud**

◄—— **Second set of code generated by Gemini for Google Cloud**

The code in listing 11.10 is not identical to the hand-written code for the get_pipeline_config function, as shown in the following listing.

Listing 11.11 get_pipeline_config function: handwritten version

```
def get_pipeline_config(path_to_yaml):
    '''ingest the config yaml file
    Args:
        path_to_yaml: yaml file containing parameters for the pipeline script

    Returns:
        config: dictionary containing parameters read from the config file
    '''
    print("path_to_yaml "+path_to_yaml)
    try:
        with open (path_to_yaml, 'r') as c_file:
            config = yaml.safe_load(c_file)
    except Exception as e:
        print('Error reading the config file')
    return config
```

◄—— **Handwritten code includes exception handling for the file opening operation**

Handwritten code includes 'r' parameter with the file open

Comparing the code generated by Gemini for Google Cloud in listing 11.10 with the hand-written code in listing 11.11, we can see two differences:

- The handwritten code includes exception handling to deal with problems opening the config file.
- The handwritten code includes the 'r' parameter in the file open operation.

The get_pipeline_config function is trivial, but, nevertheless, Gemini for Google Cloud was able to generate working code for the function.

Some additional considerations for Gemini for Google Cloud code generations are

- You don't have to accept the provisional code generations from Gemini for Google Cloud all at once. To accept the provisional code token-by-token, press CTRL + Right Arrow to accept a single token.
- To reject the entire provisional code generation and start again, press ESC, and the entire set of provisional code will be erased.
- When you ask Gemini for Google Cloud to generate code multiple times with the exact same input, you aren't guaranteed to get identical code generated. For instance, in the get_pipeline_config example, sometimes Gemini for Google Cloud generated the function in two steps, as shown in this section, and

sometimes it generated the entire function, including the `return` statement, in a single step.

Now that we have used generative AI to generate code, we'll see how we can use it to explain code in the next section.

11.4.3 *Using Gemini for Google Cloud to explain code for the ML pipeline*

Now that we have seen an example of how Gemini for Google Cloud can generate code, let's exercise its ability to interpret code.

To get Gemini for Google Cloud to interpret a code snippet, copy the code in the following listing (the `main` function from the pipeline script) into a new file in Cloud Shell Editor.

> **Listing 11.12** `get_pipeline_config` **function**

```
if __name__ == '__main__':
    start_time = time.time()
    # load pipeline config parameters
    config = get_pipeline_config('pipeline_config.yml')
    # all the arguments sent to the training
    #script run in the container are sent via
    # a yaml file in Cloud Storage whose URI is the single argument sent
    model_args = ['--config_bucket', config['config_bucket_path']]
    print("model_args: ",model_args)
    # create a CustomTrainingJob object
    job = create_job(config)
    # define TabularDataset object to use in running CustomTrainingJob
    dataset_path = \
'projects/'+config['project_id']+\
'/locations/'+config['region']+\
'/datasets/'+config['dataset_id']
    ds = aiplatform.TabularDataset(dataset_path)
    # run the CustomTrainingJob object to get a trained model
    model = run_job(job, ds, model_args,config)
    print("deployment starting")
    # deploy model to a Vertex AI endpoint
    if config['deploy_model']:
        deploy_model(model,config)
    print("pipeline completed")
    # show time taken by script
    print("--- %s seconds ---" % (time.time() - start_time))
```

Once you have pasted the code in listing 11.13 into a file, select it and then select the Gemini for Google Cloud Smart Actions icon from the Cloud Shell Editor toolbar (see figure 11.41).

Figure 11.41 Gemini for Google Cloud Smart Actions icon

In the menu that appears, select Explain, as shown in figure 11.42.

Customize (e.g. simplify my code)

🖉 Generate code
☞ Explain this
🖉 Generate unit tests

Figure 11.42   Gemini for Google Cloud Smart Actions icon

When you select this, the explanation for the code appears in the left pane of Cloud Shell Editor, as shown in figure 11.43.

The code explanation capacity of Gemini for Google Cloud can be applied to a wide variety of code, including Python, Java, and JavaScript code. You can use the code explanations to understand code that you aren't familiar with and to recommend documentation for your own code.

So far in this section, we have seen how we can use the generative AI capabilities in Gemini for Google Cloud to answer questions, generate code, and explain code. In the next subsection, we'll see how we can use Gemini for Google Cloud to help to summarize log entries.

The code you provided is an example of how to use the Google Cloud Pipeline Components SDK to create a custom training pipeline. The pipeline takes a YAML file as input, which contains the configuration parameters for the pipeline. The pipeline then creates a CustomTrainingJob object, which is used to run the training script in a container. The pipeline also creates a TabularDataset object, which is used to provide data to the training script. The pipeline then runs the CustomTrainingJob object, which returns a trained model. The pipeline then deploys the model to a Vertex AI endpoint, if specified in the configuration file. Finally, the pipeline prints a message indicating that the pipeline has completed.

Figure 11.43   Code explanation

11.4.4 *Using Gemini for Google Cloud to summarize log entries*

Google Cloud includes a log that you can use to track the behavior of your environment and debug problems. Sometimes, however, the log entries can be hard to interpret. Gemini for Google Cloud can help you understand the point of a log entry by summarizing it. In this subsection, we'll go through how you can use Gemini for Google Cloud to get the most out of Google Cloud logs.

To exercise this capability of Gemini for Google Cloud, we will try to use the foundation model tuning in Vertex AI. Foundation model tuning lets us take a pretrained model and tune it with a dataset in the JSONL (JSON Lines: https://jsonlines.org/) dataset. See the documentation for more details on tuning text models in Vertex AI: https://mng.bz/5goO.

To prepare for the example in this section, create a new folder called `staging` in the Cloud Storage bucket that you created in chapter 10.

In Vertex AI in the Google Cloud Console, select Vertex AI Studio -> Language. In the Language page, select Tune and Distill and then select Create Tuned Model, as shown in figure 11.44.

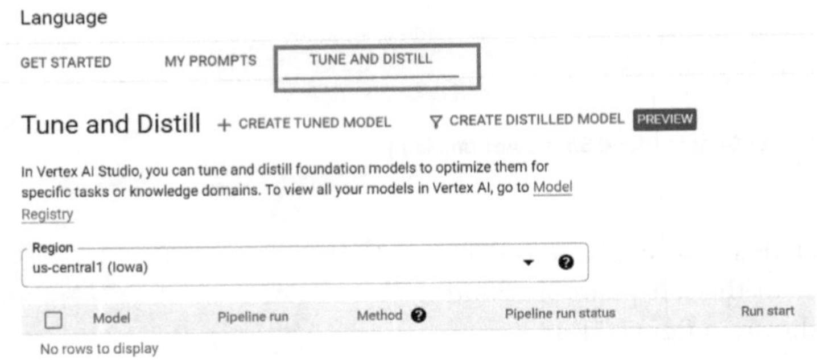

Figure 11.44 Vertex AI Studio language page

In the Tuning Method pane of the Create Tuned Model page:

- Specify a name for your model in the Tuned model name field.
- Specify the URI for the staging folder that you created at the beginning of this section in the Output Directory field.
- Click Continue.

See figure 11.45.

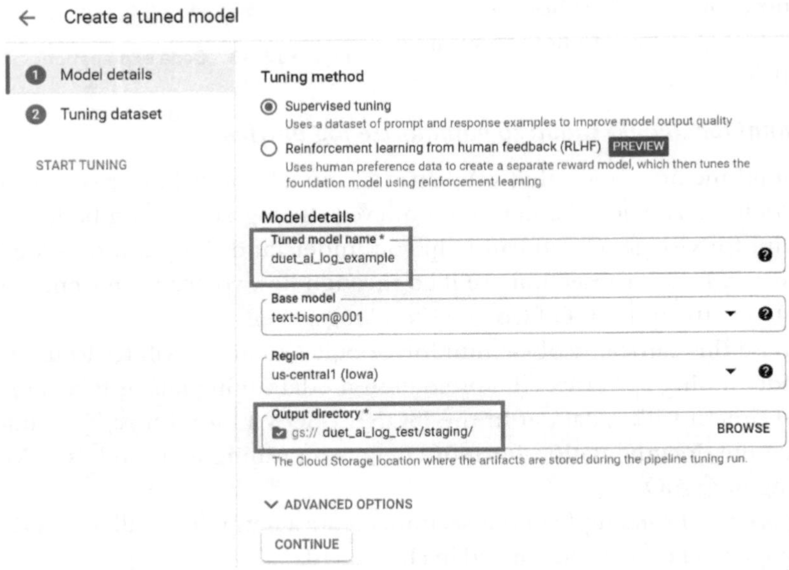

Figure 11.45 Tuning method pane of the Create a tuned model page

In the Tuning dataset pane of the Create Tuned Model page, do the following:

- Select Existing File on Cloud Storage.
- Enter the URI for this sample JSONL file `cloud-samples-data/vertex-ai/model -evaluation/peft_train_sample.jsonl` in the Cloud storage file path field. See the documentation for details about JSONL samples: https://mng.bz/6ene.
- Click Start Tuning.

See figure 11.46.

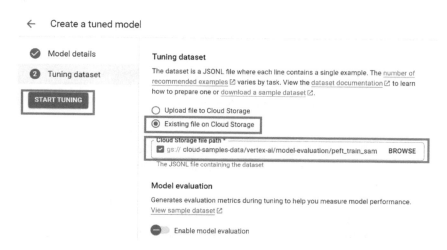

Figure 11.46   Tuning dataset pane of the Create a tuned model page

Once you click Start tuning, you will see a list of tuned models with the status of your model showing as Running, as shown in figure 11.47.

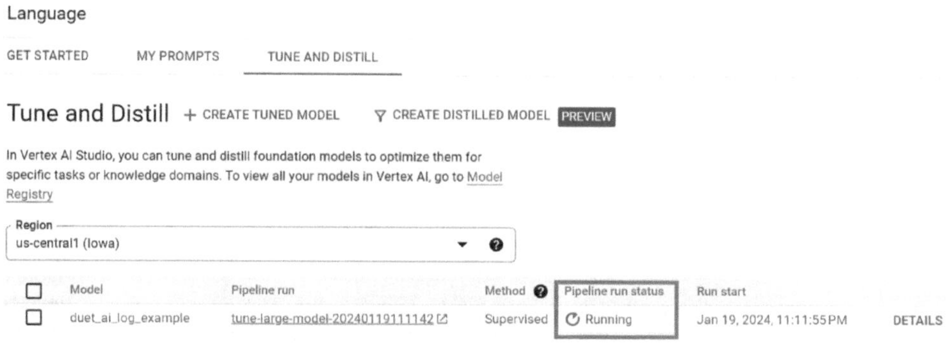

Figure 11.47   Tuning job status

When the tuning job is complete, the status will change to Succeeded, as shown in figure 11.48.

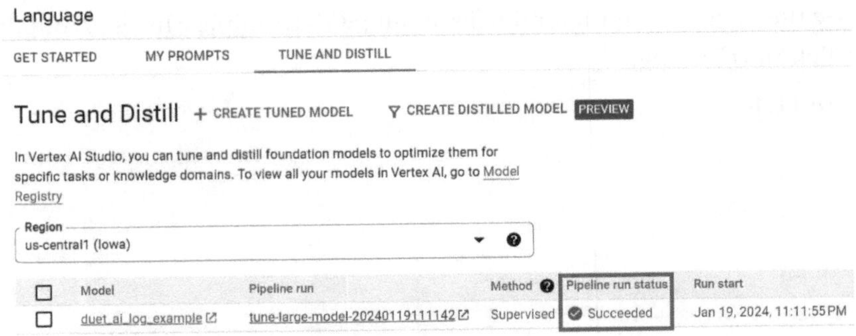

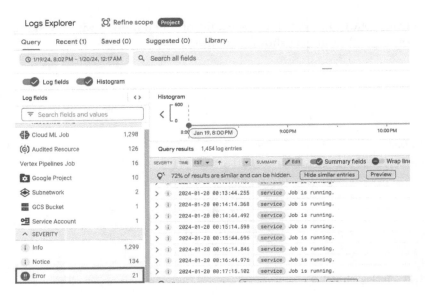

Figure 11.48   Tuning job status showing a completed tuning job

If the tuning job does not succeed, that's fine. The goal of this particular exercise is to examine an error, so it's okay if the operation fails for some reason.

Once the tuning job is complete, put "logs explorer" in the search field at the top of the Console to get to the Logs Explorer page. This page provides many options for inspecting the logs generated by Google Cloud. For now, we just want to look at one of the errors. To view the errors, select Error in the bottom left of the Logs Explorer page, as shown in figure 11.49.

Figure 11.49 Tuning job status showing a completed tuning job

The Query Results pane at the bottom of the page shows the errors, as shown in figure 11.50.

Figure 11.50 Query results pane showing errors

Select one of these error entries to expand it and click on Explain This Log Entry as shown in figure 11.51.

Figure 11.51 Expanded error entry

On the right, Gemini for Google Cloud shows an explanation of the error, as shown in figure 11.52.

The explanation provided by Gemini for Google Cloud summarizes the nested entries in the log and makes it easier to read and interpret. Note that the explanation that you will see will depend on the error that you select from the log.

11.4.5 *Tuning a foundation model in Vertex AI*

In the previous subsection, we saw how to use the generative AI capabilities in Gemini for Google Cloud to interpret error logs. It's worth taking a closer look at the action that we triggered to generate logs that we could examine with Gemini for Google Cloud. Here is a summary of what we did:

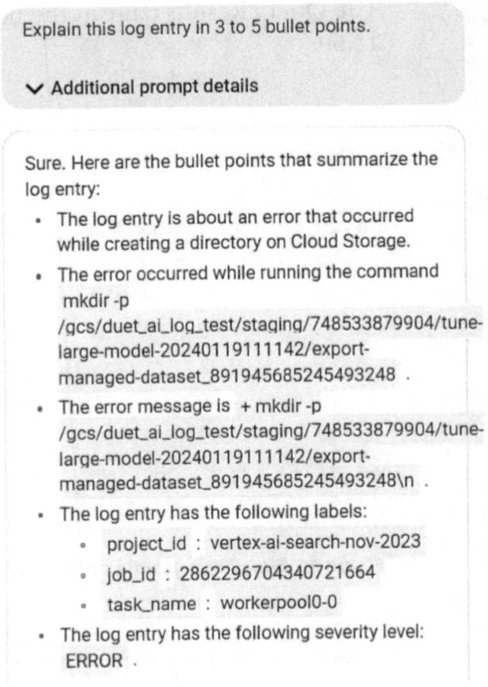

- We started with one of the foundation models available in Vertex AI, `text-bison`. This model is designed for various natural language tasks like content creation and classification. See the documentation for more details on `text-bison`: https://mng.bz/oKrZ.

- We applied supervised tuning to adapt the `text-bison` foundation model to a particular use case—our case classifying medical transcripts. To learn more about supervised tuning of foundation models in Vertex AI, see the documentation: https://mng.bz/nR15.

Explain this log entry in 3 to 5 bullet points.

⌄ Additional prompt details

Sure. Here are the bullet points that summarize the log entry:

- The log entry is about an error that occurred while creating a directory on Cloud Storage.
- The error occurred while running the command mkdir -p /gcs/duet_ai_log_test/staging/748533879904/tune-large-model-20240119111142/export-managed-dataset_891945685245493248 .
- The error message is + mkdir -p /gcs/duet_ai_log_test/staging/748533879904/tune-large-model-20240119111142/export-managed-dataset_891945685245493248\n .
- The log entry has the following labels:
  - project_id : vertex-ai-search-nov-2023
  - job_id : 2862296704340721664
  - task_name : workerpool0-0
- The log entry has the following severity level: ERROR .

Figure 11.52   Error explanation

- The dataset that we used for tuning contained medical diagnosis transcripts paired with the classification for the transcript, as shown in the following listing.

Listing 11.13   Example record from tuning dataset

```
{
"input_text":"TRANSCRIPT: \nREASON FOR CONSULTATION: ,
Loculated left effusion,
multilobar pneumonia.\n\n LABEL:",          ⟵ Medical transcript
"output_text":"Consult - History and Phy."   ⟵ Classification
}
```

- The URI for this dataset is `gs://cloud-samples-data/vertex-ai/model -evaluation/peft_train_sample.jsonl`.

Once the tuning process is complete, you can exercise the tuned model in Vertex AI Studio by selecting Language -> Tune and Distill and then selecting Test in the row for the model you tuned in the previous subsection, as shown in figure 11.53.

Language

GET STARTED   MY PROMPTS   TUNE AND DISTILL

Tune and Distill + CREATE TUNED MODEL   ▽ CREATE DISTILLED MODEL PREVIEW

In Vertex AI Studio, you can tune and distill foundation models to optimize them for specific tasks or knowledge domains. To view all your models in Vertex AI, go to Model Registry

Region
us-central1 (Iowa)   ▼   ❓

☐	Model	Pipeline run	Method ❓	Pipeline run status	Run start			
☐	duet_ai_log_example ↗	tune-large-model-20240119111142 ↗	Supervised	✅ Succeeded	Jan 19, 2024, 11:11:55 PM	DETAILS	TEST	⋮

Figure 11.53   Selecting the tuned model in Vertex AI Studio

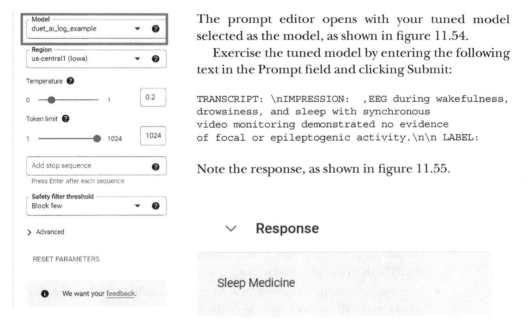

The prompt editor opens with your tuned model selected as the model, as shown in figure 11.54.

Exercise the tuned model by entering the following text in the Prompt field and clicking Submit:

```
TRANSCRIPT: \nIMPRESSION:  ,EEG during wakefulness,
drowsiness, and sleep with synchronous
video monitoring demonstrated no evidence
of focal or epileptogenic activity.\n\n LABEL:
```

Note the response, as shown in figure 11.55.

⌄ **Response**

Sleep Medicine

Figure 11.54   Prompt editor with the tuned model selected

Figure 11.55   Sleep medicine response

Now change the model back to the foundation model `text-bison@001`, as shown in figure 11.56, and click Submit again.

Model
text-bison@001   ▼   ❓

Figure 11.56   Changing the model back to text-bison@001

What's the difference between the response you get from the prompt with the tuned model and the untuned foundation model? With the tuned model, you get all the capability of the foundation model along with appropriate responses for the medical transcript classification use case.

If you examine the dataset that we used to tune the foundation model (with the URI `gs://cloud-samples-data/vertex-ai/model-evaluation/peft_train_sample .jsonl`) you will notice that it is, in fact, a tabular dataset with two columns: one containing medical transcription notes and the other containing a category for the notes, such as "cardiovascular / pulmonary," "chiropractic," or "pain management." So far in this book, we have examined how generative AI can be applied to the workflow for machine learning on tabular data. The example we used in the log interpretation exercise demonstrates a different kind of relationship between tabular data and generative AI: tabular data being part of the workflow for generative AI. A detailed examination of this subject is beyond the scope of this book, but we think that the role of tabular data in generative AI workflows is an underresearched area that could yield significant benefits in getting the most out of generative AI.

In this section, we have seen how we can use Gemini for Google Cloud's generative AI capabilities to answer questions about ML pipelines, generate some of the code required to create one, explain the code that makes up an ML pipeline, and explain log messages.

Summary

- Several set-up tasks need to be completed before setting up an ML pipeline in Vertex AI.
- A service account needs to be created, and the service account key needs to be uploaded to the directory where you run the pipeline script.
- The dataset that will be used to train the model in the pipeline needs to be uploaded to a Google Cloud Storage bucket. This bucket location then needs to be used to define a Vertex AI dataset that will be used as an argument to the Vertex AI SDK in the pipeline script.
- The training script running in a Vertex AI prebuilt container does not have access to the file system outside of the container, so the training dataset and the training config file for the ML pipeline implementation are in Cloud Storage, and their locations are passed to the training script as URIs.
- The training code from the training notebook that we ran in Colab in chapter 9 needs to be adapted to run in a container. For example, the training script needs to be updated to use the Cloud Storage locations for the config file, the training data, and the location where the trained model should be saved.
- The pipeline script invokes a series of functions from the Vertex AI SDK to create the container the training script runs in, to run the training script, and to deploy the trained model to a Vertex AI endpoint.

- You can use the same web application that you used to exercise the local deployment in chapter 10 to exercise the endpoint deployment generated by the ML pipeline.

- You can use Gemini for Google Cloud (the generative AI toolkit incorporated in Google Cloud) at various steps of the ML pipeline creation process to answer questions, generate code from text, interpret code, and explain log messages.

12

Blending gradient boosting and deep learning

This chapter covers

- A review of the end-to-end gradient boosting example from chapter 7
- A comparison of the results of the gradient boosting example from chapter 7 with a deep learning solution for the same problem
- The result of ensembling a gradient boosted model with a deep learning model

In chapter 7, we did an in-depth exploration of an end-to-end example of using gradient boosting. We explored a dataset of Airbnb listings for Tokyo, we engineered features suitable for a pricing regression task, and then we created a baseline model trained on this dataset to predict prices. Finally, applying the techniques we had learned in the book up to that point, we optimized an XGBoost model trained on this dataset and examined some approaches to explain the behavior of the model.

In this chapter, we evaluate if using deep learning would have led to different results and performance on the same problem, determine what approach works best, and discover how to use and integrate the strengths and weaknesses of each method. To do this, we begin this chapter by revisiting the gradient boosting approach to the Airbnb Tokyo problem from chapter 7. Next, we review some of the approaches we could take to apply deep learning to the same problem and share our chosen deep learning approach to this problem. Finally, we compare the two solutions and determine what we can learn from such a comparison when it comes to deciding whether to use gradient boosting or deep learning to tackle a tabular data problem, whether it's a regression or classification problem. In addition to comparing the solutions according to core performance (such as how well each solution makes predictions and their inference time), we explore how the two solutions compare according to more business-oriented metrics, such as the cost of maintenance, clarity to business stakeholders, and stability postdeployment.

This chapter pulls together themes that you have seen across this book, incorporating what we learned in chapter 7 about XGBoost and what we learned about how to approach tabular problems with deep learning in chapters 1 and 8.

In chapter 1, we reviewed some of the papers that compare tabular data applications of classical machine learning with applications of deep learning. In this chapter, we will see that the results of our comparison of XGBoost with deep learning align with the observations of one of the papers we cited in chapter 1. In chapter 8, we assessed a variety of deep learning approaches to working with tabular data. Now we will use what we learned there to help us select a deep learning approach that has the best chance of being competitive with the performance of XGBoost.

By combining the two main threads that we have explored in this book (classical machine learning approaches and deep learning approaches to solving tabular data problems), this chapter provides a summary of what we have covered so far in this book and guidance to set you up for success in your application of machine learning to tabular data. The code shown in the chapter is available at https://mng.bz/vKPp.

12.1 Review of the gradient boosting solution from chapter 7

In chapter 7, we assembled a dataset for Airbnb listings in Tokyo, analyzed the key characteristics of this dataset, and created an XGBoost model to predict the price of a listing. Starting at the Inside Airbnb Network website (http://insideairbnb.com/), we downloaded the following files related to the city of Tokyo:

- `listings.csv`, which contains the summary listings and other information about the Airbnb accommodations in Tokyo
- `calendar.csv.gz`, a zipped file containing `calendar.csv`, a dataset containing occupancy and price information for a given year for each listing

Recall that the dataset in `listings.csv` has the following columns:

- `id`—This is a unique identifier for each listing on Airbnb. It is an `int64` data type, meaning it is a numerical ID representation. In other tables, it can be referred to as `listing_id`.

- name—The description of the Airbnb listing. It is of the object data type, which typically represents a string or text.

- host_id—This is a unique identifier for each host on Airbnb. It is an int64 data type.

- host_name—The name of the host who owns the listing. It is of the object data type.

- neighbourhood_group—This field represents the broader area or region the neighborhood belongs to. It is stored as a float64 data type, but it is important to note that using a float data type to represent groups or categories is uncommon. In this case, the presence of float values indicates that the data for this field is entirely made up of missing values.

- neighbourhood—The specific neighborhood where the listing is located. It is of the object data type.

- latitude—The latitude coordinates of the listing's location. It is of the float64 data type.

- longitude—The longitude coordinates of the listing's location. It is of the float64 data type.

- room_type—The type of room or accommodation offered in the listing (e.g., entire home/apartment, private room, shared room). It is of the object data type.

- price—The price per night to rent the listing. It is of the int64 data type, representing an integer price value.

- minimum_nights—The minimum number of nights that is required for booking the listing. It is of the int64 data type.

- number_of_reviews—The total number of reviews received by the listing. It is of the int64 data type.

- last_review—The date of the last review received by the listing. It is of the object data type, which could represent date and time information, but it might require further parsing to be used effectively.

- reviews_per_month—The average number of reviews per month for the listing. It is of the float64 data type.

- calculated_host_listings_count—The total number of listings the host has on Airbnb. It is of the int64 data type.

- availability_365—The number of days the listing is available for booking in a year (out of 365 days). It is of the int64 data type.

- number_of_reviews_ltm—The number of reviews received in the last 12 months. It is of the int64 data type.

- license—The license number or information related to the listing. It is of the object data type, which typically represents a string or text.

The goal of the model we created in chapter 7 was to predict the price of a new listing. This is actually a more challenging problem for a deep learning model than the Airbnb NYC problem that we tackled in chapter 8, as we can see from the comparison in table 12.1.

Table 12.1 Airbnb NYC problem vs Airbnb Tokyo problem

	Airbnb NYC	**Airbnb Tokyo**
Rows in dataset	48,000	10,000
Columns in dataset	18	31
Target	Classification: predict whether the price is over or under the median price	Regression: predict price

In fact, the Tokyo Airbnb dataset has fewer than 25% of the records of the NYC Airbnb dataset and over double the number of columns as the NYC Airbnb dataset. With fewer data points, you may need to rely more on domain expertise (hence the role of feature engineering). Having more columns implies there's more risk of overfitting during training, and in any case, you have to deal with more complex relationships between features and the target variable itself.

Generally speaking, classical machine learning approaches can get better results on small datasets than deep learning. Techniques such as data augmentation can mitigate this downside of deep learning, but deep learning approaches will struggle with a dataset with fewer than tens of thousands of rows. Research on why deep learning requires more data is not complete, but the large number of parameters in deep learning architectures and the need for at least a certain amount of data for the model to generalize is identified as one of the reasons why deep learning struggles with problems having smaller datasets [see, for instance, "The Computational Limits of Deep Learning" by Thompson et al. (https://arxiv.org/pdf/2007.05558.pdf), which also argues how computational efficiency is necessary for the approach to progress].

The smaller number of rows in the Tokyo Airbnb dataset hence certainly presents a challenge for the successful implementation of a deep learning solution. In addition, the larger number of columns in the dataset necessitates more extensive preprocessing and feature engineering to ensure that the resulting features are relevant and usable for modeling purposes. Since we have followed the same data preparation steps as in chapter 7, we should not have to worry about having to deal with more columns for this particular application, but it is worth keeping in mind for other datasets that more columns equate to coming up with effective strategies for handling missing values, dealing with multicollinearity (as we discussed in chapter 2), and selecting the most informative features. In addition to requiring more data preparation, having more columns opens the possibility of having redundant or noisy features that could reduce the effectiveness of a deep learning solution on this dataset, although deep learning models, given their capability to capture complex relationships between features and the target variable, tend to be more robust to noise in the data.

Further, the problem we are tackling with the Tokyo Airbnb dataset is a regression (predicting the price of a listing) as opposed to a binary classification (predicting whether a given listing has a price above or below the median price) as we attempted to solve with the NYC Airbnb dataset, which has different business implications. If the goal is to provide a solution that returns business benefits, our solution should predict correctly as often as possible. With a binary classification problem, the solution is discrete (one class or the other), and the likelihood of the solution making a prediction that is correct from a business perspective is higher than it appears for a regression problem, where the business expectation is for the model to predict a price that closely matches the actual price but the outputs are continuous values that can be significantly different from the expected values. In short, a binary classification problem looks easier (from the point of view of satisfying the business need)—since it has a clear threshold for correctness—than a regression problem.

In chapter 7, after completing a set of transformations on the Airbnb Tokyo dataset, we end up with the following set of features for the dataset:

```
array(['onehot_encoding__room_type_Entire home/apt',
       'onehot_encoding__room_type_Hotel room',
       'onehot_encoding__room_type_Private room',
       'onehot_encoding__room_type_Shared room',
       'ordinal_encoding__neighbourhood_more_than_30',
       'ordinal_encoding__type_of_accommodation',
       'target_encoding__coordinates', 'numeric__minimum_nights',
       'numeric__number_of_reviews', 'numeric__days_since_last_review',
       'numeric__reviews_per_month',
       'numeric__calculated_host_listings_count',
       'numeric__availability_365', 'numeric__score',
       'numeric__number_of_reviews_ltm',
       'numeric__number_of_reviews_ltm_ratio',
       'numeric__number_of_bedrooms', 'numeric__number_of_beds',
       'numeric__number_of_baths', 'numeric__imperial_palace_distance',
       'numeric__nearest_convenience_store',
       'numeric__nearest_train_station', 'numeric__nearest_airport',
       'numeric__nearest_bus_station', 'numeric__nearest_subway',
       'binary__is_new', 'binary__is_studio', 'binary__has_shared_bath',
       'binary__has_half_bath'], dtype=object)
```

All these features are numeric, and we also properly dealt with any missing values to be able to work with a linear model baseline. In fact, we started by creating a linear regression model to act as a baseline and give us a measuring stick against which to compare further improvements to the XGBoost model.

Preparing your data for linear regression or logistic regression (depending on whether it's a regression or classification problem) automatically prepares your model for being processed by a neural network as well. However, while this is convenient, it might miss out on some specific preparations suitable only for neural networks. For instance, categorical features are commonly dealt with using one-hot-encoding in a linear model, whereas with a neural network, you can employ an encoding layer to convert categorical values into numeric ones directly during training.

After getting the baseline results for linear regression, we conducted a set of optimizations on the XGBoost model. We use that optimized XGBoost code as the basis for the gradient boosted solution to the Tokyo Airbnb problem, which we will use for the comparison with deep learning in this chapter. Listing 12.1 shows the XGBoost code that we will use to compare with a deep learning solution. This version of the XGBoost code is very close to the final XGBoost code used in chapter 7. The hyperparameters match the best hyperparameters from the notebook used in chapter 7; https://mng .bz/4a6R). In the version of the code used in this chapter, the predictions are saved in the xgb_oof_preds array so that they can be further processed or used in conjunction with the predictions we are going to obtain from a deep learning model.

Listing 12.1   Code for training the final XGBoost model

```
xgb_params =    {'booster': 'gbtree',
                 'objective': 'reg:tweedie',           ◀── Sets hyperparameters
                 'n_estimators': 932,
                 'learning_rate': 0.08588055025922144,
                 'subsample': 0.9566295202123205,
                 'colsample_bytree': 0.6730567082779646,
                 'max_depth': 7,
                 'min_child_weight': 6,
                 'reg_lambda': 6.643211493348415e-06,
                 'reg_alpha': 7.024597970671363e-05,
                 'tweedie_variance_power': 1.6727891016980427}


from sklearn.metrics import r2_score
from sklearn.metrics import mean_squared_error
from sklearn.metrics import mean_absolute_error    ◀── Imports required libraries
from XGBoost import XGBRegressor
import numpy as np
                                              Sets up an XGBoost regressor with
xgb = XGBRegressor(**xgb_params)          ◀── the specified hyperparameters

cv_splits = cv.split(X, y=neighbourhood_more_than_30)    ◀──

r2_scores = []          Defines cross-validation splits based on the
rmse_scores = []          neighbourhood_more_than_30 feature
mae_scores = []
xgb_oof_preds = np.zeros(len(X))          Generates cross-validation splits
                                          based on the neighbourhood_
                                          more_than_30 feature
for train_index, test_index in cv_splits:    ◀──
    X_train, X_test = X.iloc[train_index], X.iloc[test_index]
    y_train, y_test = y.iloc[train_index], y.iloc[test_index]
```

```
xgb.fit(X_train, y_train)
y_pred = xgb.predict(X_test)          ◀──┐  Performs cross-
xgb_oof_preds[test_index] = y_pred       └─ validated predictions

r2_scores.append(r2_score(y_test, y_pred))                        ◀──────
rmse_scores.append(np.sqrt(mean_squared_error(y_test, y_pred)))
mae_scores.append(mean_absolute_error(y_test, y_pred))
```
```
print(f"Mean cv R-squared: {np.mean(r2_scores):.3f}")    ◀──┐
print(f"Mean cv RMSE: {np.mean(rmse_scores):.3f}")
Print(f"Mean cv MAE: {np.mean(mae_scores):.3f}")
```

**Prints mean values for R-squared,
root mean squared error, and
mean absolute error**

**Calculates R-squared, root mean squared error,
and mean absolute error evaluation metrics to
assess the model's performance**

The optimizations performed on the XGBoost solution produce results that are significantly better than the linear regression baseline, as summarized in table 12.2.

Table 12.2   Summary of the results from chapter 7

Metric	Linear regression baseline	Optimized XGBoost
R-squared	0.320	0.729
Root mean squared error	17197.323	10853.661
Mean absolute error	12568.371	6611.609

As a further check, you can verify that for all three of the metrics we tracked in chapter 7—that is, R-squared, root mean squared error (RMSE), and mean absolute error (MAE)—the optimized XGBoost model is definitely always an improvement on the linear regression baseline. Now, using the XGBoost model as our reference, we will explore what kind of results we can get with the same dataset using a deep learning model in the remainder of this chapter.

12.2   *Selecting a deep learning solution*

In chapter 8, we reviewed a set of different deep learning stacks for working with tabular data, including Keras, fastai, and other libraries specifically designed for tabular data, like TabNet. If we now want to compare the XGBoost solution to the Tokyo Airbnb problem from chapter 7, which deep learning approach should we use?

As a reminder, we shared a comparison of the different deep learning approaches using the NYC Airbnb dataset, which is shown again in table 12.3.

Table 12.3   Comparison of deep learning options

	Keras	fastai	Tabular data library (e.g., TabNet)
Pro	Model details are transparent. A large community using the framework means that it's easy to find solutions to common problems.	The framework includes explicit support for tabular data models, which means the code will be more compact. It also sets intelligent defaults so we can quickly reach reasonable results.	A bespoke library explicitly created to handle tabular datasets
Con	No built-in support for tabular data	If we run into a problem, we could be on our own getting a resolution because the community is smaller than the Keras one.	Up to now, no library has emerged as an obvious choice; the fragmented community and inconsistent maintenance of some libraries make it a challenge to get the basic code to run reliably.

The differences between the dataset we used in chapter 8 and the dataset we will use now for the comparison between XGBoost and deep learning—that is, a dataset that was previously both much larger (with four times as many rows as the Tokyo Airbnb dataset) and much simpler (with less than half as many columns as the Tokyo Airbnb dataset)—for our comparison with XGBoost do not significantly weight in favor of any of the proposed solutions. In fact, Keras and fastai are general-purpose deep learning frameworks and are not specifically designed for small or complex datasets. TabNet's design gives it an edge with high-dimensional data, but when applied to smaller datasets, the advantage over Keras or fastai turns out to be less significant.

What actually weighs more in our choice is the fact that we want a fair comparison between XGBoost and a deep learning approach. As you saw in chapter 7, XGBoost shines with its ease of use, and it gets good results without a lot of tweaking. If we decide on a complex deep learning model that takes a long time to set up, tweak, and optimize, it wouldn't turn into a fair comparison for the deep learning model.

Given this, which deep learning framework should we choose? We will pass over TabNet because of the complexity of getting it to run reliably. That leaves us with a choice between Keras and fastai. As mentioned in table 12.3, Keras is indeed popular in production and boasts a larger community. However, fastai aligns better with our goals. Recall that in chapter 8 we noted that fastai is built for tabular data like ours, and it comes with smart defaults. This means you can get decent results quickly, without spending ages on optimizations. fastai handles a lot of the nitty-gritty stuff and details for you behind the scenes. As you'll see later, choosing fastai for this problem paid off. For the moment, we believe it provides a strong deep learning solution for the Tokyo Airbnb problem without much hassle, ready in a few steps to take on the XGBoost model from chapter 7.

12.3 *Selected deep learning solution to the Tokyo Airbnb problem*

So far in this chapter we have reviewed the XGBoost solution to the Tokyo Airbnb problem, reviewed options for a deep learning solution to compare it with, and selected fastai as the deep learning framework to use for the comparison with XGBoost. In this section, we'll go through the details of the fastai solution for the Tokyo Airbnb problem.

Listing 12.2 shows the core of the fastai model that we used to compare with the XGBoost solution. This code trains a fastai regression model on the Tokyo Airbnb dataset using the `TabularPandas` function (https://mng.bz/QDR6), which is a wrapper providing all the necessary transformations under the hood.

Listing 12.2 fastai model for the Tokyo Airbnb problem

```
from fastai.tabular.all import *

procs = [FillMissing, Normalize, Categorify]
cat_vars = [
    col for col in airbnb_tokyo.columns
    if "onehot_encoding__" in col
    or ordinal_encoding__" in col
    or "binary__" in col
]
cont_vars = [
    col for col in airbnb_tokyo.columns
    if "numeric__" in col
    or "target_encoding__" in col
]
dep_var = 'target'

cv_splits = cv.split(X, y=neighbourhood_more_than_30)

r2_scores = []
rmse_scores = []
mae_scores = []
dnn_oof_preds = np.zeros(len(X))

for k, (train_index, test_index) in enumerate(cv_splits):
    X_train = airbnb_tokyo.set_index("listing_id").iloc[train_index].copy()
    X_test = airbnb_tokyo.set_index("listing_id").iloc[test_index].copy()
    y_test = airbnb_tokyo["target"].iloc[test_index].copy()

    tab = TabularPandas(
        X_train, procs, cat_vars, cont_vars,          ◄──  Defines a fastai
        dep_var, y_block=RegressionBlock(),                TabularPandas object
        splits=RandomSplitter(
            valid_pct=0.2, seed=0)(range_of(X_train)),
        inplace=True,
        reduce_memory=True
    )                                            Defines a dataloaders
                                                 object based on the
                                                 TabularPandas object
    dls = tab.dataloaders(bs=128)    ◄──
```

```
y_range = torch.tensor([0, X_train['target'].max() * 1.2])
tc = tabular_config(ps=[0.001, 0.01], embed_p=0.04, y_range=y_range)
learn = tabular_learner(dls, layers=[1000,500],
                        metrics=mae,
                        config=tc,
                        loss_func=L1LossFlat())
with learn.no_bar(), learn.no_logging():
    lr = learn.lr_find(show_plot=False)
    learn.fit_one_cycle(80, lr.valley)

dl = learn.dls.test_dl(X_test)
y_pred = (
    learn.get_preds(dl=dl)[0]
    .numpy()
    .ravel()
)
dnn_oof_preds[test_index] = y_pred

r2_scores.append(r2_score(y_test, y_pred))
rmse_scores.append(np.sqrt(mean_squared_error(y_test, y_pred)))
mae_scores.append(mean_absolute_error(y_test, y_pred))
print(f"CV Fold {k} MAE: {mae_scores[-1]:.3f}")

print(f"\nMean cv R-squared: {np.mean(r2_scores):.3f}")
print(f"Mean cv RMSE: {np.mean(rmse_scores):.3f}")
print(f"Mean cv MAE: {np.mean(mae_scores):.3f}")
```

Defines a tabular_ learner object based on the dataloaders object

Trains the model

Gets predictions from the model on the test set

Saves the metrics

As you can see from the code in listing 12.2, the solution for fastai is straightforward. First, we define the preprocessing steps (procs), such as filling missing values, normalization, and categorization. Then we separate categorical and continuous variables from the dataset and choose the dependent variable (dep_var). After that, we iterate through a stratified k-fold cross-validation in the same manner as we did for the XGBoost solution.

During the iterations, the training data is preprocessed using TabularPandas, specifying categorical and continuous variables, the target variable, and data splits. DataLoader objects (dls) are created for training and validation batches. After defining a neural network model (tabular_learner) consisting of two layers, the first with 1,000 neurons and the following with 500 nodes, and their dropout rates (using tabular_ config and setting a higher dropout for the last layer), we train the model using the learning rate found by lr_find and using the one cycle (fit_one_cycle) procedure.

By combining the lr_find and fit_one_cycle procedures, we automatically tune the learning rate parameter for the best results on the type of data we are processing, thus achieving a straightforward solution without much tweaking and experimentation. The procedure lr_find (https://mng.bz/Xxq9) explores a range of learning rates on a sample of the data, stopping when the learning rate is so high that the learning diverges. While the procedure takes some time, it is relatively fast and returns the value of the learning parameter that is two-thirds of the way along the section of the loss curve where the loss is decreasing. We use that value as the upper boundary of another procedure, the `fit_one_cycle` (https://mng.bz/yWZp), which is a training method where the learning rate is not fixed or constantly decreasing but rather oscillates between a minimum and a maximum value. The oscillations allow for the network to not get stuck in a local minima, and overall the resulting network performs better than using other approaches, especially when dealing with tabular data. Both methods have been developed by Leslie Smith in a series of papers:

- "Cyclical Learning Rates for Training Neural Networks" (https://arxiv.org/abs/1506.01186)
- "Super-Convergence: Very Fast Training of Neural Networks Using Large Learning Rates" (https://arxiv.org/abs/1708.07120)
- "A Disciplined Approach to Neural Network Hyper-Parameters: Part 1—Learning Rate, Batch Size, Momentum, and Weight Decay" (https://arxiv.org/abs/1803.09820)

To our knowledge, the implementation by fastai of these methods is the most efficient and high-performing available in the open-source community.

Proceeding with the code, for each pass through the `for` loop, the predictions for the current fold and the R-squared, RMSE, and MAE evaluations are saved. The mean values for all the metrics are printed after the loop so we can get an idea of the overall values for the fastai solution. Note that we will recalculate these values as we go through the ensembling process when we compare the predictions and actual y values for an ensemble that is 100% fastai results.

12.4 *Comparing the XGBoost and fastai solutions to the Tokyo Airbnb problem*

Now that we have a deep learning solution for the Tokyo Airbnb problem, we can compare its results against the XGBoost solution. By comparing the metrics that we collected for both solutions (R-squared, RMSE, and MAE), we can get an idea of how effective each solution is at solving the Tokyo Airbnb problem. Table 12.4 contains a summary of the results of both approaches.

Table 12.4 Comparison of results from XGBoost and fastai models

Metric	XGBoost	Fastai
R-squared	0.599	0.572
RMSE	10783.027	11719.387
MAE	6531.102	7152.143

Table 12.4 demonstrates that XGBoost provides better results than fastai for all three error metrics—in fact, the R-squared value for XGBoost is significantly higher, and its RMSE and MAE values are about 8% to 9% lower.

In addition to the basic comparison of error metrics in table 12.4, we can visualize some differences relative to how the two approaches deal with the problem. For example, we can directly compare XGBoost and fastai predictions by examining each predicted data point in the Tokyo Airbnb test set. In figure 12.1, the x-axis represents the prediction from XGBoost, while the y-axis represents the prediction from fastai for each respective data point. The figure shows the relationship between XGBoost and fastai predictions.

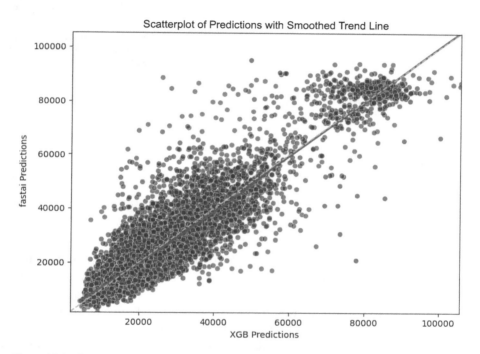

Figure 12.1   Scatterplot of predictions for XGBoost and fastai

On the diagonal of the chart, the solid trend line coincides fairly well with the dashed diagonal line, showing that, overall, there is not a huge variance in the predictions between XGBoost and fastai. The solid trend line, showing the smoothed regression line (a technique called LOWESS [LOcally WEighted Scatterplot Smoothing]) between the predictions from XGBoost and fastai, doesn't deviate significantly in comparison from the dashed line, confirming that, even if the algorithms tend to disagree in their predictions, there is no systematic over- or underestimation from one of the two in respect of the other.

In addition, we can also try to explore how their predictions relate, using the value of 70,000 on the x-axis as a pivot, since we can spot two distinct clusters of predictions. We observe that the average fastai prediction is around 81,300 against a XGBoost average at 81,550 for XGBoost predictions over 70,000 and around 23,050 against 22,500 for XGBoost predictions below 70,000.

Listing 12.3   Average fastai predictions for XGBoost predictions

```
predictions = pd.DataFrame(
    {'xgb': xgb_oof_preds, 'fastai': dnn_oof_preds}
)
                                                        Gets a pandas DataFrame with
                                                        a column each for XGBoost
                                                        and fastai predictions
avg_fastai_over_70000 = predictions.loc[
    predictions['xgb'] > 70000, 'fastai'
].mean()
                                                        Computes mean statistics for XGBoost
                                                        and fastai predictions depending on
avg_xgb_over_70000 = predictions.loc[                   XGBoost predicted value
    predictions['xgb'] > 70000, 'xgb'
].mean()
print(f"Average prediction values when xgb > 70000:",
      f"fastai:{avg_fastai_over_70000:0.2f}",
      f"xgb:{avg_xgb_over_70000:0.2f}")


avg_fastai_under_70000 = predictions.loc[predictions['xgb'] <= 70000,
    'fastai'].mean()
avg_xgb_under_70000 = predictions.loc[predictions['xgb'] <= 70000, 'xgb'].
    mean()
print(f"Average prediction values when xgb <= 70000: fastai:{avg_fastai_
    under_70000:0.2f}
    xgb:{avg_xgb_under_70000:0.2f}")
```

The differences between the two models are minimal; on average, fastai and XGBoost predictions tend to be aligned. Fastai tends to overestimate for lower predicted pricing levels and slightly underestimate for higher predicted pricing levels.

Returning to figure 12.1, now that we have examined the chart comparing the predictions, let's look at a chart comparing the error for XGBoost with the error for fastai. For each data point in the Tokyo Airbnb test set, the plot in figure 12.2 shows the error for that data point (the absolute value of the difference between the prediction and the actual value), with the x value being the XGBoost error and the y value being the fastai error.

Figure 12.2 shows that there is a large cluster of data points where the error for both XGBoost and fastai is lower than 20,000. The overall LOWESS line, in red, shows that the error for XGBoost is overall lower than for fastai most of the time.

As shown by the aggregate error metrics and the plots for predictions and errors, the XGBoost model displays better performance than the fastai model. However, given the spread of the predictions between the two models, we believe that there is an opportunity to do even better than XGBoost alone by ensembling the two models because there is a strong hint that, apart from the differences in performance, the two models operate differently in their predictions by capturing different data patterns and characteristics. In the next section, we will find out whether ensembling improves the results.

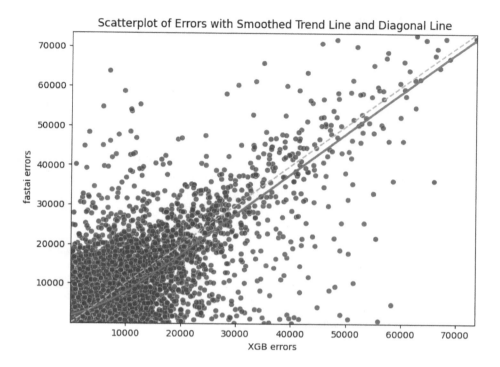

Figure 12.2   Scatterplot of errors for XGBoost and fastai

12.5   *Ensembling the two solutions to the Tokyo Airbnb problem*

Now that we have established the performance of the XGBoost and fastai solutions to the Tokyo Airbnb problem in isolation, we will look at ensembling the two solutions to see whether a combination of the two approaches provides any improvements.

The following listing shows the loop where we ensemble the results of the two models.

Listing 12.4   Code to ensemble the two models

```
blend_list = [
    [1., 0.], [0., 1.], [0.25,0.75],
    [0.75,0.25],[.5, .5]                    Ensembles ratios
]                                            to iterate through
for a, b in blend_list:
    print(f"XGBoost weight={a}, DNN weight={b}")
    blended_oof_preds = (                       Generates predictions that
        xgb_oof_preds * a + dnn_oof_preds * b   are blended according to
    )                                           the ensembling ratios
    r2 = r2_score(blended_oof_preds, y)
    rmse = np.sqrt(mean_squared_error(blended_oof_preds, y))    Gets R-squared, RMSE,
    mae = mean_absolute_error(blended_oof_preds, y)            and MAE for the
                                                               blended predictions
```

```
print(f"blended result for R-squared: {r2:.3f}")
print(f"blended result for RMSE: {rmse:.3f}")
print(f"blended result for MAE: {mae:.3f}\n")
```

The code in listing 12.4 combines results from XGBoost and fastai according to the blending values in `blend_list`. Note that these blending values are not optimized to find the absolute optimum—we are simply using a set of fixed blending values to get a general sense of the effect of blending results. Also, note that we are evaluating the results using out-of-fold predictions. Nevertheless, by combining the predictions from XGBoost and fastai according to the proportions specified by `blend_list`, we can see the effect of ensembling the two approaches across a range of values.

The output of the blending code for a typical run is

```
XGBoost weight=1.0, DNN weight=0.0
blended result for R-squared: 0.599
blended result for RMSE: 10783.027
blended result for MAE: 6531.102

XGBoost weight=0.75, DNN weight=0.25
blended result for R-squared: 0.619
blended result for RMSE: 10507.904
blended result for MAE: 6366.257

XGBoost weight=0.5, DNN weight=0.5
blended result for R-squared: 0.625
blended result for RMSE: 10527.024
blended result for MAE: 6384.576

XGBoost weight=0.25, DNN weight=0.75
blended result for R-squared: 0.618
blended result for RMSE: 10838.831
blended result for MAE: 6566.663

XGBoost weight=0.0, DNN weight=1.0
blended result for R-squared: 0.599
blended result for RMSE: 11419.374
blended result for MAE: 6959.540
```

These figures may be a bit difficult to interpret, so let's see what they look like in the form of a chart. Figure 12.3 shows the results for R-squared, RMSE, and MAE for a range of blending between the XGBoost and fastai models.

As figure 12.3 shows, we get the optimal results for R-squared evaluation when we use a 50/50 blend of the predictions from the XGBoost and fastai models. For error-based measures, RMSE and MAE, we obtain a better result weighting more XGBoost than fastai; however, if we were to use a 50/50 blend, we would obtain only slightly worse scores. The worst results are when we use 100% of prediction from fastai, as we would expect from the results we got from looking at each model in isolation, but it is interesting to notice that using only XGBoost is always worse than blending it with the other solution using a 75/25 or 50/50 share.

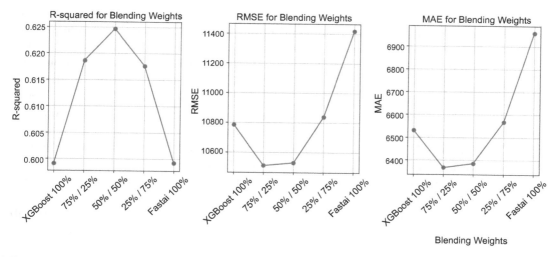

Figure 12.3   Results of blending XGBoost and fastai models

Ensembling the XGBoost and fastai models gets better results than using either model in isolation. As we will see in the next section, our observations from ensembling are consistent with the results shared in an important research paper that compared classical machine learning approaches and deep learning on tabular data problems.

12.6 *Overall comparison of gradient boosting and deep learning*

In chapter 1, we introduced the controversy over whether deep learning is needed to solve problems involving tabular data. We cited academic papers that support both sides of the argument—those that advocate for deep learning approaches and those that maintain that classical machine learning approaches, in particular gradient boosting, consistently outperform deep learning. One of the papers that we mentioned in chapter 1 is worth revisiting here: "Tabular Data: Deep Learning Is Not All You Need," by Ravid Shwartz-Ziv and Amitai Armon (https://arxiv.org/abs/2106.03253). In the Discussion and Conclusions section of this paper, the authors make the following statement:

> *In our analysis, the deep models were weaker on datasets that did not appear in their original papers, and they were weaker than XGBoost, the baseline model. Therefore, we proposed using an ensemble of these deep models with XGBoost. This ensemble performed better on these datasets than any individual model and the 'non-deep' classical ensemble.*

Their observation is not a hard and fast rule, because, in our experience, we encountered situations where using a gradient boosting solution or a deep learning one alone resulted in the best performances. However, in many of the situations we faced, we can confirm that simply averaging solutions resulted in better predictions. We are strongly convinced that this happened because the two algorithms have two different ways of optimizing predictions. Gradient boosting is based on decision trees, which are a form of analogy search because, as an algorithm, trees split your dataset into parts where the features tend to be similar in values between themselves and map to similar target outputs. The gradient part of the algorithm intelligently ensembles multiple trees together for a better prediction, although it doesn't change the basic way in which decision trees behave. Deep learning, on the other hand, is purely based on the principle of differentiation and nonlinear transformations, where the algorithm looks for the best weights to combine the transformed inputs.

These two different approaches result in quite different estimations whose errors tend to partially cancel each other out because they are strongly uncorrelated, in a similar fashion to what actually happens in a random forest algorithm when you average the results of uncorrelated decision trees. This conclusion matches our experience comparing the results of gradient boosting and deep learning on the Tokyo Airbnb problem. The ensemble of the XGBoost model with the fastai model produced the best results, as shown in figure 12.3.

Summary

- The XGBoost solution to the Tokyo Airbnb problem shown in chapter 7 provides a baseline that we can use to assess the efficacy of deep learning to solve the same problem.
- Using the XGBoost solution from chapter 7 as a starting point, we can create a deep learning solution for the Tokyo Airbnb problem. The fastai library provides a compact and relatively well-performing deep learning solution.
- By blending the predictions of the XGBoost and fastai models across a range of ratios, from 100% XGBoost to 100% fastai, we can see the effect of ensembling the models. We get the optimal results with a 50/50 ensemble of the two models.
- This result matches the recommendation from research focused on scrutinizing the claims of the efficacy of deep learning on tabular data.

appendix A
Hyperparameters
for classical machine
learning models

Table A.1 Hyperparameters for linear models

Hyperparameter	Description
C	Inversely related to regularization, smaller values correspond to stronger regularization. Search in the range `np.logspace(-4, 4, 10)`.
alpha	Constant that multiplies the regularization term, larger values correspond to stronger regularization. Search in the range `np.logspace(-2, 2, 10)`.
l1_ratio	Blending L1 and L2 regularization in Elasticnet, pick from the values [.1, .5, .7, .9, .95, .99].

Table A.2 Hyperparameters for random forests and ERTs

Hyperparameter	Description
max_features	Lower this parameter to increase bias and lower variance. Try values such as `sqrt`, `log2`, and integer numbers representing 1/10th and 1/20th of the features.
min_samples_leaf	A way to regularize trees, usually set to 1; try growing it up to 30.

Table A.2   Hyperparameters for random forests and ERTs (*continued*)

Hyperparameter	Description
bootstrap	A boolean indicating if to use bootstrap for resampling. Sometimes subsampling may be more effective than bootstrap if noise or outliers are present.
n_estimators	The more trees, the better, but you are wasting computational power beyond a certain point. Start from 100 and grow up to 1,000. It works for most problems.

Table A.3   Hyperparameters for Scikit-learn's HistGradientBoosting

Hyperparameter	Description
learning_rate	Multiplicative value for the results of the decision trees. A real number between 0.001 and 0.1.
max_iter	The maximum number of trees built in the boosting process. An integer between 100 and 1,000.
max_depth	The maximum depth of each tree acts as a regularization applied to the tree growth. Choose an integer between 1 and 12.
max_leaf_nodes	The maximum number of leaves for each tree. Related to max_depth, it also controls tree growth. Optimize this or max_depth, not both. Choose an integer between 2 and 4,096.
min_samples_leaf	The minimum number of samples per leaf is a regularization applied to the tree growth. Choose an integer between 2 and 300.
l2_regularization	L2 regularization parameter for ensembling. Choose a float between 0.0 and 100.0.
max_bins	The maximum number of bins to use in histograms. An indirect way to regularize trees. Choose an integer between 32 and 512.

Table A.4   Hyperparameters for XGBoost

Hyperparameter	Description
learning_rate	Multiplicative value to shrink the results from the decision trees. A real number between 0.001 and 0.1.
n_estimators	Number of trees in the boosting ensemble. An integer between 100 and 1,000.
max_depth	The maximum depth of a tree is a way to control the estimates' variance. An integer between 1 and 12.

Table A.4   Hyperparameters for XGBoost (*continued*)

Hyperparameter	Description
`min_child_weight`	The minimum sum of instance weight (hessian) needed in a child. The default is one. The larger `min_child_weight` is, the more conservative the algorithm will be. We suggest an integer between 1 and 10.
`max_delta_step`	Usually at zero, meaning no constraints, if set to a positive number, it acts as a regularizer because it sets a limit to the updates. It is beneficial when there is an imbalance among the classes in a classification because it prevents a class from dominating the others. We recommend a float between 0 and 10.
`max_bin`	Maximum number of bins used by histograms. An integer between 32 and 512.
`subsample`	Sampling ratio of the training instance. A real number between 0.1 and 1.0.
`colsample_bytree`	The subsample ratio of columns when constructing each tree. A real number between 0.1 and 1.0.
`reg_lambda`	L2 regularization term on weights. A real number between 1e-9 and 100.0.
`reg_alpha`	L1 regularization term on weights. A real number between 1e-9 and 100.0.
`gamma`	Another regularizer limiting the tree partitioning by setting a minimum loss reduction. Set this to a real number between 0 and 0.5.
`scale_pos_weight`	A weight value controlling the balance of positive and negative weights is useful for unbalanced binary classification problems. Set to 1 by default; a typical value to consider: number of negative instances/number of positive instances. We suggest a real number between 1e-6 and 500.

Table A.5   Hyperparameters for LightGBM

Hyperparameter	Description
`learning_rate`	Multiplicative value to shrink the results from the decision trees. A real number between 0.001 and 0.1.
`n_estimators`	Number of boosting iterations. An integer between 100 and 1,000.
`max_depth`	Limit to the maximum depth for decision trees. A way to control complexity and overfitting. An integer between 1 and 12.
`num_leaves`	An integer between 2 and 2^{max_depth}, it represents the number of final leaves a tree will have, and if set low, it acts as a regularization for tree complexity.

Table A.5 Hyperparameters for LightGBM (*continued*)

Hyperparameter	Description
min_data_in_leaf	Minimal number of data in one leaf. Setting this helps to deal with over-fitting. Zero implies no constraint. An integer between 0 and 300.
min_gain_to_split	The minimal gain to perform a split in the decision trees. A float between 0 and 15.
max_bin	Maximum number of bins used for histograms. An indirect way to deal with overfitting is by setting it lower. An integer between 32 and 512.
subsample	A random percentage of data is to be selected without resampling. A real number between 0.1 and 1.0.
subsample_freq	Frequency for subsampling: An integer between 0 and 10. If set to zero, the algorithm will ignore any setting related to the subsample and won't perform subsampling.
feature_fraction	Fraction of features to be used on each iteration. A real number between 0.1 and 1.0.
reg_lambda	L2 regularization. A real number between 0.0 and 100.0.
reg_alpha	L1 regularization. A real number between 0.0 and 100.0.
scale_pos_weight	Weight of labels with positive class used to counterbalance when in an unbalanced binary classification. A real number between 1e-6 and 500.

appendix B
K-nearest neighbors and support vector machines

In this appendix, we examine classical machine learning algorithms with a more computational nature that we didn't treat in the book because they are less frequently used nowadays and are considered outdated compared to decision tree ensembles in most applications. Overall, support vector machines (SVMs) are still a practical machine learning algorithm well suited for high-dimensional, noisy, or small-sized data applications. On the other end, k-nearest neighbors (k-NN) is well suited for running applications where the data has few features, there can be outliers, and it is not necessary to get a high degree of accuracy in predictions. For instance, SVMs can still be used to classify medical images, such as mammograms and X-rays; for vehicle detection and tracking in the automotive industry; or to detect email spam. Instead, k-NN is mainly applied in recommender systems, particularly collaborative filtering approaches, to recommend products or services based on users' past behavior.

They are suited in most tabular data situations when your data is not too small or exceedingly big—as a rule of thumb, where there are fewer than 10,000 rows. We will start with k-NN, an algorithm that data scientists have used for decades in machine learning problems and that is easy to understand and implement. Then we will complete our overview with SVMs and a brief excursus on using GPUs to have these algorithms perform when using a moderately sized dataset. All the examples need the Airbnb NYC Dataset presented in chapter 4. You can reprise it by executing the following code snippet:

```
import numpy as np
import pandas as pd
excluding_list = [
    'price', 'id', 'latitude', 'longitude',
    'host_id', 'last_review', 'name', 'host_name'    ◀── List of column names to be
]                                                        excluded from the analysis
categorical = [
    'neighbourhood_group', 'neighbourhood',          ◀── List of names of columns that
    'room_type'                                          likely represent categorical
]                                                        variables in the dataset
continuous = [
    'minimum_nights', 'number_of_reviews', 'reviews_per_month',
    'Calculated_host_listings_count'
]                                                    ◀── List of names of columns that
data = pd.read_csv("./AB_NYC_2019.csv")                  represent continuous numerical
target_median = (                                        variables in the dataset
    data["price"] > data["price"].median()
).astype(int)                                        ◀── A binary balanced target
```

The code will load your dataset and define what features to be excluded from the analysis or considered as continuous or categorical for processing purposes.

B.1   k-NN

Applicable to regression and classification tasks, the k-NN algorithm is considered one of the simplest and most intuitive algorithms for making predictions. It finds the k (where k is an integer number) closest examples from the training set and uses their information to make a prediction. For example, if the task is a regression, it will take the average of the k closest examples. If the task is a classification, it will choose the most common class among the k closest examples.

Technically, k-NN is commonly regarded as an instance-based learning algorithm because it memorizes the training examples as they are. It is also regarded as a "lazy algorithm" because, contrary to most machine learning algorithms, there is little processing at training time. During training, there is usually some processing of the distances by optimized algorithms and data structures that render it less computationally costly afterward to look for the neighboring points near a training example. Most of the computational work is done at testing time (see figure B.1).

We apply a k-NN classifier to the Airbnb NYC data, as seen in chapter 4, in listing B.1. Since k-NN works based on distances, to obtain a functioning solution, features must be on the same scale, thus assuring an equal weight to each dimension in the distance measurement process. If a feature is on a different or smaller scale, it would be overweighted in the process. The contrary would happen if a larger scale characterizes a feature. To give an idea of the problem, let's consider what happens when we compare distances based on kilometers, meters, and centimeters. Even if distances are comparable, meters and centimeters will numerically exceed kilometers measurements. This problem is usually solved by scaling features—for instance, by subtracting their mean and dividing by their standard deviation (an operation known as z-score normalization

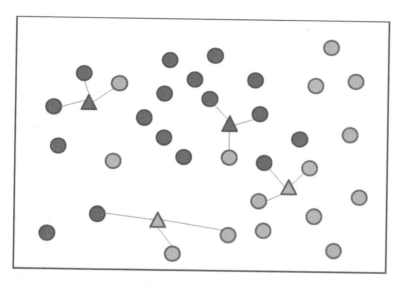

Figure B.1 Classifying new samples (the triangles) with a k-NN where k = 3

or standardization). Also, techniques such as dimensional reduction or feature selection are helpful with this algorithm because rearranging predictors or different sets of predictors may result in more or less predictive performances on the problem.

In our case, as it is often with tabular data, the situation is complicated by categorical features, which, once one-hot encoded, will turn into binaries ranging from 0 to 1, with a different scale from normalized features. The solution we propose is first to discretize the numeric features, thus effectively turning them into binary features, each representing if a feature's numeric values will fall into a specific range. Binarization of continuous features is obtained thanks to the KBinsDiscretizer class (https://mng .bz/N12N) embedded into the `numeric_discretizing` pipeline, which will turn each numeric feature into five binary ones, each one covering a bin of values. At processing time, we also apply principal component analysis (PCA) to reduce the dimensionality and make all the features unrelated. However, we might attenuate nonlinearities inside the data since PCA is a technique based on linear combinations of the variables. Having uncorrelated resulting features is a characteristic of data processed by PCA, which suits k-NN: k-NN is based on distances, and distance measurement properly works if dimensions are unrelated. Therefore, any distance change is due to changes in a single dimension, not multiple ones. The following listing shows the code implementing the data transformation process and training the k-NN.

Listing B.1   k-NN classifier

```
from sklearn.neighbors import KNeighborsClassifier
from sklearn.pipeline import Pipeline
from sklearn.compose import ColumnTransformer
```

```
from sklearn.preprocessing import OneHotEncoder
from sklearn.preprocessing import KBinsDiscretizer
from sklearn.metrics import accuracy_score

categorical_onehot_encoding = OneHotEncoder(handle_unknown='ignore')

accuracy = make_scorer(accuracy_score)
cv = KFold(5, shuffle=True, random_state=0)
model = KNeighborsClassifier(n_neighbors=30,
                             weights="uniform",
                             algorithm="auto",
                             n_jobs=-1)

column_transform = ColumnTransformer(
    [('categories', categorical_onehot_encoding, low_card_categorical),
     ('numeric', numeric_discretizing, continuous)],
    remainder='drop',
    verbose_feature_names_out=False,
    sparse_threshold=0.0)

model_pipeline = Pipeline(
    [('processing', column_transform),
     ('pca', PCA(n_components="mle")),
     ('modeling', model)])

cv_scores = cross_validate(estimator=model_pipeline,
                           X=data,
                           y=target_median,
                           scoring=accuracy,
                           cv=cv,
                           return_train_score=True,
                           return_estimator=True)

mean_cv = np.mean(cv_scores['test_score'])
std_cv = np.std(cv_scores['test_score'])
fit_time = np.mean(cv_scores['fit_time'])
score_time = np.mean(cv_scores['score_time'])
print(f"{mean_cv:0.3f} ({std_cv:0.3f})",
      f"fit: {fit_time:0.2f}",
      f"secs pred: {score_time:0.2f} secs")
```

Creates a scoring function using the accuracy_score metric

Creates a five-fold cross-validation iterator with shuffling and a fixed random state

Creates an instance of the KNeighborsClassifier with specified hyperparameters

Defines a ColumnTransformer to preprocess features, applying one-hot encoding to categorical features with low cardinality and discretization to numerical features

Creates a pipeline that sequentially applies the column transformation, performs PCA dimensionality reduction, and then fits the k-nn model to the data

Performs cross-validation on the data using the defined pipeline, with accuracy scoring

Prints the mean and standard deviation of test scores

After running the script, you will obtain a result that is close to the performance of the Naive Bayes solution:

```
0.814 (0.005) fit: 0.13 secs pred: 8.75 secs
```

The performance is good, though the inference time is relatively high. Since this algorithm works by analogy (it will look for similar cases in your training to get an idea of the possible prediction), it performs better with large enough datasets where there is a higher likelihood of finding some instances resembling those to be predicted. Naturally, the right size for the dataset is dictated by the number of features used because the more features, the more cases you will need for the algorithm to generalize well.

Though often the emphasis is placed on setting the best value to the k parameter as the key to balancing the underfitting and overfitting of the algorithm to the training data, we instead raise attention to other aspects for an effective employ of this model. As the algorithm works by analogy and distances in complex spaces, we consider two important matters about this approach:

- The dimensions to measure and the curse of dimensionality
- The appropriate distance measure and how to process the features

In k-NN, the classification or the regression estimates depend on the most similar examples based on a distance metric computed on the features. However, in a dataset, not all features can be deemed important in judging an example similar to the other, and not all of the features can be compared in the same way. Prior knowledge of the problem does count a lot when using k-NN because you have to select only the features relevant to the task you want to solve. If you assemble too many features for the problem, you will rely on too much complex space to navigate. Figure B.1 shows how a k-NN algorithm works with just two features (represented on the x and y dimensions), and you can intuitively grasp that classifying new instances (the triangles in the figure) may be difficult if there are mixed classes in an area or if there are no train examples near to a new instance. You have to rely on farther ones.

Here comes into the game the curse of dimensionality, which says that as the number of features increases, the more examples you should have available to maintain a meaningful distance between data points. In addition, the curse implies that the number of necessary examples grows exponentially with respect to the number of features. For a k-NN algorithm, it means that if you provide too many features, it will work in an empty space if the number of examples is not enough. Looking for neighbors will become daunting. In addition, if you have just assembled relevant and irrelevant features, the risk is that the algorithm will mark as neighbors some examples that are very far from the case you have to predict, and the choice could be based on features that are not useful for the problem. Hence, if you are going to use k-NN, you should choose with great care the features to be used (if you don't know which to use, you need to rely on feature selection) or be very familiar with the problem to determine what should go into the algorithm. Parsimony is essential for the proper working of a k-NN.

When you have decided about the features, regarding the distance metric you will be using, you will need to standardize, remove redundancies, and transform the features. This is because distance metrics are based on absolute measurements, and different scales can weigh in different ways. Consider using measurements in kilometers, meters, and centimeters together. The centimeters will likely predominate because they will easily have the largest numbers. Also, having features similar to each other (the problem of multicollinearity) can entail the distance measurement to overweight certain sets of features over others. Finally, a distance measurement implies having the same dimensions to measure. However, in a dataset, you may find different kinds of data—numeric, categorical, and time-based—which often need to fit together better in a distance calculation because they have different numeric characteristics.

For this reason, in addition to carefully selecting beforehand which features to use, when employing k-NN, we suggest using features that are all of the same kind (or all numeric or all categorical) to standardize them if necessary and also to reduce their informative redundancy by methods such as PCA (https://mng.bz/8OrZ), which will reformulate the dataset into a new one where features are not correlated between themselves.

B.2   SVMs

Before the 2010s, SVMs had a reputation as the most promising algorithm for tabular problems. However, in the past 10 years, tree-based models have eclipsed SVMs as the go-to approach for tabular data. However, SVMs remain a family of techniques for handling binary, multiclass, regression, and anomaly/novelty detection. They are based on the idea that if your observations can be represented as points in a multidimensional space, there is a hyperplane (i.e., a separation plane cutting through multiple dimensions) that can separate them into classes or values that, by assuring the largest separation possible between them, also guarantees the most robust and reliable predictions. Figure B.2 shows a simple example of an SVM applied to a binary classification problem with two features, represented on the x- and y-axis, as predictors. The SVM model produces a separator line with the largest slack space between the two groups, as shown in the figure, where the dashed lines delimit the slack space. In doing so, it considers only a few points near the separator, called the support vectors. Instead, it ignores the points that are near but are confusing for the algorithm because, for instance, they are on the wrong side. It also ignores the points that are far away from the separator line. Outliers have little influence on this algorithm.

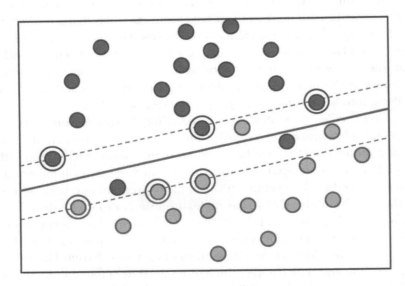

Figure B.2   A separating hyperplane from a SVM

The strong points of SVMs are their robust handling of overfitting, noise in data, and outliers and how they can successfully handle datasets that include numerous multicollinear features. Applying different nonlinear approaches to data, SVMs don't require the transformations (such as polynomial expansion) we have seen for logistic regression. However, they can use domain-based feature engineering like all other machine learning algorithms.

On the weak side, SVM optimization is complex and can be feasible only for a limited number of examples. Moreover, they are best fit for binary predictions and for just class prediction; they are not a probabilistic algorithm, and you need to wrap them with another algorithm for calibration (such as logistic regression) to extract probabilities from them. That renders SVMs valid only for a limited range of tasks in risk estimation.

In our example, we reapply our problem with Airbnb NYC data using a binary classification SVM using a radial basis function kernel, an approach capable of automatically modeling complex nonlinear relationships between the provided features.

Listing B.2 Support vector classifier

```python
from sklearn.svm import SVC
from sklearn.metrics import accuracy_score
from sklearn.impute import SimpleImputer
from sklearn.preprocessing import StandardScaler

numeric_standardization = Pipeline([
        ("imputation", SimpleImputer(strategy="constant", fill_value=0)),
        ("standardizing", StandardScaler())
        ])

accuracy = make_scorer(accuracy_score)
cv = KFold(5, shuffle=True, random_state=0)
model = SVC(
    C=1.0,
    kernel='rbf',
    gamma='scale',
    probability=False
)

column_transform = ColumnTransformer(
    [('categories', categorical_onehot_encoding, low_card_categorical),
     ('numeric', numeric_standardization, continuous)],
    remainder='drop',
    verbose_feature_names_out=False,
    sparse_threshold=0.0)

model_pipeline = Pipeline(
    [('processing', column_transform),
     ('modeling', model)])

cv_scores = cross_validate(estimator=model_pipeline,
                           X=data,
                           y=target_median,
                           scoring=accuracy,
```

Creates a scoring function using the accuracy_score metric

Creates a five-fold cross-validation iterator with shuffling and a fixed random state

Creates an instance of the Support Vector Classifier with specified hyperparameters

Defines a ColumnTransformer to preprocess features, applying one-hot encoding to categorical features with low cardinality and standardization to numerical features

Creates a pipeline that sequentially applies the column transformation and the model to the data

```
                              cv=cv,
                              return_train_score=True,
                              return_estimator=True)
```

⊳ Performs cross-validation on the data using the defined pipeline, with accuracy scoring

```
mean_cv = np.mean(cv_scores['test_score'])
std_cv = np.std(cv_scores['test_score'])
fit_time = np.mean(cv_scores['fit_time'])
score_time = np.mean(cv_scores['score_time'])
print(f"{mean_cv:0.3f} ({std_cv:0.3f})",
      f"fit: {fit_time:0.2f}",
      f"secs pred: {score_time:0.2f} secs")
```

⊳ Prints the mean and standard deviation of test scores

The results are pretty interesting, and they can probably even turn better by adjusting the hyperparameters:

```
0.821 (0.004) fit: 102.28 secs pred: 9.80 secs
```

However, the time needed for training a single fold is excessive compared to all the previous machine learning algorithms. In the next section of this appendix, we will discuss how GPU cards can speed up the process while still using the Scikit-learn API.

B.3   *Using GPUs for machine learning*

Due to the rapid rise of deep learning in the data science field, GPUs are now widespread and accessible both for local and cloud computing. Earlier, you only heard about GPUs in 3D gaming, graphic processing rendering, and animation. Since they are cheap and apt at fast matrix multiplication tasks, academics and practitioners have rapidly picked up GPUs for neural network computations. RAPIDS, developed by NVIDIA (one of the top manufacturers of GPUs), is a set of packages for doing the full spectrum of data science, not just deep learning, on GPUs. The RAPIDS packages promise to help in all phases of a machine learning pipeline, end to end. That's a game changer for many classical machine learning algorithms, especially for the SVMs, the most credible choice for more complex tasks involving noisy, outlying observations and vast datasets (having a large set of features, especially if multicollinear or sparse ones). In the RAPIDS packages (table B.1), all commands have adopted existing APIs for their commands. Such assures an immediate market adoption of the packages, and for the user, there is no need to relearn how the wheel works.

Table B.1   Rapids packages

Rapids package	Task	API mimicked
cuPy	Array operations	NumPy
cuDF	Data processing	pandas
cuML	Machine learning	Scikit-learn

This section will focus on how easy it is to replace your Scikit-learn algorithms with the RAPIDS cuML package. Currently, this package includes implementations for linear models, k-NN, and SVMs, as well as for clustering and dimensionality reduction. The following listing shows the code for testing the support vector classifier with the radial basis function kernel we just tried in the previous section in its RAPIDS implementation (using a P100 GPU).

Listing B.3 Support vector classifier from RAPIDS cuML

```
from cuml.svm import SVC
from sklearn.metrics import accuracy_score          ← Creates a scoring function using
                                                       the accuracy_score metric
accuracy = make_scorer(accuracy_score)          ←
cv = KFold(5, shuffle=True, random_state=0)     ←    Creates a five-fold cross-
model = SVC(                                         validation iterator with shuffling
    C=1.0,                                           and a fixed random state
    kernel='rbf',
    gamma='scale',                          Creates an instance of a Support Vector
    probability=False          ←            Classifier from the GPU-accelerated cuML
)                                           library with specified hyperparameters
column_transform = ColumnTransformer(
    [('categories', categorical_onehot_encoding, low_card_categorical),
     ('numeric', numeric_standardization, continuous)],
    remainder='drop',
    verbose_feature_names_out=False,        Defines a ColumnTransformer to preprocess
    sparse_threshold=0.0)          ←        features, applying one-hot encoding to
                                            categorical features with low cardinality and
model_pipeline = Pipeline(                  standardization to numerical features
    [('processing', column_transform),
     ('modeling', model)])          ←
                                            Creates a pipeline that
                                            sequentially applies the
cv_scores = cross_validate(estimator=model_pipeline,  column transformation and
                           X=data,                     the model to the data
                           y=target_median,
                           scoring=accuracy,
                           cv=cv,
                           return_train_score=True,
                           return_estimator=True)     ←
                                                         Performs cross-validation
mean_cv = np.mean(cv_scores['test_score'])               on the data using the
std_cv = np.std(cv_scores['test_score'])                 defined pipeline, with
fit_time = np.mean(cv_scores['fit_time'])                accuracy scoring
score_time = np.mean(cv_scores['score_time'])
print(f"{mean_cv:0.3f} ({std_cv:0.3f})",
      f"fit: {fit_time:0.2f}",
                                            Prints the mean and standard
      f"secs pred: {score_time:0.2f} secs") ←  deviation of test scores
```

The results we obtained are

```
0.821 (0.004) fit: 4.09 secs pred: 0.11 secs
```

As you can see, we obtained the same results by reusing the same code but relying on cuML. However, the processing time has dropped from 102 seconds per folder to 4 seconds per folder. If you calculate the time savings, that's a 25x speed increase. The exact performance benefit depends on the GPU model you use; the more powerful the GPU, the speedier the results because it depends on how fast the GPU card can transfer data from CPU memory and how fast it can process a matrix multiplication.

Based on such performances on standard GPUs accessible to the general public, we recently saw applications fusing tabular data with large embeddings from deep learning models (such as text or images). SVMs work well with numerous features (but not more than the examples) and sparse values (many zero values). In such situations, SVMs can easily obtain a state-of-the-art result, outperforming other more popular tabular algorithms at this time—namely XGBoost and other gradient boosting implementations as well as end-to-end deep learning solutions, which are weaker when you don't have enough cases to feed them with.

Having a GPU and adapting your code to use RAPIDS algorithms makes certain classic algorithms for tabular machine learning quite competitive again, as a general rule, based on the principle that there is no free lunch in machine learning (more details about no-free-lunch theorems are available at http://www.no-free-lunch.org/). Taking into account your project constraints (for instance, you may not have certain resources available in your project environment), never exclude apriori testing your problem against all available algorithms, if this is feasible.

index